The rough guide to
MEXICO

=The=
rough
guides

Other available rough guides include
**PERU, SPAIN, PORTUGAL, GREECE, YUGOSLAVIA
AMSTERDAM & HOLLAND, TUNISIA** and **MOROCCO**

Forthcoming:
CHINA, EASTERN EUROPE, KENYA, FRANCE, ITALY, ISRAEL
and **NEW YORK**

Series Editor
MARK ELLINGHAM

The rough guide to
MEXICO

Written and researched by
JOHN FISHER

Routledge & Kegan Paul
London, Boston, Melbourne and Henley

First published in 1985
by Routledge & Kegan Paul plc

14 Leicester Square, London WC2H 7PH, England

9 Park Street, Boston, Mass. 02108, USA

464 St Kilda Road, Melbourne,
Victoria 3004, Australia and

Broadway House, Newtown Road,
Henley on Thames, Oxon RG9 1EN, England

Set in Linotron Helvetica and Sabon
by Input Typesetting Ltd, London
and printed in Great Britain
by Cox & Wyman Ltd,
Reading, Berkshire

Library of Congress Cataloging in Publication Data

Fisher, John, 1958–

The rough guide to Mexico.
(The Rough guides)
Includes index.
1. Mexico—Description and travel—1981-
Guidebooks. I. Title. II. Series.
F1209.G54   1985   917.2'04834   85—1939

British Library CIP data also available

ISBN 0–7102–0059–5

My thanks for help and support to Deborah Botwood, and also to Eve and Tony Fisher, Matthew Campbell, Olga Ramirez Luna, Blanca Delmau, Javier Flores, Lucia Herrera and James Tickell. Also to Natania Jansz and especially Mark Ellingham without whom this book would never have been finished.

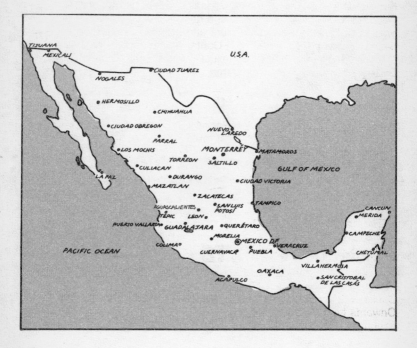

CONTENTS

Part one BASICS   1

Mexico: where to go – and when / Getting there / Red tape and entry
requirements / Cost and money / Health / Maps and information /
Getting about / Sleeping / Food and drink / Communication – post,
phones and media / Opening hours and holidays / Entertainment –
fiestas, sport, music and film / Crafts, markets and bargaining /
Trouble, police and bribery / Sexual harassment / Other things /
Glossary of common Mexican terms

Part two THE GUIDE   25

1 Baja California and the North Pacific 27
2 Between the Sierras: North-East routes 54
3 The Central Highlands 75
4 Mexico City and around 150
5 Acapulco and the Pacific Beaches 239
6 Veracruz and the Gulf Coast 262
7 Oaxaca and Chiapas 279
8 The Yucatan 311

Part three CONTEXTS   355

The historical framework 357
Monumental chronology 369
Books 372
Onwards from Mexico 374
Language 376

Index 379

Poor Mexico – so far from God,
So close to the United States.

> –Mexican Proverb

Part one
BASICS

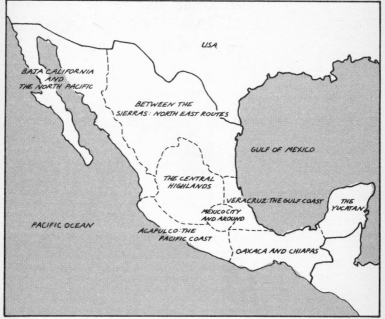

USA

BAJA CALIFORNIA
AND
THE NORTH PACIFIC

BETWEEN THE
SIERRAS: NORTH EAST ROUTES

GULF OF MEXICO

THE CENTRAL
HIGHLANDS

VERACRUZ: THE GULF COAST

THE
YUCATAN

PACIFIC OCEAN

MEXICO CITY
AND AROUND

ACAPULCO: THE
PACIFIC COAST

OAXACA AND CHIAPAS

MEXICO: WHERE TO GO – AND WHEN

Mexico enjoys a cultural blend which is wholly unique: it is an Indian country; it still seems, in places, a Spanish colony; and it has experienced an oil-based boom which has created vast modern cities and one of the fastest growing industrial powers on earth. Each aspect can be found in isolation, but far more often, throughout the Republic, the three co-exist – Indian markets, little changed in form since the conquest, thrive along-side elaborate colonial churches in the shadow of the skyscrapers of the Mexican miracle. Occasionally the marriage is an uneasy one, but for the most part it works unbelievably well. The people of Mexico reflect it too; there are communities of full-blooded Indians, and there are a few, a very few, Mexicans of pure Spanish descent. The great majority of the population, though, is *Mestizo*, combining in themselves both traditions and, to a greater or lesser extent, a veneer of urban sophistication.

Obviously there are adjustments to be made to any country which is still 'developing', and where change has been so dramatically rapid. Although the *mañana* mentality is largely an outsiders' myth, Mexico is still a country where timetables are not always to be entirely trusted, where anything that can break down will break down (when it's most needed), and where any attempt to do things in a hurry is liable to be frustrated. You simply have to accept the local temperament – that work may be necessary to live, but it's not life's central focus, that minor annoyances really are minor, and that there's always something else to do in the meantime. More deeply disturbing, perhaps, are the extremes of ostentatious wealth and absolute poverty – most poignant in the big cities where unemployment and austerity measures imposed by the massive foreign debt (and the IMF) have bitten hardest. Nevertheless, it is an easy, a fabulously varied, and an enormously enjoyable and friendly place in which to travel – despite the stories you may hear, and the lurid colour spreads of violent crime in Mexican newspapers.

Physically, Mexico resembles a vast horn, curving away south and east from the US border with its final tip bent right back round to the north. It is an extremely mountainous country – two great ranges, the Sierra Madre Occidental in the west and the Sierra Madre Oriental in the east, run down parallel to the coasts, enclosing a high, semi-desert plateau. About halfway down they are crossed by the volcanic highland area in which stand Mexico City and the major centres of population. Beyond, the mountains run together as a single range through the southern states of Oaxaca and Chiapas. Only that eastern tip – the Yucatan Peninsula – is consistently low-lying and flat.

The **north**, relatively speaking, is a dull land – arid and sparsely populated outside of a few industrial cities which are heavily American influenced. The **Baja California** wilderness has its fanatical devotees, and there are beach resorts on the Pacific, but most of the excitement lies in Central and South-Eastern Mexico. The attractions of each area are discussed in the chapter introductions. Broadly, though, **the highlands** north of and around the capital boast the bulk of the historic colonial towns, and an enticingly spring-like climate year-round. **Mexico City** itself is a choking nightmare of urban sprawl, but totally fascinating, while around it lie the chief relics of the ancient cultures of the centre – Teotihuacan, Toltec and Aztec. **Guadalajara**, to the west, is a city on a far more human scale, with some of the most gently scenic country in Mexico to the south – thickly forested hills, studded with lakes and ancient villages. The southern states of **Oaxaca** and **Chiapas** are mountainous and beautiful too, but in a far wilder way. Here, amid the jungle and impenetrable wilds, Mexico's living Indian traditions are at their strongest. In **the Yucatan** there is also Indian life, side-by-side with a tourist industry based around the magnificent Mayan cities and the burgeoning new Caribbean resorts. These do not yet compare with **Acapulco and the Pacific coast** in terms of numbers of visitors, but even there, despite the string of long-established resorts, plenty of beaches remain virtually undiscovered. Finally the Gulf coast, despite the attractions of **Veracruz** and the ruins which that state hides, is largely dominated by oil, unpleasantly humid most of the time, and its beaches on the whole a disappointment.

To a great extent, the physical terrain determines the **climate** – certainly far more than the expected indicators of latitude and longitude. You can drive down the coast all day without conditions changing noticeably, but turn inland, to the mountains, and the contrast is immediate: in temperature, scenery, vegetation, even the mood and mould of the people around you. So generalisations are difficult. Summer, from June to September, is in theory the **rainy season**, but just how rainy it is varies wildly from place to place. In the centre you can expect a heavy but shortlived downpour virtually every afternoon – in the north hardly any rain falls, ever. Chiapas is the wettest state, with many minor roads washed out in the late summer, and in the south and low-lying coastal areas summer is stickily humid too. Winter is the traditional **tourist season**, and it still is in the big beach resorts like Acapulco and Cancun, with December the busiest month of the year. Mountain areas, though, can get very cold. In effect there are now tourists all year round – sticking on the whole to the highlands in summer and the coasts in winter. Given a totally free choice, I'd pick November to come, with the rains over, the land still fresh, and the peak season not yet begun. Overall, though, the climate is so benign that any time of year will do, so long as you're prepared for some rain in the summer, some cold in winter, and for sudden changes which go with the altitude at any time.

GETTING THERE

From Britain and Europe

There are at present no direct flights from London to Mexico, and consequently it is not the cheapest place in the world to get to: fares to Mexico City are no lower than those to any other Latin American destination. Expect to pay around £460 for a return flight if you book through a 'bucket shop' or specialist agent (official fares are far higher). These will all be on **scheduled flights** – usually *KLM* via Amsterdam and Houston, occasionally *Air France* from Paris or *Iberia* from Madrid. *Aeroflot* also fly to Mexico City twice a week, if you fancy a stopover in Moscow, and will probably be the cheapest of all, as well as having a fairly convenient overnight schedule (try booking through *Sam Travel*, 01 636 2521). Otherwise the widest listings of cheap flight **operators** are to be found in the London weekly magazine *Time Out* or, nationally, in the *Sunday Times*, *Observer* and *Private Eye*. *LAM* and *TNT*, both Australian magazines distributed free in London, also have some ads. *STA* (74 Old Brompton Road, London SW7; 01 581 1022) and *Journey Latin America* (10 Barley Mow Passage, London W4; 01 747 3108) are both reliable organisations who may also be able to offer special rates for **students** or **groups**.

Package holidays, though most of the really big companies do offer them, are not on the whole good value unless you want to spend two weeks in a luxury beach hotel: *Thomas Cook*, with branches everywhere, are the leaders in this field and offer the widest selection. *Dulwich World Travel* (94 Dulwich Village, London SE21; 01 693 5224) are specialists who can plan individually tailored trips at a price. For more youth/student-oriented tours, try *STA* or *Journey Latin America* again. From Paris there are regular **charter flights** to both Mexico City and Merida – though you'd probably have to go there to book.

In any event, don't expect to find much in the way of cheap flights **back from Mexico** – you're far better off paying a bit more for an open-ended return from this end if you're unsure of your schedule, than paying full fare in Mexico.

Depending on the constantly changing fare structures, **flying to the States** might also work out cheaper – certainly if you travel down overland or plan to do some touring there anyway. **New York**, with *Virgin Atlantic* or *People's Express*, is of course the cheapest destination, but Mexico City is almost as far from New York as London is. **Los Angeles**, then, or **Houston** are the logical points from which to set off overland: both also have reasonably priced onward flights to a number of Mexican destinations, although **Miami to Merida** may work out cheaper if you're coming from Europe. Worth checking out, too, are any good deals on unrestricted **air passes** (usually cheaper if bought in Europe) offered by US airlines which cover Mexico – *Continental* or *Eastern* are the most likely.

From the States

1 By air
There are **flights to Mexico** from just about every major US city, operated by a number of American airlines and both major Mexican operators (*AeroMexico* and *Mexicana*). Cheapest and most frequent are those from the West and South-west (especially Mexicana's night service from L.A. to Guadalajara and Mexico City) but Miami to Merida is also good value. To sort out the bewildering array of competing fares and special offers you should really go to a good travel agent – or, preferably, try two or three. From close to the border, it's usually cheaper to cross into Mexico and take an **internal flight**.

2 By rail
There is no direct connection between US and Mexican passenger train services and frankly you'd have to be a real fanatic to get to the border by rail. **US trains** are on the whole inefficient and expensive, and only Europeans travelling on Amtrak passes (or Paul Theroux) are likely to be attracted. Once you've crossed the border it's a different matter – **Mexican services** from Mexicali and Nogales to Guadalajara, or from Ciudad Juarez and Monterrey to Mexico City, offer reasonably priced sleepers if you're in a hurry to get south.

3 By bus
Far better to go by bus, although it's still a pretty long haul – at least 2½ days from New York to the border, a further day's travel from there to Mexico City. Both **Greyhound** and **Trailways** run regularly to all the major border crossings, and in the larger of them their buses will take you over the frontier and into the Mexican bus station, which saves a lot of hassle. Both companies, too, should be able to book you through tickets with their Mexican counterparts.

4 By car – driving or hitching
Taking **your own car** into Mexico will obviously give you a great deal more freedom in terms of where you can go and when, but it's hedged about with problems (see driving under *Getting About*). First of all you must take out a separate Mexican **insurance** policy, which is expensive (available from numerous agencies on each side of every border post – probably more easily done in the USA); then, car drivers have a different kind of **tourist card** which ensures that they cannot leave again without the car – it is illegal to sell it, and even if your vehicle breaks down irreparably or is written off in a crash you're expected to take the bits home with you. US, Canadian and most European **driving licences** are valid in Mexico, but European ones may be unfamiliar, and it's as well to arm yourself with an International Driving Licence (in Britain, £5 from the AA – it's different from that which covers driving in the States).

Time was, you could pay for a couple of month's touring in Mexico by taking a car through and **selling it** in Belize or Guatemala. As far as I know this is still legal, but it's no longer easy, with trouble in both countries and money short. If you do try, make sure it's a simple model (preferably a Ford or Dodge) with good ground clearance – better still a pick-up.

Routes to the border are largely a matter of personal preference: if you're coming from the West Coast, though, you'll save considerable time by sticking to US highways as far as Tucson, and from there heading down through Nogales – unless, that is, you plan to go via Baja California. In Mexico, the eastern routes to the capital are shorter, but the central and Pacific coast roads more interesting. One final possibility is to **leave your car at the border** and continue on public transport – all the major US border towns have parking lots which offer long-term storage rates.

Hitching through the States should present no more than the usual problems, but it's not much of a way to get around within Mexico – certainly not in the north. Even if you have a through lift, it's probably best to walk across the border or to take a short bus ride; otherwise it will be marked on your tourist card that you came in by car and you may (although you shouldn't) have problems when it comes to leaving.

Leaving Mexico – a note
Remember if you're **flying out** of Mexico that there's an airport departure tax, equivalent to about 5 dollars but payable only in pesos. Keep enough back to

cover it. For more information on getting to **Belize**, **Guatemala** and **Central America** see the *Onwards from Mexico* section in part three.

RED TAPE AND ENTRY REQUIREMENTS

Anyone entering Mexico needs a **Tourist Card**. For US and Canadian citizens all that's required is to turn up at the border with proof of citizenship, and a card will be issued – up to 180 days for US citizens, up to ninety for Canadians. This doesn't necessarily involve even a passport, but I would strongly recommend having one anyway; it's by far the best form of identification, recognised everywhere. The Tourist Card can also be obtained in advance, from Mexican Consulates, Tourist Offices and major travel agencies – if you're flying in, the airline should arrange it. Although not necessary, this can save worry and perhaps delays. Always apply for longer than you intend to stay – getting an extension is a frustrating and time-consuming business.

Britons, Australians, New Zealanders and citizens of Ireland and most European countries must apply for a Tourist Card (valid up to ninety days) in advance from a Mexican Consulate. In theory you cannot get one at the Border, although in practice it's often possible. Since there are Mexican Consulates in most US border towns and in every major US city this is rarely a real problem. In Britain, apply to the Mexican Consulate at 8 Halkin Street, London

SW1 (01 253 6393) – they're usually issued on the spot. A **US visa** is also a sensible precaution even if you don't plan to go to the States – in Britain from the US Embassy (5, Upper Grosvenor Street, London W1; 01 499 3443); postal applications save a lot of queueing but can take up to a month.

Wherever you get it, the Tourist Card is free – despite the fact that many border guards ask for payment. Keep it with you and don't lose it; if you have to show your papers (and checkpoints on Mexican roads are not uncommon) it's more important than your passport.

At the border, you must go through Immigration (*Migracion*) and Customs (*Aduana*) checks. The entire US frontier strip is a duty-free area into which you can come and go more or less as you please: heading inland, however, there are checkpoints on every road after about 30km and you'll be sent back to have your card stamped and luggage checked if you haven't already done so.

Should you **lose** your Tourist Card, or need to have it renewed, head for the nearest office of the National Tourist Council or in big cities to the *Migracion*. In the case of **renewal**, it's often easier to cross the border for a few hours and get a new one on re-entry.

COST AND MONEY

Mexico has been hit hard by a financial crisis based largely on its massive foreign debt, exacerbated by falling oil prices and world slump. **Inflation** is rampant, and prices impossible to quote with any real accuracy. While this has forced austerity on the Mexicans themselves, however, it has made it extremely cheap for outsiders (especially those bringing dollars) and will continue to do so as long as the constant devaluation of the peso continues. In 1976 there were 12 pesos to the dollar – by 1984 the rate had almost topped 200. Consequently, prices below are quoted in

dollars – the most widely acceptable and far the easiest foreign currency to take, as well as being relatively stable.

Whatever happens, Mexico will remain substantially less expensive than anywhere in Northern Europe or the States, and at present prices are often ridiculously low. **Costs** will of course depend to some extent on where you are and when – the developed tourist resorts and big cities are invariably more expensive than more remote towns, and certain areas, too, have noticeably higher prices; among them the industrialised north, especially along the border, and all the newly wealthy oil regions. The peak tourist season – around Christmas – and any special event will also probably be marked by price hikes. Nonetheless, wherever you go you could probably get by on 8–10 dollars a day, and on 15 you'd really be living very well. **Rooms** can usually be found for around 2–5 dollars single, 3–6 double. **Food** prices can vary wildly, but you should always get a substantial meal in a plain Mexican restaurant for around 2 dollars. Other expenses are largely up to you – **drink**, especially superb Mexican beer, is very cheap; **transport** may prove to be a major expense, since distances are vast. By any standards, though, the prices are reasonable: Mexico City to Acapulco for example, a journey of over 400km, costs less than 5 dollars by first class bus. As always, if you're travelling alone you'll end up spending considerably more than you would in a group of two or more people – sharing rooms and food saves substantially. You can also cut corners by buying some of your own food and drink, hitching occasionally, and so on. If you have some kind of International **Student or Youth card**, you might also take it along for an occasional reduction – I wouldn't go out of your way to obtain one, though, as most concessions are available only to Mexican students.

The **Mexican peso** is, sometimes confusingly, written in exactly the same way as the US dollar. It's normally clear from the context (and the amount) but almost always, if you see something written as $100, it's pesos not dollars: where there's any ambiguity, pesos are written as $100 M.N. (for *Moneda Nacional*), dollars as $100 U.S. or $100dlls. The peso is divided into 100 centavos, and although you rarely come across them in prices, you may get 50 centavo coins (*tostones*) in change and need 20 centavo coins (which are in chronically short supply) to operate public phone boxes. Other coins cover 1, 5, 20 and 50 pesos, with the smallest note in common circulation being the brown $100 (though you may come across ancient 50 and even 20 peso notes).

Dollars can be changed easily at banks throughout the country, as well as in many hotels, shops and restaurants which are used to tourists (usually at a worse rate). Somewhere like Acapulco, cash dollars are almost as easy to use as pesos. **Other currencies** are much harder to change outside the big cities – and even there only a few banks can help. Although the banks have all been nationalised, each is run differently: the *Banco Nacional de Mexico* (known as *Banamex*) is always the best bet for changing pounds or other major currencies – *Bancomer*, almost as widespread, is also a possibility, while for European money the smaller *Banco del Atlantico* may also be helpful. Don't expect to change the likes of Dutch guilders or Swedish kroner anywhere, though, except at those countries' Consulates for an insulting rate. There isn't much of a **black market** in Mexico since exchange regulations are relatively free; occasionally, though, you may meet a wealthy Mexican anxious to salt away some of his reserves in cash dollars and prepared to pay slightly over the odds. It's not really worth bothering with unless it comes about through personal contacts or you want to do someone a favour. Most **banks** will change money only in the mornings, from 9–1, though many open again in the afternoon: in remote areas you may have to wait for the day's exchange rate to be wired through from the capital.

Dollar **traveller's cheques** are almost as good as cash, and can again be changed in any bank and many larger hotels and shops. Stick to the big names – *Thomas Cook, American Express, Visa* or one of the major American banks – not only because these will be recognised, but also because there will be better back-up should they be lost or stolen. Personal cheques are virtually worthless, but major **credit cards** are widely accepted and good for emergencies: *Visa/Barclaycard* and *Access/Mastercard* are the best – *American Express* and other charge cards will only be taken by very expensive places (and none are any use in the cheapest hotels or restaurants, or for bus tickets). Should you run out, it's easy enough to have **money sent** to you at any Mexican bank (*Banamex* is again the best), but check on currency regulations. You may be restricted as to the amount which can be paid out in dollars.

Most bills in Mexico will come with **I.V.A.** added on – this is a 15 per cent sales tax equivalent to VAT (Value Added Tax) and is not always included in quoted prices.

HEALTH

There are no required **inoculations** for Mexico, but most doctors will advise you to have some anyway – cholera/typhoid is a sensible precaution, as is ensuring that you're up to date with such things as polio and tetanus boosters. Some, too, recommend *gamma-globulin* against hepatitis but you should discuss this – the effects are not particularly long-lasting and if you are travelling long term you may end up more vulnerable once it's worn off than you were before you had it. Parts of the south, too, especially the jungle and coastal areas of Chiapas, are potentially malarial – you're really supposed to take malaria tablets starting about a month before you arrive and continuing for a month afterwards, though hardly anyone seems to do so.

Diarrhoea, Moctezuma's Revenge or simply *Turista* (as it's invariably known in Mexico) is a far more realistic enemy. No one, however cautious they are, seems to avoid it altogether, largely because there are no effective preventative measures. It is caused above all by the change in diet and routine and by the fact that the bacteria in Mexican food are different (and perhaps more numerous) from those found in a European or North American diet. The usual prescriptions for avoiding it (no salad vegetables, no fruit you haven't peeled yourself, no water or ice) are to my mind worse than the effects, and anyway rarely work. However, you should be cautious – don't try anything too exotic in the first few days, don't eat anywhere which is obviously dirty (easily spotted, most Mexican restaurants are scrupulously clean), and be careful with tap-water. Most people tell you never to touch the water, which is virtually impossible – however, you should always ask when you check into a hotel (*es potable*?), and if it isn't drink-able there will almost always be a supply of purified water. In restaurants stick to bottled mineral water (*agua mineral* or *agua de Tehuacan*). Taking along some simple remedy – *Kaomycin* for example – is worthwhile, but Mexican pharmacists are well used to the problem and can sell many drugs over the counter (if necessary) which would be on prescription in Europe or the States. Look for a green cross and the **Farmacia** sign, where the single word *diarrea* should be enough to communicate your problem. The most practical cures, though, seem to be to take it easy, eat nothing for 24 hours, and drink large quantities of bottled water. Or, if you've been in Mexico for some time, simply ignore it. Only if it lasts more than four or five days should you start to worry at all.

For other minor **medical problems**, head again for the Farmacia – most pharmacists are knowledgeable and helpful, and many also speak some English. One word of warning, though – in many Mexican pharmacies you can still buy drugs (*Entero-Vioform* is one) which have been banned elsewhere. For more serious complaints you can get a list of English-speaking **doctors** from the nearest US or British Consulate – every Mexican border town has hundreds of them (and dentists) since they charge less than their rivals across the border.

Medical Insurance is, in any event, a must. There are no reciprocal health arrangements between Mexico and Britain or anywhere else. In Britain, this can be arranged through any Travel Agent or Insurance Broker, and for around £10 a month will give you cover against loss or theft of your possessions as well as basic health insurance. Some US health plans may cover Mexico, but most don't.

MAPS AND INFORMATION

The first place to head for information, and for free maps of the country and many towns, is the **Mexican National Tourist Council** (in Britain at 7 Cork Street, London W1; also in at least twenty North American cities). If you know where you're going, stock up on as many relevant brochures and plans as they'll let you have – in Mexico the offices are frequently closed or have run out. These **Turismo** offices on the ground are run by both state and national organisations, and it's quite impossible to generalise about them. Some are extremely friendly and helpful, with free information and leaflets by the cart-load; others are barely capable of answering the simplest enquiry.

Better **road maps** (though still not exactly detailed) can be bought from any large bookshop – or in the States at gas stations (*Mobil* and the *AAA* both produce reasonable ones). In Britain, *Stanford's* (12 Long Acre, London WC2; 01 836 1321) and *McCarta* (122 Kings Cross Road, London WC1; 01 278 8278) both have a wide selection. In Mexico, the best are those published by *Patria*, with individual maps of each state, and

Guia Roji, who also publish a Mexican Road Atlas and a Mexico City street guide. Both are widely available – try branches of *Sanborn's* or large *Pemex* stations.

More detailed, **large-scale maps** – for hiking or climbing – are harder to come by, but the government agency *DETENAL* does print a wide variety. Details of what, and where, the stockists are, are available from them at Calle Balderas 71, Mexico 5 D.F.

GETTING ABOUT

Buses

Within Mexico, **buses** are by far the most efficient form of public transport. There are an unbelievable number of them, connecting even the smallest of villages. Long-distance services are, on the whole, in reasonably comfortable and reliable Greyhound-style coaches; remoter villages are more often connected by what look like (and sometimes are) recycled US School Buses. Although in theory there are just two classes of bus – first and second – in practice there are clearly three: first, main-road second, and those bumpy village services. Most people choose first for any reasonably long distance, second for short trips or if the destination is too small for first class buses to stop. In Mexican Spanish a bus is a *camion*, hardly ever an *autobus*.

Many towns, especially in the north, have centralised modern **bus stations** known as the *Central Camionera* or *Central de Autobuses* – elsewhere you may find separate first and second class terminals, or even individual ones for each company.

On major long-distance routes there's often little to choose between first and second class services (*Primera* and *Segunda Clase*). **First class** theoretically stop less often, have numbered, reserved seats, and will often be air-conditioned. But some **second class** lines have all this too, and air-conditioning, for one, is not necessarily a boon – there's nothing more uncomfortable than a bus with sealed windows and a broken air-conditioner. In short, although first is marginally better (and only slightly more expensive), don't be put off second class if it seems more

convenient – it may even prove less crowded. Always check the route and arrival time, though, and where possible buy tickets in advance to get the best seats. Reckon on paying about $1–1.50 (U.S.) for every 100km covered.

There is very rarely any problem getting a bus from its point of origin or from really big towns. In smaller, mid-route places, however, you often have to wait for the bus to arrive (or at least to leave its last stop) before discovering if there are any seats. Often there are too few, and without fluent and loud Spanish you may lose out in the fight for the ticket clerk's attention. You could try getting round this by chatting to the clerk beforehand and making sure he knows you want tickets (though this can backfire – some will deliberately choose to ignore the gringo) or there's almost always a bus at some time described as *local* which means it originates from where you are and tickets can be bought well in advance (the through buses are known as *de paso*). Other **terms** to look out for include *via corta* (by the short route) and *directo* (direct/non-stop). *Salida* is departure, *Llegada* arrival. A decent road map will be extremely helpful in working out just which buses are going to pass through your destination.

In almost every bus station there is some form of **left luggage** office – usually known as a *Guarderia*, *Consigna* or simply *Equipaje*. Before leaving anything, make sure that the place will be open when you come to collect. If there's nowhere, staff at the bus companies' baggage despatching offices can often be persuaded to look after things for a while.

Trains

Rail travel is by comparison far slower, although it can also be considerably cheaper. In general I would only recommend it for really long journeys – from the border to Mexico City, for example, or from there to Merida – when you can do it in style with a sleeper and restaurant car. The one exception is the amazing Copper Canyon Railway (see p. 59).

Most Mexican rolling stock is ancient (some of it fabulous 1930s US pullman cars) and none is particularly comfortable. **Second Class** (*Segunda*) is dirt cheap, and the carriages are invariably crammed to the limit with villagers, their bags, baggage and livestock – dirty, hot and uncomfortable, if fascinating for very short periods. Ordinary **First Class** (*Primera general*) is little better, though you should at least get a seat. *Primera Reservada* (or *Especial*), roughly equivalent in price to buses, gets you a reserved seat, probably reclining, possibly even in an air-conditioned carriage, and certainly with plenty of room to move around.

For **sleepers**, you pay a supplement over this top first class rate. Least expensive are pullman-style carriages with curtained-off bunks – the upper *Cama Alta* is slightly cheaper than the lower *Cama Baja*. Then there is a *Camarín*, a tiny private room either for one or two people, or ultimately an *Alcoba*, a larger room with private bathroom (probably big enough for two adults and two small kids). Any of these cost more than the bus, but you won't find cheaper sleeping cars anywhere, and it's a real slice of luxury.

Flights and ferries

Between them, *AeroMexico* and *Mexicana* have **internal flights** connecting every major city. There are direct daily flights from Mexico City to no less than thirty-five destinations within Mexico, and many others are connected less regularly or by feeder links to larger airports. Between Mexico City and Guadalajara alone there are nineteen flights every day. They offer a quick and easy, if expensive way to get around. Tijuana to Mexico City, for example, will cost about 100 dollars – Mexico City to Merida around half that.

Ferries connect Baja California with several ports on the Pacific mainland, and there are smaller boats from the Caribbean coast to Cozumel and Isla Mujeres. All are dead cheap for passengers, reasonably priced for cars – see the relevant *Travel Details* for more information.

Driving

Getting your car into Mexico properly documented (see *Getting There*) is just the start of your problems. Although most people who drive enjoy it and get out again with no more than minor incidents, driving in Mexico does require a good deal of care and concentration, and almost inevitably involves at least one brush with bureaucracy or the police. First of all, unless your car is a VW, Ford or Dodge (all of which are manufactured in Mexico), **parts** are going to be expensive and hard to come by – bring a basic spares kit. **Tyres** suffer particularly badly on burning hot Mexican roads, and you should carry at least one good spare – roadside *Vulcanizadoras* and *Llanteros* can do temporary repairs, new ones are expensive. **Parking** in big cities is always going to be a problem, too – the restrictions are complicated and foreigners are easy pickings for traffic police who usually remove one or both plates in lieu of a ticket (retrieving them can be an expensive and time-consuming business). Since theft is also a real threat, you'll usually have to pay extra for a hotel with secure parking. You may well also have to pay on the spot 'fines' for traffic offences – real or imaginary.

Mexican **roads and traffic**, though, are your chief worry – some of the new motorways are excellent, but away from the large centres of population roads are often narrow, winding and pot-holed, with animals wandering across them at unexpected moments. A good proportion of bus and truck drivers, too, are certified lunatics – get out of their way (if you indicate left on a stretch of open road, it means it's clear to overtake). Every town and village on the road, however tiny, protects its peace by a series of *Topes* (sleeping policemen) across the road: look out for the warning signs and take them seriously; these concrete or metal bumps are often huge and can be negotiated only at a crawl. Most people suggest, too, that you never drive at night, which is sound advice even if it is totally impractical. Any good road map should detail the more common Mexican road-signs.

Should you have a minor **accident**, try to come to some arrangement with the other party – involving the police will only make matters worse, and Mexican drivers will be as anxious to avoid doing so as you will. Again, if you witness an accident, don't get involved – witnesses can be locked up along with those directly implicated to prevent them leaving before the case comes up. In any more serious event you should contact your Consulate as soon as possible, and the Insurance Company.

Hiring a car in Mexico – especially if you do it just for a day or two with a specific itinerary in mind – lets you out of most of these problems, and is often an extremely good way of seeing quickly a small area which would take days to get around on public transport. In all the tourist resorts and major cities there are numbers of competing agencies, with local operations usually charging less than the well-known ones. You should check the rates carefully, though – the basic cost of hiring a VW Beetle for the day may be as little as 10-15 dollars, but by the time you have added insurance,

tax and mileage it can easily work out at three or four times that. Unlimited mileage offers are almost always a bargain. For shorter distances, mopeds and motorbikes are also available in most resorts.

Hitching

It's perfectly possible to **hitch** your way around Mexico, but as a serious means of long-distance transport it can't be recommended. Lifts are relatively scarce, distances vast, and the roadside often a surprisingly harsh environment if you get dropped by some obscure turn-off. You may also be harassed at times by the police, though this depends very much on local policy and on their mood at the time. In any case, many drivers expect you to contribute to their expenses, which rather defeats the object.

Over short stretches, though, to get to villages where there's no bus or simply to while away the time spent waiting for one, hitching is a worthwhile proposition – you'll probably come across real friendliness and certainly meet people you wouldn't otherwise.

SLEEPING

Mexican **hotels** may describe themselves as *Posadas, Paradors, Casas de Huespedes* or plain Hotels, but there's no real distinction between any of these categories. Nor is there any widely used official rating or pricing system. Price is no guide to quality – a filthy flea-pit and a beautifully run converted mansion may charge exactly the same, even if they're right next door to each other. The only answer is never to take a room without seeing it first – though you soon learn to spot which establishments have promise. There are some appalling hotels in Mexico, but there are also a great many very attractive, inexpensive places which will go out of their way to help you.

Although **prices** are supposed to be regulated to some extent by the local tourist authorities, in practice the displayed rates cannot keep up with inflation and you're not necessarily being ripped off if they charge more than the sign says. Expect to pay around $2–5 (U.S.) single, $3–6 double, for the

cheaper hotels. A little gentle haggling rarely goes amiss, and many places will have some rooms which rent for less, so ask (*Tiene un cuarto mas barato?*). For more than one person, savings can also be made by sharing rooms – most hotels have large ones with several beds in them. The charging system varies with every establishment – some have a room price which is valid no matter how many people occupy it, others charge by the bed. A double-bedded room (*con cama matrimonial*) is almost invariably cheaper than one with two beds (*con dos camas*). **Air-conditioning** (*aire acondicionado*) is another feature which always inflates prices – often you are offered a choice. Unless it is quite unbearably hot and humid, a room with a simple ceiling fan (*ventilador*) is better every time. The air-conditioning units are almost always noisy and inefficient, whereas a fan can be left running silently all night and the draught will also serve to keep insects away from the bed.

Finding a room is rarely hard – in

most old and not overly touristy places the cheap hotels are concentrated around the main plaza (the *Zocalo*) with others near the bus and railway stations. In bigger cities there's usually a relatively small area in which you'll find the bulk of the realistic possibilities. In every case, these areas, and many of the hotels within them, are detailed in the text. The more modern and expensive places have very often been built on the outskirts of towns, accessible only by car or taxi.

There are very few alternatives to staying in hotels. **Camping** is possible in places, but there are very few campsites in Mexico and those that do exist are on the whole **Trailer Parks** first and foremost, and not particularly pleasant to pitch tents in. Of course if you have a van or R.V. you can use these or park just about anywhere else – there are a good number of facilities in the well-travelled areas, especially down the Pacific coast. **Youth Hostels** are again few and far between, and in any case they normally discriminate in favour of Mexican hostellers (the one in Mexico City is an exception). For further details on either of these contact the Mexican National Tourist Council or the International Youth Hostel Association.

FOOD AND DRINK

Whatever your preconceptions about Mexican food, if you've never tried it in Mexico they will almost certainly be wrong. It bears very little relation to the concoctions served in 'Mexican' restaurants in the States or Europe – certainly you won't find *chile con carne* outside the tourist spots of Acapulco. Nor, as a rule, is it hot; indeed, a more common complaint from people who stick to standard restaurant fare is that after a while it all seems pretty bland. Some dishes are hot (if you want to avoid them ask *es picante*?), but on the whole you add your own seasoning from the bowls of home-made chile sauce on the table – these are often surprisingly mild, but they can be fiery and should always be approached with caution.

Basic meals are served at **restaurantes**, but you can get breakfast, snacks and often full meals at **cafes** too; there are **take-away** and **fast food** places serving sandwiches, *tortas* and *tacos* as well as more international style food (avoid Mexican *hamburguesas*); there are establishments serving nothing but wonderful **fruit drinks** and **salads** (usually identified by a sign saying *Jugos y Licuados*) and there are **street stalls** dishing out everything from tacos to orange juice to ready-made crisp vegetable salads sprinkled with chile salt and lime. If you're **travelling**, as often as not the food will come to you – people clamber onto buses (especially second class ones) and trains with baskets of home-made foods, local specialities, cold drinks or jugs of coffee – you'll find wonderful things this way which you won't come across in restaurants, but they should be treated with respect, and with an eye to hygiene. Traditionally, Mexicans eat a light breakfast very early, a snack of tacos or eggs in mid-morning, lunch, the main meal of the day, around 2pm (followed by a siesta) and a late dinner. There's no need to have two breakfasts, but eating a large meal at lunchtime can be a big money saver – almost every restaurant serves a set price, three course **comida corrida** (or *comida turistica*) which is extremely good value. Whenever it's eaten, the main meal is known as *comida*, and some places may also offer these set meals in the evening. Just about every **market** in the country has a cooked food section, and these are invariably the cheapest places to eat.

Vegetarians can eat supremely well in Mexico, although it does take caution to avoid meat altogether – many Mexican dishes are naturally meat-free and there are fabulous fruits and vegetables, but vegetarianism as such is not particularly common and a simple cheese and chile dish may have some meat added to 'improve' it. The basic Mexican diet, however, is essentially one of corn (*maiz*) and its products, beans and chiles. Most restaurants serve vegetable soups and rice, and will have items like *quesadillas* (tortillas wrapped around cheese and toasted or fried), *chiles rellenos* (stuffed chiles, a large mild green variety filled usually with rice and cheese and fried in batter), or *queso fundido* (simply and literally melted cheese – served with tortillas and sauce). Eggs, too, are served anywhere at any time, and many of the Fruit Juice shops (see drinks below) also serve huge mixed fruit salads to which grains and nuts can be added.

The basic corn, chile and beans take on an almost infinite variety of guises. **Beans** (*frijoles*) are of the brown kidney-bean variety and are almost always served *refritos*, that is boiled up, mashed and refried – this is an invariable accompaniment to egg dishes, and comes with almost everything else too. Even better if you can get them whole in some kind of country-style soup or stew, often with pork or bacon. There are at least a hundred different types of **chile**, fresh or dried, in colours ranging from pale green to almost black – each has a distinct flavour and by no means all are hot, although the most common, *chiles jalapeños*, small and either green or red, certainly are. **Corn**, in some form, features in virtually everything – in its natural state it is known as *elote* and you can find it toasted on the cob at street stalls or in soups and stews such as *pozole* (with meat). Far more often, though, it is ground into flour for **tortillas**, flat maize pancakes of which you will get a stack to accompany your meal in any cheap Mexican restaurant. Tortillas can also be made of wheat-flour (*de harina*), which may be preferable to outsiders' tastes, but these are rare except in the north. They form the basis of many specifically Mexican dishes, often described as *antojitos* on menus. Simplest of these are **tacos**, tortillas rolled and filled with almost anything, from beef and chicken to green vegetables – usually fried. *Enchiladas* are tacos covered in chile sauce and baked – *enchiladas suizas* are filled with chicken and have sour cream over them. *Tostadas* are flat tortillas toasted crisp and piled with ingredients – usually meat, salad vegetables and cheese: smaller bite-size versions are known as *sopes*. *Chilaquiles* are torn up and cooked together with meat and sauce – usually hot. Especially in the north, you'll also come across *burritos* (large wheat tortillas, stuffed with beef and potatoes or beans) and *gorditas* (small, fat, corn tortillas, sliced open, stuffed and baked or fried). Corn-flour too, is the basis of **tamales** – found predominantly in central and southern Mexico – which are a sort of cornmeal pudding, stuffed, flavoured,

and steamed in corn or banana leaves. They can be either savoury, with additions like prawn or *elote*, or sweet when made with something like coconut.

Breakfast (*desayuno*) can consist simply of coffee and *pan dulce* – sweet rolls and pastries which usually come in a basket, you pay for as many as you eat. Mexican **coffee** is excellent – in its basic form (*cafe solo* or *negro*) it is strong, black, often sweet (ask for it *sin azucar*) and comes in small cups. For weaker black coffee ask for *cafe americano*, though this may mean instant (if you want instant ask for Nescafe). White is *cafe cortado* or *con crema* or *con un pocito de leche*: *cafe con leche* is excellent, but made with all milk. Espresso and Capuccino are also often available, and you may be offered *cafe de olla* too – stewed in the pot for hours with cinnamon and sugar, it's thick, sweet and delicious. More substantial breakfasts consist of eggs in any number of forms (see food lists below), or at fruit juice places you can have a simple *licuado* (see drinks) fortified with raw egg (*blanquillo*). Freshly squeezed **orange juice** (*jugo de naranja*) is always available from street stalls in the early morning.

The **comida**, or main meal, will usually consist of three courses – soup, a main meat or fish course, and sweet – but there may be more. In particular there are frequently two soup courses, wet soup being followed by *sopa seca* (dry soup) – most commonly this is *sopa de arroz*, which is simply rice flavoured with tomato or chile, but it may be a plate of vegetables, pasta, beans or *guacamole* (avocado mashed with tomato, onion and maybe lime juice and chile). **Meat**, except in the north, is not particularly good – beef in particular is usually thin and tough; pork, kid and occasionally lamb are better. For fat American-style steaks look for a sign saying *Carnes Hereford* or for a description like New York Cut; these only in expensive places or in the north. **Seafood** is almost always fresh and delicious. A stack of tortillas is the usual accompaniment to any meal, but in more expensive or touristy places you'll get rolls (*bolillos*). Snack meals mostly consist of some variation on the taco theme, but **tortas** are also good: filled rolls, often with ham, cheese or both, garnished with avocado and chile and toasted if you want.

The basic **drinks** to accompany food are water or beer. Stick to bottled stuff (*agua mineral* or *agua de Tehuacan*) if you're drinking **water** – it comes either still (*sin gas*) or carbonated (*con gas*). Mexican **beer**, *cerveza*, is excellent – especially if you're comparing it to the puny US product. Most is light, lager-style *cerveza clara*, fine examples being *Bohemia*, *Superior* and *Tecate* (the last, for some reason, normally served with lime and salt); but you can also get dark beers (*oscura*) of which the best is *Negra Modelo*. **Wine** (*vino – tinto* for red, *blanco* white) is not seen a great deal, although Mexico does produce a fair number of perfectly good ones. You're safest sticking to the branded makes, like *Hidalgo* or *Domecq*.

Soft drinks (*refrescos*), including Coke, Pepsi, Squirt and Mexican brands which are usually extremely sweet, are on sale everywhere. But far more tempting are the **real fruit juices** and *licuados* sold at shops displaying the *Jugos y Licuados* sign. Juices (*jugos*) can be anything which will go through the extractor – orange (*naranja*), carrot (*zanahoria*) or whatever. *Licuados* are made of fruit mixed with water (*licuados de agua*) or milk (*de leche*) in the blender, usually with sugar added. They

Basics

Azucar	Sugar	Pescado	Fish
Carne	Meat	Pimienta	Pepper
Ensalada	Salad	Queso	Cheese
Huevos	Eggs	Sal	Salt
Mantequilla	Butter	Salsa	Sauce
Pan	Bread	Verduras/ Legumbres	Vegetables

Eggs

Fritos	Fried	con Jamon	with Ham
Revueltos	Scrambled	con Tocino	with Bacon
Tibios	Boiled		

a la Mexicana	Scrambled with mild tomato, onion and chile sauce
Rancheros	Fried and smothered in hot chile sauce
Motuleños	Fried, served on a tortilla with ham, cheese and sauce

Soups and starters

Sopa	Soup	Entremeses	Hors d'oeuvres
de Fideos	with Noodles	Caldo	Broth (with bits in)
de Lentejas	Lentil	Consome	Consomme
de Verduras	Vegetable	Ceviche	raw fish salad, marinated in lime juice
de Arroz	Plain Rice		

Fish and seafood (*mariscos*)

Anchoas	Anchovies	Lenguado	Sole
Atun	Tuna	Merluza	Hake
Calamares	Squid	Pez Espada	Swordfish
Camarones	Prawns	Robalo	Bass
Cangrejo	Crab	Sardinas	Sardines
Huachinango	Red Snapper	Trucha	Trout
Langosta	Lobster		

Meat

Alambre	Kebab	Higado	Liver
Bistec	Steak	Lengua	Tongue
Cabrito	Kid	Milanesa	Breaded escalope
Carne (de res)	Beef	Pavo	Turkey
Cerdo	Pork	Pato	Duck

are always fantastic. *Limonada* (fresh lemonade) is also sold in many of these places, as are *aguas frescas* – flavoured cold drinks most commonly found as *horchata* (white and milky, based on tiger nuts), *agua de jamaica* (flavoured with jamaica flowers) or *de tamarindo* (tamarind). These are also often found in restaurants or sold in the streets from great glass jars – though there's no guarantee that the water is pure in the latter.

Tequila, distilled from the Maguey cactus, is of course the most famous of Mexican spirits, usually served straight with lime and salt on the side. Sprinkle the salt on the lime and bite into it, followed by a swig of tequila (or the other way round – there's no correct etiquette). The best stuff is aged (*añejo*) for smoothness; try *Sauza Hornitos*, which is powerful, or *Commemorativo*, which is unexpectedly gentle on the throat. **Mescal** is basically the same drink, but less refined, rougher and younger. **Pulque**, a mildly alcoholic milky beer made from the same cactus, is the traditional drink of the poor – few Western tastes can stomach it. Drinking other **spirits**, you should always specify *nacional* as anything imported (including whisky) is fabulously expensive. Rum

Chuleta	Chop	Pechuga	Breast
Conejo	Rabbit	Pierna	Leg
Cordero	Lamb	Pollo	Chicken
Costilla	Rib	Salchicha	Sausage
Guisado	Stew	Ternera	Veal

Fruit and vegetables

Ciruelas	like yellow cherries	Platano	Banana
Coco	Coconut	Sandia	Watermelon
Frambuesas	Raspberries	Toronja	Grapefruit
Fresas	Strawberries	Tuna	Cactus fruit
Guanabana	Pear-like cactus fruit	Uvas	Grapes
Guayaba	Guava	Aguacate	Avocado
Higos	Figs	Cebolla	Onion
Limon	Lime	Col	Cabbage
Mamey	Pink, sweet and full of pips	Elote	Corn
Mango	Mango	Esparragos	Asparagus
Melocoton	Peach	Frijoles	Beans
Melon	Melon	Hongos	Mushrooms
Naranja	Orange	Lechuga	Lettuce
Papaya	Papaya	Papas	Potatoes
Piña	Pineapple	Pepino	Cucumber
		Tomate	Tomato
		Zanahoria	Carrot

Sweets

Ate	Quince paste	Ensalada de Frutas	Fruit salad
Cajeta	Caramel confection often served with	Flan	like Crême caramel
		Helado	Ice cream
Crepas	Pancakes		

Common terms

Asado	Roast	A la Parilla	Grilled
Al Horno	Baked	Empanado/a	Breaded
A la Veracruzana	usually fish, cooked with tomatoes and onions		
A la Tampiqueña	meat in thin strips served with *guacamole* and *enchiladas*		
Al Mojo de Ajo	fried in garlic and butter		
Barbacoa or Pibil	wrapped in leaves and herbs and steamed/cooked in a pit		
Con Mole	the most famous of Mexican sauces – it contains chile, chocolate and spices. Served with chicken or turkey.		

(*ron*), gin (*ginebra*) and some vodka are made in Mexico, as are some very palatable brandies (*brandy* or *coñac* – try *San Marcos*). Most of the **cocktails** for which Mexico is known – Margaritas, Piña Coladas and so on – are available only in tourist areas or hotel bars. *Sangrita* is a mixture of tomato and fruit juices with tabasco, and is often drunk as an accompaniment to tequila.

For all these, the least heavy atmosphere is in hotel **bars**, tourist areas or anything which describes itself as a Ladies' Bar. Traditional *cantinas* are for serious and excessive drinking, have a thoroughly threatening, macho atmosphere and are barred to women in 99 per cent of cases: there's almost inevitably a sign above the door prohibiting entry to 'women, members of the armed forces and anyone in uniform'. Big cities are to some extent more liberal, but in small and traditional places they remain exclusively male preserves, full of drunken bonhomie which can swing suddenly into threats and fighting.

COMMUNICATION – POST, PHONES AND MEDIA

Mexican **postal services** (*Correos*) are reasonably efficient, and you can have letters held for you at any Post Office. Air mail to Mexico City should arrive within a few days, but it may take a couple of weeks to get to anywhere at all remote. To have mail held, it should be addressed to either *Poste Restante* or *Lista de Correos* at the *Correo Central* (main post office) of any town. The two are not the same in Mexico: **Poste Restante** gets sorted alphabetically and stored behind the counter until you come to collect; mail for the **Lista de Correos** is put on a list published daily and displayed in the Post Office. Since you won't know which day your letters arrive, and will have to go back through the list for several weeks, Poste Restante is probably easier. But things are always being sorted wrongly, so you must check under all your initials (especially the middle one, which is most important in Mexico) – at least on the Lista you get a chance to go through all the names and see if any resemble yours. To collect, you need your passport or some other official ID with a photograph. **American Express** also operate a mail collection service, but they only have three or four offices in Mexico – useful in Mexico City, though, where the address is: *c/o American Express, Hamburgo 75, Mexico 6 D.F.* Officially there's a charge unless you have their travellers' cheques or a card, but they never seem to check.

Sending letters and cards home is also easy enough, if slow, but sending **parcels** out of the country is drowned in bureaucracy. There are regulations about the thickness of brown paper wrapping and the amount of string used, but most importantly, any parcel must be checked by Customs and stamped by at least three other departments, which may take all day. **Telegram** offices (*Telegrafos*) are frequently in the same building. The service is super-efficient, but international ones are very expensive – even if you use the cheaper overnight service. In most cases, you can get across a short message for less by phone.

Local **phone calls**, certainly, are ridiculously cheap – most coin boxes still take 20 centavo coins for three minutes, although they are gradually being converted. **Long-distance** and **international** costs far more – you can make such calls from anywhere displaying a blue and white *Larga Distancia* sign. They're frequently found in bus and railway stations, but in small towns it may be a bar, restaurant or shop. Most *Telefonos* offices also offer the service – 24 hours in Mexico City, Guadalajara and a few other large cities – but the procedure and cost are the same: you're connected by an operator who presents you with a bill afterwards – the cost can usually be seen clicking up on a meter. There is now **direct dialling** to the States and much of Europe, and any reasonably equipped hotel can put you through, but it will almost certainly cost more.

As for keeping in touch in other ways, a daily **English-language newspaper**, the *Mexico City News*, is published in the capital and distributed to larger towns nationwide. There are also free bulletins in English which can be picked up in Mexico City and anywhere with a sizeable tourist population – either in large hotels or from the Tourist Office – and

Time and *Newsweek* are widely available. Few domestic newspapers carry much foreign news, and what there is is mainly American: most are lurid scandal sheets full of bribery and violent crime in full colour. **Radio** stations in the capital and Guadalajara (among others) have programmes in English for a couple of hours each day, and in many places US broadcasts can also be picked up. The BBC World Service beams in this general direction 24 hours a day on various frequencies in the 19m, 25m and 49m Short Wave bands – best reception is in the early evening on 11.75MHz.

OPENING HOURS AND HOLIDAYS

It's almost impossible to generalise about **opening hours** in Mexico, for even when times are posted on museums and shops they're not strictly adhered to. The **siesta**, though, is still widely in evidence, and most places will close for a couple of hours in the early afternoon, usually from 1–3. The strictness of this, however, is very much dependent on the climate: where it's hot – especially on the Gulf Coast and in the Yucatan – everything can close for up to four hours in the middle of the day, and then re-open until 8 or 9 in the evening. In the industrial north and highland areas, hours may be the standard 9–5. **Museums** and galleries, in the most general terms, will be open from about 9–1 and again from 3–6 – many have reduced entry fees on Sundays, but may open only in the morning, and most are **closed on Mondays. Archaeological sites** are usually open right through the day.

The main **public holidays**, when virtually everything will be closed, are: New Year's Day; February 5 (Anniversary of the Constitution); March 21 (Benito Juarez Day); May 1 (Labour Day); May 5 (Battle of Puebla); September 1 (Presidential address to the nation); September 16 (Independence); October 12 (Dia de la Raza/Columbus Day); November 20 (Anniversary of the Revolution); December 12 (Virgin of Guadalupe), and Christmas.

ENTERTAINMENT – FIESTAS, SPORT, MUSIC AND FILM

Stumbling, perhaps accidentally, onto some Mexican village **fiesta** may prove the highlight of your travels. Everywhere, from the remotest Indian village to the most sophisticated city suburb, will take at least one day off a year to devote to partying. Usually it's the local saint's day, but many fiestas have pre-Christian origins and any excuse – from Harvest celebrations to the coming of the rains – will do. Traditional dances and music form an essential part of almost every one, and most include a procession behind some revered holy image or a more celebratory secular parade with fireworks, but the only rule is that no two will be quite the same. The most famous, spectacular or curious are listed at the end of each chapter, but there are many others and certain times of year are celebrated almost everywhere – especially Carnival (the week before Lent); Easter Week; Independence (Sept, 15–16); the Day of the Dead (Nov. 1–2, when offerings are made to ancestors' souls, frequently with picnics and all-night vigils on their graves); and the Christmas period. Local Tourist Offices should have details of anything going on in their area.

The **dances**, complicated and full of ancient symbolism, are often a fiesta's most extraordinary feature. Many of the most famous – including the Yaqui Indian stag dance and the dance of *Los Viejitos* (the little old men) – can be seen at performances of the **Ballet Folklorico** in Mexico City or on tour in the provinces. Many states, too, have regular spectacles put on by regional *folklorico* companies. Information, again, from Tourist Offices.

Mexican **music** has a number of different influences – Spanish, French, American, even African – and is also quite unique. **Mariachi** is the form you are most likely to come across – the sharply dressed bands of trumpeters, violinists and guitarists were traditionally hired by men anxious to serenade their lovers. Nowadays they mostly have their own vocalists and operate in set locations – notably the Plaza Garibaldi in Mexico City or Tlaquepaque in Guadalajara – but you still pay by the song, and you can still take over on vocals should the urge strike (and you know the words). In the north, **norteño** music bears a strong resemblance to traditional country and western – mournful and whining. **Marimba** bands, in the south and in Gulf Coast ports, have a far more Afro-Caribbean sound. Anything more **modern** is imported from the States or, to a lesser extent, South America: Puerto Rican teenage wonderband *Menudo* is an abiding favourite. Otherwise, there seems to be little taste or market for anything even remotely avant-garde, or even for real rock. In **discos**, it's mostly US style aural wallpaper.

As for **sport**, golf, tennis, sailing, surfing, deep-sea fishing – even riding and hunting – are laid on in all the big resorts. The chief spectator sport is of course **football** (soccer), with the 1986 World Cup in Mexico and memories of the same event in 1970, but baseball is also popular, as is American football (especially on TV). **Jai-Alai** (or *Pelota*) is common in the cities, though it's largely a gambler's sport. Mexican **rodeos** (*charreadas*) are as spectacular for their style and costume as they are for the events, while **bullfights** remain an obsession: Mexico's *toreros* are said to be the world's most reckless.

Films are extremely popular and cinemas always packed. In the capital and other major cities foreign feature films are usually in their original language with subtitles; on general release to smaller towns they'll probably be badly dubbed. Things are often released here on trial before they've been seen in the States, and certainly Hollywood films get to Mexico several months before they reach Europe. On **TV** you can watch any number of US shows dubbed into Spanish – it's distinctly bizarre to be walking through some shanty-town as the strains of *Dynasty* come floating across the air. In Mexico City and a few other places there's also **cable** service in English, which some expensive hotels provide in the rooms.

CRAFTS, MARKETS AND BARGAINING

The craft tradition of Mexico, much of it descended directly from objects which were being made long before the Spanish arrived, is still extremely powerful. Regional and highly localised specialities survive, with villages throughout the Republic jealously guarding their reputations – especially in the state of Michoacan and throughout the south, in Oaxaca, Chiapas and the Yucatan. Nowaways there is no need to visit the place of origin: with craft shops in Mexico City and anywhere else the tourists go gathering the best items from around the country. On the other hand it's a great deal more enjoyable to see where the goods come from, and certainly the only way to get any real bargains. The best stuff is rarely cheap wherever you buy it though, and there is an enormous amount of dross produced specifically for tourists. **FONART** shops, in major centres throughout Mexico, are run by a government agency devoted to the promotion and preservation of crafts – their wares are always excellent, if expensive, and they should always be visited to get an idea of what is potentially available.

Among the most popular items are: **silver**, the best of which is made in Taxco although rarely mined there; **pottery**, almost everywhere, with different techniques, designs and patterns in each region; **woollen goods**, especially blankets and *serapes* from Oaxaca, which are again made everywhere – always check the fibres and go for more expensive natural dyes; **leather**, especially tyre-soled *huaraches* (sandals), sold cheaply everywhere; **lacquerware**, particularly from Uruapan; and **hammocks**, the best of which are sold in Merida. Two more recent developments are the markets in pre-hispanic antiquities and fake **designer labels**. There's no reason why you shouldn't buy a *Gucci* handbag or *Lacoste* shirt in Mexico as long as you're aware it's not the real thing. **Antiquities** should be looked at more carefully: invariably they prove to be worthless fakes, but should you stumble on anything authentic it is illegal to buy or sell it, and even more illegal to try taking it out of the country.

For bargain hunters, the **market** is the place to head – there's a marketplace in every Mexican town, which on one day of the week, the traditional market day, will be at its busiest with villagers from the surrounding area bringing their produce in for sale or barter. On the whole, of course, markets are full of food and everyday necessities, but most have a section devoted to crafts, or in larger towns you may find a separate crafts market. Unless you're a complete no-hoper at bargaining, prices will always be lower here than in shops, but **shops** do have a couple of advantages. Firstly, they operate a degree of quality control, whereas any old junk can be sold in the market, and secondly, many established shops will be able to ship purchases home for you, which saves an enormous amount of the frustrating bureaucracy you'll encounter if you attempt to do it yourself.

Bargaining and haggling are very much a matter of personal style, highly dependent on your command of Spanish or lack of it, and to some extent on experience. The old chestnuts (never show the least sign of interest, let alone enthusiasm; walking away will always cut the price dramatically) do still hold true; but most important is to know what you want, its approximate value, and how much you are prepared to pay. And never start to haggle for something you definitely don't intend to buy – it'll end in bad feelings on both sides. In shops there's little chance of significantly altering the official price unless you're buying in bulk, and even in markets most food and simple household goods have a set price (though it may be doubled at the sight of an approaching Gringo).

For ordinary shopping and your **everyday needs**, you can buy just about anything in Mexico that would be available in Europe or the States. Food and basic items are almost always cheaper, but luxuries, electrical goods and just about anything imported will be more expensive. **Film** and camera equipment is a good example – available, but at a price. Up to twelve rolls of film can be brought in, and spare batteries are also a wise precaution. **Books** in English – a rather limited selection – are sold in all tourist areas and often in major or university bookshops (see local listings). Branches of *Sanborn's* always carry a good stock.

TROUBLE, POLICE AND BRIBERY

Despite soaring **crime** rates and some statistics which make dismal reading, you are unlikely to run into any trouble in Mexico. Even in Mexico City, which has an appalling reputation, you are far safer than you would be in most large cities in the States, and overall there is no more threat than there would be in much of Europe. Obviously there are areas of the cities where you wander alone, or at night, at your peril; but the precautions to be taken are mostly common sense and would be second nature at home. Petty **theft** and **pickpockets** are your biggest worry, so don't flash money about, try not to look too obviously affluent, don't leave cash or cameras in hotel rooms, and when travelling keep an eye on your bags (which are safe enough in the luggage compartments underneath most buses). **Drivers** are more likely to encounter problems – to avoid the worst always park legally (and preferably off the street) and never leave anything visibly lying about in the car.

Drug offences are the most common cause of serious trouble – under heavy pressure from the US government to stamp out the trade, Mexican authorities are particularly happy to throw the book at foreign offenders. You can expect a lengthy jail sentence for possession of even relatively small quantities, no sympathy and little help from your consulate. The Mexican **legal system** is based on the Napoleonic Code, and it assumes your guilt until you can prove otherwise: your one phone call should you be jailed should be to the Consulate – if nothing else they'll arrange an English-speaking lawyer. Mexican **jails** are grim, although lots of money and friends on the outside can ameliorate matters slightly, and you can be held for up to 72 hours on suspicion before charges have to be brought.

In short, always back off in any sort of

confrontation, and always be extremely polite to the police. Mexican **police** are, in the ordinary run of events, no better nor worse than any other; but they are badly paid, and graft is an accepted part of the job. It often comes hard to foreigners, but it is a system, and in its own way it works well enough. If a policeman accuses you of some violation (and this is almost bound to happen to drivers at some stage), explain that you're a tourist, not used to the ways of the country – you may get off scot free, but more likely the subject of a 'fine' will come up. Such on-the-spot fines are open to negotiation, but only if you're confident you've done nothing seriously wrong and reasonably in command of Spanish. Otherwise pay up and get out. These small **bribes** are known as *mordidas* (little bites), and they may also be extracted by border officials or bureaucrats – far more common is the *propina*, or tip, a payment which is made entirely on your initiative. There's no need to do this, but it's remarkable how often a few pesos can oil the wheels, complete paperwork which would otherwise take weeks, or open doors which before were firmly locked. All such transactions are quite open, and it's up to you to literally put your money on the table.

Should a crime be committed against you – in particular **if you're robbed** – your relationship with the police will obviously be a different one, although even in this eventuality it's worth considering whether the lengthy hassles you'll go through make it worth reporting. Some insurance companies will insist on a police report if you're to get any refund – in which case you may have practically to dictate it to the officer and can expect little action – but others will understand the situation. *American Express* in Mexico, for example, accept without a murmur the fact that your cheques have been stolen but not reported to the police.

For listings of **Embassies and Consulates**, see under *Other Things* and the details of individual cities.

SEXUAL HARASSMENT

So many oppressive limitations are imposed on women's freedom to travel together or alone that any advice or warning seems merely to reinforce the situation. That said, **machismo** is ingrained in the Mexican mentality and although to some extent it's softened by the gentler mores of Indian culture, a degree of harassment is inevitable. On the whole this will be limited to comments in the street, but even situations which might be quite routine at home can seem threatening without a clear understanding of the minutiae of Mexican Spanish. To avoid getting further in, provocation should be ignored totally – Mexican women are rarely slow with a stream of abuse, but it's a dangerous course unless you're very sure of your ground.

Any problems are amplified in the big tourist spots – especially Acapulco – where the legendary 'easy' tourists attract droves of sharks. Mexico City, too, can feel very heavy. Away from the big cities, though, and especially in Indian areas, there is rarely any problem at all – you may be treated as an object of curiosity, as an outsider (or even resented) but not necessarily with any implied or intended sexual threat. And wherever you come across it, such curiosity can also extend to great friendliness and hospitality.

Drinking – or rather the restrictions imposed on it – is the most constantly irksome symbol: women are simply and absolutely barred from the vast majority of *cantinas*, and even in so-called *Ladies' Bars* 'unescorted' women may be looked at askance or even refused service. Carry a bottle is the only answer, since in small towns the *cantina* may also be the only place which sells them.

Despite everything, there's a growing and radical **feminist movement** in Mexico – though still largely concentrated in the capital: CIDHAL (*Communicacion, Intercambio y Desarollo Humano en America Latina*; Apartado 579, Cuernavaca 62000, Morelos) is among the largest of their organisations. Other contacts include GAMU (*Autonomous Group of University Women*; Colovenes 97, Jardines de San Mateo, Maucalpan, Mexico D.F.) and the *Union Nacional de Mujeres Mexicanas* (Bucareli 12508, Mexico 1 D.F.). There's a Women's Centre at 122 Calle 17, San Pedro de los Pinos, Mexico D.F. *Revuelta* (Vicente

Tones 156, Coyoacan, Mexico 21 D.F.) is a feminist publication. Finally, from the States, *Womantour* (5314 N Figueroa Street, Los Angeles, CA 90042; tel. 213–255 1115) run **tours** to Mexico for women, in groups or individually.

OTHER THINGS

ADDRESSES in Mexico are frequently written with just the street name and number (as: *Madero 125*), which can lead to confusion as many streets are known only as numbers (*Calle 17*). *Calle* means street; *Avenida*, *Calzada* and *Paseo* are other common terms – most are named after historical personages or dates. An address such as *Hidalgo 39 8° 120*, means number 39, 8th floor, room 120.

BEGGARS are surprisingly rare in Mexico – especially when you consider that there's no social security worth mentioning and that most Mexicans are very generous towards them. What you will see, though, are people selling worthless trinkets, or who climb onto buses or trains, sing a song, and take a collection.

CONTRACEPTION Condoms (*Profilacticos*) are available in just about every Mexican *farmacia.* You can also get most brands of the pill, but only on prescription, so it's wise to bring enough – incidentally if you're suffering from relatively severe diarrhoea the pill (or any other drug) may not be in your system long enough to be absorbed, and consequently may become ineffective.

DRUGS A good deal of Cannabis – that famous Acapulco Gold – continues to be cultivated despite US-backed government attempts to stamp it out. But it's illegal, and foreigners caught in possession are dealt with harshly: with quantities reckoned to be dealable you can wave goodbye to daylight for a long time. It may also have been sprayed with Paraquat. Other naturally occurring drugs – hallucinogenic mushrooms which can be found around Oaxaca and in Chiapas, and *peyote* from the northern deserts (very occasionally found dried in markets) – still form an important part of many Indian rituals, and the authorities turn a blind eye. Though their use is theoretically illegal, too, you're unlikely to get into much difficulty over personal use – as long as you know where to find the things, and how to recognise them once you have.

ELECTRICITY in Mexico is theoretically 110 volts, with simple two pin plugs, so most US appliances can be used as they are. Anything from Britain will need a transformer and probably a plug adapter as well. Cuts in service and wild fluctuations in the current, though, are common, and in cheap hotels any sort of large appliance will blow all the fuses as soon as it's switched on.

EMBASSIES AND CONSULATES are mostly listed under the cities where they occur. As well as Mexico City, where just about every nation has an Embassy, there are British Consular services in Acapulco, Guadalajara, Mazatlan, Merida, Monterrey, Tampico, Torreon and Veracruz; US officials in all of these plus Cancun, Oaxaca, Puerto Vallarta, San Luis Potosí and most border cities; Canadian ones in Acapulco and Guadalajara.

EMERGENCIES Dial 06 for the Police emergency operator. Most phone booths should give the number for the local Red Cross (*Cruz Roja*).

GAY LIFE Apparently there are no laws at all governing homosexuality in Mexico, and hence it's legal. There are gay bars and clubs in the major resorts and in Mexico City, elsewhere you should be discreet to avoid upsetting macho sensibilities: 'of course if you wear pink satin trousers in the street', the Mexican Embassy told me, 'you'll be beaten up'.

LAUNDRY Self-service launderettes (*lavanderias automaticas*) are rare except in the big cities, but any hotel can point you to someone who takes in washing, and more expensive ones invariably offer their own laundry service. If you're doing your own, something to use as a plug is useful (they're hardly ever provided) as is some kind of concentrated liquid detergent (like *Dylon Travel Wash*) which saves on weight and leaking powder. A dry cleaner's is a *tintoreria*.

ODD ESSENTIALS Insect repellent is a must – especially for the coasts – and a flashlight and alarm clock may also be useful. Above all, toilet paper.

TAMPAX are sold at *farmacias*, usually by brand name.

TIME ZONES Most of Mexico is on the equivalent of US Central Standard Time (7 hrs earlier than London), but with no seasonal changes. Baja California, however, and the north-west coastal states of Sonora, Sinaloa and Nayarit (i.e. Chapter 1 of this book) are 1 hr earlier.

TIPS are hardly ever added to bills, and the amount is entirely up to you – in cheap places if you tip at all it's just the loose change; expensive joints tend to expect their full 12 per cent. Don't tip taxi drivers.

TOILETS Public ones are almost always filthy, and there's never any paper (though someone may sell it outside). They're known usually as *baños* (literally bathrooms) or as *excusados*, *sanitarios* or *servicios*: the most common signs are *Damas* (Ladies) and *Caballeros* (Gentlemen), though you may find the more confusing *Señoras* (Women) and *Señores* (Men).

TURISMO Tourist Offices are run by various organisations, federal, state and local. Most are helpful, some are not.

WATER A surprising amount of tap water is drinkable, but if you're not sure don't. Purified water should always be provided in hotels and restaurants. C (for *Caliente*) is hot, F (for *Fría*) cold.

WORK There's virtually no chance of finding work in Mexico unless you have some very specialist skill and have set it up beforehand. Work permits are impossible to get. Of what foreigners there are, the majority work in language schools. It would be possible, though not legal, to earn some money as an English instructor by simply advertising in a local newspaper or on noticeboards at a University.

GLOSSARY OF COMMON MEXICAN TERMS

AHORITA diminutive of *ahora* (now) meaning right now – usually a couple of hours at least.

ALAMEDA city park or promenade; large plaza.

AYUNTAMIENTO town hall/government.

AZTEC the tribe who dominated the central valleys of Mexico from the thirteenth century and whose empire was defeated by Cortes.

BARRIO area within a town or city; suburb.

CHAC Mayan god of rain.

CHARRO a Mexican cowboy.

CHURRIGUERESQUE highly elaborate, decorative form of baroque architecture (usually in churches).

CONVENTO either convent or monastery.

DESCOMPUESTO out of order.

DON/DOÑA courtesy titles (sir/madam), mostly used in letters or for professional people or the boss.

FONART government agency to promote crafts.

GRINGO not necessarily insulting, though it does imply American – said to come from invading US troops, either because they wore green coats or because they sang '*Green grow the rushes oh!. . .*'.

HUITZILOPOCHTLI Aztec god of war.

I.V.A. 15 per cent sales tax.

MALECON seafront promenade.

MALINCHE Cortes's Indian interpreter and mistress, a symbol of treachery.

MARIACHI type of music originally from Guadalajara.

MARIMBA xylophone-like musical instrument, also used of the bands based around it and the style of music.

MAYA tribe who inhabited Honduras, Guatemala and South-Eastern Mexico from earliest times, and still do.

METATE flat stone for grinding corn.

MIXTEC tribe from the mountains of Oaxaca.

MOCTEZUMA Montezuma, penultimate Aztec leader.

MUELLE jetty or dock.

NAHUATL ancient Aztec language, still the most common after Spanish.

NORTEÑO literally northern – style of food and music.

PALACIO mansion, but not necessarily royal. PALACIO MUNICIPAL is the headquarters of local government, PALACIO DE GOBIERNO of state/federal authorities.

PAN *Partido de Accion Nacional*, largest opposition party, conservative and allied to the US Republicans; recently gained surprise election victories in the north.

PASEO a broad avenue, but also the ritual evening walk around the plaza.

PLANTA BAJA ground floor – abbreviated PB in lifts.

PLATERESQUE elaborately decorative renaissance architectural style.

PORFIRIANO neo-classical architecture from the time of Porfirio Diaz's dictatorship – especially grandiose theatres.

PRI *Partido Revolucionario Institucional*, the ruling party.

QUETZALCOATL the plumed serpent, most powerful, enigmatic and widespread of all ancient Mexican gods.

STELE free-standing carved stone.

TENOCHTITLAN the Aztec capital.

TEOTIHUACAN ancient city north of the capital – the first major urban power of Central Mexico.

TIANGUIS Nahuatl word for market, still used of particularly varied marketplaces.

TLALOC Toltec/Aztec rain god.

TOLTEC tribe which controlled Central Mexico between Teotihuacan and the Aztecs, from their capital TULA.

VIRREINAL from the period of the Viceroys – colonial.

ZAPOTEC tribe which controlled the Oaxaca region to about 700AD.

ZOCALO the main plaza of any town.

Part two

THE GUIDE

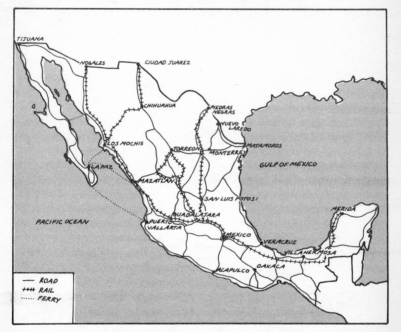

Map legend:
- ROAD
- +++ RAIL
- ...... FERRY

Place names: TIJUANA, NOGALES, CIUDAD JUAREZ, CHIHUAHUA, PIEDRAS NEGRAS, NUEVO LAREDO, LOS MOCHIS, TORREON, MONTERREY, MATAMOROS, LA PAZ, MAZATLAN, SAN LUIS POTOSI, GUADALAJARA, PUERTO VALLARTA, MEXICO, VERACRUZ, MERIDA, VILLAHERMOSA, ACAPULCO, OAXACA, GULF OF MEXICO, PACIFIC OCEAN

Chapter one
BAJA CALIFORNIA AND THE NORTH PACIFIC

Mexico's north-west is something of a bizarre – and initially uninviting – introduction to the country. Aspects of what you see here will be echoed constantly as you travel further south, yet in many ways it's resolutely untypical: at one and the same time desert and the country's most fertile agricultural area – wealthy and heavily Americanised yet drab and apparently barren.

Travelling overland from the US west coast you're clearly going to come this way, but on the whole the best advice is to hurry through the northern part at least: once you've crossed the invisible line of the Tropic of Cancer there's a tangible change – the country is softer and greener, the climate less harsh. Here you begin to come on places which could be regarded as destinations in their own right, where you might be tempted to stay some time, rather than as a night or two's relief from the rigours of constant travel: the all-out resort of **Mazatlan**, in particular, or the quieter Pacific beaches around **San Blas**. There's a straightforward **choice of routes**, down from Tijuana through the Baja peninsula and on by ferry, or around by the mainland road, sticking to the coast all the way or possibly cutting up into central Mexico, either by the magnificent railway from Los Mochis to Chihuahua, or by road from Mazatlan to Durango. The latter is quicker if your only aim is to get towards Mexico City, but the Baja route is perhaps slightly less monotonous and, surprisingly, cheaper – the ferries cost virtually nothing if you go as a simple deck passenger.

Baja California has plenty of fanatical devotees; trouble is, most of them arrive in light planes or in vehicles capable of heading off across the punishing desert tracks, laden down with fishing and scuba gear. Without these, it's impossible to get to most of the peninsula's undeniable attractions – completely isolated beaches, pre-historic cave paintings in the hilly interior, excellent fishing and snorkelling. On the bus all you can do is pound down Highway One – still a relatively new road, and low on facilities. The early colonists believed California to be an island and, after failing to find any great riches or to make much impact in converting the Indians, they left it pretty much alone – there's little of historic interest beyond a few old mission centres, and almost all you see

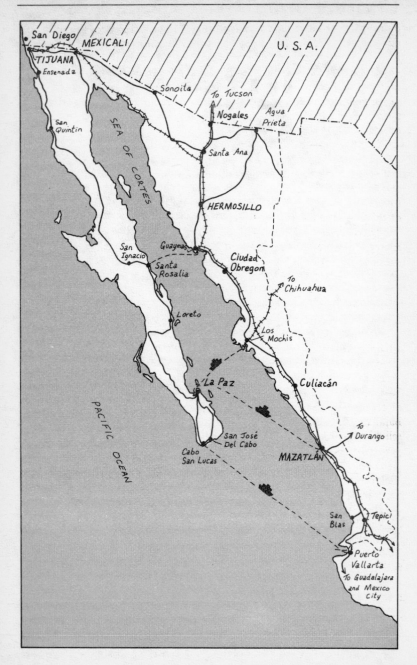

dates from the latter half of this century, in particular since the road was opened in 1973. Still, there are beautiful beaches which you can get to in the south, more crowded ones around Tijuana in the north, and if you're heading straight for the big Pacific resorts – Puerto Vallarta and on towards Acapulco – it makes a lot more sense to come this way. Early in the year you can witness extraordinary scenes at Scammon's Lagoon, near Guerrero Negro, when hordes of **whales** congregate close offshore to spawn.

On the **mainland route**, too, most people stick rigidly to the highway – over 2,000 km of it from Tijuana to Tepic where the main road finally leaves the coast to cut through the mountains to Guadalajara. But here at least you're not forced to; it's a relatively populous area and from towns all along the route there are local buses to villages in the foothills of the Sierras or down to beaches along the Sea of Cortes and, later, the Pacific. Then again you can leave the coast entirely, heading inland by road or rail over the mountains. On the whole though, the equation is a simple one, the further south you get the more enticing the land becomes and for the first stages it's a question of getting as far in one go as you can stand. By the time you reach **Mazatlan**, an enormous and growing resort, the pace becomes more relaxed and you'll increasingly come on things to detain you – village fiestas, tropical beaches, mountain excursions. **Beyond Tepic** you're faced with the choice of following the mainstream and heading inland towards the central highlands, or sticking to the coast – a perfectly feasible road all the way to Acapulco and beyond.

As everywhere, **buses** are the most efficient and fastest form of transport: they run constantly down the entire length of the coast road, and direct from Nogales or Tijuana to Mexico City, frequently down through Baja. *Tres Estrellas de Oro* has most services and is the most consistently reliable operator throughout, but none of the others is bad, with *Pacifico* perhaps having the edge when it comes to the number of buses whose air-conditioning actually works. The **train**, from Nogales and (less easily) Mexicali to Guadalajara, is practicable and perhaps more comfortable if you plan to make the journey non-stop; progress, though, is slow and sweaty – take, by preference, the 'express' *El Costeño*. If you're **driving**, it's very much quicker to head through Nogales – even if you're coming from the West Coast you'll save considerably by taking US highways via Tucson. Heading down through Baja you could be delayed for a day or two trying to get your car onto a ferry – book ahead if at all possible. **Hitching** should be regarded here only as a last resort: long-distance traffic is moving fast and reluctant to stop, and it's exceedingly hot if you get stranded by the roadside. The north is also the area where most of the 'disappearing gringo' horror stories originate.

Crossing the border, do not forget to go through immigration and customs checks. As everywhere, there's a free zone south of the frontier, and you can cross at will. Highly embarrassing, though, when you're stopped some 20 kilometers inland and sent back to get your Tourist Card stamped.

TIJUANA AND THE BAJA PENINSULA

TIJUANA

TIJUANA is *the* Mexican border town. Every virtue and every vice that that implies is here in abundance. Almost 20 million people cross the border every year – the vast majority of them staying only a few hours – so that Tijuana can boast with some justification of being the 'World's Most Visited City'. Which is not to say it's somewhere you should plan to hang around; it's the lowest common denominator they're catering for here. At the same time, if you want to stop somewhere before heading off on the long trek south, Tijuana is certainly the most practical choice and there's no shortage of reasonable hotels although, as you'd expect, most things are considerably more expensive than they are further south.

Above all the town is geared towards dealing with hordes of Californian day trippers, which means hundreds of tacky souvenir stands, cheap doctors, dentists and auto-repair shops and countless bars and restaurants, pricey by Mexican standards but cheaper than anything you'll find in San Diego. One thing you won't find any more – at least not anywhere near the centre of town – is the prostitution and the sex shows for which the border towns used to be notorious. This is partly the result of a conscious attempt to clean the city up, partly due to the changing climate in the States: indeed in many places, though not visibly here, the traffic now runs in the other direction with vast hoardings on the American side of the border offering lurid invitations to 'Total nudity – 24 hours a day'. Tijuana does still thrive on **gambling** though, with horseracing every weekend, greyhound racing every evening except Tuesday and Jai Alai every night except Thursday in the huge *Fronton Palacio*. There are also **bullfights** throughout the summer (May to September) at two rings, one right on the coast, the other in the centre of town.

The latest attraction to add to these is the **Centro Cultural Fonapas**, a spectacularly threatening globe of a building which looks like nothing so much as a huge nuclear reactor dumped in the city centre. Inside there's a museum which is supposed to be an introduction to Mexican culture and art, and is not at all bad at achieving that object despite the fact that almost everything you see is a reproduction. There are also regular exhibitions, shows and a daily multi-media spectacular: another potted introduction to Mexico, it's on in English (and very expensive) every evening, in Spanish (much cheaper) in the afternoons.

Getting to Tijuana is really no problem, although as in so many places the new **bus station** has been built miles from the centre. If you're coming from the States and plan to carry straight on through, both *Greyhound* and *Trailways* have services which will take you across the border to the bus station. On the US side the main bus terminus is right by the crossing and there's excellent local transport into Downtown SAN DIEGO – buses and trams (the brand new 'San Diego Trolley') run every few minutes. If you're heading further north in the States there's a frequent service of Mexican vans and minibuses to LOS ANGELES – wander round the car park on the Mexican side of the border and one of the drivers will accost you – it's quicker, and often cheaper, than the bus. To get from the border (LA LINEA) to the bus station take a local bus marked '*Buen Vista, Central Camionera*' – in the other direction it's '*Centro, La Linea*'.

The **centre of town** is only a short walk from the border crossing, and most of the cheaper places to stay are equally close, immediately around the main shopping street, Av. Revolucion. From the frontier simply follow the pedestrian signs which lead you to the right and over the main road on a walkway. You'll see the sign for the old *Tres Estrellas de Oro* bus station, and on the road which leads up past this – Av. Madero – there are three small **hotels**, all reasonable, and several others in the sidestreets a little further up (especially Calle 3) though these tend to be either more expensive or less enticing. Continue on Madero where it goes past the back of the Crafts Market and you'll find some more places, again small and perfectly comfortable.

If you want to get to a **beach**, the best are at **ROSARITO** about half an hour's bus ride on the road to Ensenada; beaches in Tijuana itself are invariably crowded and dirty. Rosarito, while scarcely less popular, has a far bigger, sandier strand and a much more restful atmosphere. This coast road – now supplanted by the motorway to Ensenada – is lined with seaside villas and suburban hamlets but it remains quite an attractive drive and if you're heading south you can stop over in Rosarito before continuing to ENSENADA to pick up the long-distance buses.

SOUTH TO LA PAZ

ENSENADA, just a couple of hours on from Tijuana by the new toll road, is favoured by those sophisticated Californians who are 'in the know' about where to go in Mexico. That's to say it's cheaper, raunchier, less totally geared to visitors, but still with a pretty clear idea of the value of the Yankee dollar. Certainly it's no more attractive than Tijuana, though it does at least have some life of its own as a major port and fish processing centre.

The docks are right alongside the main tourist drag, **Av. Mateos**, and this is the place to head for if you aim to stop here. Mateos and **Av. Juarez** – parallel to it on the landward side – are the centre of what limited interest there is, mostly confined to souvenir shops and outfits offering 'sport fishing' trips. On these streets, too, are all of Ensenada's **hotels** and a crowd of sleazy bars – prices tend to drop as you walk northwards with some of the cheapest places on and around C. Castelum where the clientele are largely local dockers and visiting seamen; not for nervous new arrivals to the country.

Apart from fishing enthusiasts and artefact hunters, Ensenada also attracts its share of surfers and beach boys, though as you'll find throughout Baja it really pays to have your own transport. The best beaches are at ESTERO, some 10 km to the south, off the main road. There are occasional local buses. To the south, too, is **La Bufadora**, a remarkable natural blow-hole or geyser where the action of wind, waves and tide periodically forces a huge jet of sea water up through a small vent in the roof of an undersea cavern. Again, this is more than 20km off the main road, and not easy to get to.

Beyond Ensenada and you're really into Baja California proper – barren, god-forsaken and drab. At times the road runs along the coast, but for the most part the scenery is dry brown desert, the peninsula's low mountain spine to the left, around the road nothing but sand and the occasional scrubby cactus. The towns are for the most part drab, dusty and windswept collections of single storey shacks which belie their supposed wealth. **SAN QUINTIN** is no exception, though it boasts a vast *El Presidente* hotel. **Bahia San Quintin**, however, is undeniably attractive, with a series of small sandy beaches and endless fishing. Yet again, you can't get there without your own transport and the couple of **motels**, when you do, are pricey.

From San Quintin to GUERRERO NEGRO at the border of Baja California Sur is almost 400km of unrelieved tedium, the road cutting far enough inland to deny anything but the most occasional glimpse of the ocean. Rather over halfway is the turn-off for BAHIA DE LOS ANGELES, a growing (but still very basic) resort on the Sea of Cortes; most people who get there still arrive in their own planes rather than by road. **GUERRERO NEGRO**, when it comes, offers little in the way of respite. Flat and fly-blown, it's an important centre for the production of salt and surrounded by vast salt pans and stark storage warehouses. Off the coast to the south, though, can be witnessed one of Mexico's most extraordinary natural phenomena when, in January and February above all, scores of **California Grey Whales** congregate to spawn. They can be watched (at remarkably close quarters – the young are often left stranded on the beaches) from an area which has been newly designated a national park. At the right times of year there are organised trips, otherwise you can only reach the shore here in a jeep so check with the tourist authorities first.

At any other time grab a drink in the bus station and keep going to **SAN IGNACIO**. At the very centre of the peninsula – in both directions – this is an oasis in every sense of the word; not only green and shaded but, with some of the few colonial buildings in Baja, a genuinely attractive little place. The town was founded by the Jesuits (and named after their founder) in 1728 but the area had always been populated by Guaicura Indians attracted by the tiny stream, the only fresh water for hundreds of miles. San Ignacio's church, built when the place was first settled, is probably the best example of colonial architecture in the whole of Baja California, and there are other ancient buildings around it and the shaded plaza. Early missionaries were responsible too for the palms which give the town its special character, and as well as their dates the town produces limes, grapes and olives.

In the bleak Sierras to north and south are any number of **caves**, many of them decorated with **ancient paintings**. Not much is known about the provenance of these amazing designs, beyond the fact that they were painted at different periods and bear little resemblance to any other known art in this part of the world. Indian legend, as related to the earliest colonists, has it that they are the product of a race of giants from the north. Certainly many of the human figures – most paintings depict hunters and their prey – are well over six feet tall. They are, however, extremely hard to visit, reached only by tracks or mule paths and impossible to find without a guide. If you're sufficiently determined, and prepared for some serious hiking, guides can be arranged through one of the two chief **hotels**, the *El Presidente* or the *Posada San Ignacio*. If you plan to stay, the latter is the place to head for, although by no stretch of the imagination could it be described as cheap.

The road continues to **SANTA ROSALIA** on the east coast, terminal for the ferry to GUAYMAS (see p. 40). An odd little place, built as a port to ship copper from nearby French-run mines, it still has something of a temporary look, many of its buildings strikingly un-Mexican in aspect. The mines are virtually played out (though they do still operate) but much of the paraphernalia still lies around the town, including a rusting narrow-gauge railway. **Ferries** leave three times a week for the overnight trip to GUAYMAS, and there are a couple of reasonable **hotels** if you're stuck here waiting. The *Hotel Central*, on the main plaza, is probably the best.

Some 60km to the south lies **MULEGE**, a small village on the site of an ancient mission which in many ways resembles a rather less interesting San Ignacio; pleasant enough, though, and the coast nearby has long been popular with anglers. Better if you're looking for somewhere to stay to continue to **LORETO**. Founded in 1697 as the head of the Jesuit missions to California, and later taken over by the Franciscans, it was in practice the administrative capital of the entire territory for some 150 years. Nowadays it's enjoying something of a renaissance as a resort, boosted by the development of southern Baja California, but as with so much of Baja there's more to interest fishermen and scuba enthusiasts than simple beach bums. There is, however, a **beach** of sorts in town and if you've got transport there are some great stretches of sand a few miles to the south – good camping territory too. The original **mission church** is still standing, and though heavily restored after centuries of earthquake damage its basic structure – solid, squat and simple – is little changed. Next door there's a small museum chronicling the early conversion and colonisation of California. All the **hotels** are relatively expensive, but for what you get they're not bad value, catering as they do mainly for diving buffs and people who know the area well.

From LORETO it's five more long hours on the bus before you get to LA PAZ, and if you're confined to the main road there's really nothing to detain you.

LA PAZ

Everyone ends up in **LA PAZ** eventually, if only to get the ferry out – and it seems that most of the population of Baja California Sur is gravitating here too. The outskirts are an ugly sprawl, their development outpacing the spread of paved roads and facilities. But the town centre, modernised as it is, has still managed to preserve something of its quiet colonial atmosphere and small town pace. Down by the sea you can stroll along the waterfront *Malecon*, and for once the beach in town looks inviting enough to swim from – though I make no guarantees for the cleanliness of the water.

The Bay of La Paz was explored by Cortes himself in the first years after the Conquest – drawn, as always, by tales of great wealth – but he found little to interest him and, despite successive expeditions, at first merely rapacious, later missionary, La Paz wasn't permanently settled until the end of the eighteenth century. It grew rapidly, however, thanks to the riches of the surrounding sea, and above all as a pearl fishing centre. American troops occupied the town during the Texan war, and six years later it was again invaded – by William Walker in one of his many attempts to carve himself out a Central American kingdom; by this time it was already capital of the territory of California. The pearl trade has pretty much dried up – a mystery disease having wiped out most of the oysters – but since the 1960s La Paz has continued to boom, buoyed up by tourists at first flown in, then boosted by the growing ferry service and now supplemented by the hordes pouring down Highway One.

There's not a great deal to see and if you're staying for any length of time you should aim to head for some of the beaches to the south, but if you're just hanging around for one of the ferries you can happily fill a day wandering around the centre looking in the shops (of which there are hundreds taking advantage of the duty-free zone), and the market. There are hundreds of places to eat, too, and some of the seafood is excellent. Most of the cheaper **hotels** are within a few blocks of the Zocalo. My own favourite is the *Posada San Miguel*, downhill and to the left from the Zocalo on C. Belisario Dominguez but there are others all around – try the *Hotel Yneka* near the main plaza on Francisco Madero, the *Ulloa* on C. Aguiles Serdan or the *San Carlos* on the corner of Revolucion and 16 de Septiembre. The **Tourist Office** is on the Zocalo, while the **long-distance bus station** is miles out in the suburbs. I've arrived here in the middle of the night and had to walk into town, but I wouldn't recommend it – during the day there are buses (*Centro/Camionera*) or you could try to get a taxi.

If you're leaving on the **ferry** for MAZATLAN or TOPOLOBAMPO (the port for Los Mochis) you should buy tickets at the downtown ticket office on Calle Victoria. Do this as soon as is practical if you're hoping to take a car or get a place in a cabin, as these are often oversubscribed; I've never heard of any problems for straight foot passengers. To get to the ferry itself (which sails from the terminal at Pichilingui, some 14 kms away) go to the old bus station on the *Malecon* – straight down Independencia from the Zocalo – and get there early. There are usually only two buses for each sailing – not enough to cram everyone in – and they leave at least three hours before the boat to allow time for interminable customs and immigration checks before embarkation. It's an infuriating system, not least because the bus ride is relatively expensive, but you've little choice unless you're prepared to shell out for a taxi. One consolation is that the ferry itself is ludicrously cheap if you go as an ordinary foot passenger – only about three dollars for the 16-hour ride. And this is definitely the best way to go: most of the boats seem to be Danish, designed for the icy conditions of the North Sea run, and are sealed tight, scarcely air-conditioned and get unbearably hot even at night. Half the passengers who've paid extra for cabins end up on deck with everyone else rather than stick it out in their private steam baths. Food on board is terrible, so stock up in La Paz.

LOS CABOS

LOS CABOS, the series of capes and beaches around the southern tip of the peninsula, is one of the fastest developing tourist areas in Mexico – heavily promoted by the authorities and a boom area for the big hotel chains and resort builders. Undeniably it is stunningly beautiful, but equally undeniably it's not a place for the penniless traveller to venture unprepared. Almost everything beyond La Paz is purpose-built – the one slight exception being **SAN JOSE DEL CABO** where there are some signs of a town that existed as a mission, an agricultural centre and a small port before the tourists arrived. Though fast being swamped, the old plaza and the Paseo Mijares are still more or less intact and there's a small museum in the *Casa de la Cultura*.

More than can be said for **CABO SAN LUCAS**, at the southernmost tip of California, from where the **ferry for Puerto Vallarta** sails twice a week (Sunday and Wednesday at 4pm). This is pure resort and there's nowhere reasonably priced to stay at all: you may find yourself joining many others sleeping out on the dockside or, properly equipped, you could camp on nearby beaches. It's a pity, because with its great sands and fascinating marine life Cabo San Lucas could otherwise be one of the most attractive spots in Baja. If you do stop here, or have a day to kill before the ferry, then take the excursion by small boat to the huge **rock arch** where the Sea of Cortes meets the Pacific – an extraordinary place, with a clear division between the shallower turquoise waters on the left and the profound blue of the ocean on the right. A colony of sea lions lives on the rocks round-about, and most trips, too, take in a stay on one of the small surrounding beaches.

THE MAINLAND ROUTE

EL GRAN DESIERTO: MEXICALI

If the peninsula of Baja California is desolate, the northern part of the state – to Mexicali and beyond into northern Sonora – is infinitely, spectacularly, more so. The drive from TIJUANA to MEXICALI is worthwhile for the extraordinary views alone as the mountains suddenly drop away to reveal hundreds of miles of desert and the huge salt lake below. This is '*El Gran Desierto*' and it's a startlingly sudden change: the western escarpment up from Tijuana through TECATE (where the beer comes from) and beyond is relatively fertile and climbs deceptively gently, but the rains from the Pacific never get as far as the eastern edge where the land falls away dizzily to the burnt plain and the road teeters between crags seemingly scraped bare by the ferocity of the sun. The heat at the bottom is incredible, the road down terrifying – its constant precipices made worse by the piles of twisted metal at the bottom of each one of them.

MEXICALI too is hot – unbearably so in summer – but despite its natural disadvantages it's a large, wealthy city, the capital of Baja California Norte and an important road and rail junction for the crossing into the States. There's an exotic ring to the name – Mexicali – but nothing exotic about the place and if you come looking for a movieland border town, swing-door saloons and dusty dirt streets, you'll be disappointed. There's more chance of choking to death on exhaust fumes or getting run over trying to cross the street. Even the name, it turns out, is a fake, a sweet-sounding hybrid of Mexico and California with an appalling bastard sister across the border – Calexico. I've never found any reason to stop here except possibly to prepare for the next stage south, a daunting trip of at least 9 hours to HERMOSILLO, the first place you might remotely choose to take a break.

From the **bus station** to the **centre** (or vice versa) take a *Calle 3A* bus, which passes the **rail terminus** on its way in. The border runs right alongside the commercial downtown area, and it's just a short walk from the crossing into the centre of town. You'll find no shortage of low-priced **hotels and eating places** down here in the older streets around the market; some of the best value places to stay are along Avenida de la Reforma. **Trains** leave for Guadalajara twice a day (8am and 9pm), but even in *primera reservada* it's a slow, sweaty and suffocating journey down this coastal line and I'd strongly counsel the **bus** which has regular departures day and night and is infinitely faster. If you're en route to or from the USA there's no need to go into town at all – buses run direct to and from Mexicali's bus station.

Beyond Mexicali the rail lines cut south around the northern edge of the Sea of Cortes, while the road trails the border westwards – between them rises the *Sierra del Pinacate*, an area so desolate that it was used by American astronauts to simulate lunar conditions. There's virtually no place of any size on the rail route, although the little port of **PUERTO PEÑASCO** does see a few tourists, most of whom have driven down from the States in motor homes: it boasts some good beaches, a trailer park and a couple of motels, plus one fairly cheap place – the *Hotel Peñasco*. On the road you'll pass through **SAN LUIS RIO COLORADO**, something of an oasis with a large cultivated valley watered by the Colorado river, and **SONOITA** (or Sonoyta) a minor border crossing on the river of the same name. Both are pretty dull.

Past Sonoita the road cuts inland and southwards, hitting the first foothills of the Sierra Madre Occidental whose western slopes it is to follow, hugging the coast, all the way to Tepic. At **SANTA ANA** it meets the Nogales road, and near the tiny village of BENJAMIN HILL rejoins the rail tracks. If you're travelling north you may well have to change buses at Santa Ana (especially en route to Nogales – there are far more buses to Mexicali) but it's a nothing town where there's little point venturing beyond the bus terminal.

MORE BORDER CROSSINGS: NOGALES AND AGUA PRIETA

By contrast with most of the frontier, **NOGALES** is remarkably pleasant: despite the fact that the Mexican streets are jammed with 'curio' shops and the US side with hardware, clothes and electrical stores, it never feels like a border town. There's none of the oppressive hustling and little of the frenetic nightlife which marks Ciudad Juarez, say, or Tijuana.

The **Nogales pass** (its name means walnut trees, few of which are in evidence) has been a significant staging post since man first travelled this way, with evidence of settlements several thousand years BC. After the conquest it was used by Spanish explorers and surveyors, followed in rapid succession by evangelising Jesuits (especially the celebrated Padre Kino) and Franciscans on their way to establish missions in California. Nogales itself remained no more than a large ranch, often existing in a state of virtual siege under harassment from the Apaches, until the war with the USA and the ceding of northern California, Arizona, New Mexico and Texas to the Americans in 1848. Thereafter, with the border passing straight through, the town was deliberately developed by both sides to prevent the periodic raids of the other. Yankee troops marched through a few years later, protecting Union supplies shipped in through Guaymas during the Civil War, and there was a constant traffic of rustling and raids from both sides – culminating in the activities of Pancho Villa in the years leading up to the Mexican Revolution. The railway to the coast brought the final economic spur, and the town's chief business remains that of shipping Sonora's rich agricultural produce to the States. Just over the border on the US side there's an excellent little museum of local history recording all this.

It's a sleepy, provincial little town, and not a bad place to rest up and acclimatise for a while. There are plenty of small **hotels** around the **bus stations** – cross the border, turn right and the three bus lines, *TNS*, *Tres Estrellas de Oro* and *Transportes del Pacifico*, have their offices in the first street on the right; the cheaper hotels are in the next couple of streets parallel to this. On the other side the *Greyhound* station is right by the **Customs Office** and there are about eight departures a day (from 7am to 8pm) for TUCSON. The **railway station** is, as the locals describe it, *un poco retirado* (a little retired) – or in other words it's at least an hour's walk out of town. Two trains a day leave for GUADALAJARA: take a local bus from the second street up from the border or a taxi to get there.

To the east lies one further border crossing, **AGUA PRIETA**, just across from Douglas, Arizona. A quiet town which sees few tourists, it's gradually growing thanks to new roads linking it to JANOS (for Ciudad Juarez and Nuevo Casas Grandes) and direct to HERMOSILLO. Despite the fact that these are barely marked on most maps, they're perfectly good paved highways, and Agua Prieta is thus on the only route from Central Mexico to the Pacific between the border and Mazatlan. There are several buses a day in each direction, and a couple of basic hotels if you're staying over – try the *Hotel Plaza* on the central plaza, or a nameless place in what looks like an apartment block opposite the TNS bus terminal.

SONORA

You don't pass much between NOGALES and SANTA ANA, although in the small town of **MAGDALENA**, where the bus stops briefly, there's a mausoleum containing the recently discovered remains, under glass, of Padre Kino. Kino, 'Conquistador of the Desert', was a Spanish Jesuit priest who came to Mexico in 1687 and is credited with having founded twenty-five missions and converted at least seven local Indian tribes – among them the Apaches of Arizona and the Yuma and Seri of Sonora.

HERMOSILLO is the state capital and, as such, it's a thriving city and a big ranching supply centre. The market overflows with meat and the shops are full of tack gear, cowboy hats and boots. From a distance it's an odd looking place, surrounded by strange rock formations and overlooked, right in the centre, by a tall outcrop crowned by radio masts, lit up at night like some carnival helter-skelter. Close up, though, it's less interesting – the boom of the last half century has wiped out almost everything that might have survived of the old town. And the boom in Sonora this century has been remarkable, helped no doubt by the fact that some of the earliest organised revolutionaries, including General Alvaro Obregon, were local men, as were many of the early presidents of revolutionary Mexico – Obregon himself, Huerta, whom he overthrew, Plutarco Elias Calles and Abelardo Rodriguez. Their many monuments and the streets named after them reflect the local debt.

From the rather isolated **bus station** get a town bus (marked *Ranchito* or *Mariachi*) to the centre – **hotels**, which cater largely to the newly wealthy rancheros who come here for the markets, tend to be expensive but there are any number of very basic **Casas de Huespedes**. If you get off the bus either as it turns off the broad suburban avenues into the narrower street leading into the centre or, later, at the corner of Juarez and Morelia, you'll be only a short walk from most of them.

Head, in the first instance, a couple of blocks into town, in the second, up Juarez away from the hill, and you'll come to a large Plaza. Here, the *Hotel Monte Carlo*, at the corner of Juarez and Sonora, is good (air-conditioned and elegant) but relatively pricey – standing beside it, though, you can see the *Hotel Royal* (not quite as grim as it looks) and if you walk down past it and all the way round the block back to the Monte Carlo you'll have passed four or five *Casas de Huespedes*. The *Hotel San Andres* on Calle Oaxaca (the far side of this block), is seriously over-priced, but the *Lourdes*, almost opposite, isn't too bad. On the same block, and indeed throughout the centre, there are several good **places to eat**, the best of them being the restaurant in the *Monte Carlo* – for some reason there's a small collection of **Chinese restaurants** here too, better than you'd expect a Chinese restaurant in Hermosillo to be, but not much.

BAHIA DE KINO, a growing resort on the coast some 100km west of Hermosillo, is little developed, but hard to get to. If you want to go by bus you'll have to be up early – the service is not particularly reliable but there seems to be a departure most days around 6 or 7am; it's just about practical to do this in a day – the journey takes about 2 hours, with return services in the late afternoon. Around the bay are two towns, the old fishing village of KINO VIEJO, and KINO NUEVO – the new beach resort; each is attractive but very expensive. This area used to be inhabited by Seri Indians, and despite their virtual extinction there is allegedly still a community living on the offshore **Isla Tiburon** (Shark Island). You may come across some of them hawking their traditional, and not so traditional, ironwood carvings along the beach in Kino Nuevo.

Back on the route south the next major stop is **GUAYMAS**, an important port with a magnificent, almost land-locked natural harbour where the mountains come right down to the sea. Although it claims a proud history – seemingly every adventurer whose eyes ever turned greedily to Mexico sent a gunship into the bay – there's really nothing to see beyond a couple of grandiose Porfiriano bank buildings on the main street. The Americans, the French and the British have all at one time or another attempted to take Guaymas (only the Americans had any real success, occupying the town from 1847-8), but the most extraordi-nary invader was a Frenchman, Conte Gaston Raousset de Bourbon. Attempting, with the tacit support of the then President, General Santa Ana, to carve out an empire in Sonora, Raousset invaded twice, holding the town for several months in 1852. His second attempt, in 1854, was less successful and ended with most of the pirates, the Count included, captured and shot. There are monuments to the hero of that battle – one General Yañez – all over the town.

Today, Guaymas is still a thriving fishing and naval centre and makes few concessions to tourism. The **hotels** are expensive and seem to have come to some sort of price-fixing agreement as they all charge exactly the same: given that, the best are the *Motel del Puerto* and *Hotel Impala*. There are also a couple of **Casas de Huespedes** – the *Lupita* opposite the prison very near the bus station, and another, nameless and unsavoury looking, right on the dock front in the town centre – but I can't in all conscience recommend either. The **bus stations** (*TNS* and *Tres Estrellas* share one, *Pacifico* is directly opposite) are on the block bounded by Avenidas 12 and 13 and Calles 14 and 15, about ten blocks from the centre of town. Walk in on Av. 12 past what looks like a Venetian Castle (in fact it's the jail – you can't miss its towers) and you'll pass all the places to stay mentioned above, as well as the market, before eventually hitting the **dock**. This, really, is the best part of the town – a deep bay, alive with the comings and goings of ships, scores of fishing boats at anchor. In the south of France it would no doubt be surrounded by outdoor waterfront cafes; this being Mexico the dockside looks more like a permanent building site.

The **beach** the locals use is at MIRAMAR, an upmarket suburb on Bacochibampo Bay a couple of miles to the north. A further 10 miles or so is SAN CARLOS (also hopefully dubbed *Nuevo Guaymas*) which is scheduled to become a big resort. So far there are only a couple of hotels, a yacht marina, a country club with a golf course, a clutch of villas and real estate agents and four or five half-empty trailer parks. Frankly it's not surprising because although both Miramar and San Carlos have magnificent settings – their bays set about with tall crags weirdly sculpted by the wind – neither has much of a beach. Beautiful sunsets though.

There's a much more impressive stretch of sand at ALGODONES, a further 5 miles beyond San Carlos, though there's no public transport out there and it's not exactly walking country. Algodones is where *Catch 22* was filmed and you can still see the set and the runway built for the film. For Miramar and San Carlos **buses** leave from the street by the Post Office, Calle 19, but it's probably easier to catch them on the main shopping street, Av. Aguiles Serdan, at its junction with Calle 18. The buses are marked either *Miramar* or *San Carlos*.

You may also be told (especially if you go to the not particularly helpful **Turismo**, by the waterside on C. Miguel Aleman) that there are beaches at LAS PLAYITAS, on the other side of Guaymas Bay. Don't believe it: there's a Motel/Trailer Park complex, but the beach is entirely wishful thinking. If you've a couple of hours to kill, though, it is interesting to take the bus out this way for the ride – you can stay on all the way and eventually it'll turn round and head back home. You get to see the shipbuilding industry, the fish-freezing and processing centres, and some fine views of the outer stretches of the wreck strewn bay. *Parajes* bus from C. Miguel Aleman.

The **ferry to Santa Rosalia** in Baja California leaves from the docks to the south of town – any bus heading this way on Av. Aguiles Serdan will take you there. Getting back into town is even easier; the buses turn round here so any one in either direction will get you back to the centre. There are three sailings a week (Tuesday, Thursday and Sunday mornings) and you buy tickets from the terminal – try to get them in advance if you're taking a car, otherwise there should be no problem.

Between GUAYMAS and CIUDAD OBREGON lies the valley of the Rio Yaqui, traditional home of the **Yaqui** Indians. The Yaquis were perhaps the fiercest and most independent of the Mexican Indians, maintaining virtual autonomy until the beginning of this century. Rebellions, and at times outright war against the government of the day, were frequent – the most significant coming in 1710 and again, after independence, in 1825. The last major uprising was in 1928 during the brief presidency of General Alvaro Obregon. Obregon, himself a Sonoran, was assassinated in Mexico City but his plans for the development of the North-West laid the basis for peace with the Yaquis: aided, no doubt, by the fact that earlier regimes had shipped rebels out wholesale to work on the tobacco plantations of Oaxaca. Today the Yaquis enjoy a degree of self-rule, with eight governors, one for each of their chief towns, but their cultural and political assimilation is rapid. One piece of Yaqui culture which has survived is the celebrated *Danza del Venado*, the Stag Dance. You now see it at folklore festivals throughout the Republic, and it forms one of the centrepieces of the *Ballet Folklorico* in Mexico City. The chief dancer wears a deer's head, a symbol of good (the stag being the sacred animal of the Yaqui), and he is hounded by one or more coyote dancers, falling eventually, after a gallant struggle, to these forces of evil. It's performed frequently at local festivals in the villages of this area.

CIUDAD OBREGON, founded in 1928 and named after the President, has thrived on the agricultural development which accompanied the plans to utilise the River Yaqui. Thanks to the irrigation schemes and huge dams up-river it's now a very large and uncompromisingly ugly town. About it's only attraction is for fans of cowboy clothing – locally produced straw stetsons are among the best and cheapest you'll find – but otherwise don't count on finding too much excitement.

NAVOJOA, too, is a rather dull farming town with a string of Americanised motels and restaurants along the highway and little else. But it scores over Ciudad Obregon in having a couple of cheap, basic hotels and a good market. Navojoa is also the jumping off point for ALAMOS – an old mining town which has been designated a Mexican 'National Monument'. The **bus stations** are a couple of blocks off the main road, alongside the lines of the *Ferrocarril del Pacifico*. There are a couple of **hotels** nearby – cheapest in town is the *America*, left out of the bus stations and almost opposite the railway station. If you want to pay a bit more for air-conditioning try the *Aduana* on C. Ignacio Allende. It's one block up to the right from the front of the Tres Estrellas terminal, right and right again from the others.

There are buses to **ALAMOS** every hour from the local bus depot on Guerrero, six blocks straight up from the Transportes del Pacifico terminal, past the market. Though perhaps over-rated – it certainly doesn't compare with the colonial towns of central Mexico – a ride out here does make a very pleasant respite from the monotony of the coastal road and it's nice to know that the mountains are still there, beautifully green and rugged. The town itself has suffered from its own popularity; it does have a beautiful old arcaded plaza and elegant eighteenth-century church, but most of the old stone mansions have been done up by Americans who've retired or settled here, and the whole place has a rather twee aspect. Still, it was once a very wealthy place, with silver deposits said to rival Taxco's, and some of the old mansions in the Spanish style (brooding and shuttered from the outside, but looking in on beautiful flower-filled patios) are really magnificent. Don't miss, especially, the **Casa de los Tesoros** – now a hotel where you can wander round freely inside, or rest up for a while at the bar. The one reasonably priced **hotel** in Alamos is the *Enriquez*, on the main square by the church, but unless you plan to go walking or hunting in the mountains (an exceedingly hot exercise in summer) or want simply to do nothing for a while, you can have been round the whole town in a couple of hours.

LOS MOCHIS

Continuing down the coast and crossing into the State of Sinaloa, the next place of size is **LOS MOCHIS,** another of those modern agricultural towns, broad-streeted and rather dull, but a major crossing point for road, rail and ferry and above all the western terminus of the incomparable **rail trip** down from Chihuahua through the Barranca del Cobre (see p. 59).

The various modes of **transport** into and out of this area are infuriating in their failure to connect in any way – even the bus stations are on opposite sides of town. Naturally enough the two **rail companies**, the CHP (*Chihuahua al Pacifico*) and the Nogales-Guadalajara FCP make no attempt to synchronise their schedules: the FCP station is actually in SAN BLAS, Sinaloa (not to be confused with the better known San Blas in Nayarit) some 30 miles inland, and while the CHP also stops here, at a different station, it's really not worth trying to make a direct connection between the two – there's nothing to see in the interim and nowhere you'd want to stay if you missed it. Better to use the fairly regular bus service between San Blas and Los Mochis. The **ferry**, meanwhile, leaves from the port at TOPOLOBAMPO and although again the CHP goes there (beyond Los Mochis) it's basically a freight run; go there instead by a local bus from the muddy little courtyard behind the giant *Santa Anita Hotel*. **Topolobampo** itself is a strange little place on an almost Scandinavian coastline of green deeply inset bays – there's water all around but the ocean itself is invisible and the ferry steams in through a narrow channel, appearing suddenly from behind a hill into what seems a landlocked lake. No beaches, unfortunately, and nowhere to stay, but you might persuade a local fisherman to take you out for a ride round the bay and a swim off his boat.

A final touch to all the confusion is that the **CHP station** is miles from the centre of town and operates on Chihuahua time (which is an hour earlier). Make sure you know which you're talking about when you find out when your train is leaving. There's a bus out there during the day which you can use to go and get tickets in advance (safer than relying on the agents in town) but since most trains arrive late at night and leave early in the morning you'll usually have to rely on taxis. Taxi fares here are a long-established rip-off, so grin and bear it – also, if possible, get a group of people and arrange for a driver to pick you up in advance; there's a severe rush when the train's about to leave.

What all this boils down to is that almost no matter how you arrange things, you'll have to spend the night in Los Mochis, and in peak times **hotel** space is at a premium. Best bet all round is probably the *Hotel Los Arcos*, just round the corner from the Tres Estrellas bus terminal (left out of the door and left again), although it's often full. The *Hotel Hidalgo*, on Hidalgo, is also cheap and usually has space – probably because some of its rooms are pretty foul; check yours first. Otherwise there are quite a few more expensive establishments of which the best are the places directly opposite the Hidalgo and the modern hotel across the street from the Tres Estrellas terminal. **Eating** is less of a problem: there are reasonable restaurants around all these hotels and the bus terminals, but for really superb *tacos* – enormous wheat-flour ones bulging with meat and frijoles in the local style – try *La Cabaña* on Allende one block up from the Hotel Los Arcos; it has the additional advantage of being open long after the rest of the town has closed down for the night.

The *Pacifico* and *Norte de Sonora* **bus stations**, incidentally, are next to each other on C. Morelos – turn right out the door, and right again on Zaragoza and you'll cross the aforementioned Hidalgo in about three blocks. There's a tiny *Casa de Huespedes* just by the bus entrance to these two, but it's to be avoided unless you relish the stench of diesel and the roar of the engines.

CULIACAN is actually the capital of Sinaloa, a prosperous city with a population of nearly half a million surrounded by some of the richest arable land in Mexico. It appears horribly ugly where it sprawls along the highway, but at its heart it's not too bad – mostly modern, but not unattractive. There's a lot more life in the streets, too, than in any of its near neighbours – probably thanks to the State University in the centre of town, and you can get to local **beaches** at Atlata or El Tambor, about an hour away by bus, or inspect the artworks in the local **Centro Cultural**. None of this, however, really adds up to any very compelling reason to stop, especially as Mazatlan is less than 150 miles further south. Another reason not to break your journey is that it's often extremely hard to get back on a bus: none originate here so that you frequently see little scrums of people rushing from desk to desk as the buses pull in, or fighting to get near the incoming driver to claim any empty seats. If you do stay, there are five or six **hotels** right by the Central Camionera.

MAZATLAN

About 40km from **MAZATLAN** you cross the Tropic of Cancer. I don't suppose it can be a sudden transformation but it's always struck me that way: Mazatlan is a tropical town where Culiacan was not and there's that damp airlessness about it which at first makes breathing seem an effort.

Primarily, of course, Mazatlan is a resort, and a burgeoning one at that, with hotels stretching further every year along the coast road to the north, flanking a series of excellent sandy beaches. But it's also a very large port and a thrusting town in its own right, and thanks to its situation on a relatively narrow peninsula, the centre of town has preserved much of its old, cramped and thoroughly Mexican atmosphere. The new avenues of hotels may be entirely devoted to tourism but this apart, Mazatlan is far less dominated by its visitors than its direct rivals – Acapulco or Puerto Vallarta. They tend to stay in their luxury complexes and penetrate the town itself only on brief forays.

Not that there's a great deal actually in Mazatlan – you certainly wouldn't come here for the architecture – but it is a pleasant place and the separation of town and tourism means that on the streets only a few blocks inland are some remarkably good value hotels. Mexican families mostly stay here, making the beachfront developments almost exclusively foreign preserves. There's an excellent bus service out along the coast road so staying in town doesn't mean sacrificing the sun – you can use the hotel pools and the beaches in front of them – just don't stay there.

Finding your way around is really not too hard, helped by the excellent bus system. Downtown, you can walk just about everywhere, and the rest of the resort is stretched out along the coast road northwards – some 10 miles of it, but all linked by a single bus route and patrolled by scores of taxis and little open *pulmonias*. From the **bus station** head up the hill to the main road and get on just about any bus heading to the right – they'll get you, by a variety of routes, to the **market**, very central and effectively the terminus for local buses. Arriving by **ferry** can be more of a problem: the buses from the dockside go to the same place but there are always problems getting an entire ferry-load of people and their baggage onto two of three of them. Taxis are in demand here too, so try to be among the first off the boat.

Almost all the cheaper **hotels** are within a short walk of the market: best place to start looking is on Jose Azueta where you'll find the *Hotel Vialta* and, nearby, the *Victoria* and the *Morelos*. Towards the sea there's another little cluster around the bottom of Aguiles Serdan – try the *Mexico* or the *Berlin*, or the *Lerma* (just off Serdan on Simon Bolivar). If you're determined to have a sea view the older hotels facing the **Playa Olas Altas** – *La Siesta* and *Belmar* particularly – offer the best value, but they're considerably more expensive than those above and Olas Altas isn't much of a beach to swim from; rather rocky and the waves tend to be big. To get to the northern beaches from here you have to go back into the centre of town as the buses don't follow the coast round the Cerro la Neveria.

Everything on the **northern beaches** is very much higher in price unless you're in a group large enough to consider an apartment: these can be excellent value even for short stays. Try the *Cabinas del Mar* on the Avenida del Mar about halfway to the main development at Sabalo (near the Sands Hotel) or simply wander round Sabalo looking for signs – *Apartamentos Fiesta*, about four blocks inland from the *Inn at Mazatlan* is one you might try. If you've just got off the bus and don't mind paying for a night or two's luxury, the *Sands Hotel* is air-conditioned, US motel-style with a pool, right on the beach and not badly priced for all that. Walk down the hill from the Camionera and you come out on the seafront right by it.

For **really basic accommodation** you can get a small boat from the end of the ferry docks to take you across to the **Isla de la Piedra**. On the far side here are miles more of excellent beaches where you can sleep out or sling a hammock on the terrace of one of the small restaurants. It was a very basic community but these days is increasingly included in tour itineraries and can, at times, become positively crowded.

For the best of the **mainland beaches**, the further north you go the better. They improve greatly around **Sabalo**, the 'Zona Dorada' where the earliest of the big hotels went up and where the best of them still are. It really depends from here on what you want – the beaches right in front of the hotels are clean and sheltered by little offshore islands (there are boat trips out to these from various points along the beach), while further on they're wilder but emptier. I quite like the more populous area – it never gets too crowded (most people stay by their pools and bars) and there's always a lot going on: water-skiing, sailing, parascending behind speedboats, you name it. And if you get bored there are the hotels' pools and bars and any number of tourist watering-holes and shops to

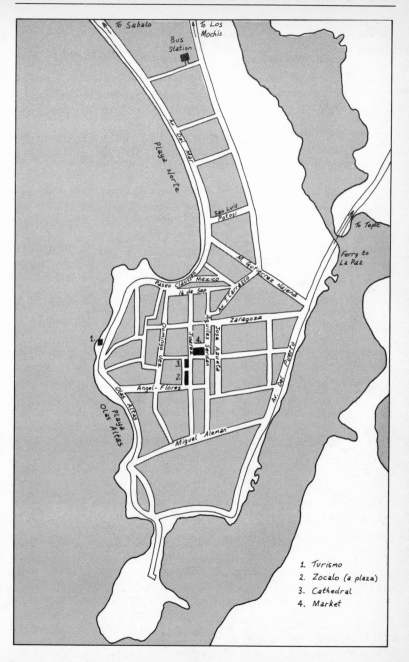

1. Turismo
2. Zocalo (a plaza)
3. Cathedral
4. Market

inspect. Stay on the bus past all this, though, and you get to an area where there's just the odd hotel, built or half built, a couple of little restaurants on the beach, and very little else but sand. Buses (marked *Sabalo* or *Cerritos*) leave from the market on the Juarez side.

The **Tourist Office** is on Avenida Olas Altas, the section of the seafront drive which goes around the **Cerro La Neveria**. As I said, the bus doesn't come round here so you'll either have to get a taxi or walk. Nearby, towards Plays Olas Altas, is the **Mirador** – an outcrop of rock from which local daredevil youth plunge into the sea. It's not as spectacular as the high-diving in Acapulco, but dangerous nonetheless. You'll see them performing whenever there are enough tourists to raise a collection from, mostly in the late afternoon when the tour buses come past.

A second, local tourist office is supposedly in the Palacio Municipal on the **Zocalo**, but I've never found it open. The Zocalo itself is very much the commercial centre of Mazatlan; aside from the Cathedral (modern and not at all attractive), there are government offices, the Post Office, main bank branches and travel agencies. This is also the **best area to eat**, avoiding the tourist traps around the coast: there are several places along Angel Flores, the street which runs past the back of the Zocalo towards Playa O!as Altas. Or, for the enforced fun of the tourist machine, you could do no better than try *El Shrimp Bucket* (sic), the restaurant in the Hotel Siesta at the bottom of this street. One of the oldest and best known in Mazatlan it certainly has atmosphere and the food, though expensive, is generally worth it.

Leaving Mazatlan you face the choice of continuing downcoast to TEPIC and from there along the main road to GUADALAJARA or to more Pacific beaches at SAN BLAS and PUERTO VALLARTA, or cutting **inland to Durango** and the colonial cities of the Mexican heartland. This road, the first to penetrate the Sierra Madre south of the border, is as wildly spectacular as any in the country; twisting and clawing its way up to the Continental Divide at over 7,000 feet. New vistas open at every curve as you climb from tropical vegetation through temperate forests of oak to the peaks with their stands of fir and pine. It can get extremely cold towards the top, so keep plenty of warm clothing to hand to cover the T-shirt and shorts you'll need for the first sweaty hour. Little over 300km, it's a very slow road, so reckon on six hours to Durango at the least.

TEPIC AND SAN BLAS

The main road below Mazatlan steers a little way inland, away from the marshy coastal flatlands. There are a few little beach communities along here, and deserted sands, but on the whole they're virtually impossible to get to without transport of your own, and fly-blown, exposed and totally lacking in facilities if you do. The first town of any size, capital of the state of Nayarit and transport hub for the area, is **TEPIC**.

Despite its antiquity – the city was founded by Cortes's brother Francisco in 1544 – there's not a great deal to be seen in Tepic. Pleasant enough in a quietly provincial way, it doesn't exactly reach out and grab you. For most it's no more than a stopover; a convenient place to spend the night before continuing across the mountains to Guadalajara or to switch buses for the coast. And this is probably the best way to treat it, for while the surrounding country can be beautiful, it's largely inaccessible and visited only by anthropologists. For them, the mountains of Nayarit, homelands of the Huichol and Cora Indians, are rich in interest: the Huichol, in particular, remain the tribe least affected by the four and a half centuries since the Spanish invasion, living in isolated mountain regions unreached by road and dotted with only the occasional mule track or landing strip for light aircraft. In these fastnesses they have preserved, virtually unaffected by attempts at evangelisation, their ancient beliefs, government and social forms. Peyote, for which a group of Huichol have to make an annual cross-country pilgrimage to Real de Catorce (p. 89), plays an important part in their ceremonials. You may occasionally see one or two in Tepic, at the market or paying homage in the church of Santa Cruz – more often at religious festivals in nearby villages. Getting to their territory is both arduous and difficult, and you'll need permission from the authorities in Tepic.

The **bus station** is some way from the centre, but local buses shuttle in and out from the main road outside. For just one night it's easiest to stay out here – two cheap **hotels**, the *Nayarit* and the *Tepic*, are immediately behind the terminal, with little to choose between them. In the centre, try the *Hotel Imperial* (Av. Mexico 208) or slightly more expensive, the *Sierra de Alica* (Mexico 180) or the *San Jorge* (Lerdo Pte. 124), all of them very near the Zocalo. If you do stay you'll want to hop on a bus to the centre anyway, to find something to eat and for something to do in the evening; the eighteenth-century cathedral, on the Zocalo, and the small regional museum, at the corner of Mexico with Zapata, are both worth a look.

If you plan to spend any time, though, head for the coast, where the obvious destination is SAN BLAS. Arriving from the north you might be tempted to leave the bus at the turn-off from the main road, avoiding the 70-km round-trip into Tepic and back out again. This is feasible, but not always wise – all too often the buses passing are full or simply refuse to stop, and you'll end up wasting time in an attempt to save it. Safer, on the whole, to carry on to Tepic and change buses there, when you're guaranteed of a place.

Beyond the junction, the road drops rapidly to the coastal plain, sultry, marshy and flat, dotted with palm trees and half submerged under little lagoons teeming with wild-life. Through this you reach **SAN BLAS**, as god-forsaken a little town as you could hope to see – at least at first impression. It was an important port in the days of the Spanish trade with the Orient, wealthy enough to need a fortress to ward off the depredations of English piracy, but though there's still an enviable natural harbour and a sizeable deep-sea fishing fleet, almost no physical relic of the town's days of glory remains. Popular in winter with the Californian surfing crowd, in summer the town is virtually deserted save for some particularly ferocious gnats.

There's an air of abandonment and of torpor about the place which extends to everything – life is very, very slow, the houses neglected, the beach a mess (especially since its bombardment by typhoons in 1983) and even many of the hotels and restaurants seem content to let things go. Among the more reasonable of the **places to stay** in town – and there are quite a few – are the *Hotel Flamingos* and the *Motel San Blas*. If you're happy with four bare stone walls and an iron bedstead, with nothing but the mosquitoes for company, you could try the *Hotel Vallarta* – basic in the extreme, but dirt cheap and right on the beach. **Eat** at one of the restaurants around the plaza – *McDonalds* (no relation to Ronald) is a slightly Americanised place which often has live music in the evenings – or on the beach: there's excellent seafood everywhere. *La Tumba*, on the street which runs from the town down to the beach, sells health food.

The **beaches** are of course the prime attraction, and by far the best are some 4km away around the *Bahia de Matanchen*. This vast, sweeping crescent of a bay is entirely surrounded by fine soft sands: at the near end is the tiny community of LAS ISLITAS on the Playa Miramar, with a few shacks on the beach serving up grilled fish and cold beers and, on the point, a group of cabins which you can rent – beautifully situated but outrageously expensive; at the far end lies the Playa de los Cocos and a new five star hotel. In between, acres of sand are fragmented only by flocks of pelicans and the occasional crab. The waves here, which rise offshore beyond Miramar and run in, past the point, to the depths of the bay, are in the *Guinness Book of Records* as the longest in the world: it's very rarely that they get up enough, though, for surfers to be able to ride them all the way in. You can walk from San Blas to Matanchen, just about, on the roads through the lagoons – it's impossible to penetrate along the coast which would be much shorter – but in the heat of the day it's far easier to get a taxi (bargain fiercely) or to cadge or hitch a lift.

The lagoons and creeks behind San Blas are almost unbelievably rich in bird and animal life of all kinds – the ubiquitous white herons, or egrets, above all, but hundreds of other species too, which no-one seems able to name (any bird here is described as a *garza* – a heron). There's no shortage of little boats offering **trips 'into the jungle'** – most leave from the river where the road crosses into town on a new bridge – and although expensive (they charge, usually, by the boat, so get a group together) it is beyond any doubt worth it. Best time to go is at dawn, before other trips have disturbed the animals, when you might even glimpse a *caiman*: most head for La Tavora, a freshwater spring where you can swim and there's a cafe. On the way back you can climb up the little hill beside the river to reach the ruins of the **fort** and a little chapel, with great views over the town and the ocean.

North of San Blas – and served only by an occasional bus from Tepic – are two more fascinating destinations. From the turn-off for SANTIAGO IXCUINTLA, a one-horse town if ever there was one, a road leads straight down to the coast and the **Playa Los Corchos**, a perfect stretch of sand lined with palm trees by the mouth of the Rio Grande de Santiago. No formal facilities, but you might find someone prepared to let you have a room, or at least space to sling a hammock under the verandah of one of the beach bars. To the right beyond Santiago, another road leads across the lagoon to the extraordinary islet of **MEXCALTITLAN**. The little town here, laid out in radiating spokes from the centre of the round island, must look something like a smaller version of Aztec Tenochtitlan before the Spanish arrived – local transport is by canoe along a series of tiny canals crossed by causeways – and indeed it's one candidate for the site from which the Aztecs set out on their long trek to the Valley of Mexico. There's no hotel, for the place sees very little tourism, but you should be able to find a guide to paddle you around the island. If you're in the area around the end of June you should definitely try to visit the island fiesta, on June 29th, when there are canoe races around the lagoons and rivers.

FIESTAS

February
3rd DIA DE SAN BLAS. The Feria in **San Blas** (Nayarit) starts on January 30th, with parades, dancing, fireworks and ceremonial.
CARNIVAL (the week before Lent, variable Feb.-Mar.) is celebrated with particular gusto in **La Paz** (Baja California Sur), **Ensenada** (Baja California Norte) and **Culiacan** (Sinaloa). The best in the north, though, is at **Mazatlan** (Sin.).

March
19th DIA DEL SEÑOR SAN JOSE. Saint's day celebrations in **San Jose del Cabo** (B.C.S.) with horse races, cockfights and fireworks, and in the hamlet of San Jose near **Guaymas**

(Sonora) where the religious fervour is followed by a fair.
PALM SUNDAY (week before Easter) sees dramatisations of biblical episodes in **Jala** (Nay.), an ancient little town between Tepic and Guadalajara.
HOLY WEEK is widely honoured. High points include passion plays in **Jala** (Nay.), processions and native dances in **Rosamorada** (Nay.), north of Tepic on the main road, and, in the Yaqui Indian town of **Cocorit** (Son.) near Ciudad Obregon, pilgrimages and Yaqui dances including the renowned *Danza del Venado*. It can also be seen in **Potam** (Son.), on the coast near here, along with curious ancient religious rites and the burning of effigies of Judas.

May

3rd DIA DE LA SANTA CRUZ celebrated in **Santiago Ixcuintla** (Nay.), north of Tepic, a fiesta rich in traditional dances.

June

1st Maritime celebrations in the port of **Topolobampo** (Sin.) with parades and a fair.

24th DIA DE SAN JUAN. **Guaymas** (Son.), **Navojoa** (Son.) and **Mochicahui** (Sin.), a tiny village near Los Mochis, all celebrate the saint's day with processions and, later, with native dancing. In **Navojoa** there's a feria which carries on to the beginning of July.

29th In **Mexcaltitlan** (Nay.) a religious fiesta in honour of Saint Peter, with processions in boats round the islet.

July

First Sunday *Romeria* in **Tecate** (B.C.N.), extremely colourful, with cowboys, carnival floats and music.

25th DIA DE SANTIAGO. Bizarrely celebrated in **Compostela** (Nay.), south of Tepic, where the men ride around on horses all day – the women take over their mounts the following morning and do the same. Also a fair with fireworks.

September

8th Formal religious processions in **Jala** (Nay.) with traditional dress much in evidence and regional dances.

16th INDEPENDENCE DAY is a holiday everywhere, and especially lively along the border. **Tijuana** (B.C.N.) has horse and motor races, mariachi, dancing, gambling and fireworks, while the much smaller crossing of **Agua Prieta** (Son.) has a more traditional version of the same, with parades and civic ceremonies.

28th DIA DE SAN MIGUEL. Pilgrimage to Boca, a community very near **Choix** (Sin.), on the railway from Los Mochis.

Dancing and parades in Choix, with a procession to Boca.

October

4th DIA DE SAN FRANCISCO is the culmination of two weeks' fiesta in **Magdalena** (Son.) attended by many Indians (Yaqui and Sioux among them) who venerate this missionary saint. Indian dances.

First Sunday in **Guasave** (Sin.), between Los Mochis and Culiacan, a pilgrimage to the Virgen del Rosario, with many dance groups.

Last Sunday Repetition of events in **Guasave** and, in **Ixtlan del Rio** (Nay.), on the road from Tepic to Guadalajara, hundreds of pilgrims arrive to observe the DIA DE CRISTO REY – more dancing here.

November

2nd DAY OF THE DEAD celebrations everywhere – **Navojoa** (Son.) one of the more impressive.

December

First Sunday Lively festival honouring el Señor de la Misericordia in **Compostela** (Nay.).

8th DIA DE LA INMACULADA CONCEPCION celebrated by the pilgrims who converge on **Alamos** (Son.), and in **Mazatlan** (Sin.) with parades, music and dancing. **La Yesca**, in a virtually inaccessible corner of Nayarit east of Tepic, has religious ceremonies and a feria attended by many Huichol Indians which lasts till the 12th.

12th DIA DE LA VIRGEN DE GUAD-ALUPE. In **Navojoa** (Son.), the climax of ten days of activities comes with a mass procession. **Tecate** (B.C.N.) and **Acaponeta**, on the main road in northern Nayarit, both have lively and varied fiestas.

TRAVEL DETAILS

Trains

The main line from Nogales to Guadalajara is operated by the *Ferrocarril del Pacifico* (FCP). It connects at Benjamin Hill with the Sonora-Baja California line to Mexicali and, badly, at San Blas (Son.) with the amazing CHP Chihuahua to Los Mochis railway.

Nogales and **Mexicali** to **Guadalajara**. *El Costeño* leaves Nogales daily 16.30. Arrives Benjamin Hill (18.30); Hermosillo (20.30), Ciudad Obregon (midnight), San Blas (Son.) (2.00), Culiacan (5.40), Mazatlan (8.35), Tepic (13.30) and Guadalajara (19.00).

Connection from Mexicali leaves 8am, arriving Benjamin Hill 17.30.

El Mexicali, much slower, leaves Mexicali (20.45), Benjamin Hill (10.30) – connection from Nogales leaves 7.15. Arrives Hermosillo (12.35), San Blas (Son.) (20.45), Mazatlan (4.55), Tepic (11.15), Guadalajara (17.20).

Return journeys leave Guadalajara 8.50 (*El Costeño*, arrives Nogales 10.20 and Mexicali 13.35 the following day) and noon, arriving Nogales 35hrs later, Mexicali 41.

Los Mochis-Chihuahua 13-hr journey, leaving daily at 8am. See following chapter (p. 61) for details.

Buses

Services on the inland highway from Tijuana or Nogales are excellent, with constant fast traffic all along the coast road. Chief operators are *Tres Estrellas de Oro*, *Transportes del Pacifico* and the second class *Transportes Norte de Sonora* (TNS).

From **Tijuana**. To La Paz 6 daily (around 22hrs). Constantly, day and night, to Guadalajara (almost 40hrs), via Mexicali (3hrs), Santa Ana (11hrs), Hermosillo (13½hrs), Guaymas (15½hrs), Cd. Obregon (18hrs), Los Mochis (21½hrs), Culiacan (25hrs), Mazatlan (28hrs), Tepic (32hrs). 4 daily to Agua Prieta (14hrs).

Nogales–Santa Ana 10 daily (2hrs) and on to Hermosillo (4½hrs), connecting with main road as above.

Agua Prieta–Hermosillo 5 daily (6hrs).

Agua Prieta–Janos 6 daily (3½hrs) – 4 to Cd. Juarez and 2 to Nvo. Casas Grandes.

Mazatlan–Durango 8 daily (7hrs).

Tepic–San Blas (Nay.) 6 daily (1½hrs).

Tepic–Puerto Vallarta 5 daily (3hrs).

Ferries

Guaymas to **Santa Rosalia** Departs Guaymas Tue., Thur., Sun., 11am, Sta. Rosalia same days 11pm. 7hrs.

La Paz to **Mazatlan** Daily departures from either end at 5pm. 16 hours.

La Paz to **Topolobampo** Dep. La Paz Tue, Wed., Sat., Sun. at 8pm; Topolobampo Mon., Wed., Thurs., Sat. 10am. 8hrs.

Cabo San Lucas to **Puerto Vallarta** Dep. Wed. and Sun. 4pm, return Tue. and Sat. 4pm. 30hrs.

Planes

Almost every town of any size has an airport, with flights, not necessarily direct, to Mexico City. Busiest are **Tijuana**, with 10 flights a day to Mexico by a variety of routings and 5 direct to Guadalajara, and **La Paz**, with flights to Mexico and many towns along the mainland coast. **Mazatlan** is the biggest of all, with 9 flights a day to Mexico City, and **International** services from Los Angeles and San Francisco, some of them via Tijuana.

Chapter two
BETWEEN THE SIERRAS: NORTH-EAST ROUTES

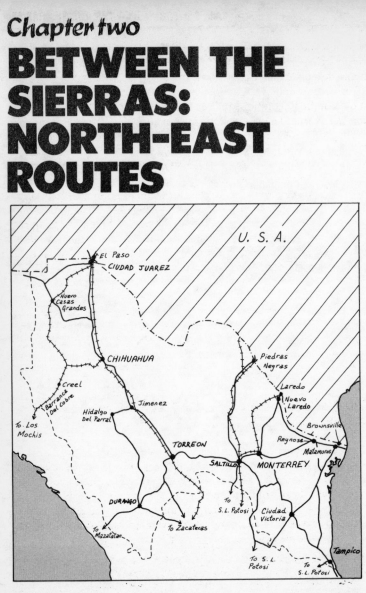

The central and eastern routes into Mexico are considerably shorter than the west coast road, and though they don't have the beaches they do offer direct access to the country's colonial heart and much of interest along the way. The high plain between the flanks of the Sierra Madre is also cool – often uncomfortably so in winter – and the highways crossing it fast.

You'll find most of interest heading down from **Ciudad Juarez**: an important archaeological site at **Casas Grandes**, and in **Chihuahua** and **Durango** a foretaste of the majesty of the colonial cities to come. There are historic connotations too, for this was the country most fiercely fought over in the Revolution, and the breeding ground for Pancho Villa's *Division del Norte*. The supreme attraction though, is the breathtaking rail journey from Chihuahua to the Pacific coast: a 13-hour ride over soaring peaks and around the walls of vast canyons down to the steamy coastal plain. To the east, along the fastest route to the capital, **Monterrey** is a heavily industrialised city which has yet managed to retain its finest sights. Nearby **Saltillo** offers escape into the tranquillity of the mountains.

Following the **Gulf Coast** is less recommended − steaming hot in summer and not particularly interesting at the best of times. It is, though, the shortest way south, and if you stick it out past the refineries you'll reach the state of Veracruz, with some fine beaches and a wealth of archaeological remains.

Crossing the border, do not forget to go through Immigration and Customs checks. *There's a free zone south of the frontier and you can cross at will. Highly embarrassing, though, when you're stopped some 20km inland and sent back to get your Tourist Card stamped.*

THE CENTRAL CORRIDOR

There are rapid and efficient bus services throughout the central area − the most efficient of the main lines probably being *Transportes Chihuahuenses* and *Omnibus de Mexico*, with *Estrella Blanca* mounting a strong challenge as you head south. Non-stop to Mexico City can be done in around 25 hours. If this is your plan you might also consider the train − *El Fronterizo* leaves Ciudad Juarez every evening at 6.25, reaching the capital some 36 hours later.

CIUDAD JUAREZ AND CASAS GRANDES

There's little doubt that the best thing to do on arriving in **CIUDAD JUAREZ** is to leave. In less than 5 hours you can reach Chihuahua or, rather closer, NUEVO CASAS GRANDES, base for excursions to the archaeological site of Casas Grandes. Juarez itself is perhaps the least attractive of all the border towns; modern, sprawling and ugly as well as extremely confusing to find your way around.

As you cross the **border** (the two bridges over the Rio Bravo are one-way, even for pedestrians, the large modern one to enter Mexico, the older one as you leave) the nature of the place is immediately apparent: on the US side blood banks and second-hand clothes emporia, in Mexico cut-rate doctors and dentists and cheap bars. It's all rather sad and sordid. However, if you're staying this is the place to be, in what's left of the old town. The **market** is straight up Lerdo a few blocks from the border and in the streets around it are most of the cheaper **places to stay** and to eat. Nothing is particularly good value by Mexican standards, but hotels here are still considerably less expensive than in El Paso: three to try are the *Juarez*, on Lerdo near the market, *Hotel Koper* on Juarez where it crosses Av. 16 de Septiembre or the *Plaza* (239 Ugarte) continuing on 16 de Septiembre and bearing right. To kill a few hours in Juarez there are two museums worth seeing: the **Archaeology Museum** (open daily 9–6.30) in the Parque Chamizal near the river and the *Pronaf* **Museum of History and Art** (open 10–7; closed Mondays) not far from the bus station. Both are basically introductions to Mexico, although the former does have some of the remarkable pottery from Casas Grandes.

Other than that there isn't a great deal of local history for them to dwell on, although the town, originally a small settlement on the Santa Fe trail known as Paso del Norte, did enjoy the brief glory of being the seat of Benito Juarez's government after he had been driven out of the south by Maximilian. It also changed hands frequently during the revolution, most notably in 1913 when Pancho Villa, having stolen a train, managed to fool the local commander into expecting reinforcements and steamed into the centre of town with 2,000 troops completely unopposed. This was one of the exploits which forged his reputation, as well as giving him access to the border and to arms from the north.

Getting out of Ciudad Juarez should present few problems: there are excellent **bus connections** to the whole of north and central Mexico from the modern Central de Autobuses. To get there take a local bus from Av. 16 de Septiembre by the market or one of the horribly cramped vans which operate a shuttle service to and from the border. There are constant departures with one company or another down the main highway and every couple of hours for Nuevo Casas Grandes (via JANOS). If you plan to head straight for Chihuahua, or straight on through to Mexico City, you can catch a Transportes Chihuahuenses bus at the Greyhound terminal in El Paso, although I have heard stories of people being held up at immigration and emerging to find that the bus had gone without them.

The *Ferrocarriles Nacionales* **railway station** is reached by going straight up Lerdo from the border – there is a bus but it is just about walking distance.

Casas Grandes

The archaeological site at **CASAS GRANDES** (open daily 9–4.30) is much the most important, and certainly the most striking, in northern Mexico. Originally an agricultural community of simple adobe houses – similar to those found throughout the south-western United States and above all in Arizona and new Mexico – it became heavily influenced by Meso-American, probably Toltec, culture. Whether this was the result of conquest or, more probably, trade is uncertain, but from around 1000–1200AD Casas Grandes flourished. **Pyramids** and **ball-courts** were constructed and the land round about irrigated by a system of **canals**. At the same time local craftsmen were trading with both south and north, producing a wide variety of elaborate ornaments and pottery. Among the finds on the site (almost all of them now in the National Museum of Anthropology) were cages in which exotic imported birds were kept to be used for making feathered ornaments; necklaces made from shell, turquoise and semi-precious stones; and other objects of copper, bone, jade and mother-of-pearl. Casas Grandes pottery, with vessels often in the shape of human or animal figures and decorated in geometric patterns of red, black and brown on a white or cream background, was particularly beautiful – remarkably similar objects are still being produced by local Indian cultures.

Surrounding the **ceremonial centre** are the remains of adobe houses: originally two or three storeys high, most survive only as foundations with an occasional wall standing to give some idea of scale. Much must have been destroyed when the site was attacked, burned and abandoned around 1340 – either by a marauding nomadic tribe such as the Apache or as a result of a more local rebellion. Either way Casas Grandes was not inhabited again, its people abandoning their already depleted trade for the greater safety of the Sierras. What is left, ruinous and unrestored as it is, remains an impressive monument and unique of its kind in Mexico.

To get to the site you have first to get to **NUEVO CASAS GRANDES**. From here take the bus from the railway station (you can't miss it) with *Casas Grandes/Col. Juarez* on its side. This will take you to the plaza in Casas Grandes in about 15 minutes and the site is signed – a bare 10-minute walk. Nuevo Casas Grandes is not, of itself, particularly interesting, but it is at least quiet and to my mind greatly preferable to Ciudad Juarez as a place to spend the night. Very small, you'll see the Hotels *California* and *Plaza* as you drive in. On the other hand if you leave Juarez early you can visit the site and continue to Chihuahua in the same day – the route is only marginally longer and certainly more interesting than the main road. Theoretically one could also get here by **rail**, and then continue to LA JUNTA to join the Chihuahua-Los Mochis railway. But at best there is only one (painfully slow) train a day and, connections being what they are, it would take at least two and possibly three days to complete a journey which can be done in one on the bus.

CHIHUAHUA AND THE BARRANCA DEL COBRE

CHIHUAHUA is the capital of the state of the same name, Mexico's largest and most productive. As such it's a big city, an industrial centre, and the base for transportation of much of the state's mineral and agricultural wealth. But it's also an attractive place, with an ancient centre surrounded by suburbs of magnificent nineteenth-century mansions in the best horror-film Gothic tradition.

At the very centre is a beautiful **Cathedral** set on a teeming plaza, opposite a wonderfully camp statue of the city's founder in the very act of pointing to the ground and saying 'right lads, we'll build it here'. The baroque, twin-towered temple was begun in 1717 but took more than seventy years to complete; work well worth it though, for it is one of the country's finest and for once the interior detail, so often despoiled elsewhere, is the equal of the facade. Also on the Plaza de Armas is the imposing, but relatively modern, Palacio Municipal – follow Calle Libertad down past this and you'll come to the Plaza Hidalgo where the **Palacio Federal** and the **Palacio de Gobierno** face each other across the square. The Palacio de Gobierno was originally a Jesuit College, converted to a military hospital after the expulsion of the Jesuits – here Padre Miguel Hidalgo y Costilla and Ignacio Allende, the inspiration and early leaders of the Mexican War of Independence, were executed in 1811, their severed heads being sent for public display in Guanajuato (see p. 129). The site of the deed is marked (despite the fact that the building has been reconstructed several times since) and you can also visit 'Hidalgo's dungeon' in the Palacio Federal where they were held beforehand.

More recent history is commemorated in the **Museum of the Revolution** (open daily 9–1 and 3–7; closed Mondays) in a former home of Pancho Villa's on Calle 10A. This enormous mansion was inhabited, until her recent death, by Villa's 'official' widow (there were allegedly many others) who used to conduct personal tours: it has now been taken over by the state and put on a more official footing. The collection is a fascinating mix of arms, war plans and more personal mementoes, including the bullet-riddled limousine in which Villa was assassinated in 1923. To get there take a bus (or walk) up Av. Ocampo as far as the huge church – the museum, which is also known as *Quinta Luz*, is two blocks to the left and one and a half further up.

Finally, a word about those revolting little short-haired, bug-eyed **dogs** to which the city has given its name. They do come from here originally, but you're most unlikely to see one, presumably because the vicissitudes of a dog's life in Mexico (and I can think of few places I'd less like to be a dog) are too great for so pathetic a creature.

Some practical details
From the **bus station** you can see the roofs of the Cathedral and the tower of the *El Presidente* hotel, also right in the centre and, incidentally, with excellent views from its top floor bar and restaurant. Simply walk towards them. If you follow Calle 10, the first going uphill, you pass several small hotels, but this is also Chihuahua's red light district and, although really very tame, it is noisy and I suspect that these hotels rent more rooms by the hour than they do by the day. Best to keep going to the top, past the *Hotel del Carmen*, where there are three small, relatively quiet places to the right. Or carry on to the *Hotel Plaza*, right behind the Cathedral. This is marginally more expensive, but it's good and couldn't be more central. For late night, exhausted arrivals there is also the *Hotel del Cobre*, right by the bus station – overpriced but modern and comfortable.

For the *Ferrocarriles Nacionales* (Ciudad Juarez-Mexico City) **railway station** take a *Villa Colon* or *Granjas Colon* bus from the centre and get someone to tell you where to get off (by the Motel del Capitan) because the station is invisible from the road. The same bus, in the other direction, will get you back into town – it's worth going out to the station in advance to buy a ticket if you want 'primera reservada'; the Zacatecas/Mexico City train leaves at 11.25 at night.

There is no shortage of good **places to eat** in Chihuahua from the basic cafes around the bus station, through the taco stalls you pass on the way up to the centre, to the fancier steak houses and American burger restaurants around the central plazas. Take your pick.

Chihuahua to Los Mochis – the Copper Canyon railway

The 13-hour rail journey which starts on the high plains of Chihuahua, fights its way up to cross the Continental Divide amid the peaks of the Sierra Madre and finally plunges down to the sweaty Pacific coast at Los Mochis must rate as one of the world's most extraordinary. Not only as an engineering feat (work started at the beginning of the century and was only completed, seventy-three tunnels and twenty-eight major bridges later, in 1961) but for the breathtaking views as it hangs over the vast canyons of the Urique river. Chief of these is the awesome rift of the *Barranca del Cobre*, with a depth, from mountain top to valley floor, of up to 12,000 feet, and broad to match. By comparison, the Grand Canyon is a midget.

Even when the bare mountain peaks here are snow covered, the climate at the bottom is semi-tropical forest: a fact which the Tarahumara Indians – driven into these mountain fastnesses after the Spanish Conquest – depend on, migrating in winter to the warmth of the deep canyons. The **Tarahumara** still live in isolated communities along the line and in the stretch of the mountains here known as the Sierra Tarahumara; and although as everywhere their isolation is increasingly encroached upon, they remain an independent people, close to their traditions. Their religious life, despite centuries of missionary work, embraces only token aspects of Catholicism and otherwise remains true to its agrarian roots – their chief deities being the gods of the Sun, Moon and rain. Above all, the tribe are renowned as runners: foot races between villages are a common feature of local festivals, they last at least a day, sometimes several days on end, the runners having to kick a wooden ball ahead of them as they go.

At first, though, as the tracks run through gentle ranching country toward the base of the mountains, the character is altogether different. Many people dismiss these first few hours of the journey as dull, but for me they have their own, albeit less spectacular, appeal. It's pioneer country which wouldn't look out of place in some gentle, romantic western: verdant grazing land where you see more horses and traps than trucks. The town of CUAHTEMOC, 130km from Chihuahua, is one of the chief centres of the **Mennonite cult**. You'll come across Mennonites throughout northern Mexico – the men looking like a series of John-Boy Walton clones in their bib-and-tucker overalls and straw stetsons, as often as not trying to sell the excellent cheese which is their main produce, the women, mostly silent, wrapped in long black nineteeth-century dresses with maybe a dash of colour from a headscarf. The sect, founded in the sixteenth century by a Dutchman, Menno Simonis, believe only in the Bible and their personal conscience: their refusal to do military service or take oaths of loyalty led to a long history of persecution. The ones here arrived in Mexico early this century, having been driven from Frisia to Prussia, thence into Russia and finally to Mexico by way of Canada – each time forced to move on by the state's demand for military tribute or secular education. Among themselves they still speak a form of German, although some Germans I met on the train claimed it was so corrupt as to be as unintelligible to them as it was to me.

Not far beyond and the train begins to climb in earnest into the first spurs of the Sierra, eventually reaching **CREEL**, almost the halfway stage and close to the highest point of the line. This is the place to stop if you want seriously to explore the Sierra Tarahumara and the canyons, and there are a couple of reasonably priced hotels, the only ones en route: the *Hotel Korachi* is by general agreement the best (it's right opposite the station) but you could also try the rather over priced *Hotel Nuevo* or the basic *Ejido*. Remember that it can get bitterly cold up here, especially in winter, but also on summer nights. All sorts of trips are organised from Creel into the surrounding country, or arm yourself with a map and set out to explore on your own: there's no shortage of expert advice around. And don't be discouraged by the fact that the journey so far, while beautiful, has not been truly spectacular – the best of the railway lies further on but from Creel you can quickly be among remarkable scenes.

Stay on the train and you clank onwards to **DIVISADERO** where there's a halt of about 20 minutes to wonder at the view. It seems a surprising choice – apparently nothing around but the mountain tops and a few Indians hawking their crafts and food (delicious *gorditas*). But walk a step down the path and you're standing suddenly on the edge of space. This is the lip of the vast chasm and below you are laid out the depths of the Barranca del Cobre and, joining it, the Barranca de Balojaque and the Barranca de Tararecua. There are a couple more places to stay here, but only for the very well-heeled, so for most it's all too rapidly back on the train for the final stage – 6 more hours which, from the rail fan's point of view, are the most exciting yet.

It was here that the original builders, the Kansas City, Mexico and Orient Railway Company finally gave up on their dream of pushing through a new route from the American mid-west to the Pacific – defeated by the sheer technical complexity of it all – and only in 1953 did the Mexicans start work on the final, linking stretch. You can see why. The train zigzags down dizzily, clinging to the canyon wall, plunging into tunnels blasted through the rock, rocking across bridges, only to find itself constantly just a short stone's drop below the track it covered 20 minutes earlier. And all the time it's getting hotter, until finally the line breaks out of the mountains onto the humid coastal plain as the air-conditioned passengers settle back in their reclining seats and the rest just sweat.

How to do it

The line is operated by the *Ferrocarril de Chihuahua al Pacifico* (**CHP** pronounced Shé Pé). To get to the CHP station in Chihuahua, take a *Sta. Rosa* or *Col. Rosalia* bus from the centre, get out at the prison (impossible to miss) and walk round behind it to the station. If you're going to get your tickets in the morning you'll have to take a taxi (the ticket office opens at 6.30) or else walk it. The **timetable** is basically as follows: on Sundays, Mondays, Thursdays and Saturdays an ordinary train leaves at 8.20am; on Mondays, Thursdays and Saturdays there's also an *autovia* (basically a bus on rails) to Creel, leaving 20 minutes earlier; on Tuesdays and Fridays an autovia leaves for the full trip at 8am and there's also a night train, setting off at 10.30. The autovia to Creel returns the same afternoon, the rest set out on the return journey the following morning, leaving Los Mochis at 8. The ordinary trains (*Tren Primera* or *VistaTren*) are the ones to go for – this is after all a rail journey and the autovia has not the slightest hint of romance about it. Nor does it have a dining car. You can get a reserved reclining seat in an air-conditioned carriage (*Primera Numerada*) but ordinary first class (*Primera General*) costs half as much and you should have no problem getting a seat, though it can get crowded as the journey wears on. Still, there are fewer Gringos and it's perfectly comfortable, if hot for the last couple of hours. The night train is not a good idea in winter – at least not if you want to see anything – but in summer it can be really spectacular, arriving at Divisadero at about 6am, just in time for sunrise. Check locally when this will be. Finally, you'll save money by taking along your own food and drink, but it's not essential; the conductors sell tepid beer and cokes, the dining car is good (though not cheap) and throughout the journey people climb on board selling *tacos*, *chiles rellenos* or whatever local produce comes to hand.

SOUTH TO DURANGO

Below Chihuahua lies a vast plain, mostly agricultural, largely uninteresting, broken only occasionally by an outstretched leg of the Sierra Madre Occidental. It's country which the train crosses at night, the buses hammer through relentlessly and where you'd be wise to follow their lead. At JIMENEZ the road divides, Highway 49 heading straight down through Gomez Palacio and Torreon, while Highway 45 curves westwards to Durango. The non-stop route for Zacatecas and Mexico City is via the former, and the railway too by-passes Durango, but if time is not your only consideration the latter offers much more of interest.

TORREON and **GOMEZ PALACIO** are virtually contiguous – there would be only one city if it weren't for the fact that the state border runs through the middle: Torreon is in Coahuila, Gomez Palacio in Durango. That said, they're as dull as each other – modern towns anyway, both were devastated by heavy fighting in the Revolution. Since you're only here to take the fast route through, I wouldn't bother stopping – though one consolation if you do is that this is the start of wine-growing country and you can sample the local produce (not the country's best) at various bodegas.

On the longer route, **DURANGO** is the first of the Spanish-colonial towns which distinguish Mexico's heartland, and while it's not a patch on some of those further south, it will certainly be the most attractive place you've come to yet. But it's a good 10 hours on the bus from Chihuahua, so you might consider breaking the journey in **HIDALGO DEL PARRAL**. Parral, as it is more simply known, is notorious now as the town where General Francisco 'Pancho' Villa was assassinated but it has a much longer history than that, if little to show for it. The stubby hills all around are rich in metals – silver above all, but also lead, copper and some gold – which attracted the Spaniards in the earliest years after the conquest. The little mining town of SANTA BARBARA, which still operates some 25km away, was then capital of the province of Nueva Viscaya, a territory which stretched as far north as Texas and southern California: the capital was transferred to Parral after its foundation in 1638. Mining is still the town's chief activity and its outskirts are grubbily industrial – at the centre, though, the old colonial plaza is pleasantly tranquil and there are a couple of remarkable buildings put up by prospectors who struck it rich. Chief of these are the **Palacio Pedro Alvarado**, an exuberantly decorated folly of a mansion built in the eighteenth century by a successful silver miner, and, across the river, the **Iglesia de la Virgen del Rayo**. Legend has it that this was constructed by an Indian on the proceeds of a gold mine he had discovered and worked in secret: the authorities tortured him to death in an attempt to find it, but the location died with him. There's also a small museum in the house from which Villa and his retinue of bodyguards were ambushed, but I've never found it open. If you want to stay, there are several small **hotels** near the plaza; the best of them on the corner by the Parish Church just along from the first class bus terminal.

DURANGO

Although the Sierra Madre still looms on the western horizon, the country around **DURANGO** itself is flat – two low hills marking out the city from the plain. The *Cerro del Mercado*, squat and black, rises to the north, a giant lump of iron ore which testifies to the area's mineral wealth, while to the west is the *Cerro de los Remedios*, its slopes given over to a peaceful city park. The old town shelters between these two, newer development straggling eastwards and southwards.

At the centre it's extremely compact – almost all the monuments clustered in a few streets around the Plaza Principal and a huge covered market just a few strides away down the city's main street. On the plaza itself is the **Cathedral**, its two robust domed towers rather dwarfing the narrow facade. It's a typical Mexican church in every way and a type you'll see throughout the country – externally imposing, weighty and baroque with a magnificent setting overlooking the plaza, and yet somehow disappointing – the interior dim and by comparison uninspired. Facing it from the centre of the plaza is a bizarre little two-storey bandstand from the top of which the town band plays on Sundays and, underneath, a small shop selling expensive local crafts.

Follow the Avenida 20 de Noviembre down from the Cathedral past the Hotel Casablanca and you come to the **Teatro Principal**, a grandiose Porfiriano theatre which has suffered the indignity of being converted into a cinema. Left here on Bruno Martinez, past the Teatro Victoria, and you come out in another beautiful plaza, its north side dominated by the porticoed facade of the **Palacio de Gobierno**. Originally the private house of a Spanish mining magnate, it was taken over by the local government after the War of Independence. The stairwells and walls of the two-storey arcaded patio inside are decorated with murals by local artists depicting the state's history. On the west side of the square is an ancient **Jesuit monastery**, now the offices of the University of Durango.

From here you can take 5 de Febrero back to the **Casa de los Condes**, the most elaborate of the Spanish-style mansions. Built in the eighteenth century by the Conde de Suchil, sometime Spanish governor of Durango, its exuberantly carved columns and wealth of extravagant detail are quite undamaged by time. History has brought some strange functions though; it was the seat of the local Inquisition for some time – and a more inappropriate setting for their stern deliberations would be hard to imagine – while nowadays it operates as a sort of upmarket shopping centre with most of the rooms off the lower courtyard given over to boutiques. For more exciting shopping, continue on 5 de Febrero to the back of the **market**. Covering a whole block on two storeys, there's just about everything you could want here, from medicinal herbs to farm equipment, as well as a series of little food stalls upstairs.

The University **Museum** is near here, a couple of blocks up Pasteur to where it crosses Aguiles Serdan; but its displays of local archaeology and history are pretty arcane and seem rarely to be disturbed by visitors. Best to head back to the plaza from where you can stroll up Constitucion, a lively shopping street with several small restaurants, to the little church and garden of Santa Ana, or along to the **Casa de la Cultura** – another old mansion converted into a cultural centre – where there are often interesting temporary exhibitions. A little further afield, take a bus from outside the Cathedral (*Remedios/Parque Guadiana*) for a walk around the hillside park. From the **Iglesia de los Remedios** at the summit there's a view which takes in the entire city.

A few practicalities
The centre may be compact, but the **Central de Autobuses** is a long way from it. Virtually any bus on the main road outside will take you down-town, direct to the plaza – look for *Centro/Camionera*. In the unlikely event that you arrive by **train**, the station (a fine example of early railway architecture) is only about 15 minutes walk from the plaza straight down Constitucion, or you can get there on a *centro* bus by a thoroughly roundabout route. Beyond any doubt, the best **place to stay** is the *Hotel Posada Duran* on Av. 20 de Noviembre right beside the Cathedral. An

old, slightly faded colonial mansion, its large rooms are set around the first floor of an inner courtyard – many of them with windows opening out over the Plaza. There's a bar downstairs and all in all it's remarkably reasonable. Nearby are the *Hotel Casablanca* (Av. 20 de Noviembre) and the *Posada San Jorge* (C. Constitucion) but they're less attractive and more expensive. If price is your only object the cheapest places are those immediately around the market and near the railway station: of the former try the *Hotel Reyes* on Av. 20 de Noviembre, or *Reforma* on the corner of Madero and 5. de Febrero; of the latter, the Hotels *Ferrocarril* and *Central*, both very basic, are directly opposite the station. There are **restaurants** throughout the central area, particularly along Constitucion, but none which seem to merit particular mention; very cheapest are the stalls upstairs in the market. Some of these serve excellent food, though the surrounding smells can make it hard to stomach at times.

Turismo is on Hidalgo, a couple of blocks west of the Palacio de Gobierno. Their full title is the *Direccion de Turismo y Cinematografia del Estado de Durango* and, though they do have useful little **maps of the town**, their main function seems to be organising the vast number of film units which come to take advantage of the surrounding area's remarkably constant, clear, high-altitude light, the desert and mountain scenery (westerns are the speciality), and, perhaps more importantly for Hollywood, the relatively cheap Mexican technicians and extras. If there's shooting in progress, the Tourist Office can normally organise a trip out to watch, and at other times there are **excursions** to see the permanent sets of CHUPADEROS or VILLA DEL OESTE. You can also get to these on the local rail line which goes to TEPEHUANES, a beautiful run up into the mountains, but frankly the journey is more enticing than the destination and it can be hard to get on a bus back. The main road from Parral runs within a few hundred yards of the movie towns and you get a pretty good view from a passing bus. Perhaps a more exciting day out is to head south to *El Saltito*, a waterfall surrounded by bizarre rock formations which has itself been a frequent film location. On any of these trips, watch out for **scorpions**. There's a genus of white scorpion unique to this area which, though rare – the only place most people see one is encased in the glass paperweights on sale everywhere as souvenirs – has a sting which is frequently fatal.

Durango's **fiesta**, on July 8th, celebrates the city's foundation on that day in 1563. Festivities commence several days before and run till the 12th – well worth going out of your way for.

On **leaving Durango** you face a simple choice – west to the Pacific at MAZATLAN over an incredible road through the Sierra Madre (see p. 48), or on south to ZACATECAS (p. 77) and the finest of Mexico's colonial cities.

MONTERREY AND THE NORTH-EAST ROUTES

The Eastern **border crossings**, from Piedras Negras to Matamoros, are uniformly dull – dedicated solely to the task of getting people and goods from one country to the other. In this they are at least reasonably efficient, although the immigration officials in MATAMOROS were the most officious and obstructive I encountered.

In all of them there are scores of hotels in every price range, but if at all possible you should press on inland – from PIEDRAS NEGRAS at least to MONCLOVA (and preferably to SALTILLO), from NUEVO LAREDO or REYNOSA to MONTERREY and from MATAMOROS, if you're taking the coastal route, to CIUDAD VICTORIA.

Direct bus services will get you from the border to Mexico City in about 16 hours, while the through train (the *Aguila Azteca*) leaves Nuevo Laredo at 6.55pm, arriving in the capital some 26 hours later.

MONTERREY

The third city of Mexico and the nation's industrial stronghold, **MONTERREY** is in many ways a remarkable place. Only in the last hundred years has it developed the vast network of factories, and the traffic, urban sprawl, pollution and ostentatious wealth which characterise the modern city; and its setting remains one of great beauty. Ringed by mountains – which sadly serve also to keep in the noxious industrial fumes – Monterrey is dominated above all by one, the *Cerro de la Silla* or Saddle Mountain.

Not that this is your first impression – that's provided by the shabby shanty-town suburbs and grimy manufacturing outskirts through which the highway roars: the city centre wears a very different aspect. Here the few old colonial relics are overshadowed by the office blocks and expensive shopping streets of the *zona commercial*. There are just two sites worth going out of your way to visit – the old Obispado on a hill overlooking the centre, and the giant Cuauhtemoc Brewery in the north. But the city itself rewards a day passed in nothing more specific than wandering and browsing.

At its heart (if not the physical centre) is the **Plaza Zaragoza**, around which lie the Cathedral and government offices. In the streets leading west from here are the smart shops, swank hotels and multi-national offices, while just beyond is the canalised – and usually dry – *Rio Santa Catarina* with the first slopes of the Cerro de la Silla rising almost immediately from its far bank. When I was last in Monterrey the plaza was a

1. Mercado Colon   4. Mercado Juarez   7. Cathedral   9. Palacio de Gobierno
2. La Purisima †   5. Bus Station   8. Plaza Hidalgo   10. Post Office
3. Independence Arch   6. City Hall

— CENTRAL MONTERREY —

vast demolition site as the city planners did away with some six complete
blocks to open up a new vista straight through from the intensely modern
City Hall to the beautiful red stone Palacio de Gobierno on what used
to be the Plaza Cinco de Mayo. This is Mexican planning at its most
extreme – when the political decision comes from the top no amount of
conservationist or social considerations are going to stand in the way,
especially as the constitution's 'no re-election' decree makes every admin-
istrator determined to leave some permanent memorial. The results can
at times be stunning as Guadalajara's new Plaza Tapatia (which
Monterrey is clearly trying to emulate) demonstrates.

In the evenings people gravitate here for no better reason than a stroll,
and there are frequently concerts, dances and other entertainments laid
on. The **Tourist Office**, in the middle of the plaza opposite the Cathedral,

can fill you in on the details. The **Cathedral**, with its one unbalanced tower, is a surprisingly modest edifice, easily dominated by the concrete bulk of the new **City Hall**, squatting on stilts at the southern end of the square. Inside there's a small archaeological collection, while in the **Palacio de Gobierno** at the other end of the square is a room devoted to local history. Off Zaragoza, and again opposite the Cathedral, opens the little **Plaza Hidalgo** – a much more traditional, shady place with old colonial buildings set around a statue of Miguel Hidalgo. The original Palacio Municipal, now superseded by the modern building, is here and acts as an occasional cultural centre. Otherwise the pavement cafes make a pleasant break in your wanderings – though food is expensive. Pedestrianised shopping streets fan out behind, crowded with window-gazing locals.

The **Obispado**, the old Bishop's Palace, tops Chepe Vera hill to the west of the city centre. Its commanding position – there are great views of the city – made it an essential objective for the city's many invaders. Originally built in the eighteenth century it became by turn a barracks, military hospital and fortress – a history recorded by the **museum** it now houses. Among its more dramatic exploits it managed to hold out for two days after the rest of the city had fallen to the Texan general Zachary Taylor in 1846. The building itself is a thoroughly elegant one and its contents an excellent example of the type of regional museum which the Mexicans seem to do so well. There's a little of everything: religious and secular art, arms from the War of Independence, revolutionary pamphlets, old carriages and displays of regional folk-ways. You get to the Obispado on Padre Mier, passing on the way the monumental modern church of **La Purisima**. There's supposed to be a bus from Av. Constitucion (by the river) but it's a complicated routing – easier to get a taxi if you can afford it, or walk (about 40 minutes).

Last, but far from least if you're thirsty after all this, a visit to the massive **Cerveceria Cuauhtemoc** is all but compulsory. This is where they make the wonderful *Bohemia* and *Tecate* beers you'll find throughout Mexico (as well as the rather drab *Carta Blanca*). And somehow it seems much more representative of Monterrey than any of its prouder settings. The brewery is open daily (except Mondays) from 10.30 to 6.30: there's a rather incongruous art museum and a much more congruous Sporting Hall of Fame, commemorating the heroes of Mexican baseball (really) – guided tours of the brewing process itself on weekdays at 11, 12 and 3pm. Your reward afterwards is **free beer** in the gardens outside. Buses run regularly up Cuauhtemoc, past the main gate.

Getting your bearings, some practical details
Monterrey's **Central Camionera** is enormous: there's even a cinema inside. The cheaper **hotels** are all nearby – mostly on the other side of

Av. Colon, safest crossed on the footbridge provided. You can see several as you stand outside the bus station, but it's best to penetrate a little further if you want to avoid the worst of the noise. Amado Nervo, heading north off Colon, has several possibilities, of which the best are probably the Hotels *Nuevo Leon* and *Virreyes*. Head to the right along Colon for a couple of blocks and you reach another cluster of very basic places between the small market and the Arco de la Independencia. Downtown, rooms are very much more expensive and the hotels, clustered in the commercial area to the west of the plazas, almost all modern and 'international'.

Getting into the centre from the bus station is no problem – there are hundreds of buses, most of which go somewhere near: pick them up heading east on Colon or south along Amado Nervo.

You'll find scores of tiny bars and rather sleazy **places to eat** in the same area as the hotels above – especially around the little market just north of Colon – but up here you might be safer sticking to one of the fast food joints which have sprung up all around the bus station. In the centre you eat better, but you also pay more. If you're craving American style food *Sanborn's*, on Morelos near the Plaza Hidalgo, is a safe bet as always – they also have a good selection of **English-language books**, magazines and guides.

Aside from the one mentioned above, there are two sizeable **markets** in Monterrey, the Mercado Juarez and the Mercado Colon (see map). The former is the one the locals use, with the typical mix, but mostly food, while the latter is much more tourist-oriented – specialising in local *artesania*.

Turismo is in the Plaza Zaragoza. They should be able to provide you with details on sidetrips into the surrounding country – often surprisingly wild. The most impressive of these is perhaps to the **Huasteca Canyon**, a mountain ravine some thousand feet deep, and the **Grutas de Garcia** – both off the road to SALTILLO. The Grutas (caves) are reached by cable car from the village of VILLA GARCIA – a popular weekend outing to see some impressive stalactites and stalagmites and an underground lake. The **Cascada Cola de Caballo** (Horsetail Falls) too is a well-worn excursion – you can hire horses and burros to ride in the hills around. Or head up to the **Mesa Chipinque** – a mountain plateau just 18km from the city with famous views back over it. Here again you can hire horses (from the enormously flash *Motel Chipinque*) to explore the hinterland.

MONCLOVA AND SALTILLO

Just 85km from Monterrey on a fast road, **SALTILLO**, capital of the state of Coahuila, is the place to head if you can't take the big city's hustle. It's infinitely quieter; cool and airy (at over 5,000 feet) with a scattering of beautiful buildings.

First though, if you're coming south from PIEDRAS NEGRAS, you pass through **MONCLOVA**. It doesn't look much now – aside from the vast steelworks – but Monclova was the capital of Coahuila in the days when the state included the whole of Texas. You wouldn't go out of your way to visit, but heading south it can make a useful staging point, some 4 hours from Piedras Negras, another three on to Saltillo. There are several small hotels near the centre; try the *Viena* or the *San Cristobal* on Cuauhtemoc, or the *Olimpia*, Hidalgo Sur.

SALTILLO itself is a much more attractive proposition: there's not a great deal to do here either, but it's a pleasant town to stroll around and soak up some atmosphere. The new **bus station** is stuck miles out in the country – there are a couple of small hotels and a restaurant directly opposite, but nothing else, and there's no point at all in staying out here unless you plan an extremely early start. Climb into one of the cramped vans instead (*Centro/Camionera*) and head for the centre. Get out in the Plaza Acuña and you're right at the heart of things. Most of the better value hotels are in the sidestreets immediately around here – head up towards Calle Victoria and the Cathedral and you pass several: the *Hidalgo* and the *Conde* are very basic, rather dingy but clean. On Victoria itself the *Hotel Arizpe Sainz* is a very fancy (and expensive) colonial-style establishment but the *Urdiñola* is more modest – in its pretensions and its price. Plaza Acuña is very much the modern centre of the town, surrounded by crowded shopping streets, the market in one corner, and with a series of little bars and cafes around the square.

The old **Plaza de Armas** is quite another story – sedate, formal, tranquil. Here the magnificent eighteenth-century **Cathedral** faces the Palacio de Gobierno across a flagged court – fountains playing in the centre. With an elaborately carved Churrigueresque facade and doorways and two strikingly tall towers, the Cathedral is one of the most beautiful in northern Mexico. The setting helps; standing in the Plaza you're well cut off from the traffic and modern development around. Around are the town's oldest streets, with some fine old houses still in private occupation. At the top of Calle Victoria, with its shopping and cinemas, is the **Alameda**, a shaded, tree-lined park. In the centre you'll find *El Estanque de la Republica*, a pond in the shape of the Mexican Republic, while the grassy areas round about tend to be peopled with students looking for a peaceful place to work: there are several language schools here as well as a University and Technical Institute, and, in summer especially, there are numbers of American students learning Spanish.

Saltillo is famous too for its **Sarapes**, and there are several small shops (especially on Calle Victoria) where you can watch the manufacturing process from hand-dying the wool to working the ancient looms. These tend to be the best quality, and their prices reflect it, but if you plan to buy one it's a good idea to look here first to get some idea of what to expect. All too many of those on sale in the market are mass-produced from artificial fibres.

For a day out from Saltillo, take a ride on the nineteenth-century carriages of the *Zacatecas and Coahuila Railway* up to CONCEPCION DEL ORO, an old silver and gold mining centre. The train runs daily and brings you back the same evening.

Beyond Saltillo you can head west to TORREON, or south to either SAN LUIS POTOSI or ZACATECAS. The direct route to Mexico City is via San Luis, passing through MATEHUALA (with the possibility of branching off to the mountain ghost-town of REAL DE CATORCE) and QUERÉTARO. Going through ZACATECAS, though slower, gives you the chance of visiting more of the beautiful colonial cities north of the capital. There's little point heading west unless you're aiming for MAZATLAN and the Pacific.

THE COAST ROUTE – CIUDAD VICTORIA AND TAMPICO

Even if you've crossed the border at **MATAMOROS**, you'd be well advised to consider following the border road west to REYNOSA and then cutting down to Monterrey. The Eastern Seaboard has little to recommend it. Unless you are determined to go straight down through Veracruz by the shortest route to the Yucatan, avoiding Mexico City altogether, there seems little point in coming this way: even the time factor is less of an advantage than it might appear from the map – the roads are in noticeably worse repair than those through the centre, and progress is considerably slower. Beyond TAMPICO, it's true, you get into an area of great archaeological interest with some good beaches around Veracruz, but this is probably better approached from the capital. Here in the North-East there is plenty of sandy coast, but access is difficult, beaches tend to be windswept and scrubby, and the whole area is marred by the consequences of its enormous oil wealth; there are refineries all the way down, tankers passing close offshore, and a shoreline littered with their discards and spillages. It's also very, very hot.

CIUDAD VICTORIA, capital of the state of Tamaulipas, is the obvious place to stop over for the first night – little more than that. It's not unattractive but nor is it interesting, and while the surrounding country is supposed to be a paradise for hunters and fishing enthusiasts, others will find little enough to detain them. Head, as always, for the Zocalo around which most of the town's facilities are concentrated. There are several hotels on the plaza itself – *Los Monteros* offers the best value –

while the cheaper places tend to be a block or two away: try the *Ritz* on Hidalgo or the hotels *Paris* and *Tampico*, both on Juarez.

Between here and **TAMPICO** the vegetation around the road becomes increasingly tropical (the Tropic of Cancer passes just south of Ciudad Victoria), lush and green, and Tampico itself is very much a tropic port. The older parts of town with their peeling, ramshackle clapboard houses and swing-door bars have a distinct feel of the Caribbean. It *is* a major port, with all the vivaciousness (and occasional heaviness) that implies, but Tampico is also a newly wealthy boom town, riding the oil surge with a welter of grand new buildings founded on the income from a huge refinery at the mouth of the Panuco. The contrasts are tangible – on one side the smart new suburbs with their supermarkets and neat planning (nowhere more so than in *CIUDAD MADERO*, Tampico's growing twin town), and on the other the run-down waterfront and the seamier sides of the city centre.

From the bus station get a bus or a collective taxi down into the centre. The two natures are instantly apparent – within a hundred yards of each other are two Plazas: the Plaza de Armas, smart and formal, ringed by government buildings, the Cathedral (built in the 1930s with money donated by American oil tycoon Edward Doheny) and the smart hotels; and the Plaza de la Libertad, raucous and randy, peopled by wandering salesmen, surrounded by cheap bars and basic hotels. This is the cheapest and the most atmospheric place to stay, but one thing you can say for Tampico is that it is not short of **hotels**, even if most are fairly expensive.

The town **beach**, *Playa Miramar*, is about a half-hour bus ride from the centre and there are several small boarding houses along it as well as a series of little restaurants serving good fresh fish – many will also let you change and shower for a small fee. This is good **camping** territory, with a stand of small trees immediately behind the beach, and if you have your own transport you can drive miles up the sand to seek out isolation. Which is one of the chief disadvantages – everyone insists on driving their cars around the beach, most local learners seem to take their first lessons here and even the bus drives on to the sand to turn round. The other is that the water, so close to the refinery and the mouth of the river, is **heavily polluted**.

FIESTAS

Carnival (the week before Lent, variable Feb.-Mar.) is at its best in the Caribbean atmosphere of **Tampico** (Tamaulipas) – also in **Ciudad Victoria** (Tam.) and **Monterrey** (Nuevo Leon).

March
19th FESTIVAL DE SAN JOSE celebrated in **Ciudad Victoria** (Tam.). 21st Ceremonies to commemorate the birth of Benito Juarez in **Matamoros** (Coahuila), near Torreon.

April
12th Processions and civic festival in honour of the nineteenth-century resto-

ration of **Tampico** (Tam.), with dress of that era.
27th FERIA DEL AZUCAR in **Ciudad Mante** (Tam.), south of Ciudad Victoria; very lively with bands, dancing, fireworks.

May
3rd DIA DE LA SANTA CRUZ. **Tula** (Tam.), between Cd. Victoria and San Luis Potosí, stages a fiesta with traditional dance. In **Gomez Palacio** (Durango), the start of an agricultural and industrial fair which lasts two weeks – many events coincide.
15th DIA DE SAN ISIDRO observed in **Guadalupe de Bravos** (Chihuahua), on the border near Ciudad Juarez, with dances all day and parades all night. Similar celebrations in **Matamoros** (Coah.) and **Arteaga** (Coah.), near Saltillo.
20th **Monterrey** (N.L.) in the midst of its Feria Comercial, a trade fair leavened with sporting events, bullfights, dances and public spectacles.

June
13th DIA DE SAN ANTONIO DE PADUA marked in **Tula** (Tam.) by religious services followed by pastoral plays and traditional dances. Colourful native dancing too in **Vicente Guerrero** (Dgo.), between Durango and Zacatecas.
25th DIA DE SANTIAGO. The start of a week-long fiesta in **Altamira** (Tam.), near Tampico.

July
4th Dancing and pilgrimages to celebrate the Dia de Nuestra Señora del Refugio in **Matamoros** (Coah.).
8th **Durango** (Dgo.) celebrates its founders' day, coinciding with the feria and crafts exhibitions.
23rd FERIA DE LA UVA in **Cuatro Cienegas** (Coah.), a spa town near Monclova.

August
6th Fiesta in **Jimenez** (Chih.) with traditional dances, religious processions and a fair. Regional dancing too in **Saltillo** (Coah.).
9th Exuberant FERIA DE LA UVA in **Parras** (Coah.), between Saltillo and Torreon.
13th **Saltillo** (Coah.) begins its annual feria, lively and varied.

September
8th DIA DE LA VIRGEN DE LOS REMEDIOS celebrated with parades and traditional dances in **Santa Barbara** (Chih.), near Hidalgo del Parral, and **San Juan del Rio** (Dgo.), between here and Durango.
10th Dancing from before dawn and a parade in the evening mark the fiesta in **Ramos Arizpe** (Coah.), near Saltillo.
11th Major Feria on the border at **Nuevo Laredo** (Tam.).
15th-16th INDEPENDENCE festivities everywhere, the biggest in **Monterrey** (N.L.).

October
25th Joint celebrations between the border town of **Ciudad Acuña** (Coah.) and its Texas neighbour Del Rio. Bullfights and parades.

November
3rd DIA DE SAN MARTIN DE PORRES is the excuse for a fiesta, with native dances, in **Tampico** (Tam.) and nearby **Altamira (Tam.)**.

December
4th **Santa Barbara** (Chih.) celebrates its saint's day.
8th Fiesta with dancing virtually non-stop till the 12th in **Matamoros** (Coah.).
12th DIA DE NUESTRA SEÑORA DE GUADALUPE is a big one everywhere, especially in **Guadalupe de Bravos** (Chih.), **El Palmito** (Dgo.), between Durango and Parral, **Cd. Anahuac** (N.L.) in the north of the state, and **Abasolo** (N.L.), near Monterrey. **Monterrey** itself attracts many pilgrims at this time.

TRAVEL DETAILS

Trains
Two rail companies operate in the region, *Ferrocarriles Nacionales de Mexico* with services between the border and Mexico City, and *Chihuahua al Pacifico* (CHP) from Chihuahua to Los Mochis. Expresses have kept to pretty

much the same schedule for years, but it's best to check anyway.

1 **Ciuded Juarez** to **Mexico City**. *El Fronterizo* leaves 18.25. Arrives Chihuahua (23.25), Jimenez (04.15), Torreon (8.00), Zacatecas (15.40), Aguascalientes (18.10), Leon (21.53), Querétaro (1.30), Mexico City (6.55).

2 **Nuevo Laredo** to **Mexico City**. The *Aguila Azteca* leaves 18.55. Arrives Monterrey (23.30), Saltillo (2.35), San Luis Potosí (10.05), Querétaro (14.40), Mexico City (20.04).

3 **Piedras Negras** to **Saltillo**. Leaves 09.00. Arrives Monclova (14.15), Saltillo (19.10). Connection to Mexico City leaves 20.25 (see below).

4 **From Monterrey**. To **Mexico City** (as well as 2 above) leaves 18.00. Arrives Saltillo (20.10), San Luis Potosí (1.50), Mexico City (09.00). To **Torreon** leaves 08.10, arrives 14.40; return leaves Torreon 12.05, arrives 18.50. To **Tampico** (second class only) leaves 08.00, arriving Cd. Victoria (13.50) and Tampico (18.45). Return leaves 7.50, arriving 18.30.

All the above are daily main-line services – there are of course local trains between various points en route, but they're very slow, unreliable, and rarely a viable alternative to the bus.

5 **Tampico** to **San Luis Potosí**, slow and second class only, leaves daily 6.30, arriving 20.20.

6 **Chihuahua** to **Los Mochis**. Six days a week, 13-hr journey – see text (p. 61) for details.

Buses

Bus services on the chief routes to and from the frontier (Ciudad Juarez-Chihuahua-Torreon/Durango and from the border to Monterrey-Saltillo-San Luis Potosí/Zacatecas) are excellent, with constant departures day and night. What follows should be taken as a minimum.

The best lines generally are, on the central route, *Omnibus de Mexico* and *Transportes Chihuahuenses*, in the east *Frontera*, *Transportes del Norte* and *Autobuses del Oriente* (ADO). *Estrella Blanca*, ostensibly a second class company, often beats them all for frequency of services and efficiency.

From **Ciudad Juarez**: hourly at least to Chihuahua (5hrs), Jimenez (8hrs) and Torreon (12hrs) or Parral (10hrs) and Durango (16hrs). 5 daily to Nuevo Casas Grandes (4hrs).

From Monterrey: hourly to Nuevo Laredo (3hrs) and Reynosa (3½hrs). Constantly to Saltillo (1hr). 12 daily to Matehuala (5hrs) and San Luis Potosí (8hrs). 5 daily to Torreon (5hrs). 6 daily to Ciudad Victoria (4½hrs). 8 daily to Zacatecas (7hrs).

From Durango: 8 daily to Mazatlan (6½hrs); 6 daily to Torreon (4½hrs); 11 daily to Fresnillo (3hrs) and Zacatecas (4½hrs).

Chihuahua–Nuevo Casas Grandes – 5 daily (5hrs).

Ciudad Victoria–Tampico – 10 daily (4hrs).

Matamoros–Ciudad Victoria – 7 daily (4½hrs).

Matamoros–Tampico – 9 daily (7½hrs).

Piedras Negras–Saltillo – 9 daily (7hrs).

Torreon–Zacatecas – 10 daily (6hrs).

Tampico–Veracruz – 8 daily (8hrs).

Plane

Frequent flights from most of the major cities to the capital – Chihuahua, Monterrey and Tampico all have several a day. From Monterrey you can also fly to Guadalajara and Acapulco, and there are international services to Dallas, Houston, San Antonio and Chicago.

Chapter three
THE CENTRAL HIGHLANDS

The Central Highlands are perhaps the most fascinating part of Mexico – certainly the richest in colonial history and the most concentrated in interest – and the country, now lofty plain, now rugged sierra, is as beautiful and varied as any. There is, too, a powerful native culture which more than compensates for the paucity of physical remains from the pre-Hispanic era; though both Chicomoztoc, near Zacatecas, and Tzintzuntzan on Lake Patzcuaro are impressive ruins.

Guadalajara is the best known destination: Mexico's second city and by far her most enticing metropolis – easy-paced, packed with elegant buildings and surrounded by beautiful country. But this is only a small part. In the centre are the great colonial cities, built on the wealth of silver. **Zacatecas** in its mountainous isolation is the most northerly, with a supremely flamboyant Cathedral, mines, and cable car ride across the city; historic **Guanajuato** is the richest and most scenic, boasting one of the finest baroque churches in Mexico, a thriving student life, and the ghoulish Museum of Mummies. Heading for the capital, Dolores Hidalgo, San Miguel de Allende and Querétaro have their own fascination, and intimate links with the struggle for Mexican Independence: **San Miguel**, in a gorgeous hillside setting, has a substantial foreign community, attracting artists and students by the hundred; **Dolores** is much smaller – a place of pilgrimage to the Independence movement; **Querétaro**, large and industrial, preserves a fine colonial quarter at its heart. Or, on the way to the more modern city of **San Luis Potosí**, there's **Real de Catorce**, a boom town burst, its mines and mansions totally deserted.

Jalisco and **Michoacan** to the south are green and mountainous states, studded with volcanoes and lakes. Here too there are colonial relics – in **Morelia** above all and in **Patzcuaro** – but it's the majesty of the country and the richness of Indian traditions therein which first call for attention. Fiestas here – and there are many – are among the most vital in Mexico, and there's a legacy of village handicrafts which survives from the earliest days of the Conquest. Restfully semi-tropical, these states are among the most serene in the country – relaxing, easy to get about, and free of urban hassle.

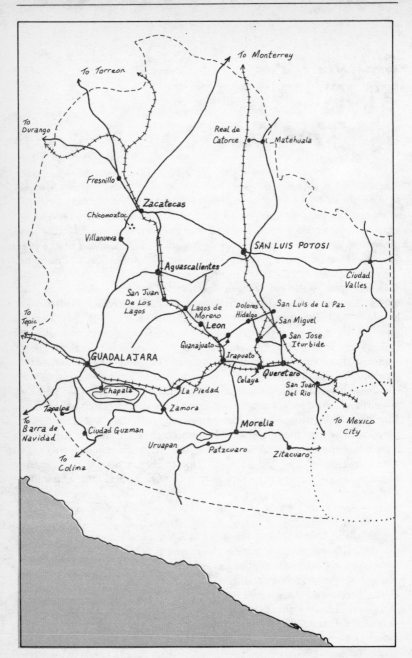

FROM THE NORTH: ZACATECAS AND SAN LUIS POTOSÍ

Coming down by the central or eastern routes you pass, inevitably, through either ZACATECAS or SAN LUIS POTOSÍ. With these begins the series of magnificent colonial cities which characterise the heartland of Mexico. Zacatecas itself is one of the most striking of all; San Luis too – though now a large modern city – has its share of monuments. En route to the latter you'll pass through MATEHUALA, close by which (see p. 89) is the strange ghost town of REAL DE CATORCE.

Making for Zacatecas there's not a great deal to hold you on any of the roads: a semi-desert landscape punctuated only by the occasional mining town or ranch where fighting bulls are bred. The one place you might want – or need – to stop over is **FRESNILLO**, but more for its location than any intrinsic interest. If you do you'll find a quiet town, long deserted by the wealth which gold-mining once brought, but retaining a few fine buildings from its heyday. There are several small hotels and frequent onward services by bus.

ZACATECAS

ZACATECAS, 8,000 feet up and crammed into a narrow gully between two hills, packs more of interest into a small space than almost anywhere in Mexico. It remains, in fact, much as the British Admiralty's *Handbook of Mexico* described it in 1905:

> . . . *irregular, and the streets very narrow, steep, and frequently interrupted by stone steps; where they are paved at all, they are roughly cobbled, and there is no wheeled traffic. There are many churches* . . .

It goes on to warn too that 'the town is much exposed to winds blowing through the gorge, and pneumonia is prevalent'. Most of the streets, sadly, are now paved and choked with traffic, but otherwise little can have changed: those winds still gust, too, bitterly chill in winter.

All views are dominated by the *Cerro de la Bufa* with its extraordinary rock cock's comb rearing some 500 feet above the city. A modern Swiss cable-car connects it with the *Cerro del Bosque* (or *del Grillo*) – a superb ride straight over the heart of the old town. From the Cerro de la Bufa itself there are commanding vistas taking in the entire city: its drab new outskirts and the bare hills all around pockmarked with old mine-workings.

It didn't take the Spanish Conquistadors long to discover the enormous lodes of silver in the hills, and after some initial skirmishes with the Zacateco Indians, Zacatecas was founded in 1546. For the next three centuries its mines disgorged fabulous wealth to enrich the Spanish crown and the city: in 1728 local mines were producing one-fifth of all Mexico's silver. The end of the boom, when it came, was brought about more by the political uncertainties of the nineteenth century than the exhaustion of the mines, some of which still operate. Throughout nearly a century of war Zacatecas found itself an important prize: there were major battles here in 1871, when Benito Juarez successfully put down local rebels, and most recently in 1914 when Pancho Villa's *Division del Norte* captured the city, completely annihilating the 12,000-strong garrison with all its baggage and supplies. Some of the destruction of that battle can still be seen.

The **Cathedral** is the outstanding relic of the years of colonial glory: built in the faintly pink stone typical of Zacatecas, it represents one of the latest, and arguably the finest, example of Mexican baroque architecture. It was completed in 1750, its facades stunningly rich and carved with a wild exuberance unequalled anywhere in the country. The interior, they say, was once at least its equal – furnished in gold and silver with rich wall hangings and a great collection of paintings – but as everywhere it was despoiled, or the riches removed for 'safekeeping', first at the time of Juarez's reforms and later during the Revolution, so that only the structure itself, with its bulky Doric columns and airy vaulting, remains to be admired. Outside, almost everything of interest lies within easy walking distance.

On each side there's a small plaza: to the north the formal **Plaza Hidalgo,** overlooked by the Palacio de Gobierno, to the south a tiny paved *plazuela* – often the scene of informal concerts and street entertainments – across which is the old market building. The **Palacio de Gobierno** is an eighteenth-century mansion built as a home by the Conde Santiago de la Laguna and subsequently bought by the State Government. As is the fashion here, the interior courtyard is embellished with a mural depicting the city's history. Opposite are more colonial mansions, now converted into more government offices and the *Hotel Reina Cristina*. On the other side, the **Mercado Gonzales Ortega** is a strikingly attractive market building, built at the end of the last century. It takes advantage of its sloping position to have two fronts: the upper level opening onto Av. Hidalgo, the lower floor with entrances on C. Tacuba – head to the right down Tacuba and you'll come to the real **market**; this place has been converted into an upmarket shopping mall, a sort of Mexican Covent Garden. There's a good pizzeria in the upper storey.

Behind and below the Cathedral is a tangle of little alleys and semi-derelict dwellings where you quickly get lost; in front, climbing up towards the Cerro del Bosque, are streets lined with more mansions – some restored, some badly in need of it, but all deserted now by the mining moguls who built them. The church of **Santo Domingo** stands raised on a platform above the Plaza of the same name, just up from the Plaza Hidalgo – its hefty, buttressed bulk a stern contrast to the lightness of the Cathedral, though it was built at much the same time. In the gloom of the interior you can just make out the gilded Churrigueresque retablos in the chapels. Next door is the new **Casa de la Cultura**, a museum (open 9–1 and 2.30–6, daily except Tuesdays) in what was originally a monastery attached to the church (both were founded by the Jesuits and known as La Compañia, for the Company of Jesus). The collection it houses is a remarkable one – almost all gathered by a local artist – with African masks, oriental statuettes, Hogarth prints and Mexican modern art alongside the more usual local archaeological finds and early religious paintings. The building itself was converted into a hospital, a barracks and a prison before its recent restoration, and one of the grimmer dungeons has also been preserved as an exhibit.

On the same street, in another converted mansion, is the main building of the Universidad Autonoma de Zacatecas, the **University Rectory** – a good place to check the noticeboards for any events that might be happening around town. Below this, on the Calle de Hierro, is the **Casa de la Moneda** – Zacatecas's mint in the days when every silver producing town in Mexico struck its own coins. There's a small exhibition inside of early coins and the history of the silver industry. Further along you come to the church of **San Agustin**, an early eighteenth-century temple which, after the Reform Laws, was converted into a casino while the adjoining monastery became an hotel. They've been working on its restoration for nearly twenty years now, but the interior is still in chaos with bits of statuary and refurbished sections of frieze lying around on the floor waiting to be put back up. It must have been very beautiful once, and there's still a very un-Mexican simplicity and charm to the place, and a magnificent relief telling the story of St Augustine. In the nave a series of before and after photographs explains the work in hand.

It's an easy climb from here up to the lower station of the **cable-car** beside the *Motel del Bosque* – though any walking around Zacatecas can be tiring until you get used to the altitude. Most people take a return trip up to the top of the *Cerro de la Bufa*, but if you only go one way the walk back down is no great strain. At the summit, after you've taken in the view, visit the little **Capilla del Patrocinio**, an eighteenth-century chapel with an image of the Virgin said to perform healing miracles, and stroll around the observatory, on the very edge of the crags. Behind, in the shadow of that great crest of rock, is the **Mausoleo de los Hombres**

Illustres where Zacatecanos who have made their mark on history are buried, or at least have their memorials. There are still a few empty places, and it would be a magnificent place to end up – as close to heaven as you could wish, and great views while you're waiting. As you look out over the city from the hilltop, notice the ruinous monastery of **San Francisco**, to your right amid rather desolate slums. It's a barracks now, as it was when it was destroyed by bombardment during Villa's assault on the city, but supposedly this too is being restored.

In quite the other direction you can follow the line of the **aqueduct** which used to carry water to the south of the city. Not much of it is left standing, but what there is can be inspected at closer quarters from the little **park** on Av. Gonzales Ortega – the continuation of Av. Hidalgo up the hill from the centre. At the back of the park stands the **Museo Francisco Goytia** (9–1.30 and 3.30–6; closed Mondays) in what was once the governor's residence. Goytia was one of Mexico's leading painters early this century, and the museum houses a permanent exhibition of his work and that of more modern local artists as well as temporary displays and travelling art shows. Surprisingly good it is too.

Finally, and perhaps the most fascinating and unusual of all Zacatecas's attractions, you can visit the **Mina El Eden**. The entrance to this old mine is right in the city, behind the modern hospital, from where a small train drives you to the beginning of the sixteenth-century shafts, right in the heart of the Cerro del Bosque some 1,000 feet below the summit. The guided tour – which takes in only a fraction of the workings – is extraordinary, and some of the statistics terrifying; if the guide is to be believed, fatalities among the workers ran to eight every day at the height of production. It seems perfectly possible when you're down there – level upon level of old galleries lie beneath you, inaccessible now, but which the miners had to reach on precarious wooden ladders, carrying their tools down with them, and their production back out. Inside now there are underground pools, chasms crossed on rickety wooden bridges and of course a ghost. Also, where the train stops, a **disco** (Thursday, Friday and Saturday nights only) and a shop where they sell rocks from the mine. The entire hill is honeycombed with tunnels, and supposedly there's a lift from the end of one shaft up to the lower station of the cable-car: plans to open this to the public are well advanced, and when it does open it should make a remarkable round trip from the depths of the mine to the top of La Bufa. You can get a bus from the Jardin Independencia up Juarez to the hospital (look for *IMSS*), but it's not far to walk, taking in a pleasant stroll along the **Alameda** and a brief climb.

Some practical details

In Zacatecas the **bus station**, for once, is just a short walk from the centre – right out the front, right again down the narrow alley beside the buses,

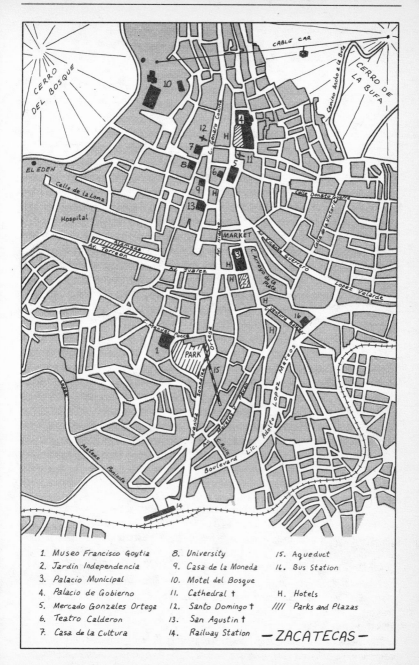

1. Museo Francisco Goytia
2. Jardin Independencia
3. Palacio Municipal
4. Palacio de Gobierno
5. Mercado Gonzales Ortega
6. Teatro Calderon
7. Casa de la Cultura

8. University
9. Casa de la Moneda
10. Motel del Bosque
11. Cathedral †
12. Santo Domingo †
13. San Agustin †
14. Railway Station

15. Aqueduct
16. Bus Station

H. Hotels
//// Parks and Plazas

— ZACATECAS —

and bear right for the Jardin Independencia. Arrive by **train** and you'll be a little further out – again you can walk, straight up Av. Gonzales Ortega, but it's mostly uphill and I'd advise getting a bus or taxi in. Both are marked on the plan.

Hotels, too, are no problem unless you're determined to go for really rock-bottom prices. I've found very few really cheap places, and none which are at all attractive – they're the closest to the bus station, though, so you could take a look on your way past. First is the *Hotel Zamora* in the tiny, traffic-choked plaza at the top of the alley (C. Ventura Salazar) which leads up from the bus station, and doubling back from here onto C. Insurgentes you'll find the *Hotel Insurgentes*. Even more basic than these, and none too clean either, is the *Hotel Reforma*, on the corner as you enter the Jardin Independencia: sooner or later, with its location right opposite the **Palacio Municipal**, someone's going to do the place up – for now it's pretty grim.

Jardin Independencia is effectively the city's main plaza; just a few paces from the market and from the important intersection of Juarez and Hidalgo, this is where people gather in the evenings or hang out between appointments – though they may take their evening *paseo* in the Alameda and more formal events occur in the Plaza Hidalgo. There are two more hotels here, just above the square on Av. Juarez – the *Condesa* and the *Posada de los Condes*. They are very similar in every way and charge much the same: better value to my mind is the *Posada de la Moneda* on Av. Hidalgo towards the cathedral, though it does cost more. The setting is great, in an old mansion almost next to the **Teatro Calderon**, a grandiose nineteenth-century theatre sadly in need of refurbishment, and virtually opposite the Merdcado Gonzales Ortega. Further down the same street, on the Plaza Hidalgo, the *Hotel Reina Cristina* falls somewhat bizarrely between these relatively deluxe establishments and the cheaper joints. It's in another colonial mansion, but barely restored at all – the lobby, for example, is a vast chamber complete with chandeliers, but empty save for a couple of cheap plastic chairs and formica-topped metal tables which serve as a dining room.

There are plenty of **restaurants** around this central area – those attached to the *Hotel Condesa* and the *Posada de los Condes* are both good for basic meals or for breakfast. *El Delfin*, in a basement on the left-hand side as you head up Av. Gonzales Ortega serves a very large, cheap *comida corrida* at lunchtimes, though it tends to be full of businessmen. For *tacos, tostadas* and sandwiches head back down towards the bus station – Ventura Salazar is lined with places serving quick snacks to travellers. While in Zacatecas, too, you should sample *tunas*, the succulent green or purple fruit of a local cactus. In season they're sold everywhere, ready peeled, by the bucket-load, or if you go out into the country you can pick your own (but see the warning under Chicomoztoc, below).

Zacatecas has one important **fiesta**, which you should definitely get to if you're in the area, at the end of August. The highlight is the battle between Moors and Christians (an import from Spain, where these stylised struggles are common) on the Cerro de la Bufa. August 27th is the main day, but festivities spill over for several days before and after, with **bullfights** – the fiercest fighting bulls are bred around Zacatecas – and all the traditional entertainments.

The **Tourist Office** is on the 3rd floor of a building on Av. Juarez, between the Jardin Independencia and Hidalgo, just up from the hotel Condesa.

AROUND ZACATECAS: GUADALUPE AND CHICOMOZTOC

Within easy striking distance of Zacatecas are two sites of great interest, and starkly contrasting nature. The **Convento de Guadalupe** is a rich, sumptuously decorated monastery, a rarity in that it has survived the centuries virtually unscathed, and for that reason one of the most important remaining in Mexico. The ruins of **Chicomoztoc** are quite unadorned, but nonetheless enormously impressive – a great fortress town in the desert. Guadalupe is now virtually a suburb of Zacatecas and can be visited in only a few hours – Chicomoztoc is further, and transport problems mean you may need a whole day, but both are well worth the effort.

El Ex-Convento de Nuestra Señora de Guadalupe

Buses run out to Guadalupe every few minutes from a courtyard right beside the Zacatecas bus station. Once there, you can't miss the enormous bulk of the church, with its dome and mismatched twin towers. You enter through a flagged, tree-studded courtyard – the church doors are straight ahead in the elaborate baroque facade, the entry to the **museum and monastery** (open daily 9–1 and 3–5) is to the right.

It's a vast and confusing warren of a place – seemingly endless rows of cells opening off courtyards, stairways leading nowhere and long corridors lined with portraits of monks. There are guided tours, but I prefer to wander alone, studying the paintings – which cover every wall – at leisure, tagging on to a group for a few minutes when our paths cross. Locked doors are everywhere, and joining a group helps get you through them, but in theory there are guards standing around with keys who will admit you individually to study the riches of the library or the various chapels. One such admits you from the body of the monastery into the *Coro Alto*, the raised choir at the back of the church with its beautifully carved and painted wooden choir stalls. Above all, don't miss the **Capilla de Napoles**, whose neo-classical domed roof is liberally plastered in gold leaf, elaborately filigreed. Presumably, 150 years ago such sights were not altogether unusual in Mexican churches – today it's by far the richest you'll see anywhere.

Chicomoztoc

The **Ruinas de Chicomoztoc** (also known, deceptively, as **La Quemada**) are some 40km from Zacatecas on the road to VILLANUEVA and GUADALAJARA. There are plenty of buses to Guadalajara (via Corta) which pass the turn-off for the site, but unfortunately no chance of persuading them to stop: even the second class operators are extremely reluctant to sell you a ticket to the ruins. If you run into this problem get a ticket on a second class bus to LA QUEMADA (the nearest village, about an hour's walk from the site), or even VILLANUEVA itself, and persuade the driver to let you off at the ruins. You'll then be faced with a 20-minute walk up a side road to the entrance – a lonely and rather wild place, with the odd rabbit darting across the road at your approach. There are cacti growing all along here, and its tempting to pick their fruit to quench your thirst – be warned, though, that these *tunas* are covered in tiny prickles which take hours to get out of your skin; they're best picked with a pair of heavy gloves and a sharp knife. The site caretaker sells cold drinks from his hut by the entrance.

The scale of the ruins themselves isn't apparent until you're right among them – from the road you can vaguely see signs of construction, but the whole thing, even the one huge restored pyramid, blends so totally into the mountain against which they are built as to be almost invisible. No two archaeologists seem able to agree on the nature of the site – its functions or inhabitants – even to the extent that many doubt that it was a fortress, though that much seems clear from its superb natural defensive position and hefty surrounding walls. Most likely it was a frontier post on the outskirts of some pre-Aztec sphere of domination – probably the Toltecs – charged with keeping at bay the southward depredations of the Chichimeca. Or it could simply have been a particularly harsh local ruling class, exacting enough tribute to build themselves these palaces, and needing the defences to keep their own subjects out. Legends which survive among the Huichol Indians seem to support that theory: there was an evil priest, the story runs, who lived on a rock surrounded by walls and covered with buildings, with eagles and jaguars under his command to oppress the population. The people appealed to their gods, who destroyed the priest and his followers with great heat, warning the people never to go near the rock again. Chicomoztoc, in fact, was burned in around 1300AD and never re-occupied thereafter, and even today the Huichols (see p. 49), in their annual pilgrimage from the Sierra Madre in the west to collect peyote in the area of Real de Catorce to the east, take a long detour around this area.

Then again, there are those who say that from here the Aztecs set out on their long trek south to the Valley of Mexico and the foundation of Tenochtitlan. Whatever the truth, you'll be in a better position to judge if you've seen for yourself: in addition to the reconstructed temple, there's a large hall with eleven pillars still standing, a ball-court, the walls, an extensive (but barely visible) system of roads heading out into the valley and many lesser, ruinous structures.

Getting back from the site is as difficult as the approach, perhaps harder since it's entirely up to the driver whether he ignores you as you try to flag down his bus, and hitching seems to be totally ineffective. Hail all the buses going in either direction – for some reason it's much easier to get to **VILLANUEVA** and then get on another bus back to Zacatecas. Villanueva's not a bad place to while away a few hours anyway, with several bars and cafes around the old plaza where the buses stop: here too you can change for a fast service on to **GUADALAJARA**. And don't worry, you will get back eventually, even if you have to wait until after dark for the bus which brings local children back from school – that stops everywhere.

AGUASCALIENTES

Lively, modern, industrial, **AGUASCALIENTES** is an important provincial capital. There are some fine colonial monuments surviving in the centre, too, and a couple of excellent museums which, while they don't put the city in the highest league as a tourist draw, do make it a pleasant place to stop over for a day or two – especially when you add a reputation for some of the finest fiestas in Mexico, and for the manufacture of excellent wines and brandy.

Both the **railway station** and the **Central Camionera** are some way from the centre on the city's ring road (Av. Circunvalacion) – there's a frequent bus service into the centre from both. Once there, almost everything of interest is in close proximity to the **Plaza de la Constitucion**. Here, and on the adjoining Plaza de la Republica, are all the important public buildings – the Cathedral and government offices – the fancier hotels and some good restaurants. Just a short walk away are two museums, the market, and all the cheaper places to stay. The **Tourist Office** has been moved out of the centre to a new building on the ring road, but you can pick up maps and leaflets from a small *Turismo* desk in the *Hotel Francia*, most expensive of the **hotels** on the main plaza. Also on the plaza itself are the *Hotel Rio Grande* and the *Imperial*: the latter, like the Francia, is in an impressive colonial building but in a state of considerable disrepair and hence relatively inexpensive. For rooms which are cheaper still head north from the plaza up Juarez towards the **market**. If you follow this all the way up to 5 de Mayo and turn left you'll end up back in the plaza beside the Imperial, having passed a series of small hotels and Casas de Huespedes – among them the *Don Jesus*, on Juarez more or less opposite the market, and the *Colonial* and *Roble* on 5 de Mayo. Right by the bus station there's also the *Hotel Continental* – noisy and rather out of the way, but not at all bad if you roll in late.

The plaza, again, is the place to go **to eat**. At the corner with Venustiano Carranza, more or less under the Hotel Imperial, there's a place which serves very good, basic Mexican food – meat and beans with vast piles of Tortillas – or, for much the same thing in a fake western atmosphere, try *El Caballo Loco* a little further down the same street on the left-hand side. Back on the plaza there are several small places for sandwiches or *quesadillas* – for a quick, simple fill the *San Francisco*, beside the Teatro Morelos, is as good as any. The restaurant in the *Hotel Rio Grande* is somewhat staid but serves a substantial and reasonably priced *comida corrida*, and there's an expensive, but occasionally reassuring, American-style soda fountain in the *Francia*. Walk up 5 de Mayo and you pass several places with chickens roasting over open fires: you can get these whole to take away or buy a quarter or a half to consume on the premises with the inevitable tortillas and chile. At some time, too, you should try some of the local wine (not always easy except in the more expensive restaurants) or at least the brandy; *San Marcos* is the best known, made here and sold all over the Republic.

The entire centre of Aguascalientes is undermined by a series of tunnels and catacombs carved out by some unknown tribe – since they're closed to the public though, the most ancient constructions you're actually going to see are the eighteenth-century Cathedral and **Palacio de Gobierno**. The latter is a remarkably beautiful neo-classical building, built in reddish volcanic rock around an arcaded courtyard with a grand central staircase, and decorated with a marvellous mural painted in the early 1960s by the Chilean Oswaldo Barra, who learnt his trade from the greatest muralist of them all, Diego Rivera. The **Palacio Municipal** has a giant mural too, a more modern work depicting Zapata, but neither it nor the building which houses it can really compare. Again in the **Cathedral** it's the artworks which stand out; the church itself is disappointing, but the *Pinacoteca Religiosa*, in an annexe, has a collection of eighteenth-century religious paintings which are well worth a look.

Across Venustiano Carranza from here is the **Casa de la Cultura**, a beautiful old mansion given over to music and dance classes and the occasional exhibition. In the patio there's a small cafe – a tranquil spot to have a drink and a rest or catch up on your postcards. Continue down the street and you come to the **Jardin San Marcos**, a tiny enclosed park with the **Templo del Carmen** to one side and the modern **Casino de la Feria** with its giant *palenque* (where cock fights are staged) just beyond. Here the ancient *Feria de San Marcos*, famous throughout Mexico, is celebrated in the last couple of weeks of April and the beginning of May. This is the most important fiesta in the city but the *Feria de la Uva* in mid-August, celebrating the grape harvest, is almost as popular, with a giant procession (the *Romeria de la Asuncion*) on the 15th. Rarely a week goes by, though, without some sort of celebration in Aguascalientes, or at least a band playing in one of the plazas at the weekend.

Four blocks south of the centre is the **Museo Jose Guadalupe Posada** (10–2 and 3.30, 3.30–7; closed Mondays), named after the lithographer whose works it houses and sited in his old home. Posada was a thoroughly Mexican artist, and his prints here mostly depict events and personages from the Revolution, grotesquely caricatured. In the other direction from the plaza, along Av. Madero then left on Zaragoza, you'll find the **Museo de Aguascalientes**. Right next door to the **Templo de San Antonio** (built around the turn of the century and way over the top) it's a typical regional museum with archaeological finds from around the state, portraits of the state governors and a substantial collection of local arts and artefacts.

If you're at all interested in local **handicrafts** – and certainly if you plan to buy anything – you should take a trip out to the **Centro de Diseño Artesanal** on Av. Adolfo Lopez Mateos. This new centre, in an impressive modern building, operates as a working craft museum, school and shop. You can watch weavers and potters at work, some on traditional designs, others resolutely modern, and buy some really excellent products – though they don't come cheap. Just over the road is the **Patio Domecq** where, supposedly, you can taste local wines and watch some of the processes involved in making them – I've never managed to get in. For cheaper shopping, as well as the aforementioned market between Juarez and 5 de Mayo, there's a Sunday **flea-market** (known as *Linea de Fuego*, 'line of fire') to the north of the centre between Av. Independencia and Zaragoza, near the top of 5 de Mayo.

Finally, if you want to visit one of the **hot springs** from which the city takes its name, head for the *Balneario Ojocaliente* just outside town on the road to San Luis Potosi. To get to the spa, which has a series of pools and bathing chambers, take a blue (*Ruta Madero*) bus from the centre.

INTO THE BAJIO: LEON

Beyond Aguascalientes the road south begins to enter the much more mountainous and fertile areas of Central Mexico known as the *Bajio*. This green belt, stretching almost from coast to coast and south as far as the capital, has always been the most heavily populated part of the country and it remains much the most consistently developed, both agriculturally and industrially. If you're heading straight for Mexico City you'll by-pass almost everywhere of interest – cutting through the industrial cities of LEON and IRAPUATO before joining the motorway past

CELAYA and QUERETARO. This would be a mistake: **Guanajato** (p. 124) and **San Miguel de Allende** (p. 133), to the east of the main road, are two of the most fascinating cities of the centre, while to the west lies **Guadalajara** (p. 95), Mexico's second city, and some of the country's finest scenery.

Buses to Guadalajara almost all follow this main road south through **ENCARNACION DE DIOS** (whose plaza boasts topiary hedges carved into the most bizarre forms) as far as **LAGOS DE MORENO**, though there are shorter routes direct from Zacatecas and from Aguascalientes. Lagos is right on the intersection where the road from Mexico City to the border at Ciudad Juarez crosses the route from Guadalajara to San Luis Potosí and the North-East, and it's always been a major staging post. Surprisingly few people stop here now though, and despite the heavy traffic rumbling around its fringes, it's a quiet and rather beautiful little town, with colonial streets climbing steeply from a small river to a hilltop monastery. Cross the bridge by the bus station and head to your left along the stream, away from the choking fumes of the main road, and it's hard to believe you're in the same place. Around the **Zocalo** are three or four run-down but comfortable little **hotels**, a couple of **bars** and **places to eat** and a massive baroque church. This is the place to head, whether you plan to stay a couple of hours or a few days: in the streets around are a scattering of colonial mansions and official buildings, including a forbidding jail which looks like something from a waxworks' chamber of horrors but is actually still in use. And once you've seen the centre you can embark on the long climb up to that hillside church – the monastery is still a monastery so you can't visit it, and the church is falling down, but it's worth it, especially towards sunset, for the views alone.

Heading west from Lagos de Moreno towards GUADALAJARA you pass through **SAN JUAN DE LOS LAGOS**, some 45km down the road. It seems just another dusty little town, yet there's an enormous bus station surrounded by scores of hotels. This is thanks to the vast parish church, and the miraculous **image of the Virgin** which it contains – one of the most important pilgrimage centres in Mexico. During the three or four major **fiestas** the place is crammed with penitents, pilgrims seeking miraculous cures, and others who are just there to enjoy it; the rest of the year San Juan slumps back into drowsiness. The chief dates of pilgrimage are February 2nd (*Dia de la Candelaria*) and December 8th (*Fiesta de la Inmaculada Concepcion*), but celebration spills over around these days and there are several lesser events round the year, notably the first fortnight of August and the entire Christmas period. There's little chance of finding a room at these times, and little point in staying long at any other so it's best treated as a stopover between Lagos de Moreno and Guadalajara or as a day trip from one of those places – less than an hour from the former, around 3 hours from Guadalajara.

Continuing south, next stop is **LEON** in the state of Guanajato – the logical jumping-off point for the city of that name. It's a teeming, industrial city with a long history of leather-work – reflected today in the fact that there are seemingly scores of shoe factories and, in the centre, hundreds of shoe shops: a good place to buy hand-tooled cowboy boots. The bus station is some way out, and most people take one look and get no further but if you're changing buses here anyway it's well worth taking a couple of hours to wander round the centre. The Plaza de los Fundadores is not at all what the rest of the city would lead you to expect – very spacious, tranquil and elegant with a fine eighteenth-century Cathedral built by the Jesuits and a typically colonial Palacio Municipal. Little else survived a disastrous flood in 1883, but the plaza is surrounded by broad boulevards lined with shops, and there are a couple of other churches which deserve a look, the baroque Templo de los Angeles and the extraordinary marble Templo Expiatorio on Av. Madero, where you can visit a series of underground chambers. There are **hotels** around the bus station, but also near the centre, especially on Av. Juarez where you'll find the *America*, the *Paris* and the *Hotel Señorial*.

MATEHUALA AND REAL DE CATORCE

Coming down from Saltillo, there's just one place of any size before you reach San Luis Potosí, and that's **MATEHUALA**. It's a pleasant enough place, with several small hotels and reasonable restaurants, but would be no more than that were it not for the proximity of the ancient and now all but deserted mining town of REAL DE CATORCE. As it is, the trip to Catorce makes a compelling reason to stop here. From the bus station, carry on down the main street, about a 5-minute walk, into the centre of town. You can't miss the grey concrete bulk of the barrel-shaped church on the main plaza, and most of the hotels and restaurants are just beyond this, still on the main street. The *Hotel Matehuala* is the most popular place with travellers, and has the advantage of being almost next door to the terminus for buses to Catorce – just up to your right. Check the schedule before you take a room, because it's far better, if you can, to stay up the mountain: the service is somewhat irregular, but there should be four buses a day, two in the morning, two in the early evening, taking a couple of hours to cover the steep 50km. If you do stay in Matehuala there are several other small hotels close by, and some good cheap local restaurants in which to while away the hours.

REAL DE CATORCE itself (or *Villa Real de Nuestra Señora de la Concepcion de Guadalupe de los Alamos de los Catorce* to give it its full title) is a quite extraordinary place. From a population of some 40,000 at the peak of its silver production (the hills around were reckoned to be the second richest source of precious metals in Mexico, after Guanajato) it declined virtually to zero by the middle of this century. A few hundred inhabitants hang on now, some prospecting for silver and hoping that the old veins can be re-opened, others in the hope that tourism offers a brighter prospect. Meanwhile the town crumbles around them, the inhabited enclave at the centre surrounded by derelict roofless mansions and, as you go further out, by houses of which only the foundations and an odd segment of wall remain standing.

The town is built in a high canyon which you approach, on the road, through a tunnel nearly 2 miles long – part of the old mine workings. It's only broad enough for one vehicle at a time, with a passing place in the middle; as you drive through, the odd mine shaft leads off into the mountain to either side – by one there's a little shrine where a lone candle seems always to be burning. Once in the town the austere, shuttered stone buildings seem to blend with the bare rocky crags which enclose them – the air is cool and clean but you can't get away from the spirit of desolation which hangs over the place. There are just two things to visit – the big baroque church of **San Francisco** and the old Casa de la Moneda, where local silver was minted into coin. It's the church which attracts Mexicans to Catorce, or rather the miraculous figure of Saint Francis (known as Panchito; Pancho being a diminutive of Francisco) which it houses. The walls are covered with hand-made retablos giving thanks for cures or miraculous escapes effected by the Saint. They are a wonderful form of naive folk art, the older ones painted on tin plate, newer examples on paper or card or even photographs, depicting the most amazing events – last minute rescues from the paths of oncoming trains, lucky escapes from horrendous car crashes, miraculous avoidance of death or serious injury in more ways than it's comfortable to contemplate – and all signed and dated with thanks to 'Panchito' for his timely intervention.

The **Casa de la Moneda** now houses a small museum with old coins, rusting mine machinery, dusty documents – anything, in fact, which has been found lying among the ruins and looks interesting. After that there's nothing to do but wander around, kick up the dust, perhaps climb up into the hills to enjoy the air and look down over the relics. These mountains, probably even before they were known to contain silver, were a rich source of **peyote**. Even now groups of Huichol Indians make the long annual pilgrimage from their homelands in and around north-eastern Nayarit to gather the precious hallucinogenic cactus, regarded by them as essential food for the soul, just as corn is essential for the body. This journey, on foot, can take up to a month.

Surprisingly there are two excellent **hotels** in Real de Catorce: not especially cheap, but very good value. They are within a few metres of each other, one on the town's main street, the other just up the hill from it to the right. Each has a restaurant. If you're really hard up there's also a very basic Casa de Huespedes on the main street right opposite the church – and for that reason occupied mostly by pilgrims.

SAN LUIS POTOSÍ

Founded in 1592 as a Francisan mission, it wasn't long before the Spaniards discovered rich deposits of gold and silver in the country around San Luis and began to develop the area in earnest. They added the name Potosí (after the fabulously rich mines of that name in Bolivia) in the expectation of rivalling the original – a hope which was never fully realised, though **SAN LUIS POTOSÍ** was a thoroughly wealthy town throughout the colonial period. Unlike its erstwhile rivals it still is – most of the silver may have gone but there are still working mines churning out zinc and lead, and a considerable modern industrial base. As a result San Luis, while preserving a little changed colonial heart, is also a large modern city.

You're likely to be staying near the centre (see *Practical Details* below) where everything is compact enough to be visited on foot, set on a tidy grid of streets around a series of little plazas. Principle focus is the **Jardin Hidalgo**, the old Plaza de Armas, around which are the state and city government offices and the Cathedral. Here too is the **Tourist Office** (open Mon.-Fri. 9–3 and 5–7; Sat. 9–2) which has maps of the town and information on any special events. The **Cathedral** is something of an architectural mish-mash – built in the early eighteenth century but so constantly tinkered with ever since that little remains of the original: certainly it's not the most elegant of the city's churches. Facing it across the square is the long facade of the **Palacio de Gobierno** with its balustraded roof. This too has been substantially refurbished over the years, but at least any alterations have preserved the harmony of its clean neoclassical lines. Inside you can visit the suite of rooms occupied by Benito Juarez when San Luis became his temporary capital in 1863. French troops supporting the Emperor Maximilian soon drove him out, but he returned in 1866, and in this building confirmed the death sentence passed on Maximilian (see Querétaro, p. 139). There's a waxworks model of Juarez with the Princess Salm Salm kneeling before him pleading for the emperor's pardon. Sensibly, he refused, 'thus' (according to the state government's leaflet) 'ending the short-lived empire and strengthening, before all peoples and the entire world, Mexico's prestige as a liberty loving nation'.

Behind the Palacio is the **Casa de la Moneda**, the old mint, one of the finest colonial mansions in San Luis. Turn left here along C. Aldama and you come to the quiet **Plaza San Francisco**, a shaded little area redolent of the city's colonial history. It's named for the Franciscan monastery whose church, the Templo de San Francisco, towers over the west side.

The monastery itself now houses the **Museo Regional** (open Tue.-Fri. 10–1 and 3–6; weekends 10–2; closed Monday), an excellent collection of pre-hispanic sculpture and other archaeological finds, displays of local Indian culture and traditions and articles relating to the history of the state of San Luis Potosí. There's a fine cloister and, upstairs, access to the lavish **Capilla de Aranzazu**, a baroque chapel with fine, exceedingly rich Churrigueresque decoration. In the entrance hall and along the stairway leading up is a miscellaneous collection of religious paintings.

At the far end of the Plaza San Francisco two more tiny churches, **Sagrado Corazon** and the **Templo del Tercer Orden**, stand side by side, while back towards the centre is the *Fonart* **Casa de la Cultura** (open 10–2 and 4–6; closed Sunday afternoon and all day Monday). Also known as the Museo de Arte Popular, this state-run shop is a show-case for crafts from all over the country. Everything on display is for sale, and if much of it is rather pricey, it is at least very high quality and worth a look before you venture to go bargaining in the markets. The same organisation runs the **Fonda Tipica Potosino**, a restaurant which specialises in authentic local food and serves a good, cheap *comida corrida* – eating here can be rather desolate, though, since it seems to be completely devoid of custom most of the time.

Returning along Aldama past the Casa de la Moneda, you reach the **Plaza de los Fundadores**, a paved open space much larger and more formal than the Jardin Hidalgo but where nothing much seems to happen. It's dominated by the enormous neo-classical building housing the State **University**, alongside which are two more small churches, **Sagrario** and **La Compañia**. The fine arcaded portals of the square are continued around the corner into Av. Venustiano Carranza.

The **Templo del Carmen**, on the little **Plazuela del Carmen** up towards the Alameda, is the most beautiful and harmonious of the churches in San Luis. Exuberantly decorated, with a multi-coloured tiled dome and elaborate baroque facade, the interior is just as flash, especially a fantastically intricate retablo, attributed to the eighteenth-century eccentric and polymath, Tresguerras (see p. 142). Beside it, where once was a monastery, is the bulky **Teatro de la Paz**, built in the last century under Porfirio Diaz and typical of the grandiose public buildings of that era. Here too is the **Museo de la Mascara**, a small exhibition of masks from around the country, those used today for fiestas and traditional dances as well as relics of pre-hispanic times. Interesting, but new when I was here and by no means certain to become a permanent fixture.

Some practical details

The modern **bus station** is some way from the centre, and although there are several **hotels** around it there's no point in staying out here. Catch a local bus instead which will bring you in across the railway tracks, round

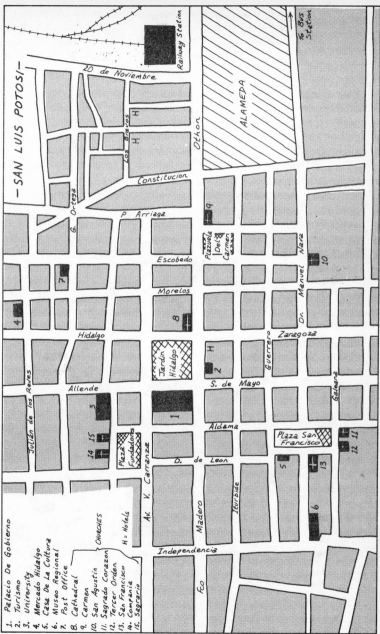

— SAN LUIS POTOSI —

20 de Noviembre
Railway Station
Los Bravos
Ortega
G. Ortega
Constitucion
Othon
ALAMEDA
To Bus Station
P Arriaga
Plazuela Del Carmen
Escobedo
Morelos
Dr. Manuel Nava
Hidalgo
Jardin Hidalgo
Zaragoza
Guerrero
Allende
S. de Mayo
Julián de los Reyes
Aldama
Plaza San Francisco
Galeana
Plaza Fundadores
D. de Leon
Av. V. Carranza
Madero
Iturbide
Independencia
Fco

1. Palacio De Gobierno
2. Turismo
3. University
4. Mercado Hidalgo
5. Casa De La Cultura
6. Museo Regional
7. Post Office
8. Cathedral
9. Carmen
10. San Agustin
11. Sagrado Corazon
12. Tercer Orden
13. San Francisco
14. Compania
15. Sagrario

CHURCHES

H = Hotels

the Alameda and eventually right into the Jardin Hidalgo. The bulk of the cheaper hotels are close to the **Alameda** and the **train** station – there are several on Calle Los Bravos, the pick of which is probably the *Hotel Jardin*. If you want to be right downtown, the *Hotel Plaza* – on Jardin Hidalgo beside the Tourist Office – is incredibly cheap considering its position. The rooms, though, tend to be rather dingy and very few have outward facing windows. Going up a bit in price, you could also try the *Hotel Progreso* on Aldama between the Plaza San Francisco and the Casa de la Moneda.

Around the centre there are plenty of reasonably priced, but rather characterless, cafe-style **places to eat**. Just about the most popular in San Luis, crowded throughout the day, is the *Cafe Tokio* on Othon facing the Alameda – good for breakfast or for a quick feed at any time. The restaurant in the *Hotel Plaza* is, like the hotel itself, almost unbelievably cheap, and though its atmosphere is thoroughly gloomy and the food no better than average you certainly won't find better value than the *comida corrida* here. Worth a try too is the *Fonda* in the Plaza San Francisco (see above).

There are also food stalls in the **Mercado Hidalgo**, but the place is too packed and noisy for anything other than a hurried snack. It's a good market, though, reached from the main plaza along the pedestrianised Calle Hidalgo – itself crammed with every kind of shop.

GUADALAJARA AND THE LAKES

The west coast route from the border to Mexico City cuts inland from TEPIC to GUADALAJARA. The land it passes through is far more than a way-station en route to the capital, though – the states of **Jalisco** and **Michoacan** contain some of the most spectacularly beautiful landscapes in Mexico, and Guadalajara is by far her most attractive big city. It's a valid destination in itself: well connected with the colonial cities of the Bajio, with the capital, and with beach resorts at **Puerto Vallarta** (p. 249), **Barra de Navidad** (p. 253) and **Manzanillo** (p. 254).

The lakes of CHAPALA, where D. H. Lawrence wrote *The Plumed Serpent*, and PATZCUARO, probably the most photographed in the country, are well known, but there are many others as well as some beautiful mountain villages and tranquil towns in a verdant sierra dotted with volcanoes. Add to this the fact that Jalisco is the home of **Mariachi** and of **Tequila** and you've got a region where you could easily spend a couple of weeks exploring without beginning to see it all.

GUADALAJARA

Guadalajara is a university town; a junction of the South-Pacific Railway; the capital of Jalisco, the richest of the ex-hacienda states; the centre of an agricultural region, the hub of the native gin manufacture, the last stronghold of Creole aristocracy and the second largest city in Mexico. It was founded almost immediately after the Conquest and is full of handsome, florid buildings of that epoch in patinaed red tezontle. The town shows dignity and powers of assimilation, appearing to be neither in decay nor straining to build itself out of sense and form, and to have escaped so far the mongrelisation of Mexico City.

Sybille Bedford wrote that on her Mexican Journey in the early 1950s, but it's just as accurate a description now. There has been a great deal of new building, but the smart new hotels and office blocks are for the most part well away from the centre, and even where the colonial heart has been tampered with – as with the Plaza Tapatia, driven straight through the heart of some of the oldest parts of the city – it's been done with discretion. Only opened in 1982, the new plaza manages to look as if it was always meant to be there, creating new sight-lines between some of Guadalajara's most monumental buildings.

For all its size, Guadalajara has a provincial elegance and relaxed pace which the crush and smog of Mexico City or the industry of Monterrey could never hope to match. And an ideal climate to go with it. They describe it as 'the city of eternal spring' and while that's somewhat exaggerated, Guadalajara *is* almost always warm – it's on much the same latitude as Bombay – yet protected from extremes by its altitude, over 5,000 feet. There are parks and little squares and open spaces throughout the city, while right downtown around the Cathedral are a series of plazas unchanged from the original colonists' town plans. Many of the more important buildings are decorated with fabulous murals by Jose Clemente Orozco, one of Mexico's greatest revolutionary artists, who lived and created his finest work in the city.

Guadalajara was founded in 1532, one of the fruits of a vicious campaign of conquest by Nuño de Guzman – whose cruelty and corruption was such that it appalled even the Spanish authorities, and who ended his life in jail in Madrid. The city named for his birthplace thrived though, being officially recognised by Charles V in 1542 and rapidly becoming one of the most Spanish of all Mexican cities – in part at least because so much of the Indian population had been killed or fled during the period of conquest and suppression. Somehow Guadalajara managed to remain relatively isolated from subsequent history – though it supported Hidalgo's Independence movement and became briefly his capital, to be rewarded when the break with Spain finally came by being named capital of Jalisco. In the 1920s the completion of the rail link with California provided the final spur for its development.

Getting your bearings – eating, drinking, sleeping

This is a very big city, but getting around is not too difficult once you have the hang of it. The central area is relatively compact and there's a comprehensive, if rather confusing, system of public transport. Taxis, too, can be relied on if you're in a hurry to get somewhere, and for three or four people shouldn't work out too expensive.

The **Central Camionera** and the **railway station** are not far from each other across the Parque Agua Azul, though the latter is considerably further from the centre. If you're not carrying too much it's a perfectly easy walk in from the bus terminal, while from the trains it seems a long haul under any circumstances. There are buses from both: go to the street running alongside the second class half of the Camionera, or straight out the front of the railway station and look for *Centro*. It's worth making doubly sure by asking the driver as you get on, since what's written on the bus is not always an accurate guide to its destination. A flat fare will take you anywhere in the city.

Arrive by air (frequent services from the western USA) and you're more or less forced to take a taxi, or at least a VW *colectivo*. Rates are fixed – and very high – so you'll just have to grin and bear it; it is a long way.

By far the greatest concentration of **cheap hotels** is immediately **around the bus station**, and while almost all of these are extremely noisy, it's certainly the easiest place to find a room. Even if you don't want to stay out here you could consider taking a room for a night to give yourself a chance to look for somewhere more congenial, or leave your luggage in the bus station's *guarderia* while you head downtown to find a place. As you come out of the front doors of the Camionera you're surrounded by hotel signs, and there are scores more in the surrounding side-streets. These tend to offer marginally more peace and slightly lower rates: the *Hotel Praga* on 28 de Enero is one of the better ones. Walk out to the Calzada Independencia – a major artery which runs up from the railway station, close by the Camionera and on up to the huge Mercado Libertad – and you'll find another string of possibilities. The *Hotel Flamingos* a couple of blocks up at No. 725, is considerably more modern and comfortable than its rivals yet charges barely any more.

In the centre, rooms at reasonable rates are much harder to find and tend to be scattered over a wide area. Considering the number of tourists Guadalajara sees there are surprisingly few expensive places either – largely because the flashy new hotels, the *Camino Real*, the *Holiday Inn* and so on, have been built out to the west of the city amid the expensive suburbs and swanky shopping centres which modern development has

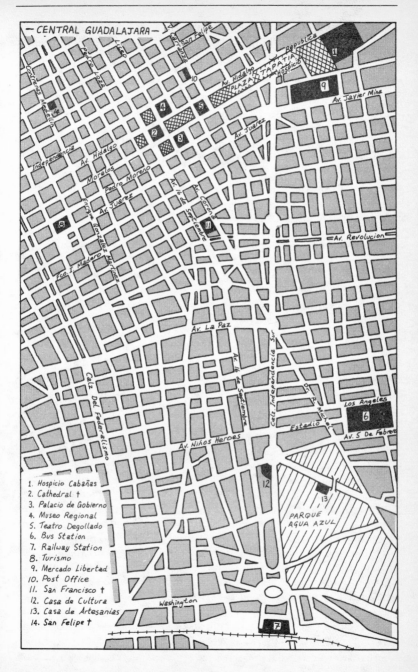

— CENTRAL GUADALAJARA —

1. Hospicio Cabañas
2. Cathedral †
3. Palacio de Gobierno
4. Museo Regional
5. Teatro Degollado
6. Bus Station
7. Railway Station
8. Turismo
9. Mercado Libertad
10. Post Office
11. San Francisco †
12. Casa de Cultura
13. Casa de Artesanias
14. San Felipe †

brought. Those that are downtown are mostly in the area just south of the cathedral, around the junction of Juarez and Corona. There's one place here which isn't too outrageously pricey – the *Hotel Morales* at Corona 243 – worth paying a bit more for the setting, a beautiful, if run down and rather gloomy, converted mansion. Off Av. Corona to the left before you reach Juarez run Francisco Madero and Lopez Cotilla, each of which offers a couple of possibilities. Most attractive of them is the *Posada de la Plata* (Lopez Cotilla 619) whose rooms, while basic, are set around a pleasant little patio in an ancient house. A little way down the same street is another Posada (at No. 594), while also nearby you'll find the *Hotel Hamilton* (Francisco Madero 381). These last three are all close to the state **Tourist Office** in the old Convento de Carmen at Juarez 638, one of the most helpful in Mexico when it comes to searching for rooms or handing out stacks of pamphlets.

Finally, as always around a market, there are a few cheap places **near the Mercado Libertad**. Try along Av. Javier Mina where you'll find the *Hotel Ana Isabel*, the *Imperio*, the *Mexico* and the *San Jorge* in that order as you walk down from the Calzada Independencia. The *Hotel Chapala* in the first side street on the right (Jose Maria Mercado 84) is good, and near it there's also the *Janeiro* at Alvaro Obregon, 95.

Eating in Guadalajara certainly doesn't present a problem – they take their food seriously in Jalisco, and there are hundreds of restaurants. *Birria*, beef or lamb in a spicy but not particularly hot sauce served with tortillas or in tacos, and *Pozole*, a stew of pork and hominy (ground maize), are both local specialities and though you probably won't find them in many restaurants you will come across them on street stalls, as food served in bars, and in the markets. For cheap basic meals the area around the bus station is again a safe bet, and the restaurant actually in the terminal is considerably better than these places usually are. The **Mercado Libertad** is a good place to head too, upstairs there seem to be hundreds of little stands with their food on display, many with their own speciality, and all eager to lure you over to them. The *Parian* in Tlaquepaque (see below) is popular too. In the centre there are plenty of places, but prices are naturally rather higher: the *Denny's* chain has a branch on Av. Juarez just below the Plaza de Armas, not cheap by any means but the place to go for authentic American and Tex-Mex food in authentically plastic surroundings. The *Copa de Leche* (Juarez 414) is expensive, but something of an institution in Guadalajara – Sybille Bedford came here ('*we ate a mixed grill, toasted tortillas, stuffed with cheese and lettuce, and some avocado pears. It was very crowded. . .*') There's a **vegetarian** restaurant, *La Zanahoria*, on Lopez Cotilla not far from the Tourist Office. And if you want to pass some time sitting outdoors watching the world go by, there's an **open-air cafe** in the little plaza at the corner of Moreno and Colon, very near the Cathedral by the old Telegrafos building.

The city's nightlife is not exactly hot, though it has perked up in recent years. Most of the new hotels have **discos**, if that's your scene, and the most central of them is in the *Sheraton*, not far from the bus station: any of these will knock a severe hole in your wallet. On the other hand you needn't spend anything at all in the **Plaza de Mariachis**. In this little area hard by the Mercado Libertad and the Church of San Juan de Dios, mariachi bands hang around or stroll between bars, playing to anyone prepared to cough up for a song. If they play for you personally you'll have to pay (check how much before they start) but there are usually several on the go anyway. You'll also find Mariachi bands in Tlaquepaque (p. 104), which some argue is now the better place to go. Certainly it's true that the Plaza de Mariachis has become increasingly commercialised.

Other entertainments include, in the summer, regular *charreadas*, or Mexican **rodeos** in the *Lienzo Charro*, out on the road to the airport near the Parque Agua Azul, and in winter **bullfights** in the *Plaza Nuevo Progreso*, a long way north on the Calz. Independencia. Right opposite this is the mighty *Estadio Jalisco*, the enormous **football** stadium where England played their preliminary rounds in the 1970 World Cup. For the more culturally minded there's a regular programme of **theatre and dance** in the beautiful *Teatro Degollado* (see below) and a series of events put on by the Tourist authorities in the old *Convento del Carmen*. Guadalajara's **Ballet Folklorico** is staged every Sunday at 10am in the Teatro Degollado (except when the company's on tour) and is definitely worth getting up for; afterwards, and every weekend, you'll find bands playing and crowds gathered somewhere round the central plaza complex and there's always entertainment of some kind laid on in the Parque Agua Azul. Turismo should be able to provide up to date details, and you'll find some further listings in the *Guadalajara Weekly* – an English language free-sheet.

The entire month of October is dominated by the famous **Fiestas de Octubre**, with some kind of event every day throughout the month, and fireworks every night. In Tlaquepaque the big day is June 29th; endless mariachis, dances, and a mass procession.

The metropolitan centre

At the very heart of the city is the Cathedral which, with the Sagrario beside it, takes up an entire block bordered by four plazas and surrounded, in the grid of streets which take these as their centre, by the most important shopping and commercial area of downtown Guadalajara.

The **Cathedral** itself is the focus, a bizarre but effective mixture of styles with its pointed, tiled twin towers. Building work began in 1561 and wasn't concluded until more than a century later – since then there have been extensive modifications, adding a new neo-classical facade, replacing the towers (which collapsed in an 1818 earthquake) and generally disguising the fact that there was ever a plan behind its design. The interior is best seen in the evening, when the lighting from huge chandeliers makes the most of its richness. In the sacristy is a picture of the Virgin, attributed to the Spanish renaissance artist Murillo.

Facing the main west entrance is the **Plaza de los Laureles**, planted with laurel trees and with a fountain in the centre. North of the Cathedral, by the porticoed **Presidencia Municipal** (only some thirty years old, though you wouldn't know it) lies the **Rotonda de los Jaliscienses Ilustres** in the centre of another plaza. This neo-classical circle of seventeen Doric columns commemorates the state's martyred heroes.

Across the Plaza the **Museo Regional** is housed in an eighteenth-century colonial mansion – originally a religious seminary, later a barracks and then a school. It's a supremely elegant setting for an extensive and diverse collection. Downstairs, you start in a section devoted to regional archaeology – from stone tools and the skeleton of a mammoth through to the finest achievements of the Mexican Western Cultures in pottery and metal-working. The peoples of the west developed quite separately from those in southern and central Mexico, and indeed there is considerable evidence that they had more contact with South and Central American cultures than with what would now be regarded as their countrymen. The deep shaft tombs found here (and displayed in the museum) are unique in Mexico, but were common down the west coast into Peru and Ecuador. Later the Tarascan kingdom, based around Patzcuaro (see p. 109), came almost to rival the strength of the Aztecs – partly due to their much more extensive use and knowledge of metals. Certainly the Aztecs tried, and failed, to extend their influence over Tarascan territory, though following Cortes's destruction of Tenochtitlan the Tarascans submitted, relatively peacefully, to the Conquistadors.

Upstairs, along with rooms devoted to the state's modern history and to the ethnography of the natives as they live now, is a sizeable gallery of colonial and modern art. Most remarkable here is the large collection of nineteenth-century portraiture, a local tradition which captures relatively ordinary Mexicans in a charmingly naive style – nowadays they'd be snapshots for the family album, and indeed many have that forced formality of early photography. Open 9–1 except Mondays.

On the other side of the Cathedral, south of the Sagrario, is the **Plaza de Armas**. In its elaborate kiosk – a present from the people of France – the state band plays every Thursday and Sunday evening. Dominating the eastern side of the square is the baroque frontage of the **Palacio de Gobierno**. Here Padre Miguel Hidalgo y Costilla (the 'father of Mexican Independence') proclaimed the abolition of slavery in 1810 and here, in

1858, Benito Juarez was saved from the firing squad by the cry of '*Los Valientes no asesinan*' – the brave are not assassins. Both those events are commemorated inside, but the overwhelming reason to penetrate into the arcaded courtyard is the first of the great **Orozco Murals** on the stairway. *Jose Clemente Orozco* (1883–1949) formed, along with Diego Rivers and David Siqueiros, the triumvirate of brilliant Mexican artists who emerged from the Revolution and who transformed painting here into an enormously powerful and populist political statement – especially through the medium of the giant mural. Their chief patrons were the state – hence the predominance of their work in official buildings and educational establishments – and their aims a national art drawing on native traditions. Almost all their work is consciously educative, rewriting – or perhaps better rediscovering – Mexican history in the light of the Revolution, casting the Imperialists as villains and drawing heavily on pre-hispanic themes.

The mural here is typical – Hidalgo blasts through the middle triumphant, brandishing his sword against a background of red flags and the fires of battle. Curving around the sides of the staircase are more scenes depicting the Mexican people's oppression and struggle for liberty, from a pre-conquest Eden to post-revolutionary emancipation.

The fourth and largest square is the **Plaza de la Liberacion**, where the back of the Cathedral looks across at the **Teatro Degollado**. Built in the mid-nineteenth century and inaugurated during the brief reign of Maximilian, the Theatre is an imposing neo-classical building, domed and with a Corinthian portico on whose pediment is a frieze depicting the muses. It still stages a full programme of drama and concerts as well as the Sunday morning *Folklorico* dances – details are posted up around the entrance. Just to see the impressively restored interior it's worth buying a show ticket – a frescoed ceiling illustrates scenes from Dante.

On either side of the theatre are two small churches, **Santa Maria** and **San Agustin**, each all that remain of a former monastery. Santa Maria was one of the oldest in the city, and where its outbuildings stood is now the **Palacio de Justicia**. Walk past here to the back of the theatre and you're at the beginning of the new **Plaza Tapatía**, with a view all the way down to the Hospicio Cabañas. It's almost entirely lined with new buildings housing expensive shops below, offices above, and swish department stores, but for all that the pedestrianised area, dotted with bits of modern statuary and fountains is undeniably attractive – a thoroughly pleasant place to wander and window-shop. It takes its name from *tapatío* – an adjective used to describe anything typical of Guadalajara, and supposedly derived from the capes worn by Spanish grandees. Guadalajarans themselves are often referred to as Tapatíos.

The **Hospicio Cabañas** (open 10–2 and 4–6; closed Sunday afternoon and all day Monday) was founded as an orphanage by the bishop Juan

Cabañas y Crespo in 1801 – taking nearly fifty years to complete, during much of which time it operated as a barracks. It was an orphanage again, however, when Orozco came to decorate the central chapel in 1939. There are no less than twenty-three separate patios – the chapel, in the form of a cross, is in the central one. The murals, in keeping with their situation, are more spiritual than those in the government palace, but you certainly couldn't call them Christian – the Conquistadors are depicted as the horsemen of the Apocalypse, trampling the native population beneath them. The Man of Fire, who leads the people from their dehumanising, mechanised oppression, is in this case a sort of strange synthesis of Christian and Mexican deities, a Christ/Quetzalcoatl figure – but his symbolic role as liberator is clearly the same as that of Hidalgo in the palace murals.

Almost alongside is the vast **Mercado Libertad**, which they claim is the world's largest market under one roof. I wouldn't argue. It's an entirely modern building, but not in the least a modern market – there are still the *curanderas* offering their herbal remedies, little stalls of basic foods and vast piles of fruit and vegetables as well as more overtly touristic sections selling leather goods, from sandals to clumpy working boots, and native *artesanias*. Before you buy, it's worth paying a visit to the **Casa de las Artesanias** in the Parque Agua Azul, or to the expensive boutiques in Tlaquepaque to get some idea of the potential quality and value of the goods (for both, see below).

Around the city

There are a couple more sites of interest, still pretty close to the centre but not actually on the network of plazas. First of these is the old **Telegrafos** building, just west of the Plaza de Armas at the junction of Pedro Moreno with Colon. Originally a church, this nineteenth-century neo-classical building later became a university lecture hall, at which time it was decorated with **murals by David Siqueiros**. Older than any of the Orozco's major work in Gaudalajara, these provide an interesting contrast – they depict the Revolution and the Zapatist movement. Only problem is that since the telegraph office has been moved to new quarters on the Calzada Federalisimo, the building is again without a role in life, and it's often locked. The little plaza here is a pleasant enough place to sit around though, with one of the few open-air cafes in the centre.

Continue west, cutting down onto Juarez, and you reach the ex-**Convento del Carmen**, where the **Tourist Office** is now sited. It was one of the city's richest monasteries, but it's wealth has largely been stripped, leaving an austere, white building of elegant simplicity. Exhibitions of modern art, dance events and concerts are regularly staged here.

Along Juarez run buses (*Par Via* or *Plaza del Sol*) which will take you out to the western side of the city where the most spectacular new development has been. Out here is the Orozco Museum. First, however, you pass the **University** where the third of his major murals (though actually the first he painted) may be seen. Head for the central hall of the main building to see the frescoed dome: again the theme fits the setting – here a paean to education for all as the means of fulfilment and redemption. Behind the university buildings, across C. Lopez Cotilla, is the **Templo Expiatorio** – a modern neo-gothic church (still not entirely complete), its chief attraction is some excellent modern stained glass. A couple of blocks further down from here is the **Instituto Cultural Norte Americano** – basically a language school, it has English-language magazines lying around and a cafe at the back. You may not be supposed to wander in off the streets, but no-one seems to mind.

Staying on the bus along Av. Vallarta (same bus as before, same street, change of name) the **Orozco Museum** is quite a bit further on by the Minerva Circle, a roundabout with a large fountain where Vallarta crosses Lopez Mateos. Housed in the artist's old studio, the museum (open 10–2 and 4–6; closed Sunday afternoon and all day Monday) houses some eighty works – sketches of the revolution, full-blown paintings and unfinished drawings.

If you want to see more of how the other half lives – most of the big new hotels are out around here – carry on down Vallarta to the *Tequila Sauza* bottling plant. You can look around during normal weekday working hours and at lunchtime get very cheap Tequila cocktails. The stuff is actually brewed in – where else – Tequila, for which see *Getting Away*, below. Alternatively get on a bus going to the left down Lopez Mateos and you'll reach the **Plaza del Sol**, a vast new commercial development said to be one of the largest in Latin America. There's an enormous shopping centre as well as new administrative offices, and inside there are a couple of good cafes and an ice-cream parlour.

Back to the centre (the same buses run back along Hidalgo) and this time south from the Plaza de Armas, you'll find the churches of **San Francisco** and **Nuestra Señora de Aranzazu** facing each other across Av. 16 de Septiembre. San Francisco lies on the site of probably Guadalajara's oldest religious foundation – a Franciscan Monastery established in the first years after the conquest. The present church was built in 1864, and has a beautiful baroque facade. Aranzazu, by contrast, is entirely plain from the outside, but it conceals one of the most elaborate interiors, with three wildly exuberant, heavily carved and gilded Churrigueresque retablos. The quiet **Jardin de San Francisco** lies across from these two, and overlooking it from the first floor is the *Cafe Junior* – a good place to break for a quick snack or a drink.

Several different bus routes run down from here to the **Parque Agua Azul** – look for *Camionera* or *FFCC*. You couldn't really describe the park as peaceful, though there are tranquil spots, because there's always something going on and it seems permanently packed with kids. A zoo, miniature train rides, playgrounds and an outdoor theatre with free performance on Sundays (rarely highbrow – the last performance I witnessed was a teeny-bop disco dancing talent contest) ensure that boredom doesn't set in too soon. However, there is also the **Casa de la Cultura** and the Casa de las Artesanias. The former hosts a permanent exhibition of modern art as well as the State Library, and is extensively covered in ultra-modern murals and frescoes. There's also an information service for cultural events in the city. The **Casa de las Artesanias** is another of those shop/museums which serve as a showcase for regional crafts: virtually everything is for sale, but a lot of it is very expensive. Outside, in an impromptu market, local tradesmen offer lesser goods at lower prices.

In the suburbs: Tlaquepaque

Guadalajara's rapid expansion has all but swallowed up several communities which were once distinct villages but are now barely distinguishable from the suburbs around them. The most celebrated is **SAN PEDRO TLAQUEPAQUE**, famous for its artesanias and for its mariachi bands. Tourism has taken over almost completely here, and the streets are lined with 'craft' boutiques selling, for the most part, pretty tacky goods at thoroughly inflated prices. Nevertheless, it's well worth seeing, and there are still quality pieces among the dross – notably some of the ceramic and glass ware on which the place's reputation was originally built. To see the best, visit the small **Ceramics Museum** (C. Independencia 237) which has displays of pottery not only from Tlaquepaque but from all over the state, notably Tonala (see below). A far more compelling reason to make the trip out, though, is to stop off at **El Parian**, the town's central plaza and in effect the biggest bar you've ever seen. Since the shops all close down for a siesta anyway, you have every excuse to hang out here for a couple of hours.

There are actually a whole series of separate establishments around this giant courtyard, but since everyone sits outside, the tables tend to overlap and strolling serenaders wander around at random, it all feels like one enormous continuum. They all charge much the same too, and offer the same limited range of food – basically *birria*, *quesadillas* and *queso fundido* (simply and literally melted cheese). Come here at the weekend and you'll see mariachi at its best, when the locals come along and offer their own vocal renditions to the musicians' backing. Buses heading south on Calzada Independencia (look for *San Pedro* or *Tlaquepaque*) will bring you out or, perhaps simpler, get a trolley bus travelling south on Federalisimo.

Some of these buses continue to TONALA a less well-known ceramics manufacturing centre some 5 miles further on. It's slightly cheaper to shop here, but the difference is no longer very significant and the trip is really only worthwhile if you do plan to buy some of the pottery. Market days are Thursday and Sunday, when there's considerably more animation about the place, but be warned that ceramics sold on stalls here tend to be rejects from the shops.

ZAPOPAN is across the city in exactly the opposite direction, but is served largely by the same buses at the other extremity of their routes. So you could go directly from one to the other, passing through the centre on the way. The **Basilica de la Virgen de Zapopan** is one of the most important churches in the city, much revered by the Huichol Indians. Pope John Paul II gave a mass in the giant plaza in front of the church during a visit to Mexico in 1979. His statue commemorates the event. The baroque temple houses the miraculous image of the Virgin which was dedicated by a Franciscan missionary, Antonio de Segovia, to the local Indians after he had intervened in a battle between them and the Conquistadors. Since then it has been constantly venerated, and is still the object of pilgrimages, especially on October 12th when it returns from the Cathedral to the church in a massive procession, having toured, and been displayed in, all the churches in Guadalajara. This is one of the highlights of the *Fiestas de Octubre*.

Beside the church is a small **museum** exhibiting clothes and objects relating to Huichol traditions, as well as a photographic display of their modern way of life. They also sell Huichol crafts here, including intricate embroideries. Open daily 9.30–1 and 3.30–7.

Also to the north of the city, out on Calzada Independencia, lies the gorgeous **Barranca de Oblatos**: 2,000 feet deep, with a cable-car to take you down, the canyon is set in a park with great views. It's enormously popular at weekends, and especially on Sundays among Guadalajara's many students – there's often a free concert here then, always plenty of life.

Listings – travel and essentials
Airlines AeroMexico, Av. Corona 196 (Tel. 14.54.00); KLM, Av. Vallarta 1390 (25.32.71); Mexicana, 16 de Septiembre 495 (13.22.22); American (30.02.60); Western (30.35.30).

Banks Main branches are mostly on Av. Corona near the Jardin San Francisco – the bigger hotels will usually change money after hours.

Books in English from *Sanborns*, Vallarta 1600 – larger bookstores around the centre mostly have a small selection too.

Buses Long-distance offices all at the *Central Camionera*, 5 de Febrero and Los Angeles. City tours by Panoramex (see Travel Agencies).

Car rental most are on Av. Niños Heroes and at the airport; Budget at 16 de Septiembre 746 in the centre.

Consulates British at Lerdo de Tejada 362 (15.14.06); Canadian,

Vallarta 1373 (25.99.32); US, Progreso 175 (25.27.00); Dutch, San Gabriel 622 (21.35.09); Belgian (15.55.55); Swiss (11.37.37); Sweden and Denmark (15.16.02); West German (13.96.23).

Hospitals Mexico-Americano at Colomos 2110 (41.31.41); Red Cross (14.33.79). Names of multi-lingual doctors from Consulates, Turismo or big hotels.

Library Benjamin Franklin Library in the US Consulate building, Libertad 1492, open 9–7 weekdays.

Markets The giant Mercado Libertad is just one – every city *barrio* has its own. Very touristy Mercado Corona near the Cathedral – crafts in Tlaquepaque and Tonala.

Post Main office at Venustiano Carranza 16.

Trains Tickets and information from the station, bottom of Calz. Independencia. Downtown reservation office at Colon 49 (12.51.86), open weekday business hours.

Travel agencies *American Express*, 16 de Septiembre 730 (14.82.28); *SETEJ* student agency, Pedro Moreno 1328; *Thomas Cook/Wagons Lits*, Vallarta 1447 (25.80.33); *Panoramex*, local tours, Vallarta 5840 (21.05.94).

Turismo Juarez 638 (14.01.56) and at the airport.

Getting away – breaking out of Guadalajara

There's some beautiful country around Guadalajara, and several short trips which you can make into it. The first two described here can be done easily in a day, the third needs, and deserves, longer.

LAKE CHAPALA, the largest lake in Mexico, lies just over 50km south of the city. Some 20,000 Americans are said to live in and around Guadalajara, and a sizeable proportion of them have settled on the lakeside – particularly in Chapala itself and in Ajijic. This mass presence has rendered the area rather expensive and in many respects somewhat twee, but it cannot detract from the beauty of the lake and does have the advantage that English is spoken widely – there's even an English newspaper produced down here.

Buses leave the Central Camionera for **CHAPALA** at least once an hour throughout the day, taking about an hour to get here – there are regular onward services to Ajijic and Jocotepec. It's a sleepy, even a dull community, but you can swim from a little beach right in the centre (though the water is none too clean) or take a boat ride around the lake, visiting one of its islands. Small sailing dinghies are also for hire. Shoreline restaurants all offer the local speciality, *pescado blanco*, famous despite its almost total lack of flavour, and street vendors offer cardboard plates of tiny fried fish from the lake, very like whitebait. Head to the left along the promenade, past streets of shuttered nineteenth-century villas, and you'll find a small crafts market. If you want to stay the best bet is the *Hotel Nido*, on the main street just up from the shore, an attractive, patioed old building which is not at all expensive. The dining room here serves a good *comida corrida*.

AJIJIC is only 6km away, but the atmosphere is very different. While Chapala does provide something in the way of entertainment, and can become positively festive on sunny weekends, Ajijic is smaller, quieter and more self-consciously arty. It is very picturesque, but you get the feeling that most of the expatriates here regard themselves as writers or artists manqués, hoping to pick up some of the inspiration left behind by D. H. Lawrence or more recent residents like Ken Kesey, and resent the intrusion of outsiders. There's not much evidence that Lawrence liked the place at all (though he may have disliked it less than the rest of the country) but then he can't have had much time to appreciate it since in just eight weeks here he turned out an almost complete 100,000 word first draft of *The Plumed Serpent* (or *Quetzalcoatl* as it was then titled). And more recently Sybille Bedford, too, passed through with barely more than a glance:

> *After another hour we came to a much larger village with proper mud houses and a market place. For three hundred yards, potholes were agreeably replaced by cobble-stones.*
> *'Now what about this place?'*
> *'Ajijic,' said the driver.*
> *'I dare say,' said E.*

But then Ms Bedford was on her way to the idyllic colonial backwater of her Visit to Don Otavio further round the lake – an experience so exquisite that anything else would be likely to pall beside it.

There are a number of luxurious but rather expensive hotels in Ajijic, as well as apartments and houses to rent for longer stays. The *Posada Ajijic*, perhaps the plushest of the lot, has a noticeboard which details many of these as well as events going on locally – especially displays of resident artists' work. Around the village you'll find numerous little arts and crafts shops.

The third major lakeside community, **JOCOTEPEC**, is larger but much less afflicted by tourists and foreign residents than the others. Its chief claim to fame is for the manufacture of serapes with elaborately embroidered motifs. You can buy them all around the main square, or there's a market on Sundays. *El Meson de los Naranjitos* here is a former staging inn (called *La Quinta* as being the fifth night's stop on the way from Guadalajara) which now houses a bar, restaurant and a small shopping complex.

North-west of Guadalajara, again around 50km distant, is **TEQUILA**, a town with a very different appeal. The quintessentially Mexican liquor to which the town lends its name is produced here in vast quantities at a series of distilleries. You approach through great fields of the spiky, blue-grey *Maguey* cactus from which the tequila – as also pulque and mescal – is produced. It's a grubby, rather dusty little town whose scattering of bourgeois mansions and fine church are overwhelmed by the trappings of a thriving modern business. But you don't come here to sightsee, you come to drink. Or at least to visit the distilleries.

They've made tequila here since at least the seventeenth century, but the oldest and most important distillery is *La Perseverancia*, the Sauza operation, founded in 1875. Cuervo is the next in size and age, and these two, which dominate the domestic and international market, are the ones which run formal tours – though other manufacturers also welcome visits. It's easy enough to get here on regular buses from Guadalajara, and heading back they pass through all the time on the run from Tepic.

To the south, on the road to Colima, lie the mountains and some of the most delightful alpine scenery in the country. The place to head for, for a couple of days relaxation amid upland pastures and pine forests, perfect rambling country, is **TAPALPA**. Buses run here from the second class side of Guadalajara's Camionera around five times a day. The village of Tapalpa, with its ancient, overhanging, wooden-balconied houses and magnificent surroundings of ranch country tree-clad hills, is beginning to be discovered as a weekend escape from the city, but for the moment its charm is little affected. There are several hotels – extremely good value – and a few restaurants serving plain country fare; you get good steaks and dairy products up here. At the weekend all the rooms can sometimes be taken (in which case head out on the road to Chiquilistlan, where there's a house with rooms to let, little known and very pleasant, about half an hour's walk) but in the week you'll often be the only outsider. The best walking is out towards Chiquilistlan, amid meadows full of wild flowers and gargantuan boulders, surrounded by fresh-scented slopes of pine – no-one seems to mind if you camp here either, though the land is farmed so it's best to ask permission. Be warned that it's very cold in winter, and even summer nights can get decidedly chilly. They brew their own tequila in the village, which may help keep out the draughts; it's sold from the barrel in some of the older shops and extremely rough.

Beyond the turn-off for Tapalpa, the main road starts to climb in earnest into the Sierra Madre, passing through SAYULA (the name chosen by Lawrence for his town on Lake Chapala) and **CIUDAD GUZMAN**, a sizeable but not particularly interesting city which does, however, have buses to Tapalpa and makes a useful staging point between there and the coast, or vice versa. Not far, too, lies **TUXPAN**, a beautiful and ancient little town which has frequent, colourful fiestas. Dominating this whole area, and the route on to COLIMA (p. 256) is the snow-capped mass of the *Nevado de Colima* – at 14,200 feet the loftiest and most impressive peak in the west.

THE STATE OF MICHOACAN: ZAMORA AND URUAPAN

From Guadalajara the direct route to Mexico City heads west through the major junction of LA PIEDAD to join the motorway outside IRAP-UATO. If you can afford to dawdle a little though, it's infinitely more rewarding to follow the slower, southern road through ZAMORA and MORELIA, taking a couple of days to cut off through URUAPAN and PATZCUARO. From URUAPAN a reasonably good road slices south through the mountains to the Pacific Coast at LAZARO CARDENAS (see p. 258).

Michoacan State, the country you'll be passing through, is one of the most beautiful and diverse in all Mexico – spreading as it does from a very narrow coastal plain with several tiny beach villages up to where the Sierra Madre Occidental reaches out eastwards into range after range of wooded volcanic hills.

Several of the towns, like the capital Morelia, are wholly colonial in appearance. But throughout the state there is a very active native tradition and a strength of Indian culture matched only in Oaxaca. This is thanks largely to Michoacan's first bishop, **Vasco de Quiroga**, one of the very few early Spanish colonists to see the Indian population as anything more than a slave-labour force. The **Tarascan kingdom**, whose chief town Tzintzuntzan lay on the shores of Lake Patzcuaro, was an advanced civilisation and a serious rival to the Aztecs before the conquest, with a widespread reputation for the excellence of their art, their metal-working and their feathered ornaments. The Tarascans submitted peaceably to the Spanish in 1522 and their leader was converted to Christianity, but it didn't prevent the massacres and mass torture which Nuño de Guzman meted out in his attempt to pacify the region and make himself a fortune. Quiroga was appointed bishop in an attempt to restore harmony – Guzman's methods going too far even for the Spanish – and succeeded beyond all expectation. Setting himself up as the champion of the Indians, his name is still revered today. He encouraged the population back down from the mountains whence they had fled, established settlements self-sufficient in agriculture and set up missions which taught practical skills as well as religion. The effects have survived in a very visible way for, despite some blurring in objects produced for the tourist trade, each village still has its own craft speciality and style: lacquerware in Patzcuaro and Uruapan, pottery in Tzintzuntzan, wooden furniture in Quiroga, guitars in Paracho.

Vasco de Quiroga also left behind him a deeply religious state. Michoacan was a stronghold of the reactionary *Cristero* movement, which fought a bitter war in defence of the church after the revolution. Perhaps too the ideals of Zapata and Villa had less appeal here; Quiroga's early championing of Indian rights against their new overlords meant that the hacienda system never entirely took over Michoacan and, unlike most of the country, it boasted a substantial peasantry with land it could call its own.

Leaving Guadalajara the road skirts the north-eastern edge of Lake Chapala before cutting south, heading into Michoacan and reaching **ZAMORA**. Though an ancient city, founded in 1540, Zamora today has little intrinsic interest. However, if you're planning to head straight down to Uruapan you may want to change buses here: it is possible to go direct from Guadalajara but there are far more buses which continue along the main road, and if you get as far as Zamora there's a much more frequent service to Uruapan. There are several small restaurants and a market very close to the bus station, but little to go out of your way to see. The old cathedral, unusually Gothic in style, is ruined and often closed, though there's a pleasant grassy plaza in front where you can while away some time.

The turn-off for Uruapan actually comes in the village of **CARAPAN**, some 40km further on. As an alternative to changing in Zamora you could get off here and flag down a bus going south, a beautiful road winding through pine-draped hills. Around half-way you pass through the village of **PARACHO** which has been famous for the manufacture of stringed instruments since Quiroga's time. Every house seems to be either a workshop or a guitar shop or both. The instruments vary enormously in price and quality – many are not meant to be anything more than ornamental, stuck on the wall rather than played, but others are serious and beautifully handcrafted. If you really want to buy, this is the place to come, with an enormous variety and all the best craftsmen. A more passing curiosity can be satisfied in Uruapan or Patzcuaro where you'll find them on display and for sale in the markets and *artesanias* museums. Paracho also plays host to a couple of fascinating **fiestas**. On Corpus Christi (the Thursday after Trinity, usually late May/early June) you can witness the dance of *Los Viejitos*. This, the most famous of Michoacan's dances, is also one of its most picturesque, with the dancers, dressed in baggy white cotton and old men's masks, alternating between parodying the tottering steps of the little old men (*viejitos*) they represent and breaking into complex routines. Naturally enough, there's a lot of music too. August 8th sees an even more ancient ceremony, whose roots go back to well before the Spanish era: an ox is sacrificed and its meat used to make a complicated ritual dish – *Shuripe* – which is then shared out among the celebrants.

URUAPAN, they say, means 'the place where flowers bloom' in the Tarascan language. It often seems that these translations of names are far too convenient to be true – fitting the modern facts rather than the ancient reality – and in this case if you look at Appleton's Guide for

1884 you'll find a different explanation: 'The word Uruapan comes from *Urani*, which means in the Tarasc language "a chocolate cup", because the Indians in this region devote themselves to the manufacture and painting of these objects.' Demand for chocolate cups, presumably, has fallen off since then. Whatever the truth, the modern version is certainly appropriate: Uruapan, lower (at just over 5,000 feet) and warmer than most of its neighbours, enjoys a steamy sub-tropical climate and is surrounded by jungly forest and lush parks.

It's a prosperous and growing town too, with a thriving commerce based on the richness of its agriculture and on new light industry. To some extent this has come to overshadow the old attractions, creating ugly new development and displacing traditional crafts. But it remains a lively place with a fine market, an abiding reputation for lacquerware, and fascinating surroundings – especially the giant waterfall and 'new' volcano of Paricutin.

You arrive at a modern bus station some way from the centre; a local bus from right outside will take you down to the Plaza Principal. There are also a couple of trains a day to Patzcuaro, Morelia and Mexico City, but it's a painfully slow way to travel unless you plan to sleep away the journey (in which case there's a sleeper train which leaves Uruapan around 7pm and reaches Mexico City at about 8 the next morning). Again, there's a bus in from the station.

The **Plaza Principal**, a long strip of tree-shaded open space, is in every sense the heart of town. Always animated, it's surrounded by everything of importance: shops, market, banks, post office, principal churches and most of the hotels. So this is the place to head first, either to find a hotel or to get some grasp of what Uruapan is about. There are several places to stay on the plaza itself – slightly cheaper are those just off it, the *Hotel Moderno*, at the bottom of Constitucion where it runs up into the market, or the *Palacio* and *Progreso*, on the same street in the other direction, for example.

On the plaza too is the town's one overt tourist attraction, *La Guat-apera*. One of the oldest surviving buildings in Uruapan, it has been restored to house the **Museo Regional de Arte Popular** (open 9–1 and 3–5 except Mondays), an impressive display of crafts from the region, especially Uruapan's own lacquer. This small courtyard with its adjoining chapel was built by Juan de San Miguel, the Franciscan friar who founded the town itself. Later it became one of Bishop Quiroga's hospitals and training centres, so its present function seems marvellously appropriate. The wares shown are of the highest quality, and are worth a close inspection if you plan to go out hunting for bargains in the market or in the shops around the park. The art of making lacquer is a complex and time-consuming one, involving the application of layer upon layer of different colours, with the design cut into the background: all too many of the goods produced for tourists are simply given a couple of coats – one for the black background and a design painted on top – which is much quicker and cheaper, but not the same thing at all.

The **market** begins right behind the museum. Walk round to the back and you come first to the *Mercado de Antojitos*, a series of long, open-air tables where the market ladies serve up meals for stallholders and visitors alike: take a look at what's on offer – this is where you'll find the cheapest, and very often the freshest and best, food in town. Around here, along C. Corregidora and spreading up Constitucion, the rest of the market sprawls – replete with herbs, fruit, trinkets, shoe stalls and hot-dog stands. It's not a particularly good place to buy **native crafts** though – the market in them is altogether more commercialised, and concentrated in a series of shops along Independencia, which leads up from here to the park. At the top of this street are several small places where you can watch the craftsmen at work – some no more than a single room with a display of finished goods on one side and a work-table on the other, others more sophisticated operations. Opposite the entrance to the park is a little 'craft-market' – mostly selling very poor quality souvenirs.

The **Parque Nacional Eduardo Ruiz** (open daily till sunset) is perhaps Uruapan's proudest asset, a luxuriant tropical park in which the *Rio Cupatitzio* rises and through which it flows in a little gorge via a series of man-made cascades and fountains. The river springs from a rock known as *La Rodilla del Diablo* (the Devil's knee), so called, runs the legend, because water gushed forth after the devil knelt here in submission before the unswerving Christian faith of the drought-ridden population. Alternatively, Beelzebub met the Virgin Mary while out strolling in the park, and dropped to his knees in respect. *Cupatitzio* means 'where the waters meet', though it's invariably translated as 'the river that sings', and again it's an appropriate, if not entirely accurate, tag. Baron Alexander von Humboldt described it as 'the most beautiful river in the world'.

Some 12km out of Uruapan, the Cupatitzio crashes over the **waterfall of La Tzararacua**, an impressive hundred-foot plunge amid beautiful forest scenery. This is a popular outing with locals, especially at weekends, and hence easy enough to get to – there are buses (marked *Tzararacua*) from the Plaza Principal, or share a taxi.

Further afield, you can take a trip out to the **Volcano of Paricutin**. On February 20th 1943 a peasant working in his fields noticed the earth begin to move and then to smoke. The ground soon cracked and lava began to flow – eventually, over a period of a year or more, engulfing the village of Paricutin and several other hamlets and forcing the evacuation of thousands of inhabitants. The volcano was active for eight years, producing a cone some 1,000 feet high and devastating an area of around

20 square km. Now there are vast fields of cooled lava, black and powdery, cracked into harsh jags, and the dead cone and crater. Most bizarrely, a church tower pokes its head through the surface – all that remains of the buried hamlet of San Juan Parangaricutiro. During its active life, the volcano drew tourists from around the world, and indeed it's partly responsible for the area's current development – less exciting now, it continues to get a fair number of visitors, though as the years pass the landscape must soften. Such events are not altogether unprecedented – Von Humboldt devoted more than ten pages of his book on New Spain to the volcano of Jorullo, south of Patzcuaro, which appeared equally suddenly in September 1759 – this was still hot enough, he reported, that 'in the year 1780, cigars might still be lighted, when they were fastened to a stick and pushed in . . .'. Jorullo is no longer the subject of any interest – indeed no-one seems to know quite where it is – so maybe Paricutin, too, will in time become no more than a folk memory.

To get to the volcano take a bus from the Central Camionera to the village of **ANGAHUAN** (the buses' ultimate destination is LOS REYES). If you plan to go all the way to the crater take some provisions along since this is an all-day journey – the trip to the *mirador* (viewing point) can be done in a morning. Best to leave your bags in the *Guarderia* at Uruapan's bus station. In Angahuan you should have no problem finding a guide – whether you want one or not. It's not really necessary if you're just going up the hill for a look, though it seems harsh not to allow these people some profit from their misfortune (although actually the volcano was not all bad news – its dust proving a fine fertiliser on the fields not actually buried by it). For the longer journey to the centre you do need a guide, and probably a horse too; not an outrageous expense, and certainly well worth it.

PATZCUARO

PATZCUARO is almost exactly halfway between Uruapan and Morelia, some 60km from each, yet strikingly different from either. Much smaller – little more than a village expanded by the tourist trade – it manages to be at one and the same time a far more colonial town than Uruapan, and infinitely more Indian than Morelia. In this it's perhaps the Mexican town par excellence; littered with Spanish-style mansions and sumptuous churches, yet owing little or nothing in its lifestyle to the colonists. Add to this the fact that it sits by the shore of probably the most beautiful lake in Mexico – certainly the most photogenic – and it's hardly surprising that it acts as a magnet for tourists, Mexicans as well as foreigners. Yet this influx has done little to dilute its attraction – prettified to some extent, the real nature of the town remains. In the vicinity, you can take trips around the lake, visit other, less developed, villages and see the site of Tzintzuntzan, one time capital of the Tarascan kingdom.

Although the outskirts straggle a kilometer or so down to the lake shore, and some of the more expensive hotels are strung out along this drive, the centre of Patzcuaro is very small indeed, with nothing more than a couple of minutes' walk from the two plazas. These are the large **Plaza Vasco de Quiroga** (or Plaza Grande) and the **Plaza Bocanegra** (Plaza Chica), named for Gertrudis Bocanegra, a local independence heroine. Not all **buses** use the same terminal, but wherever they stop you can be sure it will be near the Plaza Chica, while if you arrive by **rail** you'll want to jump on a local bus (*centro*) to take you there. None of the **hotels** – and there are packs of them – is really very cheap, but on the other hand there are some of the best reasonably priced places you'll find anywhere, and if you're prepared to pay a little extra for a lot more elegance you should get excellent value. Most are on one or other of the plazas. On Vasco de Quiroga you'll find the *Posada San Rafael*, one of the largest and fanciest with a long modern extension in colonial style behind the genuinely colonial front, the *Hotel Los Escudos* (next to the Palacio Municipal) and the *Mansion Iturbide*. Cheaper, but rowdier, are those on the Plaza Bocanegra: the *Gran Hotel* (not very grand any more), the *Posada de la Rosa*, and the *Hotel San Agustin*. Others close by include the *Hotel Blanquita* (Volador No. 4) in a narrow street just off the small plaza, and the *Hotel Valmen* (Lloreda 34) also close to this plaza towards the chief bus terminals.

Almost all of these hotels have their own **restaurants**, and the menus are fairly standard throughout – as always the *comida corrida* will be good value, if unexciting. One feature of virtually all menus is *pescado blanco*, the rather flabby, dull white fish from the lake, and *sopa tarasca* is also common – a tomato-based soup with chile and bits of tortilla in it, usually very good. For the best fish you'll want to go down to the lake itself, where there are several restaurants opposite the landing jetty: take a bus (*Lago/centro*) or walk down following the *embarcadero* signs. Considerably more expensive than most, but with a very successfully contrived colonial atmosphere and interesting Mexican food, is the dining room in the *Hotel Meson del Gallo*, up towards the basilica. On Friday nights they have a 'Fiesta Mexicana' here, with music and regional dancing, which, if you like that sort of thing, is more tastefully done than most. At the other end of the price range there are plenty of opportunities for finding something to eat in the **market**. This used to operate just one day a week in the streets leading up from the Plaza Chica, but nowadays there is some activity every day, though Mondays and Wednesdays tend to be slow. Friday is the day when most of the Indians come in from the country to trade and barter their surplus, and that's when the market is at its most colourful and animated.

Patzcuaro, more than anywhere in the state, owes its position to bishop Vasco de Quiroga's affection for the Indians (you'll find his statue in the centre of the plaza which bears his name). It was he who decided, in the face of considerable opposition from the Spanish in Morelia (then known as Valladolid), to build the cathedral here. And although subsequent bishops moved back to Morelia, a basis had been laid: indeed it's the fact that Patzcuaro enjoyed a building boom in the sixteenth century and has been something of a backwater ever since that creates much of its charm. Throughout the centre are old mansions, with their balconies and coats-of-arms, barely touched since those early years.

The finest are on the Plaza Grande – especially the seventeenth-century **Casa del Gigante**, with its hefty pillars and crudely carved figures, and another nearby said to have been inhabited by Prince Huitzimengari, son of the last Tarascan king. These, though, are both private houses and not open to visitors. There are more on the Plaza Bocanegra, but the most extraordinary thing here is the **Biblioteca**. This, the former sixteenth-century church of San Agustin, has been converted into a library and decorated with **murals** by Juan O'Gorman depicting the history of Michoacan. As well as a marvellous name, O'Gorman possessed a prodigious talent, and is one of the muralists who inherited the mantle of Rivera and Orozco (among other work, he decorated the interior of Chapultepec Castle in Mexico City). The paintings here couldn't be described as subtle, but he certainly ensures that the anti-imperialist point is taken – though even O'Gorman manages to find praise for Vasco de Quiroga.

Quiroga's cathedral, the **Basilica** or Colegiata, though never completed, is a massive church for so small a town. Even so it is often full, for the Indians continue to revere Don Vasco's name and the church possesses a miraculous healing image of the Virgin made in the traditional Tarascan method out of *pasta de caña*, a gum like modelling paste made principally from maize (other examples of the art in the museum, below). Services here, especially on saints' days or during fiestas, are extraordinary – the Indians worshipping in an intense, almost hypnotic fervour. The scrubby little park around the church becomes a fairground during local fiestas.

Between the Basilica and the Plaza Grande, at the corner of Quiroga and Lerin, is the **Museo de Artes Populares** (open 9–1.30 and 3.30–7; closed Sunday afternoon and all day Monday) in the ancient *Colegio de San Nicolas*. Founded by Quiroga in 1540, the college is now devoted to a superb collection of regional handicrafts, local lacquer and pottery, copperware from Santa Clara del Cobre, traditional masks and religious objects made from pasta de caña which, apart from being easy to work with is also very light, and hence easily carried in processions. Some of the objects on display are very ancient, others the best examples of modern work, and all in a very beautiful building. Almost opposite is the church of **La Compañia**, also built by Quiroga (in 1546) and later taken over by the Jesuits. Quiroga's remains and various relics associated with him are preserved here.

Continue in this direction, along Lerin, and you come to the **Casa de los Once Patios**, an eighteenth-century convent converted into a crafts showhouse, full of workshops and expensive boutiques. There's also a **Tourist Office** in here. As it's name suggests, the complex is set around a series of tiny courtyards, and it's a fascinating place to stroll around even if you can't afford the prices. You can watch restored treadle looms at work, admire the intricacy with which the best lacquerware is coddled, and wander at liberty through the warren of rooms and corridors.

While you're in the town itself you never actually see the lake, so, for a good view of both lake and town, climb the *Cerro del Estribo* (Stirrup Hill) up to the **chapel of El Calvario**. This is around an hour's walk, but worth it – leave the Plaza Grande on C. Ponce de Leon, past the old customs house and a little plaza in front of the church of San Francisco, and keep straight on till you start climbing the hill. Alternatively, of course, you can head down for **the lake** itself and take off to see it in a boat. Again, it's less than an hour's walk down to the jetty (follow the *embarcadero* signs) or there are buses – those marked *Lago* will drop you right by the boats, *Santa Ana* buses pass very close by.

With the completion of several new roads, the lake is no longer the major thoroughfare it once was – most locals now take the bus rather than paddle around the lake in canoes – but there is still a fair amount of traffic and regular trips out to the closest island, **JANITZIO**. The fares are fixed (get your ticket before you board) but there are almost always sundry 'extras'. Chief of these is a chance to photograph the famous butterfly nets, wielded by Indian fishermen from tiny dug-out canoes. I don't believe that anyone actually uses these nets for fishing anymore – they may be picturesque but they look highly impractical – but there's almost always a group of islanders with an eye for the main chance prepared to put on a show for the tourists. They lurk in readiness on the far side of the island and only paddle out into camera range when a sufficiently large collection has been taken. Janitzio, too, has fallen prey to commercialism, and from the moment you step ashore you're besieged by souvenir salesmen. Don't be put off though, for the lake really is very beautiful and the views from the top of the island, which rises steeply from the water to a massive statue of Morelos at the summit, are truly spectacular. Moreover, you can't blame the islanders for wanting to milk their visitors – it's their only conceivable source of income aside from fish from the lake, and they really are poor compared to the inhabitants of the mainland. Up the single steep street, between the stalls selling pottery and crude wooden carvings, are a series of little restaurants with their wares on display out front – most have good fish. Longer trips around the lake and visits to the other islands, or private hire of a boat and guide, can be arranged at the embarcadero either through the office there or by private negotiations with one of the boatmen.

The Day of the Dead (November 1st, and through the night into the 2nd) is celebrated in spectacular fashion throughout Mexico, but nowhere more so than on Lake Patzcuaro – one of the best known ceremonies in the country. Although many tourists come to watch, this is essentially a private meditation when the locals carry offerings of fruit and flowers to the cemetery and hold vigil over the graves of their ancestors all night, chanting by candlelight. It's a spectacular and moving sight, especially earlier in the evening as Indians from the surrounding area converge on the island in their canoes, each with a single candle burning in the bows. At this time of year there is little chance of getting a room in Patzcuaro without prior booking.

Tzintzuntzan and Quiroga

The remains of **TZINTZUNTZAN**, ancient capital of the Tarascans, lie 15km north of Patzcuaro on the shore of the lake. There were, the Spanish estimated, as many as 40,000 people living here at the time of the conquest, with dominion over all of what is now Michoacan and large parts of the modern states of Jalisco and Colima. Around the raised **ceremonial centre** lay their homes and markets, as well as the palaces of their rulers, but all that can be seen today is the artificial terrace on which the great religious buildings lay, and the ruins, part restored, of these temples.

Even if you do no more than pass by on the road, you can't fail to be struck by the scale of these buildings and by their elliptical design, a startling contrast to the rigid, right-angled formality adhered to in almost every other major pre-hispanic culture. Climb up to the terrace and you'll find five *yacatas*, as the temples are called, of which two have been partly rebuilt. Originally they were each some 40 feet high, tapering in steps from a broad base to a walkway along the top less than 6 feet wide: there is no ornamentation, the yacatas are in fact piles of flat stones, held in by retaining walls and then faced in smooth, close fitting volcanic stone. From the terrace, which was originally approached up a broad ceremonial ramp or stairway on the side furthest from the water, there are magnificent views across the lake and over the present-day village.

Down in the village, which has a reputation for producing some of the region's best ceramics and several shops selling it, you'll find what's left of the enormous **Franciscan Monastery** founded here around 1530 to convert the Tarascans. Much of this has been demolished, and all substantially rebuilt, but there remains a fine baroque church and a huge atrium, or courtyard, where the Indians would gather to be preached at. Vasco de Quiroga originally intended to base his diocese here, but eventually decided that Patzcuaro had the better situation and a more constant supply of water. He did leave one unusual legacy though – the olive trees planted around the monastery are probably the oldest in Mexico, since settlers were banned from cultivating olives in order to protect the farmers back in Spain. Tzintzuntzan, incidentally, means 'place of the humming-birds'. You're unlikely to see one now, but the theory is that there were plenty of them around until the Tarascans – who used the feathers to make ornaments – virtually exterminated them through hunting.

To get to Tzintzuntzan you want to take a bus from Patzcuaro which is going to **QUIROGA**. Quiroga is another village packed with craft markets, largely because it lies on the main road from Morelia to Guadalajara: the only local product seems to be painted wooden chairs, though traditionally the village makes all kinds of wooden objects and furniture. Really it's no more than a stop-over, but if you are waiting here do take time to wander down to the market for a look round. There's a regular bus service between Quiroga and Patzcuaro, and if you're coming **direct from Guadalajara** it's the most direct way of getting there (on this route, don't miss the views over the lake from the north, shortly before you reach Quiroga). Logically, this would also be the quickest way of doing the journey in reverse, **from Patzcuaro to Guadalajara**, but, things aren't always that simple: there's no guarantee that you're going to be able to get onto one of the fast buses along the main road – most pass through Quiroga full, without stopping. So although it's slightly further, you'd be much better off going from Patzcuaro direct to Morelia and from there doubling back towards Guadalajara – that way you're guaranteed a seat.

MORELIA

The state capital, **MORELIA** is in many ways untypical of Michoacan: above all it is a Spanish city. It looks Spanish and, despite a large Indian population, it feels Spanish – the streets are broad and lined with seventeenth-century mansions and sitting in the outdoor cafes of its arcaded plazas you might easily be in Salamanca or Valladolid. Valladolid was indeed the city's name until 1828, when it was changed to honour the local-born independence hero, Jose Maria Morelos. And it has always been a city of Spaniards – one of the first they founded after the conquest.

That honour fell on two Franciscan friars, Juan de San Miguel and Antonio de Lisboa, who settled here among the Indians in 1530. Ten years later they were visited by the first Viceroy of New Spain, Antonio de Mendoza, who was so taken by the site that he ordered a town to be built, naming it after his birthplace and sending fifty Spanish families to settle. From the beginning there was fierce rivalry between the colonists here and the Indian town of Patzcuaro. During the lifetime of Vasco de Quiroga it went in favour of the latter, but later the bishopric was moved here, a university founded, and by the end of the sixteenth century there was no doubt that Valladolid was predominant.

There are specific things to look for and to visit in present-day Morelia, but the city itself outweighs them: it's been declared a 'national monument' which means no new building which doesn't match perfectly with the old, and it preserves a remarkable unity of style. Nearly everything is built of the same faintly pinkish-grey stone (trachyte) which, being soft, is not only easily carved and embellished but weathers quickly, giving even relatively recent constructions a battered, ancient look. At the heart of it all is the massive **Cathedral**, whose two soaring towers are said to be the tallest in Mexico. Begun in 1640 in the relatively plain Herrerian style, the towers and dome were not completed for some hundred years, by which time baroque had arrived with a vengeance: it all harmonises remarkably though, and for all its size and richness of decoration, the perfect proportions prevent it being overpowering. The interior, refitted towards the end of the last century after most of its silver ornamentation had been removed to pay for the wars, is at least simple and preserves, in the choir and sacristy, a few early colonial religious paintings.

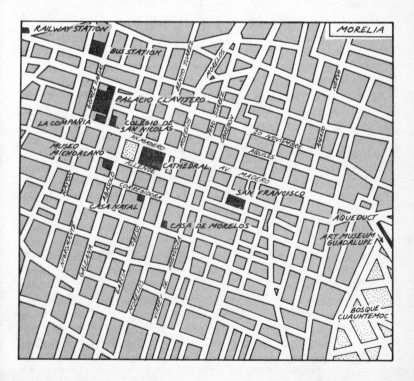

Flanking the Cathedral are the two main plazas, the **Zocalo** (Plaza de Armas or de los Martires) and the much smaller **Plaza Ocampo**. Focal point of the city, the Zocalo is the place to sit around, in the cafes under its elegant arcaded *portales*, with a coffee and a morning paper (you can buy the *Mexico City News* from the stands here) revelling in the city's leisurely pace. On the corner of Madero and Absolo, opposite the Cathedral, is the *Hotel Virrey de Mendoza*, a very expensive hotel in one of the best colonial mansions – wander in to take a look at the restaurant in what used to be the courtyard, now glassed over. On the same side of the Zocalo (corner of Allende and Absolo) the **Museo Michoacano** occupies another palatial eighteenth-century building. The Emperor Maximilian lodged here on his visits to Morelia, and it now houses a collection reflecting the state's diversity and rich history: the rooms devoted to archaeology are of course dominated by the Tarascan culture, including pottery and small sculptures from Tzintzuntzan, but also display much earlier objects, especially some small obsidian figurines. Out in the patio are two magnificent old carriages, while upstairs the colonial epoch is represented in a large group of religious paintings and sculptures and a collection of old books and manuscripts.

The Avenida Francisco Madero, which runs along the north side of the Zocalo, is very much the main street of Morelia, with most of the important public buildings and major shops strung out along it. First, facing the Plaza Melchor Ocampo and the Cathedral, is the **Palacio de Gobierno**. Formerly a seminary – Independence hero Morelos and anti-hero Agustin Iturbide studied here, as did Melchor Ocampo, a nineteenth-century liberal supporter of Benito Juarez – it's of interest now for the murals which adorn the stairway and upper level of the patio. Practically the whole of Mexican history is here, and all its heroes depicted. A little further down Madero are several **banks** which are among the most remarkable examples of active conservation you'll see anywhere: all Mexican banks are sumptuous, but they usually go in for steel and glass, marble floors and modern statuary – these are old mansions which have been refurbished in traditional style, and somehow they manage to combine reasonably efficient operation with an ambience which is wholly in keeping with the setting.

Carry on down here, past the Post Office and the baroque facade of the Templo de las Monjas, and in around quarter of an hour you reach an area of tree-lined walks and little parks on the edge of town, through the middle of which runs the old **Aqueduct**. Built between 1785 and 1789, its serried arches brought water into the city from springs in the nearby hills. On the right is the largest of the parks, the **Bosque Cuauht-emoc**, in which there's a small **Museum of Contemporary Art** as well as some beautifully laid out flower displays. To the left Calle Fray Antonio de San Miguel (named for the bishop who built the aqueduct) runs down to the vastly overdecorated **Sanctuario de Guadalupe**: there are market stalls, selling above all the local *dulces*, set out down here at weekends and during fiestas.

To get back to the centre by a different route, cut through the Bosque Cuauhtemoc and head in on C. Antonio Alzate which runs parallel to Madero. Just up to the right here, some three blocks short of the Cathedral, is the **Palacio de las Artesanias**. This is the single most comprehensive collection of Michoacan's crafts you'll find anywhere, almost all of them for sale. The main display is downstairs, where the best and most obviously commercial items are shown, while on the upper floor are a series of rooms devoted to the products of particular villages (manned by villagers rather than the Palacio's staff and hence not always open) and a collection of historic items which you can't buy. It's all housed in what used to be the Monastery of **San Francisco** whose church, facing onto the little plaza next door, can also be visited.

A couple of blocks further along Alzate, the **Casa de Morelos** is found to the left on Avenida Morelos. In this relatively modest eighteenth-century mansion *Jose Maria Morelos y Pavon* lived from 1801 – it's now a museum devoted to his life and the War of Independence. A student of Hidalgo (see p. 131) Morelos took over the leadership of the Independence movement after its instigators had been executed in 1811. While the cry of Independence had initially been taken up by the Mexican (Creole) bourgeoisie, smarting under the trading restrictions imposed on them from Spain, it quickly became a mass popular movement. Unlike the original leaders Morelos (a mestizo priest born into relative poverty) was a populist and a genuine reformer; even more unlike them he was also a political and military tactician of considerable skill, invoking the spirit of the French Revolution and calling for universal suffrage, racial equality and the break-up of the hacienda system. Defeat and execution by Royalist armies under Agustin de Iturbide came in 1815 only after years of guerrilla warfare during which Morelos had come within an ace of taking Mexico City and controlling the entire country. When Independence finally was gained – by Iturbide, now changed sides and later briefly to be emperor – it was no longer a force for change, rather a reaction to the fact that by 1820 liberal reforms were sweeping Spain itself. The causes espoused by Morelos were, however, taken up to some extent by Benito Juarez and later, with a vengeance, in the Revolution – almost a hundred years after his death.

Nearby, at the corner of Corregidora (the continuation of Alzate) and Garcia Obeso, you can see the house where the hero was born, the **Casa Natal de Morelos**. This in turn is virtually next door to the Church of **San Agustin**, from where a pedestrianised street runs up one block to the Zocalo, and opposite whose attractive facade is a tiny market area, the **Mercado Hidalgo**.

Finally, back across the Zocalo and heading just one block in the other direction along Madero, you reach the **Colegio de San Nicolas**. Originally founded at Patzcuaro in 1540 by Vasco de Quiroga, and moved here in 1580, the College is the second oldest in Mexico and hence in all the Americas – it's now part of the University of Morelia, housing administrative offices and various technical faculties. To the side, across C. Nigromante, is the public library in what was originally the Jesuit Church of **La Compañia**, while next to this is the beautiful **Palacio Clavijero**, converted into government offices. Inside here you'll find the **Tourist Office**. At the bottom of Nigromante, on a charming little plaza, is the baroque church of Santa Rosa and, beside it, the **Conservatorio de las Rosas** – a music academy founded in the eighteenth century and still functioning as such. From time to time there are concerts of classical music here – details from Turismo.

Practical details and on from Morelia

The **Central Camionera** is just around the corner from these last named places – walk one block up on Gomez Farias (to your left as you come out) and the Plaza Santa Rosa is one and a half blocks to the left along Santiago Tapia. It's little further from the **Railway Station** – a short walk up Eduardo Ruiz, directly opposite, brings you to the front of the Camionera. Heading into the centre, stop off at the department of **Turismo** (in the Palacio Clavijero, above) to pick up some information.

The cheaper **hotels** are mostly around the bus station: stand on the steps and you'll see several. Best of these are probably the *Hotel Plaza* and the *Concordia*, both of them to the left on Gomez Farias. The *Hotel Señorial*, one block up here and to the right on Tapia, is also reasonable. Carry on up to Madero and there are more places to your right – the *Fenix*, *Orozco* and *San Jorge*. More expensive, but in a position that couldn't be bettered, is the *Hotel Casino*, above a cafe on the north side of the Zocalo. Others near the centre include the *Hotel Allende* (Allende 843, about four and a half blocks west of the Zocalo, a similar distance south of the railway station), the *San Miguel* (Madero Pte. 1036) and the *Hotel Florida* towards the Casa de Morelos at Morelos Sur 161.

For a reasonably priced sit-down meal, the bus station area is again the best bet – most of the hotels there also have **restaurants** which serve a fairly standard *comida corrida*. Eating a full meal in any of the cafes on the Zocalo will prove expensive, but they're good for snacks or for a breakfast of coffee and *pan dulce*. In the evenings you can eat outdoors at places set up along Calle Hidalgo (between the Zocalo and San Agustin) and around the Mercado Hidalgo. Chief of Morelia's specialities are its *dulces*, sweets made of candied fruit or evaporated milk: cloyingly sweet to most non-Mexican tastes, but very popular here. You can see a wide selection at the **Mercado de Dulces y Artesanias**, up Gomez Farias from the bus station and on the left-hand side, around the back of the Palacio Clavijero. As it's name suggests, they also sell handicrafts here, but on the whole nothing of any class. Morelians also get through a lot of *rompope* (a drink which to a lesser extent you'll find all over Mexico) – again, it's very sweet, an egg-flip concoction based on rum, milk and egg with vanilla, cinnamon and almond added as flavouring. For healthier eating, *Señor Sol*, right opposite the Mercado de Dulces, offers fruit drinks and salads and an assortment of dairy and vegetable products. Finally, as always, there are food stalls and plenty of raw ingredients in the **market**, but Morelia's big *Mercado Independencia* is on the whole a disappointment – certainly not as large or varied as you'd expect. Sunday – market day – it perks up a little. Get there by going towards the Plaza San Francisco and then a long six or seven blocks south on Vasco de Quiroga.

Getting away from Morelia should present no problem at all: there are trains to Mexico City (including the sleeper, which leaves here around 11pm and arrives in the capital at 8am), and to Patzcuaro and Uruapan; and there are buses to just about anywhere in the state and most other conceivable destinations, very frequently to Guadalajara, Patzcuaro, Uruapan and Mexico City, regularly north to Salamanca, for Guanajuato and Querétaro. The shortest route to Mexico City, via Zitacuaro and Toluca is very beautiful – passing through the Mil Cumbres (thousand peaks) – but mountainous and slow. Some buses go round by the faster roads to the north. If only for the scenery, you should try to take the former route – these mountains are the playground of Mexico City's middle classes, and dotted with their villas, especially around the artificial lake of the VALLE DEL BRAVO. TOLUCA (see p. 220) is host to an unbelievably huge market on Fridays.

GUANAJUATO AND QUERÉTARO: THE BAJÍO

Mexico's broad central plateau narrows as it approaches the Valley of Mexico City and becomes hillier. Here in **the Bajío**, above all in the states of Guanajuato and Querétaro, are its finest and richest colonial cities, founded amid barren land and growing rich on just one thing – silver.

Before the arrival of the Spanish this was a relatively unexploited area, a buffer zone between the civilised peoples of the centre and the barbarian Chichimec tribes from the north. Though the Aztecs may have tapped some of its mineral wealth, they never began to exploit the area with the greed, tenacity and ruthlessness of the new colonists. After the conquest the mining cities grew rich, but in time they also grew restive – champing under the heavy hand of control from Spain. The wealthy *Creole* (Spanish blooded but Mexican born) bourgeoisie were free to exploit the land and its people, and forced to pay punitive taxes, but not to rule their own destinies – lucrative government posts and high positions in the church being reserved exclusively for those of Spanish birth, *Gachupines*. And the Indians and poor *Mestizos* were condemned either to landless poverty or to almost suicidal labour in the mines.

The Bajío was fertile ground for revolutionary ideas, and so it turned out. For this is also *La Cuna de la Independencia* (the Cradle of Independence) where every town seems to claim a role in the break with Spain. In Querétaro the plotters held many of their early meetings, and from here they were warned that their plans had been discovered; in Dolores Hidalgo the famous *grito* was first voiced by Father Hidalgo, proclaiming an independent Mexico, and from here he marched on San Miguel de Allende, picking up more volunteers for his armed rabble as he continued towards a bloody confrontation in Guanajuato.

This history is proudly preserved and everywhere proclaimed, attracting Mexican visitors for whom it almost constitutes a pilgrimage. It's a fascinating area, and one which is very easy to explore – towns are close together, bus services are excellent (especially on *Flecha Amarilla*, a second class company which makes up in speed and frequency of service what it lacks in comfort) and the hotels are some of the best you'll find.

GUANAJUATO

Shoe-horned into a narrow ravine, **GUANAJUATO** was for centuries the wealthiest city in Mexico, its mines pouring out silver and gold in quantities which few could hope to rival. It presents an extraordinary sight: cut off by the surrounding hills you come upon the town quite suddenly, a riot of colonial architecture dominated by the bluff (and rather ugly) bulk of the University, tumbling down hills so steep that at times it seems that the floor of one building is suspended on the roof of the last. There's a feeling, too, that Guanajuato is more than just physically isolated: it's resisted change in its architecture, in its habits, its politics (still thoroughly reactionary), in short, in its entire way of life. There's an old-fashioned, backwater feel to the place, reinforced by the students' habit of going serenading in their black capes, the brass bands playing in the plazas and the refusal to make any very special effort to accommodate the flood of tourists.

Getting your bearings, a few practicalities

Maps of Guanajuato are almost entirely incomprehensible, but in practice it is not in the least a difficult place to find your way around. The trouble with the map is that there is too much to cram into too small a space, and that if it were to be drawn accurately the streets would have virtually to be superimposed on one another, running as they do in close parallel along the sides of the valley. To confuse matters further, an underground roadway passes almost directly beneath the town's main street, Avenida Juarez. This, the *Subterraneo Miguel Hidalgo*, was originally built as a tunnel to take the river under the city and prevent the periodic flooding to which it was liable – and in the process to provide a covered sewer. The river now runs much deeper below ground; its former course, with the addition of a few exits and entrances, proving very handy in preventing the traffic from clogging up the centre entirely.

For the purposes of getting around on foot – the only practicable means of transport within the city – it's enough to know that Av. Juarez runs straight through the heart of town along the ravine floor and that everything of interest is either on it, or just off on the lower slopes. Should you get lost simply head downhill and you'll get back to Juarez. The **bus station** is right at the bottom, western end of this street, while the **rail terminus** is on its continuation just as it leaves town. It's most unlikely that you'll be arriving by train – the one daily service on the little branch line leaves Irapuato at 6.30 am, arriving here around 8, and connects very badly with main line services through Irapuato on the Mexico City-Guadalajara and Mexico City-Ciudad Juarez lines: if you do it's not too far to walk in, or get on any bus heading in the direction of the centre.

Most of the cheaper places to stay are, where else, scattered round about the bus station. First though, it's worth checking out the **Tourist Office** which is even closer. Turn left on Juarez, to where it opens out slightly and the subterranean road disappears underground, and you'll find the office on the left by the junction with 5 de Mayo. Theoretically it's open every day except Sunday from 10–2 and 4–7, but the hours do tend to be erratic – they'll give you a **free map** here, for what it's worth, and more importantly have up to date **information on hotels**; a board outside lists most with their official prices. While this doesn't guarantee what you'll actually pay, it does give a good guide and a basis for arguing if you're being overcharged. Rooms can at times be hard to come by – especially on Mexican public holidays and during the International Festival (late April-early May and again at the end of August/beginning of September), at which times the turismo people can again prove helpful.

The greatest concentration of **hotels** is in the short stretch of Juarez immediately beyond here, an area crowded with little restaurants and filled with the bustle of people coming and going between the Camionera and the market or boarding local buses in the street. Among the cheaper places, with very little to choose between them, are the *Hotel Granaditas* (No. 109), the *Central* (111) and the *Reforma* (113). Opposite these and slightly more expensive is the *Posada San Francisco* (178) and, a little further up, the *Posada del Comercio* (210) and the much pricier *Hotel Insurgente* (226). Better value than any of these, to my mind, is the *Posada Condesa*, still further up Juarez just before the Plaza de la Paz (Plaza de la Paz 60). Several other places can be found by heading towards the back of the bus station, or tracking up to the left on 5 de Mayo past the Alhondiga: the Hotels *Mineral de Rayas* and *Socavon* on C. Alhondiga, and the *Murillo* and *Alhondiga* on Insurgencia, for example. If you're prepared to pay rather more, the *Hacienda de Cobos* (Juarez 153) is very nice indeed, housed behind stout walls in what used to be a mill used for crushing and washing silver ore; it's almost opposite the bus station, you can't miss the little white-domed lodge with the name painted across it.

In town, the expensive hotels are mostly those on the Jardin de la Union, chief of Guanajuato's many little plazas, but the fanciest places are those on the outskirts where there is room for new construction and space to park cars. Very near to the former is perhaps the best of all the places to stay: the *Casa Kloster* (Calle de Alonso 32). This has something of the feel of a family-run European pension about it – it's simple, not at all expensive and often full. The disadvantage is that it's a long way to go if it is booked up – along Juarez to the Plaza de la Paz, then down to the right and it's more or less opposite the *Telefonos* building; calling in at Turismo may save you a wasted journey.

Finding **somewhere to eat** is much less likely to cause problems – it's impossible to walk more than a few yards down Juarez without passing some kind of cafe or restaurant. At the bottom end, near the bus station, are a whole series of very plain little places serving the standard Mexican staples, many of them also offering a cheap *comida corrida*, especially the hotel restaurants. Rather more adventurous, and cheaper still, are the stalls in the **Mercado Hidalgo**. The first building of note as you head up Juarez, the market is a huge iron-framed construction reminiscent of Victorian railway-station architecture, crammed with goods of every description: the place to go for food is its most modern annexe, two floors of delights (and horrors) where you'd be advised to take a good look at what's on offer before choosing where to eat – some are distinctly cleaner and more appetising than others.

Continuing on Juarez, the **Jardin de la Reforma** is just up to your left, a quiet square where you can sit outside at one of a number of Americanised establishments, popular among young locals and students. The same is true of the **Plazuela San Fernando**, also just to the left off Juarez but easiest reached from here through the Plaza San Roque, where you'll find a couple of pizza and hamburger joints as well as a vegetarian restaurant. Carry on towards the centre and you're into rather more expensive territory: pricey or not, though, few people can resist the lure of the pavement cafes in the **Jardin de la Union**, especially when there's a band playing – stick to coffee and you can't go far wrong. Finally, climb up behind here towards the **University** and you'll find another area where the students go, and where prices are consequently lower.

The town

There must be more different things to see in Guanajuato than in virtually any town of its size anywhere – churches, theatres, museums, battlefields, mines, even mummified corpses. For a couple of these you'll need to take the bus. First though head down Juarez once again. Beyond the market, to the left, you get to the **Plaza San Roque** through the Jardin de la Reforma. A small, irregular, flagged space, the plaza has a distinctly medieval feel, heightened by the raised facade of the Church of San Roque which towers over it. Here, during the **International Cervantes Festival** (Late April-early May with further events in September, after the rains) are staged the famous *entremeses*, swashbuckling one-act plays from the repertory of classical Spanish theatre. You don't need good Spanish to work out what's going on – they're highly visual and very entertaining even if you can't understand a word. There is a grandstand in which you have to book seats, but it's easy enough to join the crowds watching from the edges of the plaza for free. Groups of university students (who perform the entremeses) will quite often put on impromptu performances outside festival times, so it's worth wandering up here in the early evening just to see if anything is happening – Saturday nights especially. For details of the Festival, check with the Tourist Office – other events are held in the Teatro Juarez and the Teatro Principal (see below).

You can get back to Juarez through the Plazuela San Fernando, in which case you'll have to backtrack a little to get to the **Plazuela de los Angeles**. In itself this is little more than a slight broadening of the street, but from here steps lead up to your right into some of Guanajuato's steepest, narrowest alleys. Just off here is the **Callejon del Beso**, so called because it's so narrow that you can lean out of the windows to exchange kisses across the street – naturally enough there are any number of Canterbury Tales style legends of cuckolded husbands and star-crossed lovers associated with it. Other alleys here have equally cute names – Salto del Mono (Monkey's Leap) or Calle de las Canterranas (Street of the Singing Frogs).

The **Plaza de la Paz** comes next, reached after a short stretch of Juarez where you pass several banks and begin to feel as if you've reached the centre of town. For a while here, Juarez is not the lowest road – Calle

Alonso cuts round to the right, to rejoin it a little further up. Plaza de la Paz itself boasts some of the town's finest **colonial buildings**, among which the late eighteenth-century mansion of the Condes de Rul y Valenciana, owners of the richest mine in the country, stands out as the grandest. It was designed by Eduardo Tresguerras, undoubtedly the finest architect of his time, and played host briefly to Baron Alexander Von Humboldt, the German naturalist and writer on Mexico, an event commemorated by a plaque. On the far side of the plaza is the **Basilica de Nuestra Señora de Guanajuato**, the baroque parish church which houses the patroness of the city – an ancient image of the Virgin. This wooden statue, which now sits surrounded by silver and jewels, was given to Guanajuato in 1557 by Philip II in gratitude for the wealth which was pouring from here into the Spanish royal coffers. Even then it was very old and miraculous, having survived more than 800 years of the Moorish occupation hidden in a cave near Granada (Spain).

From here you can cut up to the university, but just a short distance further on Juarez is the **Jardin de la Union**, Guanajuato's Zocalo. It's a delightful little square, set back from the street, shaded with trees, surrounded by tables outside the cafes, and with a bandstand in the centre from which the town band regularly adds to the early evening atmosphere. Facing the Jardin across Juarez are the baroque church of **San Diego**, with a beautiful facade, and the imposing neo-classical frontage of the **Teatro Juarez**. The interior of the theatre is fabulously plush – red velvet, gilt and chandeliers – as befits its period; built at the end of the last century it was opened in 1903 by the dictator Porfirio Diaz himself. Visits from 9–2 and 4–7 daily.

Past the Jardin, Juarez changes its name to Sopeña as it leaves the centre of town and begins to climb the hill behind, eventually becoming the Paseo de la Presa. If you carry on walking up here for half an hour or so you pass through some of the fancier residential districts and eventually reach the Presa de la Olla and the Presa San Renovato, a couple of **reservoirs** with **parks** on their banks and good **views** over the city. This is a popular picnic spot, too, and you can hire boats to row around the *Presas*. There's a bus out here (look for *La Olla* or *Presa*) which goes through town on the underground street – steps near the church of San Diego will take you down to a subterranean bus-stop. Even better views can be had from the **Monument to Pipila**, on the hillside almost directly above the Teatro Juarez. You can walk up, a steep climb which takes nearly an hour (there are several routes through the alleys but the easiest, signed *Al Pipila*, leads to the right off Sopeña just beyond the Teatro Juarez), or again there's a bus (*Pipila*) which will take you round the scenic *Carretera Panoramica*.

If you want to stay in town, walk out the back of the Jardin de la Union and you'll find the **Plaza del Baratillo** up your left, a little space with another quiet cafe and a clutch of craft shops. From here the **Teatro Principal** is down to the right, while curving on round to the left there's the **Post Office** and then the church of **La Compañia** and the **University**. La Compañia, a highly decorated monumental baroque church, is just about all that's left of a Jesuit seminary founded in 1732, an educational establishment which eventually metamorphosed into the State University – now one of the most prestigious in Mexico. The University building is in fact quite modern – only some thirty years old – but designed to blend in with the town which, for all its size, it does surprisingly effectively. There's not a great deal of interest to the casual observer inside, but wander in anyway: you can catch up on any cultural events from the noticeboards, and there's often a temporary exhibition of some kind.

Among the University's more famous alumni is the painter **Diego Rivera**. For a long time Rivera, the ardent revolutionary and Marxist, went unrecognised by his conservative home town, but there is now a small **museum** (open 10–2 and 4–6 closed Sundays) in the house where he was brought up. Among more sentimental mementoes – the family furniture, the bed in which he slept – is a collection of his early works and a series of plans and sketches for later ones. This is on Calle Positos, which leads from the front of the University to emerge at the **Alhondiga de Granaditas**, perhaps the most important of all Guanajuato's monuments.

Originally a granary, now a museum, the Alhondiga achieved notoriety at the beginning of the War of Independence when it was the scene of the first real battle and some of the bloodiest butchery in all that long struggle. Just thirteen days after the cry of Independence had gone up in Dolores Hidalgo, Father Hidalgo approached Guanajuato at the head of his insurgent force – mostly peons armed with nothing more than staves and sickles. The Spanish, outnumbered but well supplied with fire-arms, shut themselves up in the Alhondiga, a redoubtable fortress. Hidalgo's troops could make no impact until a young miner, nicknamed *El Pipila*, volunteered to fire the wooden doors – with a slab of stone tied to his back as a shield he managed to crawl to the gates and start them burning, though in doing so he died. The rebels, their path cleared, broke in and massacred the defenders wholesale. It was a short-lived victory – Hidalgo was forced to abandon Guanajuato, leaving its inhabitants to face Spanish reprisals, and was eventually tracked down by the royalists and executed in Chihuahua. His head and the heads of his three chief co-conspirators, Allende, Aldama and Jimenez, were suspended from the four corners of the Alhondiga as a warning to anyone minded to follow their example, and there they stayed for over ten years, until Mexico finally did become independent. You can see the iron cages in which the heads were displayed in the museum, while the hooks from which they hung are still in evidence on the outside walls. Inside too, there's a little memorial hall devoted to the martyrs of Independence.

As for the **museum** itself (open 10–2 and 4–7; closed Sunday afternoon and all day Monday), it's a particularly well displayed version of the typical regional affair with collections devoted to local archaeology and history, to native crafts and ethnography and to a study of Guanajuato's mining industry. There is also an art gallery and, more impressively, **murals** by Chavez Morado which depict scenes from the War of Independence and from the Revolution as well as native folklore and traditions.

Close encounters

At the Alhondiga you're practically back to the bus station, and on the outskirts of town in this direction are two more sites well worth the trouble of visiting – the ghoulish Panteon and the mine and church of La Valenciana.

For **La Valenciana** carry on round to the back of the camionera, where you can pick up a bus going up the hill (*Valenciana*). Near the top of the pass here, overlooking Guanajuato where the road to Dolores Hidalgo and San Miguel heads off northwards, you'll see the elaborate facade of the church with its one completed tower: the entrance to the mine is over the road. La Valenciana was for hundreds of years the richest silver mine in Mexico, tapping Guanajuato's celebrated *Veta Madre* (Mother Lode). It just about operates still, though on a very much reduced level, and you can wander around the top of the workings, see some of the machinery and buy rocks at a small shop. The reason for coming here is not really the mine, though, but the extraordinarily sumptuous church constructed by its owner, the Conde de Rul y Valenciana, and his workers. Built between 1765 and 1788, it's the ultimate expression of the Churrigueresque style in Mexico, with a profusion of intricate adornment covering every surface – even the mortar, they say, is mixed with silver ore. Inside, notice especially the enormous gilded retablos, around the main altar and in each arm of the cross, and the delicate filigree of the roof vaulting, especially around the dome above the crossing.

Halfway up the hillside opposite, the **Panteon** (**Museo de la Momias**) offers a very different sort of attraction. Here, lined up against the wall in a series of glass cases, are more than a hundred mummified human corpses exhumed from the local public cemetery. All these bodies had originally been laid out in crypts in the usual way, but here, if after five years the relatives are unable or unwilling to meet the payments, the remains are removed. Many are found to have been naturally preserved, presumably by some quality of the air, and the 'interesting' ones are put on display – others, not properly mummified or too dull for public titilation, are burned or transferred to a common grave. The wasted, leathery bodies on display vary from a few over a hundred years old (including a smartly dressed mummy said to have been a French mining engineer) to relatively recent fatalities – there's a small child wearing plastic pants – who presumably have surviving relatives. The burial clothes hang off the corpses almost indecently – others, completely naked, seem far less luridly lewd – and the guides delight in pointing out their most horrendous features: one twisted mummy, its mouth opened in a silent scream, is 'the woman who was buried alive'; another, a woman who died in childbirth, is displayed beside 'the smallest mummy in the world' – the foetus which cost her her life. It is absolutely gross, but the Panteon exercises a macabre fascination which few are able to resist. Outside, hawkers sell mummy models and sticks of rock in the shape of mummies. To get there, either walk, following the signs out past the railway station, or take the bus (*Panteon/La Rocha*) which goes up the hill past the main entrance.

ON THE ROAD: DOLORES HIDALGO, SAN LUIS DE LA PAZ, SAN JOSE ITURBIDE

Almost exactly midway between Guanajuato and San Miguel de Allende, **DOLORES HIDALGO** is as ancient and as historically rich as either town. This was Father Hidalgo's parish, and it was from the church in the main plaza here that the historic *Grito* of Independence was first issued. Perhaps because of its less spectacular situation, though, or perhaps because there is no university or language school here, Dolores hasn't seen a fraction of the tourist development which has overtaken its neighbours.

It's a good bet, too, for a one night stopover, and certainly if you can't find accommodation in either Guanajuato or San Miguel its the place to head; you'll get a better room here for half the cost. True, there is less to see, but it's an elegant little town and thoroughly Mexican – which in many ways is more than can be said for the others. There are regular, rapid bus connections with both San Miguel and Guanajuato, so that most people treat Dolores as a day trip from one of them – for Mexicans it's something of a pilgrimage – but there's no cause to follow the herd.

On the night of September 15th 1810, *Padre Miguel Hidalgo y Costilla* and some of his fellow plotters, warned by messengers from Querétaro that their plans to raise a rebellion had been discovered (see p. 139), decided to go ahead immediately. At dawn on the 16th Hidalgo, tolling the church bell, called his parishioners together and addressed them from the balcony of the church with an impassioned speech ending in the *Grito de la Independencia* (Cry of Independence) – '¡*Mexicanos, Viva Mexico*!'. That cry is repeated year after year by the President in Mexico City and by politicians all over the country at midnight on September 15th, the sign for Independence Day celebrations to begin. The 16th remains the one day of the year when the bell in Dolores Hidalgo's parish church is rung – though the bell you see is a copy of the original which was either melted down for munitions or hangs in the Palacio Nacional in Mexico City, according to which story you believe.

Just a block or two from the bus station as you walk towards the central plaza is the **Casa Hidalgo** (open Tuesday-Saturday 9.30–5.45; Sunday 9–4.45; closed Monday). This, the house in which Hidalgo lived, has been converted into a museum devoted to his life: long on copies of letters he sent or received and on tributes from various groups to the Father of Independence, but interesting nonetheless. Elsewhere there's a beautifully laid out plaza, overlooked by the exuberant facade of the famous church, a couple of other graceful churches, and little else but the attraction of the dilapidated old streets themselves.

The best **place to stay** is the *Posada Cocomacan* on the main square, a lovely old inn with a patio draped in bougainvillea; just up the road from here, and marginally cheaper, you'll find the *Hotel El Caudillo*. In the unlikely event of both of these being full, try the *Hotel Hidalgo* on Calle Veracruz – leave the main square in the direction of the church with the impressive spire and you'll pass it. No need to stray far from the plaza to eat well either – both the hotels here have **restaurants**, or sample the *Restaurant Plaza*. There's also a good seafood place on the way to the Hotel Hidalgo. As you wander around, look out for the locally made ceramics – hard to miss, they're on sale everywhere and are a very ancient tradition here. The bigger shops are near the Casa Hidalgo.

If you carry straight on through Dolores rather than turning right for San Miguel, you hit the San Luis Potosí to Querétaro road at SAN LUIS DE LA PAZ. From here a road runs south, parallel to the main road, to SAN JOSE ITURSIDE, not far from San Miguel. Both are typically Mexican provincial towns – one main street, a colonial plaza, and horses tied up alongside the farmer's pick-up trucks outside the market. SAN LUIS is the larger of the two, a major junction where, if you're travelling between San Luis Potosí and Guanajuato, Dolores or San Miguel de Allende, you'll want to change buses: there are regular connections with all these as well as express services to Mexico City passing by on the main road. It's also a good place to buy rugs and serapes at reasonable prices, though most of what is made here is sent off to the markets in larger towns. If you need to stay there are a couple of small hotels on the main street just up from the bus terminal.

SAN JOSE is distinguished by the massive behemoth of a neo-classical church on its Plaza dedicated, appropriately, to Agustin de Iturbide, a local opportunist who started the War of Independence as a general loyal to Spain – inflicting major defeats on Morelos – later changed sides and, having helped secure Mexico's Independence without any concomitant reform, briefly declared himself emperor in 1822. The plaque says, accurately enough, 'from the only town in Mexico which still honours your memory'. There's a frequent bus service between San Jose and San Luis de la Paz (and occasional buses on from San Jose to San Miguel). On the road between the two you pass through **POZOS**, which describes itself as a ghost town. Don't expect to find swing doors flapping in the breeze and tumbleweed gusting through the streets, though. For although Pozos, which was once, as Real de Pozos, a rich and flourishing mining community, does have vast areas of crumbling masonry inhabited only by the odd burro, there are still quite a number of people living here. It's far from dead, and indeed seems recently to be undergoing something of a revival in its fortunes.

SAN MIGUEL DE ALLENDE

Set on a steep hillside overlooking the Rio Laja, **SAN MIGUEL DE ALLENDE**'s rooftops and domed churches seem at first sight little different from those of any other small colonial town. Its character, though, is immediately distinct – dominated by and invariably crowded with North Americans. There's a very high profile colony of 'artists and writers' here, fleshed out with less ambitious retirees from the States and by flocks of students drawn to the town's several language schools. Like such a community anywhere, it's inward looking, bitchy and gossip ridden, but also extremely hospitable and much given to taking newcomers under its wing.

There are good reasons why this should have happened in San Miguel – chiefly that it's a very picturesque town with a perfect climate and, for the artists, good light throughout the year. What got it started, though, was the foundation in 1938 of the Instituto Allende, an arts institute which enjoyed an enormous boost after World War II when returning GIs found that their education grants could be stretched much further in Mexico. Its fame established, San Miguel has never looked back, and for all its popularity remains one of the most pleasant places you could pick to rest up for a while in comfort.

There are few specific sights, but the whole town (which has been a National Monument since 1926, hence no new building) is crowded with old seigneurial mansions and curious churches. It was founded in 1542 by a Franciscan friar, Juan de San Miguel, and as San Miguel El Grande became an important supply centre for the big mining towns, later changing its name to honour Ignacio Allende, a local who became Hidalgo's chief lieutenant. The country roundabout is still ranching territory, though increasingly being taken over by the tourists and foreigners: there is a traditional spa at TABOADA, and less lasting attractions nearby – a golf course, water skiing on the new reservoir and horse riding at a couple of dude ranches.

In the very centre of town is the **Zocalo**, or Plaza Allende, and the most famous of the city's landmarks, **La Parroquia** – the parish church.

This was rebuilt towards the end of last century by a self-taught Indian stone-mason, Zeferino Gutierrez, who supposedly learned about architecture by studying postcards of the great French cathedrals and then drew diagrams in the dust to explain to his workers what he wanted. It seems a likely enough explanation for the towering pseudo-Gothic facade, bristling with turrets and spires. The **Tourist Office** – extremely helpful – is more or less next door to the Parroquia; beside it is an expensive cafe with tables set outside from which you can keep an eye on events. It is in the Zocalo that everyone seems to gather in the evenings, to take the air, to stroll, to check out what's going on, and it's here that you should gravitate first too. Two sides of the square are lined with covered *portales*, under whose arches vendors of drinks and trinkets shelter from the sun, with a row of shops behind them – look out here for the guy who sells heroic black-and-white postcards of Pancho Villa and Zapata and of 1930s Mexican movie stars. The Parroquia takes up a third side, and opposite is a block containing the **Palacio Municipal**, the **Galeria San Miguel**, one of the most prestigious of the many galleries showing local artists' work, and the **Posada San Francisco**, an expensive hotel with a fairly ritzy restaurant, well worth looking at for its fine reconstruction of colonial luxury.

On the Zocalo too are a couple of San Miguel's most distinguished mansions. The **Casa de Don Ignacio de Allende**, on the corner of Allende and Umaran, was the birthplace of the Independence hero: a plaque notes '*Hic natus ubique notus*' – 'here was born he who is famous everywhere'. On the next corner, Hidalgo and Canal, you can see the **Casa de los Condes de Canal**, with an elaborately carved doorway and elegant wrought-iron grilles over the windows. Near here too, just half a block down Umaran, is the **Casa de los Perros**, its balconies supported by little stone dogs. All of these houses – indeed almost every home in San Miguel – are in the Spanish style; forbidding, even grim, from the outside, they mostly conceal patios decked with flowers or courtyards with a fountain playing. If you want to see inside some, and if you think you could take it, the English-speaking community organises a '**House and Gardens Tour**' every Sunday, leaving the Instituto Allende at noon. You'll see details on posters around the town: proceeds go to charity.

Leave the Zocalo uphill on San Francisco, and you get to an area around the market which seems less affected by outsiders – Spanish or Norte Americano. The architecture, it's true, is still colonial, but the life which continues around the battered buildings seems cast in a more ancient mould. Behind the church of **San Francisco**, whose elaborate Churrigueresque facade contrasts sharply with its neo-classical towers, tiled dome and plain interior, and quite overshadows the modest simplicity of its smaller neighbour, **Tercer Orden**, the **market** begins. Spilling over from a tiny plaza into the surrounding streets, it's managed to remain almost entirely traditional – fruit, vegetables, medicinal herbs, pots and pans are all on display, but there's little specifically for the tourist among the cramped tables with their low canvas awnings. Officially, market day is Sunday, but no-one seems to have told the people here and it's pretty busy all week.

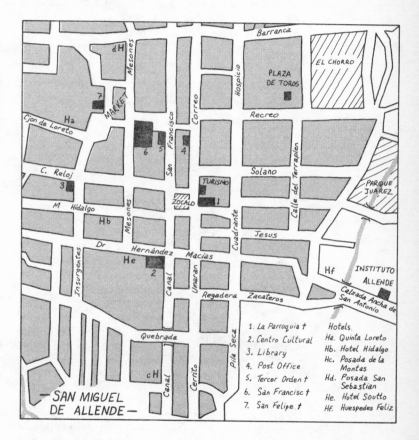

Across the market square from San Francisco, up a few steps from the street, the **Oratorio de San Felipe Neri** sits in the centre of a little group of churches and chapels. The baroque facade shows signs of native influence – presumably the legacy of Indian labourers – but the main interest lies within in a series of paintings, including a group depicting the life of St Philip Neri, attributed to Miguel Cabrera. Next door, off the Callejon de Loreto, you'll find the **Santa Casa de Loreto**, a copy of the Holy House at Loreto, Italy. It was put up by the Conde Manuel de la Canal, and in its gilded octagonal interior there are statues of the count and his wife, below which lie their tombs.

From here, pushing down through the market stalls which crowd the top of Calle Insurgentes, you can get to the **Biblioteca Publica** (open 10–2 and 4–7 daily except Sunday), a public library which lends **books in English**. There's quite a substantial collection, with quiet space to sit down and read, and they also sell a certain number of second-hand books – either duplicates or those deemed too lightweight for preservation in the library. A couple of houses further down (Insurgentes 21) is the **Academia Hispano Americana**, a language school which specialises in high-pressure, total immersion techniques. Less prestigious than the Insti-tuto, but probably better if you want to speak Spanish in a hurry.

The **Centro Cultural 'El Nigromante'** – also known as Bellas Artes – is around the corner from here on Hernandez Macias, or just one block downhill from the Zocalo. Housed in the beautiful cloistered courtyard of the old Convento de la Concepcion, it's an arts institute run by the State Fine Arts Organisation – concentrating on music and dance, but to a lesser extent teaching visual arts too. Mexicans can take courses here for virtually nothing, foreigners pay rather more. Around the courtyard there are various exhibitions, and on the upper floors several murals, including one by David Siqueiros. The church of **La Concepcion**, part of the complex, is lovely too, but noted mainly for its tall dome raised on a drum, again said to be the work of the untrained Zeferino Gutierrez.

To get to the famous **Instituto Allende**, simply keep going downhill on Hernandez Macias from here: on the way, at the corner of Cuadrante, you pass the **Casa del Inquisidor**, an eighteenth-century mansion with a particularly fine facade, and opposite it the old building which served as a jail for the Inquisition. The Instituto itself, on the edges of the old town, occupies a former hacienda of the Condes de la Canal – it was moved here in 1952 when the government recognised its success and made it part of the University of Guanajuato. There are courses in all kinds of painting and sculpture, crafts like silverwork and weaving, photography as well as Spanish language courses, and all in a very beautiful, park-like setting. There's a cafe down here, even a hotel, and the noticeboards are covered with offers of long-term accommodation, requests for and offers of rides through Mexico and up to the States, and information about what's going on in San Miguel.

At the back of the Institute is the **Parque Benito Juarez**, a beautiful shaded park created out of what used to be the fruit orchards of many of the old families; from here you can walk uphill to **El Chorro**, the little hill whose springs supply the city with water, and site of the town originally founded here by Juan de San Miguel. There are good views of the town from here, but if you've the energy to climb on higher still to

El Mirador, the viewing point on the road to Queretaro, you'll find really tremendous panoramas: San Miguel below, the broad plain and the ridge of mountains before Guanajuato in the distance.

Some practicalities

San Miguel, for a change, has a reasonably good **rail service,** on the main line from Mexico City to Nuevo Laredo. The *Aguila Azteca* express sets off from the border daily at about 7pm, arriving here just after 1pm the next day, and getting to Mexico City some 7 hours later: in the other direction it leaves Mexico City at 8am, gets here at 2.30pm and reaches the border early the following morning. The station, though, is a considerable distance from town and while there's supposed to be a bus you may well find a taxi is the only practicable solution. For relatively short journeys it's far easier to arrive by bus. The **bus terminal** is currently a dusty little square on the edge of town where the road to the station leaves; before that they used to stop opposite the Instituto Allende and there are plans to build a more permanent home – so check. Wherever it is, the centre is easy enough to find – walk uphill towards the unmistakable tower of La Parroquia. If you're heavily laden, and if you're going to one of the hotels across town, you might again consider a taxi – it won't cost much and saves a lot of sweat on the steep climb.

The *Quinta Loreto*, certainly, is a long haul from where the buses stop, at Callejon de Loreto 13. **Rooms** here are definitely the best value in San Miguel – you'd be hard pressed to find anywhere cheaper and the Quinta Loreto has a swimming pool, quiet grounds of its own and one of the best value restaurants in town. Unfortunately, though hardly surprisingly, it's often full – you could try phoning first (on 2.00.42). Nearby, the *Posada San Sebastian* (Mesones No. 7) is also peaceful, costs marginally less and tends to have a more Mexican clientele (the Quinta Loreto has many long-term residents, staying for a month or more while they attend courses) – though they do have the strange habit of parking cars in the courtyard, right outside the rooms. The *Posada de Las Monjas* (Canal 37) is one of the first places you'll pass as you walk up from the buses – it's very pleasant, an old convent converted into a colonial style hotel, but costs nearly twice as much as the others listed here. Nearer the centre the *Hotel Hidalgo* (Hidalgo 22) is cheap, and very close to the Zocalo, but rather gloomy and with distinctly dodgy plumbing. Not far away is the *Hotel Sautto* (Hernandez Macias 59, next to the Centro Cultural) which is far more cheerful, with a bright flowery garden, but more expensive and liable to charge more than they ought. In the passageway beside the Parroquia, Allende, you'll find the *Posada Allende*, cheapest place of all in San Miguel and rightly so – there are also two more expensive hotels here, the *Posada Carmina* and the *Vista Hermosa*. Down by the Instituto, the *Huespedes Feliz* is very reasonably priced but has two major drawbacks – it's at the bottom of the hill and it's almost always booked up. Also down here but much more expensive are the *Parador San Miguel* in the Institute's grounds and the *Posada La Aldea* directly opposite the gates.

It's surprising, in so touristy a town, that there should be so many low-priced hotels. No such luck with **restaurants**: there are plenty of them, but they tend to be fancy and expensive. One exception, for a substantial if rather bland *comida corrida*, is the restaurant in the *Quinta Loreto*. Near here too, in a little shopping mall which goes through from Mesones towards the market, is *La Hierba Buena*, a tiny health food place. Otherwise you might as well go for the enforced liveliness of one of the places favoured by the younger set hereabouts, *Mama Mia* (Umacan 5) for spaghettis, pizzas and salads, or *Carrusel* (on Canal near the Zocalo) for its bizarre decor. San Miguel even has **nightlife**, though apart from the free entertainment of the fiestas it can come expensive: liveliest discos are *Ring* (Hidalgo 15) and *Laverintos* (more or less opposite the Instituto).

Out of San Miguel – two trips

To the north of San Miguel, off the road to Dolores, lie two destinations which merit an afternoon away from the town – the spa of Taboada and the shrine of Atotonilco. The warm thermal waters of **TABOADA** are a really delightful place to head for a swim, either in the luxurious surroundings of the *Hotel Hacienda Taboada* or at the public baths just beyond. The hotel runs regular buses from San Miguel (leaving from the corner of Hidalgo and Insurgentes) and three days a week puts on a magnificent outdoor buffet – very expensive but the swimming comes as a free extra; other days there's a small charge for use of the pool. The public area is cheaper, just a short walk from where the bus drops you beyond the hotel. Details, prices and bus timetables from the *Hotel Vista Hermosa*, run by the same people as the Hacienda.

To get to Atotonilco, which is slightly further, check bus details at the Tourist Office. **ATOTONILCO EL GRANDE** is a rural Indian community whose church has come to be a centre of pilgrimage for two reasons – it was founded by Padre Felipe Neri, later to be canonised, and it was from here that Padre Hidalgo, marching from Dolores to San Miguel, took the banner of the Virgin of Guadalupe which became the flag of the Mexicans in the War of Independence. Allende was married here too. The six chapels of the church are liberally plastered with murals demonstrating every kind of Mexican popular art, from the naive and amateurish to the highly sophisticated, and freely interspersed with poems, biblical passages and painted statues.

QUERÉTARO

Most people seem to hammer straight past **QUERÉTARO** on the motorway to the capital, seeing only the expanding industrial outskirts and the rowdy modern bus station. Yet of all the colonial cities in the Bajío this is perhaps the most surprising, preserving at its heart a tranquil colonial town which boasts magnificent mansions and some of the country's finest ecclesiastical architecture. Little over 2 hours from Mexico City, and the junction of every major road and rail route from the north, it is also a wealthy and booming city.

There's a history as rich and deep here as anywhere in the Republic, starting before the conquest when Querétaro (rocky place) was an Otomi Indian town subject to the Aztecs; many Otomi still live in the surrounding area. In 1531 the Spanish took control relatively peacefully, and under them it grew steadily into a major city and provincial capital before becoming, in the nineteenth century, the setting for some of the most traumatic events of Mexican history. It was here, meeting under the guise of Literary Associations, that the Independence conspirators laid their earliest plans. In 1810 one of their number, Josefa Ortiz de Dominguez, wife of the town's Corregidor (or governor – she is known always as *La Corregidora*) found that her husband had learned of the movement's intentions. Although locked in her room, the Corregidora managed to get a message out warning the revolutionaries and precipitating an unexpectedly early start to the struggle for Independence.

Later in the century, less proud events. The Treaty of Guadalupe Hidalgo, which ended the Mexican-American War by handing over almost half of Mexico's territory – Texas, New Mexico, California and more – to the USA, was signed in Querétaro in 1848. In 1867 the Emperor Maximilian made his last stand here: defeated, he was tried by a court meeting in the theatre and finally faced a firing squad on the hill just to the north of town – the *Cerro de Las Campañas*. The same theatre hosted an important assembly of revolutionary politicians in 1916, leading eventually to the signing here of the 1917 Constitution, still in force today.

Getting your bearings, some practicalities

For all its sprawl, Querétaro is an easy place to find your way around – the centre remaining firmly set into the grid laid down by the Spanish. There are local buses to anywhere you might want to visit, and taxis here are extremely cheap, but on the whole walking will prove simpler. One very good way of getting to grips with the layout of the old town, and at least a brief glimpse of most of the important buildings, is to join the **walking tour** which sets off from the Regional Museum every morning – details from the museum or from the *Tourist Information* booths

—QUERÉTARO—

CERRO DE LAS CAMPAÑAS

Av. Hidalgo
Av. Fco. Madero
Av. Pino Suarez
Av. Pino Suarez
Calzada
Zaragoza
Alameda
ALAMEDA
Panamericana
Carretera
Circunvalación
Guerrero
Juarez
Corregidora
Av. 16 de Septiembre
Av. 5 de Mayo
Independencia
Paseo

1. Bus Station
2. Market
3. Palacio de Gobierno
4. Teatro de la Republica
5. Casa de Los Perros
6. Casa de la Corregidora
7. Casa de la Culture
8. Juarez Statue
9. Museo Regional
10. Convento de la Cruz †
11. Cathedral †
12. Santa Clara †
13. Santa Rosa †
14. Palacio Federal (P.O.)
15. Plaza Principal

just round the corner. It's in Spanish and costs only what you have in refreshments along the way – Sangria is laid on.

Querétaro's **Central Camionera** is one of the busiest there is, but even so it's relatively central. A bus (*Burocrata*) will take you up to the Plaza Principal, or it's an easy enough walk, around or across the Alameda park and then up C. Corregidora. The **railway station** is slightly further out, in the opposite direction, but again you could walk it – straight down Allende and then left on Madero – or take a local bus.

For **hotels**, head straight for the Plaza Principal (also known as Jardin Obregon) where you'll find, first of all, the *Gran Hotel*. The Gran has undoubtedly seen better days, but it's very central and cheap with some (slightly more expensive) rooms at the front which remain genuinely elegant. Charging slightly more for its comforts since it was done up in a rather characterless international style is the *Hotel Plaza*, on the left-hand side of the Plaza Principal. On the way up from the bus station you'll have passed others – the large, modern *Hotel Impala* overlooking the Alameda is not quite as pricey as it looks, though still expensive. At the bottom of Corregidora the Hotels *Corregidora* and *San Francisco* are both reasonable, but definitely not such good value as those on the plaza. Heading up Juarez, which runs parallel to Corregidora towards the centre, you pass two *Casas de Huespedes* which are the cheapest places to stay in town – absolutely no frills, but acceptable. Others include the *Hotel Hidalgo* (Av. Madero Pte. No. 11), on Madero less than a block from the plaza, and the *Hotel San Agustin* (Pino Suarez 12) which more or less backs on to it. Opposite this latter is the *Posada de la Academia*, another place with very basic, no-nonsense accommodation.

Finding **somewhere to eat** is as straightforward as ever – there's certainly no shortage. The main plaza is again the place to start – here both the restaurant in the *Gran Hotel* and (better) *La Flor de Querétaro* towards the Hotel Plaza provide good *comidas corridas* and straightforward local food. For fast food, *tacos*, hamburguesas or ice cream try the alleys which lead up from here to the right towards the Plaza Independencia, or the *bus station cafeteria* – better than most, certainly for a quick bite between buses, if you can stomach the accompaniment provided by Don Pedro and his electric organ. Rather more elegant and expensive than these is the *Fonda del Refugio* in the little Jardin Corregidora just up from the plaza – the place to sit outside, drink, and watch the time pass. There's quite a good pizzeria here too. If you want to get together something of your own, head for the **market** – in a huge new setting off Zaragoza, not far from the Alameda.

The city

Dominating the Plaza Principal is the beautiful facade of the church of **San Francisco**, one of the earliest founded in the city. The dome is covered in *azulejos*, coloured tiles imported from Spain around 1540, but for the most part San Francisco was rebuilt in the seventeenth and eighteenth centuries. Adjoining, in what used to be its monastery, is the **Museo Regional** (open 10–2 and 4–6; closed Mondays). The building alone is reason enough to visit, built around a large cloister and going through in the back to a lovely chapel, it's far bigger than you imagine from the outside. The contents are wildly varied: there's the keyhole through which La Corregidora passed on her news; early copies of the Constitution; the table on which the Treaty of Guadalupe Hidalgo was signed, and quantities of ephemera connected with Emperor Maximilian whose headquarters was here for a while. Then too there are more usual collections relating to local archaeology, and a sizeable gallery of colonial art – altogether well worth an hour or two.

Down to the left, at the back of the *Gran Hotel*, is the **Plaza de la Constitucion**, a raised paved square which used to house the market and is now left bare, seemingly without much of a role in life: there are a few sleazy bars and downmarket restaurants scattered around it. To the right, up the alley beside the church where there's a **Tourist Information** booth (with maps and pamphlets), you reach the **Plaza Independencia**, a very pretty, arcaded open space. The little alleys which lead up here, closed to traffic, are some of the city's most interesting; crammed with ancient houses, with little restaurants, and with shops selling junky antiques and the opals and other semi-precious stones for which the area is famous. If you buy, make sure you know what you're getting. In the centre of the plaza stands a statue of *Don Juan Antonio Urrutia y Arana*, Marques de la villa del Villar del Aguila, the man who built Querétaro's elegant aqueduct, providing the city with drinking water. Around the square are the **Casa de la Cultura**, with exhibitions of local crafts, and the **Casa de la Corregidora**, now the Palacio Municipal. It was here, on September 14th 1810, that the Corregidora was locked up while her husband made plans to arrest the conspirators, and here that she managed to get a message to Ignacio Perez who carried it to San Miguel and Dolores, to Allende and Hidalgo. It's a very fine colonial mansion, too, so wander in and take a look.

The commercial centre of Querétaro nowadays is in the other direction, leaving the Plaza Principal on Avenida Madero. This is where you'll find the **banks** and most of the shops, on formal streets lined with stately mansions. At the corner of Madero and Allende is the little Jardin de Santa Clara with its famous **Fountain of Neptune**, designed by Tresguerras in 1797. *Francisco Eduardo Tresguerras* (1765-1833) is rightly regarded as one of Mexico's greatest architects – though he was also a sculptor, painter and poet – and was almost single-handedly responsible for developing a native Mexican style diverging from (though still close to) its Spanish roots. His work, seen throughout central Mexico, is particularly evident here and in nearby Celaya, his birthplace. Beside the fountain rises the deceptively simple church of **Santa Clara**, once attached to one of the country's richest convents. Inside it's a riot of baroque excess, gilded cherubs and angels swarming all over the profusely decorated altarpieces. Also here is the **Meson de Santa Clara**, an old cloister in which plays are staged by a group from the university every Friday and Saturday night. Mostly comedies from the classical Spanish repertoire, they're spiced with plenty of music and thoroughly enjoyable – you sit at large tables, cabaret style, and there's food and drink to keep the mood flowing.

Carry straight on down Madero and you get to the **Palacio de Gobierno** and the **Cathedral**, eighteenth-century buildings neither of which, by Querétaro's standards, is particularly distinguished. Cut down Calle Guerrero, however, and you'll find the **Palacio Federal** – home of the main **Post Office**. Once an Augustinian monastery, this is one of the most exuberant mansions in a town full of them: in the cloister, at its most extreme, every surface of the two storeys of portals is carved with grotesque figures, no two quite alike, of men, monsters and abstract designs. The sculptures, which they attribute locally to Tresguerras although most books date the monastery from before his birth, are full of religious symbolism which, if possible, you should try to get someone to explain to you: for example the large figures supporting the arches all hold their fingers in different positions – three held up to represent the Trinity, four for the Evangelists and so on. Around the corner from here at Allende and Pino Suarez, the **Casa de los Perros** is almost as exotic, a mansion named for the ugly dog gargoyles which line its facade.

The church of **Santa Rosa de Viterbo** is further out in this direction, at the junction of Arteaga and Montes. Its interior rivals Santa Clara for richness of decoration, but here there is no false modesty on the outside either. Two enormous flying buttresses support the octagonal cupola – remodelled by Tresguerras – and a blue and white tiled dome. The needling tower, too, is Tresguerras's work, holding what is said to be the first four–sided public clock erected on the American continent.

Back to the Plaza Principal and heading north now on Corregidora, you pass the **Jardin Corregidora** with its statue of the heroine and reach, on the left, the **Teatro de la Republica**. The theatre is a striking example of nineteenth-century public building – small but nonetheless pompously imposing. Inside it has been wonderfully restored to its original glory and contains little memorials to the historic events which took place here: the trial and sentencing to death of Maximilian and the Congress which determined the shape of the Mexican constitution.

Slightly further afield, but still in easy walking distance, lies the **Convento de la Cruz**. This monastery is built on the site of the battle between the Spanish and the Otomi in which the Conquistadors gained control of Querétaro – according to legend the fighting was cut short by the miraculous appearance of St James (*Santiago*) and a dazzling cross in the sky which persuaded the Indians to concede defeat and become Christians. The **Capilla del Calvarito**, just opposite the monastery entrance, marks the spot where the first mass was celebrated after the battle. The monastery itself was founded in 1683 by the Franciscans as a college for the propagation of the faith (*Colegio de Propaganda Fide*) and grew over the years into an important centre for the training of missionaries with a massive library and rich collection of relics.

Because of its hilltop position and hefty construction, the monastery was also frequently used as a fortress – one of the last redoubts of the Spanish in the War of Independence, it was also Maximilian's head-quarters for the last few weeks of his reign; he was subsequently imprisoned here to await execution. Nowadays there are guided tours round the monastery, and the proudest exhibit is the *Arbol de la Cruz*, a tree whose thorns grow in the shape of little crosses. The tree grew, according to the story, from a walking stick left behind by a mysterious saintly traveller who slept here one night – certainly it does produce thorns in the form of the cross, though whether this is particularly rare I don't claim to know.

Beyond the monastery you can see the **Aqueduct,** a beautiful series of arches up to 93 feet high which still brings water into the city from springs nearly 6 miles away. Spotlit at night, it looks magnificent from a distance, especially as you drive into town.

North-west of town, the **Cerro de las Campañas** (Hill of Bells) commands better, if rather less scenic, views over the town and its industrial outskirts. Maximilian and his two generals, Miguel Miramon and Tomas Mejia, faced their firing squad here, and there is supposed to be a chapel commemorating the ill-fated emperor at the spot where the execution took place. I've never found it though, and anyway the hill is dominated by a vast stone statue of the victor of that particular war, Benito Juarez, glaring down over the town from its summit. Parts of the new university campus sprawl up one slope too.

On to Mexico City

From Querétaro you can race straight into the capital on the motorway, one of the fastest roads in the country. There are hundreds of buses a day passing through, and it's infinitely quicker and easier than the train – although there is also a new fast rail link under construction, still several years off by the look of it.

Almost all the buses pull in for a stop at **SAN JUAN DEL RIO.** It looks like nothing at all from where the bus drops you, but is in fact a major market centre, and a popular weekend outing from the capital. Among the crafts they specialise in are gemstones – mostly local opals but also imported jewels which are polished and set here – basket weaving and the manufacture of wine and cheese. If you are going to buy gems be very careful – it's easy to get ripped off without expert advice; other purchases are safer, though not particularly cheap on the whole. The best known wine here is Hidalgo – a brand name sold all over the country and usually reliable – you can visit their cellars (*Cavas de San Juan*) a short distance out of town on the road to Tequisquiapan.

TEQUISQUIAPAN, some 18km away, was an Otomi village, but is now overrun by hotels and villas catering mainly for escapees from Mexico City who come here for the hot springs. It remains very picturesque, though, and like San Juan del Rio has a big crafts market, especially active on Sundays. At the end of May running into June, Tequisquiapan hosts a major wine and cheese festival, the *Feria Nacional de Queso y Vino* which is well worth going a bit out of your way for – plenty of free food and drink, and no shortage of other entertainments laid on. There are buses direct from Querétaro (with extra ones for the feria) or local services from San Juan. Both are also stops on the rail line from Mexico City to Querétaro. If you want to stay, there are numerous hotels in both, though very few cheap ones – try the *Layseca* (Juarez 9) or the

Hotel San Juan (Hidalgo Sur 6) in central San Juan or the *Posada Casa Blanca* (5 de Mayo 6) in Tequisquiapan.

Two more places off this route, covered in the following chapter, are the ancient Toltec capital of TULA (see p. 217) and TEPOTZOTLAN with its magnificent Baroque architecture (p. 219). Tula is some way from the motorway and means changing buses, but it is on the railway, while Tepotzotlan is very close to the road, but also so close to Mexico City that unless you're driving yourself it's probably easier done as an outing from there.

FIESTAS

The central highland area is one of the most active in Mexico when it comes to celebrations. The states of Guanajuato, Jalisco and above all Michoacan with its strong native traditions, are particularly rich in fiestas: the list below is by no means exhaustive, local tourist offices will have further details.

January
1st NEW YEAR's DAY widely celebrated. Fair in **Dolores Hidalgo**.
6th DIA DE LOS SANTOS REYES (Twelfth Night). Many small ceremonies – **Los Reyes** (Michoacan), south of Zamora and west of Uruapan, has dancing and a procession of the Magi. **Cajititlan** (Jalisco), on a tiny lake near Guadalajara, also has traditional dances. On the same day the Feria begins in **Matehuala** (San Luis Potosí), lasting till the 15th.
8th **San Juan de las Colchas** (Mich.) commemorates the eruption of Paricutin with a dance contest and traditional dress. Many of the homeless villagers moved to this village near Uruapan.
15th **La Piedad** (Mich.). Traditional dances and a major procession for local saint's day.
20th DIA DE SAN SEBASTIAN. In **San Luis Potosí** (S.L.P.) the climax of ten days of pilgrimages, in **Leon** (Guanajuato) the religious festival coincides with the agricultural and industrial fair. **Tuxpan** (Jal.), a beautiful village between Ciudad Guzman and Colima, has traditional dances including the unique *Danza de los Chayacates*. Start of the mass pilgrimages to **San Juan de Los Lagos** (Jal.) which culminate on Feb 2nd.

February
1st **Cadereyta** (Que.), north-east of Querétaro, holds a festival famous for its cockfights – also religious processions, dancing and mariachi. In **Tzintzuntzan** (Mich.) the start of a week-long fiesta founded in the sixteenth century by Vasco de Quiroga.
2nd DIA DE LA CANDELARIA (Candlemas). Celebrated in **Lagos de Moreno** (Jal.) with pilgrimages, but much more so in nearby **San Juan de Los Lagos**, one of the largest in Mexico.
CARNIVAL (the week before Lent, variable Feb.-Mar.) particularly good in **Zinapecuaro** (Mich.), near Morelia, with pretend bulls chasing people through the streets, **Copandaro** (Mich.), also near Morelia on the shores of Lake Cuitzeo, with similar fake bullfights, rodeos and marathon dances, and **Charapan** (Mich.), near Uruapan, where you can see the dance of *Los Viejitos*. All these best on Carnival Tuesday. On the Sunday **Yuriria** (Guanajuato), between Celaya and Morelia, has real bullfights, processions and dances.

March
First Friday **San Miguel de Allende** (Gto.) Fiesta del Señor de la Conquista.
PALM SUNDAY (week before Easter) is the culmination of a week's celebration in **Uruapan** (Mich.) – the Indians collect palms from the hills and make ornaments from the leaves, sold here in a big *tianguis*. Similar events in **San Miguel de Allende** (Gto.) with a pilgrimage to Atotonilco.
HOLY WEEK is observed everywhere. In **Copandaro** (Mich.) they celebrate all week, especially on the Thursday with the ceremony of Washing the Apostle's Feet, and Good Friday when they act

out more scenes from Christ's passion. These passion plays are quite common: you'll see them at nearby **Iramuco** (Gto.) where the villagers act on the shores of Lake Cuitzeo, and at **Tzintzuntzan** (Mich.) and the hamlet of Maya near **Lagos de Moreno** (Jal.). In **Ciudad Hidalgo** (Mich.), between Morelia and Zitacuaro, they add firework displays and burning effigies of Judas. In **Patzcuaro** (Mich.) there's a huge procession, while in **San Miguel de Allende** every family constructs an elaborate altar, proudly displayed in the house. The Saturday sees the beginning of the spring feria in **Jerez** (Zac.), near Zacatecas, where after they've hung Judas they get on with the bullfighting and motor races.

April
In early April (variable) **Irapuato** (Gto.) holds its FERIA DE LA FRESA (Strawberry fair) in honour of the region's principal cash crop.
25th The FERIA DE SAN MARCOS in **Aguascalientes** (Ags.) runs for around a week either side of this date. One of the largest and most famous in Mexico, there's dancing, bullfights, music, *charrerias* and great wine.

May
3rd DIA DE LA SANTA CRUZ. Native dances in **Ciudad Hidalgo** (Mich.), mariachi and tequila in **Tequila** (Jal.).
24th **Empalme Escobeda** (Gto.), near San Miguel de Allende, has a fiesta lasting until the next Sunday, with traditional dances including that of *Los Apaches*, one of the few in which women take part.
Last Sunday, DIA DEL SEÑOR DE LA MISERICORDIA, fiesta in honour of this highly venerated image in **Tuxpan** (Jal.) – native dances.
CORPUS CHRISTI (variable – the Thursday after Trinity) is celebrated in **San Miguel de Allende** (Gto.) and, very beautifully, in the neighbouring villages of **Cheran** and **Paracho**, in Michoacan. The following Wednesday sees a very ancient fiesta in **Juchipila** (Zac.), between Zacatecas and Guadalajara, with flowers and dances including the famous *Jarabe Tapatio*, the Mexican Hat Dance.
The FERIA NACIONAL DE QUESO Y VINO in **Tequisquiapan** (Que.) runs from late May through early June.

June
23rd Festival de la Presa de Olla in **Guanajuato** (Gto.).
24th DIA DE SAN JUAN. **Purepero** (Mich.), between Uruapan and La Piedad, starts a week-long fiesta.
29th DIA DE SAN PEDRO. In **Tlaquepaque** (Jal.) a highly animated festival with mariachi, dancing and processions. **Chalchihuites** (Zac.), between Zacatecas and Durango, stages a 'Battle of the Flowers' in which local kids take part.

July
First Sunday. Torchlit religious processions in **Quiroga** (Mich.).
4th **Acambaro** (Gto.), a very ancient town between Celaya and Morelia, has a fiesta with religious processions, music and many traditional dances.
16th DIA DE LA VIRGEN DEL CARMEN celebrated in **Celaya** (Gto.).
22nd DIA DE MARIA MAGDALENA. Fiesta in **Uruapan** (Mich.) – processions of animals.
25th DIA DE SANTIAGO widely observed. Mass pilgrimages to **San Luis Potosí** (S.L.P.); saint's day celebrations in **Santiago Maravatio** (Gto.), near Irapuato; stylised battles between Moors and Christians in **Jesus Maria** (Ags.), near Aguascalientes.
26th Culmination of a week-long Feria in **Acatlan de Juarez** (Jal.), south of Guadalajara: regional dress, dances and fireworks.
28th FIESTAS DEL SEÑOR DEL CALVARIO in **Lagos de Moreno** (Jal.) last until August 6th.

August
8th Very ancient 'pagan' fiesta in **Paracho** (Mich.).
15th DIA DE LA ASUNCION (assumption) coincides with three large fairs – the FERIA DE LA UVA in **Aguascalientes** (Ags.); the FERIA DE LA CAJETA in **Calaya** (Gto.) celebrating the syrupy confection made here, and in **Santa Clara del Cobre** (Mich.), near Patzcuaro, markets of the renowned handmade copperware.
25th DIA DE SAN LUIS hugely enjoyed in **San Luis Potosí** – giant procession and fireworks.
27th In **Zacatecas** (Zac.) battles between Moors and Christians on the Cerro de la Bufa are the highlight of several days' celebrations.

September

1st DIA DE LA VIRGEN DE REMEDIOS justifies a fiesta in **Comonfort** (Gto.), near San Miguel de Allende. Traditional dances.

8th In **Jerez** (Zac.) the start of a festival lasting till the 15th. Similarly in **San Juan de las Colchas** (Mich.), where it lasts to the 22nd, its climax on the 14th.

14th Ten days of pilgrimages to the Señora del Patrocinio start in **Zacatecas** (Zac.), coinciding with the FERIA NACIONAL and all sorts of secular entertainments, especially bullfights.

15th-16th INDEPENDENCE CELEBRATIONS everywhere, above all in **Dolores Hidalgo** (Gto.) and **Querétaro** (Que.) where they start several days early.

28th Start of three-day festival of San Miguel in **San Felipe** (Gto.), north of Dolores Hidalgo, with Otomi dances and battle between Moors and Christians.

30th In **Morelia** (Mich.), celebrations for the birthday of Morelos.

DIA DE SAN MIGUEL (variable, a Friday around the end of September) is the most important of **San Miguel de Allende's** many fiestas: two days of processions, concerts, dancing, bullfights and ceremonial.

October

Guadalajara's FIESTAS DE OCTUBRE run throughout the north.

3rd DIA DE SAN FRANCISCO DE ASIS. Major pilgrimage to **Real de Catorce** (S.L.P.) and festivities in the town.

4th DIA DE SAN FRANCISCO. Saint's day celebrations culminate a week of pilgrimages to **Talpa** (Jal.), near Guadalajara, where the faithful come bearing flowers and candles. Celebrated, too, in **Jiquilpa** (Mich.), between Zamora and Lake Chapala, and in **Uruapan** (Mich.) where it's one of the year's biggest. **Nochistlan** (Zac.), between Aguascalientes and Guadalajara, starts a feria lasting to the end of the month.

12th DIA DE LA RAZA commemorates Columbus's discovery of America. Feria in **Uruapan** (Mich.) and, in **Guadalajara**, the highlight of the Fiestas comes with an enormous pilgrimage to the Virgin of Zapopah.

16th Native dances and an all-night procession honour a much revered image of Christ in **Cuitzeo** (Mich.), on Lake Cuitzeo north of Morelia.

21st DIA DE SAN JOSE. In **Ciudad Guzman** (Jal.), the climax of a lively feria which lasts from the 12th to the 23rd.

22nd **Apatzingan** (Mich.), in beautiful mountain country south of Uruapan and the end of the railway through there, has a fiesta which includes dance competitions and rodeos on the rather flimsy excuse of the anniversary of the 1814 Constitution.

23rd **Coroneo** (Gto.), south of Querétaro, begins a three-day feria.

24th-26th The FESTIVAL DE COROS Y DANZAS in **Uruapan** (Mich.). A competition between Tarascan Indian choirs and dance groups. Great.

DIA DE CRISTO REY. On the last Sunday in October, an ancient series of dances in honour of Christ the King in **Contepec** (Mich.), south of Querétaro, east of Morelia. Also processions and regional costume.

November

2nd DIA DE LOS MUERTOS (All Souls). The Famous Day of the Dead is celebrated everywhere, but the rites in **Patzcuaro** (Mich.) and on the island of **Janitzio** are the best known in Mexico. Highly picturesque, too, in **Zitacuaro** (Mich.).

7th-14th FIESTA DE LAS ILLUMINACIONES in **Guanajuato** (Gto.).

Last Sunday Fiesta and crafts markets in **Comonfort** (Gto.).

December

8th DIA DE LA INMACULADA CONCEPCION. In **San Juan de Los Lagos** (Jal.), the high point of a massive feria which attracts thousands of pilgrims and boasts an enormous crafts market. **Dolores Hidalgo** (Gto.) combines a religious fesitval with a feria and traditional dancing, while **Sayula** (Jal.), between Guadalajara and Ciudad Guzman, also has impressive displays of native dance. In **Tequila** (Jal.), not surprisingly, the celebrations are more earthy, with rodeos, cockfights and fireworks. On the same day **Patzcuaro** (Mich.) celebrates La Señora de la Salud, an event attended by many Tarascan pilgrims and the scene of Tarasc dances including *Los Viejitos*.

12th DIA DE LA VIRGEN DE GUADALUPE. Large fiesta in **Jiquilpan** (Mich.) with fireworks and a torchlight procession in which locals dress in the Mexican colours, green, white and red.

Tanalpa (Jal.) attracts pilgrims from a wide area, with regional dances in front of the church.

16th-25th The traditional Christmas **Posadas** are widely performed – particularly good in **Celaya** (Gto.). In **Querétaro** (Que.), on the 23rd, there's a giant procession with bands and carnival floats, and in **Aranza** (Mich.), a tiny village near Paracho, they perform pastoral plays on Christmas Eve. On Christmas Eve too, in **Tuxpan** (Jal.), there are very ancient dances and a large religious procession.

TRAVEL DETAILS

Trains

1 **From Zacatecas**. To **Mexico City**: *El Fronterizo* leaves Zacatecas 15.48, arriving Aguascalientes (18.10), Lagos de Moreno (20.55), Leon (21.50), Irapuato (23.00), Querétaro (1.30), Mexico (6.55); also at 5.15 arriving Aguascalientes (8.00), Lagos de Moreno (10.55), Querétaro (16.15) and Mexico (22.30). Returns leave Mexico City at 19.50 and 7.10, arriving Querétaro (1.00 and 13.00), Aguascalientes (8.00 and 20.30), Zacatecas (10.30 and 23.50). To **Ciudad Juarez**: leaves 10.30, arriving Chihuahua (1.45) and Ciudad Juarez (7.20) the following morning.

2 **From San Luis Potosí**. To **Mexico City**: The *Aguila Azteca* leaves S.L.P. at 10.30, arriving San Miguel de Allende (13.10), Celaya (14.00), Querétaro (14.45) and Mexico (20.05); also at 21.20, arriving 6.25, and 2.00, arriving 9.00. Returns leave Mexico City at 8.00, 18.00 and 21.15, arriving S.L.P. 17.10, 1.00 and 6.40. Departures for **Monterrey** at 17.40, 1.05 and 7.15, arriving 2.20, 9.00 and 18.00. To **Tampico** (1 daily, second class only) leaves S.L.P. 7.50 arriving 20.45. For **Aguascalientes** (second class only) leaves 10.00, arriving 16.30 – return leaves Aguascalientes 7.40, arriving S.L.P. 14.05.

3 From **Guadalajara**. To **Mexico City**: *El Tapatio* leaves 20.55, arriving Querétaro (3.30) and Mexico (8.45); also daily at 19.30, arriving 8.30. Returns leave Mexico City at 20.30 and 18.05, arriving Querétaro (1.40 and 23.40) and Guadalajara (8.20 and 7.20). Departures for **Nogales** and **Mexicali** daily at 8.50 and 12.00 arriving Nogales 10.20 and 23.15 following day, Mexicali 13.30 following day and 7.20 the second morning. For **Manzanillo** daily departure at 10.00 arriving Ciudad Guzman (13.45), Colima (16.15) and Manzanillo (18.15).

4 **Uruapan** to **Mexico City**. Twice daily, leaving Uruapan (6.30 and 19.15), arriving Patzcuaro (9.05 and 21.30), Morelia (10.30 and 23.00) and Mexico City (20.50 and 7.50). Return leaves Mexico City at 6.55 and 21.30, arriving Morelia (17.10 and 6.10), Patzcuaro (18.50 and 7.40) and Uruapan (21.05 and 10.10).

Buses

Relatively densely populated, this area is criss-crossed by thousands of services, locally between towns and villages, and long-distance runs which call in at all major towns on their routes. It can occasionally be difficult to pick up a seat on the latter: they're not normally sold until the bus has arrived. Nevertheless what follows is a minimum, covering the major stops only – it should be assumed that these buses also cover the towns en route. As the roads converge on major destinations – so the number of buses increases – there's a constant stream calling in at Querétaro, for example, before the last 2½-hour stretch to Mexico City.

In general the fastest and most efficient operators are *Omnibus de Mexico* and *Tres Estrellas de Oro*, though there's little to choose between the first class companies. *Flecha Amarilla* run many of the local runs and are fairly reliable – *Estrella Blanca* is better but less frequent.

From **Zacatecas**: At least 15 daily to Mexico City (8hrs upwards); 8 daily to Guadalajara (7hrs); 10 to San Luis Potosí (2½hrs).

From **Aguascalientes**: 8 daily to Guadalajara (5½hrs); 7 to San Luis Potosí (2½hrs).

From **San Luis Potosí**: At least 15 daily to Mexico City (5½hrs); 9 daily to Guadalajara (6hrs).

From **Guadalajara**: At least 20 a day to Mexico City (around 9hrs); 5 daily to Tepic and Puerto Vallarta (5/8hrs); 4 to Barra de Navidad and Manzanillo (6½hrs); 7 daily to Colima (5hrs); 11 to Morelia (6hrs), and 4 a day to Uruapan (5hrs).

From **Morelia**: 10 daily to Mexico City (6hrs); 9 to Patzcuaro (1½hrs).

From *Uruapan*: 7 a day to Patzcuaro (1½hrs) and 4 to Lazaro Cardenas (6hrs).

From **Guanajuato**: 10 daily to Leon (1hr); 7 to Dolores and San Miguel (1/2hrs); 5 to San Luis de la Paz (2½hrs).

Planes

Zacatecas, Aguascalientes, San Luis Potosí and Uruapan all have airports with flights to and from the capital. By far the most important, though, is **Guadalajara**, with regular services to destinations throughout the Republic (and more than 20 flights a day to Mexico City) as well as international services to most of the south-western USA.

Chapter four
MEXICO CITY AND AROUND

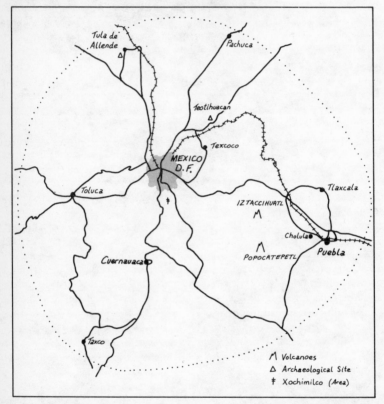

The **Valley of Mexico** has been the centre of gravity of the Mexican nation since earliest pre-history – long before the concept of such a nation existed. In this mountain-ringed basin – 100km long, 60km wide, 7,000 feet high, dotted with great salt and fresh water lagoons and dominated by the vast snow-capped volcanic peaks of Popocatépetl and Ixtaccíhuatl – were based the most powerful civilisations the country has seen. Today the lakes have all but disappeared and the mountains are shrouded in smog, but it continues in every sense to be the heart of Mexico: its physical centre, the generator of every political, cultural and economic pulse.

At the crossroads of everything sprawls the vibrant, elegant, choking, crime-ridden fascination of **Mexico City**. Arguably now the largest city in the world – and certainly set soon to become so – its lure is irresistible. Beside the mansions of the colonial centre lie excavated pyramids, and over them tower the concrete and glass of thrusting development: the city today has fabulous museums and galleries, but above all it's alive – exciting, sometimes frightening, always bewildering – but boldly alive. You can't avoid it, and if you genuinely want to know anything of Mexico you shouldn't try – even if the attraction does sometimes seem to be the same as that which draws onlookers to the site of a particularly nasty accident. Round about there's escape, and interest, in every direction: to the north Tula and Teotihuacan and the magnificent baroque treasures of **Tepotzotlan**; to the east the market town of **Toluca** and mountainous national parks which are the rural retreat of the wealthy; to the south **Cuernavaca** with its ancient palaces and **Taxco**, where the silver comes from; in the west the volcanoes, **Cholula**, and ultra-colonial, thriving **Puebla**.

It is above all the **Aztecs**, whose warrior state was crushed by the armies of Cortes, who are associated with the area in modern minds. But they were relative newcomers, forging their empire by force of arms in less than two centuries and borrowing their culture, their science, their arts, even their language from Valley societies which had gone before. The metropolis today owes virtually nothing to them: the Aztec capital was smashed and in its place, from its stones, arose colonial Mexico. **Teotihuacan**, whose mightly pyramids still stand some 50km north-east of the modern city, was the predominant culture of the Classic period and the true forebear of the Aztecs – a city of some 200,000 people whose influence spread throughout the country, south to the Mayan lands in the Yucatan and beyond into Guatemala and Central America. Their style, though never so militaristic as later societies was adopted everywhere: *Quetzalcoatl*, the plumed serpent, and *Tlaloc*, the rain God, were Teotihuacan deities.

For all its pre-eminence, though, Teotihuacan was neither the earliest, nor the only settlement in the Valley; the pyramid at **Cuicuilco**, now in the south of the city, is probably the oldest stone structure in the country, and there were small agricultural communities all around the lakes. Nor did the Aztecs, arriving some 500 years after the destruction of Teotihuacan, acknowledge their debt. They regarded themselves as descendants of the **Toltec** kingdom, whose capital lay at **Tula** to the north, and whose influence – as successors to Teotihuacan – was almost as pervasive. The Aztecs consciously took over the Toltec military based society, and adopted many of their gods: above all Quetzalcoatl who assumed an importance equal to that of their own tribal deity, *Huitzilopochtli*, the God of War who had brought them to power and demanded human sacrifice to keep them there. In this, in many respects, they were right, for the Toltecs, like the Aztecs themselves, had arrived in Central Mexico as a marauding tribe of *Chichimeca* (sons of dogs) from the north, absorbing the local culture even as they came to dominate it.

THE CAPITAL

And when we saw all those cities and villages built in the water, and other great towns on dry land, and that straight and level causeway leading to Mexico, we were astounded. These great towns and cues and buildings rising from the water, all made of stone, seemed like an enchanted vision from the tales of Amadis. Indeed, some of our soldiers asked whether it was not all a dream.

Bernal Diaz

It is hardly surprising that Cortes and his followers should have been so taken by their first sight of *Tenochtitlan*, capital of the Aztecs. For what they found, built in the centre of a lake traversed by great causeways, was a beautiful, strictly regulated, stone-built city of 300,000 people – easily the equal of anything they might have experienced in Europe. The Aztec people (or more properly the *Mexica*) had arrived at the lake, after years of wandering and living off what they could scavenge or pillage from settled communities, in around 1345. Their own legends have it that Huitzilopochtli had ordered them to build a city where they found an eagle perched on a cactus devouring a snake, and this they duly saw on an island in the middle of the lake (the nopal, eagle and snake motif forms the centrepiece of the modern Mexican flag and is seen everywhere, from coins and official seals to woven designs on rugs). Reality was probably more desperate – driven from place to place, the lake seemed a last resort – but for whatever reasons it proved an ideal site. Well stocked with fish, it was fertile too once they had constructed their *chinampas*, or floating gardens of reeds, and virtually impregnable; the causeways, when they were completed, could be flooded and the bridges raised to thwart attacks (or escape, as the Spanish found to their cost on the *Noche Triste*, see p. 176).

The **island city** eventually expanded to cover an area of some 5 square miles, much of it reclaimed from the lake, and from this base the Aztecs were able to begin their programme of expansion. First, by a series of strategic alliances, war and treachery, dominating the valley, and finally, in a period of less than a hundred years before the conquest, establishing an empire which demanded tribute from and traded with the furthest parts of the country. This was the situation when **Cortes** landed on the east coast in 1519, bringing with him an army of only a few hundred men, and began his long march on Tenochtitlan. Three things assured his survival: superior weaponry, and above all the shock effect of horses (never having seen such animals, the Indians at first believed them to be extensions of their riders) and firearms; the support of tribes who were either enemies or suppressed subjects of the Aztecs; and the unwillingness of **Moctezuma II** (Montezuma) to resist openly.

The Aztec emperor, who had suffered heavy defeats in campaigns against the Tarascans in the west, was a broodingly religious man who believed Cortes to be the pale-skinned, bearded god Quetzalcoatl, returned to fulfil ancient prophecies. Accordingly he admitted him to the city – fearfully, but with a show of ceremonious welcome. By way of repaying this hospitality the Spanish took Moctezuma prisoner, and later attacked the great Aztec temples, killing many priests and placing Christian chapels alongside their altars. Meanwhile there was growing unrest in the city at the emperor's passivity and at the rapacious behaviour of his guests. Moctezuma was eventually killed – according to the Spanish stoned to death by his own people while trying to quell a riot – and the Spaniards driven from the city with heavy losses. Cortes and a few of his followers, however, escaped to the security of Tlaxcala, most loyal of his native allies, there to regroup and plan a new assault. Finally, reinforced and re-armed, swelled by Indian allies and with ships built in secret, they laid a three-month siege – taking the city in the face of suicidal opposition in August 1521.

It is still a harsh memory – Cortes himself is hardly revered, but the Indians who assisted him, and in particular Moctezuma and Malinche, the Indian woman who acted as Cortes's interpreter, are non-people. You won't find a monument to Moctezuma in the country, though Cuauhtemoc, his successor who led the fierce resistance, is commemorated everywhere; Malinche is represented, acidly, in some of Rivera's more outspoken murals. More telling, perhaps, of the bitterness of the struggle, is that so little remains: 'all that I saw then', wrote Bernal Diaz, 'is overthrown and destroyed; nothing is left standing'. The victorious Spanish systematically smashed every visible aspect of the old culture and built, where the great temples had stood, their Cathedral, and on the site of the Aztec emperor's palace, a palace for Cortes. As often as not the very stones of the old city were used to construct the new. Only in recent years, particularly during construction of the Metro, have some remains of Tenochtitlan been brought to light.

The **new city** developed slowly in its early years, only attaining the level of population which the old had enjoyed at the beginning of this century. It spread far wider, however, as the lake was drained, filled and built over – only tiny vestiges remain today – and grew with considerable grace. In many ways it's a singularly unfortunate place to site a modern city. Pestilent from the earliest days, the inadequately drained waters harboured fevers, and the Indian population was constantly swept by epidemics of European diseases. Many of the buildings, too, simply began to sink into the soft lake bed – a process not helped by regular earthquake activity. They say it's stabilised now – and demonstrate that confidence by studding the city with skyscrapers – but you'll see old churches and mansions leaning at crazy angles throughout the centre.

Such problems fade into insignificance, however, compared to the horrors which recent growth and industrialisation have brought. Estimated at around 16 million, the city's **population** is the fastest growing in the world (from fewer than 5 million in 1960) and at present rates will reach 35 million by the end of the century. **Pollution**, churned out by industry but even more by the chaotic traffic, is trapped in the bowl of mountains, hanging permanently in a pall of smog over the city. This is not mere rhetoric – as you fly in, and often, even, as you arrive by bus over the mountains, you descend from clear blue skies into a thick greyish-yellow cloud: Popocatépetl and Ixtaccíhuatl, the volcanoes on which every visitor used to comment ('Japanese contoured shapes of pastel blue and porcelain snow, and thin formal curls of smoke afloat in a limpid sky' – wrote Sybille Bedford in the 1950s), are now visible from the centre on just two or three days a year. Within hours of arriving your eyes smart and your throat is sore – just breathing is said to be the equivalent of smoking forty cigarettes a day (it's a good place to give up) and chronic bronchitis is endemic among residents. At 7,400 feet, there wasn't much oxygen to begin with. Not surprisingly, Mexico is also the city with the most petty crime, and where you feel least secure walking the streets at night: the centre is safe enough, and the luxurious suburbs, but you should avoid taking risks away from these.

All of which you should know, but which should not deter you – a certain seaminess amid the elegance of the new quarters and the genteel decay of the old is part of the charm. Mexico is very much a living city, and while it might not be one you'd choose to live in, it's a compelling place to visit. There's a wealth of great buildings – the **Cathedral** and **National Palace** in the colonial centre around the Zocalo, **Maximilian's castle** in Chapultepec, daring modern architecture throughout the city; there are superb museums – the **Anthropology Museum** ranks with the world's best, Diego Rivera's **Museo Anahuacalli** with its most bizarre; there's art in galleries but above all in **murals** adorning public buildings everywhere, particularly the startling **University City**; and a diverse, dynamic **street-life** unequalled in Latin America. On the whole you won't see the shantytowns, and you'll soon get used to the atmosphere, but it's as well to remember they're there. Exercise the sort of caution you would in any major city and you'll enjoy it a lot more.

ORIENTATION
Getting your bearings

First, disabuse yourself of the notion that you're in Mexico City. As far as a Mexican is concerned you're not, you're in *México*, or possibly *El D.F.* (Day Effé). It's a source of infinite confusion to visitors, but the fact is that the country took its name from the city and *México*, in conversation, almost always means the latter (it's written Mexico D.F. – the *Distrito Federal* being the administrative zone which contains most of the urban areas). The nation is *La Republica*, or in speeches *La Patria*, very rarely Mexico.

For all its size and the horrors of its traffic, Mexico, once you're used to it, is surprisingly easy to find your way around. Certainly there is more logic in its plan than in any European city and given an efficient and very cheap, if horrendously crowded, public transport system, and reasonably priced taxis, you should have no trouble getting about. Remember the altitude – walking can get tiring quickly, especially for the first day or two.

Traditional centre of the city is the **Zocalo**; the heart of ancient Tenochtitlan and of Cortes's city, it's surrounded by the oldest streets, largely colonial and unmodernised. In practice, as a visitor, this is the furthest east you're likely to go, except to get to the airport or the eastbound bus station. Westwards, Avenidas **Madero** and **Juarez** lead to the **Alameda**, the small park which marks the extent of the old city centre. Here is the Palacio de las Bellas Artes, the main Post Office, the enormous Torre Latino-Americano, and a clutch of large hotels. Carry straight on past here and you get into an area, between the ugly bulk of the Monumento a la Revolucion and the railway station, where you'll find many of the cheaper hotels. Turn slightly to the left, however, and you're on the **Paseo de la Reforma** which leads down to the great open space of **Chapultepec Park**, recreation area for the city's millions, and home of the National Museum of Anthropology and several other important **museums**. Off to the left as you head down Reforma is the **Zona Rosa** with its chic shopping streets, expensive hotels, fancy restaurants and constant tourist activity. On the right is a more sedate, upmarket residential area where many of the old-established embassies are based. Beyond Chapultepec, Reforma runs out of the city through the ultra-smart suburb of **Las Lomas**.

The **Avenida de los Insurgentes** crosses Reforma about halfway between the Alameda and the park. Said to be the longest continuous city street in the world, Insurgentes runs straight through the city, more or less from north to south. It's perhaps the city's most important artery, lined throughout with modern commercial development. In the south it runs past the suburb of **San Angel** and close by **Coyoacan**, to the **Univer-**

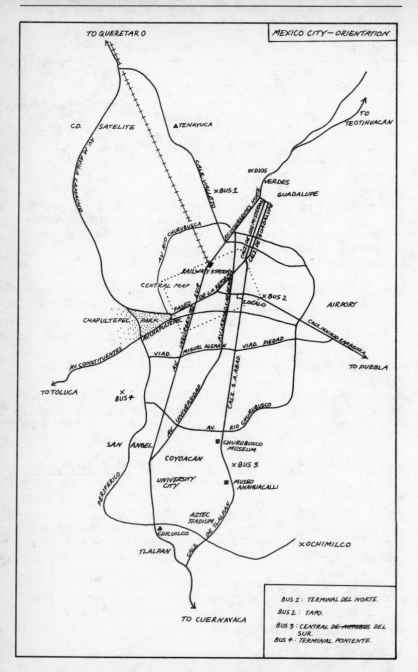

sity City, and on out of Mexico by the **Pyramid of Cuicuilco**. Also in the southern extremities of the city are the **Floating Gardens of Xochimilco** – virtually the last remains of the great lagoons. Right in the outskirts Insurgentes meets another important through-route, the **Calzada de Tlalpan**, which heads back to the Zocalo, passing the Rivera Museum and the other side of Coyoacan. To the north, Insurgentes leaves the centre past the railway station, and close by the north-bound bus station, to leave the city via **Guadalupe** and **Indios Verdes**. The northern extension of Reforma, too, ends up at the great shrine of Guadalupe, as does the continuation of the Calzada de Tlalpan beyond the Zocalo.

These, then, are the chief areas of the city. Around the cramped streets of the old part you'll want to walk, and the ancient city itself was quite small enough to make that the most practicable method. Heading for Chapultepec, though, or the Zona Rosa, you're better off taking the bus or metro – it's an interesting walk all the way down Reforma, but a very long one. And for the further suburbs you've clearly got no choice but to rely on taxis or public transport: as far as practicable, bus and metro details are contained within the text. One further point to remember is that many **street names** are repeated over and over again in different parts of the city – there must be hundreds of streets called Morelos, Juarez or Hidalgo, and a good score of Cinco de Mayos. If you're taking a cab, or looking at a map, you should always be clear which area you mean – it's fairly obvious in the centre, but searching out an address in the suburbs can lead to a series of false starts unless you're clear of its general location or the name of the *barrio*. Also useful to know that you can get **news in English**, and extensive **listings**, from the *Mexico City News*, sold on news-stands throughout the centre, or from the free *Daily Bulletin* which you can pick up in the lobbies of big hotels.

Comings and goings: buses, trains and planes

Arriving unprepared in the vastness of Mexico can be a disconcerting experience, but in fact it's not hard to get into the centre, or to a hotel, from any of the major points of arrival. No luggage of any size is allowed on the Metro, which effectively rules that out as a means of transit – the guards are very strict about this during rush hours, when even a large briefcase may be looked at askance, less so in the evening or during the quieter period in the middle of the day. You can take anything on a bus, but they tend to be very crowded, and getting bags on and off can prove a nightmare. Even if only this once, you should seriously consider a taxi, certainly if you are at all heavily laden. Special systems operate at the bus stations and the airport to prevent rip-offs; they're outlined below. The railway station is pretty central anyway.

There are four chief **LONG-DISTANCE BUS STATIONS** in Mexico, one for each point of the compass, though in practice the north-bound terminal handles far more than its share, while the west-bound one is tiny. With all the direct routes to and from the US border, and serving every major city which is even slightly **north** of Mexico (including the fastest services to Guadalajara and Morelia), the *Terminal del Norte* (Av. de los Cien Metros 4907) is by far the largest of the four. You leave from here for any destination in the first three chapters. There's a metro station (*Terminal de Autobuses del Norte*, line 5), or you can get a bus heading south on Insurgentes, about four blocks away – anything which says *Metro Insurgentes* will take you down Insurgentes, past the railway station, across Reforma, and on through the edge of the Zona Rosa. Alternatively, in the vast lobby, you'll see government-run booths which sell tickets for **collective taxis**. It's the same procedure in all the bus stations – there's a large map of the city marked out in zones, with a standard, set fare for each: you pick where you're going (almost certainly *Centro*) and buy a ticket, then walk outside and you'll be hustled into a cab going your way – once it's full you leave and supposedly get dropped at any address you choose within the stated zone. There are just two problems; firstly the driver may drop you a block or two from your hotel rather than take a major detour through the one-way systems (best to accept this unless it's very late at night), and secondly he may demand a large tip which you're in no way obliged to pay. Or you can pick up an ordinary taxi outside the terminal and take your chances with the meter.

East-bound services use the most modern of the termini, the *Terminal de Autobuses de Pasajeros de Oriente*, always known as TAPO. Buses for Puebla, for the Gulf Coast state of Veracruz, and for places which you might think of as south, Oaxaca, Chiapas and the Yucatan, even Guatemala, leave from here. Located on Av. Ignacio Zaragoza, out towards the airport, there's a metro station very close by (*San Lazaro*, line 1) or regular buses up Zaragoza towards the Zocalo and on to Reforma. Buses **south to the Pacific Coast** – for Cuernavaca, Taxco, Acapulco and Zihuatanejo in particular – leave from the *Central de Autobuses del Sur* (Av. Taxqueña 1320). It's at the end of Metro line 2 (*Taxqueña*) which is also a big terminus for local buses from the centre – the 7D will take you in to the junction of Juarez and Reforma, or in the streets around the Zocalo look for *Metro Taxqueña*, *La Villa/Tlalpan*, or *La Villa/Xochimilco*. If you arrive here by metro, ignore the signs which point to the *Central de Autobuses* – they lead to the city bus stands – the long-distance terminal is immediately obvious when you go out the front of the Metro station. Finally, for **the west**, there's the *Terminal Poniente*, at the junction of Calles Sur and Tacubaya. The smallest of them, it basically handles traffic to Toluca, but it's also the place to go for the slower, more scenic routes to Morelia and Guadalajara, via Toluca. Hard by the *Observatorio* Metro station, there are also buses

heading south on Reforma (look for *Observatorio*) or from the stands
by the entrance to Chapultepec Park.

All of these bus stations are used by hordes of competing companies,
and the only way to get a full idea of the timetable for any given destination is to check out every one: different companies may take different
routes and you can sometimes waste hours by choosing the wrong one.
Though it's rare not to be able to get on any bus at very short notice, it
can be worthwhile booking in advance for long-distance journeys or for
express services to popular destinations – that way you'll have a choice
of seat and be sure of getting the fastest service going. If you're uncertain
which bus station you should be leaving from, simply get into a taxi and
tell the driver what your ultimate destination is – he'll know where to
take you. You'll find places to eat, and stalls selling food and drink for
the journey, in all the termini, and you may also see hotel reservation
desks, both for Mexico City and for the major destinations served. These
are privately run, and are on the whole not in the least interested in you
if you're looking for somewhere cheap.

All mainline **TRAINS** arrive at the *Estacion Central de Buenavista*,
just off Av. Insurgentes Norte about nine blocks from its junction with
Reforma. There's no metro station particularly near, but you'll find a
large taxi rank right outside, and buses and taxis heading south on
Insurgentes towards Reforma and the Zona Rosa, or west on Mosqueta
towards the Zocalo. Being fairly central, many of the cheaper hotels are
in any case in easy walking distance. If you're planning to leave by train,
you should get your tickets as far in advance as possible – certainly don't
leave it to the last minute as you often have to queue for hours. The first
class ticket office is open from 6am to 11.30pm, Mondays to Saturday,
and on Sunday from 6 to 9.30 – second class closes a couple of hours
earlier and enjoys a siesta (from 10 till 2) on Sundays.

The **AIRPORT** is some way from the centre, but it is still very much
within the city limits and you get some amazing views as you come in
to land, low over the houses. There's a **tourist information** desk here,
and several **banks** which change money 24 hours a day. As you emerge
from Customs and Immigration, or even off an internal flight, you'll be
besieged by offers of a taxi into town. Ignore them. By the main exit
doors you'll find a booth selling tickets for the official SETTA airport
transit – there's a scale of fares posted according to how you want to
go: the bus, which may take some time to fill and then does a tour of all
the major hotel areas; smaller VW *colectivos*, or individual taxis. The
system has been set up to avoid rip-offs, and although it is itself overpriced
(an ordinary taxi with a meter would be far cheaper, but they're not
allowed to operate here), you won't do any better. If you go with one of
the unofficial drivers – as often as not it turns out to be a private car –
you're very unlikely to pay less, whatever extravagant claims they may

make, and there's always the remote possibility that you could find yourself relieved of your money and luggage and dumped by the roadside somewhere. If you're travelling extremely light you could also go in on the Metro (*Terminal Aerea*, line 5, up to the left from the main terminal building – **not** *Aeropuerto*) or walk up to the main road and catch a bus.

To get **to the airport** it's easiest to take a regular taxi, but you can also catch the green and silver SETTA bus as it goes on the rounds of the hotels (it travels most of the way up Reforma) or phone SETTA the day before (on 571 6317) to arrange to be picked up from your hotel. If you're leaving the country bear in mind that there's an airport **departure tax** (of around five dollars) so keep a few hundred pesos to hand: it can only be paid in Mexican currency.

Getting about – handling public transport

Even if you have **your own car**, you'd be better off getting around within the city by bus, metro or taxi. Driving is a nightmare, compounded by confusing one-way and through-route systems, by the impossibility of finding anywhere to park and by traffic police who can spot foreign plates a mile off and know a potential 'fine' when they see one. Best to choose a hotel with secure parking (see lists below) and to leave it there for the duration of your stay, except possibly to do the tour of the south of the city. Public transport is, in any case, almost ludicrously cheap.

Certainly that's true of the **METRO**, on which the flat fare must cost far more to collect than it raises in revenue. Tickets come in blocks of five or ten at one peso each, or individually for slightly more – getting five will save a lot of queueing and messing about with tiny quantities of change. It's a superb modern system, French-built, fast, silent and expanding all the time, but there are problems. Worst of these are the crowds – unbelievable at rush hours when the worst stations in the centre designate separate entries for women and children only, patrolled by armed guards to protect them from the crush. At such times it can also get unbearably hot. Then, once you've got into the system, there are no maps, just pictographic representations of the line you are on. So before you set off you need to work out where to change, and which way you'll be travelling on each line: these are indicated by the last station in each direction (thus on line two you'll want either *Direccion Tacuba* or *Direccion Taxqueña*), transfers by the word *Correspondancia* and the name of the new line – each has a different colour code to make matters slightly simpler. You may be able to pick up a complete map of the system from the ticket office – clearer than our black and white plan – but more often than not they've run out. Remember, too, that no luggage of any size is allowed. The rules vary to some extent with where you board and the time of day – at rush hour in the centre even a small bag may be regarded as excessive, while in the evening in the suburbs you can get away with quite a lot – but certainly a full-size backpack would never be allowed on. Trains run till around midnight every night, later at weekends.

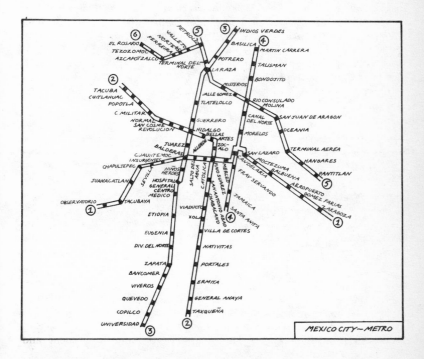

MEXICO CITY – METRO

Rush hour crowds may be worst on the Metro, but the situation is little better with buses and taxis: it's virtually impossible to get a taxi and the buses, once they're full, simply don't stop to let passengers on. You'll save a lot of hassle, then, if you avoid travelling between about 7 and 9am and 5 and 7pm.

BUSES in Mexico are unmistakable, not so much because they're painted yellow as for their deafening roar and the vast plumes of choking black smoke they leave behind them. Some on the central routes have very much smartened up their acts, but on the whole they're still grimy machines with hard seats and maniacs behind the wheel – though also very efficient if you know where you're going. As far as possible they're outlined in the text, but the two most useful routes are along Reforma from Chapultepec to the Zocalo, and along Insurgentes, from Indios Verdes in the north, past the Terminal del Norte, the railway station,

Metro Insurgentes and on eventually to the University in the south. The former, *Ruta Cien, Expreso Reforma* buses, set off from 16 de Septiembre opposite the Gran Hotel, run through the Zocalo, down Cinco de Mayo and Juarez (past Bellas Artes and the Alameda) and on down Reforma to Chapultepec where some stop, while others continue to Las Lomas or Observatorio – in this direction they're marked *Toreo, Lomas Km. 13* or *Metro Observatorio*; going back, look simply for *Zocalo*. Most useful bus on Insurgentes is the No. 17, which goes all the way from Indios Verdes to San Angel, but there are many others which also cover large sections of the route. The area just by Chapultepec metro station and the entrance to the park is also a major downtown bus terminus, from where you can get to almost any part of the city. Buses charge slightly more than the metro, but are still very cheap.

Also running down the major through routes, especially on Reforma and Insurgentes, you'll find **PESEROS**, or collective taxis, which charge more than the bus but far less than a regular taxi, and will let you on and off anywhere along their set route. They're mostly VW vans or large American saloons, usually white, and have their destination displayed on the windscreen – the driver will cruise by the side of the road holding up a number of fingers to indicate the number of free seats.

Ordinary **TAXIS** come in a variety of forms. Cheapest and best are the white and yellow cabs which cruise the streets looking for custom. These should have a meter (make sure it's switched on) and are extremely good value compared to anywhere in Europe or North America – go for the smaller ones, which seem to charge less and can negotiate the traffic much more easily. Be warned that they can't adjust taxi meters fast enough to keep up with inflation – there should be a chart to convert the reading into what you actually pay. The orange cabs which wait at *sitios* (taxi ranks) charge slightly more, but in general work in the same way as the above. The ones to look out for are the *turismo* taxis with their notorious hooded meters. Simply by slipping a black bag over the meter and lying in wait outside the big hotels, these think they have the right to at least treble their rates. In the normal course of events you should avoid them, but they do have a couple of advantages, namely that they're almost always around and that many of the drivers speak some English. So they can be worth it if, for example, you need to get to the airport in a hurry (for which they charge no more than a SETTA cab would) or if you want to go on a tour for a few hours. In the latter case, with some ferocious haggling, you might even get a bargain.

Hotels

There must be thousands of hotels in Mexico. On any street, in any unlikely corner of the city, there seems to be at least one. But in the centre, while you're still spoilt for choice, it can be hard to find anywhere which is both well situated and reasonably priced. The vast majority of tourists nowadays stay in the expensive modern places of the Zona Rosa, or in the even more costly, still flashier hotels overlooking Chapultepec Park. If you want to pay less you'll have to look in older, less fashionable areas.

The greatest concentration of cheap rooms is to be found in the area **between the railway station and the Plaza de La Republica**. It's not, for the most part, an attractive part of the city, but it is highly convenient – close to the Alameda, within walking distance past that of the Zocalo (or in the other direction of the Zona Rosa) and in easy reach of the buses and taxis on Reforma or Insurgentes and the Metro at Hidalgo or Revolucion. Richest pickings are just behind the **Plaza San Fernando**, which you'll find a couple of blocks from the Alameda along Puente de Alvarado. Just before this, on Heroes Ferrocarrilleros, is the *Hotel Marconi*, cheap and very close to the Alameda, but noisy: on the plaza itself the *Monaco* (Guerrero 12, with parking) and the *Managua* opposite have more pretensions to luxury and consequently charge more than most around here. Better choices line Orozco y Berra, the street which runs past the back of the plaza, and Mina, the one behind that. The *Hotel Polly* (Orozco y Berra 35 at the corner of Zaragoza) is particularly good, or try the *Miño* (across the street on Zaragoza) which is slightly cheaper. Zaragoza itself is a pleasant street with a market on Thursday mornings – the *Savoy*, towards the bottom, charges more than it deserves. Back on Orozco y Berra, both the *El Dorado* (No. 131), back towards the Alameda, and the *Hotel Riviera* (in the other direction at the corner of Aldama) have parking space and are hence rather more expensive. Opposite this latter, the *Pigal* is a bizarre modern-looking place, but much cheaper. On Mina try the *Hotel Mina*, the *Iberia*, the *La Paz* or the *Astoria*.

For absolutely the **cheapest places** here – or probably anywhere in the centre – head west a couple more blocks to the two streets immediately before Insurgentes: Bernal Diaz and Bernardino de Sahagun. This is a pretty grim, industrial little backwater, but the *Hotel Buenavista*, the *Diaz* and the *Estaciones* among others are certainly not overpriced. On the main roads here, Insurgentes, Central and Puente de Alvarado, are a whole series more, though these are very noisy and considerably more expensive. South of here, **between Alvarado and the Plaza de la Republica**, the hotels are slightly more upmarket, but it's a quieter and pleasanter place to stay. There are several large, pricey places around the Plaza de la Republica itself of which the *Principado* (Jose Maria Iglesias 55) is the pick if you want to stay in some luxury in a tall, modern, international-type hotel. They charge around $12 double, and you'll be surrounded by businessmen. Better value, and also with parking, is the *Hotel Edison*

(Edison 106) – just around the corner, modern, small and often full, but about half the price. Behind here too, on a tiny peaceful square, are the Hotels *Oxford* (Ignacio Mariscal 67) and *Carlton* (32) – both old-fashioned and comfortable, but more expensive than they ought to be.

Between Republica and the Paseo de la Reforma there's nowhere which is particularly good value, but it has the advantage, like the Plaza itself, of being on the route of the airport bus if you've just arrived. Best known is the *Mayaland* (Antonio Caso 23) which tends to be full of Americans and, for what you get, is seriously overpriced. Cheaper are the *Marin* (at the corner of Antonio Caso and Leon) or the *Uxmal* (Madrid 13). Or, **on Reforma** itself right opposite the fancy *Fiesta Palace*, try the *Hotel Francis*, an old place which offers remarkable value considering where it is. These are the fringes of the **Zona Rosa**, where prices rise rapidly, but if you want to stay close to the action the *Premier* (Atenas 72) is one of the cheapest. Right on the other side of the Zona Rosa you'll find the **Youth Hostel** at Cozumel 57 – it's the cheapest bed you'll find in Mexico, but you need a YHA or student card and it's rather out of the way, not easy to get to on public transport (nearest Metro station is *Sevilla*).

The other area to look is in the old **streets surrounding the Zocalo**. Hotels here are very much more scattered, and tend to be old and often dilapidated with prices slightly higher than those around San Fernando, but once you start to look there are a surprising number of them. Start around Calles Republica del Salvador and Republica de Uruguay, a couple of blocks south of the Zocalo. On Uruguay you'll find the *Concordia*, the *Roble*, the *Ontario* and the *Capitol*, as well as the *Monte Carlo* (Uruguay 69) which was originally an Augustinian Monastery, was later lived in briefly by D. H. Lawrence, and now has a car park – for one or all of which reasons it costs more than the others. Among others on Salvador are the *Hotel Paris* (Rep. del Salvador 91), the *El Salvador* (16), and the *Hotel Isabel*, at the corner of Isabel La Catolica. Elsewhere, the *Hotel Ambos Mundos*, on Bolivar between Tacuba and Cinco de Mayo, is the most basic and cheapest of all these, full of elderly Mexican salesmen who probably used to come here when it and they were successful thirty years ago, and atmospheric if not comfortable. Not far from here, on Bolivar between Madero and 16 de Septiembre, you'll find the *Hotel Principal*. In the unlikely event that you want to blow large amounts of money, try the *Gran Hotel de la Ciudad de Mexico*, on 16 de Septiembre just off the Zocalo. It's infinitely more stylish, and costs considerably less (around $25 double) than any of the skyscrapers in the Zona Rosa. Even if only to gawp you should wander in for a look at its art-deco interior, complete with Tiffany stained-glass dome, wrought-iron lift cages, and exotic stuffed birds pouring out recorded warbles.

Finally if you arrive by bus at the **Terminal del Norte** and are concerned only with getting some sleep in luxurious silence, head for the *Hotel*

Brasilia (Av. de los Cien Metros 4823). It's a tall, modern, skyscraper which you can't miss as you leave the terminus, and while expensive, is good value for what you get – TV, tiled bathrooms, a decent restaurant and all.

THE SIGHTS

Around the Zocalo: the central zone

The vast paved open space of the **Zocalo** – second largest in the world after Moscow's Red Square – is the city's political and religious centre in a very literal sense. Here stand the great Cathedral, the National Palace with the offices of the President, and the city administration – all of them magnificent colonial buildings. But it also reflects other periods of the country's history – this was the heart of Aztec Tenochtitlan, and beside the Cathedral they're excavating what remains of the great temples. There are echoes of the country's present economic plight, too, in the lines of unemployed who queue up around the Cathedral looking for work, each holding a little sign with his trade – plumber, electrician or mechanic – and a box with a few scavenged tools. By them, as often as not, wait a rather shabby group of Indians in gaudy, wilting head-dresses and feath-ered robes, ready to perform their sad dances for the next group of tourists. Each evening at 6 you can watch the National Flag being ceremoniously lowered from its giant pole in the centre of the plaza. A troop of presidential guards march out from the palace, strike the enor-mous banner, and perform a complex march routine at the end of which the flag is left, neatly folded, in the hands of one of their number. You get a great view of this, and of everything else happening in the Zocalo, from the rooftop bar in the *Hotel Majestic* at the corner of Madero.

It's the **Cathedral**, flanked by the parish church of **El Sagrario**, which first draws the eye, with its heavy, grey baroque facade and squat, bell-topped towers. Like so many of the city's weightier, older structures the Cathedral has settled over the years into the soft wet ground beneath it – you can see the tilt. The first church on this site was constructed only a couple of years after the Conquest using stones torn from the Temple of Huitzilopochtli, but the present structure was begun in 1573 to provide Mexico with a cathedral more suited to its wealth and status. The towers weren't completed until 1813 though, and the building incorporates a plethora of architectural styles throughout. Even the frontage demon-strates this clearly; relatively austere at the bottom where work started in a period when the Conquest was still recent, flowering into full baroque as you look up, and topped by neo-classical cornices and clock tower. Inside, it was seriously damaged by fire in 1967 and is still not fully recovered – the chief impression is of vast and rather gloomy open space.

CENTRAL MEXICO CITY

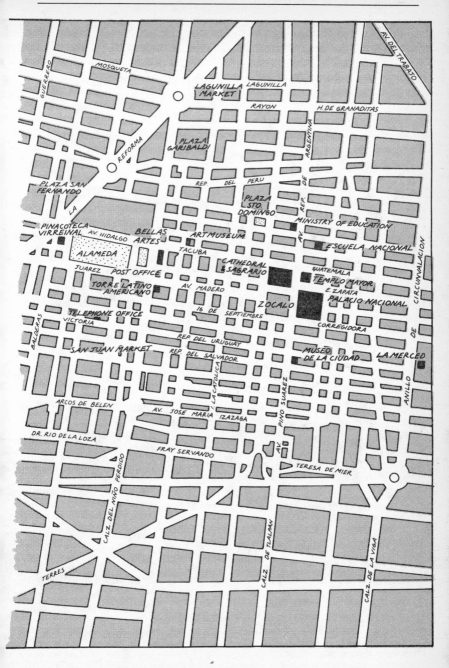

By contrast El Sagrario seems far richer, though that's largely a false impression created by liberal use of gold paint and exuberant Churrigueresque carving.

The other dominant structure is the great **Palacio Nacional**, its facade taking up a full side of the Zocalo – more than 200 yards. The so-called New Palace of Moctezuma stood here, and Cortes made it his first residence too, but the present building, for all its apparent unity, is the result of centuries of agglomeration and rebuilding. Most recently, a third storey was added in 1927. From 1562 the building was the official residence of the Spanish Viceroy, and later of Presidents of the Republic, and it still contains the office of the President, who makes his most important pronouncements from the balcony – especially on September 15th, when the *Grito de Dolores* signals the start of Independence celebrations around the country. Benito Juarez died here in 1872, and his living quarters have been turned into a tiny museum in his honour (open Mon.-Fri. 10–3 and 4–6; free).

The overriding attraction, however, is the series of **Diego Rivera murals** which decorate the stairwell and upper storey of the main courtyard (there are fourteen courts in all). *Diego Rivera* (1886–1957) was arguably the greatest of the 'Big Three' Mexican artists who interpreted the Revolution and Mexican history through the medium of enormous murals and put the nation's art onto an international footing in the first half of this century. Though currently not particularly fashionable, the works of Rivera (along with those of Jose Clemente Orozco and David Siqueiros see pp. 101 and 189) remain among the country's most striking sights. Rivera himself studied from the age of ten at the San Carlos Academy in the capital, later moving to Paris where he flirted with many of the new trends, and in particular cubism. More importantly, though, he and Siqueiros planned, in exile, a popular, native art to express the new society in Mexico. Almost from the moment of his return he began work, for the Ministry of Education, on the first of his massive, consciousness-raising murals: a political art whose themes – Mexican history, the oppression of the natives, post-revolutionary resurgence – were initially more important than their techniques. Many of the early murals are deceptively simple, even naive, but in fact Rivera remained close to the major trends and, following the lead of Siqueiros, took a seriously scientific view of his work – looking to industry for new techniques, better materials, fresh hope. Their view of industrial growth as a panacea (particularly in their earlier works) is perhaps simplistic, but their use of technology, their experimentation with new methods and original approaches, has often startling results – look, in particular, at the University City or the *Polyforum Cultural*.

The series of murals here, which Rivera began in 1929, are classics; ranking with the best of his works anywhere. The great panorama of

Mexican history around the **main staircase** combines an unbelievable wealth of detail with savage imagery and a masterly use of the space available. On the right-hand wall Quetzalcoatl sits in majesty amid the golden age of the Valley of Mexico, with an idealised vision of life in Teotihuacan, Tula and Tenochtitlan going on around him. The main section depicts the conquest, oppression, war, inquisition, invasion, Independence and eventually revolution. Almost every major personage and event of Mexican history is here, from the grotesquely twisted features of the Conquistadores, to the heroes – balding white-haired Hidalgo with the banner of Independence; squat, dark Benito Juarez with his Constitution and laws for the reform of the church; Zapata, with a placard proclaiming his cry of *Tierra y Libertad*; Pancho Villa, moustachioed and swaggering. On the left is post-revolutionary Mexico and the future, with Karl Marx pointing the way to adoring workers, and businessmen clustered over their tickertape: a somewhat ironic depiction in the modern city with its swank, skyscraper offices and grim industrial wastes. Rivera's wife, the surrealist artist Frida Kahlo, is depicted too – behind her sister Cristina in a red blouse with an open book.

Around the walls of the **upper storey** are a whole series of smaller panels. Originally intended to go all the way round – a project never completed and perhaps always over-optimistic – you can still see a few sketches on unpainted walls. The ones here mostly depict the idyll of various aspects of life before the conquest – market day, hunting scenes and so on – while the last couple show the arrival of the Spanish.

Continuing round the Zocalo clockwise, the third side is taken up by the City Hall, the **Ayuntamiento**, while sheltering under the arcades of the fourth is a series of shops. Almost all of these sell either hats or jewellery. This practice – a whole street given over to one particular trade – is one that you'll still find to some extent throughout the city: even very near here there are places where you can buy nothing but stationery, other blocks packed with shoe shops. It's probably the most concrete hangover of Aztec life – their well-regulated markets were divided up according to the nature of the goods on sale, and the practice was continued by colonial planners. For strange shopping experiences, though, you can't beat the **Monte de Piedad**, at the corner of the Zocalo with 5 de Mayo. This huge building, supposedly the site of the palace in which Cortes and his followers stayed as guests of Moctezuma, is now the National Pawn Shop. The most unbelievable variety of stuff put up for hock is displayed here – a better selection than you'd find in the average mail order catalogue and including office machinery, beds, jewellery, artworks, dentists' chairs – anything, in fact, that will go through the doors. From time to time they hold major auctions to clear the place out, but this is really a place to look at – always full of milling crowds – rather than to buy.

Just off the Zocalo, in the corner between the Palace and the Cathedral, lies the site where the **Templo Mayor** has been excavated. What you see are the bare ruins of the foundations of the great temple and one or two buildings immediately around it – highly confusing since, as was normal practice, a new temple was built over the old at the end of every fifty-two-year calendar cycle (and apparently even more frequently here) so that there were a whole series of temples stacked inside each other like Russian dolls. Arm yourself with a cutaway diagram (free from the ticket office) or a look at the models and maps in the City Museum (see below) and it all makes more sense.

Although it's been known since the beginning of this century that the ceremonial area lay under this part of the city, work only began in earnest in 1978 after workmen uncovered a vast stone disc weighing about 8 tons and depicting *Coyolxauhqui*, goddess of the moon. Logic demanded that this must lie at the foot of the temple of Huitzolopochtli, and so the colonial buildings were cleared away and excavation began. The goddess was the elder sister of Huitzlopotchli who, on discovering that her mother was miraculously pregnant, vowed to wipe out the dishonour by killing her. Huitzilopochtli, however, sprung fully armed from the womb (like Athena in Greek mythology), decapitated and dismembered his sister, throwing her body down a mountain, and killed his 400 other brothers who had gathered to help. Coyolxauhqui is thus always portrayed with her head and limbs cut off, and was found here at the foot of the Temple of Huitzilopochtli symbolising her fall from the mountain. The sacrifices carried out in the temple were in part a re-enactment of this – the victims being thrown down the steps afterwards – and in part meant to feed Huitzilopochtli with the blood he needed as sun god to win his nightly fight against darkness. The Great Temple was also dedicated to Tlaloc, the infinitely more peaceful God of Rain, and at its summit were two separate sanctuaries, reached by a monumental double stairway.

Work on the Templo Mayor site is not entirely complete, and there's talk of installing a museum to exhibit some of the many objects from all parts of Mexico that were found here. For the moment the best have gone to the National Anthropology Museum, while some others, including the great Coyolxauhqui disc, lie where they were found: you walk round the excavations on raised wooden walkways, looking down on them. It's open, currently, from 10–1, closed on Mondays. Right beside the archaeological zone, on Calle Moneda, is the **Museo de las Culturas** (open Mon.-Sat. 10–6), a collection devoted to the archaeology and anthropology of other countries, and not one of the city's most interesting.

Follow Seminario past the Templo Mayor away from the Zocalo and in a couple of blocks you reach the **Ministry of Education**, where Rivera painted his first murals on returning from Paris. The inspiration behind them was *Jose Vasconcelos*, revolutionary Minister of Public Education but better known as a poet and philosopher, who promoted educational art as a means of instilling a sense of history and cultural pride in a widely illiterate population. As such, he is the man most directly responsible for the murals in public buildings throughout the country. Rivera created 235 frescoes here, spread over three floors, and rising from a series celebrating everyday Mexican life, its traditions and festivals (in particular the celebrated *Dia de los Muertos*), to more overtly political themes. There are also murals, painted at much the same time (around 1923), by Jean Charlot, Amado de la Cueva and Carlos Merida among others. You can visit the SEP (*Secretaria de Educacion Publica*) during weekday business hours.

More murals, for which Vasconcelos was also responsible, adorn the **Escuela Nacional Preparatoria** (National Preparatory School), very nearby in the eighteenth-century Jesuit seminary of San Idelfonso. Turn right out of the SEP and then first left to get there – it's at San Idelfonso 33. Many artists are represented, including Rivera and Siqueiros, but the most famous here are the works of Jose Clemente Orozco which you'll find on the main staircase and around the first floor of the main patio. As everywhere, Orozco, for all his enthusiasm for the Revolution, is less sanguine about its prospects, and modern Mexico is caricatured almost as savagely as the pre-revolutionary nation.

Head down this street in the other direction (it changes its name from San Idelfonso to Republica de Cuba) and you reach the little plaza of **Santo Domingo**, one of the city's most wholly colonial. There's a fountain playing in the middle and eighteenth-century mansions lining the sides, with the fine baroque church of Santo Domingo on the site of the country's first Dominican monastery. Under the arcades you'll find clerks sitting at little desks with portable typewriters, carrying on an ancient tradition of public scribes. It's a sight you'll find somewhere in most large Mexican cities – their main function is to translate simple messages into the flowery, sycophantic language essential for any business letter in Spanish, but they'll type anything from student theses to love letters. In a more modern reflection of this you'll also find printing shops around here, churning out posters and business cards. Avenida Brasil leads back to the Zocalo.

Leaving the Zocalo to the south, Pino Suarez heads off from the corner between the Palacio Nacional and the Ayuntamiento towards the Mexico City Museum. First though, right on the corner of the square, is the colonial-style modern building housing the **Supreme Court** (*Suprema Corte de Justicia*). Inside are three superb, bitter murals by Orozco – *Proletarian Battles*, *The National Wealth* and *Justice*. The latter, depicting justice slumped asleep on her pedestal while bandits rob the people of their rights, was not surprisingly unpopular with the judges and powers that be, and Orozco never completed his commission here.

The **Museo de la Ciudad de Mexico** (open Tues.-Sun. 9.30–7.30; free) is a couple of blocks further down, housed in the colonial palace of the Condes de Santiago de Calimaya. Its contents trace the history and development of the city from pre-historic to modern times, through everything from fossil remains to photographs of Villa and Zapata entering in Triumph to architectural blueprints for the future. Perhaps most interesting, though, are the models of Tenochtitlan at its peak, and the old maps and paintings showing the city and the lake as they were, the gradual spread of development and disappearance of the water. There are also plans which superimpose the map of ancient Tenochtitlan onto the modern streets – giving some idea of its location and extent. On the topmost storey is preserved the studio of the landscape artist Joaquin Clausell, its wall plastered in portraits and little sketches which he scribbled between working on his real paintings. The Museum also presents a multi-media show (in Spanish) which describes the city's evolution – supposedly every morning at 11, but cancelled last time I went for lack of customers.

If you continue down Pino Suarez (notice the museum's cornerstone – a hefty plumed serpent obviously dragged from the ruins of some Aztec temple) you'll reach **Pino Suarez Metro station**, remarkable for the huge Aztec shrine which was uncovered here during construction and has been preserved as an integral part of the concourse. It dates from around the end of the fourteenth century, and was dedicated to Quetzalcoatl in his guise of Ehecatl, God of the Wind. From here a **subterranean walkway** runs back to the Zocalo metro station – there are almost always exhibitions down here, or market stalls, and thousands of people.

Before this, though, you should cross the road from the museum for a look at the church and hospital of **Jesus Nazareno**. The **hospital**, which is still in use and you're not really allowed to visit, was founded by Cortes himself in 1524 on the site where traditionally he first met Moctezuma. As such it's one of the oldest buildings in the city, if not anywhere in the country, and exemplifies the severe, fortress-like construction of the immediate post-Conquest years. The church, which contains the tomb of Cortes, has been substantially remodelled over the years. Its vaulting was decorated by Orozco with a fresco of the apocalypse, and around the upper walls with murals relating the Spanish Conquest.

Head east from here on Salvador or Uruguay and you get to the giant **market** area of La Merced, passing, on Uruguay, the beautiful cloister which is all that's left of the seventeenth-century **Convento de la Merced**. Westwards you can stroll down some fairly tatty old streets and eventually find yourself approaching the Zona Rosa, passing several smaller markets. It's much more interesting, however, to return to the Zocalo and strike down towards the Alameda from there.

Westwards: the Alameda and the Paseo de la Reforma

The streets which lead down from the Zocalo towards the Alameda – Tacuba, Cinco de Mayo, Madero, 16 de Septiembre and the lanes which cross them – are the most elegant in the city: least affected by any modern developments and lined with ancient buildings, with traditional cafes and shops, and with mansions converted to offices, banks or restaurants. Few of these merit any particular special attention, but it's a pleasant place simply to stroll around, lingering at whatever catches the eye.

On Madero you'll pass several former aristocratic palaces, given over to a variety of uses. At the corner of Bolivar stands the mansion built by mining magnate Jose de la Borda (see p. 227) for his wife, with a magnificent balcony. Close by on Bolivar, the **Spanish-Mexican Club** is a fine example of how the wealthy used to amuse themselves, and how some apparently still do. If you can talk your way in, the interior is superb – fitted out with Moorish-style dining rooms, vast ballrooms, enormous chandeliers and endless works of art, it's hard to believe it was only built at the beginning of this century: the sort of extreme which led to the downfall of the Diaz regime. Still further down Madero you'll find the **Palacio de Iturbide**, now occupied by *Banamex* and thoroughly restored (the banks seem to have the money for all the best restoration work). Originally the home of the Condes de Valparaiso in the eighteenth century, it was from 1821–23 the residence of the ill-fated 'emperor' Augstin de Iturbide.

In the next block, the last before you emerge at Bellas Artes and the Alameda, the Churrigueresque church of San Francisco lies opposite the famous **Casa de los Azulejos**. This is now a branch of *Sanborn's*, inside which, as well as the usual shopping, you'll find a restaurant in the glassed-over patio and a giant Orozco mural on the staircase. Most remarkable, though, is the exterior – clothed entirely in blue and white tiles from Puebla.

At the end of Madero you're at the extent of the colonial city centre, and standing between two of the most striking buildings in modern Mexico – the Torre Latino-Americano and the Palacio de las Bellas Artes – both, though it seems incredible to draw any comparison, products of this century. The steel and glass skyscraper of the **Torre Latino-Americano** was until very recently the tallest building in Mexico and, indeed, in the whole of Latin America. It's now been overtopped by the *Hotel de Mexico* (on Insurgentes Sur and still incomplete) and doubtless by others in South America, but it remains the city's outstanding landmark and a point of reference no matter where you are. In the unlikely event of a clear day, the views from the top are outstanding; if it's averagely murky you're better off going up after dark when the lights delineate the city far more clearly. There's a charge to go up to the top two floors (open 10 am – midnight) where there's a caged-in observation deck, a cafe, permanent crowds and, for some inexplicably bizarre reason, an aquarium – or you can go to the *Muralto* restaurant and bar on the 42nd floor for nothing. If you're really mean you could do this, catch the view, study the menu and decide not to eat after all, but if you have a drink you'll be able to sit in luxury and take it all in at your leisure for only two or three times what it costs to get to the *mirador*. On the way up you'll see plans explaining how the tower is built, and the proud boast that it is the tallest building in the world to have withstood a major earthquake. The general principle appears to be similar to that of an angler's float, with enormously heavy foundations bobbing around in the mushy soil under the capital, keeping the whole thing upright.

It's certainly a more successful engineering achievement than the **Palacio de Las Bellas Artes**, which has very obviously subsided. On the other hand Bellas Artes is extremely beautiful, which you certainly couldn't say of the Tower. It was designed in 1901, at the height of the Diaz dictatorship, by the Italian architect Adamo Boari and constructed, in a grandiose Italian style of art-nouveau, of white marble imported from Italy. Building wasn't actually completed, however, until 1934, with the Revolution and several new planners come and gone. Now it's the headquarters of the National Institute of Fine Arts, venue for all the most important performances of classical music, opera or dance, home of the **Ballet Folklorico** (who perform here on Wednesday evenings and Sunday mornings), and a major Art Museum. It's worth getting to some performance in the theatre (preferably the Ballet Folklorico – see *Nightlife and Entertainment*) if only to see the amazing Tiffany glass curtain depicting the Valley of Mexico and the volcanoes.

The **art collections** (open Tues.–Sun. 11–7) are on the upper floors. In the galleries you'll find a series of exhibitions, permanent displays of Mexican art and temporary shows which can be anything from local art school graduates' work to major international extravaganzas. Of constant and abiding interest, however, are the great murals surrounding the central space. On the first floor are *Birth of our Nationality* and *Mexico Today* – dreamy, almost abstract works by Rufino Tamayo (for whom see under *Chapultepec*, below). Going up a level you're confronted by the unique sight of murals by Rivera, Orozco and Siqueiros gathered in the same place – along with the work of one Jorge Gonzales Camarena entitled *Liberation*. Rivera's *Man in control of the Universe* (or *Man at the Crossroads*), celebrating the liberating power of technology, was originally painted for the Rockefeller Centre in New York, but destroyed for being too leftist. This is Rivera's own copy. *Catharsis*, a huge, vicious work by Orozco, is in some ways a counterpoint to this. Siqueiro's three panels on the theme of *Democracy* are perhaps more powerful and original than either of them.

Around the back of Bellas Artes, at the corner of Tacuba and Lazaro Cardenas, you'll find the **Correo Central**, the main **Post Office**. Completed in 1908, this too was designed by Adamo Boari, but in a style much more consistent with the buildings around it. Look closely and you'll find a wealth of intricate detail, while inside it's full of richly carved wood. Directly behind the Post Office on Tacuba is the **Palacio de Mineria**, a neo-classical building completed right at the end of the eighteenth century, and now housing the mining authorities and a school for mining engineers. It makes an interesting contrast with the Post Office and with the National Art Museum (formerly the Palacio de Comunicaciones) directly opposite, the work of another Italian architect, Silvio Contri, in the first years of this century.

The **Museo Nacional de Arte** (open Tues.-Sun. 10–6) is set back from the street on a tiny plaza in which stands one of the city's most famous sculptures, *El Caballito*, portraying Carlos IV of Spain. This enormous bronze, the work of Manuel Tolsa, was originally erected in the Zocalo in 1803. In the intervening years it has graced a variety of sites and despite the unpopularity of the Spanish monarchy, and of the effete Charles IV in particular, is still regarded affectionately. The latest setting is appropriate, since Tolsa also designed the Palacio de Mineria. As for the museum itself, it's a massive collection of more than 1,000 works of Mexican art from pre-hispanic times to the present. If you're interested in art, this is a must – by far the most comprehensive presentation in the city – but there are few really great works and a lot of very average painting to wade through to find them. The city certainly has other art collections which are more exciting for the amateur.

From behind Bellas Artes, Lazaro Cardenas runs north towards the **Plaza Garibaldi** (see *Nightlife and Entertainment*) through an area crowded with seedy cantinas and eating places, theatres and burlesque shows. Walk on down Tacuba, though, which here becomes Av. Hidalgo, and you finally reach the **Alameda**. First laid out as a park at the end of the sixteenth century, and taking its name from the *alamos* (poplars) then planted, the Alameda had originally been an Aztec market and later became the site where the Inquisition burned its victims at the stake. Most of what you see now – formally laid-out paths and flowerbeds, ornamental statuary and fountains – recalls the last century when it was the fashionable place to stroll. It's still popular, always full of people, the haunt of ice-cream and sweet vendors, illuminated at night, and particularly crowded at weekends, but Chapultepec is where everyone goes now by choice. Here it's mostly a transient population – office workers taking lunch, shoppers resting their feet, messengers taking a short cut.

Overlooking the park from Av. Juarez are several large hotels, grand looking but also no longer as fashionable as they once were. In the main lobby of the *Hotel del Prado* is one of Rivera's most celebrated **murals**:

Dream of a Sunday Afternoon in the Alameda. It is an impressive tour de force – comprising almost every famous Mexican character from Cortes, his hands stained red with blood, to Rivera himself, portrayed as a child between his mother and daughter, out for a stroll in the park – but one suspects that its popularity with tour groups is as much to do with its relatively apolitical nature as for any superiority to Rivera's other works. The hotel organises lectures (free; check times at reception) which explain and describe the whole thing in great detail.

Also in the *Del Prado* is a small **crafts shop** run by *Fonart*, a government agency which promotes quality arts and crafts and helps the artisans with marketing and materials. There are two bigger locations very close by, one a short distance up Juarez towards Bellas Artes, the second on the opposite side of the road just beyond the park. On Juarez too, across from the park's semi-circular monument to Benito Juarez, is the **Museo de Artes y Industrias Populares** (open Mon.-Sat. 10–6; free), housed in the chapel of the former convent of Santa Clara. It has displays of craftworks, native art and traditional techniques, some ancient, most contemporary, and much of what is shown is also on sale.

Beyond the Alameda, Avenidas Juarez and Hidalgo lead on to the Paseo de la Reforma. Between them, at the far end of the park, lies the **Pinacoteca Virreinal** (open Tues-Sun. 10–5; free), a collection of colonial painting (*Virrey* being the Spanish Viceroy) in the glorious seventeenth-century monastery of San Diego. The galleries are mostly filled with florid religious works of the seventeenth and eighteenth centuries, but some are exquisitely executed while others are fascinating for their depiction of early missionary work, and all are superbly displayed around the church, chapel and cloister of the old monastery. There are occasional concerts here in the evening – mostly chamber music or piano recitals – and it's a very lovely setting for them too.

On Hidalgo along the north side of the Alameda are the churches of **Santa Veracruz** and **San Juan de Dios**, and behind the latter a small Mercado de Artesanias. Recently, though, this area has been boarded off while construction work goes on – presumably in an effort to shore the churches up and prevent any further subsidence. Continue along Hidalgo westwards and you'll find the *Hotel de Cortes* at the corner with the Paseo de la Reforma. The Hotel occupies a fine eighteenth-century mansion, stern from the outside but enclosing a lovely, tranquil patio: sadly it's far more expensive than it looks. Beyond Reforma, Hidalgo becomes the **Puente de Alvarado**, and it follows the line of one of the main causeways which led into Tenochtitlan, and along which the Spanish fled the city on the *Noche Triste* (Sad Night), July 10th 1520. Following the death of Moctezuma, and with his men virtually under siege in their quarters, Cortes decided to try to escape the city under cover of darkness. It was a disaster: the Aztecs cutting the bridges and attacking constantly from their canoes, killed all but 440 of the 1,300 Spanish soldiers who set out, and more than half their Indian allies. Greed, as much as anything, cost the Spanish troops their lives, for in trying to take their gold booty with them they were, in the words of Bernal Diaz, 'so weighed down by the stuff that they could neither run nor swim'. The street takes its name from Pedro de Alvarado, one of the last conquistadors to escape, crossing the broken bridge 'in great peril after their horses had been killed, treading on the dead men, horses and boxes'. Recently a hefty gold bar – exactly like those made by Cortes from melted-down Aztec treasures – was dug up here.

The church of **San Hipolito**, at the corner of Reforma and Puente de Alvarado, was founded by the Spanish soon after their eventual victory, both as a celebration and to commemorate the events of the *Noche Triste*. The present building dates from 1602, though over the years it's been damaged by earthquakes and rebuilt, and has taken on a distinct list. A little further down is the baroque, eighteenth-century church of **San Fernando**, by the plaza of the same name. Once one of the richest churches in the city, San Fernando has been stripped over the years like so many others, and the chief interest is the highly decorative facade. Continuing on the same street you'll find, at number 50 on the left-hand side, the **Museo de San Carlos** (open Tues.-Sun. 10–5; free) which houses the country's oldest art collection, started in 1785 by Carlos III of Spain, and comprising largely European works of the seventeenth and eighteenth centuries. Travelling exhibitions are also frequently based here. The building itself is a very beautiful neo-classical design of Manuel Tolsa's, and has had something of a bizarre history. Its inhabitants have included the French Marshal Bazaine, sent by Napoleon III to advise the Emperor Maximilian – who presented the house to him as a wedding present on his marriage to a Mexican beauty – and the hapless Mexican general and sometime dictator, Santa Ana. Later it served for a time as a cigarette factory.

Leaving the Alameda on Juarez, you can see the massive, ugly bulk of the **Monumento a la Revolucion** ahead of you. The first couple of blocks, though, are dull enough – commercial streets heavy with banks, offices, travel agents, expensive shops. The junction with Reforma is a major crossing of the ways, and is surrounded by modern skyscrapers and one older one – the marvellous **National Lottery building**. In here, at 8 pm on Mondays, Wednesdays and Fridays, you can watch the winning tickets being drawn in a wonderful carnival atmosphere, although the Lottery offices have been moved to a much duller steel and glass building opposite. Beyond Reforma, Juarez continues in one long block to the **Plaza de la Republica** and that vast monument. Originally intended to be a new home for the *Cortes* (or parliament) its construction was interrupted by the Revolution and never resumed – in the end they buried a few heroes of the Revolution under the mighty columns (including Presidents Madero and Carranza) and turned the whole thing into a memorial. Among the offices and large hotels around the plaza you'll find the **Fronton Mexico** where *Fronton* matches are held most evenings (see *Nightlife and Entertainment*).

The **Paseo de la Reforma** was laid out by Emperor Maximilian to provide Mexico with a boulevard to rival the great European capitals and as a ceremonial drive from his palace in Chapultepec to the city centre. Along the way it provided a new impetus, and direction, for the growing metropolis. The original length of the broad avenue ran simply from the park to the junction of Juarez, and although it has been extended in both directions, this stretch is still what everyone thinks of as Reforma. Reforma Norte, as the extension towards Guadalupe is known, is almost a term of disparagement – and while the street is just as wide and the traffic just as dense, you won't find people strolling here for pleasure. Real Reforma, though, remains *the* smart thoroughfare – ten lanes of traffic, lines of trees, imposing statues at every intersection. There are perhaps three or four of the original French-style, nineteenth-century houses surviving along its entire extent. Elsewhere even relatively new blocks are torn down to make way for yet newer, taller, more prestigious towers of steel, glass and mirrors.

It's a long walk – some 4 miles – from the Zocalo to the gates of Chapultepec, made more tiring by the altitude and the constant crush, noise and fumes of the traffic. You'd be well advised to take the bus – they're cheap enough and frequent enough to hop on and off at will. The *Glorietas*, roundabouts at the major intersections, each with a distinctive statue, provide easy landmarks along the way. First is the **Glorieta Colon**, with a statue of Christopher Columbus (*Cristobal Colon* in Spanish). Around the base of the plinth are carved various friars and monks who assisted Columbus in his enterprise or brought the Catholic faith to the Mexicans. The Plaza de la Republica is just off to the north here. Next comes the crossing of Insurgentes, nodal point of all the city's traffic, with **Cuauhtemoc**, last emperor of the Aztecs and leader of their resistance, poised aloof above it all in a plumed robe, clutching his spear, surrounded by warriors. Bas-relief engravings on the pedestal depict his torture and execution at the hands of the Spanish, desperate to discover where the Aztec treasures lay hidden. **El Angel**, a golden winged victory atop a column nearly 150 feet high, is the third to look out for – the place to get off the bus for the heart of the Zona Rosa. Finally, right by the entrance to the park, but shifted to one side of Reforma to make way for more traffic, stands a bronze **Diana**.

The **Zona Rosa** runs parallel to Reforma to the south – an area delineated by Reforma and Avenida Chapultepec, the park to the west and spilling across Insurgentes in the east. You can spot it by the street

names, famous cities all: Hamburgo, Londres, Genova, Liverpool. . . .
Packed into a tiny area here are hundreds of bars, restaurants, hotels and
above all shops, teeming with the city's wealthy and would-be elegant and
with vast numbers of tourists. You'll also find the highest concentration of
beggars and rip-offs here – there are official multi-lingual policemen
wandering around specifically to help the tourists (they wear little flag
emblems to denote which languages they speak) but there are also quantities of impressively uniformed unofficial guides whose only task is to
persuade you to go to whichever shop or market employs them. You
should come and look – for the constant activity (**street entertainers**,
especially around the corner of Hamburgo and Florencia), flash hotels
like the *Galeria Plaza* and incredible diversity of shops and places to eat
and drink, but remember that everything is very expensive. On the fringes
of the Zona you'll find the **Wax Museum** (*Museo de Cera*, Londres 6:
open daily 10–8), thoroughly and typically tacky, with a basement
chamber of horrors which includes Aztec human sacrifices. Entrance here
costs around ten times as much as any other museum in the city, but
that's still less than a dollar.

On the other side of Reforma, where the streets are named after rivers
(Tiber, Danubio etc.) is a much quieter, upmarket residential area where
many of the older embassies are based. You can spot the US embassy
(which is actually on Reforma) by the vast queues snaking around it
throughout the day. Near the British Embassy is the **Museo Venustiano
Carranza** (Lerma 35; open Mon.-Fri. 9.30–2.30; free). Housed in the
mansion which was the Mexico home of the revolutionary leader and
president, shot in 1920, it contains exhibits relating to his life and to the
Revolution. Not far away, just north of the junction of Reforma and
Insurgentes, the **Parque Sullivan** hosts open air exhibitions and sales of
paintings every Sunday: nothing of great quality, but a pleasant holiday
atmosphere prevails.

Chapultepec and the National Anthropology Museum

Chapultepec Park, or the *Bosques de Chapultepec*, is a vast green area –
some 1,000 acres in all, dotted with trees, scattered with fine museums,
with boating lakes, gardens, playing fields, a zoo – and a resort from the
pressures of the city for seemingly millions of Mexicans. Sundays, when
at least a brief visit is all but compulsory and many of the museums are
free, you can barely move for the throng. They call it, too, the lungs of
the city, and like the lungs of most of the inhabitants, its health leaves a
lot to be desired. Large areas of the park, towards the back where it's
less frequented, have been fenced off to give them a chance to recover
from the pounding they take from the crowds. There has even been talk

of sealing the whole place off for three years to give the grass a chance to grow back, the plants to recover their equilibrium. Whatever the hopes or fears of the authorities, though, this is never likely to happen – public outrage at the very suggestion has seen to that. Meanwhile it still manages to look pretty good and remains one of Mexico's most enduring attractions: some of the fanciest new developments in the city are going on around the edges, including the vast Hotels *Camino Real* and *El Presidente Chapultepec*, two of the most modern, elaborate and expensive you could find.

The rocky outcrop of **Chapultepec** (the Hill of the Locust), which lends its name to the entire area, is mentioned in Toltec mythology, but first gained historical significance in the thirteenth century when it was no more than another island among the lakes and salt marshes of the valley. Here the Mexica, still a wandering, savage tribe, made their first home – a very temporary one before they were defeated and driven off by neighbouring cities, provoked beyond endurance. And here they returned once Tenochtitlan's power was established, channelling water from the springs into the city, and turning Chapultepec into a summer resort for the emperor, with plentiful hunting and fishing around a fortified palace. Several Aztec rulers had their portraits carved into the rock of the hill: most were destroyed by the Spanish soon after the conquest.

The hill, crowned by Maximilian's very peaceful looking 'castle', confronts you as soon as you enter the park. In front of it stands the strange, six-columned monument to the **Niños Heroes**, commemorating the cadets who attempted to defend the castle (then a military academy) against the American invaders in 1847. According to the story, probably apocryphal, the last six flung themselves off the cliff wrapped in Mexican flags rather than surrender. The **Castillo** itself had been built only in 1785 as a summer retreat for the Spanish viceroy – until then it was the site of a hermitage established on the departure of the Aztec rulers. Its role as a military school followed Independence, but the present shape was dictated by Emperor Maximilian who remodelled it in the image of his Italian villa. Today it houses the National History Museum.

First, though, as you climb the hill, you pass the modern **Gallery of History** devoted to 'the Mexican people's struggle for liberty' (open Tues.-Sun. 9–5; free). Through the use of models, maps and dioramas, it tells the history of the constant wars which have beset the country – from Independence, through the American and French interventions to the Revolution. There are also murals by Siqueiros and Juan O'Gorman. The **Museo Nacional de Historia** (open daily 9–5), in the castle, is a much more traditional collection spread over two floors. The setting is very much part of the attraction, with many rooms retaining the opulent furnishings left behind by Maximilian and Carlota, or by later inhabitants with equally expensive tastes – notably Porfirio Diaz. Downstairs the

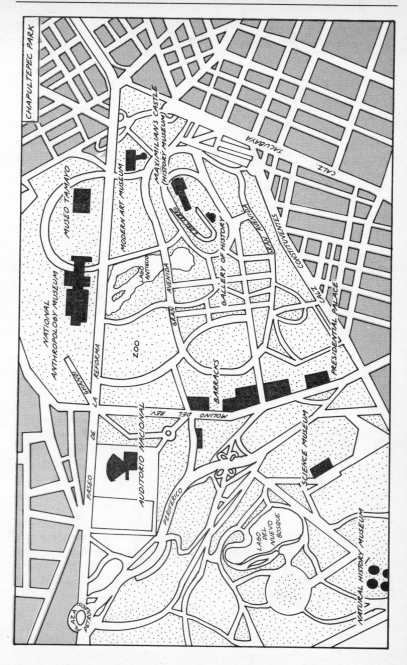

exhibits follow a straight historical progression, from a small collection of pre-hispanic objects and reproductions of Aztec codices, through weapons and paintings of the conquest and on to documents, pictures, memorabilia and patriotic relics from every era of Mexican development. There are several murals here too, including works by Orozco and Siqueiros, but the ones by Juan O'Gorman most directly attract attention for their single-minded, straight down the line political message. Upstairs is a more miscellaneous collection of objets d'art, jewellery, period costume, furniture, clocks and a host of other things – Maximilian's fabulously pompous state carriages among them. Traditionally there should also be wonderful views from here, across the city to Popocatépetl and Ixtaccíhuatl, but of course there never are.

The park's outstanding attraction – for many people the main justification for visiting the city at all – is the *Museo Nacional de Antropologia*, the **NATIONAL ANTHROPOLOGY MUSEUM**. It is beyond doubt one of the world's great museums, not only for its collection, which is vast, rich and diverse, but for the originality and practicality of its design. Opened in 1964, the exhibition halls surround a patio with a small pond shaded by a vast square concrete umbrella supported by a single slender pillar around which splashes an artificial cascade (or 'inverse fountain' as the architect describes it). The halls in turn are ringed by gardens, many of which contain outdoor exhibits. If you plan to rush it, or to spend most of a day here, you can follow the logical progression round from one to the next – but each room is devoted to a separate period or culture, and all open separately onto the central space, so it's easy enough, and far more satisfactory, to pick one or two to take in on each of several separate visits. Located about half a mile into the park beside the Paseo de la Reforma, you can take the bus virtually to its entrance, or walk easily from *Chapultepec* Metro station or any of the other museums at this end of the park. The entrance from Reforma is marked by a colossal statue of the Rain God Tlaloc – the story goes that its move here from its original home in the east of the city was accompanied by furious downpours in the midst of a drought. **Opening hours** are from 9–7 Tuesday to Saturday, 10–6 Sundays, closed every Monday – on Sundays the small entrance charge is reduced; cameras cost extra.

As you come into the **entrance hall** there's a bookshop selling postcards, souvenirs, books in several languages on Mexican culture, archaeology and history, and detailed guides to the museum – some of these are slightly dated (the Mexica room in particular has been rearranged to accommodate new finds from the Templo Mayor, and theories are constantly changing) but they do provide detailed descriptions of most of the important pieces. Straight ahead is a small circular space with temporary exhibitions, usually devoted to the latest developments in archaeology and often very interesting. More of these lie to the right, beyond Rufino Tamayo's mural of a battling jaguar and serpent, and here also are the library and museum offices as well as the small **Sala de Orientacion** which presents an audio-visual overview of the major ancient cultures. The ticket office, and the entrance to the museum proper, is by the huge glass doors to the right. You can get tickets here too for the regular guided tours – free in Spanish, or for a fee in English, French or German. They're very rushed, but do get you round the whole thing with some form of explanation: labelling inside is meagre and in Spanish only.

The full **tour of the museum** starts on the right-hand side with three **introductory rooms** explaining what anthropology is, the nature of and relationship between the chief Meso-American cultures, and the region's pre-history. Skip or skim them if you're in a hurry. They're followed on the right-hand side by halls devoted to the pre-Classic, Teotihuacan and Toltec cultures. At the far end is the vast **Mexica** (Aztec)* room, followed around the left wing by Oaxaca (Mixtec and Zapotec), Gulf of Mexico (Olmec), **Maya*** and the cultures of the North and West. The first floor is given over to the ethnography collections – devoted to the life and culture of the various Indian groups today: stairs lead up from the first and last rooms on each side. Downstairs, behind the hall devoted to the cultures of the North and West, is a cafeteria/restaurant – expensive but welcome.

The **Pre-Classic** room covers the development of the first cultures in the Valley of Mexico and surrounding highlands – pottery and clay figurines from these early agricultural communities predominate. Notice especially the small female figures from Tlatilco (a site in the suburbs), probably related to some form of fertility or harvest rites, and the amazing acrobat, also from Tlatilco. Later, with the development of more formal religion, images of gods begin to appear. Several of these, from Cuicuilco in the south of the city, depict Huehueteotl, the Old God or God of Fire, as an old man with a brazier on his back. A small model of the circular pyramid of Cuicuilco stands in the garden outside.

The next hall is devoted to **Teotihuacan** (see p. 212), the first great city in the Valley of Mexico. Growing sophistication is immediately apparent in the more elaborate nature of the pottery vessels and the use of new materials, shells, stone and jewels. There's a full scale reproduction of part of the Temple of Quetzalcoatl, brightly polychromed as it would originally have been, and copies of some of the frescoes which adorned the city, including *The Paradise of Tlaloc*, a depiction of the heaven reserved for warriors and ball players who died in action. Many new gods appear too – as well as more elaborate versions of Huehueteotl there are representations of Tlaloc, of his companion Chalchiutlicue,

---

* These two, if you have limited time, are the highlights: what else you see should depend on where you're going to go. But every hall has at least one outstanding feature.

goddess of rivers and lakes, of Mictlantecuhtli (a stone skull, originally inlaid with gems) God of Death and of Xipe Totec, a God of Spring, clothed in the skin of a man flayed alive as a symbol of regeneration.

The **Toltec room** actually begins with objects from Xochicalco, a city near modern Cuernavaca which flourished between the fall of Teotihuacan and the heyday of Tula. The large stone carvings and pottery show distinct Mayan influence: particularly lovely is the simple stone head of a macaw, similar to ones found on Mayan ball-courts in Honduras. Highlights of the section devoted to Tula itself are the large stone carvings, including one of the Atlantean columns from the main temple, representing a warrior. Also of note are the *Chac-mool*, a reclining figure with a receptacle on his stomach in which sacrificial offerings were placed, symbolising the divine messenger who delivered them to the gods; the small human figures which acted as flag poles when a standard was inserted into the hole between their clasped hands; the stone relief of a dancing jaguar; and the exquisite mother-of-pearl and clay mosaic of a coyote's head with a bearded man emerging from its mouth – possibly a warrior in a head-dress.

Next comes the biggest and richest of them all, the **Mexica**, characterised above all by massive yet intricate stone sculpture, but also displaying pottery, small stone objects, even wooden musical instruments. Many of these objects have been or are being rearranged to make way for new finds from the Templo Mayor. At the entrance, at least until recently, are two of the finest pieces: the *Ocelocuauhxicalli*, a jaguar with a hollow in its back in which the hearts of human sacrifices were placed; and the *Teocalli de la Guerra Sagrada* (Temple of the Sacred War) a model of an Aztec pyramid decorated with many of the chief gods and with symbols relating to the calendar. There are hundreds of other powerful pieces – most of the vast Aztec pantheon is represented – with everywhere snakes, eagles and human hearts and skulls as prominent themes, but the centrepiece is the massive (24-tonne) **Stone of the Sun**, the *Aztec Calendar Stone*. The latter, popular name is not strictly accurate, for this is much more a vision of the Aztec cosmos, completed under Moctezuma only a few years before the Spanish arrived. It was dug up in the Zocalo in 1790 and for years was propped up against the walls of the Cathedral. For a detailed description, wait till a guided tour comes past, but briefly: in the centre is the Sun God, Tonatiuh, with a tongue in the form of a sacrificial knife and claws holding human hearts on each side, representing the need for human sacrifice to nourish the sun. Around him are symbols for the four previous incarnations of the sun – a jaguar, wind, water and fiery rain; this whole central conglomeration forming the sign for the date on which the fifth world would end (as indeed, with defeat by the Spanish, it fairly accurately did). Encircling all this are hieroglyphs representing the twenty days of the Aztec month and other symbols of cosmic importance, and the whole thing is surrounded by two serpents. One final statue to notice, if only as a counterpoint to the viciousness and hopelessness of most of the Aztec gods, is Xochipilli, the god of love and flowers, dance and poetry. You'll come across him just before the exit, wearing a mask and sitting cross-legged on a throne strewn with flowers.

Moving round to the third side you reach the halls devoted to cultures not based in the highlands of the centre, starting, in the corner of the museum, with the Zapotec and Mixtec people of **Oaxaca**. Although the two cultures evolved side by side, the Zapotecs flourished earliest (from around 900BC to 800AD) as accomplished architects with an advanced scientific knowledge, and also as makers of magnificent pottery with a pronounced Olmec influence. From around 800 many of their chief sites were taken over by the Mixtecs whose over-riding talents were as crafts-men and artists, working in metal, precious stone and clay. The great site for both is Monte Alban (see p. 288). Of the Zapotec collection notice above all the fine sense of movement in the human figures: the reproduction of part of the carved facade of the *Temple of the Dancers* at Monte Alban; a model of a temple with a parrot sitting in it; vases and urns in the form of various gods; and the superb jade mask representing the bat god. Among the Mixtec objects are many beautifully polychromed clay vessels including a cup with a hummingbird perched on its rim, and jewellery of gold and turquoise. There are also repro-ductions of Zapotec and Mixtec tombs, showing how many of the finer small objects were discovered.

Next the **Gulf of Mexico room**, in which are displayed some of the treasures of Olmec art – considered the mother culture of Mexico for its civilisation as early as 1500BC, which provided much of the basic for later Teotihuacan and Maya development – as well as objects produced in this region during the Classic period. Olmec figures are delightful, but display many puzzling features, in particular their strongly negroid (or childlike as some would have it) features: nowhere better displayed than in one of the famed colossal Olmec heads (see p. 357) in the garden outside. You can also see evidence of the deliberate deformation of the skull and teeth in many pieces. Outstanding are the statue known as *The Wrestler* – arms akimbo as if on the point of starting a bout – and the many tiny objects in jade and other polished stones: notice the group of sixteen little figures and six ceremonial axes arranged to represent some religious ceremony. Of the later cultures many fine figures and excellent pottery survive. The two most celebrated are a statue of Huehueteotl, looking thoroughly grouchy with a brazier perched on his head, and the so-called *Huastec Adolescent*, a young Huastec Indian priest of Quetzal-coatl (perhaps the God himself) with an elaborately decorated body and a child on his back.

The Hall devoted to the **Maya** (see pp. 312 and 332) is perhaps the most varied of all, reflecting the longest lived and widest spread of the Meso-American cultures. In many ways it's a disappointment, since their greatest achievements were in architecture and in the decoration of their temples – many of which, unlike those of the Aztecs, are still standing. Nevertheless, there are reproductions of several buildings, or parts of them, friezes and columns taken from them, and substantial collections of jewellery, pottery and minor sculpture. Steps lead down into a section devoted to burial practices, including a reproduction of the Royal Tomb at Palenque (p. 306) with many of the objects found there – especially the prince's jade death mask. Outside, several small temples from relatively obscure sites are reproduced, the Temple of Paintings from Bonampak among them. Three rooms are entirely covered in frescoes representing the coronation of a new prince, a great battle, and the subsequent punishments and celebrations: very much easier to visit than the originals, and in far better condition.

Finally, on the ground floor, there's a large room devoted to the **North** and the **West** of the country. Northern societies on the whole developed few large centres, remaining isolated nomadic or agricultural communities – the small quantities of pottery, weapons and jewellery which have survived show a close affinity with Indian tribes of the American southwest. The west was far more developed, but it too has left relatively few traces and many of the best examples of Tarascan culture (see p. 109) remain in Guadalajara.* Among the highlights here are some delightful small human and animal figurines in stone and clay, a Tarascan *Chac-Mool*, and a copper mask of Xipe Totec representing a flayed human face.

To get to the **Ethnography Section**, cross the courtyard back towards the beginning of the museum before climbing the stairs – otherwise you'll be going round in reverse order. The rooms relate as far as possible to those below them, showing through photographs, models, maps and examples of local crafts the lifestyle of surviving Indian groups in the areas today. Regional dress and reproductions of various types of hut and cabin form a major part of this inevitably rather sanitised look at the poorest people in Mexico, and there are also objects relating to their more important cults and ceremonies.

The rest of the park: and more museums

The enormous success of the Anthropology Museum has led to a spate of other audacious modern exhibition halls being set up in the park. Two are very close by.

---

* In Mexico itself, the Museo Anahuacalli too has a collection of Tarascan objects at least the equal of those here.

The **Museo de Arte Moderno** (Modern Art Museum – open Tues.-Sun. 10–6) is not far from the entrance to the park between Reforma and the Niños Heroes monument. Two low circular buildings linked by a corridor house a substantial permanent collection of twentieth-century Mexican and Latin American art including works by Rivera, Orozco and Siqueiros, as well as landscapes of the Valley of Mexico by Jose Velasco (one of Rivera's teachers) and hauntingly surreal canvasses by Frida Kahlo (Rivera's wife). Often though, it's the temporary exhibitions which prove more arresting. The garden outside, fenced off from the rest of the park, has been turned into a sculpture park.

Nearby, on the other side of Reforma and up towards the Anthropology Museum, another collection of modern art graces the **Museo Rufino Tamayo** (same hours) – this time an internationally-based show. It was built by, and stocked with the collection of, *Rufino Tamayo*, an artist whose work in murals and on smaller projects is far more abstract and less political than the Big Three, but who was nevertheless more or less their contemporary and enjoys an international reputation almost as high. There is much of his own work here, and exhibits of his techniques and theories, but also an impressive collection of European and American twentieth-century art – most of it from Tamayo's private collection. Artists represented include Picasso, Magritte, Francis Bacon and Henry Moore.

Less highbrow diversions are on offer at the **Zoo**, on Reforma beyond the Anthropology Museum, which retains the distinction of being the only place outside China to have successfully bred Giant Pandas (at least naturally – several others now have test-tube pandas). Indeed there seems to be a veritable production line of the beasts – every time you visit the city there are posters advertising a new baby bear (*Osito Panda*). This must prove something: Chapultepec Zoo owes nothing to modern theories of creating a natural environment and everything to the old-fashioned view that the animals are there to be put in cages and stared at. Perhaps, when you add the altitude and the pollution, it's simply that pandas thrive in hostile conditions. Near here too is a small Children's Zoo, the largest lake, and, a little further up Reforma, the **Botanical Gardens**.

On the far side of the gardens Reforma crosses Molino del Rey, a street named for the major battle here during the Mexican-American War, passes the *Auditorio* and leaves the park past the Plaza Petroleos, a complex of modern skyscrapers surrounding a monument to the nationalisation of the oil industry. Beyond, it heads into Las Lomas, an expensive suburb whose luxury villas are mostly hidden behind high walls and heavy security gates. The **Auditorio Nacional** is a major venue for dance, theatre and music events, with a couple of small theatres and the enormous National Auditorium.

If you head south on Molino del Rey you get towards the new section of the park (*Nuevo Bosques de Chapultepec* or *Chapultepec, Segunda seccion*) which, while considerably less attractive, does offer two more museums, an amusement park and a restaurant which is one of the city's more daring pieces of modern architecture. On Molino del Rey itself though, you first pass the **Presidential Palace**, *Los Pinos*, surrounded by barracks full of presidential guards. This, plus the fact that much of the surrounding park is also fenced off to recuperate, makes it extremely difficult to walk from one side to the other, especially when you add the impossibility of crossing the Periferico. It's much easier to either take the Reforma bus out to the Plaza Petroleos and walk down from there, or to get a bus (No. 30) from Metro Chapultepec along Av. Constituyentes, which skirts the southern edge of the park.

Right by where this bus drops you is the **Museo de Historia Natural** (Museum of Natural History – open every day from 10 to 5), ten interconnecting domes filled with displays on nature and conservation, biology and geology, and breakdowns of Mexico's mineral wealth, flora and fauna. Modern and well presented, it's particularly popular with kids. From here there's a miniature 'railway' which will take you round the new part of the park, or it's not far to walk. Head away from the road and you'll pass the artificial lake by which stands the remarkable *Restaurante del Lago*, stunning on the inside with its huge windows looking out over the fountain, but pricey (and the sort of place where men are expected to wear a jacket and tie). Underneath the fountain (the *Fuente Lerma*) is an underwater painting by Rivera. Beyond the lake you can see the rollercoaster and giant wheel of the **Amusement Park**, and beside this the **Museo Tecnologico** (Science Museum – open Tues.-Sat. 9–5, Sun. 9–2; free).

South to the suburbs

Mexico spreads itself furthest to the south, and here, among a series of old villages swallowed by the urban sprawl, are some of the most enticing destinations outside the centre. The colonial suburbs of Coyoacan and San Angel, each with a couple of worthwhile museums, make a tranquil respite from the city centre's hustle, and a startling contrast to the ultra-modern bravado of the architecture of the University and the residential area of the Pedregal. There are echoes of ancient Mexico too in the archaeological sites of Copilco and Cuicuilco, in the 'floating gardens' of Xochimilco, final remains of the great valley lakes, and in Diego Rivera's remarkable collection of antiquities in the Museo Anahuacalli.

It's not at all difficult to get out to any of these sites on public transport (detailed below), but getting from one to the other can be tricky if you're cutting across the main north-south routes. It's not impossible, but it can be worth taking a few short taxi rides – from San Angel to Coyoacan for example, or from Coyoacan to the Rivera Museum. If you're really pushed, and want to see as much as possible in a day or even an afternoon, you could consider getting a tourist taxi to take you round the lot. If you bargain furiously this may not be as expensive as it sounds, indeed it sometimes seems that you can barely be paying for the petrol used. Alternatively, of course, there are coach tours run by several of the bigger travel agencies in the Zona Rosa.

The main approach is along **Insurgentes Sur**, where you'll find a constant stream of buses and peseros heading for San Angel and the University City. Their main destinations should be chalked up, or on a card, on the windscreen – look for *San Angel* or *Ciudad Universitaria* (often simply *C.U.* or *UNAM* for *Universidad Autonomia de Mexico*) in the first instance. Other main terminals for heading south are the bus stands by Metro Chapultepec or at Metro Taxqueña (the end of Line 2) for services along the Calzada de Tlalpan and to the south-west of the city, above all to Xochimilco.

Insurgentes, however, is interesting in its own right and the most direct approach: leaving behind the Glorieta de Insurgentes (the roundabout surrounding Insurgentes Metro station) it runs almost perfectly straight all the way out to the University, lined throughout with huge department stores and shopping malls, cinemas, restaurants and office blocks. Not far from the centre you pass, on the right, the enormous **Hotel de Mexico** and the garish **Polyforum Cultural Siqueiros**: the hotel is the tallest building in the city and the complex taken as a whole is surely the ugliest. The Polyforum, designed and decorated by David Siqueiros, is certainly way over the top: its exterior plastered in brash paintings designed by Siqueiros and executed by some thirty young artists, the interior containing what is allegedly the world's largest mural (about 4,500 square meters of it) painted by Siqueiros alone. If you go in (open 10–9 daily; expensive) there's no excessive effort involved in seeing this massive work – entitled *The March of Humanity on Earth and Towards the Cosmos* – since the floor revolves to let you take it all in. A complete explanation is provided by the daily Son et Lumière performance (4pm in Spanish, 6pm in English) which brings out the full impact of the changing perspectives and use of sculptural techniques. Elsewhere, the building also houses visiting art exhibitions and a sizeable display of crafts, on sale but very expensive. The whole thing was financed by one Manuel Suarez, an extremely wealthy businessman who intended it as a further attraction for his gargantuan hotel, along with enormous conference and sports facilities. Unfortunately the hotel is not yet open and shows no signs of completion in the near future, although the revolving rooftop restaurant and disco (both extremely expensive) have been operating for years.

Beyond this monster you shortly pass, on the same side, a large sports centre where the **Estadio Nacional**, a 65,000-seat soccer stadium, and the **Plaza Mexico**, the largest bullring in the world (holding 50,000) are situated. Finally, just before you reach San Angel, comes the **Teatro de los Insurgentes**, its facade covered in a huge mosaic designed by Diego Rivera depicting assorted personalities from Mexican history and culture. Along the top are ranged *Los Insurgentes* (the insurgents of Mexico's War of Independence) Hidalgo and Morelos, along with Benito Juarez and Emiliano Zapata.

San Angel and the Pedregal

From the choked traffic of Insurgentes at its junction with Avenida La Paz it's only a short walk up to the colonial charm of **San Angel** with its markets and ancient mansions around flower-draped patios. A very exclusive place to live, it's also a highly popular spot to visit (especially on Saturdays for the Bazar Sabado) and is packed with little restaurants and cafes where you can sit outside and watch the crowds go by.

Climb La Paz up to Av. Revolucion and you'll find, on the left, the old Carmelite Convent – now the **Museo del Carmen** (open Tues.–Sun. 10–6). There's a collection of colonial religious paintings and sculpture here, and mummies in the crypt, but the convent itself is the chief attraction, a lovely example of early seventeenth-century architecture with domes covered in multi-coloured (predominantly yellow) tiles and an almost tropical garden in the cloister. Heading up Revolucion to the right, past a small flower market, you reach the **Museo de Arte Alvar y Carrillo Gil** (open Tues.-Sun. 11–7), a small, somewhat incongruous and surprisingly good museum of modern art. There are works by Mexicans including Rivera, Orozco and Siqueiros, and an international collection which takes in Rodin, Picasso, Kandinsky and Paul Klee.

If you cross straight over Revolucion from the Convent and continue up the hill, the centre of San Angel and the oldest mansions lie ahead. **Plaza San Jacinto** is the target, a delightful square which is the centrepiece of the **Bazar Sabado** and animated throughout the week. Initially the Saturday market was based in one of the mansions on the square, and this still opens every weekend selling upmarket crafts and artworks, but nowadays there are stalls spilling over into all the surrounding streets with fairground rides and freak shows (the half man/half shark when I was last there as well as assorted tattooed and bearded ladies). Also on the Plaza is the **Casa del Risco** (sometimes known as the *Centro Cultural Isidro Fabela* – open Tues.-Sun. 10–6) an eighteenth-century mansion in which is displayed the said Isidro Fabela's collection of antique furniture and paintings, with an extraordinary fountain in the patio made from old porcelain plates and cups, broken and unbroken.

Not far away, on the Avenida Altavista, is the famous *San Angel Inn*, a luxurious restaurant in the restored **Hacienda de San Angel**. Expensive, and tending to be packed with tourists since it's included on many day tour itineraries, it's nevertheless worth visiting for the lovely gardens and courtyards. The food, if you decide you can afford it, is very good too. Beyond San Angel you can head south through the *Jardines del Pedregal de San Angel*, more often known simply as **El Pedregal**. The Pedregal of the name is actually a vast lava flow which spreads across from here through the University City and on to the south of Coyoacan, but the section south of San Angel is the thickest, the most craggy and dramatic. It was regarded as a completely useless stretch of land, the haunt of bandits and brigands, until in the early 1950s an architect named Luis Barragan began to build extraordinarily imaginative houses here, using the uneven lava as a feature. Now it's filled with the most amazing collection of luxury homes – you're not allowed to build here unless you can afford a sufficiently large piece of land and an architect to design your house – which have become a tourist attraction in themselves. Coach parties ride through in much the same way as they do in Beverly Hills or Hollywood, spotting the homes of the famous. Public transport up here is hard, though there are buses from San Angel, so if you're really into modern architecture you might try getting a taxi to drive you round for half an hour or so.

Coyoacan: Trotsky and Frida Kahlo

On the other side of Insurgentes from San Angel, some distance away, lies **Coyoacan** – another colonial township which has been swallowed by the city. Even before the Spanish Conquest it was a sizeable place, the capital of a small kingdom on the shores of the lake which had been subjugated by the Aztecs in the mid-fifteenth century. Cortes based himself in Coyoacan during the siege of Tenochtitlan, and continued to live here while the old city was torn down and construction began on the new capital of Nueva España. It remains very peaceful, far less visited than San Angel, and with a couple of lovely plazas on which stand the ancient church of San Juan and a small Palacio Muncipal said to have been built by Cortes himself. You can get to Coyoacan from San Angel on buses heading down Altavista by the San Angel Inn (or more easily by taxi) or from the centre from Metro Chapultepec, Insurgentes, or Av. Cuauhtemoc. In each case look for *Coyoacan* or *Colonia del Valle/ Coyoacan*. There's also a new metro station (*Bancomer*) on the extension of line 3.

The **Museo Frida Kahlo** (open Tues.-Sun. 10–6) is just a few minutes walk from the centre, six blocks along Av. Centenario and then down Calle Londres to the right – it's painted bright blue and hard to miss. Kahlo was an artist whose morbid, dream-like works reflect the pain of her own life – a polio victim who suffered severe injuries in an accident, she spent much of her later life confined to a wheelchair or to bed or in hospital. The products of that experience – grisly, self-obsessed canvasses

– almost always feature Kahlo herself: a fixed, almost beatific expression on her face above a body always sliced open, mutilated or crippled in some way. This was her family home (where she was born in 1910) and she later returned to live here with Diego Rivera from 1929 to 1954. As well as her own paintings – the best of which are frequently off in touring exhibitions – the museum contains early Rivera drawings and many mementoes of their life together and their joint interest in Mexico's artistic heritage. It reflects too, in its extraordinary decoration, littered with pre-hispanic artefacts and more modern folk items (in particular bizarre papier-mâché animals and figures), the coterie of artists and intellectuals of which they were centre in the 1930s and 1940s. Trotsky stayed here for a while and later settled nearby (see below), and D. H. Lawrence too was a frequent visitor to friends in Coyoacan, though he had little political or artistic sympathy with Rivera and Kahlo – or with Trotsky for that matter. Taken as a whole, the house is a fascinating insight into the social and intellectual background of Mexican art in the aftermath of the revolution.

Trotsky's House (the *Casa de Trotsky*) is not far away at Viena 45 near the corner of Morelos – about three blocks down and a couple to the left. Here the genius of the Russian revolution and organiser of the Red Army lived and worked in exile, and here Stalin's long arm finally caught up to him, to stifle the last fears of opposition. It's a bizarre story, with a suitably chilling setting, the house a veritable fortress behind steel gates and shutters, high blank walls and watch-towers. Incongruously surrounding it now are the bourgeois homes of a prosperous suburb, but to enter Trotsky's house you still have to ring at those great steel gates and wait to be admitted, almost as if even now they feared a fresh assault on the great man. The place is as he left it, if rather dustier and more depressing: the books on the shelves, his glasses smashed on the desk, and all the trappings of a fairly comfortable ordinary life. Except for the bullet holes: and the steel shutters and bullet proof doors.

The first attempt on Trotsky's life here, which left more than seventy scars in the plaster of the bedroom walls, came at 4am on the 24th May 1940. A heavily armed group (led allegedly by the painter David Siqueiros, who had been a commander in the Spanish Civil War) overcame the guards and pumped more than 200 shots into the house: an attack which Trotsky, his wife and son survived by the simple expedient of hiding under their beds. After this, the house, already heavily guarded, was fortified still further. But the assassin was already a regular visitor who had been carefully building up contacts for nearly two years: posing as the businessman boyfriend of a trusted Trotskyist who was being slowly converted to the cause, bringing presents for the wife and kids. Although never wholly trusted, it seemed natural when he turned up on the afternoon of August 20th with an article which he wanted Trotsky to look over: Trotsky invited him into the study. About 30 seconds later, the notorious ice-pick (the blunt end), which had been concealed under the killer's coat, smashed into Trotsky's skull. He died some 24 hours later, in hospital after an operation. His brain, they say, was vast. The killer, who called himself Frank Jackson and claimed to be Belgian, never explained his actions or even confessed to his true indentity – Jaime Ramon Mercader del Rio.

This house is virtually the only memorial to Trotsky anywhere in the world – his small tomb stands in the gardens – and it's a fairly sad one. Rarely visited, suffering from neglect and the lack of funds for its upkeep, it gathers dust behind its impregnable, ineffectual defences.

Copilco, Cuicuilco and the University City

Beyond Coyoacan and San Angel, Insurgentes enters the great lava field of the Pedregal. On the left here, shortly before the University, lies the archaeological site of **Copilco** (open Tue.-Sun. 10–5; easiest reached by Metro Line 3 to *Copilco*). Digging through the lava here, archaeologists discovered some of the earliest remains in the Valley of Mexico – several tombs and evidence of a simple community (pottery, clay figurines, stone implements) dating from around 1500BC and abandoned well before it was buried by the volcano. The tunnels created by the excavations have been turned into a small museum in which you can see the skeletons – some crushed by the weight of the lava – and many of the objects found. Among them are *Metates*, small slabs of stone for grinding corn, virtually identical to those used in rural areas today for preparing tortillas.

Continuing down Insurgentes you emerge in the **University City** (*Ciudad Universitaria*) dominated by the astonishing twelve-storey **library**. Each face of this rectangular tower is covered in a mosaic fresco designed by Juan O'Gorman – mostly natural stone with a few tiles or glass to supply colours which would otherwise have been unavailable. It represents the artist's vision of the country's progression through history: on the larger north and south faces pre-hispanic and colonial Mexico; on the west wall the present and the University coat-of-arms; on the east the future ranged around a giant atom. It's altogether remarkable how this has been incorporated as an essential feature of the building – at first it appears that there are no windows at all, but look closely and you'll see that in fact they're an integral part of the design, appearing as eyes, mouths or as windows of the buildings in the mural.

More or less beside this are the long, low **administration buildings** (*Rectoria*) with a giant mural in high relief (or a 'sculptural painting') by Siqueiros, intended to provide a moving perspective as you walk past or drive by on Insurgentes. At the front here too are the University Theatre and the **museum** (*Museo Universitario de Ciencias y Artes*; open Tues.-Sun. 10–2 and 4–9), a wide-ranging general collection which often has interesting temporary exhibits. Behind them spread out the enormous grounds of the main campus, starting with a large esplanade known as the Plaza Mayor, with sculptural groups dotted around a shallow artificial pond. Towards the back there are more murals adorning the Faculties of **Science** and **Medicine** and if you continue past these you reach another grassy area where are the **Botanical Gardens** and several large free-standing walls against which the students play fronton.

After some thirty years of use, parts of the campus are beginning to show their age: certainly it's no longer the avant-garde sensation it was when it opened – but it remains a remarkable architectural achievement. The whole thing was built in just five years (1950–5) under the Presidency of Miguel Aleman, and is now one of the largest universities in the world. It's also the oldest on the American continent. Granted a charter by Philip II in 1551, the University of Mexico occupied a succession of sites in the city centre (including the Hospital de Jesus Nazareno and what is now the Escuela Nacional Preparatoria), was closed down several times in the nineteenth century and was finally granted its present status as the *Universidad Nacional Autonoma de Mexico* in 1929.

Directly across Insurgentes from the main University buildings is the sculptured oval of the 100,000 seater *Estadio Olimpico*. The main facade is decorated with a mosaic relief by Diego Rivera, representing the development of human potential through sport, and any taxi driver will tell you that the **Olympic Stadium's** curious shape was deliberately designed to look like a giant Mexican sombrero. This I don't believe for a second, but it is undeniably odd – half sunk into the ground as if dropped here from a great height, and slightly warped in the process.

Ciudad Universitaria buses stop at a terminus right in front of the main complex. You can also get here by the Metro (*Universidad*; line 3) in which case you'll be right at the back of the campus, barely in sight of some modern blocks housing schools of engineering and physics, and have to walk all the way through, past the fronton courts and medical faculty, to reach the library.

To get to the pyramid of **Cuicuilco** you want to carry on down Insurgentes (buses marked *Tlalpan*) to where it crosses the great *Periferico* ring-road – the site is just beyond the junction (there are also buses round the Periferico, look for *Perisur* or *Villa Olimpica*). If you follow the Periferico round here, you'll see pieces of sculpture at regular intervals by the roadside – each was a gift from a different country at the time of the 1968 Olympics – and the old Olympic Village is also out here, now a high-rise residential area. The site itself, however, is dominated by the circular temple clearly visible from the road. This is much the oldest construction of such scale known in Central Mexico, abandoned at the time of the eruption of Xitle (the small volcano which created the Pedregal – around 100–300AD) just as Teotihuacan was beginning to develop.

Not a great deal is known about most of the site, much of which has been buried by modern housing, completing the work of the lava, but other structures have been uncovered, notably at the Olympic Village. The pyramid itself is composed of three sloping tiers (of a probable original five) about 17 meters high by 100 in diameter, approached by a ramp and a stairway. A small museum on the site (open daily 9–5) displays objects found here and at contemporary settlements.

Xochimilco – lazy Sunday afternoons

The 'floating gardens of Xochimilco' can provide one of the most memorable experiences in the city – for all that the canals are heavily polluted, their level dropping alarmingly year by year – it remains the most popular Sunday outing for thousands of Mexicans and a place filled every weekend with the most intense carnival atmosphere. It's also the one place where you get some feel of the ancient city (or at least an idealised view of it) with its waterborne commerce, thriving markets and dazzling colour. **Hire a boat**, its superstructure decorated with an arch of paper flowers, and you'll be punted around miles of canals, continually assaulted by Indian women in tiny canoes selling flowers or fruit, or with a precarious charcoal brazier burning under a pile of tortillas, chicken and chile, or by larger vessels bearing entire mariachi bands in their full finery who, for a small fee, will grapple alongside you and blast out a couple of numbers.

The floating gardens themselves are no more floating than the Titanic: following the old Aztec methods of making the lake fertile these *chinampas* are formed by a raft of mud and reeds, firmly rooted to the bottom by the plants. As well as amusing the hordes of visitors, the area is still a very important market gardening and flower producing centre for the city – if you wander the streets of the town you'll find garden centres everywhere, and wonderful flowers and fruit in the market (though whether it's healthy to eat food raised on these filthy waters is open to question). Off the huge central plaza is the lovely sixteenth-century church of **San Bernardino**, full on Sundays of a succession of people paying homage and leaving offerings at one of its many chapels, and in the plaza itself there are usually bands playing, or mime artists entertaining the crowds.

For the easiest approach to Xochimilco, take the Metro to *Taxqueña* (line 2) and from there a bus, pesero or the red tram. There are also buses direct from the centre, down Insurgentes and around the Periferico or straight down the Calzada de Tlalpan: on Sundays many extra services are laid on. To get a boat follow the *embarcadero* signs: what you pay depends on the size of the punt, how long you want to go for, and most importantly your skill at bargaining (especially on a weekday when there are few people about). Since you pay by the boat it's much cheaper to get a group together, and probably more enjoyable too – remember that there are likely to be sundry extras including the cold beers thoughtfully provided by the boatman, and any flowers, food or music you're hustled into accepting on your way. While Sunday is by far the most crowded and animated day, Saturdays are lively too, and you can hire a boat any day of the week for a little solitary cruising.

Down the Calzada de Tlalpan
The **Calzada de Tlalpan** is the other main approach to the south, running down more or less from the Zocalo to cross the Periferico not far from Xochimilco. Along the way there are two interesting museums – both of them also quite close to Coyoacan.

The first, the *Museo Nacional de las Intervenciones* (Tues.-Sun. 9–7), occupies the old Franciscan **Monastery of Churubusco**. It owes its present role to the 1847 battle in which the invading Americans led by General Winfield Scott defeated the Mexicans under General Anaya – the exhibits are devoted to the history of foreign military adventures in Mexico. Skeletons in the cupboards of Britain, Spain, France and the USA are all loudly rattled. There's also a transport museum in one wing, and lovely grounds. The museum is very close to *General Anaya* Metro station (line 2), one stop before Taxqueña, and not far from the heart of Coyoacan – buses leaving the centre (from 5 de Febrero near the Zocalo) pass by en route to Coyoacan, or take a taxi.

The bizarre **Museo Anahuacalli** (open Tues.-Sun. 10–6; free), designed and built by Diego Rivera, lies further south, on Calle Museo a little way off the Calzada. It's an extraordinary structure, a sombre mass of volcanic stone inspired by Toltec and Aztec architecture, housing Rivera's own huge collection of pre-hispanic artefacts. The ground floor is devoted to objects from the main cultures of the Valley of Mexico, Teotihuacan, Toltec and Aztec, which provided Rivera with such an important part of his inspiration. On the first floor, rooms devoted to the west of Mexico (arguably the best such collection in the country) surround the huge airy room which Rivera, had he lived, would have used as a studio. It's been fitted out as if he had anyway, with an unfinished portrait on the easel and many sketches and mementoes of the artist lying around. On the top floor are more Aztec objects, along with pottery and small figures from Oaxaca and the Gulf Coast. To get to the Museum, take a *Colonia Ruiz Cortines* bus from Metro Taxqueña, or a taxi from Coyoacan or Churubusco.

Heading north

There's less to see and do north of the centre, but without going far afield there are two sites of compelling interest – the great Basilica of Guadalupe and the emotive Plaza de las Tres Culturas – which well deserve the afternoon it will take to cover both. Further out, and harder to get to, you'll find the pyramids of Tenayuca and Santa Cecilia, the two most dramatically preserved remains of Aztec architecture in the city.

Site of the ancient city of *Tlatelolco*, the **Plaza de las Tres Culturas** will be your first stop. Today, in the midst of the excavated ruins stands a lovely colonial church, the whole surrounded by the high-rise housing complex of *Nonoalco-Tlatelolco*: all three great cultures of Mexico side by side. **Tlatelolco** was a considerably more ancient city than Tenochtitlan, based on a separate but nearby island in the lake. For a long time, under independent rule, its people existed in close alliance with the *Mexica* of Tenochtitlan and the city was by far the most important commercial and market centre in the Valley – even after its annexation into the Aztec empire in 1473 Tlatelolco retained this role. By the time the Spanish arrived much of the swampy lake between the two had been filled in and built over: it was here that Cortes and his troops came to marvel at the size and order of the market. Cortes estimated that 60,000 people, buyers and sellers, came and went each day, and Bernal Diaz wrote (after several pages of detailed description):

> *We were astounded at the great number of people and the quantities of merchandise, and at the orderliness and good arrangements that prevailed . . . every kind of goods was kept separate and had its fixed place marked for it. . . . Some of the soldiers among us who had been in many parts of the world, in Constantinople, in Rome, and all over Italy, said that they had never seen a market so well laid out, so large, so orderly, and so full of people.*

In 1521 the besieged Aztecs made their final stand here, and a plaque in the middle of the plaza recalls that struggle: 'On the 13th of August 1521', it reads, 'defended by the heroic Cuauhtemoc, Tlatelolco fell under the power of Hernan Cortes. It was neither a triumph nor a defeat, but the painful birth of the mixed race that is the Mexico of today.'

The **ruins** are a pale reflection of the original, whose temples rivalled those of Tenochtitlan itself: some idea of their scale can be gained from the size of the bases. The chief temple, for example, had by the time of the conquest reached its eleventh rebuilding – what you see now corresponds to the second stage, and by the time nine more were superimposed it would certainly have risen much higher than the church which was built from its stones. On top, probably, was a double sanctuary like that on the Great Temple of Tenochtitlan. The smaller structures include a square *Tzompantli*, or Wall of Skulls, near which nearly 200 human skulls were discovered, each with holes through their temples – presumably the result of having been displayed side by side on long poles around the sides of the building.

Dedicated to Santiago, the present **church** was erected in 1609 on the site of an earlier Franciscan monastery. Parts of this survive, arranged about the cloister. Here, in the early years after the Conquest, the friars established a college at which they instructed the sons of the Aztec nobility in European ways, teaching them Spanish, Latin and Christianity: Bernardino de Sahagun was one of the teachers, and it was here that he collected and wrote down many of the customs and traditions of the Indians, the most important existing record of daily Aztec life.

The **modern buildings** which surround the plaza – mostly a rather ugly 1960s housing project but including the Ministry of Foreign Affairs – represent the third culture. The current state of Mexico was rather more brutally represented on October 2nd 1968, when troops and tanks were ordered to fire on almost a quarter of a million students demonstrating here. It was the culmination of several months of student protests over the government of the day's social and educational policies, which the authorities were determined to subdue with only ten days left before the ceremonial opening of the Olympic Games in the city. Estimates of deaths vary from an official figure at the time of thirty to student estimates of more than 500, but it seems clear that hundreds is closer than tens. The Mexican philosopher Octavio Paz saw it all as part of the cycle of history – a ritual slaughter to recall the Aztec sacrifices here – but it's perhaps better seen as an example of at least one thread of continuity between all Mexico's civilisations: the cheapness of life and the harsh brutality of their rulers.

You can get to the Plaza de las Tres Culturas either on the Metro (line 3, *Tlatelolco*) which continues to Guadalupe, or by bus. It lies between Insurgentes Norte and Reforma Norte: on the former take any bus north (*Indios Verdes*) and get off shortly before the black A-shaped skyscraper which marks the Monumento a la Raza; on the latter *La Villa* buses pass within about three blocks on their way to Guadalupe.

The **Basilica de Nuestra Señora de Guadalupe** is in fact a whole series of churches, chapels and shrines, set around an enormous stone-flagged plaza and climbing up the rocky hillock where the miracles which led to its foundation occurred. The Virgin of Guadalupe, Mexico's first indigenous saint, is still her most popular – the image recurs in churches throughout the country, and the Virgin's banner was fought under by both sides in almost every conflict the nation has ever seen: most famously when Hidalgo seized on it as the flag of Mexican Independence. According to the legend, a christianised Indian, *Juan Diego*, was walking over the hill (formerly dedicated to the Aztec earth goddess Tonantzin) on his way to the monastery at Tlatelolco one morning in December 1531. He was stopped by a brilliant vision of the Virgin who ordered him, in *Nahuatl*, to go to the bishop and tell him to build a church on the hill. Bishop Juan de Zumarraga was unimpressed until, on December

12th, the Virgin reappeared, ordering Diego to gather roses from the top of the hill (in December!) and take them to the bishop. Doing so, he bundled the flowers in his cape, and when he opened it before the bishop found the image of the dark-skinned Virgin imprinted into the cloth. The cloak today hangs above the altar in the gigantic modern Basilica: it takes its name, presumably, from the celebrated (and equally swarthy) Virgin in the Monastery of Guadalupe in Spain.

The **first church** was built in 1533, but the large baroque basilica you see was completely reconstructed in the eighteenth century and again remodelled in the nineteenth and twentieth. Impressive mostly for its size, it is anyway closed to the public while being shored up – around the back you can go into a small **museum** (open Tues.-Sun. 9–4) which contains some of the Virgin's many treasures of religious art. To the left of the great plaza is the **modern home of the image** – a huge church with space inside for 10,000 worshippers and for perhaps four times that when the huge doors all round are thrown open to the crowds. It's always crowded and there seems to be a service permanently in progress. The famous cloak hangs above the main altar, and to avoid constant disruption there's a passageway round behind the altar which takes the devout to a spot right underneath – strips of moving walkway are designed to prevent anyone lingering too long here, but they never seem to be working.

From the plaza you can walk round to the right and up the hill past a series of little chapels associated with the Virgin's appearance. Loveliest of them is the little **Capilla del Pocito**, in which is a well, said to have sprung forth during one of the apparitions. Built in the eighteenth century, it actually consists of two linked elliptical chapels, a smaller and a larger, with colourful tiled domes and magnificently decorative interiors. On the very top of the hill, another chapel marks the spot where the miraculous roses grew.

All around all of this there is a constant stream of humanity – pilgrims, sightseers, priests, and salesmen offering candles, souvenirs, pictures of the Virgin, snacks, any number of mementoes which make Guadalupe a vast industry as well as a religion. On December 12th, anniversary of the second apparition, their numbers swell to hundreds of thousands – many covering the last miles on their knees in an act of penance or devotion, but for others it is little more than a vast fiesta, with dancing, singing and drinking throughout the day.

Tenayuca and Santa Cecilia – two Aztec pyramids

In the extreme north of the city lie the two most wholly preserved examples of Aztec-style architecture. They're hard to get to by public transport but, if you have a strong interest in the Aztecs, thoroughly repay the effort involved. Tenayuca is just off the Calzada de Vallejo, which cuts off to the left from Insurgentes Norte at the Monumento a la Raza: you could try getting a bus heading north along here, or go to the *Terminal del Norte* from where some of the buses to Tula (or even long-distance services through Querétaro) will pass nearby – make sure that they'll be prepared to let you off. Santa Cecilia is just about in walking distance of here, or a very short taxi ride. Some coach tours take both in on their way to Tula and Tepotzotlan.

Tenayuca is another site which pre-dates Tenochtitlan considerably, indeed there are those who claim that it was the capital of the tribe which destroyed Tula. In this its history closely mirrors almost all the other valley settlements: a barbarian tribe from the north invades, conquers all before them, settles in a city and becomes civilised – borrowing much of their culture from their predecessors – and is in turn overcome by the next wave of migrants. There's little evidence that Tenayuca ever controlled a large empire, but it was a powerful city and provides one of the most concrete links between the Toltecs and the Aztecs. The pyramid which survives dates from the period of Aztec dominance and is an almost perfect replica – in miniature – of the great temples of Tlatelolco and Tenochtitlan. Here the structure and the monumental double stairway are intact – only the twin sanctuaries at the top and the brightly painted decorations would be needed for it to open for sacrifices again tomorrow. This is the sixth superimposition; five earlier pyramids (the first dating from the early thirteenth century) are contained within it (and revealed in places by excavation), while originally there was a seventh layer built on top, of which some traces remain. Its most unusual and striking feature is the border of interlocking stone **snakes** which must originally have surrounded the entire building – well over a hundred of them survive. Notice also the two coiled snakes (one a little way up the north face, the other at the foot of the south) known as the 'turquoise serpents': their crests are crowned with stars and aligned with the sun's position at the solstice.

A poor road leads some 2 miles north to **Santa Cecilia Acatitlan** where there's a second pyramid – much smaller and simpler but wholly restored and remarkably beautiful with its clean, very modern looking lines. Originally, this was a temple with a double staircase very similar to the others, but it was discovered during excavation that one of the earlier structures inside was almost perfectly preserved. The ruined layers were stripped away to reveal what, after some reconstruction, is the only example of a sanctuary more or less as it would have been seen by Cortes. It's a very plain building, rising in four steps to a single roofed shrine approached by a broad ramped stairway. The studded decorations around the roof represent either skulls or stars.

THE FACTS
Eating and drinking

Starvation is unlikely to be staring you in the face in Mexico City. There are restaurants, cafes, taquerias, juice stands on every block and since eating out seems to be the city's main pastime many of them are very reasonably priced. Even in the heart of the Zona Rosa, or along Reforma, or just off the Zocalo, good, cheap food is never far away.

For a start there are several **chains** with branches throughout the city – dull on the whole but reliable. *Sanborn's* is the best known, not particularly cheap but good for a breakfast of coffee and *pan dulce* or for reasonably authentic Mexican food tailored to foreign tastes: chief outlets are in the Zona Rosa on Hamburgo opposite American Express; just off Reforma next to the Sheraton and on the street leading up to the Plaza de la Republica; the House of Tiles by Bellas Artes; 16 de Septiembre just down from the Zocalo; and in San Angel. *VIPs* is cheaper and serves a filling *comida corrida* as well as standard Mexican and American dishes – branches just off the Plaza de la Republica and in the Zona Rosa. For tacos which you can be confident are palatable while still pretty authentic, *El Porton* (Zona Rosa at the corner of Hamburgo and Niza and in the Pl. de la Republica) is a safe bet, while *Tacos Beatriz* (at the railway station and on Londres in the Zona Rosa among others) has a less sanitised atmosphere. Burger places are on the whole to be avoided – if you want thoroughly American food try *Denny's* (on Londres in the Zona Rosa and on Reforma near Colon; overpriced).

While these are always safe standbys, you'd have a pretty dull time if you restricted yourself entirely to their fare. The choice elsewhere is almost limitless, ranging from traditional coffee-houses to fast food lunch counters and taking in Chinese, Japanese, French, Spanish, expensive international and rock-bottom Mexican cooking along the way. A few possibilities in the main areas are set out below, but it's the bare beginnings of a list: a comprehensive selection could easily fill the book.

Some of the more interesting places are in the old zone **around the Zocalo**. In particular there are several long-established **cafes** which offer superb coffee and pastries for breakfast but also have full menus of basic egg and enchilada-style Mexican meals: the *Cafe la Blanca* on 5 de Mayo is one of the most traditional, or try the *Cafe Paris* on the same street or the *Cafe Tacuba* on Tacuba. Since there are so many office workers in this area, cheap *comidas corridas* are on offer everywhere – for really rock-bottom prices look for the handbills flyposted onto lampposts or empty shopfronts. These places, which rarely seem to survive long, are often unsigned and on the first or second floors of unlikely buildings – they'll serve a very plain lunch (usually soup, some kind of meat dish with piles of tortillas and a very sweet sweet) for next to nothing: one

such is the *Pension Española*, at Isabel La Catolica 10 between Tacuba
and 5 de Mayo. Moving slightly upmarket, you're spoilt for choice: the
Restaurante Catalan at 31 Calle Bolivar is not the cheapest, but you'll
get a massive Spanish meal on the second floor of an old patioed mansion
full of businessmen taking a long afternoon break; *El Cardenal* (Moneda
2) is also on the second floor, but this time some of the tables have a
view over the Zocalo. As you get slightly further away from the Zocalo
prices tend to come down – many of the hotels around Uruguay and
Salvador have restaurants attached (try the one in the *Hotel Salvador* on
Salvador), and there's a succession of *taquerias* and cheap lunch counters
in the area around Cuba and Allende. The *Hosteria de Santo Domingo*,
not far from here on Belisario Dominguez just off the Plaza Santo
Domingo, claims to be the oldest restaurant in the city. For healthier
food, there are **fruit juice** bars here as there are everywhere: one of the
best is on 16 de Septiembre more or less opposite the Gran Hotel, offering
massive fruit salads and reinforced health drinks as well as the standard
jugos and *licuados*.

Moving down to the **Alameda**, you'll find a whole series of Mexican-
style fast food places in the streets leading off Juarez and those crossing
them. At the bottom of Dolores here there's a veritable Chinatown –
some ten **Chinese** restaurants which are neither particularly good nor
especially cheap but interesting to see what Mexican Chinese food tastes
like, and acceptable if you have a sudden craving for Chop Suey.

The greatest number of cheap places to eat are found in much the same
area as the cheap hotels, around the **Plaza San Fernando** and towards
the Plaza de la Republica. The *Cafe Paris*, on the corner of the Plaza San
Fernando, is similar to the cafes around the Zocalo, and a very good
place for breakfast. Just down from it, on the same side of the plaza,
is a rather strange restaurant where you are served very ordinary and
inexpensive Mexican food with enormous formality by uniformed waiters
who were obviously intended for better things. Across the square, by way
of contrast, is a thoroughly downmarket establishment where they serve
up the tasty chickens you can see roasting in the window with a minimum
of ceremony. Continuing down Puente de Alvarado you'll find a clutch
of basic restaurants and several fruit places around the bottom of Buenavista – the street which leads up to the railway station – and again on
this section of Insurgentes, while around Revolucion Metro station there's
a group of **bakeries** and sweet shops.

Heading from here to the **Plaza de la Republica**, Arriaga has a
succession of rather unsavoury looking taquerias, as well as stalls in the
street selling orange juice and more tacos. *El Porton*, on the Plaza itself,
is safer if less exciting. This is again an area of office workers and
again you'll find many places catering for them at lunchtimes. Between
Republica and the Paseo de la Reforma, Antonio Caso is a good place

to look for tacos and tortas, or for something more substantial try the cafeteria in the *Hotel Mayaland*. On this stretch of Reforma there are many rather more expensive places: *Shirley's* with American-style food and a set price lunchtime buffet is one of the most popular – pricey though. Another of those old-style cafes, one of the best, is not far from here – the *Cafe Habana* at the corner of Morelos and Bucareli. As well as serving great coffee here they sell it, fresh ground or as beans, to take away.

In the **Zona Rosa** you can barely move for restaurants, but most are expensive and many are extremely expensive. You can eat cheaply at some of the taquerias squeezed in between fancier places or try *Parri-Pollo* (Hamburgo 154) for roasted chicken with excellent side dishes. Alternatively head for **Insurgentes Metro** station (at the junction of Genova, Insurgentes and Chapultepec) where the concourse around the station is crowded with reasonably priced places serving up tacos, tortas and pizzas, mostly packed with young Mexicans.

If you're prepared to spend rather more freely, *Kineret*, at the corner of Hamburgo and Genova, is a **Jewish** restaurant where you can sit outside with a beer and New York-style pastrami sandwiches – just one of a whole series of places on Genova and nearby Copenhague with tables set out on streets closed to traffic. Others include the rather cheaper *Pizza Real* (Genova 20) and the *Meson del Perro Andaluz* (Copenhague 28) for really excellent **Spanish** food. There are several small **Japanese** restaurants on Londres which are reasonably cheap if not terribly authentic; better but more expensive examples are *Kabuki* (Rio Tiber 91 near the Sheraton) and *Kyoto* (Arkansas 38 near the Polyforum). For **seafood** in the Zona Rosa try *La Marinera* (Liverpool 183), very popular with locals and not too outrageously priced.

Vegetarians can, as always, rely on finding something meat free almost anywhere (with the exception of the most expensive international or French places), but in the capital there are also several enterprising vegetarian restaurants. The biggest is *Las Fuentes*, at the corner of Rio Tiber and Panuco near the Sheraton, and you'll find others, mostly identified simply by a *Restaurante Vegetariano* sign, in the Zona Rosa at Varsovia 3 and on Londres near its junction with Amberes; close to the Zocalo at Madero 56; near Bellas Artes at Filomata 17 (between Madero and 5 de Mayo), and off the Alameda at Dolores 10.

Very fancy French and international restaurants are thick on the ground in the Zona Rosa but if you've got the money to spare there are a couple of places further afield which are genuinely **special**. The *San Angel Inn* in San Angel must have the most beautiful setting – in a colonial hacienda – of any of the city's restaurants and food, Mexican and international, to rival the best. And in the new section of Chapultepec Park, the *Restaurante del Lago* is also spectacular: this time in an ultra-modern building overlooking a floodlit lake – French food and a very formal atmosphere. For a more down to earth, raucous evening out try *Las Comerciales* (Insurgentes Sur 1373 in San Angel) or *Anderson's* (Reforma 400, Zona Rosa) which both have music and much enforced jollity: the former is popular with young Mexicans, and while the food's not up to much there are singing, roller-skating waiters to compensate; the latter has better food but a largely tourist clientele.

Bars in Mexico, as in the rest of the country, are very much a male preserve, but here at least things are beginning to change. Even so it's safer for women to stick to hotel bars (which most in the centre are anyway) or to the established night spots (see *Entertainment* below). One traditional watering hole which is quite tame – though still predominantly male – is the *Bar L'Opera* on 5 de Mayo near Bellas Artes. It's worth going in just to see the magnificent fin-de-siècle decor – ornate mahogany panelling, a brass-railed bar and gilt-framed mirrors in the booths.

Markets and shops

The big advantage of shopping in Mexico is that goods from all over the country can be found somewhere in the city: the disadvantage is that they will be considerably more expensive here. By far the greatest concentration of shops aimed at the tourist can be found in the **Zona Rosa** – pricey leather goods, jewellery, clothes, handicrafts and souvenirs abound, and there's a roaring trade in fake designer labels. Gucci and Lacoste are particularly popular, sold everywhere and very rarely genuine. These places are worth a look, but certainly don't offer good value by Mexican standards.

For anything you really need – clothes and so on – you're better off going to one of the big **department stores**. *Liverpool* and *El Palacio de Hierro* both have branches on 20 de Noviembre just off the Zocalo. *Sanborn's* sell large quantities of tacky souvenirs, but they're good for local guide books and pulp reading in English and every branch also has a sizeable drug-store. More serious **books in English** can be found at branches of the American Book Store (see under *Listings*). Much the best **crafts** outside the markets are sold at the various government-run *FONART* shops – there are three on Av. Juarez, see text for the *Alameda* (p. 176). You should come here anyway to get an idea of price and quality before venturing into any serious bargaining in the markets.

Every area of the city has its own **MARKET** selling food and essentials, and many others operate for just one day a week with stalls set up along a suburban street. The most interesting are set out below.

La Merced is the city's largest, a collection of huge modern buildings which for all their size can't contain the vast number of traders who want to set up here. Fruit, vegetables and other foods take up most space, but somewhere there's almost anything you could conceive of finding in a Mexican market. Metro *Merced*.

La Lagunilla comes closest to rivalling it in size and variety, but is best visited on a Sunday when the Thieves' Market (see below) takes over the surrounding streets. On Rayon, a couple of blocks north of the Plaza Garibaldi, La Lagunilla is easiest reached by buses (*La Villa*) heading north on Reforma.

The **Centro Artesanal de San Juan** is a modern complex primarily aimed at tourists: one of the best places to see crafts nevertheless (silver in particular) and to bargain the prices down. Located about five blocks south of the Alameda along Dolores, or close to Metro *Salto de Agua* (down Arcos de Belen and second right).

Flower Markets. Very close to San Juan, at the corner of Luis Moya and E. Pugibet, is a small market selling nothing but flowers – loose, in vast arrangements and wreaths, growing in pots, even paper and plastic. Similar smaller markets can be found in San Angel and Xochimilco.

Crafts Markets. Several other markets, aimed more or less directly at tourists, rival San Juan. Best of them is probably the modern complex in the **Plaza de la Ciudadela** (Metro *Balderas*) on Balderas about eight blocks south of Reforma. Others include the **Bazar Sabado** (Saturdays only) in San Angel; a commercially run **Mercado de Artesanias** at Aldama 187 near the railway station; a covered market in the heart of the **Zona Rosa** (insignificant entrance on Londres between Amberes and Florencia) which is surprisingly authentic in its grime and smells but generally poor quality; and a large open-air market at **Indios Verdes** (Metro *Indios Verdes* or *Indios Verdes* buses north on Insurgentes).

Flea Markets. Most famous and still the most interesting is the Sunday **Thieves' Market** which spreads over the streets north of La Lagunilla, especially Calle Comonfort: it gets its name because here, traditionally, stolen goods would be on offer to give their owners a chance to buy them back, especially items which might have more sentimental than real value! Few real bargains any more, but a vast and bizarre collection of goods are on offer including thousands of books, a fair number of which are in English. Not far from here, along Av. del Trabajo, is a very basic junk market in one of the city's heaviest areas, **Tepito**. It operates every day – especially on Sundays – and here most of what's on sale probably has been stolen; don't venture in alone or flashing large wads of money. The **Tianguis Dr Vertiz** falls somewhere between these two – relatively safe, but still with an aura of risk about it and a place you feel you might stumble across a genuine antique among the junk. Mostly on Sundays, it covers the backstreets around the corner of Calles Dr Vertiz and Dr Ugarte, not far from Metro *Niños Heroes*.

Nightlife and entertainment

There's a vast amount going on in Mexico, the nation's cultural and social centre just as much as its political capital. Much of the obvious nightlife, though, is rather tame in its attempt to be sophisticated – Mexicans themselves favour discos with a bland diet of recorded American sounds, while for the tourists they lay on piano bars or 'typical' Mexican bands, Herb Alpert style. Two events, however – the Ballet Folklorico and the mariachi music in the Plaza Garibaldi – transcend this dramatically; although both are unashamedly tourist events, they have an enduring appeal, too, for Mexicans.

The **Ballet Folklorico** is a long-running, internationally famed compilation of traditional dances from all over the country, superbly choreographed and designed and interspersed with Mexican music and singing. And much better than that brief description might sound. The best place to see it is in the traditional setting of the Palacio de Bellas Artes, with performances (usually) on Sundays and Wednesdays. Tickets for this, however, can be hard to come by and pressure of other events occasionally forces a move to the Auditorio Nacional in Chapultepec Park. You should try to get tickets at least a couple of days in advance – either from the Bellas Artes box office or through the *Boletronico* ticket agency which has booths set up throughout the city (including inside Bellas Artes – they handle most big theatre and sporting events). If it's sold out, you can always try at reception in one of the big hotels or go with an organised tour, for either of which you'll pay a considerable premium. A rival troupe, every bit as good, performs on Sundays and Tuesdays in the Teatro de la Ciudad (Donceles 36), just round the corner from the Bellas Artes.

Entertainment in the **Plaza Garibaldi** is rather less sedate. Here in the evenings gather hundreds of competing **mariachi** bands, all in their tight, silver-spangled charro finery and vast sombreros, to play for anyone who'll pay them among the crowds wandering the square and spilling in and out of the bars which surround it. A typical group will consist of two or four violins, a brass section of three trumpeters standing some way back so as not to drown out the others, three or four men on guitars of varying sizes and a vocalist – though the truly macho serenader will hire the band and do the singing himself. They take their name, supposedly, from the French word *mariage* – it being traditional during the nineteenth-century French intervention to hire a group to play at weddings. You may also come across *norteño* bands from the border areas with their Tex-Mex brand of country music, or the softer *marimba* musicians from the South.

Simply wander round the square and you'll get your fill of music – should you want to be individually serenaded, pick out a likely looking group and negotiate your price. At the back of the square a whole series of stalls are set up serving simple food – mostly to the musicians themselves – or there are several fairly pricey restaurants around the square. These include *Tlaquepaque* and *Guadalajara de Noche*, but a much more atmospheric place is *Tenampa*, a traditional saloon with heavies guarding its swing doors against drunks and undesirables, and several bands playing around the tables inside. The walls are decorated with portraits of the mariachi greats and the lyrics of their most popular numbers. The Plaza Garibaldi is on Lazaro Cardenas about five blocks north of Bellas Artes – a walk up through a thoroughly sleazy area of cheap bars and cafes, streetwalkers, grimy hotels and several brightly lit theatres offering burlesque and strip shows. As the night wears on and the drinking continues it can get pretty rowdy around the square: despite a high-profile police presence you'd be better off not coming laden down with expensive camera equipment or an obviously bulging wallet.

For high quality mariachi in a far more genteel atmosphere, the first floor bar in the **Hotel Alameda** (Av. Juarez opposite the Alameda) has a nightly show: expensive drinks and a cover charge but the music is good and virtually non-stop. **Hotel bars** generally are the scene of much of the action in the centre and around the Zona Rosa – most have a tame pianist or a band playing muted 1960s hits. All are expensive but some offer compensating attractions: the lobby of the *Gran Hotel* (16. de Septiembre off the Zocalo) for its amazing decor; the *Del Prado* (Juarez by the Alameda) for the murals; and the *Muralto* bar (top of the Torre Latino Americano) or the top floor of the *Fiesta Palace* (or Reforma) for their views of the city. For serious drinkers, the bar in the *Hotel Continental* (at the junction of Reforma and Insurgentes) opens 24 hours a day.

Most of the popular **discos** are in hotels too, and are again very expensive. Of these perhaps the best, and the most reasonably priced, are at the *Hotel Aristos* in the Zona Rosa (Copenhague just off Reforma). Among the flashiest and most popular (as well as most expensive) are those in the newest hotels – *CeroCero* in the *Camino Real*, *Club 84* at the *El Presidente Chapultepec*, and the revolving top floor of the *Hotel de Mexico*. *Marrakesh* in the Zona Rosa at Florencia 36 is a complex of several nightspots including a disco, very pricey, or try the more down to earth *Catacumbas* (Dolores 16 near the Alameda) with its horror movie theme.

The **gay scene**, though perfectly tolerated, is not exactly well developed in Mexico. Most of the action centres on the Zona Rosa, where you'll find the capital's one well known gay club, *Disco 9*, at Londres 156.

Listings for current cinema, theatre and other **cultural events** can be found in the English-language *Mexico City News* or to a lesser extent in the *Daily Bulletin*: local newspapers in Spanish will have more detail (certainly for films), or you could try the weekly magazine *Tiempo Libre*. While Mexican theatre tends to be rather turgid, there are often excellent classical music **concerts** and performances of **opera** or **ballet** by touring companies. Bellas Artes and the Auditorio Nacional are again the main venues, but other downtown theatres as well as the Polyforum and the Teatro de los Insurgentes may also have interesting shows. Most Sundays there's a free concert in Chapultepec Park near the lake. **Movies**, at least in the city centre, are almost always in English with Spanish subtitles (assuming, that is, they were made in English in the first place); major films open here up to a year before they reach Europe and are sometimes released even before they've been seen in the States. If you go to the cinema arrive early, as popular screenings frequently sell out.

Both America (the *Instituto Mexicano Norteamericano de Relaciones Culturales* at Hamburgo 115 in the Zona Rosa) and Britain (*Instituto Anglo-Mexicano de Cultura*, Antonio Caso 127) have **cultural institutes** in the city which frequently organise events – film shows, lectures, concerts – open to the public. Both also run language courses in Spanish and English and have library facilities. They can be useful places for **contacts**, and if you're looking for work or long-term accommodation or travelling companions their noticeboards are good places to start.

Sport is probably the city's biggest obsession, and **football**, throughout its winter season, the most popular. The big games are held either at the *Estadio Azteca* or the *Estadio Mexico* – check local papers for fixture details. Throughout the year you can watch **fronton** (*pelota* or *jai alai*) right in the city centre: it's a pretty dull game unless you're betting but you can wander in and out freely throughout the evening sessions (every day except Sunday). Men play at the *Fronton Mexico* on the Plaza de la Republica, women at the *Fronton Metropolitano*, Bahia de Todos Santos 190 (get there on a bus heading up Calz. Melchor Ocampo from the entrance to Chapultepec). There's **horse racing**, too, throughout the year (Tuesday, Thursday and weekend afternoons) at the *Hipodromo de las Americas* – buses and peseros heading west on Reforma will take you there – look for *Hipodromo*. More exciting horsey action is involved in the *Charreadas*, or **rodeos**, put on by amateur but highly skilled afficion-ados most weekends; venues and times vary, but these are usually spec-tacles worth witnessing so check the press to find out what's going on. Devoted cowboy fans might also be interested in the *Museo de la Char-reria* (open Mon.-Fri. 10–7), a small museum devoted to the cult of the charro with a collection of costumes, saddles, wagons and paintings – it's at the corner of Isabel la Catolica and Izazaga, near Metro *Isabel la Catolica*. Finally, there are **bullfights** every Sunday afternoon in the winter season at the giant *Plaza Mexico*, largest bullring in the world. Any bus heading south on Insurgentes will pass close by.

Other things

Airlines almost all have their offices on Reforma. The main ones are *AeroMexico*, Reforma 64 (Tel. 546 9840); *Aeroflot*, Reforma 46 (566 5388); *Air France*, Reforma 76 (566 0066); *American*, Reforma 314 (566 2500); *British Airways*, Reforma 332 (533 6375); *Iberia*, Reforma 24 (592 2988); *KLM*, Reforma 87 (566 0100); *Mexicana*, corner of Juarez and Balderas (582 2666); *PanAm*, Reforma 35 (566 2600).

American Express is at Hamburgo 75 in the Zona Rosa (511 0309).

Baggage If you want to leave bags somewhere, all the long-distance bus terminals have lock-ups (*Guarderias*).

Banks throughout the city are open normal hours (24-hour branches at the airport). Many will only change money in the morning. Best bet for currency other than dollars are branches of *Banamex*. Most large hotels and shops will change travellers cheques and cash dollars.

Books in English can be bought at the *American Book Store* – Madero 25 downtown and Revolucion 1570 in San Angel. Pulp paperbacks and local guides are sold at *Sanborn*'s and in many big hotels. French books from the *Librairie Française*, at the corner of Reforma and Niza. Large quantities of second hand books, many in English, are sold at the Sunday *Thieves' Market*.

Buses The four long-distance terminals are: *Terminal del Norte*, Av. de los Cien Metros 4907, for northbound services, Guadalajara and the US border (Metro *Terminal de Autobuses*); *TAPO* on Av. Ignacio Zaragoza for the east and south-east (Metro *San Lazaro*); *Central del Sur* for buses south to the Pacific coast, Av. Taxqueña 1320 (Metro *Taxqueña*); and the *Terminal Poniente* for Toluca (Metro *Observatorio*). See *Comings and Goings* and *Getting About* in the Orientation section.

Car rental Thousands of agencies throughout the city – small local operations are often cheaper. Try *Rent-a-Volks*, Hamburgo 7 (566 8802) or *Combi Rent*, Tonala 255, for vans (584 2120). *Avis* (761 5796), *Budget* (533 0450), *Hertz* (511 5686), *Quick* (533 4908).

Embassies *American*, Paseo de la Reforma 305 (533 3333 24hrs); *Australian*, Reforma 195 (566 3055); *British* Rio Lerma 71 (511 4880); *Canadian*, Schiller 529 (254 3288); *Dutch*, Avila Camacho 1 (557 9192); *French*, Liverpool 67 (525 0181); *Irish* (consulate), Chapultepec 18 (510 3867); *Swedish*, Avila Camacho 1 (540 6393).

Emergencies Police emergency number is 06; Red Cross 557 5758.

Hospital The *British-American Cowdray Hospital* (ABC) is at Calle Sur 136 – phone 515 8359 in emergency, 515 8500 for information. Your embassy should be able to provide a list of multi-lingual doctors if necessary.

Language schools Many places run Spanish courses, try the *Instituto*

Mexicano Norteamericano, Hamburgo 115 (525 6248), or the *Instituto Anglo-Mexicano*, Antonio Caso 127 (566 6739).

Laundry Self-service launderettes are rare in Mexico, try: *Lavanderia Liverpool*, Liverpool 41; *La Espuma*, Plaza Melchor Ocampo 32 (at the junction of Rio Mississipi and Rio Nazas); or *Las Artes*, Antonio Caso 82. There are several dry cleaners around the top of Rio Mississipi near *La Espuma*.

Maps of the city are rarely good. Best are those produced by *Guia Roji*, from news-stands or *Sanborn's*.

Newspapers The *Mexico City News* can be bought from kiosks in the centre, the *Daily Bulletin* free in hotel lobbies. *Sanborn's* have a fair number of English-language magazines, the *American Book Store* even more.

Opening hours for most businesses are from 10 till 7. Some, but increasingly few, close for a siesta from around 2 to 4.

Police In emergency dial 06. Local headquarters is 588 5100.

Post The main post office is at the corner of Lazaro Cardenas and Tacuba, behind Bellas Artes.

Telephones Local calls can be made from booths throughout the city – *Sanborn's* always has a couple somewhere quiet and also a supply of the irritating 20 centavo coins you need to operate them. For international services look for the blue *Larga Distancia* signs – you can dial direct from most big hotels. The central office, open 24 hours, is on Calle Victoria near its junction with Luis Moya.

Tourist cards Should you lose yours, or want an extension, apply to the *Consejo Nacional de Turismo* at Mariano Escobedo 726 near the entrance to Chapultepec (533 0540).

Tourist information can be had by phoning 250 0123 between 8am and 8pm. The *Turismo* office is at Presidente Mazaryk 172, Colonia Polanco – perfectly helpful but a long way from the centre.

Trains run from the *Estacion Central Buenavista* on Insurgentes Norte. See *Comings and Goings* for details. For rail freaks, they run Sunday excursions by steam train from here.

Travel agencies *American Express*, Hamburgo 75 (511 0309); *Wagons Lits/Thomas Cook*, Juarez 88 (521 4528); *Viajes Bojorquez*, Juarez 97 (585 4466); tours of the city and surrounds from *Grey Line*, Londres 166 (533 1540), or *London Tours*, Londres 101 (533 0766).

Visas are needed for onward travel to certain Central American countries. The *Guatemalan* Consulate is at Vallarta 1 (546 4876); *Honduras*, Juarez 64 (512 0620); *El Salvador*, Galileo 17 (531 7995).

Women's groups *FINALIDM* is a support group for many women's rights movements – Margaritta E. Magana A.A. No. 70–564, Mexico 20 D.F.; university women's group *GAMU* is at Colovenes 97, Jardines de San Mateo, Maucalpan, Mexico; or try the *Union Nacional de Mujeres*

Mexicanas, Bucareli 12508, Mexico 1 D.F.; *Revuelta* is a feminist magazine.

Work is very hard to come by – there's some chance of finding a job teaching English, maybe Au Pair type work. Look in the *Mexico City News* classifieds, or advertise your services to give private lessons in one of the Spanish papers.

AROUND THE CITY

Breaking out of the capital in any direction, there are targets of interest within a couple of hour's drive. First, and the one-day trip which everyone seems to take, are the massive pyramids and ancient city of **Teotihuacan**, about 50km to the north-east. Directly *north*, on the road to QUER-ÉTARO and the colonial cities, lies **Tula**, the centre which succeeded Teotihuacan as the valley's great power. Its site is perhaps slightly less impressive, but imposing nonetheless, and on the way you can stop in **Tepotzotlan**, with some of the finest baroque and colonial art in the country.

To the *west*, **Toluca**, on the old road to Morelia, hosts a colossal market every Friday, and the country around it is full of mountain retreats where Mexicans escape the pressures of their city. **Cuernavaca** has long been a sought-after refuge – full of colonial mansions and gardens it's also close to several important archaeological sites, while beyond lies the road to ACAPULCO and the tourist mecca of **Taxco** with its silver jewellery. *East* towards the Gulf Coast, **Puebla** stands on the plain behind the great **volcanoes**, one of the most colonial towns in the country but also one of its most crowded, and a major industrial centre. Nearby **Cholula** was an important ally of the Aztecs when Cortes marched this way from the coast – a church was erected on the site of each pagan temple here, and they claim there's a chapel for every day of the year.

SAN JUAN TEOTIHUACAN

It really does seem that every visitor to Mexico heads out to Teotihuacan at some stage – there's a constant stream of tours, buses and cars heading this way, and the site itself is crawling with people, increasingly so as the day wears on. Joining them all is easy enough: there are buses every half hour or so throughout the day (6am–8pm) from the *Terminal del Norte* direct to the site. Head to the second class (left-hand) side of the bus station and look for the *Autobuses Teotihuacan* stand. It takes about an hour, and it's worth getting an early start to arrive before the worst of the crowds (the site opens at nine).

On the way you pass a couple of places which, if you're driving, are certainly worth a look, but barely merit the hassle involved in stopping over on the bus. First, at **TEPEXPAN**, is a museum (open Tues.-Sun. 10–6) housing fossils of mammoths dug up in the surrounding plain (then marshland) over the years. This whole area is a rich source of such remains – the Aztecs knew of their existence which is one of the reasons they believed that the huge structures of Teotihuacan had been built by a race of giants. A little further on lies the beautiful sixteenth-century monastery of **SAN AGUSTIN ACOLMAN** (closed Fridays). Built on a raised man-made terrace (probably on the site of an earlier, Aztec temple), it's a stern looking building, lightened by the intricacy of its sculpted facade. In the nave and around the cloister are preserved portions of early murals depicting the monks, while several of the halls off the cloister display colonial religious painting and pre-hispanic artefacts found here. **CHICONCUAC** is rather more of a detour, but on Tuesdays when there's a large market here (specialising in woollen goods, sweaters and blankets) it's included in the itinerary of many of the tours to the pyramids. Again this is hard to do on a regular bus and if you want to visit the market it's easier to do so as an entirely separate trip – buses, again, from the *Terminal del Norte*.

The site of **TEOTIHUACAN** is open every day from 9 to 5 (free on Sundays), and again in the evening for the Son at Lumière performances (six nights a week, at 7pm in English and 8.15 in Spanish; not during the rainy season, June-Sept). A road, the *Carretera de Circunvalacion*, surrounds the main structures with parking spaces at intervals and several restaurants. If you arrive by bus it'll drop you at the *Unidad Cultural*, by the principal entrance, where there's a **museum**, a restaurant, several shops and market-type stalls: from here the *Street of the Dead*, chief thoroughfare of the ancient city, leads north through the ceremonial centre to the great pyramids – about 1½ miles in all. The restaurants, incidentally, are expensive, so it's worth bringing some food with you – there are normally vendors offering drinks, sandwiches or tortas, but it's not entirely to be relied upon. To see the entire site and its outlying buildings could take a full day, but the most important can be looked over in a few hours: involving a lot of climbing and walking, this can be exhausting at such altitude.

Teotihuacan is not, on first sight, the most impressive site in Mexico – it lacks the dramatic hilltop setting or lush jungle vegetation of those in the south – but it is a city planned and built on a massive scale, the great pyramids so huge that before their refurbishment one would have passed them by without a second glance, as hills. At its height this must have been the most imposing city ever seen in pre-hispanic America, with a population approaching 200,000 spread over an area of some 60 square miles (as opposed to the 1½ square miles of the ceremonial centre) and every building – grey hulks now – covered in bright polychrome murals. The **rise and fall** of Teotihuacan is almost exactly contemporary with Imperial Rome: from around 600BC there is evidence of small agricultural communities in the vicinity and by 200BC a township had been established on the present site. From then until 0AD (the period known as *Teotihuacan I*) the population began to soar, and the city assumed its most important characteristics: the great Pyramids of the Sun and Moon were built, and the Street of the Dead laid out. Development continued through *Teotihuacan II* (0-350 AD) with more construction, but most importantly with evidence of the city's influence (in architecture, sculpture

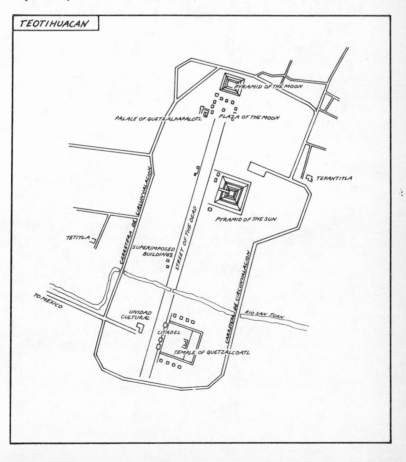

and pottery) occurring at sites throughout modern Mexico and into Guatemala and Honduras. From 350 to around 650 (*Teotihuacan III*) it reached the peak of population and power, with much new building and addition to earlier structures. Already by the end of this period, however, there were signs of decline, and the final period (*Teotihuacan IV*) lasted at most a century before the city was sacked, burnt and virtually abandoned. This, presumably, was the result of attack by northern tribes, probably the Toltecs, but the disaster may in the end have been as much ecological as military. Vast forests were cut down to build the city (in columns, roof supports, door lintels) and huge quantities of wood burnt to make the lime plaster which coated the buildings: the result was severe soil erosion which left the hillsides as barren as they appear today. In addition, the agricultural effort needed to feed so many people (with no form of artificial fertiliser or knowledge of crop rotation) gradually sapped what land remained of its ability to grow more.

Whatever the precise causes, the city was left, eventually, to a ruination which was advanced even by the time of the Aztecs. To them it represented a holy place from a previous age, and they gave it its present name: *The Place where Men became Gods*. Although Teotihuacan features frequently in Aztec mythology, there are no written records – what we know of the city is derived entirely from archaeological and artistic evidence. What you see, too, is to some extent conjecture, for everything here has been dug up and at least partly reconstructed.

From the Cultural Centre you emerge at the bottom of the restored Street of the Dead (which originally extended some 2 miles further south) opposite the **Citadel** – *La Ciudadela*. This enormous sunken square, surrounded by stepped platforms and with a low square altar in the centre, was the city's administrative heart, with the houses of its chief priests and nobles arranged around a vast meeting place. Across the open space stands a tall pyramid construction inside which, during excavation, was found the **Temple of Quetzalcoatl**. With the back of the newer pyramid demolished, the elaborate (*Teotihuacan II*) temple structure stands revealed. It rises in four steps (of an original six), each sculpted in relief and punctuated at intervals by the stylised heads of Quetzalcoatl, the plumed serpent, and Tlaloc, the rain God. Traces of the original paint can be seen in places. This theme – with the goggle-eyed, almost abstract mask of the god and the fanged snake, its neck ringed with a collar of feathers – recurs in later sites throughout the country.

The **Street of the Dead** (*Calle de los Muertos*) forms the axis around which the city was planned. A broad causeway linking all the most significant religious and administrative buildings, it was conceived to impress with the low buildings which flank most of its length serving to heighten the impact of the two great temples at the northern end. Other streets, leading off to the rest of the city, originally intersected it at right angles, and even the river San Juan, which you cross just beyond the Citadel, was canalised so as not to disturb the symmetry (the bridge which then crossed it would have extended the full width of the street). Its name is something of a misconception, since it is neither a simple street – rather a series of open plazas linked by staircases rising some 100 feet between the Citadel and the Pyramid of the Moon – nor in any way linked with the dead. The Aztecs believed the buildings which lined it, then little more than earth-covered mounds, to be the burial places of kings. They're not, and although the exact function of most remains unclear, all obviously had some sacred significance. The design, seen in the many reconstructions, is fairly uniform: low, three- or four-storey platforms consisting of vertical panels (*tableros*) supported on sloping walls. In many cases several are built on top of each other – nowhere more clealy demonstrated than in the *Edificios Superimpuestos* (**superimposed buildings**) on the left-hand side shortly beyond the river. Here you can descend a metal staircase to find excavated structures underneath the present level.

The great **Pyramid of the Sun** is Teotihuacan's outstanding landmark, a massive structure second in size only to Cholula of Mexico's ancient buildings (and Cholula is a total ruin). Its base is almost exactly the same size as that of the great Pyramid of Cheops, but since this is not a true pyramid it is very much lower. There are wonderful views from the top nonetheless, and the bulk is all the more remarkable when you consider that the 2½ million tons of stone and earth used in its construction were brought here without benefit of the wheel or any beast of burden, and shaped without use of any metal tool. The pyramid you see was reconstructed by Leopoldo Batres in 1908, in a thoroughly cavalier fashion. He blasted, with dynamite, a structure that originally abutted the south face, and stripped much of the surface in a search for a more complete building under the present one. In fact the Pyramid of the Sun, almost uniquely, was built in one go at a very early stage of the city's development (about 100AD), and there is only a very small older temple right at its heart. As a result of Batres's stripping the stone surface, the temple has eroded considerably more than it might otherwise have done. He also added an extra terrace to the original four.

You approach by a short staircase leading to the right off the Street of the Dead onto a broad esplanade where stand the ruins of several small temples and priests' dwellings. The main structure consists of five sloping layers of wall divided by terraces – the large flat area at the top would originally have been surmounted by the sanctuary, long disappeared. Evidence of why this massive structure came to be raised here emerged in 1971 when archaeologists stumbled on a tunnel (closed to the public) leading to a clover-leaf shaped **cave** directly under the centre of the pyramid. This, clearly, had been some kind of inner sanctuary, a holy of holies, and may even have been the reason for Teotihuacan's foundation and the basis of its influence. Theories abound as to its exact nature, and many fit remarkably with legends handed down through the Aztecs. Perhaps most likely the cave was formed by a subterranean spring, and came to be associated with Tlaloc, god of rain but also a bringer of fertility, as a sort of fountain of life. Alternatively, it could be associated with the legendary 'seven grottoes', a symbol of creation from which all later Mexican peoples claimed to have emerged, or have been the site of an oracle, or associated with a cult of sacrifice – in Aztec times the flayed skins of victims of Xipe Totec were stored in a cave under a pyramid.

At the end of the Street of the Dead rises the **Pyramid of the Moon**, a smaller structure built slightly later (but still *Teotihuacan I* and one of the oldest you see) whose top, thanks to the higher ground on which it's built, is virtually on a level with that of the Pyramid of the Sun. The structure is very similar, four sloping levels approached by a monumental stairway, but for some reason this seems a very much more elegant building: perhaps because of the smaller scale, perhaps as a result of the approach, through the formally laid-out **Plaza of the Moon**.

The **Palace of Quetzalpapalotl** lies to the left of this square, behind the low temples which surround it. Wholly restored, it's virtually the only example of a roofed building in Central Mexico and a unique view of how the elite lived at Teotihuacan. The rooms are arranged around a patio whose elaborately carved pillars give the Palace its name – their stylised designs represent birds (the brightly coloured *Quetzals*, though some may be owls) and butterflies. In the galleries around the patio several frescoes survive: very formalised and symbolic, with the themes reduced almost to geometric patterns. **Mural art** was clearly very important in Teotihuacan, and almost every building has some trace of decoration, though much has been removed for preservation and restoration. Two earlier buildings, half buried under the Palace, still have substantial remains: in the **Palace of the Jaguar**, jaguars in feathered head-dresses blow conch shells from which emerge curls of music, or perhaps speech or prayers to Tlaloc (who appears along the top of the mural); in the **Temple of the Plumed Shells** you see a motif of feathers and sea-shells along with bright green parrots. Other murals, of which only traces remain, were found in the temples along the Street of the Dead between the two pyramids.

Such art was not reserved for the priesthood – indeed some of the finest frescoes have been found in outlying 'apartment buildings'. At **Tepantitla**, a residential quarter of the old city across the road from the back of the Pyramid of the Sun, the famous *Paradise of Tlaloc* mural (reproduced in the National Museum of Anthropology, see p. 183) was discovered. Only a part of it survives here, but there are others in the complex depicting a procession of priests and a ball game. All have a great vitality and an almost comic-strip quality with the speech bubbles emerging from the figures' mouths, but their themes always have a religious rather than a purely decorative intent. More can be seen at **Tetitla** and **Atetelco**, both a little way to the west of the main site.

TULA AND TEPOTZOTLAN

In legend at least, the mantle of Teotihuacan fell on *TOLLAN* (**TULA**) as the next great power to dominate Mexico. History, legend and archaeological evidence, however, are here almost impossible to disentangle, and often flatly contradictory. The Aztecs regarded their city as the descendant of Tula and hence embellished its reputation – the streets, they said, had been paved with gold and the buildings constructed from precious metals and stones; the Toltecs were the inventors of every science and art. In reality it seems unlikely that this was ever as large or as powerful a city as Teotihuacan had been – or as Tenochtitlan was to become – and its period of dominance (about 950 to 1150AD) was relatively short. Yet all sorts of puzzles remain about the Toltec era, and in particular the extent of their influence in the Yucatan – at Chichen Itza much of the architecture is clearly Toltec (see p. 333). Few people believe that the Toltecs could actually have had an empire stretching so far: however warlike (and the artistic evidence is that Tula was a grimly militaristic society, heavily into human sacrifice), they would have lacked the manpower, resources or any logical justification for such expansion. Nevertheless, they were there.

The answer lies, perhaps, in the legends of **Quetzalcoatl** which surround the city. Adopted from Teotihuacan, the plumed serpent attained far more importance here in Tula, where he is depicted everywhere. Again fact and legend are almost impossible to extricate, but at some stage Tula certainly had a ruler regarded as Quetzalcoatl who was driven from the city by the machinations of the evil god Texcatlipoca. In legend Quetzalcoatl fled to the east where he either burnt himself to become the morning star or set sail across the ocean on a raft of snakes, promising one day to return (a prophecy which Cortes turned skilfully to his advantage). What may actually have happened is that the ruler was defeated in factional struggles within Tula and, in exile with his followers, eventually reached Mayan territory where they established a new Toltec regime.

Of **the** site itself (open daily 8–6), only a small part is of interest: though the city spreads over some considerable area only small parts have been excavated, and the outlying digs are holes in the ground, meaningful only to the archaeologists who created them. The ceremonial centre, however, has been partly restored. Centrepiece is the low five-stepped pyramid of the **Temple of Tlahuizcalpantecuhtli** (Morning Star), atop which stand the famous **Atlantes of Tula**. These giant, 15-foot tall figures originally supported the roof of the sanctuary: they represent Quetzalcoatl in his guise as the morning star, dressed as a Toltec warrior. They wear elaborately embroidered loincloths, sandals, and feathered helmets, with ornaments around their necks and legs – for protection, sun-shaped shields on their backs and chestpieces in the form of a stylised butterfly. Each carries an *atlatl*, or spear-thrower, in his right hand (Eric von Daniken claims these are ray guns) and a clutch of arrows or javelins to use in them in the left. Other pillars are carved with more warriors and gods.

These relief carvings are one of the constant themes in Tula: the entire temple was originally faced in sculpted stone, and although this was pillaged long ago you can see some remnants from an earlier incarnation of the temple – prowling jaguars and eagles devouring human hearts, symbols of the two great warrior groups. In front of the temple is a great L-shaped collonade, where the partly reconstructed pillars originally supported a huge roof under which, perhaps, the priests and nobles would review their troops or take part in ceremonies in the shade. Part of a long bench (or *banquette*) survives, with its relief decoration of a procession of warriors and priests. More such benches survive in the **Palacio Quemado** (Burnt Palace – it was destroyed by fire), next to the temple on the western side. In the middle of its three rooms – each a square roofed area with a small central patio to let light in – is the best preserved of them, still with much of its original paint, and two *Chac-mool* statues.

The main square of the city stood in front of the temple and palace, with a low platform in the centre and the bulky, now ruinous, pyramid to the left. The larger of two **ball courts** in the central area delineated a third side: although overgrown, this is one of the closest links between Tula and Chichen Itza – of identical shape and orientation to the great ball court there, and displaying many of the same features. To the north of this plaza, behind the temple, stands a wall known as the **Coatepantli** (serpent wall), elaborately carved in relief, and beyond this, across an open space, a second ball court, smaller but in better order.

The modern town of **TULA DE ALLENDE** lies in the valley just below the ruins; easily reached by bus from Mexico's *Terminal del Norte* (*Autobuses del Valle de Mezquital*, less than 1½hrs journey). Tula is also on the rail line from Mexico to Querétaro, but this is slower and more complicated: when the new fast rail link is opened, though, there will be a station right by the site. For some reason, the **entrance to the site** is on the far side from the town, a considerable walk all the way round the perimeter fence. Either get off the bus just as it enters the town by a bridge and the railway lines, where a road (signed *Zona Arqueologica*) branches off to the right towards the entrance, or take a taxi from the Zocalo. There's a small **museum**, with statues and artefacts from the site, just inside the gate. To get back into town, follow one of the broader tracks which leads down the hill (slightly to the left) from the chief monuments towards the town. At the bottom you should find a hole in the fence, or a gate, which local people use to get in and out: the centre of town is easy enough to find, and this is much quicker than going back via the entrance (where there's little chance of finding a taxi unless you've asked one to wait or pick you up). In Tula itself it's worth taking a few minutes to look over the impressive, fortress-like **Franciscan monastery and church** (built around 1550), after which you'll find several reasonable cafes and **restaurants** around the main square where you can kill any spare time before heading back.

TEPOTZOTLAN lies, logically, en route from Tula to the capital, but if you're relying on public transport the problem will be getting from one to the other. It may be easiest to visit the two separately – Tepotzotlan is easily close enough to the city to be a morning's excursion (buses from the *Terminal del Norte* or go to Metro *Indios Verdes* and take a local bus on from there) – but you could also try hitching from Tula or persuade a bus to drop you at the motorway exit and hitch, or take a local bus, for the last couple of miles. The attraction of this small colonial backwater is simple: the magnificent baroque **church of San Francisco Javier** and the *Museo Nacional de Arte Virreinal* which it houses.

The church and seminary here were founded by the Jesuits in the sixteenth century, but what you see dates from the eighteenth, having been completed only a few years before the Jesuits were expelled from the country. The **church** is considered one of the finest examples of Churrigueresque architecture in the country, with a fabulously elaborate facade and an even more dazzling interior. Dripping gold, and profusely carved with a bewilderment of saints and cherubim, it strikes you at first as some mystical cave of treasures. Nowhere more so than in the octagonal *camerino* (little room) where the hand of native craftsmen is clearly evident in the crude but exuberant riot of carving – fruit and flowers, shells and abstract patterns crammed in between the angels. In the main body of the church and its chapels are five huge gilded retablos, stretching from ceiling to floor, each more gloriously flourished and curlicued than the last.

From the cloisters to the right of the church you enter the old seminary, restored to all its colonial richness and now housing the **National Museum of Viceregal Art** (open 10–6; closed Monday and Tuesday). This is the country's most extensive collection or religious art from the colonial period, and includes a great wealth of painting and statuary – native and European – as well as more exotic treasures: silver reliquaries with bones of St Peter and St Paul; embroidered vestments; pictures created from inlaid wood. The setting, too, is lovely, with many of the rooms (the infirmary, kitchens and refectory) recreated, and gardens in which you can see more statues.

The *pastorelas* (**nativity plays**) staged here in the week before Christmas are very famous – and booked up long in advance – but there are often concerts in the church or cloisters at other times of the year. The *Hosteria del Convento*, in the seminary's grounds, often has music too (weekends especially) and excellent food. Cheaper places to eat can be found all round the plaza – try the *Restaurant Virreyes* for a good *comida corrida*.

WEST TO TOLUCA

TOLUCA, capital of the State of Mexico and at nearly 9,000 feet the highest city in the country, is today a large modern industrial centre with few attractions in terms of buildings or atmosphere. It is, however, surrounded by beautiful mountain scenery – dominated by the white-capped Nevado de Toluca – and the site of what is allegedly the largest single **market** in the country. This, held every Friday (and to a lesser extent throughout the week), is the overriding reason to visit, attracting hordes of visitors from the capital. It is so vast that there can be no question of its being overwhelmed by tourists – quite the opposite, many outsiders find themselves crushed by the scale of the place, lost among the thousands of stalls and crowds from the state's outlying villages. There's a substantial selection of local crafts – woven goods and pottery above all – but also vast areas selling more humble everyday domestic items. For an idea of what quality and prices to expect, head for the **Casa de Artesanias**, on the main Paseo Tollocan a few blocks east of the market area.

An almost uninterrupted stream of **buses** leaves Mexico's *Terminal Poniente* for Toluca throughout the day – a journey lasting about an hour. On arrival, the market is right by the modern Central Camionera, and around here too are a number of places to eat (or try the market itself) and several cheap *hotels*. There's little point though, and less pleasure, in staying in Toluca unless you plan to stop over Thursday night, get to the market early, and continue westwards – and on Thursdays it can be hard to find a room.

The country around Toluca is of course easiest explored by car, but most villages do have a bus service, if only once or twice a day. One trip you will miss out on without your own transport is to the volcano, the **Nevado de Toluca** (or *Xinantécatl*). A rough dirt road – not practicable during the rainy season or in mid-winter – leads all the way to two small lakes in the heart of the crater: from its lip the views are breathtaking – below you the lakes, eastwards a fabulous vista across the Valleys of Toluca and Mexico, and to the west a series of lower, greener hills ranging towards the peaks of the Sierra Madre Occidental. You need a tough vehicle to get up here, and healthy lungs to take even a short climb at 14,000 feet.

Easier, closer to Toluca and accessible by local bus, is a visit to the archaeological site of **Calixtlahuaca** just north of the city. This was the township of the *Matlazinca* people, inhabited from pre-historic times and later subjugated by the Aztecs, who established a garrison here in the fifteenth century. Calixtlahuaca was not a willing subject, and there were constant rebellions; after one, in 1475, the Aztecs took over 11,000 Matlazinca prisoners to be sacrificed on the temples of Tenochtitlan. The most important buildings on the site are those of the Aztec ceremonial centre, and in particular the circular Temple of Quetzalcoatl. Dedicated to him in his role as Ehecatl, god of wind, its circular design is typical — allowing the wind to blow freely around the shrine. See also the remains of the pyramid devoted to Tlaloc, and the nearby *Tzompantli* (skull rack), both constructed of the local pink and black volcanic stone.

Leaving Toluca westwards, the road towards MORELIA and the State of Michoacan is a truly spectacular one. Much of this wooded, mountainous area — as far as ZITACUARO — is given over to villas inhabited at weekends by wealthy refugees from the capital, and nowhere more so than **VALLE DE BRAVO**, reached by turning off to the left about halfway. Set in a deep pine-clad valley, the town sits on the eastern shore of an artificial lake, the *Presa Miguel Aleman*. There's everything here for upmarket relaxation — sailing, swimming and water-skiing on the lake (the remarkable yacht club moves up and down according to the level of the water, which can vary dramatically); riding, hiking and even golf on dry land. It's expensive despite the number of hotels, but does make for a very relaxing break — especially if you come during the week, when fewer people are about. There's a reasonable bus service from Mexico, via Toluca, or you should be able to hitch the last 30km without too much difficulty.

One of the strange things about this route is that as you descend from Toluca, so the country becomes more mountainous — where Toluca is on a very high plateau, broken only by the occasional soaring peak, the lower country to the west is constantly, ruggedly hilly. It's also warmer, and far more verdant. Much the same happens as you head **south to TAXCO**, although here you head across the plateau for some way until you start to go down into the mountains. There are four or five buses a day along this road, and several places of interest on the way. The first village, less than 10km out of Toluca, is **METEPEC**, famed as a pottery-making centre. Brightly coloured local wares can be found at craft shops throughout the country — supposedly the figures were originally inspired by the saints on the facade of Metepec's sixteenth-century Franciscan Monastery, and in this century Diego Rivera taught the villagers new techniques of colouring and design. There's a market here on Mondays. After some 25km you pass **TENANGO** where there was a fortified Malatzinca township (*Teotenango*) whose excavated remains can be visited (from 9–5 except Mondays). Also on the site is a small museum with objects found here and at Calixtlahuaca.

TENANCINGO, the next village of any size, is perhaps more inter-esting, and here there are a couple of small hotels – try the *San Carlos* – which can make a quiet place to stop over if you want to avoid the dull modernity of Toluca or the tourist trappings of Taxco. Liqueurs made from the fruit which grows in abundance on the surrounding plain, and finely woven traditional *rebozos* (shawls) are sold here, many of them produced at the lovely monastery of El Santo Desierto, but the chief attraction is the proximity of the amazing Aztec ruins at **MALINALCO**. Carved, mostly, from the raw rock of a steep mountainside, this was a garrison and sanctuary for the Aztec warrior elite from which they could maintain control of the local population. Still incomplete at the time of the conquest, and relatively small, it is nonetheless the most spectacular and evocative Aztec site in the country. The main structures and the stairways up to them are part cut out of the rock, part constructed from stone blocks, but the most remarkable aspect is the circular inner sanctuary of the main temple (the House of the Eagle), hewn entirely from the face of the mountain. With its thatched roof replaced, the natural light effects inside are wonderful, and give some idea of the mystic atmosphere which must have surrounded the place at its height, although then the sculpted figures would all have been painted. You approach up a broad staircase on either side of which sit stone jaguars – in the centre the broken human statue would originally have held a flag. The doorway of the sanctuary itself, cut through a natural rock wall, represents the giant mouth of a serpent – you walk in over its tongue, and around the entrance traces of teeth are still visible. Right in the centre of the floor lies the figure of an eagle, on the raised horseshoe-shaped bench behind two more eagles and the pelt of a jaguar, all carved in a single piece from the bedrock.

Few people get to Malinalco, presumably because of the difficulties of transport, but is is by no means impossible. The **village of Malinalco** (which has a lovely Augustinian monastery, largely built with stone plun-dered from the site) is only about 20km from Tenancingo, but over an atrocious road. There is an occasional bus along this route, but you might have more luck hitching. Alternatively you can approach from the other direction, via Chalma, on buses from either CUERNAVACA or MEXICO itself (*Flecha Roja* from the *Central del Sur*; check with them on 271 0333). **CHALMA** is an important centre of pilgrimage, attracting vast crowds every Sunday, and at times of special religious significance (especially the first Friday in Lent, Holy Week and September 29th) so many people that the tiny village is entirely overwhelmed and it's imposs-ible to get anywhere near the church. The permanent population is only a couple of hundred, but at such times pilgrims are camping out for miles around to take part in the rituals which are a fascinating mix of Christian and more ancient pagan rites: before the Spanish arrived the deity Otzoc-teotl, god of caves, was venerated in a natural cavern here, but he was 'miraculously' replaced by a statue of Christ when the first missionaries arrived. In the seventeenth century this crucifix was moved to a new church. As well as paying their devotions to Christ the pilgrims bathe themselves in the healing waters which flow from the cave.

Back on the main road from Toluca to Taxco, **IXTAPAN DE LA SAL** is a long-established spa whose mineral rich waters are supposed to cure a plethora of muscular and circulatory ills. You can swim in the pools here – cheaper in the old town, but much more elegant at the *Balneario Nuevo* – and there are several reasonably priced hotels (*Guadalajara, Reforma, Ideal*) as well as some very expensive ones. Further south, and almost at Taxco, you pass close to the vast complex of caves known as the **GRUTAS DE CACAHUAMILPA** (open daily 10–3). This network of caverns, hollowed out by two rivers, extends for some 43 miles – although the guided tour (which is obligatory) obviously takes in only a fraction. Among the graffiti you're shown a rather prim note by the Empress Carlota, wife of Maximilian – 'Maria Carlota reached this point'. Alongside, Lerdo de Tejada, who became president in 1872 five years after Maximilian's execution, has scrawled 'Sebastian Lerdo de Tejada went further'. There's a swimming pool by the entrance to the caves, as well as a restaurant and several food stalls, and buses on to Taxco or Cuernavaca (*Flecha Roja* again).

CUERNAVACA AND TAXCO

The old road to ACAPULCO ran out from the capital via Cuernavaca and Taxco, and although the modern route skirts the former and gives Taxco a wide berth, both remain firmly established on the tourist tread-mill. The journey starts well: a steep, winding climb out of the Valley of Mexico into refreshing pine forests, and then gently down, leaving the city pollution behind. It's a fast road too, and, smog permitting, offers lovely views back over Mexico.

CUERNAVACA has always been a place of escape from the city – the Aztecs called it *Cuauhnahuac* ('place by the woods') and it became a favourite resort and hunting ground for their kings. Cortes seized and destroyed the city during the siege of Tenochtitlan, but he too ended up building himself a palace: the Spanish corrupting the name to Cuernavaca ('cow horn') for no better reason than their inability to cope with the original. The fashion then established has been followed ever since – among others by the Emperor Maximilian and the deposed Shah of Iran – but for the casual visitor the modern city is in many ways a disappointment. Its spring-like climate remains, but as capital of the state of Morelos, Cuernavaca is rapidly becoming industrialised and the streets in the centre are permanently clogged with traffic and fumes. The gardens and villas which shelter wealthy Mexicans and expatriates are almost all hidden behind high walls, or so far out in the suburbs that you won't see them: it seems an ill-planned and widely spread city, certainly not easy to get about on foot. Food and lodging, too, come expensive, in part thanks to the large foreign contingent, swelled by tourists and by students from the many language schools. On the other hand, the centre of town is attractive enough and there are a few sights which deserve, at least, half a day.

The first of these, right on the central plaza, is **Cortes's Palace** (Tues.-Sun. 9.30–5) which now houses the **Museo Regional Cuauhnahuac**. Building began as early as 1522 when, although Tenochtitlan had fallen, much of the country was still not under Spanish control, and the fortress-like aspect of the earlier parts reflect this period: over the centuries, though, it's been added to and modified substantially – first by Cortes himself and his descendants, later by the state authorities to whom it passed. What you see today is very much a palace. The museum is a good one, covering local archaeology and history, with a substantial collection of colonial art, weaponry and everyday artefacts, but the high-light is the series of Diego Rivera murals* around the gallery. Depicting Mexican history, they concentrate in particular on the atrocities committed by Cortes and on Emiliano Zapata – the revolutionary who was born in nearby Cuautla, raised most of his army from the peasants of Morelos, and remains something of a folk hero to them. From the balcony here, if you're lucky, there are wonderful views to the east, with Popocatépetl in the far distance. Around the main entrance, you can see excavated traces of the Aztec pyramid which originally occupied this site.

Right next to the Palace, on the right as you face it, is a small *FONART* craft shop – the best of many catering to the tourists here – and around the twin plazas you'll find a series of **cafes** where you can sit outdoors. If you stick to simple stuff, these are not unreasonably priced. Head out of the plaza on Hidalgo and you'll reach the **Cathedral**, founded by Cortes in 1529. Bulky and threatening from the outside (at one stage there were actually cannons mounted along the battlemented roofline), it has been remarkably tastefully refurbished within: stripped almost bare and painted in plain gold and white. Traces of murals, discovered during the redecoration, have been uncovered in places – they have a remarkably Oriental look and are believed to have been painted by a Christian Chinaman or Filipino in the days when Cuernavaca Cathedral was the

---

* More murals, by David Siqueiros, can be seen in the *Hotel Casino de la Selva* (Leandro Valle 1001), and you can also visit his studio at Calle Venus 2 (open Tues.–Sun. 10–2 and 4–6). Both are a taxi ride away from the centre.

centre for missions to the Far East. The main Spanish trade route then came through here, with goods brought across the Pacific to Acapulco, overland through Central Mexico, and on from Veracruz to Spain. The present bishop of Cuernavaca is one of the country's most liberal and, apart from doing up his cathedral, is renowned for his outspoken sermons, and for the *Mariachi Mass* which he instituted here. Every Sunday morning at 11, this service is conducted to the accompaniment of traditional Mexican music and usually attracts large crowds.

A few yards beyond the Cathedral is the entrance to the **Jardin Borda**, a large formal garden laid out by the Taxco mining magnate Jose de la Borda (see p. 227) in the eighteenth century. Open daily from 9–2 and 4–7, both the gardens and Borda's mansion are in a rather sorry state but they remain delightfully tranquil and a reminder of the haven which Cuernavaca once was – and no doubt still is behind the walls of its exclusive residences. Maximilian and Carlota adopted Borda's legacy as their weekend home before moving to a house further out. The latter can also be visited – with more impressive grounds and a small **Museum of Medicinal Plants** – but again it's rather too far out to walk. The small **Tourist Office** at the entrance to the Borda Gardens has maps of the town on which you can find this and the other sites in the outskirts: the **Salto de San Anton**, a small waterfall in another park where there's a crafts market, is also worth visiting if you enjoy gardens.

Just one significant reminder of the pre-colonial period survives in the city, the **Pyramid of Teopanzolco**, and even that was so effectively buried that it took an artillery bombardment during the Revolution to uncover it. To the north-east of the centre beyond the railway station (which is what the gunners were aiming at), it's a small temple with a typically Aztec double stairway.

Buses run every few minutes to Cuernavaca from Mexico's *Central del Sur*: of the three lines you can take, *Flecha Roja* is probably the best since its Cuernavaca terminal, on Calle Morelos, is central and easy to find. *Pullman de Morelos* also stops quite close to the centre, at the corner of Abasolo and Netzahualcoyotl; simply walk up the latter and you find yourself at the heart of things. First class *Estrellas de Oro* may be more luxurious, but their terminus is miles out – worth getting to though, if you're continuing on the long ride south to Acapulco and the coast. If you want to stay, what cheap **hotels** there are are mostly between the centre and the Flecha Roja station – walk down Morelos, turn left on Aragon y Leon after about three blocks, then right onto Matamoros and you'll reach the main plazas. On the way you should pass the Hotels *America* and *Buen Vecino* and the *Casa de Huespedes Marilu* on Aragon y Leon, and the Hotels *Royal* and *Roma* on Matamoros. There's little to choose between them.

One of the most interesting side trips from Cuernavaca is to

TEPOZTLAN, just 20km away but, until recently at least, an entirely different world. In a narrow valley spectacularly ringed by volcanic mountains, the village was an isolated agrarian community, inhabited by *Nahuatl*-speaking Indians whose life can have changed little between the time of the Conquest and the beginning of this century. It was on Tepoztlan that Oscar Lewis's classic study of *Life in a Mexican Village*, and the effects of the Revolution on it, was based: the village was an important stronghold of the *Zapatista* movement. New roads and a couple of luxury hotels have changed much – a turning of the tables noted by James Tickell in his *American Express Guide* who recommends that you come here to 'gaze at the bright costumes and beads of the foreign hippies' – but the stunning setting survives, as does a reputation for joyously boisterous fiestas (especially the drunken revelry of the night of September 7th). On the central plaza, where the market is held on Sundays and Wednesdays, stands the massive, fortress-like **Dominican Monastery**. It was indeed a fortress for a while during the revolution, but is now given over to a museum (open Tues.–Sun. 10–2 and 4–6) with a remarkably good archaeological collection. Several pre-hispanic temples have been found on the hilltops roundabout and you can reach one, atop the artificially flattened **Cerro del Tepozteco**, with an exhausting climb of an hour or more along a well-signposted path from the village. The pyramid here was dedicated to Tepoztecatl, a god of *pulque* and of fertility, represented by carvings of rabbits. There were so many pulque gods that they were known as the 400 rabbits, since the drink was supposedly discovered by rabbits, nibbling at the agave plants from which it is made (and presumably then acting as crazily as our own mad march hare). This one gained particular kudos when the Spanish flung the idol off the cliffs only for his adherents to find that it had landed quite unharmed – the big September fiesta is in his honour.

Not much further from Cuernavaca, this time to the south, lie the ruins of **XOCHICALCO**. While not much is known of the history of this site or the peoples who inhabited it, it is regarded by archaeologists as one of the most significant in Central Mexico, forming as it does a link between the Classic culture of Teotihuacan and the later Toltec peoples. Xochicalco flourished from around the seventh to the tenth century AD – thus overlapping with both Teotihuacan and Tula – and it also shows clear parallels with Mayan and Zapotec sites of the era. The setting, high on a bare mountain top, is immediately reminiscent of Monte Alban (p. 288), the great Zapotec site near Oaxaca and, like Monte Alban and the great Mayan sites (but unlike Tula or Teotihuacan), Xochicalco was an exclusively religious and ceremonial centre rather than a true city. The style of many of the carvings, too, recalls Zapotec and Mayan art. Their subjects, however, and the architecture of the temples, do seem to be a transitional stage between Teotihuacan and Tula: in particular Quetzalcoatl first appears here in human guise, as he was to feature at Tula and almost every subsequent site, rather than simply as the feathered serpent of Teotihuacan. The ball-court is almost identical to earlier Mayan examples, and very similar to those which later appeared in Tula. For all these diverse influences, however, or perhaps because there are so many of them, it's almost impossible to say which was dominant: some claim that Xochicalco was a northern outpost of the Maya, others that it was a subject city of Teotihuacan which survived (or perhaps precipitated through revolt) the fall of that empire.

In any case, much the most important surviving monument is the **Pyramid of Quetzalcoatl** on the highest part of the site. Around its base are carved wonderfully elaborate plumed serpents, coiling around various seated figures and symbols with astronomical significance – all clearly Mayan in inspiration. On top, part of the walls of the sanctuary remains standing. Not far from here, to the left and slightly down the hill, you'll find the entrance to the subterranean passages, a couple of natural caves which have had steps and tunnels added to them by human hands. In one a shaft in the roof is so oriented as to allow the sun to shine directly in at times of equinox: any other time you'll need a torch to make out remains of frescoes on the walls.

Both Xochicalco (twice a day) and Tepoztlan (frequently) have a **bus service** from Cuernavaca with *Flecha Roja*. If you're driving, or if you go with a tour, you can continue down the road beyond Xochicalco to the caves of CACAHUAMILPA (p. 223) from where TAXCO is only a short distance further.

Silver has been mined in **TAXCO** since before the Spanish Conquest, and although the sources have long been virtually exhausted, silver is still the basis of the town's fame and its livelihood. Nowadays, though, it's in the form of jewellery made here in hundreds of workshops to be sold throughout the country but especially in a bewildering array of shops (*platerias*) catering to the tourists in Taxco itself. More indirectly, silver wealth has created the town itself, a mass of narrow cobbled alleys lined with red-roofed, white-washed houses straggling steeply over the hills. At intervals the pattern is broken by some larger mansion, by a courtyard filled with flowers, or by the twin spires of a church rearing up – above all the famous baroque wedding cake of Santa Prisca.

Taxco's development, for all that it might seem a prosperous place now, has not been a simple progression – indeed on more than one occasion the town has been all but abandoned. Although the Spaniards came running at the rumours of mineral wealth here (Cortes himself sent an expedition in 1522), their initial success in finding silver was short-lived, and it wasn't until the eighteenth century that *Jose de la Borda* struck it fabulously rich by discovering the San Ignacio vein. It is from the short period of Borda's life that most of what you see dates – he spent one large fortune on building the church of Santa Prisca, others on more buildings and a royal lifestyle here and in Cuernavaca – but by his death in 1778 the boom was already over. In 1929 a final revival started with the arrival of the American *William Spratling* who set up a jewellery workshop in Taxco, drawing on the town's traditional skills and designs. With the completion of a new road around the same time the massive influx of tourists was inevitable, but the town has handled it well, becoming rich without losing too much of its charm.

The one outstanding sight in Taxco is the church of **Santa Prisca**, a building so florid and expensive that it not surprisingly arouses strong feeling. Aldous Huxley, in his journey *Beyond the Mexique Bay*, regarded the town, and the church in particular, with less than affection:

> *Taxco is a sort of Mexican Saint-Paul largely inhabited by artists and by those camp followers of the arts whose main contribution to the cause of Intellectual Beauty consists in being partially or completely drunk for several hours each day. In the eighteenth century, Borda, the mining millionaire, built for Taxco one of the most sumptuous churches in Mexico – one of the most sumptuous and one of the most ugly. I have never seen a building in which every part, down to the smallest decorative detail, was so constantly ill-proportioned. Borda's church is an inverted work of genius.*

But that is the minority view – most would follow Sacheverell Sitwell (who loves anything frilly) in his view that

> *its obvious beauties in the way of elegance and dignity, and its suitability to both purpose and environment are enough to convert those who would never have thought to find themselves admiring a building of this kind. It is of course much helped by the beautiful little town in which it stands ... [which] could qualify as the National Monument of Latin America. Its red tiled roofs, steep winding streets and pebbled pavements in mosaic give to it the aura of some old forgotten town in Italy or Spain.*

Which is probably enough said about the church. Its hyper-elaborate facade towers over the Zocalo, and inside there's a riot of gilded Churriguresque altarpieces and other treasures including paintings by Miguel Cabrera, a Zapotec Indian who became one of Mexico's greatest religious artists.

The **Museo Guillermo Spratling**, which houses William Spratling's personal collection of antiquities and a small display devoted to the history of Taxco, can be found by going round to the back of the church on Calle Veracruz. Impressively displayed over three floors, it's open from 10–2 and 4–7 daily. Not far from here on Juan Ruiz de Alarcon, the street parallel to Veracruz, is the **Casa Humboldt**, an old staging inn named for the German explorer who spent one night here in 1803. A beautiful colonial building, it now houses an excellent state-run crafts shop and exhibition which frequently displays prize-winning pieces by local silversmiths. In the other direction, above the Zocalo, you'll find the **Casa Figueroa** (open daily 10–1), another fine mansion converted into a small art gallery and museum. It was originally known as the *Casa de Lagrimas* (House of Tears) because the magistrate who built it employed the forced labour of Indians unable to pay the fines he imposed on them. Beyond these few sights the charm of Taxco is to be found in simply wandering the streets, nosing about in the *platerias*, stopping occasionally for a drink. If you're buying silver you can be fairly sure it's the real thing here (check for the hallmark – .925 or 'sterling'), but prices are much the same as they would be anywhere and quality and workmanship can vary enormously: there's everything from mass-produced belt buckles and cheap rings to designer jewellery which will set you back thousands of dollars.

By **staying in Taxco** you'll find a far more pleasant side to the town: there are some excellent hotels, and when most of the day-trippers have left the place settles into a calmer mode. In the evening everyone gathers around the Zocalo to see and be seen, to stroll in front of the church, or to sit outdoors with a coffee or a drink. You can join in from one of the famous bars – *Berta's*, the traditional place to meet right next to the church, or *Paco's*, more fashionable nowadays, across the square. The best value place to stay in town is the *Hotel Jardin*, right next to the church of Santa Prisca in the little alley on the left as you face it: small and quiet. The *Hotel Melendez*, on Calle San Agustin between the Zocalo and the Plazuela San Juan, is considerably more expensive but also much larger and more formally run – its restaurant is reasonable, and especially good for breakfast. Or try the *Casa Grande*, cheap but run down, which you'll find by going through to a courtyard behind the cinema on the Plazuela San Juan. Moving upmarket you're swamped with choices, though the most expensive tend to be some way out of town. Centrally the *Hotel Los Arcos* (Juan Ruiz de Alarcon 2), the *Posada de los Castillo* (Juan Ruiz de Alarcon 7) and the *Hotel Santa Prisca* (Cena Obscuras 1, near the Melendez) are all converted colonial buildings and good value considering the luxury. Finding somewhere to **eat** is no problem at all, though the enticing places around the Zocalo do tend to be expensive. For rock-bottom food the **market** (down the steps beside the Zocalo and full of rather tacky tourist goods) has a section given over to food stalls which are better than they look, or carry on right through to emerge on the street below the market where you'll find a couple of reasonable local restaurants. All except the cheapest of the hotels, too, have their own dining rooms.

Both **bus stations** are on the main road which winds around the side of the valley below the town. To get in from *Flecha Roja* turn to your left up the hill and then turn left again to climb even more steeply past the church of Veracruz to the Zocalo. From *Estrella de Oro* (which has a small **Tourist Office** opposite) head straight up the steep alley directly across from you until you come, on your right, to the Plazuela San Juan, and from there down Cuauhtemoc to the Zocalo.

PUEBLA, CHOLULA AND THE VOLCANOES

East of the capital, a fast new road climbs steeply, past glorious views of the snow-decked heights of Popocatépetl and Ixtaccíhuatl (the best are looking back, for the last wisps of smog are only left behind at the very brow of the pass) to **PUEBLA**. Little over an hour on the bus – *ADO*, *Cristobal Colon* or *Estrella Roja* from the TAPO terminal – this is the Republic's fourth largest city, and one of its hardest to pin down. On the whole it's a disappointment, with the initial impression of industrial modernity imparted by the huge Volkswagen works on the outskirts never quite dispelled in streets which are permanently clogged with traffic, raucous and rushed. There are few good places to stay, with rooms expensive and often booked up. Yet this is as historic a city as any in Mexico, and certainly in the centre there's a remarkable concentration of interest – fabulous cathedral, 'hidden' convent, museums and colonial mansions. Nevertheless, Puebla is unlikely to tempt you into staying particularly long, and in a packed day both the city and nearby Cholula can be seen, either returning to Mexico or continuing overnight to Veracruz or Oaxaca.

The city was founded by the Spanish in 1531 and, rare for this area, was an entirely new foundation – preferred to the ancient sites of Cholula and Tlaxcala because there, presumably, the memories of Indian power remained too strong. It rapidly assumed great importance as a staging point on the journey from the capital to the port at Veracruz, and for the trans-shipment of goods from Spain's far-eastern colonies, delivered to Acapulco and transported across Mexico from there. Wealth was brought, too, by the reputation of its ceramic and tile manufacture (still very much in evidence) which was in part due to the abundance of good clays, in part to its settlement by Spaniards from Talavera who brought traditional skills with them. The city did well out of colonial rule, and perhaps not surprisingly it took the wrong side in the War of Independence, preserving to this day a name for conservatism and traditional values. Military defeat seems to play an even larger part in Puebla's history than it does in most of Mexico – the city fell to the Americans in 1847 and to the French in 1863 – but what's remembered is the greatest victory in the country's history, when a force of some 2,000 Mexicans defeated a French army three times the size in 1862 – to this

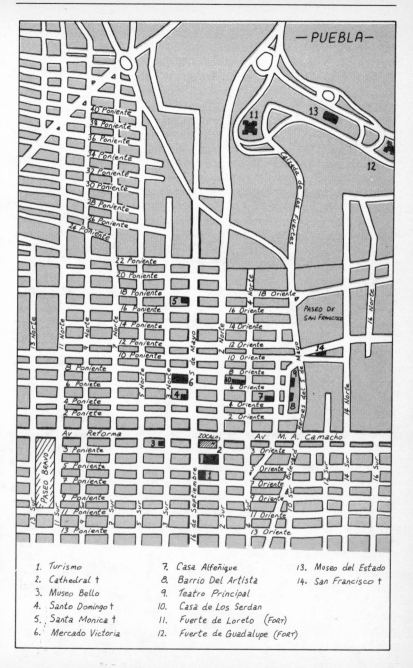

- PUEBLA -

1. Turismo
2. Cathedral †
3. Museo Bello
4. Santo Domingo †
5. Santa Monica †
6. Mercado Victoria
7. Casa Alfeñique
8. Barrio Del Artista
9. Teatro Principal
10. Casa de Los Serdan
11. Fuerte de Loreto (FORT)
12. Fuerte de Guadalupe (FORT)
13. Museo del Estado
14. San Francisco †

day the 5th of May is commemorated with a massive fiesta here, and with a public holiday throughout the country.

Any tour of the city must start in the **Zocalo**, centre of the numbering system for the ancient grid of streets, where stands the great **Cathedral**, second largest in the Republic. Under construction from 1562 until the middle of the following century, its ornamentation – especially the interior, decked out in onyx, marble and gilt – is amazing. There are frequent free guided tours. Immediately behind the Cathedral, at the corner of 16 de Septiembre with 5 Oriente, you'll find the **Tourist Office**, which has free maps and details of city tours – worth taking if you want to see everything in a hurry. Here too is the old **Archbishop's Palace** – converted to a library in the seventeenth century and now housing this (the *Biblioteca Palafoxiana*) upstairs, with a fabulous collection of ancient books, and the city's Casa de la Cultura downstairs. There are regular exhibitions of local arts and crafts.

Head north from the Zocalo along Avenida 5 de Mayo and you reach the church of **Santo Domingo** at the corner of 4 Poniente. Its *Capilla del Rosario* is a quite unbelievably lavish orgy of gold leaf and baroque excess: dedicated to a revered image of the Virgin, there's a constant hushed, shuffling stream of devotees lighting candles and praying for miraculous cures. Puebla's main **market**, the *Mercado Victoria*, lies just beyond on 5 de Mayo, while continuing for another five or six blocks brings you to the remarkable 'hidden' convent of **Santa Monica**. Here, from the suppression of the church in 1857 until their discovery in 1934, several generations of nuns lived hidden from the public gaze behind a smokescreen of secret doors and concealed passages. Just how secret they were is a matter of some debate – many claim that the authorities simply turned a blind eye – and certainly several lay families were actively supportive, providing supplies and new recruits. But it makes a good story, embellished by the conversion into a museum which preserves the secret entries along with many religious artworks and a beautiful cloister. In the same general direction, at 3 Norte and 14 Poniente, is the convent of **Santa Rosa**, whose main claim to fame is that the great *Mole Poblano* was invented in its kitchens. You can sample this extraordinary sauce – made of chocolate, chile, and any number of other herbs and spices – in the kitchens at Santa Rosa, but it's also served with chicken or turkey at every restaurant in Puebla.

The rest of the interest is mostly concentrated west of here, north-west of the Zocalo. On 6 Oriente, heading west from the market, is the **Casa de los Serdan** – the ancient home of the Serdan family whose liberal struggles against the dictatorship of Porfirio Diaz are recorded in a museum here. The assassination of Aguiles Serdan in this house was one of the most important steps in the fall of Diaz and the start of the Revolution – the bullet holes have been lovingly preserved, even down to the huge smashed mirror, still on the wall where it appears in contemporary photos of the carnage. At the end of 6 Oriente lie the **Mercado Parian** – mostly given over to rather tawdry tourist souvenirs – and the **Barrio del Artista**, traditionally the artists' quarter but now with artworks on sale which are again aimed squarely at the tourists. The **Teatro Principal**, nearby, is a fine eighteenth-century theatre, said to be the oldest on the continent, which still hosts occasional performances. Walking back to the Zocalo, you can stop in at the **Casa Alfeñique**, an elaborate old mansion covered in Puebla tiles which now houses the regional museum (open Tues.–Sun. 10–5). There are period furnishings, Puebla ceramics, a small archaeological section, and upstairs an excellent display of colonial artworks.

Also worth seeing is the **Museo Bello**, just east of the Zocalo at 3 Norte. It's an eclectic private collection (open Tues.–Sun. 10–5) of paintings, furniture, ceramics and just about anything else which caught Señor Bello's eye. Further afield, the historic forts of **Guadalupe** and **Loreto**, and the modern **State Museum**, crown a hill to the north-west. They mark the site of the constant battles and sieges of the nineteenth century, and the Fuerte Loreto contains a small military museum: the State Museum is largely devoted to the area's archaeology and ethnology. A local bus (marked *Fuertes*) will get you out there from the Zocalo.

Finding somewhere reasonable **to stay** in Puebla can be a real problem, but at least the bulk of the possibilities are not far from the Zocalo, mostly just to the west and north. The *Hotel Embajadores*, on 5 de Mayo more or less opposite the church of Santo Domingo, is basic but has large rooms and fair prices. Walk down 2 Oriente or 4 Oriente from here and you'll pass several others – the *Ritz* on 2 Norte, the *Palacio*, and slightly higher in price the *Posada de los Angeles* and the *Hotel Latino* on 4 Norte and 6 Norte respectively. The *Hotel Colonial*, just one block from the Zocalo at the corner of 4 Sur and 3 Oriente, is considerably more expensive, but worth it if you can afford a little colonial luxury: those actually on the plaza are much pricier still. **Eating**, at least, is no problem, and you should really try a *pollo con mole poblano* at one of the restaurants on the Zocalo or at any of the many *fondas tipicas* around the central area. For cheaper food, head for the area around the Mercado Victoria, or if you crave the familiar there's a *Sanborn's* on Av. 2 Oriente, just off 5 de Mayo.

Plans to build a **Central Camionera** in Puebla are so old, and so constantly delayed, and I doubt it will ever happen. For the moment every company has a separate terminal and your best bet is to note down where you arrive if you want to go back the same way. *ADO* is currently the handiest, on 6 Norte just a couple of blocks west of the Zocalo.

Cholula and Tlaxcala

The ruins of **CHOLULA**, and the largest pyramid in Mexico, are just 15km from Puebla. At the time of the conquest this was a vast city of some 400 temples, famed as a shrine to Quetzalcoatl and for the excellence of its pottery (a trade dominated by immigrant Mixtecs, see p. 288). But the city paid dearly for its attempt – inspired by its Aztec allies – to ambush Cortes on his march to Tenochtitlan: the chieftains were slaughtered, their temples destroyed, and churches built in their place. The Spanish claimed to have constructed 365 churches here, one for each day of the year, but although there are an awful lot, the figure certainly doesn't approach that. There may well, though, be 365 chapels, which is already a few hundred more than the village population nowadays could reasonably need.

Even the **Great Pyramid** is not much to look at these days – at least as a building. Still covered in earth, it makes a not inconsiderable hill; a stiff climb up which will take you to the church of *Nuestra Señora de los Remedios* and a viewing position from which you can attempt to count the churches. Within the pyramid/hill a series of tunnels dug during excavations can be explored: over 8km of them in all wind through the various stages of construction, but only a small proportion is open to the public: poorly lit but fascinating. The entrance is at the bottom near the railway station – guided tours only.

In **the town**, the great multi-domed Capilla Real is the most interesting of the churches. Most of the rest seem to have been left quietly to crumble away. It's a pleasantly tranquil place to decay, at least, and there are a couple of basic cafes on the plaza where you can sit and join the endless inactivity. **Buses** leave Puebla for Cholula every half hour or so from the terminal at 8 Poniente and 9 Norte: heading onwards you can get a slow, stopping, second class service straight back to Mexico City, though it might actually save time to go via Puebla.

TLAXCALA, capital of the tiny state of Tlaxcala, is also close to Puebla – about 30km. As Cortes's closest ally in the struggle against the Aztecs, the town suffered a very different fate from that of Cholula, but one that in the long run has led to an even more total disappearance of its ancient culture. For although the Spanish founded a town here – now restored and very beautiful in much of its original colonial glory – to the Mexicans Tlaxcala was a symbol of treachery, and to some extent it still is (in much the same way as Malinche is bitterly remembered in the commonly used insult *hijo de la chingada*; son of the whore). Siding with Spain in the War of Independence didn't help greatly either, and whether for this reason, or whether for its genuine isolation, development has passed Tlaxcala by. Nowadays it's a genuine backwater, quiet and rarely visited.

There are buses from Puebla and occasionally from Mexico City. If you're driving you could also stop in at the ancient site of CACAXTLA, where a series of murals, depicting battle scenes which are clearly Mayan in style, continue to baffle archaeologists.

Popocatépetl and Ixtaccíhuatl

Although you get excellent views of the snowy volcanic peaks throughout this area, actually climbing the volcanoes, or at least spending some time in the National Park which encompasses their gentle lower slopes, is an exceptional experience. *Popo*, at 17,845 feet, is the taller of them and theoretically still active (though the last eruption was in 1802); *Ixta*, 17,295 feet, is the more challenging climb for serious mountaineers – they're the second and third highest mountains in Mexico, after the Pico de Orizaba.

Their strange names stem from an Aztec Romeo and Juliet style legend – **Popocatépetl** (Smoking Mountain) was a warrior, **Ixtaccíhuatl** (White Lady) his lover, the beautiful daughter of the emperor. Believing Popocatépetl killed in battle, she died of grief, and when he returned alive he laid her body down on the mountain, where he eternally stands sentinel, holding a burning torch. From the west, Ixta does somewhat resemble a reclining female form and the various parts of the mountain are named accordingly – the feet, the knees, the belly, the breast, the neck, the head and the hair.

To climb the volcanoes (or to visit the park) take a *Cristobal Colon* bus from Mexico City or Puebla to **AMECAMECA**. It's a lovely little town, with breathtaking views of the mountain peaks set bizarrely against the palms in the Zocalo, and there are a couple of good hotels. From here the **Tlamacas hut,** base for climbing Popo, can be reached at weekends by minibus, at other times either by taxi or hitching. As long as you're acclimatised to the altitude, adequately dressed (it's extremely cold), properly equipped (gear can be hired at the Tlamacas hut) and the weather conditions are all right (best in mid-winter when the snow is hard), anyone in reasonable physical condition can manage the climb to the rim of the crater – from where Cortes lowered some of his men down to gather sulphur for gun powder. But even so it's not to be undertaken lightly – you need a dawn start and will be on the move all day – and is probably best done with experienced climbers. At weekends it's normally easy enough to link up with a Mexican climbing party (everyone stays at either the hostel or the hotel in Tlamacas), but you might consider getting in touch with a mountaineering club beforehand. The *Club de Exploraciones de Mexico* (Juan Mateos 146, Mexico 8 D.F.) or the *Mountain Rescue Club* (San Juan de Letran 80, Mexico D.F.) should be able to put you in touch with someone. Ixta is a far more serious climb, and not for amateurs or anyone without full equipment. More information on routes and detail can be gleaned from Hilary Bradt's *Back-*

packing in Mexico and Central America, or much more fully from R. J. Secor's *Mexico's Volcanoes* (see p. 374).

FIESTAS

January

6th DIA DE LOS SANTOS REYES (Twelfth Night). The Magi traditionally leave presents for children on this date: many small ceremonies include a fiesta with dancing at **Nativitas** (Distrito Federal), a suburb near Xochimilco, and at **Malinalco** (Mexico state).

17th BENDICION DE LOS ANIMALES. Children's pets and peasants' farm animals alike are taken to church to be blessed. A particularly bizarre sight at the Cathedral in **Mexico** and in **Taxco**, where it coincides with a fiesta running over into the following day.

February

2nd DIA DE LA CANDELARIA is widely celebrated, especially in **Cuernavaca** (Morelos).

CARNIVAL (the week before Lent, variable Feb.–Mar.) is especially lively in **Cuernavaca** (Mor.) and nearby **Tepoztlan** (Mor.). Also in **Chiconcuac** (Mex.) on the way to Teotihuacan. In **Xochimilco** (D.F.), for some reason, they celebrate Carnival two weeks after everyone else.

March

On the Sunday following March 9th a large feria with traditional dances is held at **San Gregorio Atlapulco**, near Xochimilco (D.F.)

PALM SUNDAY (the week before Easter) sees a procession with palms in **Taxco** (Guerrero), where representations of the Passion continue through Holy Week.

HOLY WEEK itself is observed everywhere. There are very famous passion plays in the suburb of **Itzapalapa** (D.F.), culminating on the Friday with a mock crucifixion on the *Cerro de la Estrella*, and similar celebrations at **Chalma** (Mex.) and nearby **Malinalco**. In **Cholula** (Puebla), with its host of churches, the processions pass over vast carpets of flowers.

April

Cuernavaca's flower festival, the FERIA DE LA FLOR, usually falls in early April.

May

1st Mayday, a public holiday, is usually marked by large marches and demonstrations in the capital. In **Cuautla** (Mor.) the same day sees a fiesta commemorating an Independence battle.

3rd DIA DE LA SANTA CRUZ is celebrated with fiestas, and traditional dancing, in **Xochimilco** (D.F.), in **Tepoztlan** (Mex.) and in **Valle de Bravo** (Mex.)

5th Public holiday for the Battle of Puebla – celebrated in **Puebla** (Pue.) itself with a grand procession and re-enactment of the fighting.

15th DIA DE SAN ISIDRO. Religious processions and fireworks in **Tenancingo** (Mex.), and a procession of farm animals through **Cuernavaca** (Mor.) on their way to be blessed at the church.

On the third Monday of May there's a large religious festival in **Tlaxcala** (Tlax.) as an image of the Virgin is processed around the town followed by hundreds of pilgrims.

CORPUS CHRISTI (variable – the Thursday after Trinity). Thousands of children, rigged out in their Sunday best, gather in **Mexico City's** Zocalo to be blessed.

June

29th DIA DE SAN PEDRO observed with processions and dances in **Tepoztlan** (Mex.) and traditional dancing in **San Pedro Actopan** (D.F.), on the southern outskirts of Mexico.

July

16th DIA DE LA VIRGEN DEL CARMEN. Dancers, and a procession with flowers to the convent of Carmen in **San Angel** (D.F.).

25th DIA DE SANTIAGO particularly celebrated in **Chalco** (Mex.), on the way to Amecameca. The following Sunday sees a market and regional dances at the **Plaza de las Tres Culturas** and dances too in **Xochimilco**.

29th DIA DE SANTA MARTA in **Milpa Alta** (D.F.), near Xochimilco, celebrated with Aztec dances and mock fights between Moors and Christians.

August
13th Ceremonies in **Mexico** commemorate the defence of Tenochtitlan, with events in the Plaza de las Tres Culturas, around the statue of Cuauhtemoc on Reforma and in the Zocalo.
15th DIA DE LA ASUNCION (Assumption) honoured with pilgrimages from **Cholula** (Pue.) to a nearby village, and ancient dances in **Milpa Alta** (D.F.).

September
8th A very ancient ceremony in **Tepoztlan** (Mor.), a Christianised version of homage to the Pyramid of Tepozteco, and more usual candle-lit religious processions in **Cuernavaca** (Mor.).
15th-16th INDEPENDENCE CELEBRATIONS everywhere, above all in the Zocalo in **Mexico** where the President proclaims the famous *grito* at 11pm on the 15th.
21st DIA DE SAN MATEO celebrated in **Milpa Alta** (D.F.).
29th DIA DE SAN MIGUEL provokes huge pilgrimages to both **Taxco** (Gro.) and **Chalma** (Mex.)

October
4th DIA DE SAN FRANCISCO sees a feria in **Tenancingo** (Mex.), with much traditional music-making, and is also celebrated in **San Francisco Tecoxpa** (D.F.), a village on the southern fringes of the capital.

12th In **Tlaxcala** (Tlax.), a fiesta centring around one of the ancient churches.

November
1st–2nd DIA DE LOS MUERTOS (All Souls) is observed by almost everyone and the shops are full of chocolate skulls and other ghoulish foods. Tradition is particularly strong in **San Lucas Xochimanca** (D.F.) and **Nativitas** (D.F.), both to the south of the city.
22nd DIA DE SANTA CECILIA. Santa Cecilia is the patron saint of musicians, and her fiesta attracts orchestras and mariachi bands from all over to **Santa Cecilia Tepetlapa** (D.F.), not far from Xochimilco.

December
1st FERIA DE LA PLATA – the great silver fair in **Taxco** (Gro.) runs for about ten days from this date.
12th DIA DE NUESTRA SEÑORA DE GUADALUPE – a massive pilgrimage to the **Basilica of Guadalupe** (D.F.) runs for several days round about, combined with a constant secular celebration of music and dancing.
CHRISTMAS. In the week leading up to Christmas *posadas* – nativity plays – can be seen in many places. Among the most famous are those at **Taxco** (Gro.) and **Tepotzotlan** (Mex.).

TRAVEL DETAILS

The capital is the centre of the nation to such an extent that any attempt at a comprehensive list of the comings and goings would be doomed to failure. What follows is no more than a survey of the major services on the main routes: it must be assumed that intermediate points are linked at least as frequently as those mentioned.

Trains
To **Ciudad Juarez**. Leaves daily 19.50, arriving Querétaro (01.00), Aguascalientes (08.00), Zacatecas (10.30), Chihuahua (02.15) and Ciudad Juarez (07.20).
To **Monterrey**. Fast train (first class only) leaves 18.00, arriving 09.00. Slower services leave 08.00, arriving Querétaro (13.05), San Luis Potosí (17.30), Saltillo

(00.15) and Monterrey (02.00); and at 21.15, arriving San Luis Potosí (07.00), Saltillo (15.30) and Monterrey (18.00)
To **Guadalajara**. Departures at: 18.05, arriving Querétaro (23.45) and Guadalajara (07.20); and 20.30, arriving Querétaro (01.40) and Guadalajara (08.10).
To **Uruapan**. Departures at 06.55, arriving Morelia (17.15) and Uruapan (21.05), and at 21.30, arriving Morelia (06.10) and Uruapan (10.05).
To **Veracruz**. Departures at 07.34, arriving Orizaba (15.30) and Veracruz (19.00), and at 21.30, arriving at 07.00. Second class service via Jalapa leaves 07.20, arriving Jalapa (15.30) and Veracruz (19.25)
To **Puebla**. Second class departures at 07.05, arriving 15.50, and 08.15, arriving 16.55.

To **Oaxaca**. Leaves at 17.30, arriving 08.05.
To **Coatzacoalcos**. Leaves 20.10, arriving 12.40.
To **Merida**. Leaves daily at 20.10, arriving Palenque (22.00 next day), Campeche (06.00) and Merida (09.05).

Puebla to **Oaxaca**. Leaves 06.40, arriving 17.50.

Buses

Thousands of buses leave Mexico every day, and you can get to just about any town in the country, however small, whenever you want. Those below are a bare minimum of the main road routes.
From the Terminal del Norte To all destinations in the first three chapters – there are regular departures for all the major US border crossings. At least 20 buses a day head for Guadalajara (about 9hrs), slightly fewer than that to Zacatecas (8hrs) and San Luis Potosí (5½hrs). There's an almost constant flow to Querétaro (1½hrs), some 10 daily to Morelia (6hrs) and several direct services to the Pacific Coast at Manzanillo and Puerto Vallarta (upwards of 12hrs).
Eastbound from TAPO to destinations in Chapters 6, 7 and 8: to Puebla (constantly; 2hrs), Veracruz (at least 15 daily; 8hrs), Jalapa (6; 6½hrs) and Poza Rica (8; 5hrs). Very frequent too to Oaxaca (upwards of 8hrs) and a few daily services on towards Merida and the Yucatan.
From the Central del Sur to most places in Chapter 5: to Acapulco at least hourly (6½hrs), and 8 daily to Zihuatanejo (8–9hrs). Also for Cuernavaca (every 15mins or so; 1½hrs) and Taxco (7; 3½hrs).
The **Terminal Poniente** basically serves Toluca, with constant departures (1½hrs). Also occasional departures on the scenic route to Morelia.
From Cuernavaca. To Taxco (8; 2hrs) and Acapulco (7; 6hrs).
From Taxco to Acapulco (2; 5hrs).
From Toluca to Morelia (8; 4hrs).
From Puebla. To Oaxaca (10; 7hrs) and Veracruz (12; 6½hrs)

Planes

There are direct daily flights to no less than thirty-five **internal** destinations, and 20 a day to Guadalajara alone. If you're leaving on an *international* flight, don't forget the departure tax of around 5 dollars, payable only in pesos.

Chapter five

ACAPULCO AND THE PACIFIC BEACHES

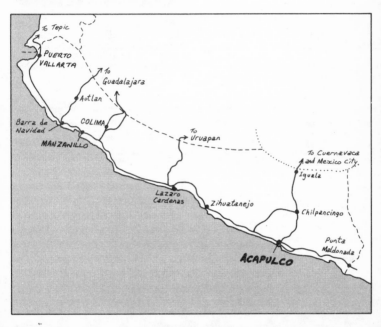

From **Acapulco**, the original, the biggest, and still for many the best, resorts and beaches stretch in both directions along a coastline where for the most part the mountains of the Sierra Madre reach out to the ocean, leaving a series of coves, bays and narrow stretches of sand. Acapulco is the classic example – a steep-sided, tight curving bay which for all its excesses of high-rise development remains breathtakingly beautiful. This is still the stamping ground of the wealthy whose villas, high around the wooded sides of the bay, offer isolation from the packaged enclaves below. But it's not necessarily expensive, and the old town is still very Mexican: run-down and often rather tawdry.

If Acapulco is the model, its younger rivals have all diverged from the pattern in their various ways. **Puerto Vallarta**, second in size and reputation, feels altogether smaller, more like the tropical village it claims to be, while in fact spreading for miles along a series of tiny beaches. More chic, younger, more overtly glamorous and certainly far more single-mindedly a resort, it lacks Acapulco's great sweep of sand but makes up for it with cove after isolated cove. Heading south from here, **Barra de Navidad** is still relatively little known by foreigners, a lovely crescent of sand, backed for once by flatlands and lagoons, with a village at either end. By contrast **Manzanillo**, also well connected with Guadalajara, is first and foremost a port and naval base – its beaches, strung out along a spit outside the town, largely an afterthought and fronted mostly by private villas and suburban homes. **Zihuatanejo** and its purpose-built neighbour **Ixtapa** are the most recently developed: Ixtapa so much so that there's nothing there but brand new hotels. Zihuatanejo is a far more attractive proposition; almost, to look at, a miniature Acapulco with magnificent villas mushrooming on the slopes overlooking the bay.

All along this coast, though, between the major centres, you'll find beaches – sometimes completely underdeveloped, or with a village where a few rooms are let and a makeshift bar on the sand, occasionally with an isolated, maybe even a luxurious hotel. The ocean breakers can be wild, even positively dangerous at times, and there are minor discomforts to bear – unreliable or non-existent water and electricity supplies, vicious mosquitoes – but the space and the simplicity often only an hour's drive from a packed international resort are an unbelievable escape.

Inevitably, most people arrive on the well-travelled route from Mexico City to Acapulco, but the **coast road**, whatever some old maps may say, is perfectly feasible all the way from the US border to Guatemala – if a little rough in the final stretches. Between Puerto Vallarta and Acapulco, it's a good modern stretch and unrelentingly spectacular as it forces its way south, sometimes over the narrow coastal plain, more often clinging precariously to the fringes of the Sierra where it falls away into the ocean. You can also fly in of course, with international services to Acapulco, Puerto Vallarta and Zihuatanejo and domestic flights to various points in between. In the state of Guerrero (of which Acapulco lies at the heart) military checkpoints on the roads are frequent and all traffic is stopped and searched. Tourists usually assume that these are for drugs, which may be at least partly true, though the check rarely amounts to more than a peremptory prod at the outside of your case: more importantly the hills inland remain wild and relatively undeveloped, retaining a reputation for banditry and guerrilla activity. This is not something you need expect to come across, but travelling along these roads you should keep your passport and papers handy and not carry anything you wouldn't want discovered in your possession.

ACAPULCO

Everyone – even if they've not the remotest idea where it is – has heard of **ACAPULCO**, but few people know what to expect. Certainly it is not the Mexican Benidorm which its notoriety leads many to fear, but nor is it the Pacific paradise for which the less worldly might hope. Truth is that as long as you don't expect to get away from it all, you'll find almost anything you want here to some degree, from magnificent beaches by day to clubs and discos by night.

First, there's the bay itself which is stunning: a sweeping scythe-stroke of yellow sand backed by the white towers of the high-rise hotels and, behind them, the jungly green foothills of the Sierra. And, though there are hundreds of thousands of people here throughout the year – the town itself has a population of some half a million and even out of season (busiest months are from December to February) most of the big hotels remain nearly full – it rarely seems oppressively crowded. Certainly there's always space to be found somewhere along the beach, partly because of its sheer size, partly because of the number of rival attractions from hotel pools to parasailing, 'romantic' moonlight cruises to all-night discos. Which is not to say that everything is perfect: inevitably Acapulco is very, very commercialised and prices out along the beach where the package tourists stay are frequently outrageous. Hustlers, too, are everywhere, most of them easy enough to handle – there's no need to go shopping in Acapulco, simply lie on the beach and a string of goods will be paraded in front of you – but occasionally irritating or even heavy. For women, and women alone in particular, the constant pestering of would-be gigolos can become maddening, and for anyone the derelict downtown backstreets can be dangerous at night. It's worth remembering that this is still a working port of considerable size and that in the midst of all the tourist glitz real poverty remains: don't leave things lying about on the beach or too temptingly displayed in hotel rooms.

There's little to show for it now beyond the star-shaped Fuerte de San Diego and a few rusty freighters tied up along the quayside, but Acapulco was from the sixteenth century one of Mexico's most important ports, the destination of the famous *Nao de China* which brought silks and spices from Manila and returned laden with payment in Mexican silver. Most of the goods were lugged overland to Veracruz and from there shipped onwards to Spain. Mexican Independence, Spain's decline and the direct route around southern Africa combined to kill it off, but for nearly 300 years the trade between Acapulco and the Far East was among the most prized and preyed upon in the world, attracting at some time or other (and if you believe all the stories) every pirate worth the name.

In one such raid, in 1743, Lord Anson (the 'Father of the British Navy') picked up silver worth as much as £400,000 sterling from a single galleon and altogether, with the captured ship and the rest of its cargo and crew, collected booty worth over a million even then. With the death of its major trade, Acapulco went into a long slow decline – only reversed with

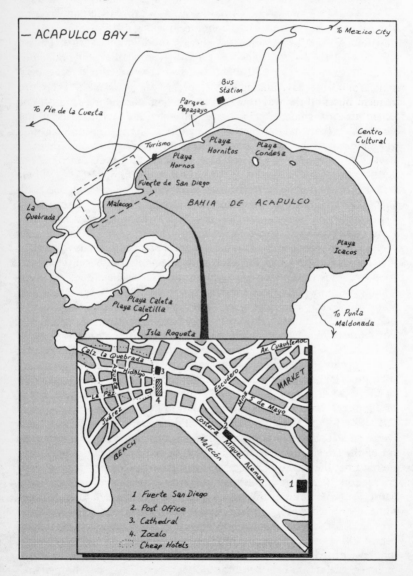

— ACAPULCO BAY —

To Mexico City

Bus Station

Parque Papagayo

To Pie de la Cuesta

Centro Cultural

Turismo

Playa Hornitos

Playa Condesa

Playa Hornos

Fuerte de San Diego

Malecon

BAHIA DE ACAPULCO

La Quebrada

Playa Icacos

Playa Caleta
Playa Caletilla

To Punta Maldonada

Isla Roqueta

Calz la Quebrada

Av. Cuauhtemoc

Hidalgo

Escudero

MARKET

La Paz

3

5 de Mayo

Juárez

4

Costera Miguel Aleman

BEACH

Malecón

1

1 Fuerte San Diego
2. Post Office
3. Cathedral
4. Zocalo
.... Cheap Hotels

the completion of a road to the capital in 1928. Even so, but for tourism it would still be no more than a minor port.

Practicalities – getting about, finding a room
Acapulco divides fairly simply into two halves: the **old town** which sits at the western end of the bay, with the rocky promontory of La Quebrada rising above it and curving round to protect the most sheltered anchorage; and the new **resort area** consisting of hotels and tourist services following the curve of the bay all the way round to the east. A single sea-front drive, the Costera Miguel Aleman, runs from the heart of the old town right around the bay, linking almost everything of interest. There are frequent **buses** all the way round (look for *Cine Rio/La Base*, *Zocalo* or *Caleta directo*) which, from the east, run along the Costera past all the big hotels, turn inland onto Av. Cuauhtemoc where they pass the *Estrella de Oro* **bus station**, the **market** and the *Flecha Roja* terminal, then back onto the Costera just before the Zocalo. *Caleta* buses continue round the coast to Caleta beach.

As usual, everything is very much cheaper in the old town, and it's here that you should head to **look for a room**. From the Flecha Roja terminal you can just about walk into the centre (and there are a few cheap, if rather grim hotels nearby – try the *Hotel Beatrix* on calle Balboa) but if you arrive first class you'll have to take a local bus – anything going down the hill to the left as you come out. On arrival, beware the extremely friendly and official-looking **guides** who hang around the bus stations. They'll offer to phone your hotel and book you in, but inevitably it will be 'full' and they'll direct you instead to somewhere of their choice: not necessarily bad but probably not what you would have chosen for yourself. Taxi drivers, too, have something of a reputation for taking you where they want to go regardless, but I've never experienced this personally.

The area to look (outlined on the map) is in the streets immediately to the left and slightly inland of the Zocalo, particularly in Calles La Paz and Teniente Jose Azueta and at the bottom of Calzada La Quebrada where it leads up the hill. Azueta has the most choice, with the *Casa Anita*, near its junction with La Paz, and the *Hotel Fiesta*, towards the top of the street, probably the best among many. The *Hotel Lucia*, up the hill from the Fiesta, is also good. On La Paz you could try the Hotels *California* and *Isabel* or the *Casa de Huespedes Ramon*, though being nearer the Zocalo these are more often full. Assuming that the town is not too crowded – when rates can rocket – all of these charge much the same; costing rather more, but a very definite step up in class, is the *Hotel Mision* at Felipe Valle 12. In a narrow street parallel to Azueta but closer to the Zocalo it is, quite unexpectedly for Acapulco, an old colonial-style house with rooms spread out around the patio.

If you plan to **stay longer** and want more comfort or to be closer to the beaches, there are a surprising number of reasonably priced places about, particularly on the slopes above Caleta and Caletilla beaches where the hotels are rather older and tend to be patronised by Mexican families. Trouble is, they're scattered and often booked up in advance so the best plan is probably to stay at least one night in the centre, work out where you'd ideally like to be based, and then head out to the **Tourist Office** (Costera Miguel Aleman 187) where they have complete lists of hotels and should help you ring round until you've found something.

Just as there are hundreds upon hundreds of hotels in Acapulco, there are thousands of **restaurants**, but to eat cheaply you're confined to much the same area around the Zocalo. *El Flor de Acapulco*, right on the Zocalo, is not the cheapest but it's a pleasant spot to linger over breakfast at an outdoor table and a popular meeting place for travellers. Just off the Zocalo on La Paz you'll find the *Restaurant San Carlos* and next door to it a well-used *taqueria*. Carry on down the street and you'll find many others: *El Amigo Juan* offers a good cheap *comida corrida*. For seafood, the three places at the bottom of Azueta, *Mariscos Nacho*, *Silvia* and *Milla* are all reasonable. In the other direction from the Zocalo, along the seafront beyond Woolworth's and the main branch of *Banamex*, are a couple more places, more animated and touristy, but still reasonably inexpensive. Alternatively, for blander, more westernised food, there's a branch of *Sanborn's* on the Costera down here, and a *Denny's* on the Zocalo itself. Eating on the beach, where there's some kind of restaurant every few hundred yards, is of course very much more expensive – and increasingly so as you head east – but if you have the cash to spare many of these places, and the fancy tourist traps between the hotels, are really good.

The beaches

To get to the best of the sands from the centre you're going to have to get on the bus: there is a tiny beach right in front of the town but it's not in the least inviting, grey sand made greyer by pollutants from the boats moored all around it.

Playas **Caleta** and **Caletilla** have a very different atmosphere from those in the main part of the bay: very small – the two are divided only by a rocky outcrop and breakwater – they tend to be crowded with Mexicans, but the water is almost always calm and, by Acapulco's standards, the beach is clean. Most enticingly, though, you can sit at shaded tables on the sand, surrounded by Mexican matrons whose kids are paddling in the shallows, and be brought drinks from the cafes behind; not particularly cheap, but considerably less than the same service would cost at the other end of the bay. There are showers here too, and small boats plying regularly to the islet of **La Roqueta** where there are more beaches (and beer drinking burros, one of the town's less compelling attractions).

The main beaches, despite their various names, are in effect a single sweep of sand and it's best to go some considerable distance round to Playa **Condesa** or Playa **Icacos,** in front of hotels like the *Hyatt Continental* and the *Holiday Inn* or opposite the Centro Acapulco, where the beach is much less crowded and considerably cleaner. Here too, it's easy enough to slip in to use the hotel showers, swimming pools and bars – there's no way they're going to spot an impostor in these thousand-bed monsters. This is also the place to come if you want to try being towed around the bay on the end of a parachute, waterskiing, or sailing – you'll find outfits offering all of these at regular intervals along the beach; charges are standardised though the quality of the equipment and the length of the trips can vary.

Beyond this end of the bay to the south are two more popular beaches, **Puerto Marques** and **Revolcadero.** On the way you'll pass some of the fanciest hotels in Acapulco: *Las Brisas*, overlooking the eastern end of the bay, is probably the most exclusive of all, its individual villas offering private swimming pools and pink jeeps to every occupant. Puerto Marques is the first of the beaches, a sheltered, deeply indented cove overlooked by two more deluxe hostelries – very calm, very upmarket. You can continue by road to Revolcadero (though only an occasional bus comes this far) or go by boat down a narrow inland channel. The beach, a long exposed stretch of sand, is beautiful but frequently lashed by a surf which makes swimming impossible.

Pie de La Cuesta, north of the town, is still more open to the vicissitudes of the ocean. Definitely not for swimming – even if it weren't for the massive breakers there are said to be sharks offshore – but as good a place as you can imagine to come and watch the sun sink into the Pacific. The sand extends for miles up the coast, but at the end nearer Acapulco where the bus drops you there are several rickety bars and beach restaurants. Behind lies the **Laguna de Coyuca,** a shallow marsh rich in bird and animal life, and a huge palm forest. The bus (*Pie de la Cuesta*) runs east past the Zocalo along the Costera, turns inland by the very touristy Mercado de Artesanias and passes the market and Flecha Roja terminal before heading north for the beach. Coming back, check the times in advance since you can have a very long wait in the dark if you miss the early evening service.

Entertainment and nightlife
If you were so inclined, and perhaps more importantly if you were extremely rich, you could spend several weeks in Acapulco doing nothing more than touring its scores of nightclubs and bars, discos and dinner dances. There are people who claim never to have seen the town during

daylight hours. However, these places are all very expensive and anywhere with music or dancing will demand a hefty cover charge before they even consider letting you spend money at the bar.

Not everything costs money, though, and you can watch Acapulco's most celebrated spectacle – the **high divers** – for virtually nothing. The divers plunge some 140 feet from the cliffs of **La Quebrada** into a tight, rocky channel, timing their leap to coincide with an incoming wave. Mistimed, there's not enough water to stop them hitting the bottom, though the chief danger these experts seem to face is in getting back out of the water without being dashed against the rocks. It's an impressive spectacle, especially at night when the divers grasp lighted torches – evening performances are at (approximately) 7.15, 8.15, 9.15, 10.30 and 11.30. From the road you can see them for nothing, but you'll get a much better view if you pay a few pesos to go down the steps to a viewing platform more or less opposite the divers. Alternatively you can sit in the bar of the *Mirador* Hotel if you arrive early enough or watch from the (expensive) *Restaurant La Perla*. To get there, simply climb the Calzada La Quebrada from the centre of town, about 15 minutes walk from the Zocalo.

Still on the water, as well as the parasailing, waterskiing and sailing from the beaches, there are assorted **boat trips** to choose from. You can hire your own cruiser along the Malecon to go sea-fishing or diving, but this inevitably is very pricey; more popular are the various **bay cruises** or outings in glass-bottomed boats. You'll see details and prices posted up all over town and you can book in any big hotel or simply go down to the quayside at departure time. Again, these are probably better at night with the lights of the town shining out from all around the bay. At night, too, most of the boats lay on some kind of entertainment as they cruise.

By day, if people aren't at the beach or asleep, they're mostly scouring the expensive shops – it's that sort of place. And in reality there are few enough sights; the **Cathedral**, on the Zocalo, is modern and uninteresting and the **Fuerte de San Diego** is not open to the public. If you have **kids** to amuse the **Parque Papagayo**, opposite Playa Hornos has various amusements or the *Centro Infantil* **CICI**, round the bay near the Centro Acapulco, offers dolphin shows and water-based rides. The **Centro Acapulco** itself is an amazing place, ultra-modern in design, packed with upmarket shops and pricey restaurants, the home of a futuristic disco and Las Vegas-style shows: there's a small **archaeology museum** too, open daily from 10–2 and 5–9. Entrance to the complex is free in the mornings, but in the afternoon, when there's a **show** in the grounds with traditional dances, you pay to get in. There's an extra charge to sit in the grandstand or at any of the outdoor tables, but you can stand around on the sidelines for nothing. Although it's aimed four-square at the American package tour market – with an appallingly cheery presenter keeping up a constant running commentary – the spectacle is well worth seeing, especially the acrobatic *Voladores de Papantla* (see p. 272), and as authentic as one could reasonably hope.

Just about any of the above, and anything from a 2–hour city tour to a day-trip to Mexico City can be done through a **guided tour** from one of the hundreds of local travel agents or any large hotel, but obviously you'll be paying more. You can even take a Slumming Tour (their description) which takes in a visit to *La Huerta*, a plush, walled and heavily guarded club in the midst of Acapulco's sickeningly sleazy red light district. As for the mainstream **clubs and discos** – virtually all of which are out along the Costera in the hotel district – they move in and out of fashion with such bewildering rapidity that recommendations are virtually impossible. Some, like *Baby-O*, try to maintain a spurious exclusivity by turning people away if they appear insufficiently glamorous, but most can afford to do this only at the height of the season. Look for queues outside if you want to know where you really should be going. Among the more consistently popular discos are *Baby–O* itself, *Le Dome*, *Magic*, and *Plus 1*. Gay hang-outs include *9* and *Gallery*, both on the Av. de los Deportes near the Holiday Inn. If you're not easily intimidated you could also try some of the downtown **bars** and cantinas: you'll find a couple which aren't too heavy around the bottom of Calle Azueta – *La Sirena* for example.

Getting to Acapulco and moving on

There's a constant stream of **buses between Acapulco and the capital:** Estrella de Oro run eighteen first class services and thirteen *Expresos de Lujo* daily while Flecha Roja have second class buses leaving virtually hourly day and night. Even so it's worth getting your ticket at least a short while in advance: there's little point paying the supplement for the express, they all take around 6½–7 hours (usually with a meal stop) and the bigger buses tend to be more crowded and less mechanically reliable. Unless you're going to detour into Cuernavaca (p. 223) or Taxco (p. 227), each of which has several buses on to Acapulco every day, there's really nothing worth breaking the journey for. CHILPANCINGO, capital of the state of Guerrero and the only large town en route, is a fairly dull, provincial place. All along this coast in fact, until you get as far north as the state of Colima, the Sierra Madre forms a formidable barrier and there's virtually no settlement away from the coast, and fewer roads.

Leaving Acapulco, then, you either head back to the capital or **along the coast**. Flecha Roja has half-hourly services in each direction, north as far as Lazaro Cardenas (p. 259), south to Puerto Escondido (p. 293). The **southern route**, as far as PUNTA MALDONADA is described immediately below; **northern destinations** are dealt with in reverse order (i.e. from Puerto Vallarta southwards) in the latter half of the chapter.

SOUTH OF ACAPULCO: THE COSTA CHICA

Highway 200 south of Acapulco is little travelled, at least by tourists, and in some ways that's not surprising; there's little in the way of facilities between here and Puerto Escondido – a good 7 hours on the bus. But it is an interesting and sometimes bizarre coastline and there are a few great beaches along it, especially if you have your own means of transport.

The people who inhabit the area towards the border of Oaxaca are for the most part either Amuzgo Indian or black – the descendants of African Bantu slaves who escaped and settled here. And to look at the land is vaguely reminiscent of Africa – flat grazing country in which many of the villages consist of thatched huts. In COAJINICUILAPA the impression is reinforced by the predominance of round constructions – though these are in fact as much a local Indian tradition as an African one. From here a road runs some 20 miles down to the coast at **PUNTA MALDONADA**, with a *Parador Turistica* offering expensive rooms about halfway along. Punta Maldonado itself, along with nearby San Nicolas, has some beautiful beaches but virtually no facilities and only one or two buses a day. Above all it's famed for clear water and for perfect skin diving and snorkelling opportunities – many of the people who you'll find here have come down in campers to take advantage.

If you want to break your journey along this coastline in rather more comfort than camping out on the beaches at Punta Maldonado could offer, there are two possibilities. **OMETEPEC**, an old gold-mining town a few miles inland of the main road before it reaches Coajinicuilapa, has several small hotels of which the *Hotel Riviera Lopez* is the best, but also the most expensive. Although this is off the highway, there are hourly buses to Acapulco so it's easy enough to get back to the junction and pick up transport heading south from there. The second option is **PINOTEPA NACIONAL**, across the border in the state of Oaxaca, where again there are a number of basic places to stay. Pinotepa's Sunday market is one of the best in the region, a meeting place for local Amuzgo, Mixtec and Chattino Indians.

THE COAST ROAD FROM THE NORTH

Coming down from Northern Mexico there are a number of ways of approaching the coast. Most buses heading down from the Pacific from **MAZATLAN** head inland to Guadalajara, but by changing at **TEPIC** you can continue to **Puerto Vallarta,** and from there on down Highway 200 towards Acapulco. GUADALAJARA itself has very frequent bus connections with Puerto Vallarta, **Barra de Navidad** and **Manzanillo,** while from **Lazaro Cardenas** you can head inland to central Michoacan. **Zihuatanejo** offers direct bus services to Mexico City.

There are, too, plentiful buses between all these resorts, although since few of them are long-distance routes it's often quicker and more convenient to change buses: getting from Puerto Vallarta to Barra de Navidad, and from there to Manzanillo and from Manzanillo to Lazaro Cardenas, for example, is easy enough – but there are few direct services from Puerto Vallarta all the way down.

PUERTO VALLARTA

By reputation the second of Mexico's beach resorts, **PUERTO VALLARTA** is very different from Acapulco: smaller, quieter and younger. In its own way it is actually every bit as commercial – perhaps more so since here tourism is virtually the only source of income – but appearances count for much, and Puerto Vallarta appears far less developed. Its hotels are scattered along several miles of coast – the greatest concentration in Nuevo Vallarta, north of the town and invisible from it; there are no tall or obviously modern buildings in the centre; and the tropical village atmosphere, an asset assiduously exploited by the local tourist authorities, does indeed survive to a remarkable degree. The package tourists stay, on the whole, in the beach hotels around the bay, coming into town only on shopping expeditions or to eat out: downtown hotels are small and reasonably priced.

Arrival: food and rooms

The **Rio Cuale**, spanned by two small bridges, divides Puerto Vallarta in two. Most of the town lies on the northern side – the main square, official buildings, market, and the bulk of the shops and restaurants. South, however, you'll find the bus stations, the town beach, and most of the cheaper hotels. It's a very small place, hemmed in by the ocean and by the steep slopes behind – downtown, you can walk just about anywhere and there are frequent buses around the edge of the Bahia de Banderas

1. Plaza Aguiles Serdan
2. Plaza de Armas
3. Guadalupe (†)
4. Turismo
5. Museo

— CENTRAL PUERTO VALLARTA —

to the north, rather less efficient services southwards to the smaller beaches. The **Cabo San Lucas ferry** docks at the new marina, to the north in Nuevo Vallarta – again, there's a regular bus service into the centre.

Although there's no centralised *Camionera* in Puerto Vallarta, all the **bus companies** have their offices within a block of each other around the junction of Insurgentes and Madero. From here you can walk easily to any of the cheaper **hotels**. There are a couple of places right by the *TNS* terminal, but quite apart from being extremely noisy these are overpriced and, thanks to their position, tend to fill up early. If you head up Madero, away from the sea, you'll find more tempting possibilities: first, the *Hotel Lina*, which is expensive, then in the next block the *Hotel Analiz* (Madero 425) and the *Bernal* (Madero 429), virtually next door to each other, and the *Villa del Mar* (Madero 440) opposite. All three charge the same rates for very similar facilities, and there's little to choose between them, though the last named is the biggest. Two blocks across from here, at Venustiano Carranza 466, the *Hotel Mexico 70* is probably the cheapest in town – basic but acceptable. Alternatively, if you want to be closer to the beach, head down Basilio Badillo. Here the *Posada Roger* (Basilio Badillo 237) is very popular with American backpackers and hence frequently booked up, but offers noticeboards for rides and messages, and a lovely patio in which to sit around and meet people, while the *Hotel Yasmin* (Basilio Badillo 168 just off Av. Olas Altas) is very near the sand. Both are more expensive than those on Madero. Finally, for a group of four or more, an apartment in the *Hotel Marsol* can work out less than even the cheapest rooms elsewhere, and you'll be right on the beach, with ocean views, cooking facilities in the room and a small pool outside. Ordinary rooms are less good value and don't look out over the sea, but they're still probably the cheapest place so close to the beach. It's at the bottom of Francisca Rodriguez, next door to the *Hotel Playa Los Arcos* (Av. Olas Altas 270) which is much the nicest of the more expensive places in the centre. **Camping** on any of the more popular beaches around the centre of the bay is out, but if you're reasonably well provisioned and protected against mosquitoes you could try hiking out to Punta Mita, at the northern end of the bay, or south to Boca de Tomatlan (where the main road turns inland), each of which from time to time sees small communities establishing themselves on the sand. At Yelapa, a southern beach to which there are boat trips from town (see below), there's a small but rather pricey hotel or you might be able to rent a hut or find somewhere to sling a hammock.

Finding somewhere to eat in Puerto Vallarta is no problem – tourist restaurants offering cocktails by candlelight are everywhere – but eating cheaply is rather less easy. For anything other than the dull basics you really do have to join the gringos. However, basic places first: as always the area around the bus stations is a good bet for plain, fast food, and as usual the market – on the north bank of the river by the upper bridge – also has a few food stalls. There are, too, taco and hot dog stands in the streets and kids on the beach offering fresh caught fish, roasted on sticks. On the whole, though, for reasonable, straightforward restaurants you're better off on the north bank in the centre of town: *Tutifruti*, at Morelos 552 near the Post Office, serves up good fruit juices, *licuados* and *tortas*, as does *Frutilandia* on the seafront not far away. *Mi Tierra*, at the corner of Matamoros just below the market, is a good standard Mexican diner, while *Benito's*, on Zaragoza just off the Plaza de Armas, is a very popular pizzeria – touristy but not outrageously priced. South of the Rio Cuale along Av. Olas Altas there are several restaurants which bridge the gap between the out and out tourist traps and the plain eating houses, especially those around the Hotels Marsol and Los Arcos – the restaurant in the *Marsol*, too, is reasonable if dull. Several beach-front cafes on the Playa de Los Muertos were swept away by typhoons in 1983, but they used to offer good value and should do again if they've been rebuilt. Of the more expensive places you can really take your pick: most offer some form of music or entertainment along with their food, or at least a good view while you eat – almost all, too, display their menus outside so you know what you're letting yourself in for. *Las*

Cazuelas (Lazaro Cardenas 263) is small, with good Mexican and Spanish food; the *Cafe Franzi*, on the Isla Rio Cuale, has **English books** and magazines to look through at the bar (they'll also swap one for two of yours) and classical guitar in the evenings; *Carlos O'Brien's* (Gustavo Diaz Ordaz 786) is much loved by young Americans for its rowdy 'fun' atmosphere.

Filling the day
Apart from the beaches, outlined below, and the tourist shops which pack the centre of town, there's not a great deal to do; certainly nothing in the way of great sights or architecture. You could fill an hour or two, though, wandering around the area between the two plazas and on the island in the river. The **Tourist Office** is just off the **Plaza de Armas** in the modern city administration buildings; they have maps of the town and surrounding area and copies of the English language 'newspaper' *Vallarta Today* which can be picked up for nothing. The Plaza itself is where everyone gathers in the evenings and at weekends: the Church of Guadalupe is here, and from the bandstand in the centre there's frequently music blaring out. Just down from here on the Malecon, the old seafront, is the **Plaza Aguiles Serdan**, with a strange little amphitheatre looking out over the sea: again, there's often entertainment laid on. On the **Isla Rio Cuale** a small park surrounds a clutch of boutiques and restaurants. At the seaward end there's a tiny local **archaeology museum** (open 10–3 and 5–7; closed Sundays) and a couple of benches looking out over the ocean – the best place in town from which to watch the sun set – while inland a children's playground is overlooked from the hillsides by the fancy villas of 'Gringo's Gulch'.

Puerto Vallarta's **beaches** vary in nature as you move round the bay: those to the north, out towards Nuevo Vallarta and the airport and beyond, are long flat stretches of sand often pounded by surprisingly heavy surf; south, a series of steep-sided coves shelter tiny, calm strands. The town beach, **Playa de los Muertos** (Beach of the Dead), or Playa del Sol as the local Tourist Office would like it known, falls somewhere between the two extremes – not very large and reasonably calm, yet facing apparently open water. This is the most crowded of all, where locals and Mexican holiday-makers go too, and in many ways it's the most enjoyable – plenty of people and activities on offer, food and drink close at hand. But don't leave anything of value lying about.

To the **north**, the best beaches tend to front the big hotels, and since the hotels all have pools and poolside bars the sand is virtually deserted. It only really makes sense to make a special journey out here if you too plan to sneak in and use the pool – easily enough done – since on all but the calmest days there's sand blowing around and waves which are great for surfers but not so good for swimming. The beaches can be rather dirty too, except right in front of the fancier hotels where there are staff keeping a patch cleared.

The smaller stretches of sand to the **south** are far more popular, and though the bus service in this direction is less regular there's no real problem in getting out to them. Best bet, rather than waiting in town for the bus, is to climb up to the highway as it heads out of town southwards and start hitching – there's a fair amount of traffic and if the bus comes past it will stop for you. There are small beaches every few hundred yards, most with a hotel nearby, but the best known and most convenient is **Mismaloya**, some 7 miles out of Puerto Vallarta. Here John Huston filmed *The Night of the Iguana* with Richard Burton (an event which many credit with having made Puerto Vallarta an international resort) and you can wander out to parts of the crumbling film set on the point. There are a couple of small, reasonable restaurants on the beach, and a stream running across it which leads inland to *Chino's Paradise*, a restaurant by a waterfall with a natural pool in which you can swim.

There are also **boat trips** out to Mismaloya, and for the beaches further round in this direction – Quimixto and Yelapa are the most common destinations – a boat is the only means of access. Travel agents all over town tout a variety of excursions, mostly leaving from the new marina: compare prices and what's on offer in the way of food and drink – if meals are not included it's worth taking your own food along. At **Yelapa** there's a small Indian village not far from the white sand beach, and a waterfall a short distance into the jungle: it's no longer really deserted – there's a hotel and several tourist cabins – and nor is it cheap, but with luck you might be able to rent a hut for very little, or at least you can always find somewhere to sleep out. To get there more cheaply try going down to the dock early in the morning, when there are various supply boats which might give you a ride. The others, **Quimixto**, **Las Animas** and so on, are beaches pure and simple.

SOUTH TO BARRA DE NAVIDAD AND MANZANILLO

In the 200-odd km from Puerto Vallarta to Barra de Navidad there's not a great deal to delay you. For much of the way the road runs away from the coast, and where it finally does come in striking distance of the ocean it's either for a fabulously expensive resort development, as at COSTA CAREYES, or a beach, as at TENACATITLA, which is easily outshone by those on the Bahia de Navidad.

BARRA DE NAVIDAD is, for me, the most enchanting place on this entire stretch of coastline. It's not undeveloped or totally isolated – indeed families from Guadalajara come here by their hundreds, especially at weekends – but nor is it at all heavily commercialised: it's a small, simple, very Mexican resort. The entire Bay, the Bahia de Navidad, is edged by fine sands and, if you're prepared to walk, you can easily leave any temporary crowds behind. Barra de Navidad itself lies towards the southern end of the bay, where the beach runs out and curves back round into a lagoon behind the town. Coming from the north, you first pass SAN PATRICIO (or MELAQUE), at the other end of the same beach. Perhaps slightly less attractive and more commercial, San Patricio is nonetheless a good second choice if you can't find a room in Barra. Both have several small, cheap hotels as well as a couple of more upmarket but not outrageous places: in Barra de Navidad as you walk from the bus station along the beach-front you'll pass the *Hotel Barra de Navidad* and the *Tropical* – turn inland past the latter and you'll find a couple of the cheapest places in the backstreet, Hotels *Jalisco* and *Kukulkan* for example. Twenty minutes is quite long enough to walk all the way round town and check out all the rooms on offer. San Patricio is slightly larger, but again by walking down the Avenida Las Palmas and from there into the centre of town, you'll have seen virtually everything: the *Posada Legazpi* on Las Palmas is a safe bet, and here there's a Tourist Office (on Las Palmas by the *Hotel Melaque*) which can help out.

Just an hour down the road, MANZANILLO is a very different sort of place; a working port where tourism – although highly developed – very definitely takes second place to trade. Downtown, it has to be said, the place is not at all attractive – criss-crossed by railway tracks, rumbling with heavy traffic and surrounded by a bewildering array of inner harbours and shallow lagoons which seem to cut the place off from the land. You can easily imagine that a couple of hundred years ago plague and pestilence made sailors fear to land here and it's not surprising to read in an 1884 Guide to Mexico that 'the climate of Manzanillo is unhealthy for Europeans, and the tourist is advised not to linger long in the vicinity'. Few tourists do stay in the town even now – most are concentrated in the hotels and club resorts around the bay to the west – but for all that the streets are narrow and none too clean, the town is healthy enough nowadays and there's a certain romance in staying in the centre. Certainly it's a lot more interesting than the sanitised resort area, and much cheaper too, while buses out to the beach are frequent and efficient.

Head for the main square, the Jardin Alvaro Obregon, which is right on the harbour front opposite the main outer dock. This is the commercial centre of town, and all the hotels and restaurants, shops, banks and offices are within a very short walk. The local Tourist Office is here too, in the Town Hall (Presidencia Municipal). From the Central Camionera, some way out, there are buses (marked *Centro*) or taxis to get you there. Best of the hotels is the *Miramar* on Juarez, just off the Jardin Obregon at the bottom left-hand corner if you stand with your back to the sea. This street changes its name to Davalos as it runs past the back of the plaza, and at the other end, again just off the square, are two more possibilities, the *Hotel Savoy* and the *Emperador*. Others in the immediate area include the *Hotel Colonial*, a rather more expensive place one block down Mexico from the Plaza at the corner with 10 de Mayo, and the *Hotel Flamingos*, cheap but dingy, also just off the Plaza on the street which runs down by the side of the Presidencia Municipal. If you're really desperate there are also two cheap dives very close to the Central Camionera: the *Casa de Huespedes Central* on Suarez, right and right again out of the terminal, and the *Casa de Huespedes Ibarra* on Guadalupe Victoria – a further right turn onto the street which runs past the back of the bus stands. I wouldn't recommend either.

Places to eat are concentrated largely in the same area, with several good cafes overlooking the Jardin Obregon itself – the *Savoy*, under the hotel of the same name, and the *Reymar*, on the corner diagonally across the plaza, both serve reasonable meals. If you head down Mexico, which is Manzanillo's main commercial and shopping street, you'll find a whole series of further possibilities, from take-away *taquerias* to the fancy restaurant in the Hotel Colonial. The *Mi Tierra*, on the left about five blocks down, is simple and unpretentious, while in the sidestreet just below it you'll find, to the right, the *Restaurant Tomy* and to the left a place labelled simply as *Carnes Asadas El Norteño*, which has excellent northern-style meat if you're tiring of the seafood which dominates local menus. Along the harbour front on your way into the centre you'll probably have noticed a couple of restaurants with terraces hanging out over the water – they're not bad but the view could hardly be described as stunning, and of course they're more expensive. At the other end of the scale, there are several very cheap places – grimy and raucous on the whole – at the bottom end of Juarez by the railway tracks.

While locals might go **swimming** from the tiny harbour beach of San Pedrito and in the Laguna de Cuyutlan behind the town, both are thoroughly polluted. Far better to head for those in the bay proper, where the tourist hotels are. The nearest of these, at **Las Brisas**, are in fact very close to town, just across the entrance to the inner harbour, but to get there by road you have to go all the way round the Laguna de San Pedrito before turning back towards Manzanillo along the narrow strip of land which forms Las Brisas. There are frequent buses from the centre *(Las Brisas)* which run all the way along the single seafront drive: it's a rather strange area, as much suburb as resort, and the beach, steeply shelving and often rough, is perhaps not as good as those in the other direction round the bay, but as the original seaside strip its hotels and restaurants are older and considerably cheaper. If you want to stay right by the beach, take the bus out here and have a look – the Hotels *Las Brisas* and *Star* are among the cheapest, or for larger groups there are several places offering cabins or apartments, *Bungalows La Joya* for example, or the *Motel Rancho Luna*.

Better and more sheltered swimming can be found along the coast further round, where the bay is divided by the rocky Peninsula de Santiago. *Miramar* buses run all the way round to the far side of the bay, past the settlements of **Salahua** and **Santiago** and a string of beaches. The best are around the far edge of the Peninsula, getting off the bus at Santiago. There are several restaurants here, both in the village and down on the beach and if you're prepared to walk a little way out onto the peninsula you can reach the beautiful cove of **La Audiencia**, with calm water and tranquil sand. From here, feeling reasonably energetic and looking smart enough to get past the guards, you can climb over the hill to **Las Hadas** – the amazingly flashy, glistening white hotel/villa complex where Dudley Moore and Bo Derek frolicked in *10* – worth seeing even if you can't afford a drink at any of the many bars. There's more of how the other half lives at the *Club Maeva*, further round the bay on the **Playa Miramar**, but on the whole the hotels round here are thoroughly middle of the road, and certainly Manzanillo can't claim to be the liveliest of international resorts. Nightlife, such as it is, is confined to a few discos strung out along the coast road.

The inland routes: Colima

There are two roads heading to Guadalajara from this part of the coast: the direct looking route from Barra de Navidad is indeed reasonably fast, although any route has to tangle spectacularly with the Sierra Madre, but it's also very dull, with just one town of any size at AUTLAN and that dusty, provincial and untempting. The journey up from Manzanillo via COLIMA is considerably more interesting, not only for the city itself but for the spectacular snow-capped volcanoes which come beyond.

Surprisingly after so much that is modern, **COLIMA**, the state capital, is a distinctly colonial city, and a very beautiful one too, famed for its parks and overlooked by the Volcan de Colima and in the distance the Nevado de Colima. It doesn't offer a whole lot in the way of excitement, but it is a pleasant place to stop over for a night or two; cooler than the coast, but never as cold as it can get in the high mountains. As in all these old cities, life centres on the Zocalo – the Jardin Libertad – where you'll find the Cathedral, the government offices and a couple of mid-priced **hotels**, the *Casino* and the *Ceballos*. Slightly cheaper places to stay nearby include the *Hotel San Cristobal*, one block down Reforma, the *Hotel Madero*, four blocks along Madero, and the *Impala* and *Moctezuma* on 16 de Septiembre at its junction with Moctezuma. There's a second, smaller plaza behind the Cathedral and the Palacio de Gobierno, the Jardin Torres Quintero, and on Madero just beyond this you'll find the **Tourist Office**. **Restaurants**, too are concentrated around here – *La Fuente* opposite the Tourist Office is a good start and there are others all along Madero, the chief shopping street, and around the Plazas. *Los*

Naranjos, to the left up the street before the Tourist Office, is one of the best around, and not as expensive as it looks. The Bus Station is on Reforma, three blocks south of the Jardin Libertad.

While you're in Colima, there are two **museums** worth visiting. The *Museo de Las Culturas de Occidente* (open 9–1 and 4–6; closed Mondays) has a substantial collection of local archaeology, and in particular numbers of the lovely figurines and animal statuettes which characterise Western Mexican cultures: the site of Colima itself was inhabited probably as early as the eleventh century and has been permanently settled since – the modern town being one of the earliest Spanish foundations, started by Cortes's Lieutenant Gonzalo de Sandoval in 1522. The other museum, bizarrely, is a collection of antique cars (*Museo Zaragoza*; open 9–1.30 and 4–7), and a very extensive one too. You can get details of both, and maps of the town, from the Tourist Office, who can also advise on local excursions – to COMALA, for example, a village famous for its handicrafts, or up into the National Park around the **Volcan de Colima**. The volcano, which smokes from time to time, is still active but there seems little imminent danger: if you can get transport up high enough it's a relatively easy hike on to the summit at about 12,000 feet. By contrast the **Nevado de Colima**, northwards into the state of Jalisco and standing over 14,500 feet, is extinct, but its snowy peak needs real mountaineering skills to reach.

POINTS SOUTH – THE ROAD TO ACAPULCO

Once you've got beyond the Manzanillo area – there are beach villages at CUYUTLAN and BOCA DE PASCUALES on the lagoons south of the town – you run into an area which appears on the map and is, indeed, virtually uninhabited. There are occasional beaches, but for the most part the mountains drop straight into the ocean; spectacular, but no reason to stop. In spring this coast is subject to the *Ola Verde*, vast waves up to 30 feet high: at other times of year the surf is impressive, but quite easy to handle.

CALETA DE CAMPOS, some 70km short of Lazaro Cardenas, is the first and in many ways the best place to stop. It's a small village, barely electrified and with distinctly dodgy plumbing, but with two lovely beaches and an impressive ocean view. The streets are still dirt, and there are horses standing at hitching posts alongside the campers of dedicated American surfers and the fancy new cars of visitors from the city. Yet there's one good hotel, with its own generator and water supply, and a string of makeshift bar-restaurants down at the beach. For much of the year it's virtually deserted, but in winter, when the Californian beach boys come down in pursuit of sun and surf, and at weekends, when families pile down from Lazaro Cardenas, it enjoys a brief season. If the hotel is full, which at such times it can be, they'll direct you over the road to a place which rents rooms though this, frankly, is worse than sleeping on the beach – no electricity or running water, none-too-clean beds, and unbelievably voracious mosquitoes. Better to beg a hammock under the thatch of one of the beach bars: most are happy enough as long as you eat there too, and though you may still be bitten, at least you're not paying for the privilege. The beach, too, should definitely be seen at night, when if the conditions are right the ocean glows bright, luminous green. This is not a product of the excellent local beer, or of the Acapulco Gold which allegedly grows in the surrounding mountains, but a naturally illuminated, emerald-green plankton: go swimming in it and you'll come out covered in sparkling pinpoints. In fact the phenomenon is common to much of this coast, and also seen in Baja California – but nowhere so impressive as here. One word of warning: the second beach, cut off by a narrow, rocky point, looks like an unspoilt paradise (which it is) but you can only get there by boat or a stiff climb over the rocks. Try to swim round and you'll be swept out to sea by a powerful current – locals are well used to picking up tourists who suddenly find themselves several hundred yards offshore.

Getting from here to **LAZARO CARDENAS** is simple enough, local buses do the trip several times a day in addition to the rarer long-distance services. But there's little reason to go there except to get somewhere else – it's strictly industrial, dominated by a huge, British-funded steelworks (which the Queen visited in 1983 – 'checking up on her investments' according to the locals). If you need to stay you'll find several small hotels around the bus terminals (all close to each other on the outskirts of town), but you'd be much better off getting a local bus down to **PLAYA AZUL**. Once a small-time, slow-moving beach not far removed from Caleta de Campos, it's been rather over-run by the growth of the city, but there are still numerous, reasonably priced hotels and not a bad beach. The *Hotel Playa Azul* on Calle Principal is easy enough to find and boasts a swimming pool – cheaper places nearby include the *Hotel Delfin* and the *Casa de Huespedes Silva*.

Although it's only about 3 miles from IXTAPA to ZIHUATANEJO, the two places could hardly be more different. **IXTAPA**, a purpose-built, computer-planned paradise resort is quite simply the most soulless town I have ever visited. To say nothing of being one of the most expensive. While this will probably change over the years, as the place mellows and becomes worn in, for the moment it's a single coastal drive past a series of concrete boxes of varying heights. And while you might want to visit for the beaches, or maybe in the evening to go to a disco, you will definitely not want to stay. **ZIHUATANEJO** on the other hand, for all its growth and popularity in recent years, has at least retained something of the look and feel of the village it once was – what building there has been is small scale and low-key. Here too, there are still a fair number of small, reasonably priced hotels (though it is noticeably more expensive than the lowest rates in Acapulco). For some it's the ideal compromise, quiet – almost dead by night – yet with the more commercial excitements of Ixtapa in easy reach.

The one real problem is its popularity – with strictly controlled development rooms can be hard to find. The centre of Zihuatanejo, and the area with all the cheaper places to stay, consists of just about ten small blocks hemmed in by the beach, the Yacht Marina, and the main roads into town. Since many of the cheaper **hotels** are often full, its probably easiest to head straight down to the **Tourist Office,** on the waterfront, for up to date information, a map, and a list, but you could also check out a few places on the way down. If you arrive on a second class bus you'll be some way from the centre, and if you don't fancy a walk it's worth grabbing a taxi or getting on the local bus. The *Hotel Villa Vera*, right opposite the bus terminal, is good value but of course a long way from the sea. Better is the *Posada Laura*, on the main road towards the beach just beyond the market. First class buses drop you much further in: if you walk down to the beach from here along Av. Cuauhtemoc you'll pass the *Hotel San Pablo*, about five blocks inland and one of the cheapest in town, and the *Hotel El Dorado*, practically on the beach and much more expensive. Also near the first class bus stop (one block further from the sea) are the *Casa de Huespedes Guadalupe* and the *Casa Aurora*.

Opposite these last two are a couple of good, cheap **places to eat**, as there are also around the market, but eating should be no problem – you can barely move for restaurants here. If you want to get into Ixtapa, for the beaches or a boat trip out to one of the islands, buses leave regularly from the stop opposite the market, and there are also slightly more expensive VW vans or collective taxis. Closer at hand, you can take a boat across from the pier to **Playa Las Gatas,** a strip of sand facing Zihuatanejo from across the bay where there's calm swimming, showers, and a line of good but rather pricey restaurants.

From here to ACAPULCO, a fast road with regular buses, the aspect of the coast changes again – it's flatter, more heavily populated and more regularly cultivated. At **PAPANOA,** some 50km on, there's a beautiful beach, some 15km long, overlooked from the point at its far end by the *Papanoa Beach Club Hotel.* This was obviously someone's plan for a luxurious, Club-Med-style development which never quite panned out – there's still considerable comfort, a pool, and stairway down to the beach through manicured gardens, but the place has a distinctly run-down air. It's not exactly cheap, but nor is it in the high luxury bracket, and a room costing about 15 dollars a night is easily large enough for four. You could, too, camp out quite easily on this stretch of sand, getting supplies from the nearby village of EL MORRO DE PAPANOA. The hotel restaurant is also good value, and the staff friendly.

Beyond Punta Papanoa the road again leaves the coast for a while –
although with sturdy transport of your own there are several places where
you could find your way down to a surf-pounded beach – not to rejoin
it until shortly before Acapulco itself. **COYUCA DE BENITEZ**, the last
village of any size, has pleasant restaurants overlooking the Rio Coyuca,
and you can arrange boat trips down-river into the Laguna de Coyucan.
The place is of little intrinsic interest though. Nearby **PLAYAS DE SAN
JERONIMO** has huts on the beach which you could probably rent, and
where you could certainly find somewhere to camp or sling a hammock,
but again it's an exposed, windswept and wavy stretch of sand.

FIESTAS

January
1st NEW YEAR's DAY is celebrated
everywhere. In **Cruz Grande** (Guerrero),
on the coast road about 120km east of
Acapulco, the start of a week-long feria.
26th In **Tecoman** (Colima), on the
coast road, a colourful religious
procession.
2nd Tuesday DIA DE JESUS AGONIZ-
ANTE marked in **Colima** (Col.) by a
mass pilgrimage to a nearby hacienda.

February
2nd DIA DE LA CANDELARIA
celebrated in **Colima** (Col.) and
Tecoman (Col.) with dances,
processions and fireworks. Similar
events in **Zumpango del Rio** (Gro.), on
the road from Acapulco to Mexico, and
particularly good dancing in **Atzacu-
aloya** (Gro.), off this road near
Chilpancingo.
5th Fiesta Brava – day of bullfights and
horse races – in **Colima** (Col.).
CARNIVAL (the week before Lent – variable Feb.-Mar.). **Acapulco** (Gro.) and
Manzanillo (Col.) are both famous for
the exuberance of their celebrations –
rooms can be hard to find.

March
6th Local fiesta in **Zumpango del Rio**
(Gro.) lasts through the night and into
the following day – traditional dances.
19th DIA DE SAN JOSE is the excuse
for fiestas in **Tierra Colorada** (Gro.),
between Acapulco and Chilpancingo,
and **San Jeronimo** just outside
Acapulco.
HOLY WEEK is widely observed: the
Palm Sunday celebrations in **Petatlan**

(Gro.) just south of Zihuatanejo, are
particularly fervent.

May
3rd DIA DE LA SANTA CRUZ. Saint's
day festival in **Cruz Grande** (Gro.).
5th The victorious battle of Cinco de
Mayo commemorated – especially in
Acapulco.
8th In **Mochitlan** (Gro.), near Chilpancingo, the Festival de las Lluvias has
pre-Christian roots: pilgrims, peasants
and local dance groups climb a nearby
volcano at night, arriving at the summit
at dawn to pray for rain. Also a local
fiesta in **Azoyu** (Gro.), just off the coast
road south of Acapulco.
15th DIA DE SAN ISIDRO provokes a
week-long festival in **Acapulco**.
Celebrations too in **San Luis Acatlan**
(Gro.), south along the coast, where you
might see the rare *Danza de la Tortuga*,
and in **Tierra Colorada** (Gro.).
31st **Puerto Vallarta** (Jal.) celebrates
its Founder's Day.

June
1st DIA DE LA MARINA (Navy Day) in
the ports, particularly **Manzanillo** and
Acapulco.
13th DIA DE SAN ANTONIO. A Feria in
Tierra Colorada (Gro.).
3rd Sunday. Blessing of the Animals at
the church of Jesus Agonizante outside
Colima (Col.)

July
25th At **Coyuca da Benites** (Gro.),
festival of the patron saint: very near
Acapulco. A colourful fiesta too in **Mochitlan** (Gro.).

August
6th A fiesta in **Petatlan** (Gro.) distinguished by dances and mock battles between Indians and Spaniards.
23rd DIA DE SAN BARTOLOME. In **Tecpan de Galeana** (Gro.), between Acapulco and Zihuatanejo, religious processions the preceding night are followed by dancing, music and fireworks.

September
15th–16th INDEPENDENCE CELEBRATIONS almost everywhere.
28th DIA DE SANTIAGO celebrated in several villages immediately around **Acapulco**
29th DIA DE SAN MIGUEL exuberantly exploited in **Azoyu** (Gro.) and **Mochitlan** (Gro.).

November
First week **Colima's** major Feria lasts from the last days of October until November 8th.
2nd DAY OF THE DEAD is widely observed, with particularly picturesque traditions in **Atoyac de Alvarez** (Gro.), just off the Acapulco-Zihuatanejo road.

December
12th DIA DE NUESTRA SEÑORA DE GUADALUPE, patroness of Mexico. In **Atoyac de Alvarez** (Gro.) and **Ayutla** (Gro.) there are religious processions and traditional dances, while **Acapulco** enjoys more secular celebrations. In **Manzanillo** (Col.) the celebrations start at the beginning of the month, while in **Puerto Vallarta** (Jal.) they continue to the end of it.

TRAVEL DETAILS

Trains
From **Manzanillo** to **Guadalajara**. Leaves Manzanillo at 08.00 daily, arriving Colima (10.35), Ciudad Guzman (13.30) and Guadalajara (16.45). Return leaves Guadalajara at 10am. A slow and sweaty journey.

Buses
Bus services all along the coast are frequent and fast, with the possible exception of the stretch between Manzanillo and Lazaro Cardenas, and there are almost constant departures on the major routes heading inland. The southern sector – Acapulco and Zihuatanejo – is served largely by Estrella de Oro (first class) and Flecha Roja (second class, noted for their manic drivers). In the north there's more competition, but since everywhere of size has a unified Central Camionera this is rarely a problem. Tres Estrellas de Oro, Transportes del Pacifico and Omnibus de Mexico are the first class standbys, while Autobuses de Occidente, TNS and Flecha Amarilla are the most widely seen second class outfits.
From **Acapulco**. To Mexico City (6½hrs) at least hourly throughout the day and most of the night. To Taxco (twice daily; 5hrs) and Cuernavaca (7; 6hrs) with Estrella de Oro. 7 a day to Zihuatanejo (4½hrs) and 5 to Lazaro Cardenas (6hrs) on Estrella de Oro,

more frequently on Flecha Roja. To Puerto Escondido with Flecha Roja half hourly throughout the day (8hrs).
From **Puerto Vallarta**. To Guadalajara at least 5 daily (8hrs). To Tepic (for the north; 3hrs) at least 8 daily. To Barra de Navidad (4hrs) at least 10 daily.
From **Barra de Navidad**. 5 at least to Guadalajara (6½hrs). 10 or more to Manzanillo (1½hrs).
From **Manzanillo**. To Guadalajara (7hrs) at least hourly throughout the day. Several every hour to Colima (2½hrs). Direct to Mexico about 8 daily (at least 12hrs). Four daily to Lazaro Cardenas (7hrs).
From **Colima**. Around 12 daily to Guadalajara (5hrs).
From **Lazaro Cardenas**. 4 daily to Uruapan (6hrs).
From **Zihuatanejo**. Hourly to Lazaro Cardenas (2½hrs) with Flecha Roja. 8 daily direct to Mexico City (8–9hrs).

Ferries
From **Puerto Vallarta** to **Cabo San Lucas** leaves Tuesday and Saturday at 4pm, 18hrs.

Planes
Puerto Vallarta, Manzanillo, Ixtapa/Zihuatanejo and Acapulco all have at least one flight a day to Guadalajara and to the capital, and all, too, have scheduled connections with many US cities.

Chapter six
VERACRUZ AND THE GULF COAST

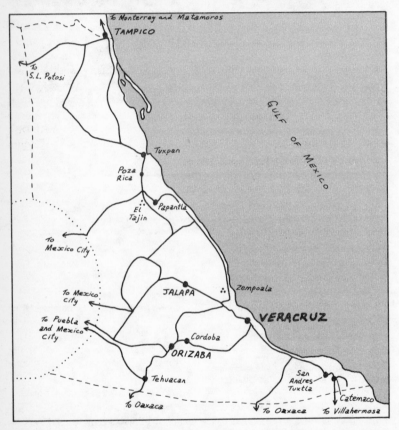

The central Gulf coast is among the most distinct, atmospheric areas of Mexico. From the capital you descend through the southern fringes of the Sierra Madre Oriental, past the country's highest peaks, to a broad, hot, wet, lush and jungly coastal plain. In this fertile tropic zone the earliest Mexican civilisations developed, and it remained densely populated throughout the pre-hispanic era. Cortes himself began his march on the capital from Veracruz, and the city remains, as it was throughout colonial history, the busiest port in the country. Rich in agriculture –

coffee, vanilla, tropical fruits and flowers grow everywhere – the Gulf coast is further enriched by oil and natural gas deposits.

Surprisingly few tourists come here, and those who do are mostly passing through. In part, at least, this is because the area doesn't need them and makes no particular effort to attract them; in part the weather can be blamed – it rains more often and more heavily than just about anywhere else. Yet even in the rainy season the torrential downpours are shortlived, and within a couple of hours of the rain starting, you can be back on the steaming streets in bright sunshine. There are long, wind-swept Atlantic beaches all down the coast, and although many suffer pollution from the busy shipping lanes and the oil industry, and none are up to the standards of the Pacific or Caribbean shores, enough remain to make a real attraction. More importantly, **Veracruz** is among the most welcoming of Mexican cities – too busy with its own affairs to create a separate life for visitors, you're drawn instead into the atmosphere of a tropical port with strong echoes of the Indies. Within a couple of hours lie **La Antigua**, where Cortes established the first Spanish government in the Americas, and **Zempoala**, ruined site of the first civilisation he subdued. **El Tajin**, near the coast in the north of the state, is among the most important archaeological sites in the country – surrounded now by oilfields, but also in an area where Totonac Indian culture retains powerful influence. South, **Lake Catemaco** again reflects the mixing of the cultures – middle-class Veracruzanos have their villas overlooking the water, but the lake is also renowned as a meeting place for Indian *brujos* and *curanderos*, witches and healers.

The food, too, is great – not only local coffee, fruit and vanilla (Mexicans inevitably take home a plastic bottle of vanilla essence as a souvenir), but also the seafood. *Huachinango a la Veracruzana* (Red Snapper Veracruz style) is served throughout the country, and is of course on every menu here. But there are many more exotic possibilities, from langoustines and prawns to *jaiba*, a large local crab: look out for anything made with *Chile Chipotle*, a hot, dark brown chile with a very distinctive (and delicious) flavour – *Chilpachole de Jaiba* is a sort of crab chowder which combines the two. Sweet *tamales*, too, are a speciality, and to go with them all the brewery at Orizaba produces several local beers – cheaper on the whole, and better, than the big national brands.

FROM THE CAPITAL

If you take the direct bus from Mexico to Veracruz (much quicker and cooler than the train) you'll by-pass every major town en route. If time is short this is no bad thing – for Veracruz and the coast are very much the outstanding attractions· – but there are at least three cities in the mountains which merit a stop if you're in no hurry. This is, however, the rainiest area of all, and while it brings bounties in terms of great coffee and a luxuriance of flowers, rain can become a problem. Particularly irritating – especially in October and November – is what they call locally the *chipichipi*: a persistent fine drizzle caused by warm airstreams from the Gulf hitting cooler air as they reach the eastern face of the Sierra.

The vast majority of buses follow the motorway, which now runs virtually all the way to Cordoba, the bulk of the high mountain trip. ORIZABA, first major town in the state of Veracruz, is largely an industrial city in spite of its colonial centre. What it lacks in innate charm, though, it makes up for by being positioned at the foot of the **Pico de Orizaba** (or *Citlaltepetl*), a perfectly formed volcano and, at 18,260 feet, the highest peak in Mexico. There's further comfort in that the most important industry here is brewing, and that the giant *Cerveceria Moctezuma* produces some of the best beer in the Republic – ask at the Tourist Office for details of tours. Seeing the town need only take a couple of hours even so, and there are more attractive places to spend the night further down the road at Fortin and Cordoba. If, however, you plan to tackle the Pico de Orizaba – and the climb, once again outlined in detail in R. J. Secor's *Mexico's Volcanoes*, is only for serious mountaineers – you should change here for the second class bus to the villages of SERDAN or TLACHICHUCA from where the main trails start. Again, the **Tourist Office**, on Oriente 6 at the junction of Sur 5 not far from the *ADO* bus station, can help with further information. Should you need to stay the *Gran Hotel de France*, above the Turismo, offers rooms with a degree of class, or there are cheaper accommodations along Norte 4 – the *Hotel San Cristobal* among them.

FORTIN DE LAS FLORES (Fortress of the Flowers) lies on the main road towards Cordoba, where a beautiful minor route cuts across country to Jalapa. For once, it's a singularly appropriately named town, for here more than anywhere in the state there are flowers everywhere – in the plaza, in the hotels, on the hillsides all around. Rain, which is frequent from May to December, and constant warmth ensure their growth – with the coming of the rains in May wild orchids bloom freely. The fortress of the name has all but disappeared, but you can visit the **Hacienda de las Animas**, once a residence of Maximilian and Carlota, now part of the luxury *Hotel Ruiz Galindo*. A couple of miles out of town the **Barranca de Matalarga** exemplifies the luxuriance of the vegetation: above the ravine you can see plantations of coffee and fruit trees, while the banks of the torrent itself are thick with a stunning variety of wild plants, and with humming birds and insects. It's a small town, but there are a number of reasonable places to stay: the *Posada La Marina*, on Avenida 1 at the corner of Calle 5, the *Casa de Huespedes Virginia*, almost next door, and the slightly more expensive *Hotel Mayorga*, on the same street at the junction of Calle 7, among them.

Second class buses take the mountain road to Jalapa fairly regularly, but on down the main road it's only a few miles further to **CORDOBA**, a somewhat decaying colonial city and the centre of the local coffee trade. Its main claim to fame is that here, in 1821, the last Spanish viceroy Juan O'Donoju signed a treaty acknowledging Mexican Independence with General Iturbide, soon to become emperor. This was in the Palacio de los Condes de Zeballos – now ignominiously reduced to the crumbling *Hotel Zevallos* – on the main square. There's not a great deal to do beyond sitting in the plaza, sampling the coffee and listening to the music, but it's a pleasant enough place to do that. As well as the expensive hotels around the Zocalo, you'll find plenty of cheap places scattered about, especially along Av. 2 – closest to the action are the *Hotel Virreinal*, by the side of the Cathedral at the corner of Avenida Uno and Calle 5, and the *Posada Ruiz*, just down Calle 5 from here.

Although it's slower, a number of buses also go from Mexico to Veracruz via **JALAPA** – second class ones especially. The state capital, Jalapa (or Xalapa as locals frequently spell it) is remarkably attractive despite its relative modernity. This is largely due to a tumbling hillside setting overlooking the *Cofre de Perote* and a richness of vegetation almost the equal of Fortin's (with which it also shares a warm, damp climate), but also thanks to civic leaders who have promoted the place as a cultural centre. There are frequent music festivals here, and the modern State University (on the outskirts of town) has an excellent **Archaeology Museum** (open daily 9–6). This is the outstanding sight of the city – easily rivalling the Gulf Coast collection in Mexico City's National Museum and an important introduction to the sites along the coast if you haven't seen that. Cultures represented range from the earliest Olmec to Totonac objects from the time of the Conquest: among them several of the colossal Olmec heads (displayed, too, in the gardens outside), and some glorious Man/Jaguar figures. In the final rooms there are ethnological displays of contemporary Indian life.

Downtown, the small colonial area is the main attraction – the eighteenth-century **Cathedral** and **Palacio de Gobierno** (with murals by the Chilean *Jose Chaves Morado*) both deserve to be seen, and you can check out what's going on in the way of cultural events at the **Teatro del Estado**. If you're feeling energetic you could also climb **Macuiltepec**, the highest of the hills on which the town is built, where there's a *Mirador* from which, if you're lucky, you might catch a glimpse of the Gulf. Most of the cheaper hotels are along Av. Revolucion, which leads down from the second class bus station to the central Parque Juarez – the *Limon* and *Dulcelandia* among them. Heading on from Jalapa to Veracruz you'll pass through Zempoala (see p. 270), and if you have a couple of hours it's well worth breaking the journey here to visit the ruins.

VERACRUZ

VILLA RICA DE LA VERACRUZ was the first town founded by the Spanish in Mexico; a few days after Cortes's arrival on Good Friday, 1519.

> *As soon as we had made this treaty of alliance with the Totonacs . . . we decided with their ready help at once to found the city of Villa Rica de la Veracruz. So we planned a church, a market-place, arsenals and all the other features of a town, and built a fort.*

This first development – little more than a wooden stockade – was in fact some way to the north, later being moved to LA ANTIGUA (see p. 270) and subsequently to its present site in 1589. But the modern city is very much the heir of the original; still, as it has been since its foundation, the most important port in Mexico and with a history which reflects every major event from the Conquest on. 'Veracruz' states Paul Theroux, 'is known as "the heroic city". It is a poignant description: in Mexico a hero is nearly always a corpse.'

And if the modern city is far from dead, then certainly its past has been a series of 'invasions, punitive missions and local military defeats . . . humiliation as history'. It started even before the Spanish Conquest was complete, when Panfilo Narvaez landed here on his ill-fated mission to bring Cortes back under the control of the Governor of Cuba; and continued intermittently for the next 400 years. Throughout the sixteenth and seventeenth centuries Veracruz, and the Spanish galleons which used the port, were preyed on constantly by English, Dutch and French buccaneers. In the War of Independence the Spanish made their final stand here – holding the fortress of San Juan Ullua for four years after the country had been lost. In 1838 the French occupied the city, demanding compensation for French property and citizens who had suffered in the years following Independence; in 1847 US troops took Veracruz, and from here marched on to capture the capital; in 1862 the French, supported by Spanish and English forces which soon withdrew, invaded on the pretext of forcing Mexico to pay her foreign debt, but ended by staying five years and setting up the unfortunate Maximilian as emperor; and finally in 1914 US marines were back, occupying the city to protect American interests during the Revolution. These, then, are the *Cuatro Veces Heroica* of the city's official title, and the bulk of the history displayed with a certain bitterness in the museums.

The first, and the lasting, impression of Veracruz, however, is not of its history or its bitterness, but of its life now. It's one of the most enjoyable places in the Republic in which simply to be, to sit back and watch, or join, the daily round. This is especially true in the evenings when the tables under the *Portales* of the plaza fill up, and the drinking and the marimba music begin – to go on through most of the night. *Marimba* – a distinctively Latin-Caribbean sound based around a giant wooden xylophone – is *the* local sound, but at peak times there are mariachi bands too, and individual strolling crooners, all striving to be heard over each other. When the municipal band strikes up from the centre of the square, confusion is total.

Some practicalities – buses, rooms, food

Although Veracruz is a large and rambling city, the downtown area, once you've got to it, is relatively straightforward and small – anywhere further afield can be reached by local bus from somewhere very near the **Zocalo**. This, to an even greater extent than usual, is the epicentre of city life – not only the site of the Cathedral and the Palacio Municipal (in which you'll find a helpful **Tourist Office**) but the place where everyone gathers, for morning coffee, lunch, afternoon strolls and night-time revelry.

The **bus stations**, both *ADO* first class and *AU* second class, are a long way from the centre on Av. Diaz Miron. Any bus heading to the right as you come out should take you to the centre – most will have *centro* on the windscreen, or ask. They head straight to the end of Diaz Miron, round a confusing junction at the Parque Zamora, and on by a variety of routes mostly ending up on Independencia which runs past the Zocalo. To get back head for 5 de Mayo, parallel to Independencia one block inland, and take any bus marked *Camionera*. The **railway station** is right downtown, just about five blocks from the Zocalo along the dock-front.

There's a **hotel**, the *Central*, right next to the first class bus station, and several very cheap and rather grim places around the back of the second class terminal, but unless you've arrived very late at night there's no point in staying this far out. The other cheap places are mostly within a couple of blocks of the plaza; they're nothing to write home about, and noise can be a real problem, but at least you should find a clean room with a fan. Sandwiched between the expensive hotels on the Plaza itself, alongside the *Prendes* and the *Colonial*, is the *Hotel Imperial* (Miguel Lerdo 153) – not the cheapest, but given its relative comfort and position probably the best value. Carry on down this street past the side of the Palacio Municipal and you come out into a small park facing the Customs House (*Aduana Maritima*) and other port authority buildings: to your right is the rather expensive *Hotel Oriente*, a little way down to the left (opposite the *Aduana*) the *Hotel Ria* and next to it a basic, nameless *Casa de Huespedes*. A little further in this direction, more or less opposite the Post Office, you'll find the *Hotel Rex*. In the other direction, right from the back of the Zocalo, there's another group of cheaper places near the market: try the *Hotel Amparo* or *Mallorca*, at the junction of Zaragoza and Serdan, or the *Hotel Vigo*, on the corner of Molina and Landero y Cos.

As for **eating**, there are seafood restaurants all over Veracruz, although by no means all are particularly good value. The plaza itself is ringed by little bars and cafes, but these really are places to drink, and though most do serve food, or at least sandwiches, it's generally overpriced and not up to much. One place you should definitely try here, though, is the *Cafe La Parroquia*, just off the plaza on Independencia opposite the Cathedral, which claims its locally grown coffee is the best in the country. Certainly it is extremely good, and the cafe, which is cavernous inside, is permanently packed: if you can fight your way to a table you'll be presented with a menu, but most people simply drink the coffee – maybe, at breakfast time, with a *pan dulce*. For more substantial meals there are a whole series of small fish restaurants around the **market**, and the top floor of the market building itself is given over to cooked food stalls. Between here and the Zocalo (leave the square through the passageway, *Portales Miranda*, behind the Cathedral) is another small square with a group of restaurants. *La Gaviota* serves good plain meals 24 hours a day (which can be useful after an evening under the Portales), and next to it are two small places which serve nothing but fruit – fruit salads, fruit drinks, fruit cocktails, fruit juices. Try a *Jaiba rellena* – half a melon stuffed with fresh seasonal fruit and ice cream. These are all just off Zaragoza at its junction with Molina: for a slightly more luxurious seafood restaurant head up Zaragoza towards the museum and you'll find *El Pescador*, a good place to sample a coctel of real *jaiba* (crab).

Getting around – sights and beaches

The outstanding sight in Veracruz is the **Castillo de San Juan de Ullua** (open daily 9–5), the great fortress which so signally failed to protect the harbour. Actually, in most cases, this was hardly the fault of its defenders, since every sensible invader landed somewhere on the coast nearby, captured the town, and having cut the fort off by land and sea called for its surrender. Certainly the fortifications are impressively massive despite their dire state of disrepair, and from the walls there are superb views over the harbour and city. A bus runs out regularly, past the busiest part of the docks and along the great harbour bar which joins the mainland to the former reef on which the castle stands. Catch it on Av. Landero y Cos, in front of the tacky souvenir stands which line the dockside.

The place is thoroughly run-down – watch out for unguarded 30-foot drops and take a torch if you really want to penetrate the dingy, dripping depths – but fascinating nonetheless. You can still see the gun emplacements on the great walks around the ramparts, overseeing now the work of a busy port, and within the defences the arsenals (some still with a few rusting cannon lying around), barracks and dungeons, partially submerged at high tide.

Back in town, there are two museums worth seeing. The **Museo de la**

Ciudad (open daily 10–6, but part closed for restorations) covers local history and folk¹˙ ˙e from the earliest inhabitants to the 1914 US invasion. Inevitably, it's rather a potted version, and many of the exhibits go completely unexplained, but there's some beautiful Olmec and Totonac sculpture, including one of the giant Olmec heads, and fascinating photographs of more recent events as well as relics of the city's various 'heroic defenders'. The City Museum occupies an old mansion on Zaragoza, about five blocks from the Palacio Municipal, and from here it's an easy walk, down past the market, to the Malecon at the side of the harbour. Here the **Museo Venustiano Carranza** is in the old *Faro* (lighthouse) alongside the huge Banco de Mexico building. Venustiano Carranza established his constitutionalist government in Veracruz in 1915 (with the support of US President Woodrow Wilson, whose troops then still occupied the town); living in the Castillo de San Juan and running his government – and the war against Villa and Zapata – from this lighthouse building. There's a fine statue of Carranza outside, looking exactly as John Reed describes him in *Insurgent Mexico* – 'a towering, khaki-clad figure, seven feet tall it seemed . . . arms hanging loosely by his side, his fine old head thrown back' – and inside assorted memorabilia of his government's term here. Opening hours, though, seem at the whim of the Navy, whose local headquarters the building also houses.

You wouldn't make a special trip to Veracruz for its **beaches** – although for Mexicans from the capital it's a relatively cheap and handy resort, and there are hotels catering to them for miles to the south – but for an afternoon's escape to the sea they're quite good enough. Avoid **Villa del Mar**, which is the closest, most crowded and least clean, and head instead to **Mocambo** or **Boca del Rio**. Buses (marked *Boca del Rio*) head out to both from the corner of Zaragoza and Serdan: both are lined with small hotels and restaurants, and each has warm, calm swimming – though from time to time the water can be pretty filthy. Better than either, but more expensive, is to take a boat trip out from the dock to the **Isla de Sacrificios**.

This was named by Juan de Grijalva, whose expedition sailed up this coast a full year before Cortes arrived: Bernal Diaz explains that, on landing,

> *we found two stone buildings of good workmanship, each with a flight of steps leading up to a kind of altar, and on those altars were evil-looking idols, which were their gods. Here we found five Indians who had been sacrificed to them on that very night. Their chests had been struck open and their arms and thighs cut off, and the walls of these buildings were covered with blood.*

Hence the name.

NORTH ALONG THE COAST – LA ANTIGUA TO TUXPAN

Heading north from Veracruz there's a short stretch of motorway as far as CARDEL, junction of the coast road and the route up to Jalapa. **LA ANTIGUA** lies just off this road, and although it does see an occasional bus you'll find it much easier and quicker to take one heading for Cardel (very frequent from the second class terminal) and get off at the toll-booths. From here it's only about a 20-minute walk up a signed road.

For all its antiquity, there's not a great deal to see in La Antigua, but it is a beautiful, broad-streeted tropical village on the banks of the **Rio La Antigua** (or *Rio Huitzilapan*) and at weekends makes a popular excursion for Veracruzanos who come to picnic by the river and to swim or take boat rides on it. There are lots of seafood restaurants catering to this local trade. In the centre of the village, semi-ruinous, stand a couple of the oldest surviving Spanish buildings in Mexico: the Edificio de Cabildo, built in 1523, housed the first *Ayuntamiento* (local government) to be established; the Casa de Cortes was built for Cortes himself a few years later – a fairly crude construction of local stone; and the parish church too dates from the mid-sixteenth century, though altered and restored several times since. On the river-bank stands a vast old tree – the *Ceiba de la Noche Feliz* – to which, according to local legend, Cortes moored his ships when he arrived here.

That Cortes came here at all, after first landing near the site of modern Veracruz, was thanks to the invitation of the Totonac Indians of **ZEMPOALA** (or Cempoala), then a city of some 25 or 30,000 inhabitants. It was the first native city visited by the Conquistadors ('a great square with courtyards', wrote Bernal Diaz, 'which appeared to have been lime coated and burnished during the last few days ... one of the horsemen took the shining whiteness for silver, and came galloping back to tell Cortes that our quarters had silver walls') and quickly became their first ally against the Aztecs. Zempoala, which had existed in some form for at least 800 years, had been brought under the control of the Aztec empire only relatively recently – around 1460 – and its people, who had already rebelled more than once, were only too happy to stop paying their tributes once they believed that the Spanish could protect them from retribution. This they did, although the 'Fat Chief' and his people must have begun to have second thoughts when Cortes ordered their idols smashed and replaced with crosses and Christian altars.

Cortes left Zempoala in August 1519 for the march on Tenochtitlan, taking with him 200 Totonac porters and fifty of the town's best warriors, but the following May was forced to return in a hurry by the news that Panfilo Narvaez had come after him with a large force. The battle took place in the centre of Zempoala, where despite the fact that Narvaez's force was far larger and had taken up defensive positions on the great temple, Cortes won a resounding victory – the enemy leaders were captured and most of the men switched sides, joining in the later assaults on the Aztec capital.

The archaeological site dates largely from this period, and although obviously the buildings have lost their decorative facings and thatched sanctuaries, it's one of the most complete examples of an Aztec ceremonial centre surviving – albeit in an untypically tropical setting. The pyramids with their double stairways, grouped around a central plaza, must resemble those of Tenochtitlan, though on a considerably smaller scale. Apart from the main, cleared site, consisting of the **Templo Mayor** (the largest and most impressive structure, where Narvaez made his stand), the Great Pyramid and the Templo de las Chimeneas, there are lesser ruins scattered throughout, and around, the modern village. Most important of these are the Templo de las Caritas, a small temple on which a few carvings and remains of murals can still be seen, in open country just beyond the main site, and the Temple of Ehecatl, on the opposite side of the main road through the village.

There are buses (second class) to Zempoala from both Veracruz and Jalapa, but it can be quicker – certainly if you plan to continue northwards – to go back to **CARDEL** and change there for a first class service. From La Antigua you can go back to the main road, get a bus on to Cardel, and another from there to Zempoala. Cardel itself is not of much interest, but there are several restaurants and a couple of small hotels around the plaza if you need them, and from here you can head down to a good beach at **CHACHALACAS** (another short bus journey), a small fishing community where you'll also find excellent seafood.

Continuing northwards up the coast, there's very little in the long stretch (some 4 hours on the bus) from here to Papantla. The village of QUIAHUITZLAN, about 70km from Veracruz, bears the name of a fortified Totonac town visited by Cortes, but the ruins lie unexcavated nearby. At LAGUNA VERDE there's a new nuclear power station, and at NAUTLA the largest town you'll see, surrounded by coconut groves. Although there are long, flat stretches of sand much of the way, they are pretty uninviting – desolate, windswept, and raked by heavy surf. Only in the final stretch does the beach offer much temptation, with several motels dotted between Nautla and **TECOLUTLA,** a low key resort a few miles off the main road. If you crave the beach you can stay here (try the *Hotel Playa* or the *Marsol*) and still get to Papantla and El Tajin with relative ease.

As a town, though, **PAPANTLA** is far more attractive – flower-filled and struggling over an unexpected outcrop of low, jungly hills. It's one of the most important centres of the Mexican vanilla industry – the sweet, sticky odour frequently hangs over the place and vanilla products are on sale everywhere – and also one of the surviving strongholds of Totonac Indian life. You'll see Totonacs wandering around in their loose white robes and bare feet – especially in the market – but, more significantly, Papantla (with El Tajin) is the one place where you can regularly witness the amazing **dance-spectacle** of the *Voladores de Papantla*. The dance is performed each Sunday (weather permitting) from the huge pole by the church: it involves five men, a leader who provides music on flute and drum, and four performers. These represent the five earthly directions – the four cardinal points and straight up, from earth to heaven. After a few preliminary ceremonies, the five climb to a small platform atop the pole where the leader resumes playing – and directs prayers for the fertility of the land in every direction. Meanwhile the four dancers tie ropes, coiled tightly around the top of the pole, to their waists and at a signal fling themselves head first into space. As they spiral down in ever-increasing circles the leader continues to play, and to spin, on his platform until the four hit the ground (or hopefully land on their feet, having righted themselves at the last minute). In all they make thirteen revolutions each, symbolising the fifty-two-year cycle of the Aztec Calendar. Although the full significance of the dance has been lost – originally the performers would wear bird costumes for example – it has survived much as the earliest chroniclers reported it largely because the Spanish thought of it as a sport rather than a pagan rite. In Papantla and Tajin it has become, at least partly, a tourist spectacle (though no less hazardous for that) as the permanent metal poles attest: if you can see it at a local village fiesta there is still far more ceremonial attached, particularly in the selection of a sufficiently tall tree and its erection in the place where the dance is to be performed.

There are several reasonably priced **hotels** in Papantla, of which the *Hotel Papantla* – in the main plaza – is probably the best choice. The Hotels *Tajin* and *Totonaca* are also fair. The *Cafe La Terraza*, overlooking the plaza from the first floor, is a lively place from which to watch the evening action, and if the food's not up to much, it's as good as any you'll find here.

However charming and peaceful Papantla may be, the main reason anyone comes here is to visit the ruins of **EL TAJIN**, by far the most important archaeological site on the Gulf Coast, and a much more interesting and impressive collection of buildings than the more recent remains of Zempoala. The city flourished – extending to occupy an area of some 10 square km – during the Classic, or Teotihuacan, period of Mexican pre-history from around 600–900AD, and although it survived several centuries after, Tajin eventually suffered the fate of its contemporaries, being invaded, burned and abandoned around 1200. By the time of the Conquest it had been forgotten, and any knowledge of it now comes from archaeological enquiries since the accidental discovery of the site in 1785. Although it is generally called Totonac, after the present inhabitants of the region, few experts believe that it was the Totonacs who created El Tajin – though none can agree on just who did.

Only a small part of the huge site has been cleared, and even this limited area is constantly in danger of being engulfed by the jungle: stand on top of one of the pyramids and you see green mounds in every direction, each concealing more ruins. They say that the work of exploration is advancing gradually, and that the whole area should have been uncovered by some time in the next century – in fact, old photographs of the place make it quite clear that over recent years the jungle has reclaimed mounds which formerly were cleared. The temptation to go and discover one of these for yourself is a powerful one, but should be resisted, as one look at the rogue's gallery of poisonous snakes and insects in the site museum will doubtless convince you. All of these preserved specimens were killed during clearance of the site, and although the nastier ones are rare, there are plenty of irritating little bugs about. Stick to the cleared areas and paths, and if you do wander into the longer grass or into the jungle make sure that your feet and legs are well covered: Totonac trousers lace at the ankle for added protection.

The site (open daily 9–6) divides broadly into two areas: *Tajin Viejo*, the original explored area centring on the amazing Pyramid of the Niches, and *Tajin Chico*, a group of administrative buildings built on an artificial terrace. From the entrance (where there are a couple of stalls selling cold drinks and occasionally sandwiches or *tortas*) a track leads up past the **museum** – where you can buy guides to the site – through a small group of unexcavated buildings, and into *Tajin Viejo*. Before you reach the square in front of the Pyramid you pass several **ball-courts**, the most important of which, on your left, is the South Court or *Juego de Pelota Sur*. There are at least ten such courts, probably many more, and the game must have assumed an importance here far greater than in any other known site: we know little of the rules, and courts vary widely in size and shape, but the general idea was to knock a ball through a ring or into a hole without use of the hands. Clearly, too, there was a religious significance, and at Tajin the game was associated closely with human sacrifice – the superb bas-relief sculptures which cover the walls of the South Court show aspects of the game, and they also portray a decapitated player, and another about to be stabbed with a ritual knife by fellow players. These bas-reliefs are another constant feature of the site, adorning many of the ball-courts and buildings while others are stacked in the museum, but these in the South Court are much the most striking and best preserved.

The unique **Pyramid of the Niches** is the most famous building at Tajin, and indeed one of the most remarkable and enigmatic of all Mexican ruins. It rises to a height of about 60 feet in six receding tiers, each face punctuated with regularly spaced niches; up the front a steep stairway climbs to a platform on which the temple originally stood. If you total up the niches, including those hidden by the stairs and those, partly destroyed, around the base of the temple, there are 365 in all. Their exact purpose is unknown, but clearly they were more than mere decoration: perhaps each would hold some offering or sacrifice, one for each day of the year, or they may symbolise caves – the dwellings of the Earth God. Originally they were painted deep red, with a blue surround, to enhance the impression of depth. Around the plaza in front of the Pyramid stand all the other important buildings of **Tajin Viejo**: opposite, Monument 3, a similar pyramid without the niches, and behind it Monument 23, a strange steep-sided bulk, one of the last to be built here; to the right Monument 2, a low temple, squats at the base of Monument 5, a beautiful truncated pyramid with a high decorative pediment broken by a broad staircase; on the left Monument 4, one of the oldest in Tajin and only partly restored.

From the back of Monument 4 the path continues, past the *Juego de Pelota Norte* with its worn relief sculptures, up onto the levelled terrace of **Tajin Chico**. Originally this raised area was supported by a retaining wall, part of which has been restored, and reached by a staircase opposite the ball-court. Now, only parts of the buildings survive, making a rather confusing whole. **Building C**, and the adjoining structure B, are the most impressive remains: building C has stone friezes running around its three storeys, giving the impression of niches – in this case, presumably, purely decorative, a chiaroscuro (light and shade) effect which would have been heightened by the original, brightly coloured stucco finish. It has, too, the remains of a concrete roof – originally a huge single slab of poured cement, unique in ancient Mexico. **Structure A** also had a covered interior, and you can still get into its central terrace via a narrow staircase, the entrance covered by a false arch of the type common in Mayan buildings. Above Tajin Chico on the hill stood the *Edificio de las Columnas*, which must originally have dominated the entire city. Although this has been excavated, however, it had been reclaimed by the jungle and was quite inaccessible on my last visit.

To get to El Tajin from Papantla take a second class bus to CHOTE from the terminal by the market – halfway down the hill from the plaza (ask, because buses to numerous destinations pass through this crossroads). From Chote it's another 5km through oil-rich country – nodding-donkey wells dot the skyline – to the entrance of the ruins. Assuming the buses connect, the entire journey takes only about 20 minutes. There are also buses direct from El Tajin to **POZA RICA**, where you can connect with services to Mexico City as well as up or down the coast. In itself, though, Poza Rica is not a place of any delights – a dull, oil-boom city with something of a reputation for violence.

If you are continuing northwards you'd be much better off in **TUXPAN** (or Tuxpam, pronounced Toosh-pam), about an hour up the coast. Though this too has been swollen by the oil boom, its tank farms and half-completed oil rigs cannot entirely disguise what is still, in places, a beautiful riverside town. What's more, there are excellent beaches nearby. As you walk towards the centre from the bus station, along Av. Juarez, you'll pass several hotels. The first, the *Hotel Colon*, is the cheapest and virtually the only place in town with views over the river: which is not to say I'd recommend it – it's really very basic and in the height of summer the heat and mosquitoes can be unbearable. Better to continue past this and the fancy places beyond it to the Zocalo, where there's the *Hotel Parque* and, just behind it, the *Hotel Huastecas*.

The beaches at **Barra de Tuxpan**, by the river mouth, are the real attraction: buses shuttle out there from beneath the giant bridge (near the market and bus station), driving down the river-bank, past tankers and fishing boats, and ending up about 20 minutes later on a huge stretch of sand. There are restaurants and changing rooms here, a couple of basic rooms for rent in the first restaurant on the right, and any number of shaded hammocks under little palapas – or sling your own under the trees behind the beach. As long as the wind keeps up to drive the worst of the insects away – and it's usually fairly breezy here – you could sleep out or **camp** here, no problem. There are plenty of showers around which you can use for a few pesos.

Between Tuxpan and TAMPICO (see p. 72) there's nothing of great interest: a slow, bumpy and sweaty road across a plain whose thick tropical vegetation quickly becomes monotonous. Only the ferry crossing of the Panuco, just before Tampico, livens things up a little – and you'll miss even that if your bus takes the longer, inland route via TEMPOAL, as most seem to do.

SOUTH OF VERACRUZ

Leaving Veracruz to the south, Highway 180 traverses a long expanse of plain, a country of broad river deltas and salt lagoons, for nearly 150km until it hits the hills of the **Sierra Tuxtla**. Beyond, it's more low, flat, dull country all the way to VILLAHERMOSA (p. 303). While few tourists come this way, it is a heavily travelled route, with plenty of buses and trucks thundering through. In the first stretch there are a few interesting fishing towns, and in the hills some really attractive scenery and a welcome dose of cool, fresh air: a definite incentive for an overnight stop before the tedious haul to follow. This was Olmec country, the first real civilisation of Mexico, but the Olmec sites are virtually impossible to get to without your own transport, and largely disappointing when you do. Unless for some special reason, it's best to reserve your studies to museums and to the reproduction of the site of La Venta in Villahermosa.

ALVARADO is the first stop, a sizeable fishing port some 70km from Veracruz. Not surprisingly, the attraction is fish, and Alvarado's Port Authority restaurant is famed for its excellence: it's also cheap, since it genuinely is used by port workers and fishermen. There are several hotels and other restaurants here, and the Laguna de Alvarado stretches away from the town, but for anything more than a meal-break it is not a particularly attractive place. If you want somewhere small, quiet, and entirely off the tourist circuit, try instead **TLACOTALPAN**, some 20 minutes further on. Still on the edges of the Rio Papaloapan close to the lagoon, it's a very pretty village, and although there's absolutely nothing laid on you can hire boats on the river, and fish or swim. There are a couple of small hotels on the main street near where the buses stop.

Once the mountains start (in a region which Alexander von Humboldt described as *the Switzerland of Veracruz*, an overblown and overused claim) things become much more interesting, and the cooler climate an infinite relief. There are two lovely townships here, **SANTIAGO TUXTLA** and **SAN ANDRES TUXTLA**, each with several hotels. San Andres has an excellent market, too, and Santiago is not far from the important Olmec site of **Tres Zapotes** (occasional buses).

CATEMACO, however, is a far more attractive place to stay than either. Squatting on the shore of a large, mountain-ringed lake – by tradition a centre of Indian witchcraft – it would be hard to envisage a more tranquil and picturesque spot to break the journey before the long leg south. Veracruzanos arrive in force at weekends, but it's little spoiled for all that. On the whole, hotels right on the lake are expensive, but you could try the *Tio Tin*, on the lakefront very close to the centre and the best value in town, or the nearby *Hotel Julita*. Barring these you're better off finding a room in one of the places a couple of streets inland – the *Hotel Los Arcos*, for example, just down from where the buses stop. There isn't a great deal to do: haggle at the dock over the price of a boat trip round the lake; visit the local waterfall (*Salto de Teoteapan*) or one of the lake beaches; sample *Mojarra*, a small fish from the lake, at one of the restaurants on the shore or around the plaza; but it's an ideal place not to do a great deal. A local bus from the plaza (marked *La Margarita*) goes round much of the shore, passing a couple of beaches and the beautiful Rio Cuetzalpan. While Catemaco is slightly off the main road, there are some direct buses from Veracruz – don't make a special effort to get one, though, as local services from San Andres cover the short journey regularly.

FIESTAS

January
In the last week of January **Tlacotalpan** has a fiesta with dances, boat races and bulls let loose in the streets.

February
2nd DIA DE LA CANDELARIA. Colourful Indian fiesta in **Jaltipan** on the main road south of Catemaco, which includes the dance of *La Malinche* (*Malintzin*, Cortes's Indian interpreter, known to the Spanish as Malinche, is said to have been born here), recreating aspects of the Conquest. Also the final day of celebrations in **Tlacotalpan**.
4th Agricultural festival in **Otatitlan**, near the Oaxaca border off the road from Alvarado to Oaxaca, where many Indians attend a midnight mass to bless their crops.
CARNIVAL (the week before Lent, variable Feb.-Mar.) is riotously celebrated in **Veracruz** – other places too, but go to Veracruz.

March
On the first Friday, the FERIA DEL CAFE in **Ixhualtan**, a coffee-growing town near Cordoba – both Trade Fair and popular fiesta.
18th-19th FIESTAS DE SAN JOSE. In **Naranjos**, between Tuxpan and Tampico, a fiesta with many traditional dances celebrates the local patron saint. Similar events in **Espinal**, a Totonac village on the Rio Tecolutla not far from Papantla and El Tajin, where with luck you can witness the spectacular *Voladores*.
HOLY WEEK is widely observed, and in this area recreations of the Passion are widespread. You can witness them in **Papantla** – where you'll also see the *Voladores* – in **Coatzintla**, a Totonac village near Tajin, in **Cotaxtla**, between Veracruz and Cordoba, and in **Otatitlan**. **Naolinco**, a beautiful village near Jalapa, stages a mock crucifixion on Good Friday. Also celebrations in **Catemaco**, and in the port of **Alvarado** – a far more ribald Fish Fiesta following hard on the heels of the Veracruz Carnival.

April
15th–17th (approx.) FERIA DE LAS FLORES flower festival in **Fortin de las Flores**.

May
3rd Hundreds of pilgrims, mostly Indian, converge on **Otatitlan** to pay homage to the village's *Cristo Negro*.
27th DIA DEL SAGRADO CORAZON – the start of four days' festivities in **Naranjos**.
CORPUS CHRISTI (variable, the Thursday after Trinity) sees the start of a major four-day festival in **Papantla** and in particular regular performances by the *Voladores*.

June
13th DIA DE SAN ANTONIO. Fiesta in **Huatusco**, between Cordoba and Veracruz.
24th DIA DE SAN JUAN celebrated in **Santiago Tuxtla**, with dancing, and in **Martinez de la Torre**, on the road inland from Nautla, where the *Voladores* perform.

July
15th DIA DE LA VIRGEN DEL CARMEN – a massive pilgrimage to **Catemaco** is accompanied by a fiesta which spills over into the following day.
24th DIA DE SANTIAGO celebrated with fiestas in **Santiago Tuxtla** and **Coatzintla**; each lasts several days.

August
14th **Teocelo**, a village in beautiful country between Jalapa and Fortin, celebrates an ancient fiesta with dance and music.
15th In **Tuxpan**, a week-long feria begins – dancing and *Voladores*.
24th **Cordoba** celebrates the anniversary of the signing of the Treaty of Independence.

September
15th–16th Independence celebrations everywhere.
21st DIA DE SAN MATEO sees secular as well as religious celebration in **Naolinco**.
30th **Coatepec**, between Jalapa and Fortin, celebrates its patron's day – processions and dances.

October
7th FIESTA DE LA VIRGEN DEL ROSARIO, patroness of fishermen. In **La Antigua** she is honoured with processions of canoes on the river, while

Alvarado enjoys a more earthly fiesta, filling the first two weeks of the month.

NOVEMBER
2nd DAY OF THE DEAD is honoured everywhere – the rites in **Naolinco** are particularly strictly followed.

December
12th DIA DE LA VIRGEN DE GUAD-ALUPE widely observed, especially in **Huatusco**, **Cotaxtla**, and **Amatlan de los Reyes**, near Cordoba.
24th Christmas, of course, celebrated in **Santiago Tuxtla** with a very famous festival which lasts until Twelfth Night – January 6th.

TRAVEL DETAILS

Trains
From **Veracruz** to **Mexico City**. *El Jarocho* sleeper leaves 21.30, arriving 7.30 next morning (exactly the same times in the opposite direction). Also at 08.00, arriving Cordoba (10.25), Orizaba (11.30) and Mexico (19.12), and at 07.25, arriving Jalapa (11.40) and Mexico (19.45). Returns leave Mexico at 07.30 (Orizaba 15.30, Cordoba 16.30 and Veracruz 19.00) and 07.20 (Jalapa 15.30 and Veracruz 19.25).

From **Veracruz** to **Tapachula** (Guatemalan border). Leaves Veracruz 09.05, arriving Juchitan (22.30) and Tapachula (08.30).

Buses
First class buses are mostly operated by *Autobuses de Oriente* (ADO) – remarkably slick and efficient. Second class is dominated (at least on long hauls) by *Autobuses Unidos* (AU), more of a mixed bag.

From **Veracruz**. At least 15 daily to **Mexico City** (8hrs), via Cordoba (2½hrs) and Orizaba (3½hrs) – less frequently via Jalapa, but Veracruz-Jalapa (2½hrs) and Jalapa-Mexico (6½hrs) are both well-run routes. To Papantla (4hrs) and **Poza Rica** (4½hrs) not less than 10 a day. A similar number south to **Villahermosa** (7hrs) via San Andres Tuxtla (3hrs) and Coatzacoalcos (5hrs). Also direct services to **Oaxaca** (8hrs upwards, 4 daily) via Tuxtepec, though the route through Orizaba and Tehuacan may be preferable.
From **Poza Rica**. To Mexico City (5hrs) about 8 a day. To Tuxpan (1hr) very frequently.
From **Tuxpan**. To Tampico (5hrs) at least 10 daily.

Planes
There are four flights a day from Veracruz to Mexico City, and three a week from Poza Rica.

Chapter seven
OAXACA AND CHIAPAS

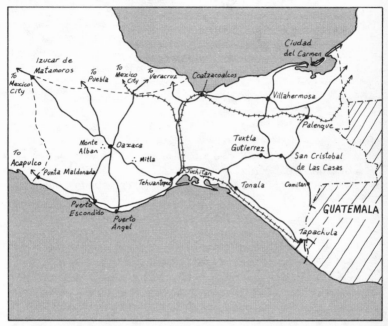

Oaxaca and **Chiapas,** along with the Gulf Coast state of **Tabasco,** form
the break between North American Central Mexico and Central America.
Here the two chains of the Sierra Madre converge, to run on as a single
range right through into South America and the Andes. Here too, the
often barren landscapes of northern Mexico are left firmly behind,
replaced by thickly forested hillsides, or in low-lying areas by jungle. It
is all very much closer to a Central American experience than anything
that has gone before – a feeling compounded by the relative lack of
development: the 'Mexican miracle' has yet to transform these states.
Chiapas was actually administered by the Spanish as part of Guatamala
until the early nineteenth century when it seceded to join newly independent Mexico.

Indian traditions and influence, too, remain more powerful in this area
than anywhere else in the country. The old tongues are still widely spoken,
and in the villages are scenes which seem to deny that the Spanish

Conquest ever happened. For the colour and variety of its markets, and the fascination of its fiestas, there is no rival in Mexico. Less enticingly, but arising out of the same traditions and geographical accidents, Chiapas and to a lesser extent Oaxaca have been troubled states of recent years. There are refugee camps along the Guatemalan border for Indians fleeing the terror there, and the occupants have clashed with Mexican troops trying to relocate them further inland and to prevent any more crossing the border to swell their numbers. You hear too, occasional stories of guerrilla activity in the border zone, and there have also been internal conflicts, in particular at Juchitan. Nevertheless, you are most unlikely to run into any of this – even news of such events leaks out only rarely – and the mountains of Oaxaca and Chiapas remain among the most compelling of Mexican experiences.

Oaxaca itself is the prime destination, close enough to the capital and the mainstream to attract large numbers of tourists to its markets, constant fiestas, and occasionally bizarre mix of colonial buildings and Indian street-life. Nearby are the most important Zapotec/Mixtec sites of **Monte Alban** and **Mitla**, and from here too you can head across the mountains to the growing Pacific resorts of **Puerto Escondido** and **Puerto Angel**.

On into **Chiapas** there's a direct coastal route **to Guatemala**, but the road through the mountains – the delightful market hill town of **San Cristobal de las Casas** and on to the sublime lakes of **Montebello**, right by the border – is infinitely more attractive. Heading for **the Yucatan**, **Palenque** should not be missed – the most beautiful of all Mexican archaeological sites; **Villahermosa**, despite its name, is not a particularly attractive city, but it's an almost unavoidable stop on the way, and the archaeological park of La Venta provides a glimpse of the otherwise barely accessible Olmec culture.

OAXACA: THE STATE

There are a number of ways of approaching Oaxaca. The main route from Mexico City, and the one followed by the majority of the buses (*ADO* or *Cristobal Colon* from the TAPO terminal), is on the Pan-American Highway via Puebla and IZUCAR DE MATAMOROS. You can also get to this road by heading south of the capital to CUAUTLA (birthplace of Emiliano Zapata, and a spa town with a climate similar to Cuernavaca's) and on from there. Either way, this is a ride of at least 8 hours through some impressive mountain scenery – cactus and scrub in the early stages giving way to thicker vegetation as you approach

Oaxaca. Most people do this non-stop, which is in all honesty the best policy, though ACATLAN – almost exactly halfway – does produce beautiful black pottery, on sale throughout the town. Some 50km further you enter the state of Oaxaca near HUAJUAPAN DE LEON – a town of no great interest in itself, but marking the beginning of *mescal* producing territory, with spiny, bluish-green Maguey cactuses cultivated all around the road. On the side road which leads from here to TEHUACAN, you pass through one of the largest and most impressive **cactus forests** in the Republic.

The newer road from Puebla to Oaxaca **via TEHUACAN** is also served by plenty of buses – if anything even more spectacularly mountainous, it's also slightly quicker. Tehuacan itself is the source of the bulk of the bottled **mineral water** (*Agua de Tehuacan*) consumed throughout Mexico, and a spa town of some antiquity. It's relaxing and easy paced, temperate in every way, and the best place to break the journey if you do decide to stop overnight. There are several hotels between the bus station and the central plaza – try the *Hotel Iberia* on Independencia – and you can head off to one of the springs in the outskirts to sample the waters. Worth seeing downtown is the elegant church of Carmen, with a brightly coloured tiled dome, and the *Museo del Valle de Tehuacan* (closed Mondays) housed in its former monastery, which has relics of the valley's pre-historic life – among the earliest evidence of settled habitation in Mexico.

The chief route **from the Gulf Coast** to Oaxaca – from Veracruz via Orizaba – again passes through Tehuacan, but if you're coming this way the other road, up from the coast at Tlacotalpan **via TUXTEPEC**, is far more exciting. It's a slow journey, bumpy and uncomfortable in the bus, but one of the most scenic and varied in the country. From steaming jungle in the broad valley of the Rio Papaloapan, you climb to a complex tangle of mountains (the very meeting place of the Atlantic and Pacific ranges) before dropping precipitously into the valley of Oaxaca. There are a couple of reasonable hotels in Tuxtepec.

From the direction of Acapulco, it's probably easier to go through Mexico City, but there are occasional buses up **from the Pacific Coast** at PINOTEPA NACIONAL; more frequently, and equally uncomfortably, from PUERTO ESCONDIDO or PUERTO ANGEL.

OAXACA

The city of **OAXACA**, capital of the state, sprawls across a grand expanse of deep-set valley, 5,000 feet above sea level, some 500km south-east of Mexico City. Its colour, its folklore, the huge extent of its Indian market and its thoroughly colonial centre combine to make this one of the most popular destinations for travellers, but still one of the most rewarding.

Increasingly Oaxaca is becoming an industrial city – the population is well over 100,000, the streets choked and noisy – yet it seems set to remain one which is easy to handle. In the centre, thanks to strict building regulations, the provincial charm is little affected and just about everything can be reached on foot. Provincial it remains, too, in its habits – by 11 at night the city is asleep – and in a leisurely atmosphere where the big excitements are sitting in a cafe watching life pass or gathering in the plaza to stroll and listen to the band.

From earliest times the valley was inhabited by the same Zapotec and Mixtec Indians who form the bulk of its population now. Their ancient centres – at Monte Alban, Yagul and Mitla – are less well known than their contemporaries in Central and Eastern Mexico, but every bit as important and impressive: all are easily reached from Oaxaca. In more

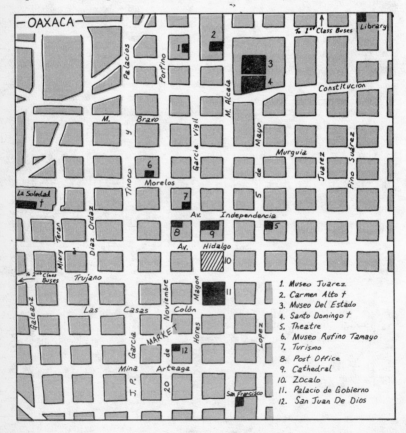

1. Museo Juarez
2. Carmen Alto †
3. Museo Del Estado
4. Santo Domingo †
5. Theatre
6. Museo Rufino Tamayo
7. Turismo
8. Post Office
9. Cathedral
10. Zocalo
11. Palacio de Gobierno
12. San Juan De Dios

recent history, the city played a lesser role. Cortes, attracted by the area's natural beauties, took the title of *Marques del Valle de Oaxaca* and until the Revolution his descendants held vast lands hereabouts. But for practical purposes Oaxaca was of little interest to the Spanish, with no mineral wealth and no great joy for farmers (though coffee was grown). The indigenous population was left to get on with their lives far more than was generally the case, with only the interference of a proselytising church to put up with. The city's most famous son, Benito Juarez, was himself a Zapotec Indian. Adopted and educated by a wealthy Oaxacan priest, he became a lawyer, state governor, and eventually president on a platform of smashing the power of the church. His Reform Laws — most importantly promoting secular education and expropriating church land — sparked off civil war and the intervention of the French and Emperor Maximilian, but the liberals eventually won the struggle, most of their reforms remain law, and Juarez himself stands out as one of the shaping hands behind modern Mexico. He is commemorated everywhere in Oaxaca, a privilege not shared by Porfirio Diaz, the second most famous Oaxaqueño, whose dictatorship most people choose to forget.

Practical details

Both **bus stations** in Oaxaca are a good way from the centre – at least 20 minutes' walk. First class is on the Calzada Heroes de Chapultepec, north of the centre, from where your best bet is to get a taxi in: if you're determined to walk, turn left along the main road about four blocks to Av. Juarez, left again for nine of ten blocks to Independencia or Hidalgo, then right to the Zocalo. On Juarez you can start to pick up city buses. The second class terminal is west of the centre by the new market buildings – walk past these, across the railway lines and the *Periferico*, and on up Calle Trujano towards the centre. The **railway station** is still further out, but from here there is a good bus service (*Estacion/Centro*) which will take you right into the Zocalo. From the **airport** there's a *colectivo* service (*Transportaciones Aeropuerto*) which again will drop you right by the Zocalo. On **leaving**, you should buy tickets in advance wherever possible – especially for early morning departures on popular routes, to Mexico City or to San Cristobal.

Although there are hundreds of **hotels** in Oaxaca, there are thousands of visitors, and if you arrive late you may well have difficulty finding a room. Under such circumstances it's best to take anything that's offered, and look for better things the next morning. The bulk of the cheaper places are in the streets south and east of the plaza, around the market and along Calle Trujano. Among the better places here **on Trujano**, between the second class bus station and the centre, are the *Hotel del Pacifico* (No. 420, corner of Mier y Teran), *Hotel Jimenez* (just up Mier y Teran from here), *Hotel Fortin* (among others on Diaz Ordaz, just off

Trujano) and, around the Junction with 20 de Noviembre, the *Hotel Francia* (where D. H. Lawrence stayed), *Meson del Rey*, and *Hotel Plaza*, all three more expensive but very close to the Zocalo. Heading down **towards the market** you'll find the *Hotel Riviera* at the corner of 20 de Noviembre with Las Casas, and nearby the *Hotel Rex*. Slightly cheaper, basic and noisy, places around the market include the *Hotel Chayo* (20 de Noviembre), *Hotel America* (Aldama 513), *Hotel Pasaje* (Mina 302) and *Hotel Yalalag* (Mina 108). A short walk to the east from here are the *Hotel Colon* (Colon 120) and the *Guelaguetza* (Rayon 205). Several more expensive hotels also cluster around the Zocalo – you could try the *Monte Alban* (Alameda de Leon 1), *Hotel Ruiz* (Bustamante 103), the *Central* (20 de Noviembre just north of the plaza), the *Hotel Pombo* (Morelos 601 behind the Cathedral) or a little further north the *Hotel Principal* (5 de Mayo 208). Though it's often full and by no means cheap, the *Hotel Veracruz*, right by the first class bus terminal, is worth trying if you roll up late. Finally, if money were no object, the *El Presidente* would be the ultimate place to stay – a beautifully converted sixteenth-century convent with a swimming pool in the cloister. It's worth visiting anyway, just for a look, at Calle 5 de Mayo 300, about five blocks north of the plaza.

Food is not one of Oaxaca's more noted attractions; you can eat perfectly well, but on the whole it's rather dull. The two things which come closest to being local specialities are *Tamales* – in just about any form – and *Mole Oaxaqueño*, which is not significantly different from *mole* anywhere else. The cheapest places to eat are in the markets – either a section of the main market around 20 de Noviembre and Aldama, or the new one by the second class bus station. More formal, but still basic, restaurants are found in the same areas as the hotels, especially along Trujano. The *Hotel Paris* here serves a good *comida corrida*, or try the *Restaurant Colonial* on 20 de Noviembre. The Zocalo is ringed by cafes and restaurants where you can sit outside, but not surprisingly they tend to be expensive – *El Jardin* is the best of them for coffee or breakfast; *Guelatao* is the cheapest overall, with a reasonable *comida corrida*. Of the expensive options, *El Asador Vasco* serves excellent Spanish-style food. *Bum-Bum*, also on the Zocalo, is the place to go for fruit juices and *licuados*. The *Cafe El Sol y La Luna* (Murguia 105 near the *El Presidente*) serves a mixture of health food and American-style junk food popular with local students, while you can get **vegetarian** fare at the *Restaurant Pisces*, on Hidalgo near the church of La Soledad. **Mescal** (or mezcal) is *the* local drink, sold everywhere in bottles with a dead worm in the bottom – this creature lives on the Maguey cactus and is there to prove it's genuine: you don't have to drink it, though people are constantly taking a swig from the bottle to discover they have without coming to any apparent harm. Basically, mescal is a rougher, less refined version of Tequila, and is drunk the same way.

The **Tourist Office** (open 9–3 and 5–7, except Sundays), for maps or any problems, is just off the Zocalo on Independencia opposite the Cathedral; the **Post Office** is almost opposite. *Aerovias Oaxaqueñas*, for **flights to Puerto Escondido**, is at Armenta y Lopez 209, though you can buy tickets at any downtown travel agent. **Books in English** can be borrowed from the Library – run by expatriate Americans – on Pino Suarez, or bought from a limited selection at the *Libreria Universitaria* (Guerrero 108, just off the Zocalo).

The city

Simply being in Oaxaca, absorbing its life and wandering through its streets is enough, especially if you happen to catch the city during a fiesta (they happen all the time – the most important are listed at the end of the chapter), but you should definitely take time out to visit the State Museum and the churches of Santo Domingo and La Soledad, and to get out to Monte Alban or the longer excursion to Mitla.

The Zocalo is the place to start, closed to traffic now and constantly animated. Beggars, hawkers, businessmen, tourists and at some stage every day most of the local population pass through, and on Sundays and many weekday evenings there's a band playing in the centre. The neo-classical, *Porfiriano* **Palacio de Gobierno** is here, on the south side, while you reach the **Cathedral** from the north-west corner, opposite. Begun in 1544, its construction was only completed in the eighteenth century, and it has been repeatedly pillaged and restored since then: as a result, despite a fine baroque façade, it's not the most interesting of Oaxaca's churches.

Walk past the Cathedral and the Alameda, then right onto Independencia, and you reach the **Teatro Macedonia de Alcala** in a couple of blocks. Still operating as a theatre and concert hall, it is typical of the grandiose public buildings which sprang up across Mexico around the turn of the century – the interior, if you can see it (try going to a show, or sneaking in before one), is a magnificent swathe of marble and red plush. At the end of 5 de Mayo, left from here and up past the *El Presidente*, stands the church of **Santo Domingo**. Considered by Aldous Huxley 'one of the most extravagantly gorgeous churches in the world', this sixteenth-century extravaganza is elaborately carved and decorated both inside and out – the external walls solid, defensive and earthquake-proof, the interior really delicate. Parts – especially the chapels, pressed into service as stables – were damaged during the Reform Wars and the Revolution, but most have been restored. Notice especially the great gilded main altarpiece, straight ahead, and the family tree of the Dominican order, with leafy branches and tendrils, busts and a figure of the Virgin for fruit and flowers on the underside of the raised choir, above you as you enter. The adjoining **Capilla del Rosario** is also richly painted and carved.

Behind the church, the old Dominican Monastery has been restored to house Oaxaca's **Museo del Estado** (open 10–1 and 4–7; closed Mondays) in a series of beautiful chambers on two floors around a cloister. Downstairs, there's a collection of colonial religious artworks and an extensive display devoted to the state's various Indian groups – their art, crafts, costumes and so on. Upstairs is the archaeological collection, and above all one room containing the magnificent **Mixtec jewellery** discovered in Tomb 7 at Monte Alban. This constitutes a substantial proportion of all known pre-hispanic gold, since anything the early Spanish found they melted down or plundered: it includes a couple of superbly detailed gold masks and breastplates. There are also smaller gold jewels, and objects of a wide variety of precious materials – mother of pearl, obsidian, turquoise, amber, and jet among them. Other rooms contain further Mixtec and Zapotec relics.

The church of **Carmen Alto** is on Calle Alcala just above the Museum: head down the narrow street beside it and you'll come out just below the **Casa y Museo Benito Juarez** on Calle Garcia Vigil (open 10–1 and 4–7; closed Mondays). The house belonged to the priest who took Juarez in and educated him, and although Juarez himself only lived here for a couple of years in his youth, some of its rooms have been preserved as they were in the middle of the last century, and others given over to a small collection of mementoes of the ex-president. From here you can head straight back down Garcia Vigil towards the Cathedral. To the right along Morelos, fifth block along the way, lies the **Museo Rufino Tamayo** (open 10–2 and 4–7; closed Tuesdays), a private collection of pre-hispanic artefacts, gathered by the abstract artist who is now considered (since Rivera and Orozco are out of fashion) one of the greatest Mexican painters of the century. The objects come from all over Mexico and all periods – all of them superb of their kind, and all excellently displayed.

The **Basilica de la Soledad**, not far away to the west along Independencia, contains an image – the *Virgen de la Soledad* – which is not only Oaxaca's patron saint, but one of the most revered in the country. The sumptuously decorated seventeenth-century church is set on a small plaza surrounded by other buildings associated with the Virgin's cult, including a small museum. The only local church to compare with it, in terms of the crowds of worshippers it attracts, is the ancient **San Juan de Dios** right in the heart of the old market area. Here villagers who've come to town for the day and market traders drop in constantly to pay their devotions – often in curiously corrupted forms of Catholic ritual.

Saturday, by tradition, is **market day** in Oaxaca and although nowadays the markets operate every day of the week, Saturdays are still the time to come here if you want to see the old-style *Tianguis* at its best. This is when Indians flood in from the villages in a bewildering variety of costumes, and when Mixtec and Zapotec dialects replace Spanish as the Lingua Franca. The bulk of this activity, and of the serious business of buying and selling everyday goods, has moved out to the **new market** by the second class bus station. The **old market**, downtown, has been somewhat displaced by this, but it still sells the bulk of village **handicrafts**; somewhat touristy – you're harassed far more by the vendors here and have to bargain fiercely – the quality of the goods is also often suspect. *Serapes*, in particular, are often machine-made of chemically dyed artificial fibres: these look glossy, and you can also tell real wool by plucking out a thread – artificial fibres are long, thin and shiny, woollen threads short, rough and curly. If you hold a match to it a woollen thread will singe and smell awful, an artificial one will melt and burn your fingers. There's a *Fonart* shop at the corner of Garcia Vigil and Bravo, between the Zocalo and the *Casa Juarez*, which will give you a good idea of the potential quality, and there are many more expensive craft shops scattered about, as well as a small handicrafts market just beyond the main section around 20 de Noviembre and Zaragoza.

You could also, with time to spare, go out to one of the villages from which the goods originate – each has a different speciality (TEOTITLAN DEL VALLE, for example, for serapes, or SANTA ROSA COYOTEPEC for black pottery) and each has a market one day of the week. The Tourist Office has more information on this, and although there's no guarantee that you'll be able to buy better or cheaper, a **village market** is an experience in itself.

ZAPOTEC AND MIXTEC

The Valley of Oaxaca, or rather the three valleys which abut each other here, saw the development of some of the earliest and most accomplished civilisations in Mexico. A small and relatively peripheral regional power, to be sure, but one which survived in a degree of peace far longer than any other, and whose craft skills – in pottery and metal-working – were unrivalled. There is evidence of settled population in the valleys dating back to several millenia BC, but the earliest concrete remains are at **Monte Alban**, founded around 700BC. Its impractical, mountain-top site raises several problems: pre-eminently, why should the **Zapotecs** have abandoned the fertile valley which supported them? In all probability, the bulk of the population never did, and Monte Alban reflects rather the growing sophistication of their society: it was a religious and political centre, physically dominating all three valleys from a neutral vantage point. Until about 700AD Monte Alban was clearly the most important centre in the region – trading over long distances with both Teotihuacan and the Maya, waging war where necessary to preserve its hegemony.

From 700, though, Monte Alban was suddenly deserted. This, probably, was a knock-on effect of the fall of Teotihuacan – in the period of uncertainty which followed, and especially with the loss of an important trading partner, the non-productive elite simply became too much of a burden. At the same time incursions of mountain-dwelling **Mixtecs** began to disturb the life of the valleys as through war and intermarriage Mixtec influence grew and eventually came to dominate. The style of **Mitla**, successor to Monte Alban, is Mixtec, although whether it was inhabited by Mixtecs or by Zapotecs under Mixtec control is impossible to say. They maintained control right through to the fifteenth century, developing above all the arts of the potter and the goldsmith to new heights. Moctezuma is said to have eaten only off plates made by Mixtec craftsmen – Aztec forces having conquered (although by no means pacified) the area in the years before the Conquest.

Monte Alban

> *Imagine a great isolated hill at the junction of three broad valleys; an island rising nearly a thousand feet from the green sea of fertility beneath it. An astonishing situation. But the Zapotecs were not embarrassed by the artistic responsibilities it imposed on them. They levelled the hill-top; laid out two huge rectangular courts; raised pyramidal altars or shrines at the centre, with other, much larger, pyramids at either end; built great flights of steps alternating with smooth slopes of masonry to wall in the courts; ran monumental staircases up the sides of the pyramids and friezes of sculpture round their base. Even today, when the courts are mere fields of rough grass, and the pyramids are buried under an obscuring layer of turf, even today this high place of the Zapotecs remains extraordinarily impressive . . . Monte Alban is the work of men who knew their architectural business consummately well.*
>
> Aldous Huxley, Beyond the Mexique Bay

In the fifty years since Aldous Huxley visited, little has changed at **Monte Alban**. The main structures have perhaps been cleared and restored a little more, but it's still the great flattened mountain top (750m by 250), the overall lay-out of the ceremonial centre and the views over the valley which impress more than any individual aspect. Late afternoon, with the sun sinking behind Oaxaca, is the best time to see it.

The **site** (open daily 9–6) is just 9km from town, up a steeply switch-backing road. Buses run three or four times a day from the *Hotel Meson del Angel* (Mina 518, at the corner of Mier y Teran) giving you a couple of hours at the site – if you want to return on a later one you have to pay twice; the first up leaves at about 9, the last down at 5.45. You could also take a taxi, which for four or five people is not much more expensive, and it's perfectly possible to walk back to Oaxaca, downhill almost all the way. Get a guard or one of the kids selling 'genuine antiquities' to show you the path. There's a car park, restaurant and souvenir shop by the entrance.

It seems almost madness to have tried to build a city here, so far from the obvious livelihood of the valleys and without even any natural water supply (water was carried up and stored in vast urns). Yet that may have been the point – to demonstrate the Zapotecs' mastery of nature. Certainly the rulers who lived here must have commanded a huge work-force, first to create the flat site, later to transport materials and keep it supplied. What you see today is just the very centre of the city – the religious and political heart later used by the Mixtecs as a magnificent burial site. On the terraced hillsides below lived a population which, at its peak, reached over 25,000 – craftsmen, priests, administrators and warriors, all, presumably, supported by tribute from the valleys. Small wonder that so top-heavy a society was easily destabilised.

You enter the **Great Plaza** at its north-eastern corner, with the ball-court to your left and the bulky north platform to your right. Sombre, grey and formal as it all appears now, in use, with its roofs and sanctuaries intact, the whole place would have been brilliantly polychromed. The **North Platform** may well have been the most important of all the temples at Monte Alban, although now the ceremonial buildings which lined its sides are largely ruined. What survives is a broad monumental stairway (with a carved obelisk at its foot) leading up to a platform enclosing a square patio with an altar at its heart. At the top of the stairs are the remains of a double row of six broad columns which would originally have supported a roof to form a colonnade dividing this plaza off from the main one.

The **eastern side** of the Great Plaza consists of an almost continuous line of low buildings, reached by a series of staircases from the plaza. The first of them looks over the **Ball-Court,** a simple I-shaped space with no apparent goals or target rings, and obviously an early example. Otherwise, the platforms on the east side are relatively late constructions – dating from around 500AD onwards. Facing them from the **centre of the plaza** is a long building which must have taken an important role in any rites celebrated here: its central section has broad staircases by which it can be approached from east or west – the lower end temples have smaller stairways giving to the north and south. A complex of tunnels runs under the site from here, emerging in several of the other temples, presumably to allow the priests to emerge suddenly and miraculously in any of them. Part of one of these has been cleared on the east side.

South of this central block, the **Observatory**, or Building J, stands alone in the centre of the plaza. Both its alignment – at 45° from everything else – and its arrow-shaped design mark it out from its surrounds. Although the orientation is almost certainly for astronomical reasons, there's no evidence that this was actually an observatory – more likely it was built (around 250AD, but on the site of an earlier structure) to celebrate a military victory. Relief carvings and hieroglyphs on the back of the building apparently represent a list of towns captured by the Zapotecs. In the vaulted passage which runs through the heart of the building can be seen several more panels carved in relief, mostly *danzante* figures (see below) – these, often upsidedown or on their sides and in no particular order, were obviously re-used from an earlier building.

The southern end of the mountain top is dominated by its tallest structure, the **South Platform**. Unrestored as it is, this vast square pyramid still offers the best overview of the site. Heading back from here up the western side of the plaza, there are just three important structures – the inexplicably named and almost identical **System M** and **System IV**, and the great Dancers Group between them. Each of the System buildings consists of a rectangular platform reached by a stairway from the plaza. Behind it is a small sunken square from which rises a much larger pyramid, originally topped by a roofed sanctuary.

The gallery and building of **Los Danzantes** (the dancers) are probably the most interesting at Monte Alban. A low wall extending from System M to the base of the Danzantes building forms the **gallery** – originally faced all along with blocks carved in relief of Olmec or negroid featured 'dancers'. Only a few of these *danzantes* remain in situ, and they are among the oldest (around 500BC) and most puzzling features of the site. Quite what the nude male figures represent is in dispute – many of them seem to have been cut open and may represent sacrificial victims or prisoners: others suggest that the entire wall was a sort of medical text-book, or that the figures really are dancers, or ball-players, or acrobats. Whatever the truth they show clear Olmec influence, and many of them have been pressed into use in later buildings throughout the site – the Danzantes **building** itself is one such, built over and obscuring much of the wall. It's a bulky, relatively plain rectangular platform with three temples on top – tunnels cut into the structure by archaeologists reveal earlier buildings within, and more of the dancing figures.

Several lesser buildings surround the main plaza, and although they're not particularly interesting, many contained tombs in which rich treasures were discovered (as indeed did some of the main structures themselves). **Tomb 104**, reached by a small path behind the North Platform, or from the car park area, is the best preserved of them. One of several in the immediate vicinity, this vaulted burial chamber still preserves excellent remains of murals. **Tomb 7**, where the important collection of Mixtec jewellery now in the Oaxaca Museum was found, lies a few hundred yards down the main road from the site entrance. Built underneath a small temple, it was originally constructed by the Zapotecs towards the end of Monte Alban's heyday, but was later emptied by the Mixtecs who buried one of their own chiefs here along with his magnificent burial trove.

Mitla

MITLA, some 45km from Oaxaca just off the Pan-American Highway as it heads towards Guatemala, involves a slightly longer excursion. It's easy enough to do, though, with buses leaving from the second class terminal every half hour or so throughout the day. On the way are several of the more easily accessible Indian villages: if you want to stop at one, check with the Tourist Office which one has a market on the day you're going – there will be more buses and much more of interest once you get there. One of the best is the Sunday Market at TLACOLULA, a village which also boasts a beautiful sixteenth-century church. En route, too, are a couple of smaller ancient sites.

At **SANTA MARIA DEL TULE** you pass the famous *Arbol del Tule* in a churchyard by the road. This mighty tree, said to be at least 2,000 years old (some say 3,000), is a good 40m round and slightly fatter than it is tall. A noticeboard gives all its vital statistics: suffice it to say that it must be one of the oldest living (and flourishing) objects on earth, and that it's a species of Cypress (*Taxodium Mucrunatum*) which has been virtually extinct since the colonial era. There's a drink stand and a couple of stalls for visitors by the tree, but if you're on the bus (left-hand side heading for Mitla) you get a pretty good view as you pass.

The most important of several small archaeological sites on the way to Mitla are YAGUL and DAINZU. **DAINZU**, an ancient Zapotec township, lies just a kilometer off the main road, almost exactly halfway to Mitla. Although quite extensive, only a small part has been excavated – notably a large pyramid structure built against a hill. The most important feature is the façade of this pyramid, covered in relief carvings like those of the *danzantes*, except that here the figures are undeniably ball-players. **YAGUL** lies off to the left of the road after about 34km – it's a much larger site, and although probably occupied by the Zapotecs its main features show strong Mixtec influence. Beautifully set, on a small hill studded with cactus, the ruins include a large ball-court and a couple of palaces demonstrating typically Mixtec mosaic decoration. At the top of the hill are the remains of a fortress.

The town of **MITLA** (*Place of the Dead*), which is where the bus drops you, is some 4km off the main road, and just 10 minutes' walk from the ruins. It's an unattractive, dusty little place where you'll be harassed by would-be guides and vendors of handicrafts (there's also a distinctly second-rate crafts market by the ruins): there is, however, a good **archaeological museum**, and next door to it the *Posada La Sorpresa* with a reasonable restaurant and a few good rooms (also, cheaper, the *Hotel Mitla*). **The site** (open daily 8–6) is pure Mixtec in style – largely secular palace complexes, decorated with elaborate stone mosaics – and dates probably from as late as the thirteenth century: the problem is that the area is a Zapotec one, inhabited by Zapotecs before the Mixtecs arrived, and inhabited by them again when the Spanish arrived. It may well be that Mitla was always Zapotec, but built by them under Mixtec direction or in a period when their own culture had been totally swamped.

You come first to the **Church Group**, so called because the Spanish built a church over, and from, much of it. Two of its three original courtyards do survive, and in the smaller of them the mosaic decoration bears traces of the original paint, indicating that the patterns were picked out in white from a dark red background. The **Group of the Columns**, however, is by far the best preserved and most impressive of the palace complexes at Mitla. The only other site that these long, low, fabulously decorated buildings recall in any way is Uxmal in the Yucatan, and there may well have been some contact between Mixtec and Maya. Even there, though, pyramids rise among the palaces and much of the decor has a clearly religious significance – here there is no such evidence of the spiritual importance of the buildings – their designs are purely geometric patterns (*petrified weaving*, as Aldous Huxley saw it). The first large courtyard has buildings on three sides – its central **Palace of the Columns** is a magnificent building, precision engineered and overpowering in effect. Up the broad stairway and through one of three entrances in its great façade, you find yourself in the **Hall of the Columns**, named after the six monolithic, tapered columns of volcanic stone which supported its roof. A low, dark and very narrow passageway (probably deliberately restricted so as to be easily defensible) leads from here into the small **inner patio**, with more intricately assembled geometric mosaics. Four dark rooms opening off it continue the patterned mosaic theme.

The second courtyard of the Columns Group, adjoining the south-west corner of the first, is similar in design though perhaps less impressive in execution. Known as the **Patio of the Tombs**, it does indeed contain two cross-shaped tombs – long since plundered by grave robbers. In one the roof is supported by the **Columna de la Muerte** (Column of Death); embrace this, and the gap left between your outstretched fingers tells you how long you have left to live. Three other groups of buildings, the **Adobes Group**, the **Arroyo Group** and the **South Group** (across a narrow *barranca*) complete the site – all are much less well preserved and far less interesting.

THE COAST: PUERTO ESCONDIDO AND PUERTO ANGEL

The Oaxacan coastal resorts of PUERTO ESCONDIDO and PUERTO ANGEL have a reputation – passed by word of mouth between travellers – for being unspoilt beach paradises. This is no longer entirely justified, and Escondido in particular attracts crowds of Californian surfers in winter and is developing rapidly, but an element of truth remains. Partly because they're so far from the States and not at all easy to get to, these are some of the emptiest and best Pacific beaches in Mexico. Puerto Angel sees fewer tourists, but Escondido has better swimming, surf and sand.

Both resorts are around 250km from Oaxaca, but hairy mountain roads which can take anything from 6 to 12 hours to traverse, and may even be impassable in the rainy season. Although there are regular **buses** to both (more frequently, and on a better road, to Puerto Angel) it's an uncomfortable and occasionally heart-stopping journey. Many people prefer to fly down in *Aerovias Oaxaqueñas* daily DC3 to Escondido – an experience in itself. There are also regular buses from Acapulco to Puerto Escondido.

Puerto Escondido

Once you've described the laid-back fishing village atmosphere, the huge swathe of magnificent beach, much of it pounded by heavy surf, and a rather scattered collection of houses, restaurants and hotels, there's not much left to say about **PUERTO ESCONDIDO**. Except that the pace of development is almost tangible – with the main street being paved and shops aimed strictly at the tourist springing up all along it.

Beaches are stretched out around the bay for miles in each direction. Those directly in front of town are perhaps a little overused, and shared, too, with local fishermen and the activities of the port; others are there for the taking. To the south-east they're exposed surfers' dreams where the currents can be strong and occasionally dangerous – to the north are a couple of sheltered coves. **Puerto Angelito** is the closest of these, just 20 minutes' walk down a path which heads off the main street by the *Cafe Colas*. Small boats also ply the coast round here and to many other local beaches.

Finding somewhere to stay should present no problem, with the majority of hotels lined up along the main drag and down towards the beach. Sleeping rough is not recommended – mosquitoes are likely to be the least of your troubles – but there are a couple of **trailer park/campsites** (one right on the beach in town, the other a few kilometers out on the coastal highway) where you can sling a hammock in relative security. The **hotels** *Nayar*, *Loren* and *Roca Mar* are all on the main street, getting more expensive as you get nearer the water – here too you'll see a sign advertising *Habitaciones Amuebladas* (furnished rooms) which can be very good value for a stay of more than a few days. The *Hotel Rincon del Pacifico* on the beach right in town is more expensive but very good; the *Hotel de las Palmas* slightly less good value. Recent development has seen the arrival of several more expensive places in the surrounds – if you wanted to pay more the *Paraiso Escondido*, on a hill overlooking the town (still on the main street) is the oldest established and the best – the *Viva* and *Rancho El Pescador* are both some way out and more expensive, while the *Hotel Bugambilia* is the first to be built in an area out towards Puerto Angelito which has been designated the luxury hotel zone. *Cabañas de Cortes*, on the highway as it leaves the town to the south, and *Bungalows Villa Marinero* both rent **beach-front cabins** – the latter with some pretensions to luxury.

As for **eating**, there's no problem at all, with superb seafood on offer everywhere. *La Posada* is the most popular of the places down by the beach, with good fish, cold beer, and a long-distance phone. There are many others like it, or you'll find cheaper food by heading inland to the old village (such as it is).

Puerto Angel

Just 70km further down the coast, **PUERTO ANGEL** still goes about its business as a small fishing port with little fuss. On a bay beautifully ringed by mountains and fringed by white sand, it attracts fewer visitors partly because the beaches are slightly less good, partly because the currents and undertow here really can be dangerous – don't venture too far out. Of the nearby beaches, **Zipolite** is the most popular – a long-standing hippy haven which to some extent it still is. None too clean to camp on, but the beach here is relatively sheltered and safe, and there are cabins to rent.

Downtown there are several small **hotels** or private rooms on offer, and other places where you can hire a hammock. The *Hotel Sonaya*, rather more expensive, is the only one which seems at all formally organised. A good long walk up the hill, and very much pricier, the *Hotel Angel del Mar* is positively luxurious, with panoramic vistas over the bay. Also expensive, the *Posada Cañon de Vata*, behind the town, is American run and has a good communal atmosphere if you like that sort of thing.

ON TO THE ISTHMUS

The **Isthmus of Tehuantepec,** where the Pacific and the Atlantic are just 210km apart and the land rises nowhere to more than 250m above sea level, is the narrowest point of Mexico. For years, until Panama got there first, there were plans to cut a canal through here: as it is the coast-to-coast railway (still a link in the line to Guatemala) was, in the late nineteenth century, an extremely busy trade route, the chief point of communication between the continent's east and west coasts. It's a hot and steamy region, long run-down and not in any way improved by the trappings of a recent oil boom, and one where the only good reason to stop is if there's a fiesta going on: they're among the most colourful in the country. Otherwise you can go straight through – from Oaxaca to TUXTLA GUTIERREZ and from there on to SAN CRISTOBAL – within the day. Only if you plan to head straight for the YUCATAN is there any particular cause to cross the Isthmus – it's considerably quicker to stick to the lowlands, though a lot duller than going via Chiapas.

TEHUANTEPEC has the best of the fiestas, and it's also the most pleasant of the towns to stop at; with a fine plaza at the centre and several cheap hotels around it (try the *Oasis*). A fortress on the river here was Porfirio Diaz's headquarters during the wars against the French. By tradition the Indians of this region have a matriarchal society, but though you'll still find women dominating trade in the market, this is a tradition that is dying faster than most others in macho Mexico. Nevertheless, at least some truth remains: the women are as notoriously tall and handsome as they are made out – fabulously dressed, too, for fiestas; it's still the mother who must give away a child at a wedding (and occasionally still the eldest daughter who inherits any land); and on feast days the women prove their dominance by climbing to the roof-tops and throwing fruit down on the men (the *Tirada de Frutas)*.

Due south of here on the coast, SALINA CRUZ was the Pacific terminus of the railway and the port through which everything was shipped. Now it again exports oil in large quantities and is frankly unattractive. As a further discouragement the place has a reputation for crime and brawling violence. La Ventosa, the nearby beach village, is as windy as its name implies and nowadays polluted too. JUCHITAN, just 26km from Tehuantepec, and the point where the road meets the railway to Guatemala, was an Indian town with traditions similar to those of Tehuantepec and every bit as attractive, with a good market and rather sleazy tropical port atmosphere. In recent years, however, there has been considerable political trouble and some violence after the town somehow managed to elect a reforming socialist government. The PRI didn't take kindly to their activities, and eventually the state governor found a pretext to remove local officials from power and replace them with party faithfuls. This may well have blown over – and if it hasn't events will no doubt make the front pages of local newspapers – but if not, Juchitan's fiestas are likely to become political demonstrations, and potentially violent.

The northern shore of the Isthmus is still less attractive, with a huge industrial zone stretching from MINATITLAN to COATZACOALCOS (formerly *Puerto Mexico,* the Atlantic terminus of the railway), which is itself dominated by a giant oil refinery. If you need to stay somewhere, the best place to do so is ACAYUCAN, the junction of the Gulf Coast and the Trans-Isthmus roads, where there are a number of reasonably priced hotels. Better still, press on to VILLAHERMOSA.

CHIAPAS AND TABASCO

From Juchitan the quick route **to Guatemala,** and the international railway, follows the Pacific coast down to TAPACHULA. The Pan-American Highway, however, is infinitely more interesting – striking as it does through the highlands of Chiapas and some of the most beautiful, least developed country in Mexico. By this route, too, the approach to GUATEMALA CITY is more direct once you've crossed the border. If sheer speed is your motive, though, the road to Tapachula can be covered in a long day from Oaxaca (about 10 hours by bus). There's little to detain you on the way, although ARRIAGA and TONALA are attractive enough, and each has a couple of small hotels; from Tonala, you could head off to the quite undeveloped (but rough) coastline around PAREDON and PUERTO ARISTA.

TAPACHULA itself boasts a lovely setting at the foot of the 13,000ft Volcan Tacana, a hot and very humid climate, plenty of local coffee and bananas, but little else. There are, however, Guatemalan and El Salvadorean **Consulates** where, if necessary, you can still get a visa (it would be a mistake to wait this long, though – you may have to hang around for days), and plenty of hotels. For somewhere to stay, look around the bus station and the Zocalo – the Hotels *Central, Colon, Internacional, Puebla* and *Tazacepec* all appear reasonable, though given a captive clientele they do tend to overcharge. Frequent second class buses run the 20km beyond Tapachula to the border at the **Talisman Bridge** *(Puente Talisman)*, which you cross on foot to pick up *Transportes Galgos* services the other side (four or five daily to Guatemala City). The Guatemalan **train** from the border leaves at 6am, but it doesn't come recommended. En route to the bridge the road passes through the archaeological site and ruins of IZAPA.

On the coast just half an hour from Tapachula, **PUERTO MADERO** is your last chance to see the Mexican Pacific. Which is virtually its sole attraction. Built up and being developed as a port, the beach is dirty and the sea normally rough. There are, however, some good fish restaurants along the front, and a number of cheap, dingy hotels.

SAN CRISTOBAL AND THE CHIAPAS HIGHLANDS

There is nowhere in Mexico so rich in scenery or in Indian life as inland Chiapas. The forested uplands and jungly valleys are studded with rivers and lakes, waterfalls and unexpected gorges, and flush with the rich flora and fauna of the tropics – wild orchids, brilliantly coloured birds and monkeys. Even now the network of roads, though growing, is skeletal, and for much of its history the isolation of the state allowed its Indian population to carry on their lives little affected. In the villages you'll see the trappings of Catholicism and of economic progress, but in most cases external form is all they are: daily life is still run in accordance with ancient customs and beliefs.

TUXTLA GUTIERREZ, the capital of the state, does its best to deny this – a fast growing, modern and not overly attractive city which offers little to stop for. The drive up, though, has already been spectacular and the landscapes around the city are no less so. As the transport hub of the state, and the place where most buses get to in the end, you almost inevitably have to pass through, but in normal circumstances the best bet is to carry straight on to San Cristobal. If you are stranded here, or have time to kill, head out to the **Parque Madero:** here there's not only a good regional museum (*Museo del Estado de Chiapas;* closed Mondays) but some botanical gardens and a zoo with plants and animals native to the Chiapas jungle which you are otherwise unlikely to see. The road past the park continues to the **Sumidero Canyon,** or rather to a *Mirador* looking into this spectacular cleft in the earth, as much as a mile deep in places. According to legend, hundreds of Indian warriors flung themselves in rather than submit to the Spanish. To get out here, either take a taxi, or check with the local Tourist Office (on Av. Central near the park) about a VW *colectivo* service which may or may not be running.

You could also head out to **CHIAPA DE CORZO,** an elegantly colonial village overlooking the Rio Grijalva, just 20 minutes away on the road to San Cristobal (frequent buses from the main square in Tuxtla). Here there's a small museum of regional handicrafts, especially the painted or lacquered gourds which are the local speciality, and, in the Zocalo, an amazingly elaborate sixteenth-century fountain. Local boatmen offer impressive rides down the river and into the Sumidero Canyon – of which you also catch glimpses from the road on the way here. If you have to stay in Tuxtla Gutierrez there are a couple of **hotels** opposite the first class bus terminal – *Santo Domingo* and *Maria Teresa* – which aren't bad, and several rather poor places around the second class station. Others are around the plaza and on Av. Central, but none seem to be particularly good value.

Just beyond Chiapa de Corzo, the **road to Villahermosa** – a spectacular wind down to the Gulf plain – cuts off to the north. Ahead on the Pan-American Highway, however, lies **SAN CRISTOBAL DE LAS CASAS.** Just 80km from Tuxtla Gutierrez, San Cristobal is almost 6,000 feet higher – a cool place with an unrivalled provincial colonial charm. Its low, white-washed red-tiled houses seem huddled together on the plain as if to keep out imaginary enemies. And there is a frontier feel to the town, too, a real sense that it may be intruding, as a Spanish-speaking enclave, into country in which the Indians still predominate. The people who get here tend to be travellers, with a much higher proportion of Europeans than is usual (though perhaps less so since the Central American trail has become less inviting) and with relatively simple requirements and demands – so although it's an increasingly popular destination, it's not touristy in any obviously obtrusive way. The atmospheric tranquillity, rich tradition of local crafts, and the Indian life are what draw people here – the last a fact not always appreciated by the Indians themselves, who not surprisingly resent being treated as tourist attractions or objects of amateur anthropology. Nevertheless, the life of the town depends on the life of the Indians from surrounding villages, who fill its streets and dominate its trade.

It took the Spanish four years to sufficiently pacify the area to establish a town here, in 1528. Officially named San Cristobal, it was more widely known as *Villaviciosa* (evil city) for the oppressive exploitation of its colonists. In 1544 Bartolome de Las Casas was appointed bishop, and promptly took an energetic stance in defence of the native population –

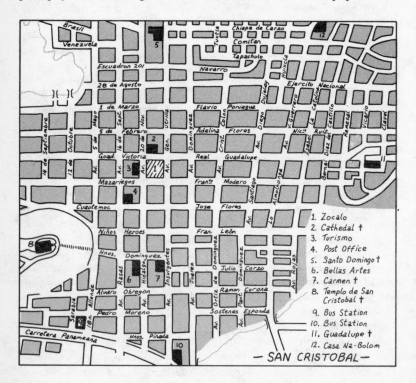

1. Zocalo
2. Cathedal †
3. Turismo
4. Post Office
5. Santo Domingo †
6. Bellas Artes
7. Carmen †
8. Templo de San Cristobal †
9. Bus Station
10. Bus Station
11. Guadalupe †
12. Casa Na-Bolom

— SAN CRISTOBAL —

playing a similar role to that of Bishop Vasco de Quiroga in Patzcuaro (see p. 109). His name – added to that of the town – is still held in something close to reverence by the Indians. Throughout the colonial era San Cristobal was the capital of Chiapas, then administered as part of Guatemala, and it lost this rank in 1890 only as a result of its reluctance to accept the union with Mexico.

Whether you **arrive** by first or second class bus you'll be just off the Highway at the southern edge of town: from the first class terminal walk straight up to the Zocalo along Insurgentes, about seven blocks; from the other, head a couple of blocks east on Pedro Moreno, then left along Hidalgo or Insurgentes to the Zocalo. The **Tourist Office** (open Mon.-Sat. 9-2 and 4-7) is in the Palacio Municipal on the Zocalo. You'll already have passed a couple of **hotels** by the time you get there – the *Casa de Huespedes Pola,* the *Hotel San Francisco* and more expensive *Posada San Cristobal* are all on Insurgentes. Better, to my mind, are those on Calle Real de Guadalupe – right from the opposite corner of the Zocao. The *Hotel San Martin,* the *Posada Tepeyac* and best of all the *Posada Margarita* between them, are all good and cheap. More expensive places include the *Ciudad Real* and the *Santa Clara,* both on the Zocalo, or the *Hotel Español,* two blocks north at 1 de Marzo, where every room has its own fireplace. The *Posada Abuelita,* at the corner of Tapachula and Tuxtla Gutierrez not far from the church of Santo Domingo, is some way out, but its dormitory-style accommodation is just about the cheapest in town. Wherever you stay, make sure that you have an adequate supply of blankets – the nights can get really cold.

Calle Real de Guadalupe not only has some of the best cheap hotels, it also offers several good plain **restaurants,** and the bulk of the shops selling Indian crafts. The *Casa Blanca* is the pick of the places to eat here, though for more elaborate Mexican food you should head a couple of blocks down Juarez, to its corner with Jose Flores, and *La Normita.* With a sizeable permanent population of young American outcasts, a popular language school, and a constant stream of travellers it's hardly surprising that San Cristobal should have places which cater to them – here though, there seem to be hundreds. The *Olla Podrida* is the longest established: everyone's hang out and serving a rather bizarre (but good) mix of healthy food and yoghurts with wholemeal burgers, salads, pies and even Mexican food. On Diego Mazariegos at the corner of 5 de Mayo, two blocks east of the Zocalo, it's a popular meeting place with noticeboards offering rides, goods for sale, travelling companions etc. Other similarly oriented restaurants include *La Galeria* (on Navarro between General Utrilla and Belisario Dominguez, near Santo Domingo) and *El Trigal* (at the corner of 1 de Marzo and 20 de Noviembre, between the Zocalo and Sto. Domingo).

There aren't a great many specific things to do in San Cristobal – the true pleasures lie simply in wandering the streets and in getting out to some of the nearby villages – but a couple of sights are worth mentioning. Chief of these is the **Casa Na Bolom,** a Museum and Library of local anthropology, devoted especially to the isolated Lacandon Indians (see p. 307). It was the home of Danish explorer and anthropologist Franz Blom, and is still run by his widow as a centre for the study of the region – a few rooms are let, but they are expensive and exclusive, mostly occupied by working archaeologists or ethnologists. Visits every afternoon except Monday, from 4–6.

Two churches dominate views of the town from their hilltop sites, Guadalupe to the east and San Cristobal to the west. Neither offers a great deal architecturally, but the climbs are worthwhile for the views – **San Cristobal,** especially, is at the top of a dauntingly long and steep flight of steps. **Santo Domingo,** to the north of the plaza, is the most intrinsically interesting of the churches, with an elaborate plateresque façade and richly gilded interior. This is close to the market, and consequently often full of traders and Indians, but the **Templo de Carmen,** south of the Zocalo by the Moorish arch across the road, seems more popular with locals. The Instituto de **Bellas Artes,** very near here, often has interesting displays of local art. Finally, the **Zocalo** itself is worth seeing – not so much for the sixteenth-century Cathedral, externally dull, as for some of the Conquistadors' mansions, and in particular the *Casa de Mazariegos,* built by the town's founder and now the Hotel Santa Clara.

The **market** is beyond Santo Domingo along General Utrilla, and trades every morning except Sunday, when most of the villages have markets of their own. It's a fascinating place, if only because here you can observe Indian life and custom without causing undue offence – your presence is entirely natural. What's on sale is mostly local produce and household goods, although there are also good tyre-soled leather *huaraches* and rough but warm sweaters which you might well feel the need of. For craft objects, though, you're really better off in the shops on Calle Real de Guadalupe.

It's possible to see Indian life at closer quarters by visiting some of the nearby villages, but such **excursions** should be treated with extreme sensitivity. You are an intruder, and will be made to feel so – be very careful about taking photographs, and certainly never do so inside churches (theoretically you need a permit from the tourist authorities in Tuxtla Gutierrez for any photography in the villages). I don't know if it's true, but there's an oft-repeated traveller's tale of two gringos being lynched for photographing the interior of the church at San Juan Chamula. The ride out, though, and the countryside, make some kind of escape worthwhile, even if when you reach a village you find doors shut in your face and absolutely nothing to do (or, obversely, are mobbed by begging kids). On market and fiesta days you'll be less out of place.

The Indians in the immediate vicinity are all **Tzotzil** speaking, but each village has developed its own trademarks in terms of costumes, craft specialities and linguistic quirks: as a result they are often sub-divided by village and referred to as *Chamulas, Zincantecos, Huistecos* (from Huistan) etc. **SAN JUAN CHAMULA** is the closest to San Cristobal, the most frequently visited and consequently the least threatening and disruptive. If you take a bus or taxi up, the 6 miles back is an easy and delightful walk. Even though it's the most important of the Chamula villages, San Juan is little more than a collection of civic and religious buildings with a few huts – most of its 'population' actually live isolated in the country around. **ZINCANTAN** is also reasonably close, and there are a number of others which can be reached by early morning buses from the market area, although you may have some difficulty getting back. Seek further information from the Tourist Office, who can also advise on a much more pleasant way to get about the valley – on horseback. Several places rent out **horses** and guides (*El Recoveco* bookshop on the plaza is good) for trips to the villages or to the local caves.

ON FROM SAN CRISTOBAL: COMITAN, MONTEBELLO AND THE BORDER

Leaving San Cristobal, if you're heading towards the Yucatan the best advice is to go via VILLAHERMOSA. There is a direct **road to PALENQUE** via OCOSINGO (with a couple of grimy hotels if you get stuck) but it's in appalling condition, frequently impassable during the rainy season and takes at least a full day to cover. If you do decide to go this way, though, don't miss the series of beautiful waterfalls at **AGUA AZUL,** on the paved stretch about 60 km from Palenque. There are a couple of restaurants here, and good opportunities to camp.

The Pan-American Highway continues to the border, and even if you don't plan to cross into Guatemala it also leads to some of Chiapa's most scintillating scenery. You pass on the way AMATENANGO DEL VALLE, a pottery-producing Indian village, but **COMITAN** is the jumping-off point for the Lagunas de Montebello National Park. It's a pretty enough town in its own right, spectacularly poised on a rocky hillside and surrounded by country in which wild orchids bloom freely, and it is too the final place of any note before the border (inaptly named Ciudad Cuauhtemoc is no more than a collection of mean shacks). There's a **Guatemalan Consulate** here (last chance for visas) and a collection of reasonable hotels: try the *Rio Escondido* or *Montebello,* or slightly more expensive the *Delfin, Internacional* or the *Motel Morales* – all of them very near the main square and the bus stations. The Casa de La Cultura, on the main square, has a small museum with archaeological finds from the area – once a major Mayan centre of population (Bonampak and

Yaxchilan, even Palenque, are not far away as the parrot flies across the jungle).

The **LAGUNAS DE MONTEBELLO,** and the entrance to the **National Park,** are a further 50 kms or so – almost two hours by a regular service of buses and vans from Comitan. If you hope to see anything much in a single day, leave early – the last return is at 5.30pm, and there's frequent afternoon rain. They say there are as many as a hundred lakes in the forest here, and sixteen large ones, but only two or three are in easy reach if you come by bus: even these, though, more than reward the effort involved in reaching them – shimmering through an unbelievable variety of colours lent them by mineral deposits and the changing weather and landscape conditions. The best views are reached by following the side road (3km) to the *Lagunas de Colores*. At the hamlet where the bus drops you, *Maria's* (or the *Restaurant Orquedia*) has a few rooms, and there's also a campsite on the road to the *Lagunas de Colores*. Hilary Bradt's *Backpacking in Mexico and Central America* outlines an amazing eight-day **hike** through the jungle from here to Bonampak.

Continuing **to Guatemala,** there are three or four buses a day from San Cristobal to **CIUDAD CUAUHTEMOC** via Comitan, and regular vans on from there to the border – try to reach it during weekday working hours, which will simplify the passage considerably. On the other side, pick up *Rutas Limas* services; you can go direct to Guatemala City, but there are places to stay in HUEHUETENANGO or, much more attractive, in QUETZALTENANGO (known as Xela).

One **WORD OF WARNING** – with Guatemalan refugees pouring in, and occasional trouble along the border, I have heard of the Montebello Park being closed: check with the tourist authorities in San Cristobal or Tuxtla Gutierrez.

TOWARDS THE YUCATAN – VILLAHERMOSA

VILLAHERMOSA, capital of the state of Tabasco, is a major and virtually unavoidable road junction: a large and prosperous city, an expensive one too, and extremely hard to define. I was tempted to hate the place – which is certainly confusing, unpleasantly hot, hard to get around and not initially welcoming – but couldn't quite bring myself to do so. For among the modern urban blight one keeps coming on attractive plazas or quiet ancient streets, and sudden unexpected vistas of the broad sweep of the Rio Grijalva. And, above all, there is the Park of La Venta to brighten any enforced stopover.

Things are at their oil-booming worst where you arrive, as the new highway thunders through the concrete outskirts and past the bus stations: the centre is a vast improvement. The two **bus stations** are pretty close to each other – second class a ramshackle affair actually on the highway, first (known as *El ADO*) a spectacularly ugly but efficient modern building just off it on Javier Mina. Your best plan is probably to buy an onward ticket on arrival, giving you a few hours to see the city and then escape. To Palenque, second class buses are much more frequent. To get from first to second, turn left on Mina, walk a couple of blocks down to the highway, and cross it on the overpass – the terminal is to your right. There's no *Consigna* or *Guarderia* here, but a small tip should persuade the staff at one of the despatching offices to look after your bags. The best way to get about would be by taxi, but taxis are almost impossible to get outside the bus stations – there's also a bus from outside the second class terminal which will take you, after a long excursion round various concrete *urbanizaciones*, to the Parque La Venta (which is also on the main highway, round to the west of town). It's a good half-hour walk from either terminus to the centre.

Should you have to stay, be prepared to pay well over the odds for **a room** and perhaps to look long and hard to find one. Av. Madero, the long street which leads from the main plaza down (eventually) to the highway more or less opposite the second class terminal, has the greatest concentration. Among the places to look out for here are the *Hotel La Paz*, *Los Arcos*, *Palma de Mallorca*, and *Manzur*. Perhaps more pleasant are the pedestrianised streets behind the plaza, where you'll find hotels especially around the junction of Juarez and Lerdo: the *Tabasco* and *San Miguel* aren't too bad. The **Tourist Office**, should you need help, is on the riverside Malecon at the corner of Zaragoza, right by the plaza. At least **eating** should present no problems – there are a number of good places where you can sit outdoors around the plaza, and several restaurants, too, opposite the ADO bus station. One of these – just down to the left – is *norteño*-style, with particularly good steaks and wonderful bowls of soupy beans.

The **plaza** itself, with river views and vestiges at least of the colonial city, is a pleasant enough place to while away some time, but to spend it to real purpose you should head out to the **Parque La Venta**. To this open-air museum most of the important finds from the Olmec site of *La Venta* have been transferred. Although hardly the reproduction of that site which it claims to be, it does give you a chance to see a superb collection of artefacts of the earliest Mexican civilisation in a beautiful jungle park setting. The most important and famous are of course the gigantic basalt heads (three of them here) which present such a bizarre puzzle with their flattened, negroid features. There are a whole series of other Olmec stone sculptures too and also in the park a zoo, and boating on the Laguna de Ilusiones. The park is open daily except Mondays from 8.30–5. Also worth seeing is the massive modern **CICOM museum** complex (*Centro Internacional de las Culturas Olmeca y Maya*; open

10–1 and 5.30–8 except Mondays) on the riverside south of the centre. It displays Mayan and Olmec antiquities – especially some lovely jewellery – in an extremely well laid-out setting.

The journey from Villahermosa **to CAMPECHE by the coast road** is an extraordinarily beautiful one, involving a series of ferry rides across broad river mouths and over the great lagoon at whose centre CIUDAD DEL CARMEN sits on an island. There are a number of inviting looking beaches along the way, and you pass too through FRONTERA, where Graham Greene landed on his voyage of discovery in 1938:

> *Shark fins glided like periscopes at the mouth of the Grijalva River*
> *. . . three or four aerials stuck up into the blazing sky from among*
> *the banana groves and the palm-leaf huts: it was like Africa seeing*
> *itself in a mirror across the Atlantic. Little islands of lily plants*
> *came floating down from the interior, and the carcases of old stranded*
> *streamers held up the banks. And then round a bend in the river*
> *Frontera . . . the Presidencia and a big warehouse and a white*
> *blanched street running off between wooden shacks.*

But undeniably attractive as this route is, almost no tourists travel it, for the simple reason that PALENQUE lies off the inland road, and if you were to see just one ancient site in Mexico, Palenque is the one you should see.

PALENQUE

PALENQUE is the first, and for me at least, the best of the Mayan sites in Mexico. It's not large – you can see everything in a couple of hours – but it is extraordinarily beautiful. Some people choose to visit as a day trip from Villahermosa, but while this is perfectly possible it seems a strange way of going about things: **Palenque village** may be totally uninteresting, but it does offer reasonable food and accommodation, is less oppressively hot than the coast, and is a great meeting place for backpacking travellers. Apart from the ruins, too, there are some fine swimming holes and waterfalls in the hills roundabout.

Arriving by bus you'll be in the village: first class is on Av. Juarez right behind the Zocalo, second on the dusty road where the highway comes into town, between the centre and the road to the ruins. Av. Juarez runs downhill from the Zocalo to emerge here, and this section is really the only part of town you need to know – almost everything of importance is either on the plaza or on this street. The **train**, too, is for once a really promising alternative: Palenque lies on the main Mexico-Merida line. From the capital the train arrives at 10pm, but it's especially good as a means of getting from here to Merida – leave at 10 and arrive there at 9 the following morning, having spent the night in a wonderfully antiquated sleeper for little more than the first class bus fare (similarly, from Merida, you reach Palenque at 8am, in time for a quick breakfast and an early start at the ruins). From the station take a bus (if you're lucky) or taxi into town.

Your search for **somewhere to stay** starts on the Zocalo, where you'll find the long-established *Hotel Palenque* and the *Lacroix*: just below the plaza on Juarez are several more hotels, of which the *Regional* and the more expensive, modern *Misol-Ha* are worth a try. On the road which leads down from the corner of the plaza by the *Restaurant Maya* (towards the market) is the *Hotel Leon*, one of the cheapest in the centre. Still cheaper, if a little noisy and grimy, are the *Hotel Avenida* and the *Posada Alicia*, both more or less opposite the second class bus stop. A series of more expensive motels line the highway out of town and the road to the ruins – *La Cañada*, down a dirt track from the junction of the two, is probably the best of them. Also on the road to the ruins is *Camping Mayabel*, a long-established back-packers meet with reasonable facilities and good food. You could also **camp** at the *Motel/Trailer Park Nututum*, with a swimming pool and lovely riverside setting: this, though is some 3km down the road to Ocosingo (and San Cristobal) and hence only really practical with your own transport or if you're prepared to take a lot of taxis. **Eating**: the two restaurants on the Zocalo – *Maya* and *Nicte-Ha* – are as good as any.

To get to the ruins, either take the local bus which runs every half-hour or so down Juarez, past the second class buses and out to the site, or share a taxi. Open every day from 8–5, you should arrive early if you want to avoid the worst of the heat and the crowds. There's a small cafe by the entrance, where for a fee you can leave any bags while you explore.

Palenque's style is unique – it bears a closer resemblance, superficially, to the Mayan sites of highland Guatemala than to those of the Yucatan, but its towered palace and pyramid tomb are like nothing else, and the setting, too, is a remarkable one. Surrounded by hills covered in impenetrable jungle growth, Palenque is at the same time right at the edge of the great Yucatan plain – climb to the top of any of the structures and you look out, across the dark green of the hills, to an endless stretch of low, pale-green flatland. The city flourished during the classic period from around 300–900AD, but its peak apparently came during a relatively short period of the seventh century under two rulers – *Pacal* and *Chan-Bahlum*. Almost everything you see (and that's only a tiny, central part of the original city) dates from this era.

As you enter **the site**, the Great Palace, with its extraordinary watch-tower, stands ahead of you. To the right, and first, comes the **Pyramid of the Inscriptions**, an eight-stepped pyramid, 75 feet high, built up against a thickly overgrown hillside. Reached either by the broad stairway up the front, or by paths up the hill, the temple on top contains a series of stone panels carved with hieroglyphic inscriptions relating to Palenque's history. Most remarkable, though, is the **tomb** which lies at the heart of this pyramid. Discovered in 1952, this is the only such pyramid burial found in the Americas, and it's certainly an impressive one: although the smaller objects – the skeleton and the jade death mask – have been moved to Mexico City where the tomb is reproduced in the Anthropology Museum, the crypt itself is still here, with the massive, intricately carved stone sarcophagus. The burial chamber, and the narrow, vaulted stairway leading down there (only open for a couple of hours daily – check at the entrance) are dank and eerie, but well worth the slippery descent. The deified king buried here was probably **Pacal**, and in order that he should not be cut off from the world of the living a hollow tube, in the form of a snake, runs up the side of the staircase from the tomb to the temple.

The **Great Palace** is in fact a complex of buildings constructed at different times to form a rambling administrative or residential block. Its square **tower** is quite unique, and no-one knows exactly what its purpose was – perhaps a look-out post or an astronomical observatory. Bizarrely, the narrow staircase which winds up inside it starts only at the second level – you reach it now along the top of a wall constructed later. Throughout you'll find delicately executed relief carvings – most remarkable of which are the giant human figures on stone panels in the grassy courtyard.

From here, the lesser buildings of the **North Group**, and the **Ball-Court**, are slightly downhill across a cleared grassy area. Beyond them is the **Museum**, small and not particularly well laid out, but containing a good number of carved panels removed from various parts of the site. On higher ground in the other direction, across the narrow stream which runs through the site and half obscured by the dense vegetation around them, lie the Temples of the **Sun**, of the **Cross**, and of the **Foliated Cross**. All are tall, narrow mounds surmounted by a temple with an elaborate stone roof comb. Each, too, contains carved panels representing sacred rites – the cross found here is as important an image in Mayan iconography as it is in Christian, representing the meeting of the heavens and of the underworld with the land of the living. The **Temple of the Jaguar** is reached by a small path which follows the brook upstream – a delightful shaded walk. Downstream, there's a small pool just beyond the museum, although swimming is theoretically forbidden.

Around Palenque and on

Of many **waterfalls** and streams in the hills around Palenque, the most accessible are MISOL-HA and AGUA AZUL, both off the road to Ocosingo and San Cristobal (see p. 301). There are a couple of buses along this route every day, or you could share a taxi for the 20km ride to Misol-Ha. Closer, but less impressive, are swimming spots at Nututum, and the small waterfall of Motiepa (reached by a signed path off the road about 1km from the ruins).

Palenque is also the most common starting point for trips by light plane to the sites of **BONAMPAK** and **YAXHILAN**. Bonampak, famous for its murals, is frankly disappointing in the flesh – you'll get a better impression from the reproductions in Mexico City's National Museum of Anthropology. Yaxchilan, crumbling away beside the broad Rio Usumacinta, is beautiful but very desolate and thickly overgrown. Both are in territory inhabited by **Lacandon Indians** – the most remote and elusive of all Mexican tribes, impressively wild-looking with their uncut hair and simple, hanging white robes. Trips can take in one of their villages – most commonly LACANJA – but representatives are likely to meet any planes anyway, looking for news or supplies. Further information from the Tourist Office in Palenque, or at the airstrip.

Leaving by bus, you should book well in advance if you hope to get out on first class, and especially if you want to get one of the early morning departures for MERIDA or VILLAHERMOSA. If necessary, be prepared to take a second class service to somewhere out on the main road, and hope to pick up onward transport from there. Campeche is about 5 hours away, Merida at least 8.

FIESTAS

This chapter covers one of the richest areas of all for festivities. Local Tourist Offices should have more information on what's happening in your vicinity.

January
1st NEW YEARS DAY is celebrated everywhere – particularly good in **Oaxaca** (Oax.), and **Mitla** (Oax.). **San Andres Chamula** (Chiapas) and **San Juan Chamula** (Chis.), both near San Cristobal, have civil ceremonies to install a new government for the year.
14th Fiesta in **Niltepec** (Oax.), on the Pacific coast road.
20th DIA DE SAN SEBASTIAN sees a lot of activity. In **Chiapa de Corzo** (Chis.) a large fiesta with traditional dances lasts several days, with a re-enactment on the 21st of a naval battle on the Rio Grijalva. Big, too, in **Tehuantepec** (Oax.), in **Jalapa de Diaz** (Oax.), near Tuxtepec, in **Pinotepa de Don Luis** (Oax.), near the coast and Pinotepa Nacional, and in **Zincantan** (Chis.), near San Cristobal.

February
2nd DIA DE LA CANDELARIA.

Colourful Indian celebrations in **Santa Maria del Tule** (Oax.) and in **San Mateo del Mar** (Oax.), near Salina Cruz.
11th Religious fiesta in **Comitan** (Chis.).
22nd–25th Feria in **Matias Romero** (Oax.), between Juchitan and Coatzoacoalcos.
27th In **Villahermosa** (Tab.), a fiesta commemorates the anniversary of a battle against the French.
CARNIVAL (the week before Lent – variable Feb.-Mar.) is at its most frenzied in the big cities – especially **Villahermosa** (Tab.) and **Oaxaca** (Oax.) – but is also celebrated in hundreds of villages throughout the area.

March
21st **Gueletao** (Oax.), near Oaxaca, celebrates the birthday of Benito Juarez, born in the village.
25th Fiesta in **Acatlan** (Pue.) with many traditional dances.
HOLY WEEK is widely observed – particularly big ceremonies in **Pinotepa Nacional** (Oax.) and nearby **Pinotepa Don Luis** (Oax.), as well as in **Jamiltepec** (Oax.) on the road from here to

Puerto Escondido. **Ciudad Hidalgo** (Chis.), at the border near Tapachula, has a major week-long market.

April
1st–7th A feria in **San Cristobal de las Casas** (Chis.) celebrates the town's foundation.

May
3rd DIA DE LA SANTA CRUZ celebrated in **San Juan Chamula** (Chis.) and in **Teapa** (Tab.) between Villahermosa and San Cristobal. In **Salina Cruz** (Oax.), the start of a week-long feria.
8th DIA DE SAN MIGUEL. In **Soyaltepec** (Oax.), between Oaxaca and Huajuapan de Leon, festivities include horse and dog races, as well as boating events on a nearby lake; processions and traditional dances in **Mitontic** (Chis.), near San Cristobal.
15th DIA DE SAN ISIDRO sees peasant celebrations everywhere – famous and picturesque fiestas in **Juchitan** (Oax.) and in **Huistan** (Chis.), near San Cristobal.
19th Feria in **Huajuapan de Leon** (Oax.).
CORPUS CHRISTI (variable – the Thursday after Trinity) sees a particularly good feria in **Izucar de Matamoros** (Pue.).

June
13th DIA DE SAN ANTONIO celebrated in **Simojovel** (Chis.), near San Cristobal, and **Cardenas** (Tab.), west of Villahermosa.
14th–16th Fiestas for the patron saint of **Ciudad del Carmen** (Campeche).
24th DIA DE SAN JUAN is the culmination of several days' celebration in **San Juan Chamula** (Chis.) and in the midst of festivities (22nd–26th) in **Tehuantepec** (Oax.).
28th DIA DE SAN PEDRO. Fiestas in **Huistan** (Chis.), in **San Pedro Amuzgos** (Oax.) on the mountain road inland from Pinotepa Nacional, and especially in **Tepantepec** (Oax.) on the coast at the border of Chiapas, and **Tehuantepec** (Oax.).

July
On the first Wednesday of July, **Teotitlan del Valle** (Oax.), near Oaxaca, holds a fiesta with traditional dances and religious processions.

7th Beautiful religious ceremony in **Comitan** (Chis.), with candle-lit processions to and around the church.
20th Heavily Indian festivities in **Las Margaritas** (Chis.), near Comitan.
23rd Feria in **Huajuapan de Leon** (Oax.).
25th DIA DE SANTIAGO provokes widespread celebration – especially in **San Cristobal de las Casas** (Chis.), where they begin a good week earlier, and in nearby villages such as **Tenejapa** and **Amatenango del Valle**. Also good in **Izucar de Matamoros** (Pue.), in **Niltepec** (Oax.) and in **Juxtlahuaca** (Oax.).

In **Oaxaca** itself, the last two Mondays of July see the famous festival of **GUELAGUETZA** (or the *Lunes del Cerro*), a mixture of traditional dancing and Catholic rites on the *Cerro del Fortin*. Highly popular, tickets for the good seats are sold at the Tourist Office.

August
6th Images from the churches of neighbouring villages are brought in procession to **Mitontic** (Chis.), for religious ceremonies there.
10th FIESTA DE SAN LORENZO in **Zincantan** (Chis.), with much music and dancing.
13th–16th Spectacular festivities in **Juchitan** (Oax.) and lesser fiestas in **Nochixtlan** (Oax.), between Oaxaca and Huajuapan de Leon, and on the 15th in **Tehuantepec** (Oax.).
22nd–29th Feria in **Tapachula** (Chis.).
24th Fiestas in **Venustiano Carranza** (Chis.), south of San Cristobal, and **San Bartolo Coyotepec** (Oax.), near Oaxaca.
30th DIA DE SANTA ROSA celebrated in **San Juan Chamula** (Chis.).
31st Blessing of the animals in **Oaxaca** – locals bring their beasts to the church of La Merced to be blessed.

September
3rd–5th **Juchitan** (Oax.) once again hosts a series of picturesque celebrations.
8th Religious ceremonies in **Teotitlan del Valle** (Oax.), in **Putla** (Oax.), on the road inland from Pinotepa Nacional, and in **Tehuantepec** (Oax.).
25th FIESTA DE SAN JERONIMO in **Ixtepec** (Oax.) lasts until October 2nd.
29th DIA DE SAN MIGUEL is

celebrated in **Huistan** (Chis.) and **Soyaltepec** (Oax.).

October

1st Several *barrios* of **Tehuantepec** (Oax.) have their own small fiestas.
On the first Sunday in October, the DIA DE LA VIRGEN DEL ROSARIO is celebrated in **San Juan Chamula** (Chis.) and **San Pedro Amuzgos** (Oax.). On the second Sunday there's a large feria in **Tlacolula** (Oax.), near Oaxaca, and on the second Monday the Feria del Arbol based around the famous tree in **Santa Maria del Tule** (Oax.).
18th Indian fiesta in **Ojitlan** (Oax.), near Tuxtepec, with a large, formal candle-lit procession.
24th In **Acatlan** (Pue.), a fiesta with processions and traditional dances.

November

2nd DAY OF THE DEAD is respected everywhere, with particularly strong tradition in **Salina Cruz** (Oax.), **Chiapa de Corzo** (Chis.), **Comitan** (Chis.), and in **San Gabriel Chilac** (Pue.), near Tehuacan.
25th Patron Saint's day in **Mechoacan** (Oax.), on the coast near Pinotepa Nacional.
29th DIA DE SAN ANDRES celebrated in **San Andres Chamula** (Chis.) and in **San Juan Colorado** (Oax.), on the coast road near Pinotepa Nacional.

December

8th DIA DE LA INMACULADA CONCEPCION is widely observed – especially with traditional Indian dances in **Juquilla** (Oax.), not far from Puerto Escondido, and **Zacatepec** (Oax.), on the road inland from Pinotepa Nacional.
12th DIA DE LA VIRGEN DE GUAD-ALUPE is an important one throughout Mexico. There's a particularly good fiesta in **San Cristobal de las Casas** (Chis.), and the following day another in nearby **Amatenango del Valle** (Chis.).
17th–22nd **Pijijiapan** (Chis.), on the road to Tapachula, organises a feria and cheese expo.
16th–25th The pre-Christmas period is a particularly exciting one in **Oaxaca**, with posadas and nativity plays nightly. The 18th is the FIESTA DE LA VIRGEN DE LA SOLEDAD, patroness of the state, with fireworks, processions and music. The 23rd is the FIESTA DE LOS RABANOS (Radishes) when there's an exhibition of statues and scenes sculpted from radishes – don't ask me why. On Christmas Eve there's more music, fireworks and processions before midnight mass. Throughout it all, **buñuelos** are served from street stalls – crisp pancakes which you eat before smashing the plate on which they are served.

TRAVEL DETAILS

Trains

From **Oaxaca** to **Mexico City**. Leaves daily 18.20, arriving Tehuacan 1.15, Puebla (3.30) and Mexico City (8.55).

From **Tapachula** to **Veracruz**. Leaves daily 18.10, arriving Juchitan (04.00) and Veracruz (17.20).

From **Coatzacoalcos** to **Mexico City**. Leaves daily 15.55, arriving Mexico City 9.15.

From **Palenque**. Departures at 22.00, arriving Campeche (06.00) and **Merida** (9.05); Slow train at 20.45, arriving Campeche (12.15) and Merida (17.10). For **Mexico** departure at 8.05, arriving 9.15 (25hrs).

Buses

From **Oaxaca**. Very frequently to Mexico City (8hrs upwards). At least 10 daily to Tehuacan (4½hrs) and Puebla (7hrs). To Tuxtepec and Veracruz (4; 4 and 8hrs): to Tehuantepec (8; 4hrs); to Tapachula (4; 10hrs): to Puerto Angel (7; 7½hrs) and Puerto Escondido (6; 8hrs).

6 a day to Tuxtla Gutierrez (9hrs), just one through to San Cristobal (11hrs).

From **San Cristobal**. Constantly to Tuxtla Gutierrez (2hrs). To Comitan (4; 2hrs); to Villahermosa (6; 6hrs): to Palenque (1; 8hrs at least).

From **Villahermosa**. At least 10 daily to Coatzacoalcos (3hrs) and Veracruz (7hrs). To Palenque (5; 2hrs) and Campeche (12; 8 hrs).

From **Palenque**. 3 a day to Campeche (5hrs) and Merida (8hrs).

Planes

Villahermosa has the busiest airport in the region, with several daily flights to the capital, but there are daily direct services too from **Oaxaca**, Tuxtla Gutierrez, Ciudad del Carmen, Coatzacoalcos and Tapachula. Also Aerovias Oaxaqueñas fly from Oaxaca to Puerto Escondido every morning, and several companies operate light planes – from Palenque or San Cristobal to Bonampask, for example.

Chapter eight
THE YUCATAN

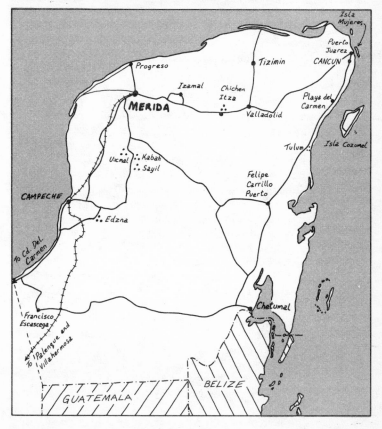

Both physically and historically, the three states which comprise the **Yucatan peninsula** – Campeche, Yucatan and Quintana Roo – are distinct from the rest of Mexico. The interminably flat, low-lying plain is one of the hottest and most tropical feeling areas of the country, but in fact it lies further north than you imagine – Merida is actually north of Mexico City. Until the 1960s, when proper road and rail links were completed, the Yucatan lived out of step with the rest of Mexico – there was almost as much contact with Europe and the US as with the centre. Now tourism has made major inroads, especially in the north around the great **Mayan sites** and on the route from **Merida** to the new 'super-resort' of **Cancun**, and new investment in the area has brought it closer to the heart of things, but a unique character remains. In the south, where townships are sparsely scattered in thick, jungly forest, there's still a distinct pioneering feel.

The modern boom is, in fact, a re-awakening – for this has been the longest continuously civilised part of the country, with evidence of Mayan inhabitants as early as 2,500BC, already producing good pottery and living in huts virtually identical to those you'll see in the villages today. **The Maya** are not a specifically Mexican culture – their greatest cities, indeed, were not in Mexico at all but in the highlands of modern Guatemala and Honduras – but they did produce a unique style in the Yucatan and continued to flourish here long after the collapse of the 'Classic' civilisations to the south. This they did despite natural handicaps – thin soil, heat, humidity and lack of water – and in the face of frequent invasion from Central Mexico. And here the Mayan peasantry still live, remarkably true to their old traditions and lifestyle despite the hardships of the intervening years: ravaged by European diseases and forced to work on vast colonial *encomiendas* or later, through the semi-slavery of debt peonage (rivetingly described in the novels of B. Traven) on the henequen plantations or in the forests, hauling out timber.

The florescence of Mayan culture, throughout their extensive domains, came in the **Classic period** from around 300–900AD: a period in which the cities grew up and Mayan science and art apparently reached their height. The Mayan calendar, a complex interaction of solar, astronomical and religious dates, was far more complicated and accurate than our own, and they had developed a sophisticated mathematical and (still largely undeciphered) hieroglyphic system. In the ninth century, though, their cities suddenly became abandoned – the result perhaps of revolt by a population from whom the knowledge of the elite had become too arcane and remote, brought about by some natural disaster. Whatever the reason, in Guatemala and Honduras they were never to be re-populated; in the Yucatan the abandonment was less total, and in many places shortlived. Instead there was a renaissance stimulated by contact with Central Mexico, initially perhaps through trade, later by a direct Toltec invasion; a new society fusing the Toltec stress on militarism and new gods with Maya traditions sprang up – with its ultimate achievements at **Chichen Itza**, dominant until the twelfth century.

From the twelfth century on, **Mayapan** became the new centre of power, controlling the entire peninsula in an era when artistic and architectural standards went into sharp decline. But by the time the Spanish arrived their power, too, had been broken by revolt and the Maya splintered into tribalism – although still with coastal cities and long-distance sea-trade which awed the Conquistadors. It proved the hardest area of the country to suppress. Despite systematic attempts to destroy all trace of the ancient culture, there was constant armed rebellion against the

Spanish and later the Mexican authorities – the last the **Caste Wars** of the nineteenth century, during which the Maya, supplied with arms from British Honduras, gained brief control of the entire peninsula. Gradually, though, they were again pushed back into the wastes of southern Quintana Roo, where the final pockets held out until the beginning of this century.

CENTRAL YUCATAN: THE GREAT MAYAN SITES

There's really only one route around the Yucatan: the variation comes in where you choose to break the journey or to make side-trips off the main trail. Whether from Palenque or by road and ferry along the beautiful coast from Ciudad del Carmen, the trail heads up to **Campeche**, from there to **Merida**, and on via **Chichen Itza** to the Caribbean coast. From Merida the best of the **Mayan sites** – Uxmal, Chichen Itza and a trove of smaller, less well explored ruins – are in easy reach. Most people head there first, avoiding Campeche altogether. This is strongly to Campeche's advantage (even if locals don't see it that way), for while the attractions in and around the city can't compare with Merida's, it is at least spared the blight of tourist overkill.

The road across the south of the peninsula, from FRANCISCO ESCARCEGA to Chetumal, is a new one, and although it passes through jungle in which there are many Mayan remains, these are largely unexplored and hard to reach (see p. 352). There's little traffic along it, and little incentive to add to it, although as a quick route back it can complete a circular tour.

CAMPECHE

CAMPECHE, capital of the state which bears its name, is something of a bizarre mixture of ancient and ultra-modern. At its heart, relatively intact, lies a colonial port still surrounded by hefty defensive walls and fortresses: around, the trappings of a city which is once again becoming wealthy. Nowhere is this more obvious than along the seafront – originally the city defences dropped straight into the sea, now they face a reclaimed strip of land on which stand the spectacular new Palacio de Gobierno and State Legislature (spectacularly ugly in the eyes of most locals) and the big hotels – the *El Presidente* and the *Baluartes*.

A Spanish expedition under Francisco Hernandez landed outside the

Mayan town *Ah Kin Pech* – in 1517, only to beat a hasty retreat on seeing the forces lined up to greet them, and it wasn't until 1540 that Francisco de Montejo founded the modern town, and from here set out on his mission to conquer the Yucatan. From then until the nineteenth century it was the chief port in the peninsula, exporting above all logwood (source of a red dye known as *Hematein*) from local forests. It became, too, an irresistible target for the pirates who operated with relative impunity from bases in the untamed coast roundabout. Hence the fortifications, built between 1668 and 1704 after a particularly brutal massacre of the population. Although large sections of the walls have gone, seven of the eight original fortresses (*baluartes*) survive, and you can still trace the line of the ramparts between them around the Avenida Circuito de los Baluartes.

Both the **railway station** and the **Central Camionera** are some distance out of the centre – the railway station right at the end of Av. Gobernadores, the buses about halfway in. From either you can get a bus (marked *Gobernadores* or *Centro*) which will take you in and round the circuit of walls, passing the Zocalo. Almost everything of interest is gathered within the perimeter of the old walls, and all the cheaper **hotels**, too, are within a couple of blocks of the Zocalo. Best value all round is probably the *Hotel Castelmar*, on Calle 61 just up from the corner of Calle 8 (even numbered streets run parallel with the sea, starting for some reason with Calle 8 just inside the walls – odd streets run inland: the Zocalo is bordered by 8, 10, 55 and 57). On the Zocalo itself, the Hotels *Campeche* and *Cuauhtemoc* are surprisingly reasonable and nearby on Calle 8 you'll find the *Hotel Reforma*, or, on 10, the *Roma* and the more expensive *America*. The *Hotel Central*, on Gobernadores right opposite the bus station, is also perfectly good – though its name is hardly appropriate. As for **eating**, you'll find good seafood almost everywhere in Campeche, and by general agreement the *Restaurant Miramar*, at the corner of Calle 8 and 61 by the Hotel Castelmar, is the best place to try it, if not the cheapest. There are also several places around the Zocalo, of which the Hotel Campeche's restaurant is the best value, or you could try the stalls in the **market** – just outside the city walls by the Alameda, top of Calle 57.

Though your time is really as well spent wandering the old streets or seafront as in seeking out any particular sight, the **Tourist Ofice**, prominently signed in the new seafront Plaza Moch Couoh (and actually in the *Baluarte San Carlos*), has maps and is generally very helpful on what to do. The **Baluarte San Carlos** also houses a small library and armaments museum (open 9–12 and 5–7 weekdays): there are cannon on the battlemented roof and, underneath, the beginnings of a network of tunnels which undermines much of the town. Mostly sealed off now, these provided a place of refuge for the populace from pirate raids, and before that were probably used by the Maya too. The **Museo de Campeche** is back around the walls from here, facing the Zocalo in the *Baluarte de la Soledad*. Open Monday-Saturday 9–2 and 4–8, Sundays 9–1, it traces the region's history from early Mayan relics – especially from the nearby sites of Edzna and the island of Jaina – to collections of colonial art, weapons and marine trophies. The **Cathedral**, also on the Zocalo, was founded in 1540 and is hence one of the oldest churches on the peninsula – the bulk of the construction, though, took place much later and what you see is a not particularly striking plain baroque building.

Other sights are a little further out. About 20 minutes walk to the right (north-east) along the seafront you'll reach the **Iglesia de San Francisco**, the only surviving remnant of a sixteenth-century Franciscan monastery – on this site, supposedly, the first Mass to be heard in Mexico was celebrated in 1517. Not far beyond lies the **Pozo de la Conquista** (Well of the Conquest) where the same Spanish expedition, under Francisco Hernandez, gathered water to fill their leaking casks. In the other direction, again along the waterfront Malecon, the *Baluarte de San Miguel* houses Campeche's **Archaeological Museum** (open Tues.–Sat. 9–2 and 3–8; Sun. 9–1; closed Mon.). It's not a particularly large collection, but there are some fine Olmec and Maya pieces and the fort itself, on a low rise just inland of the road, offers great views across the Gulf. Objects from Edzna and Jaina again predominate – some of the fine Jaina figurines are cross-eyed, a feature which the Mayans considered a mark of beauty (and was also, presumably, a badge of rank since it must have been a considerable handicap in most forms of work). As with straightened noses and flattened foreheads, this was often brought about by deliberate deformation – Bernal Diaz noted that the first two prisoners taken by Hernandez were both cross-eyed.

A *Playa Bonita* bus along the waterfront will take you past the museum and beyond to the **beaches** at PLAYA BONITA and LERMA, a fishing village just beyond the city. They look pleasant, if a little rocky, but both the water and the beach can be pretty filthy here – in 1979 an offshore rig blew out, causing massive pollution which is still not entirely cleared.

EDZNA AND OTHER NEARBY SITES: THE ROAD TO MERIDA

Some 50km from Campeche by road lie the ruins of **EDZNA**, not the most impressive in Yucatan, but important as the main example of the *Chenes* style (closely related to the Puuc of Uxmal – see p. 326) and certainly the only *Chenes* site practically accessible by bus. Even this is not particularly easy – best to head out early (there's a bus at 7) which will enable you to return by lunchtime.

The most important building here is the great **Templo Mayor**, a palace-pyramid at the highest point of the raised platforms of the Acropolis. It takes the form of a stepped pyramid, over 65 feet high on a base 200 feet square, topped by a broken roof-comb set at the back of the highest level – highly unusual, though, in that each of its five storeys contains chambered 'palace' rooms. Up the front, a steep monumental staircase leads to the top level, a three-roomed temple. While solid temple pyramids and multi-storeyed 'apartment' complexes are relatively common, it is extremely rare to see the two combined in one building. Lesser buildings surround the ceremonial centre, including one, a palace on the north-west side, which has a room used as a steam bath, with stone benches and hearths over which water could be boiled. Near here, too, is a ball-court. Although Edzna was a large city, on the main trade route between the Mayas of the highland and the coast, the rest still lies unexcavated – including a large system of drainage (and possibly irrigation) canals. By the entrance is a large stela carved with the image of a local noble wearing a huge head-dress and with Maya hieroglyphs: others have been taken to the museums in Campeche.

Edzna bears a much greater resemblance to the Puuc sites (especially the lesser ones, Sayil and Kabah) than do the sites further inland. These, though, are only accessible with a car and a considerable degree of determination. *Chen* means 'well' and is a fairly common suffix to place names hereabouts – the chief **Chenes sites**, though, are reached on a poor road from **HOPELCHEN**, a village about 100km from Campeche on the long route to Merida. A bus follows this road as far as DZIBALCHEN and ITURBIDE, but it's not much use for visiting the sites as it turns straight round on arrival and there's nowhere to stay. The best of the ruins are, in any case, some way from the paved road and substantially buried in the jungle: **HOCHOB** has an amazing three-roomed temple (low and fairly small as are most *Chenes* buildings) with a façade entirely covered in richly carved, stylised snakes and masks. The central chamber is surmounted by a crumbling roof-comb, and its decoration forms the effect of a huge mask – with the doorway as a gaping mouth. This is reproduced in the Museum of Anthropology in Mexico City, a much easier way of getting to see it. **DZIBILNOCAC**, close to ITURBIDE, is slightly easier to reach, and its buildings, too, demonstrate the ultra-decorative façades typical of *Chenes* style.

There are two roads from CAMPECHE to MERIDA. First class buses, and all *directo* services, will take the shorter route via **Highway 180** – the colonial Camino Real. This old Spanish route is lined with villages whose plazas are laid out on the traditional plan around a massive old church: if you want to stop, **HECELCHAKAN** (about 65km on) has a small archaeology museum on the main square with figures from Jaina and objects from other nearby sites, and **BECAL** (a further 35km) is one of the biggest centres for the manufacture of basketwork products and the ubiquitous Yucatecan *Jipis*, or 'Panama' hats (real panama hats, as everyone knows, come from Ecuador). There's a *Centro Artesanal* by the road where you can buy them, but it's more interesting to go into the village and watch this cottage industry at work.

Better, if you have the time, is to take the long route **via HOPELCHEN and MUNA,** for this road goes past the great sites of SAYIL, KABAH and UXMAL (see pp. 330–2). With a car you could easily visit all three, perhaps stopping also at **BOLONCHEN DE REJON,** with its nine wells (**Bolonchen** means nine wells) and nearby caves, and still get to Merida within the day. By bus it's slightly harder, but if you set out early and check the timetable carefully you should have time for a reasonable look at at least one – Kabah is the easiest since its ruins lie right on the main road.

MERIDA

Even if practically every road didn't lead here in the end, **MERIDA** would still be an inevitable stop. The 'White City', capital of the state of Yucatan, is in every sense the leading town of the peninsula: remarkably calm and likeable for all its thousands of visitors. It's the ideal base for excursions to the great Mayan sites – to Uxmal and Chichen Itza above all – and whilst the city itself has little in the way of sights, you can live well and there are good beaches in easy reach.

Practical details: arrival and getting about

Merida is laid out on a simple grid of numbered streets: even numbers run north-south, odd from east to west, with the central Plaza Mayor, or Zocalo, bounded by Calles 60, 61, 62 and 63. Arriving by train or bus you'll be within walking distance (about 15 minutes) of the centre. The **railway station** is at the junction of Calles 48 and 55 – to get to the plaza head down 48 and take the third right (61) under the Arco Dragones (an archway which, with two others, is the only remaining evidence of the city walls) to reach the Zocalo in six blocks. From the chief **Terminal de Autobuses,** on Calle 69 between 68 and 70, turn right along 69 until you reach the church and small plaza of San Juan de Dios, then left up 62 to the Zocalo. Some short-haul buses use other terminals (dealt with where relevant under excursions from Merida), but on first arrival you're almost bound to be at this main stop. From the **airport** you can get in by local bus – look for the *Autobuses Urbanos* sign outside the terminal, you'll arrive on Calle 60 near the market – or share a taxi or VW bus for the 20-minute ride. The **Tourist Office** is miles out on the Av. de los Itzaes, but there's an information booth on the Zocalo (in front of the Palacio de Gobierno) which dishes out maps and advice.

There are hundreds of **hotels** in Merida, a fair number of them very

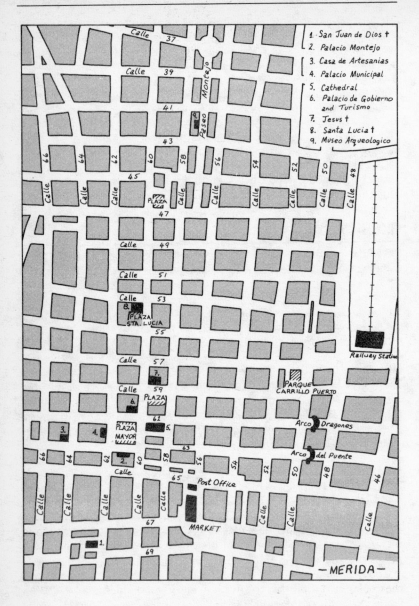

1. San Juan de Dios †
2. Palacio Montejo
3. Casa de Artesanías
4. Palacio Municipal
5. Cathedral
6. Palacio de Gobierno and Turismo
7. Jesus †
8. Santa Lucia †
9. Museo Arqueologico

— MERIDA —

close to the centre, so that although the city can get crowded at peak times you should always be able to find a room with a little trudging around. It seems, in any case, to be the expensive places which fill up first. Some of the very cheapest are **near the bus station**, though be warned that this is a noisy and grimy part of town: virtually opposite you'll see the *Hotel San Jorge* and the smaller, cheaper *San Fernando*; the *Hotel Alamo* (Calle 68 No. 549), right and right again from the terminal, is quieter and probably better value. A couple of blocks closer to the centre, the *Posada del Angel* (Calle 67 between 68 and 66) is more pleasant but more expensive. The *Posada Central*, on Calle 55 in front of the railway station, is **handy for trains** but not particularly well-positioned or good value – better but more expensive is the *Hotel Chac-Mool*, three blocks from the station (Calle 54 No. 474, corner of 55).

For my money, though, it's worth paying more here to be close to the centre of things, and the *Hotel Caribe*, on the tiny **Plaza Hidalgo** (or Plaza Cepeda Peraza) just one block from the Zocalo at the corner of 59 and 60, is definitely the best of the medium-priced choices. In an old convent with a tiny rooftop pool and a good restaurant downstairs in the patio, it has some rather dingy rooms, but get one facing inwards and with a fan rather than air-conditioning (noisy, ineffective, and you pay more) and you'll be well set. The *Gran Hotel*, next door, is less good value, while the *Hotel Regis*, half a block up on the other side of Calle 60 is very basic and barely noticeable – but cheap given its position. Better alternatives if you want some luxury are the *Hotel Reforma*, one block from the Zocalo at the corner of 59 and 62, a once fancy place fallen on hard times with a pool which is often closed, or the *Hotel Mucuy*, on Calle 57 between 56 and 58. Cheaper places **close to the centre** include, on Calle 62 just south of the Zocalo, the Hotels *Sevilla* (No. 511), *Oviedo* (515) and *La Paz* (520) as well as a tiny nameless *Casa de Huespedes* (507); **near the Market** the *Hotel America* (Calle 67 between 58 and 60) and the more upmarket *Hotel Dolores Alba* (Calle 63 at the corner of 54); and **near the Casa de Artesanias** the Hotels *Margarita* and *Latino* (both on Calle 66 between 61 and 63) and the *Casa Bowen* (Calle 66 between 63 and 65). If you're totally broke – and this is definitely not a recommendation – you could always try the *Casa del Pueblo*, a municipal doss-house on Calle 65 about ten blocks from the centre: early to bed here (and best to have your own bedding) and you're thrown out at 7.

Good **restaurants**, too, are plentiful in the centre, with a number of cheap places on Calle 62 just north of the Zocalo, and more expensive places further up here and on Calle 60. In the Plaza Mayor itself there are several wonderful **juice bars** – notably *Jugos California* – which serve all the usual range of fruit *jugos* and *licuados* as well as concoctions of more exotic local fruits: try *Mamey* or *Guanabana*. Combined with something from the **bakery** at the corner of Calles 62 and 63 this can make a great breakfast. For more substantial meals the *Cafeteria Erik* and *Le Louvre*, just north of the plaza on 62, are both basic but reasonable, or you can get good *tortas* from *Las Mil Tortas*, one block down 62 in the other direction. Other cheap places to look are around the market, especially the restaurant in the *Hotel America*, and near the bus station – try the *Restaurant la Terminal*.

Slightly more expensive, and much more pleasant, is to head for the Plaza Hidalgo, where you can either sit outside at the *Cafe Express* – a good place to mull over a coffee and a copy of the *Mexico City News* from the news-stand opposite – or in the patio of the Hotel Caribe at *El Rincon*. Across the road, and half a block further up, *Los Balcones* is on the first floor of the same building as houses the Hotel Regis. A health food place, it has excellent yoghurt-based drinks (*smoothies*) and a selection of **vegetarian** dishes as well as run-of-the-mill Mexican standards – good views, too, if you get a balcony table and popular with students from the nearby University. The *Cafeteria Pop*, left at the next corner onto Calle 57, is even more of a student hang-out; a westernised, plasticky snack bar. Also in this area are several more expensive and tourist-oriented places, particularly *Pancho Villa's Follies*, on Calle 59 opposite the Hotel Reforma. With fun decor, lots of giant photos of Mexican revolutionaries, and a pricey Tex-Mex menu, it's aimed squarely at Americans homesick for 'Mexican' food – good steaks though. *Yannig*, round the corner on Calle 62, has surprisingly good **French** food.

Few of these places serve food which is specifically Yucatecan, a pity since much of it is excellent. For that you should try *Los Almendros* in the Parque Carrillo Puerto (or Plaza Mejorada), at Calle 59 between 50 and 52. This is a branch of a restaurant from Ticul which claims to have invented *Poc-Chuc*, a delicious combination of pork with tomatoes, onions and spices. The menu is vast, and fully explained in English, including **typical Yucatan dishes** such as *Sopa de Lima* (not actually lime soup, but chicken broth with lime and tortilla chips in it), *Pollo* or *Cochinita Pibil* (chicken or suckling pig wrapped in banana leaves and cooked in a *Pib*, basically a pit in the ground, though restaurants cheat on this), *papadzules* (tacos stuffed with hard boiled eggs and covered in red and green sauce) and anything *en relleno negro*, a black, burnt-chile sauce. Little of this is hot, but you should watch out for the *Salsa de Chile Habanero* which most restaurants here have on the table – pure fire. *Los Almendros* has all of these and more, but it's best to avoid the real exotics like venison (*venado*, another local tradition) since things which are served less often tend to be lukewarm and arrive looking as if they've sat on the plate for hours. Best time to go is Sunday lunch, when it's packed with locals. *Los Tulipanes*, a long way out on Calle 42 near its junction with 45 (take a taxi), is a much touted dinner-dance place with a 'Mayan Spectacle' while you eat. Tacky and expensive, but the food's traditional and it's housed in an amazing underground *Cenote*, complete with mini-lake, which makes it all worthwhile. Evenings only – information from any travel agent.

The city

Founded by Francisco de Montejo (the Younger) in 1542, Merida is built over, and partly from, the ruins of a Mayan city known as Tiho. Although like the rest of the peninsula it had little effective contact with central Mexico until the completion of road and rail links in the 1960s, trade with Europe brought wealth from the earliest days. In consequence the city looks more European than almost any other in Mexico – many of the older houses, indeed, are built with French bricks and tiles, brought over as tradeable ballast in the ships which exported *henequen*. Yucatecan henequen (or sisal) produced a substantial proportion of the world's rope until the advent of artificial fibres, a business which reached its peak during World War I. Around the turn of the century it was an extraordinarily wealthy city – or at least a city which had vast numbers of extremely rich landowners riding on the backs of a landless, semi-enslaved peonage – a wealth which went into the grandiose mansions of the outskirts (especially along the Paseo de Montejo) and into European educations for the children of the *hacendados*. Today, with that trade all but dead, it's a quieter place – elegant and businesslike still, but imbued too with the calm resignation of the Maya who fill the streets.

Any exploration begins in the **Plaza Mayor**: as ever the centre of interest, and ringed by some of Merida's oldest buildings. The **Cathedral**, built in the second half of the sixteenth century, dominates the scene. Although most of its valuables were looted in the Revolution, the *Cristo de las Ampillas* (Christ of the Blisters) in a chapel to the left of the main altar remains worth seeing. This statue is carved, according to legend, from a tree in the village of Ichmul which burned for a whole night without showing the least sign of damage; later, the parish church at Ichmul burned down and the statue again survived, though blackened and blistered. The image is the focal point of a local fiesta at the beginning of October. Beside the Cathedral, separated from it by the Pasaje San Alvarado, the old Bishop's palace has been converted into shops and offices. On the south side stands the **Casa de Montejo**, a palace built in 1549 by Francisco de Montejo himself and inhabited until 1980 by his descendants. It now belongs to *Banamex*, and much of the interior is open to the public (weekdays 10–12 and 4–6, but erratic): the facade is richly decorated in the Plateresque style, and above the doorway Conquistadors are depicted trampling savages underfoot. The **Palacio Municipal**, on the third side, is a further impressive piece of sixteenth-century design with a fine clock tower, but the nineteenth-century **Palacio**

de Gobierno, completing the square, is actually more interesting to visit. Inside you'll find murals depicting modern Mexican history and, on the first floor, a small museum devoted to the same subject,

Walk north from the plaza up Calle 60 and you'll eventually reach the Paseo Montejo. Calle 60 is one of the main commercial streets of the city, and on the way you'll pass several of the fancier hotels and restaurants – the *Hotel Casa del Balam* has a particularly pleasant bar if you get thirsty along the way, with mariachi crooners in the evening. You pass, too, a series of colonial buildings, starting with the seventeenth-century Jesuit **Iglesia de Jesus** between the Plaza Hidalgo and the Parque de la Madre. Beside it on Calle 59 is the **Cepeda Peraza Library**, full of vast nineteenth-century tomes, while continuing up 60 you reach the **Teatro Peon Contreras**, a grandiose neo-Classical edifice built by Italian architects in the heady days of Porfirio Diaz and recently restored, with the **University** opposite. One block further, the sixteenth-century Iglesia **Santa Lucia** stands on the elegant plaza of the same name – a collonaded square which used to be the town's stagecoach terminus. Finally, three blocks further, the **Plaza Santa Ana**, a modern open space where you turn right and then second left to reach the **Paseo Montejo**.

To either side of this broad, tree-lined boulevard stand the magnificent, pompous mansions of the grandees who strove to outdo each other's style (or vulgarity) around the turn of the century. In one of the grandest, the Palacio Canton at the corner of Calle 43, is Merida's **Museo Arqueologico** (open Mon.-Sat. 8–8; Sun. 8–1). The house was built for General Canton, state governor at the turn of the century, in a restrained but very expensive elegance befitting his position. The collection it houses is perhaps something of a disappointment given the archaeological riches which surround the city, but it's a useful introduction to the sites nonetheless, with displays covering everything from pre-historic stone tools to modern Mayan life. Obviously there are sculptures and other objects from all the main sites, but more interesting are the attempts to fill in the background and give some idea of what life was like in a Maya city. Topographical maps of the peninsula, for example, explain how *cenotes* are formed and their importance to the ancient population; a collection of skulls demonstrates techniques of facial and dental deformation, and there are displays of jewellery, ritual offerings and burial practices as well as a large pictorial representation of the workings of the complex Maya calendar.

The walk out here is quite a long one, and the tour agencies and hotels press their clients to take a *Calesa* – one of the increasingly rare **horse-drawn taxis** – instead. This is not altogether a bad idea, especially if you fancy the romance of riding about in an open carriage, and if times are slack and you bargain well it need cost no more than a regular taxi: there are usually a couple waiting at the stand in the Parque Hidalgo. If you do this, take time out to head a little further out on the Paseo Montejo where the homes are more modern and interspersed with big new hotels and pavement cafes. The **Monumento a la Patria**, about ten long blocks beyond the museum, is a spectacularly tasteless titan of a monument, covered in neo-Mayan sculptures of Mexican history – you'll also pass it if you take the bus out to Progreso. Should you decide really to do the Grand Tour of the city, you can also visit the **Parque de las Americas**, on Avenida Colon, which is planted with trees from every country on the American continent, and get back to the centre via the **Parque Centenario**, Av. de los Itzaes and Calle 59, where there's a zoo, botanical gardens, and a children's amusement park.

The **market** is for most visitors a major attraction, and certainly you shouldn't miss it, but it has to be said that it is very much dominated by the tourist trade. As far as quality goes, you're almost always better off buying in a shop, and market prices are no great shakes either unless you're an unusually skilful and determined bargainer. Before buying anything head for the **Casa de Artesanias**, on Calle 63 west of the Zocalo, where you'll get an idea of the potential quality and price of the goods. Run by the state-sponsored *Fonapas* organisation, it has crafts from all over the state on display – virtually all of them for sale – and the quality is consistently good, right down to the cheapest trinkets and toys.

Merida is definitely the best place in the country to buy a **hammock**, but if you want something you could realistically sleep in a degree of care should be exercised. There are plenty of cheap ones about, but comfort is measured by the tightness of the weave (the closer packed the threads the better) and the breadth: since you're supposed to lie in these things diagonally, in order to be relatively flat out, this is far more crucial than the length (although obviously the central portion of the hammock should be at least as long as you are tall). A decent sized hammock (*doble* at least, preferably *matrimonial*) with cotton threads (*hilos de algodon* – more comfortable and less likely to go out of shape than artificial fibre) will set you back at least 10 dollars – more if you get a fancy multi-coloured version. Rather than mess about with dubious dealers in the market, head for *Tejidos y Cordeles Nacionales*, very nearby at Calle 56 No. 516 B; more of a warehouse than shop, it has hundreds upon hundreds of the things stacked against every wall, divided up according to size, material and price. Buy several and you can enter into serious negotiations over the price. Other good local buys are tropical shirts (*Guayaberas*), panama hats known here as *Jipis*, and the long, white, embroidered dresses worn by Mayan women (*Huipiles*). The last named in particular vary wildly in quality, from factory made, machine-stitched junk to ones which are not only hand-embroidered but of home-spun cloth too. Even the best, though, rarely compare with the antique dresses which can occasionally be found; identical in style (as they have been for hundreds of years) but far better made and very expensive.

Finally, one of the most pleasant things of all about the city is the **free**

entertainment laid on by the authorities most evenings. **Thursdays** are best, with a performance of traditional music and dance in the Plaza Santa Lucia, starting at 9pm – there are a couple of bars with tables outside from which you can watch, or just hang around under the arcades. On **Friday evenings**, again from 9pm there's a 'Noche Romantica' with serenading guitarists in the **Ermita de Santa Isabel**. This old chapel, once a way-station for travellers outside the city walls, is worth visiting anyway for its beautiful garden with reproduction Mayan statuary and, during the day, piped Mayan muzak. **Sunday** mornings (from around 10–2) there are market stalls set up in the Plaza Santa Lucia with everything from fake antiques to more hammocks, and meanwhile the local *Ballet Folklorico* perform in the Teatro Peon Contreras (11am, not free). **Mondays** see a smaller dance and music festival in the Jardin de los Compositores (behind the Palacio Municipal), while on **Wednesdays** there's a concert of classical music in the Plaza Santa Ana (both at 9pm). The town band quite often plays in the Plaza Mayor, too, although not on any apparent schedule.

NORTH TO THE COAST – DZIBILCHALTUN AND THE BEACHES

From Merida to the port of PROGRESO, the closest point on the coast, is just 33km – half an hour on the bus. On the way you pass through flat country where the henequen industry seems still to be flourishing – about 10km out there's a giant *Cordemex* processing plant, and nearby a shop run by the same company selling goods made from the fibre.

The ruins of **DZIBILCHALTUN** lie about halfway, a few kilometers off the main road. Their importance for archaeologists – there's evidence of settlement here from 1000BC right through to the Conquest, the longest continuous occupation of any known site – is hardly reflected in their interest on the ground, but it's a very easy excursion from Merida or an interesting stop on the way to the coast. What's more you can swim in the Cenote at the very centre of the ancient city, fed with a constant supply of fresh water from a small spring. This was, apparently, an extremely large city – its major points linked by great causeways – but little has survived, in particular since the ready-dressed stones were a handy building material, used in several local towns and in the Merida-Progreso road. What there is is the **Cenote**, in which over 6,000 offerings have been found, including human remains, and a causeway leading from there to a ramshackle group of buildings around the **Templo de las Siete Muñecas** (of the seven dolls). The temple itself was originally a simple square pyramid, subsequently built over with a more complex structure. Later still a passageway was cut through to the original building and seven deformed clay figures (dolls) buried, with a tube through which their spirits could commune with the priests. In conjunction with the buildings which surround it, the temple is aligned with various astronomical points and must have served in some form as an observatory. The dolls, and many of the finds from the Cenote, can be seen in a small museum by the site entrance.

PROGRESO is not at first sight a particularly prepossessing place, a working port with a vast (mile-long) concrete pier; but penetrate to the beach and its image changes. Along the shorefront are ranged the mansions of the old henequen exporters, more modern holiday villas, and a fair smattering of small hotels and restaurants – and there's a beach which stretches for miles in each direction. The water may not be the cleanest, and visually it can't compare with the Caribbean sands of the eastern Yucatan, but it's a very pleasant day out from Merida. Good for kids too, as the sand shelves away unbelievably gently (which is why the pier's so long) and always crowded at weekends with day-trippers. There are changing rooms and showers here, and excellent seafood to be had everywhere. If you want to get away from it all, simply strike out along the coast – there are further, smaller resorts at PUERTO CHICXULUB to the west and YUCALPETEN to the east, with deserted sands beyond and between them.

To the east beyond Yucalpeten, the coast road is barely practicable, but there are empty beaches along it all the way round to CELESTUN, on the point east and slightly south of Merida. **SISAL** was Merida's chief port in colonial times – though you'd hardly guess it from the semideserted pueblo today, barely surviving despite its road to the capital. **CELESTUN**, too, is a one-boat fishing village, but behind it is an amazing bird-filled lagoon which even boasts a colony of flamingoes. There are a couple of tiny pensions here and although the swimming isn't up to much you should be able to persuade a local to take you out on the lagoon or the sea, or even hire a boat and do it yourself. Don't come during the winter duck-hunting season, though, unless that sort of thing appeals to you.

Buses run from Merida to Progreso every 15 minutes from 5 am until 9 pm and to Dzibilichaltun four times a day (5, 7.15, 12.15 and 16.15), leaving from the terminal on Calle 62 between 65 and 67. Obviously if you have a car it's dead easy to do both in one go, but even on the bus it's not hard – head out to the ruins early and from there either hitch or wait for the lunchtime bus back to the main road where you can flag down a Progreso bus. Both Sisal (1¼hrs) and Celestun (1½hrs) have regular services too – about twelve buses a day to each – leaving from the *Lineas Unidas del Sur* terminal on Calle 50, a couple of blocks behind the market (between Calles 65 and 67 again).

UXMAL AND OTHER NEARBY SITES

South of Merida in the Puuc hills lie a group of the peninsula's most important archaeological sites. UXMAL (pronounced Oosh-mal) is chief of them, second to Chichen Itza in size and significance, but perhaps greater in its initial impact and certainly in the beauty and harmony of its distinctive architectural style. KABAH sits astride the main road not far beyond, SAYIL nearby down a side track and LABNA further down this same rough track. All of them are sites with just one important structure, but each is beautiful and, although related, quite distinct from the others. From Labna you could continue to OXKUTSCAB on the road from MUNA to FELIPE CARILLO PUERTO. Near here are the caves of LOLTUN, and a minor road which heads back to Merida via the ruins of MAYAPAN.

Obviously, it's impractical to do more than a fraction of this by bus, unless you're prepared to spend several days over it and endure a lot of waiting around. Uxmal and Kabah are perfectly feasible, but getting to both in a single day requires an early start and careful conning of the timetable. For once, then, an **organised tour** is well worth considering – it may not give you as long at the sites as you'd like, but at least you'll see them. For upwards of 10 dollars, most take in Uxmal in the morning, with lunch and a chance to swim at one of the hotels there; Kabah, Sayil and maybe Labna in the afternoon. Any tour agency or large hotel in Merida can arrange one. There has in the past been a special day-trip bus run by *Autotransportes del Sureste* from the bus station in Merida, calling at all these sites long enough for an independent inspection – no guide or lunch, but far cheaper than a tour. This may operate again, so check while you're in the bus station or ask at the Tourist Office. Better still, if you can afford it, is to hire a car: in two days you can explore thoroughly everything below, either returning overnight to Merida or finding a room in MUNA, TICUL or BOLONCHEN DE REJON. This way you could even include the Uxmal son-et lumière.

UXMAL ('*thrice-built*') represents the finest achievement of the *Puuc* architectural style, in which buildings of amazingly classical proportions are decorated with broad stone mosaic friezes of geometric patterns or designs so stylised and endlessly repeated as to become almost abstract. As in every Mayan site, the face of *Chac*, the rain god, is everywhere. The god must have been more crucial here than almost anywhere, for Uxmal and the other Puuc sites, almost uniquely, have no cenote or other natural source of water, relying instead on artificially created underground cisterns, jug-shaped and coated with lime, to collect and store rainwater. In recent years these have all been filled in, to prevent mosquitoes breeding.

Little is known of the city's history, and what can be gleaned from

Mayan chronicles is not only confusing and contradictory, but in direct opposition to the archaeological evidence. What is clear is that the chief monuments, and the city's peak of power and population, fall into the Late Classic period (600–900AD) and that it was probably founded only slightly earlier than this. Later the *Xiu* dynasty settled at Uxmal, which

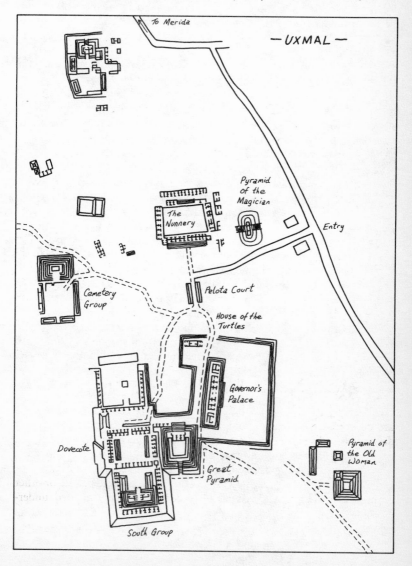

became one of the central pillars of the League of Mayapan, and from here in 1441 the rebellion originated which finally overthrew the power of Mayapan and put an end to any form of centralised Mayan authority over the Yucatan. All the significant surviving structures, though, date from the Classic period.

On entering **the site** (open daily from 6 am to 5pm) the back of the great **Pyramid of the Magician** rises before you. The most remarkable looking of all Mexican pyramids, it soars at a startling angle from its oval base to a temple some 120 feet above the ground, with a broad but terrifyingly steep stairway up either side. It takes its name from the legend that it was magically constructed in a single night by a dwarf, though in fact at least five stages of construction have been discovered, six if you count the modern reconstruction which may not correspond exactly to any of its earlier incarnations. Two of the older structures are entirely buried within the pyramid, visible only through tunnels punched in the facade — two others form an integral part of what you see.

The rear (east) stairway leads directly to the top, past a tunnel which revealed Temple III, and a platform going around the sides of the temple which crowns the pyramid. Even with the chain to help you, the climb up the high, thin steps is not for the unfit, nor for anyone suffering from vertigo: standing near the unguarded edges on top is a sure recipe for heart failure (especially on windy days) and coming down is even worse. The views, though, are sensational, particularly looking westwards over the rest of the site and the green unexcavated mounds which surround it. Here you're standing at the front of the temple, its facade decorated with interlocking geometric motifs. Below it, the west stairway runs down either side of a second, earlier sanctuary in a distinctly different style. Known as the *Edificio Chenes* (or temple IV), it does indeed reflect the architecture of the *Chenes* region — the entire front forming a giant mask of Chac. At the bottom of the west face, divided in half by the stairway, you'll find yet another earlier stage of construction (the first) — the long, low facade of a structure apparently similar to the 'Nunnery'.

The **Nunnery Quadrangle** a beautiful complex of four buildings enclosing a square plaza, is one of many buildings here named quite erroneously by the Spanish, to whom it resembled a convent. Whatever it may have been, that wasn't it, though theories range from its being a military academy to a sort of earthly paradise where intended sacrificial victims would spend their final months in debauchery. The four buildings are in fact from different periods, and although they blend superbly, each is stylistically distinct. The **North building**, raised higher than the others and even more richly ornamented, is probably also the oldest: approached up a broad stairway between two colonnaded porches, there's a strip of plain stone facade from which doors lead into the vaulted chambers within, surmounted by a slightly raised panel of mosaics — geometric patterns, human and animal figures with representations of Mayan huts above the doorways. The **west building** boasts even more varied themes, with the whole of its ornamentation surrounded by a coiling, feathered rattlesnake, the face of a warrior emerging from its jaws. All of them display growing Mayan architectural skills – the false Mayan vaults of the interiors are taken about as wide as they can go without collapsing (wooden crossbeams provided further support), and the frontages are slightly bowed, in order to maintain the proper horizontal perspective.

An arched passageway through the centre of the South building provided the square with a monumental entrance directly aligned with the **ball-court** outside. Now a path leads through here, between the ruined side walls of the court, and up onto the levelled terrace on which stand the Governor's Palace and the **House of the Turtles**. This very simple, elegant building, named for the stone turtles (or tortoises) carved around the cornice, demonstrates well another constant theme of Puuc architecture – stone facades carved to appear like rows of narrow columns. These represent, probably, the building style of the Mayan huts still in use today – walls of bamboo lashed together. The plain bands of masonry which often surround them mirror the cords which tie the hut walls in place.

It is the **Governor's Palace**, though, which marks the finest achievement of Uxmal's builders. John L. Stephens, arriving at the then virtually unknown site in June 1840, had no doubts as to its significance: 'if it stood this day on its grand artificial terrace in Hyde Park or the Garden of the Tuileries,' he later wrote, 'it would form a new order ... not unworthy to stand side by side with the remains of Egyptian, Grecian and Roman art.' The palace faces east, away from the buildings around it, probably for astronomical reasons – its central doorway aligns with the column on the altar outside and the point where Venus rises. Long and low, it is lent a remarkable harmony by the architect's use of light and shade on the facade and by the strong diagonals which run right through its broad band of mosaic decorations – particularly in the steeply vaulted archways which divide the two wings from the central mass, like giant arrow-heads fired at the sky. Close up, the mosaic is equally impressive, masks of Chac alternating with grid and key patterns and with highly stylised snakes. Inside, the chambers are, as ever, narrow, gloomy and unadorned; but at least the great central room, 65 feet long and entered by the three closer-set openings in the facade, is grander than most. At the back, rooms have no natural light source at all.

Behind the palace stand the ruinous buildings of the **South Group**, with the partially restored **Great Pyramid** and **Dovecote**. You can climb the rebuilt staircase of the pyramid to see the temple on top, decorated with parrots and more masks of Chac, and look across at the rest of the site. The dovecote was originally part of a quadrangle like that of the nunnery, but the only building to retain any form is this one – topped with a great wavy, latticed roof-comb from which it takes its name. The **Pyramid of the Old Woman**, probably the earliest structure here, is now little more than a grassy mound with a clearly man-made outline and the **Cemetery group**, too, is in a state of ruin – low altars in the centre of this square bear traces of carved hieroglyphs and human skulls.

At the **entrance to the site** there's a small snack bar selling drinks and sandwiches, as well as a shop with guides to the site, souvenirs, film and other tourist indispensables. There are also three expensive hotels nearby, the *Villa Arqueologica*, the *Hacienda Uxmal* and, a short distance up the road, the *Mision Uxmal* – lunch at any of them is costly (least so at the Hacienda) but it does give you a chance to cool off in the pool. Uxmal's **Son et Lumière** performance is put on daily (except Mondays) at 7pm in Spanish and at 9pm in English (more expensively) – the commentary is pretty crass, but the lighting effects are undeniably impressive. From Merida there are about four buses a day direct to the site, but any bus heading down the main road towards HOPELCHEN will drop you just a short walk from the entrance – none, though, run late enough to get you back after the Son et Lumière.

Some 20km south, the extensive site of **KABAH** stretches across the road. Most of it, though, is unexplored – the one great building, the **Codz Poop** or Palace of Masks, lying not far off the highway to the left. The facade of this amazing building is covered, all over in ludicrous profusion, with goggle-eyed, trunk-nosed masks of Chac. It may not sound much, but even in its present state – with most of the long, curved noses broken off – this is the strangest and most striking of all Mayan buildings, decorated so obsessively, intricately and repetitively that it seems almost mad. Even the steps by which you mount to the doorways and the interior are more Chac noses. There are a couple of lesser buildings grouped around the Codz Poop, and on the other side of the road an unusual circular pyramid – now simply a green, conical mound – and beyond it a sort of triumphal arch at the point where the ancient causeway from Uxmal entered the city.

SAYIL is reached by a minor road heading east from the highway 5km further on; the site itself is another 4–5km along this. Here again there's just one really important building, the extensively restored **Great Palace**. On three storeys, each smaller than the one below, and some 250 feet long, it's a sober, restrained contrast to the excesses of Kabah. Although there are several large masks of Chac around the top of the middle level, the decoration mostly takes the form of bamboo-effect stone pillaring – seen here more extensively than anywhere. The interiors of the middle level, too, are lighter and airier than is usual, thanks to the use of broad openings, their lintels supported on fat columns. The upper and lower storeys are almost entirely unadorned, plain stone surfaces with narrow openings.

The minor road continues, paved but in poor condition, past some ruined walls which are all that is to be seen of a site known as XLAPAK, to **LABNA**. Near the entrance to this ancient city is a palace, similar to but less impressive than that of Sayil, on which can be seen traces of sculptures including the inevitable Chac, and a crocodile (or snake) with a human face emerging from its mouth – symbolising a god escaping from the jaws of the underworld. Remnants of a raised causeway lead from here to a second group of buildings, of which the most important is the **Arch of Labna**. Originally part of a complex joining two great squares like that of the Nunnery at Uxmal, it now stands alone as a sort of triumphal arch. Both sides are richly decorated: on the east with geometric patterns; on the west (the back) with more of these and with niches in the form of Mayan huts or temples. Nearby is El Mirador, a low pyramid with the remains of a tall, elaborate roof-comb.

Beyond Labna, almost at OXCUTSCAB, the **GRUTAS DE LOLTUN** also lie close to the road. This network of caves, studded with stalactites and stalagmites, were revered by the Maya as a source of water long before they built their cities. There are troughs and cisterns carved out of the rock and traces of ancient paintings and carvings on the walls. Nowadays the caves are lit, and guided tours are led through three times a day (at 9.30, 11.30 and 1.30, though it depends to some extent on who turns up and when; not on Mondays, when they're closed).

From **OXKUTSCAB** you can head back north to Merida via TICUL and MUNA. **TICUL** is an important pottery-producing centre, full of shops selling reproduction Mayan antiquities. It also boasts the original branch of the *Restaurant Los Almendros*, with excellent local food, and a couple of small hotels. Alternatively, you can go straight on at Oxkutscab, towards MANI and MAYAPAN. Although both of these places played a vital role in the decline and fall of Mayan civilisation, neither is frequently visited: frankly there's not a whole lot to see, but if you have a car this makes an interesting alternate route to Merida. There are occasional buses from Oxkutscab to Mani and a couple every day from Merida down the minor road past Mayapan.

MAYAPAN was, from the eleventh to the fifteenth century, the most powerful city in the Yucatan. Its history is somewhat vague, but according to Mayan chronicles it formed (with Chichen Itza and Uxmal) one of a triumvirate of cities which as the **League of Mayapan** exercised control over the entire peninsula from around 987 to 1185. This broke up when the *Cocom* dynasty of Mayapan attacked and overwhelmed the rulers of Chichen Itza, establishing themselves as sole controllers of the peninsula. Mayapan became a huge city by the standards of the day, with a population of some 15,000 in a site covering 2 square miles in which traces of over 4,000 buildings have been found – here, rulers of subject cities were forced to live where they could be kept under control, perhaps even as hostages. This hegemony was maintained until 1441 when *Ah Xupan*, a Xiu leader from Uxmal, finally led a rebellion which succeeded in overthrowing the Cocom and destroying their city: thus paving the way for the disunited tribalism which the Spanish found on their arrival and which made their conquest so much easier. What can be seen today is a disappointment – the buildings anyway were crude and small by Mayan standards, at best poor copies of what had gone before. This has led to its widespread dismissal as a 'decadent' and failing society, but a powerful case can be made for the fact that it was merely a changing one. Here the priests no longer dominated – hence the lack of great ceremonial centres – and what grew instead was a more genuinely urban society: highly militaristic, no doubt, but also far more centralised and more reliant on trade than anything seen previously.

After the fall of Mayapan, the Xiu abandoned Uxmal and founded **MANI**. Hard to believe in what is simply a small village now, but at the time of the Conquest this was the largest city the Spanish encountered. Fortunately for the Spanish its ruler, Ah Kukum Xiu, converted to Christianity and became their ally. Here in 1548 was founded one of the earliest and largest **Franciscan Monasteries** in the Yucatan: surrounded now by thatched Mayan huts, about the only evidence of past glories are the ancient stones used in its construction. In front of the church in 1562, Bishop Diego de Landa held the notorious auto-da-fe in which he burned the city's ancient records (because they 'contained nothing in which there was not to be seen the superstitions and lies of the devil') effectively destroying the vast bulk of all surviving original Mayan literature.

CHICHEN ITZA

Chichen Itza, the most famous, the most extensively restored, and by far the most visited of all Mayan sites, lies conveniently astride the main road from Merida to Cancun and the Caribbean, about 120km from Merida and a little over 200km from the coast. There's a fast and very regular bus service all along this, making it perfectly feasible to visit as a day's excursion from Merida or en route from Merida to the coast (or even as a day out from Cancun, as many tour buses do). The site, though, deserves better, and both to do the ruins justice and to see them when they're not entirely overrun by tourists, an overnight stop is well worth considering – either at the site itself or, less extravagently, at the nearby village of Piste or in Valladolid.

The country you pass through is not of any outstanding interest – dead flat plain with only the occasional pueblo, the larger of them marked by the inevitable colonial church and, as often as not, by a semi-ruinous hacienda complete with abandoned henequen processing factory. **IZAMAL**, though, does merit a detour if your trip is a fairly leisurely one: now a quiet backwater whose colonial air is denied by its inhabitants' allegiance to their traditional dress and lifestyle, it was formerly an important Mayan religious centre. Here they worshipped *Itzamna*, one of the gods of creation, at a series of huge pyramid-temples. Most are now no more than low hillocks in the surrounding country, but two survive in the town itself. One, dedicated to the Sun God, has been partly restored just a couple of blocks from the central plaza: the other had its top lopped off by the Spanish and replaced with a vast monastery. The porticoed atrium, or square, in front of this church encloses a vast 80,000 square metres, and inside is the Virgen de Izamal, patron saint of the Yucatan. Painted pale yellow, like much of the town, and really staggering in its sheer size, the monastery complex is well worth seeing. Buses run out here from Merida every 45 minutes (from the *Unidas del Sur* terminal on Calle 50 between 65 and 57; just over an hour's journey) and there are a few onward services to Valladolid, passing Chichen Itza. Izamal is also 2 hours from Merida by rail, two trains a day. To continue eastwards, though, it's easier to get a Merida bus back as far as HOCTUN, on the main road, and pick up a mainline bus from there.

The Highway, which once cut straight through the centre of **CHICHEN ITZA**, has now been re-routed around the ruins: if you're on a through bus it will drop you at the junction of the by-pass and the old road, about 10 minutes' walk from the entrance. Although blocked off by gates at each side of the fenced-in site, the old road still exists, conveniently dividing the ruins in two: Old Chichen to the South, New or Toltec Chichen to the North.

In most minds the image of Chichen Itza *is* the image of the Maya – an image repeated everywhere including on the cover of this book. In fact, it is its very divergence from Mayan tradition which makes it such a fascinating site, and one so important to archaeologists. For at Chichen Itza the stamp of an outside influence – that of the **Toltecs** – is clearly marked across all the most famous structures. The history is a curious and a hotly disputed one, but its broad outlines are accepted by most authorities. A city was founded around the fifth century, and flourished along with all the great Classic Maya sites until about 900: much of Old Chichen reflects this era. Thereafter it appeared, like many Maya centres, to decline – but at Chichen there was a startling renaissance in the following century. New and magnificent buildings appear which clearly employ the themes and style of central Mexico: new gods, a new emphasis on militarism and, apparently, human sacrifice on an unprecedented scale. The city had, it seems, been conquered and taken over by the Toltecs under their God/King **Quetzalcoatl** (Kukulkan to the Maya) and a dynasty established in which Mayan and Toltec art were to be fused into a new synthesis. There are all sorts of problems with the theory – some claim that Tula, the Toltec capital, was a Mayan colony from the start, others

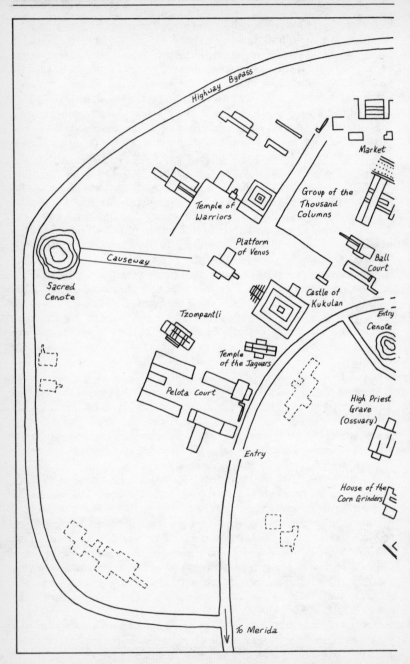

Highway Bypass

Market

Temple of Warriors

Group of the Thousand Columns

Platform of Venus

Ball Court

Causeway

Sacred Cenote

Castle of Kukulan

Entry Cenote

Tzompantli

Temple of the Jaguars

Pelota Court

High Priest Grave (Ossuary)

Entry

House of the Corn Grinders

To Merida

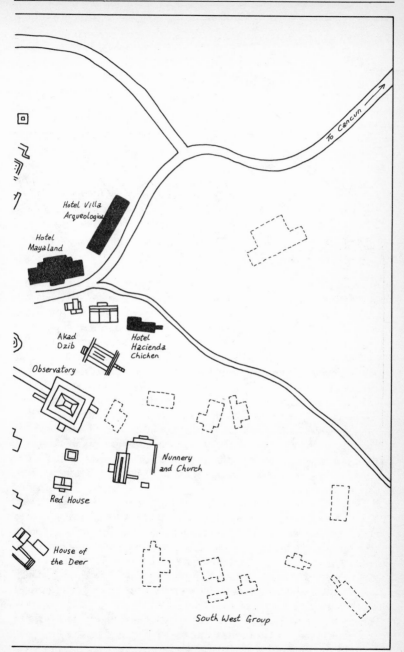

To Cancun

Hotel Villa Arqueologica

Hotel Mayaland

Akad Dzib

Hotel Hacienda Chichen

Observatory

Nunnery and Church

Red House

House of the Deer

South West Group

point to similar tales of an invasion by the Itza, who may or may not have been the same people as the Toltecs – but it fits remarkably with both Mayan and Aztec accounts of the banishment of Quetzalcoatl from Tula in 987 and his subsequent journey to the east, and with a good deal of the archaeological evidence.

The main **entry to the site** (open from 6am to 5pm, though the process of getting everyone out starts at least an hour earlier) is in the west, at the Merida end: there are bus and car parks here, drink and snack stands, a *Consigna* where you can leave any bags, and shops selling souvenirs, film and guides (best are the *Panorama* series); but you can also buy tickets and get in at the eastern gate. Keep your ticket, you may be asked for it and it also permits re-entry if you go out for lunch. Also check the timetable for admissions to the insides of the various buildings – most open only for a couple of hours each day, and you'll want to plan your wanderings around them.

If it's still reasonably early, head first for **El Castillo** (or the Pyramid of Kukulkan), the structure which dominates the site. This should allow you to climb it before the full heat of the day, and get a good overview of the entire area. It is a simple, relatively unadorned square building, with a monumental stairway climbing each face (though only two are restored), rising in nine receding terraces to a temple at the top. Each staircase has ninety-one steps, which, added to the single step at the main entrance to the temple, amounts to 365: other numbers relevant to the Mayan calendar recur throughout the construction. Most remarkably, at sunset on the Spring and Autumn equinoxes, the great serpents' heads at the foot of the main staircase are joined to their tails (at the top) by an undulating body of shadow – an event which draws spectators, and awed worshippers, by the thousand. Inside the present structure, an earlier pyramid survives almost wholly intact – an entrance has been opened at the bottom of the pyramid by which you can enter and climb a narrow, dank, claustrophobic stairway (formerly the outside of this pyramid) to its temple. In its outer room is a rather crude Chac-mool, but in the **inner sanctuary**, now railed off, one of the greatest finds at the site: an altar, or throne, in the form of a jaguar, painted bright red and inset with jade 'spots' and eyes – the teeth are real jaguar teeth. This discovery created endless problems for archaeologists, since these are clearly Toltec relics yet the temple apparently predates their arrival – most would say now either that the original dating was wrong, or that the Toltecs discovered the original pyramid just as modern investigators did. The interior is open for just a couple of hours in the middle of the day, starting at 11am (but check the current times).

The Castillo stands on the edge of a great grassy plaza which formed the focus of Toltec Chichen Itza: all its most important buildings are here, and from the northern edge a *sacbe*, or causeway, leads to the great sacred cenote. The **Temple of the Warriors**, and the adjoining **Group of 1,000 columns**, take up the eastern edge. These are the structures which most recall Tula, both in design and in detail: in particular the colonnaded courtyard (which would originally have been roofed with some form of thatch) and the use of 'Atlantean' columns, representing warriors in armour, their arms raised above their heads. Throughout, the temple is richly decorated with carvings and sculptures (originally with paintings too) of jaguars and eagles devouring human hearts, feathered serpents, Toltec warriors and, the one undeniably Mayan feature, masks of Chac. On top are two superb Chac-mools: the exact purpose of the reclining figures is unknown, but probably offerings were placed on their stomachs and they represent the messengers who would take the sacrifice to the gods, or perhaps the divinities themselves. Once again, the Temple of the Warriors was built over an earlier temple, in which (during set hours) some remnants of faded **murals** can be made out. The '1,000' columns alongside originally formed a square, on the far side of which is the building known as **the Market**, although there's no evidence that this actually was a market-place. Near here too is a ruinous small ball-court.

Walking across the plaza from here towards the main ball-court you pass three small platforms. The **Platform of Venus** is a simple, raised, square block, with a stairway up each side guarded by feathered serpents, on which rites associated with Quetzalcoatl, in his role of Venus, the morning star, must have been carried out. Slightly smaller, but otherwise virtually identical in design, is the **Eagle and Jaguar** platform, on which are relief carvings of eagles and jaguars holding human hearts. The jaguar and the eagle were symbols of the Toltec warrior classes, one of whose duties was to capture sacrificial victims – the human sacrifices may even have been carried out here, judging by the proximity of the third platform, the **Tzompantli**, or skull rack, on which victims' skulls were hung on display. It is carved on every side with grotesquely grinning stone skulls.

Chichen Itza's **ball-court**, on the western side of the plaza, is the largest known – over 270 feet long – and again its design recalls Tula: a capital I shape surrounded by temples with the goals, or target rings, halfway along each side. Along the bottom of each side wall runs a sloping panel decorated in low relief with scenes of the game and its players. Although the rules and full significance of the game remain a mystery, it was clearly not a Saturday afternoon kick-about in the park: the players are shown processing towards a circular central symbol, the symbol of death, and one player (presumably the losing captain – just right of the centre) has been decapitated, while another (to the left, surely the winner) holds his head and a ritual knife. Along the top runs the stone body of a snake, whose heads stick out at either end of this 'bench'.

At each end of the court stand small buildings with open **galleries** overlooking the field of play – the low one at the south may simply have been a grandstand, that at the north (known as the *Temple of the Bearded*

Man after a sculpture inside) was probably a temple – perhaps, too, the umpires' stand. Inside, there are several worn relief carvings and a whispering gallery effect which enables you to be heard clearly at the far end of the court, and to hear what's going on there. The **Temple of the Jaguars** also overlooks the playing area, from the side: to get to it, though, you have to go back out to the plaza. At the bottom – effectively the outer wall of the ball-court – is a little portico supported by two pillars between which a stone jaguar stands sentinel. Inside are some wonderful, rather worn, relief carvings of Mayan priests, Toltec warriors, and animals, birds and plants. Beside this, a very steep, narrow staircase ascends to a platform overlooking the court and to the **Upper Temple** (restricted opening hours) with its fragments of a mural depicting battle scenes – perhaps the fight between Toltec and Maya for control of the city.

The **Sacred Cenote** lies at the end of the causeway which leads off through the trees from the northern side of the plaza – about 300 yards away. It's a remarkable phenomenon, an almost perfectly round hole in the limestone surface of the earth some 200 feet in diameter and over 100 feet deep – the bottom half full of water. It was thanks to the presence of this natural well (and another in the southern half of the site) that the city could survive at all, and it gives Chichen Itza its present name, *At the edge of the well of the Itzas*. Into the well the Maya would throw offerings – incense, statues, jade and especially metal disks (a few of them gold), engraved and embossed with figures and glyphs – and also human sacrificial victims. People who were thrown in and survived emerged with powers of prophecy, having spoken with the gods.

Buildings in the southern half of the site, **Old Chichen**, are on the whole in less good condition. Less restoration work has been carried out here, and the ground is less extensively cleared. A path leads from the road by the Castillo to all of its major structures, passing first the ruinous pyramid known as the **High Priest's Grave** (or *Osario*). Externally it is very similar to the Castillo (or would be if it were in better condition) but inside, most unusually, were discovered a series of **tombs**. Explored at the end of the last century, a shaft drops down from the top through five crypts, in each of which were found a skeleton and a trap door leading to the next. The fifth is at ground level, but here too there was a trap door, and steps cut through the rock to a sixth chamber which opens onto a huge underground cavern – the burial place of the High Priest.

Near here, also very ramshackle, are the **House of the Deer** and the **Red House**, with a cluster of ruins known as the **South-west group** beyond them. Follow the path round, however, and you arrive at the **Observatory** (or *El Caracol*, the snail), a circular, domed tower standing on two rectangular platforms and looking remarkably like a twentieth-century observatory in outline. No telescope, though, was mounted in the roof (whatever Eric von Daniken might think) which instead has slits aligned with various points of astronomical observation. Four doors at the cardinal points lead into the tower, where there's a circular chamber and a spiral staircase leading to the upper level, from where the sightings were made.

The Observatory is something of a Maya-Toltec mix, with few of the obvious decorative features associated with either: the remaining buildings are pure Maya. The so-called **Nunnery** is the largest and most important of them – a palace complex showing several stages of construction. It's in rather poor condition, the rooms mostly filled with rubble and inhabited by flocks of swallows, part of the facade blasted away by a nineteenth-century explorer, but is nonetheless a building of grand proportions. Its **annexe** has an elaborate facade in the *Chenes* style, covered in masks of Chac which combine to make one giant mask, with the door as a mouth. The **Church** (*la Iglesia*), a small building standing beside the monastery, is by contrast a clear demonstration of *Puuc* design – a low band of unadorned masonry around the bottom being surmounted by an elaborate mosaic decoration and roof-comb. Hook-nosed masks of Chac again predominate, but above the doorway are also the figures of the four *Bacabs*, mythological creatures which held up the sky – a snail and a turtle on one side, an armadillo and a crab on the other.

Beyond the Nunnery, a path leads in about 15 minutes to a further group of ruins – among the oldest on the site, but unrestored. Nearer at hand is the **Akad Dzib**, a relatively plain block of palace rooms which takes its name ('*Obscure writings*') from some undeciphered hieroglyphs found inside. There are, too, red palm prints on the walls of some of the chambers – a sign frequently found in Mayan buildings, whose significance is not understood. From here you can head back to the road past the Observatory and the Cenote de Xtoloc.

Staying near the ruins and moving on

The village of **PISTE** is about half an hour's walk from the ruins along a footpath beside the road. If you want to stay cheaply near Chichen Itza, this is where you should head – to the *Posada Novelo*, the *Hotel Cunanchen* or *La Picuda*. There are also several reasonable restaurants here, rather overpowering at lunchtimes when they tend to serve up set meals and musical entertainment to coach trips, but better in the evening. A taxi between Piste and the site usually works out very cheap. Or you can take a taxi in the **other direction** (east) from the ruins and get to the tiny isolated *Hotel Dolores Alba* – the best value here if you don't mind being stuck by the road in the middle of nowhere (but still much less than an hour's walk from the site). Rooms here can be booked in advance at the hotel of the same name in Merida (Calle 63 No. 464).

If you can afford to splash out, though, there are three excellent hotels virtually **on the site**. The *Hacienda Chichen*, indeed, has a couple of small ruins within its grounds, and if it's open (the whole shebang is sometimes taken over by archaeological expeditions) is the cheapest and most atmospheric of the three. The *Hotel Mayaland*, too, is beautiful – most of its rooms are luxurious thatched huts dotted about the gardens. Least attractive, but still pretty good, is the *Villa Arqueologica*, a modern place run by Club Med with its rooms set out round a patio enclosing the pool and cocktail bar: it boasts a library of archaeological and architectural tomes, which by night doubles as a disco (usually empty). All three have pools, and all three offer an expensive lunch which includes use of it – in the Villa Arqueologica you could probably get away with just having a drink at the poolside bar.

The nightly **Son et Lumière** is worth seeing if you do decide to stay at any of these – it's not particularly well done but there's nothing else to do in the evening. Stick to the established routes, though, if you do wander around at night: as I walked back from the performance a group of site workers produced an enormous rattlesnake which they claimed to have just killed. Whether they had, or whether the poor creature is drugged and produced for the tourists' benefit every night I don't know, but it worried me.

As an alternative which is not quite so close, but offers better value rooms and more of interest, you could take a bus east as far as **VALLA-DOLID**, some 40km away. The town is worth visiting anyway (and all the buses do pull in, at least briefly) for its colonial elegance, which persists despite the place's almost total destruction in the nineteenth-century Caste War, the sixteenth-century Church of San Bernardino, which survived, and for its two cenotes, *Sis-Ha* and *Zaci*. The latter has been converted into a real tourist attraction, in which you can swim (for a small fee) and with an open-air restaurant at the entrance. There are numerous hotels on and around the Zocalo, and near the bus station and market. There's a daily train service between Valladolid and Merida: painfully slow but fascinating.

On the way (or as a trip by taxi from Chichen Itza, 5km away) you can visit the **Caves of Balankanche**, where in 1959 a sealed passageway was discovered leading to a series of caverns in which the ancient population had left offerings to Tlaloc, the Toltec equivalent of Chac. There are guided tours roughly every hour, past stalactites and stalagmites, an underground pool, and many of the original offerings. Be warned that in places it can be cold, and damp, and thoroughly claustrophobic. Charles Gallenkamp's book *Maya* has an excellent final chapter devoted to the discovery of the caves, and to the ritual of exorcism which a local *h-man* (or traditional priest) insisted on carrying out to placate the ancient gods and disturbed spirits.

QUINTANA ROO AND THE CARIBBEAN COAST

The coastal state of **Quintana Roo** was a forgotten frontier for most of modern Mexican history – its lush tropical forests exploited for their mahogany and chicle (from which chewing gum was made), but otherwise unsettled, a haven for outlaws and pirates and for Maya living beyond the reach of central government. Now tourism has brought a dramatic upsurge of interest: new roads have been built, new townships settled, and the place finally became a full state (as opposed to an externally administered Federal Territory) in 1974. It is still a duty-free zone in an attempt to promote development (shops selling luxury goods are everywhere, though the prices are still high by US or European standards) and it is still thinly populated. In the north there is Cancun, the islands, and no shortage of tourists, but the south remains thickly forested, with only an occasional tourist.

From Valladolid you could head north to the coast, south to FELIPE CARRILLO PUERTO, or south east to **Coba** (the easiest way to get there by bus – see p. 350); but the vast majority of traffic heads straight on, to **Cancun** and the embarkation points for **the islands**. You'd be well advised to follow them, and especially to head for **Isla Mujeres** for some well-earned relaxation before perhaps checking out the rest of the Caribbean coast and the magnificent site of **Tulum**. To the north, though, **RIO LAGARTOS** does exercise a certain pull – on the marshy coastal flats nearby live vast colonies of pink flamingoes, and there's talk of turning the area into a new tourist centre, with at least one hotel already built. Trouble is, swimming is said to be dangerous and the waters shark-infested. There are regular buses to **TIZIMIN**, a town with an elegant colonial plaza, from both Valladolid and Merida, and onward services from there to Rio Lagartos several times a day – also a daily train from Merida to Tizimin.

CANCUN

Hand-picked by computer, **CANCUN** is, if nothing else, proof of the rise and rise of Quintana Roo, and of Mexico's remarkable ability to get things done in a hurry if the political will is there. Fifteen years ago there was nothing here but an island sand-spit and a fishing village of some 120 souls. Now it's the only close rival to Acapulco as a massive resort. To some extent the computer obviously picked its location well: if you come on an all-in package tour (Cancun is marginally closer to Miami than it is to Mexico City) the place would have a lot to offer – striking modern hotels, white sand Caribbean beaches right outside them, entertainment from golf to scuba-diving laid on, and much of the rest of the Yucatan relatively easily accessible. For the casual arrival, though, it is fantastically expensive, and, excluded from the resort enclave, both frustrating and unwelcoming. You may well be forced to spend the night here – in which case you should definitely take time out to see how the other half lives down by the beach – but without pots of money the true pleasures of the place will elude you.

There are, in effect, two quite separate parts to Cancun, the *Zona Commercial* – downtown, the commercial, shopping and residential centre – and the *Zona Hotelera,* a string of hotels and tourist facilities around the 'island' (actually a narrow strip of sandy land now connected to the mainland at each end, but , because it encloses a huge lagoon, with water on both sides). All the vaguely affordable hotels and restaurants are in the **Zona Comercial,** and even here they're surrounded by very expensive places. The *bus stations* (two of them, but next door to each other) are in the heart of this area, just by a roundabout at the major junction of Avenidas Tulum and Uxmal. Tulum is Cancun's main street, and heading south along it you pass the bulk of the shops, banks, restaurants and travel agencies as well as many of the hotels – up side-streets, but in view. If you completed a square by walking down Tulum to the next large roundabout, right on Av. Coba (which in the other direction heads out to the *Zona Hotelera*), right again on Av. Yaxchilan and finally back down Av. Uxmal, you'd have seen practically everything the town has to offer. From the **airport** there's a system of taxis and VW buses which will take you to any part of town for a fixed price.

The **Tourist Office,** such as it is, is in the City Hall, just a couple of blocks down Tulum on the left as you walk from the bus station – they have free maps and leaflets, as does just about every travel agency and hotel reception desk. **Hotels** here are frequently full, so it may take some wandering (around the block outlined before) to find a room: the cheapest are on Av. Yaxchilan, but they're not particularly pleasant. Right on the roundabout by the bus station, at the corner of Tulum and Uxmal, is the *Novotel* – fairly pricey and usually booked up, but the best in its range by some way. Almost opposite, between here and the City Hall, is the *Hotel Parador,* while in the other direction from the bus station lie the *Plaza Caribe* and the better value *Tropical Caribe* (Cedro 10). Head up Tulum to Tulipanes, about the third on the right, and you come to the *Hotel Colonial,* the closest the town gets to having a decent, reasonably priced hotel. If you continue to the end of this street, across the rather sad, deserted plaza, and on up Gladiolas, you'll reach the cheaper places on Av. Yaxchilan. Alternatively, carry on down Tulum and there are several more modern, soulless possibilities. Cancun also boasts a 600-bed **Youth Hostel,** out on the beach in the *Zona Hotelera*. It's often full with Mexican student groups – and like all Mexican Youth Hostels is reluctant to admit foreigners at the best of times – but if they have room, and you have a valid student card, there's just a chance of a very cheap, dormitory-style bed.

As for **eating,** it's the same streets once again – Tulum has the bulk of the places devoted to tourists, while there are a number of more basic alternatives around the bus station and on Uxmal and Yaxchilan. Claveles, an alley off Tulum, has several 'fun' restaurants if you want to get into the tourist swing with seafood and blaring disco sounds: *Chocko's y Tere* is the most over the top and, in this, the best. Town buses run every few minutes along Tulum heading for the *Zona Hotelera* and the **beaches:** you're free to go anywhere, although some of the hotels do their best to make you feel a trespasser. *Panchos,* by the Hotel Maya Caribe on the Playa Tortugas, is a good place to eat out here, and not too outrageously priced.

The same buses continue in the other direction to **PUERTO JUAREZ,** where the boats for Isla Mujeres leave from, and some go on to **PUNTA SAM,** from where there's a car ferry. Each of these places has a couple of small, cheap hotels (try *Los Faroles* near the jetty in Puerto Juarez) and there's also a campsite on the road, but there's no real reason to stay in either place – hardened travellers who've missed the last ferry sleep out on the beach (and are bitten to death by mosquitoes). To **hire a car** or motorbike for trips along the coast, Av. Tulum is once again the place – *Econorent* for bikes, *Budget* and many others for VW Beetles.

ISLA MUJERES

ISLA MUJERES, just a couple of miles off this easternmost tip of Mexico in a startlingly clear Caribbean, is an infinitely more appealing prospect. Its attractions are simple: first there's the beach, then there's the sea. And when you've tired of them, you hire a bike or a moped to carry you around the island to more sea, more beaches, a coral reef and the tiny Mayan temple which the Conquistadors chanced upon, full of female figures, to give the place its name. Why it isn't more developed is a mystery – not enough beaches, perhaps, to support a really large tourist population, no room for an airport, and too little fresh water – but for the moment it's a place to be taken advantage of. Even now Mujeres is no desert island, but for anyone who has been slogging their way down through Mexico and around the Yucatan, it's the great final haven; everyone you've met along the way seems to turn up here eventually.

The entire island is no more than five miles long, and, at its widest point, less than a mile across. A lone road runs its length past the dead calm waters of the landward coast – the other side, east facing, is wind-swept and exposed; there is a small beach on this side in the town, but the currents even here can be dangerous. The most popular beach, just 5 minutes' walk from the town plaza, is **Playa Los Cocos** – at the northern tip of the island but protected from the open sea by a little promontory on which stands the lone luxury hotel, the *El Presidente Zazil-Ha*. The beach takes its name from the tall coconut palms which stood in ranks behind it: sadly, most of these are now dead, killed by a disease (brought from America, say the locals) which has swept not only the island but much of this Caribbean coast. New strains have been planted but most are still young and even when full-grown lack the sweeping majesty of the towering originals.

In half an hour you can have completed a grand tour of the town, which spreads from coast to coast (about four blocks) at the northern end of the island. **Looking for a room,** head first up Calle Madero (one block to the left from the ferry dock, then right) which cuts straight across the island, and on or near which are most of the cheaper downtown places – the *Martinez, Maria Jose, Osorio* and *Caribe Maya* (pricier with a pool), all on Madero itself, or the *Berny,* one block away at the corner of Juarez and Abasolo. Overlooking the sea at the far end of Madero is the *Rocas del Caribe:* it's more expensive, and the management are stupefyingly rude, but the best rooms are worth it, with huge picture windows and balconies over a rocky little beach. The *Rocamar,* to the right from here along the seafront, has similar views but charges slightly more. As you walk up Madero, the second street you cross is Hidalgo, and the third Guerrero: both lead in one direction to the plaza, in the other to the beach. Most of the good restaurants are on one or the other. Following Guerrero towards the beach you pass the **market** (not up to much) and then have to turn right and left to continue to the beach. Here is *Poc-Na,* a sort of private Youth Hostel, modern and white-washed, where all the long-term travellers seem to meet up and sleep in bunks in semi-private dormitories. If you carry full camping equipment it's much the cheapest place to stay, if not, by the time you've hired sleeping bags, sheets and mattresses, it can work out more expensive than a hotel. No doubt, though, that it's the place to meet people, with a good restaurant and communal areas. The nearby *Hotel Caracol* often takes up Poc-Na's overflow, but much better, indeed by far the most attractive place to stay on the island, is *Las Cabañas,* right on the beach. There's no sign, but if you follow the sandy track which leads from Poc-Na towards the beach, you'll see a group of white-washed concrete huts on your left just before you get there. This was obviously part of a more ambitious project which went wrong: what you get is a cavernous room with nothing in it but a huge bed or two, maybe a wardrobe, and a bathroom with cockroaches in the shower. Outside, each has a palapa-fringed terrace, probably shared with your neighbours and ideal for slinging a hammock, and the beach. Unfortunately, the Cabañas are often full. There are also two **campsites** just down from here – *Las Hamacas* and *Los Cocoteros,* both of which seem to close for much of the year – or you could always camp out on the beach, easily enough done, but a move which could prove unpopular if there are more than one or two people already there.

Ciro's Lobster House and *Gomar* (on Guerrero and Hidalgo respectively) are the two most popular **restaurants** on the island: *Gomar* is over-rated, but if you can afford it you should sample the self-explanatory delights of *Ciro's* at least once. *El Bucanero,* nearby, is a better bet for standard meals – vast fruit breakfasts, seafood and, the island speciality, turtle in a bewildering variety of guises. There are also several good restaurants around the *Hotel Rocamar,* or the very cheapest food comes from the stalls set up near here in the area beyond the Zocalo beneath the water tower. *Buho's* is a sort of open-air disco-bar on the beach just across from Las Cabañas – it plays the best music on the island, which isn't saying a great deal.

If you've had enough of the beach and exhausted the possibilities of trying to hire a windsurfer, rent a bike or a moped (loads are on offer) to explore the south of the island. **El Garrafon** is the most obvious destination, but to see this coral reef at its best you should set out early: by 11 day-trip launches from Cancun have arrived, and although this doesn't seem to worry the fish, it can get unpleasantly crowded. There are an enormous number of completely tame, fabulously coloured tropical fish swimming about here (and waterproof underwater fish-spotting guides are on sale to help you recognise them): at times it seems you need the snorkel and mask not so much to help you find the swarms of Mohican-styled parrot fish, as to dodge them. Small and commercialised as El Garrafon is (entrance fee, souvenir stands, showers and crowds), you shouldn't miss it. To get just to El Garrafon and back, a taxi is cheapest, but moped rates are better by the day than they are by the hour, so make it part of a day's exploration: hire mask and flippers in the town too, they cost the same as at El Garrafon and you'll be able to use them all day.

El Garrafon is almost at the southern end of the island – beyond, the road continues to the lighthouse, and from there a short rough track leads to the **Mayan Temple** at the southernmost tip. It's not much of a ruin, but it is very dramatically situated, on low rocky cliffs below which you can often spot worryingly large fish basking. On the way back, stop at **Playa Lancheros,** a palm-fringed beach which is virtually deserted except at lunchtimes when the Cancun daytrippers pile in. There's a turtle pen here, full of beasts which stay remarkably docile despite the abuses they're subjected to, and a gaggle of geese on the beach. Inland, in the jungly undergrowth, lurk the decaying remains of the **Hacienda Mundaca:** an old house and garden to which scores of romantic (and quite untrue) pirate legends are attached.

More adventurously, there are day-long boat trips to the island bird sanctuary of **CONTOY** (some, with special permission, stay overnight) where you can see colonies of pelicans and cormorants and occasional more exotic sea-birds, as well as a sunken Spanish galleon. Or, with more sang-froid, you can take the scuba-diving trip to the '**Cave of the Sleeping Sharks**'. In these underwater caverns bask groups of Nurse Sharks, lulled into a semi-comatose state by the heavily oxygenated, almost fresh water which has a medicinal effect on them. Apparently they don't bite, but even so this close encounter with the sharks is not, as the local guide puts it, an adventure for 'Neophyte aquanauts', nor one that I've ever attempted.

Getting to Mujeres is dead easy, with boats from Puerto Juarez very frequently (officially at 5.30, 9.00, 10.30, 12.00, 1.15, 2.30, 3.30, 6.00 and 7.00, but in practice even more often than this) and car ferries from Punta Sam five times a day (7.00, 10.00, 1.00, 3.00 and 5.00). There's also a more expensive hydrofoil, which leaves from the dock by the convention centre in Cancun's *Zona Hotelera* at 7.15am and 5pm, returning about an hour later. *AeroCaribe* and others also occasionally fly out in light planes to Cancun or Cozumel.

COZUMEL

The **ISLA COZUMEL** is a far larger island than Mujeres, and it *has* been developed: up to and beyond its potential. Before the Spanish arrived, Cozumel appears to have been one of the most flourishing centres of the Maya, carrying on sea trade around the coasts of Mexico and as far south as Honduras and perhaps Panama – after the Conquest it was virtually deserted for 400 years. This ancient community – one of several around the Yucatan coast which survived the collapse of 'Classic' Mayan civilisation – is usually dismissed as being the decadent remnants of a moribund society. But that was not the impression the Spanish received when they arrived, and nor is it necessarily the right one: architecture might have declined in the years from 1200 to the Conquest, but large-scale trade, specialisation between centres and even a degree of mass production are all in evidence. Cozumel's rulers may have enjoyed a less grand style than their forebears, but the rest of an increasingly commercialised population were probably better off. Cozumel itself may even have been an early free-trade zone, where merchants from competing cities could trade peaceably.

Whatever the truth, you get little opportunity to judge for yourself: a US air base built here during World War II has erased all trace of the ancient city, and lesser ruins scattered across the island are unrestored and hard to get to in the roadless interior. The airfield did, at least, bring new prosperity – converted to civilian use it remains the means by which most visitors arrive. In the 1950s and 1960s the island boomed: now, overshadowed by Cancun, its luxury hotels wear an air of decay while it's still overpriced for most Mexicans and less attractive than Mujeres for the non-packaged traveller. The town (officially San Miguel, but always called Cozumel) is drab, and the cheaper central hotels some way from the beaches. Only for diving enthusiasts is there compelling reason to come here, with miles of offshore reef, and water which is crystal clear all the way down.

Arriving by boat you'll be right in the town centre, with the Zocalo just one block inland – from the airport you have to take the VW Combi service. The cheaper **hotels** are all downtown and fairly close to the centre, though none on Cozumel offers particularly good value. Best of the bunch is probably the *Hotel Aguilar,* three blocks from the plaza at the corner of Calle 3 Sur and 5a. Av. (Fifth Avenue), but there are several more on 5a. Av. between here and the square: the *El Marques* and the modern *Suites Colonial* among them. Others include *El Pirata,* also on 5a. Av., the *Posada Letty* and *Hotel Pepita,* both a couple of blocks behind the plaza at the corner of Calle 1 Sur and 15a. Av., or more expensive places on the waterfront Malecon like the *Hotel Bahia,* the *Vista del Mar,* and the *Maya Cozumel* (bottom of Calle 5 Sur). **Eating** is pretty expensive wherever you go – the most popular places are *Pepe's,* just off the plaza, and *Las Palmeras,* on the waterfront by the jetty. Of the out-and-out tourist traps, *Acuario,* on the waterfront at the southern edge of town, is worth a try – expensive but good food, tanks full of tropical fish, and a couple of sharks swimming around in a pool.

The downtown area is almost entirely devoted to tourists – restaurants, souvenir shops, tour agencies and 'craft markets' are everywhere. All of them sell **black coral,** a rare product of the reefs which can be extremely beautiful. Until Jacques Cousteau discovered it off Cozumel about twenty years ago, it was thought that the last sources of black coral, in the Indian Ocean and the Red Sea, had been exhausted. Even now there's not a great deal of it (it grows at little more than an inch every fifty years) so it's expensive and heavily protected – don't go breaking it off the reefs.

As on Isla Mujeres, only the west coast is really suitable for swimming – protected as it is by a line of reefs and the mainland. The eastern shoreline is often impressively wild. The easiest **beaches** to get to are north of the town in front of the older resort hotels – there's a bus service which runs regularly out to these along the Malecon. Much more pleasant, though, are the less exploited places to the south, for which you'll have to hire some kind of vehicle. The *Hotel Aguilar* rents both mopeds and VW jeeps as do many other agencies in the centre. You pass first a clutch of more modern hotels by the car ferry dock: offshore here, at the end of the Paraiso reef, you can see a wrecked airliner on the bottom, apparently a movie prop rather than a real crash. For better beaches carry on to the **Parque Chankanaab** ('Little Sea'), a beautiful if rather over-exploited lagoon full of turtles and brightly coloured fish. Around it botanical gardens have been planted, and there's a beach and a tiny reef just a few feet offshore: there are also changing rooms and showers here, and a restaurant. Further towards the south of the island are more authentically deserted sands, a couple of them with beach restaurants – **Playa San Francisco** is the best for lounging and swimming. From here you can complete a circuit by following the road round and up the windswept eastern shoreline. There are a couple of good restaurants here at Punta Chiqueros and Punta Morena. The road cuts back across the centre of the island to the town, but if you have a sturdy vehicle (not a moped, which probably won't have enough petrol anyway) you could continue up a rough track to the northern point – off here is the most significant ruin, El Real.

The boat from **PLAYA DEL CARMEN** to Cozumel runs three times a day (at 6am, noon and 6pm, returning at 4am, 9.30, and 4pm) and the car ferry from **PUERTO MORELOS** once (at 6am, returning at noon – not on Mondays). There's also a hydrofoil service every day except Sunday direct from Cancun. All of these, however, can be cancelled for days at a stretch during bad weather (for some reason the rainy season is far harsher in Cozumel than in Cancun or Mujeres), in which case you're left to the tender mercies of AeroCaribe or AeroCozumel who fly light planes in and out almost hourly during the day. Most go to Cancun, but you can also fly to Playa del Carmen or even Tulum (a popular day trip) – all are very short hops so that although they cost far more than the ferry, they're not entirely prohibitive. The bus service from Playa del Carmen to Cancun (via Puerto Morelos) is pretty regular, to the south slightly less so: you can stay here, but on the whole people who do so are stuck waiting for bus or ferry – the hotels know this and charge accordingly. Least avaricious is the *Posada Lily,* by the ADO bus station, next the *Hotel Molcos* by the jetty – expensive but comfortable.

SOUTH ALONG THE COAST: XEL-HA, TULUM AND COBA

Getting to the marvellous seaside ruins of Tulum and from there back towards Cancun or on to Chetumal, can be done within the day on local buses. But if you can afford to do so, hiring a car in Cancun will give you far more freedom: the chance to stop at one of several beaches along the way or to return via the very different site of Coba. Some people try it on mopeds, but it's a long trip, the bikes are underpowered, and Mexican bus and truck drivers will show scant respect as they pass. Worth noting too, that there's no petrol to be had between Cancun and Tulum.

Leaving Cancun behind, you pass PUERTO MORELOS and PLAYA DEL CARMEN. Between the two lies **PUNTA BETE**, the first of the worthwhile beaches, on which, separated by several miles of sand, are a couple of luxurious cabin-style hotels, the *Capitan Lafitte* and the *Marlin Azul*. Still more attractive, and still more expensive, is the palm-fringed strand at **AKUMAL**, some 35km beyond Playa del Carmen. Here there are two new luxury hotels – with good beach bars for a cocktail or a sundowner on your way back – empty sands, and an offshore reef with a series of easily accessible wrecks (scuba equipment for hire). The next signed turning is to **XEL-HA**, a rocky *caleta* (round, sheltered cove) where fresh water from a lagoon mixes with the sea. It's now a park, with changing rooms and a rotten restaurant; thoroughly exploited, but still lovely, and teeming with all kinds of marine life among which you can swim, or row, in designated areas. Avoid lunchtimes, however – apart from the poor food it's full of tour buses. Between all these, you could also take virtually any of the dirt tracks heading towards the sea from the main road, to find a small beach or *caleta*, maybe with a few huts, probably (if you don't mind mosquitoes) with a chance to camp out.

TULUM, 130km south of Cancun, is at first sight the most beautiful of all Mayan sites – small, but exquisitely poised on 40-foot cliffs above the Caribbean. When the Spanish first set eyes on the place, in 1518, they considered it as large and as beautiful a city as Seville. They were, perhaps, misled by their dreams of Eldorado, by the glory of the setting and by the brightly painted facades of the buildings, for architecturally Tulum is no match for the great cities. Nevertheless, it sticks in the memory as no other.

The site (open 8–5 daily; about 1km from the main road) is entered through a breach in the wall which protects it on three sides – the fourth was defended by the sea. This wall, some 15 feet high with a walkway around the top, may have been defensive, but more likely its prime purpose was to delineate the ceremonial and administrative centre (the site you see now) from the residential enclaves spread out along the coast in each direction. These houses – by far the bulk of the ancient city – were mostly constructed of perishable material, and little or no trace of them remains. As you go through the walls the chief structures lie directly ahead of you, with the Castillo rising on its rocky prominence above the sea. You pass first the tumble-down **House of Chultun**, a porticoed dwelling whose roof collapsed only in the middle of this century, and immediately beyond it the **Temple of the Frescoes**. The murals, partly restored, which can be seen inside the temple depict Mayan gods and symbols of nature's fertility – rain, corn and fish: they in fact adorn an earlier structure and have been preserved by the construction around them of a gallery and still later (fifteenth-century) by the addition of a second temple on top with walls which, characteristically, slope, outwards at the top. On the corners of the gallery are carved masks of Chac, or perhaps of the creator god Itzamna.

The **Castillo**, on the highest part of the site, commands imposing views in every direction. It may well have served, as well as a temple, as a beacon or lighthouse – even without a light it would have been an important landmark for mariners along an otherwise monotonously characterless coastline. You climb first to a small square, in the midst of which stood an altar, before tackling the broad stairway to the top of the castle itself. To the left of this plaza stands the **Temple of the Diving God**. The diving or descending god appears all over Tulum as a small, upsidedown figure – depicted here above the narrow entrance of the temple and his exact meaning is not known; he may represent the setting sun, or rain or lightning, or he may be the Bee God since honey was one of the Maya's most important exports. Opposite is the **Temple of the Initial Series** – so called because in it was found a stele (now in the British Museum) bearing a date well before the foundation of the city, and presumably brought here from elsewhere. Right beside the castle to the north is a tiny cove with a beautiful white-sand beach, and on the promontory beyond it the aptly-named **Temple of the Wind** – a small, single-roomed structure. This is reflected by a similar chamber – the **Temple of the Sea** – overlooking the water at the southern edge of the site.

You can swim from the beach on site, or there are others strung out along the sandy road which runs south along the coast. This track continues, though practicable only in a sturdy (and preferably four-wheel drive) vehicle, all the way to PUNTA ALLEN – a beautiful and deserted coastline. Along the first few kilometers are several **hotel/campsites** where you can rent huts or perhaps space to hang a hammock. All of them, though, are plagued by mosquitoes and tend to overcharge severely. *El Paraiso* and *El Mirador* are the worst in this respect, but on the other hand they're much the closest – it's as much as an hour's walk to the better *Cabañas Chac-Mool* or basic *La Riviera*. There are also a couple of small motels in the village of Tulum, on the main road.

At the crossroads in the village you can pick up buses along the main road easily enough, but they may be crowded – the last to Chetumal is at about 7pm, though this will get you there late and you'll have difficulty finding a room. Heading inland on the road to COBA there are hardly any buses, but if you're driving you can see the ruins and continue past them to come out on the Cancun-Valladolid road at the village of Chemax, completing the tour from there. If you want to get to Coba by bus, you'll have to go to Valladolid (or Chemax) from where there are three or four a day..

COBA itself is little visited and still only partly excavated, but it's a fascinating site in a muggy rain-forest dotted with lakes. Its most surprising feature is a resemblance, not to the great ruins of the Yucatan, but to those of the Highland Maya in Guatemala and Honduras. This was clearly a very important centre in the Classic period (600–900AD), and its remains are scattered about between two lakes, linked by more causeways than have been found at any other site. Seeing it all requires at least a couple of hours wandering in the jungle, along sparsely signed paths. Most important of the structures is the part-restored Pyramid of Nocoh Mul, the tallest in the Yucatan and strikingly similar, in its long, narrow and precipitous stairway, to the famous Guatemalan ruins of Tikal. Were you in the mood to blow a lot of money, you could do little better than stay at the *Villa Arqueologica*, the only hotel anywhere near the site, and a wonderful bit of tropical luxury complete with swimming pool and archaeological library. Otherwise, you have little choice but to grab a drink and something to eat from one of the stalls by the entrance, and press on.

CHETUMAL

South of Tulum the road continues good and fast all the way to Chetumal and the border of Belize. But it runs here well away from the coast, and the initial fascination of the steaming forest fast degenerates into tedium. A little under halfway lies **FELIPE CARRILLO PUERTO**, a major crossroads for the routes to Valladolid and Merida, but a town otherwise of strikingly little interest. You could get stuck here overnight if you plan to circle back towards Merida, in which case there are several reasonable hotels around the main plaza – try the *Chan Santa Cruz* or the *Esquivel*. The former is named after a cross, much venerated by the Maya in the nineteenth century, which allegedly spoke and gave orders during the Caste Wars.

CHETUMAL itself, though a much larger city and the capital of the state of Quintana Roo, is not much better. Its broad modern streets (the town was levelled by a hurricane thirty years ago) are lined with a series of rather dull overpriced hotels and restaurants, and with shops doing a brisk trade in duty-free goods – Dutch cheese, Taiwanese Hi-Fi, American peanuts, Scotch whisky – to be smuggled into Belize or back into Mexico. Most visitors are here for this, or on their way across the border. The surroundings, however, do offer the opportunity of some beautiful excursions, and if you're not heading on to Belize the waterfront gives some idea of the more sleazily tropical atmosphere to be found down there.

The **bus station** is at the top of the Avenida de los Heroes, the town's main street, which runs down from a big electricity generating plant to the waterfront. The **market** (which like everything else here sells mostly duty-free imports) is virtually next door, and walking down Heroes you'll pass virtually all the **hotels**. There are loads of them, which is just as well since rooms can be hard to find, especially if you arrive late: the best value seem to be around the junction of Heroes and Obregon – especially the *Baroudi* and the *Maria Dolores*. The **Tourist Office** is also here on Obregon, and there's a good bakery next to the Maria Dolores. On the waterfront near the bottom of Heroes you could, alternatively, try the *Hotel Bahia*. With its ramshackle wood-frame construction it looks very much like a Belizean hotel – if it is (and I've never stayed here) it'll be appalling in terms of hygiene and comfort, but deeply romantic. There are restaurants all along Heroes, but for cheap **food** stick to the area around the bus station and market, or eat in the market itself. For high luxury, try the *El Presidente* hotel.

Near Chetumal are any number of refreshing escapes from the heat and dull modernity. At weekends, the town descends en masse on **Calderitas**, a small seaside resort just 6km north around the bay: there's a good campsite on the beach here and the opportunity (at least in the week when its uncrowded) to find somewhere to sling a hammock for free. The **Laguna Bacalar**, too, is a popular outing, a vast and beautiful lake some 35km north up the main road – you pass it as you drive in from Tulum. Near the village of Bacalar there's a semi-ruinous **fort**: built by the Spanish for protection against British pirates from Belize (then British Honduras), it became a Mayan stronghold in the Caste Wars, and was the last place to be subdued by the government, in 1901. There are several lakeshore restaurants, and nearby is the **Cenote Azul**, an inky-blue 'bottomless' well which is again crowded with swimmers and picnickers at weekends. **Laguna Milagros** is rather closer to Chetumal off the road towards Francisco Escarcega – perhaps less spectacular than Bacalar but emptier, and superb for swimming and birdwatching. Local buses and VW Combi *colectivos* run out to all of these – more frequently at weekends – from the area by the market, mostly around the junction of Colon and Belize. You may also find a local bus to the ruins of Kohunlich. Keep your passport and tourist card with you – as in all border areas there are checkpoints on the roads.

The most direct route **from Chetumal** back towards Central Mexico is on the new road across the bottom of the peninsula to FRANCISCO ESCARCEGA. This on the whole is virgin forest where the sparse settlements bear a desperately pioneer air, but in the Classic Mayan era it was relatively populous. With a car you could visit several **sites** along the way – by bus (just two or three a day) it's scarcely practicable to do so. First, and most impressive, is KOHUNLICH (60km from Chetumal, then another 9km off the road), a cleared and partially restored site which, like Coba, owes more to the traditions of Mayan Guatemala than to the Yucatan. Its most impressive structure is the Temple of the Masks, with great sculpted faces of the Mayan Sun God. Others near the road and open to the public include XPUJIL, with a towering pyramid visible as you pass, BECAN, and CHICANNA.

For BELIZE, there is theoretically a daily bus direct from the Chetumal bus station to Belize City (*Batty's* or *Bluebird*). Otherwise you can get a local bus to the somewhat chaotic border post and pick up erratic local transport, or hitch, from the other side.

FIESTAS

January
The first week of January sees the festival of the Magi in **Tizimin** (Yucatan), an important religious and secular gathering.
6th   FIESTA DE POLK KEKEN in **Lerma** (Campeche), near Campeche, with many traditional dances.
21st   In **Dzitas** (Yuc.), north of Chichen Itza and on the rail line from Merida to Valladolid, an ancient festival with roots in Mayan tradition.
In **Temax** (Yuc.), between Merida and Tizimin, the last Sunday of the month is celebrated with a fiesta – the culmination of a week's religious celebration.

February/March
CARNIVAL (the week before Lent, variable Feb.-Mar.) is at its most riotous in **Merida**, though it's celebrated too in **Campeche** and on **Isla Mujeres** and **Cozumel**.
20th   FERIA DE LAS HAMACAS in Tecoh (Yuc.), near Merida, a hammock-producing village.

April
13th   The traditional festival of honey and corn in **Hopelchen** (Cam.) lasts until the 17th.

May
3rd   DIA DE LA SANTA CRUZ is the excuse for another fiesta in **Hopelchen** (Cam.).
20th   FERIA DEL JIPI in **Becal** (Cam.), the town where many of these hats are made.

June
26th–30th   The Festival of San Pedro and San Pablo celebrated on the island of **Cozumel** and in **Panaba** (Yuc.), north of Tizimin.

July
At **Edzna** (Cam.; date variable) a Mayan ceremony to the god Chac is held, to encourage, or celebrate, the arrival of the rains.

August
10th–16th   Feria in **Oxkutscab** (Yuc.)

September
14th   DIA DE SAN ROMAN. In **Dzan** (Yuc.), near Ticul, the end of a four-day festival with fireworks, bullfights, dances and processions – in **Campeche** (Cam.) the Feria de San Roman lasts on to the end of the month.
29th   DIA DE SAN MIGUEL celebrated with a major festival in **Maxcanu** (Yuc.), on the road from Merida to Campeche.

October
The first two weeks of October in **Merida** see processions and celebrations associated with the miraculous statue of Cristo de las Ampillas.
18th   A pilgrimage centred on **Izamal** (Yuc.) starts ten days of celebration, culminating in dances on the night of the 28th.

November
8th–13th   Feria in **Tekax** (Yuc.), on the road from Merida to Felipe Carrillo Puerto, with dances and bullfights.

December
3rd–8th   Popular fiesta with traditional dances in **Kantunilkin** (northern Quintana Roo).
8th   DIA DE LA INMACULADA CONCEPCION is widely celebrated, but especially in **Izamal** (Yuc.) and **Champoton** (Cam.), each of which has a fiesta starting several days earlier.

TRAVEL DETAILS

Trains

From **Merida** to **Mexico City**. Through train leaves daily at 20.00, arriving Campeche (23.20), **Palenque** (08.00) and Mexico City (09.15; 37 hours).

From **Merida** to **Campeche**. Slow trains daily at 05.00, arriving 11.35 (and, Mon.-Fri. on to Palenque at 01.40) and 23.00, arriving 03.40. Returns leave Campeche at 06.00 (fast train), 12.15 and 16.30, arriving 09.00, 17.10 and 21.30.

From **Merida** to **Valladolid** departs daily at 15.10, arriving 20.00. Return leaves Valladolid 03.00, arriving 08.00.

From **Merida** to **Tizimin** departs daily at 05.30, arriving 10.25. Return leaves at 12.40, arriving 17.40.

Buses

From **Campeche**. At least 14 daily to Merida (3hrs). To Villahermosa (8hrs) at least 12.

From **Merida**. To Cancun (6hrs) via Chichen Itza (2½hrs) and Valladolid (3hrs) 12 first class services daily. To Uxmal (1½hrs) about 5 daily, and to Chetumal (8hrs) at least 6.

From **Cancun**. To Playa del Carmen (1hr) about 12 services daily; to Tulum (2hrs) around 8, and to Chetumal (6–7hrs), 6.

From **Chetumal**. To Francisco Escarcega (5hrs) 2 or 3 a day.

Ferries

From **Puerto Juarez** to **Isla Mujeres** a minimum of 9 daily.

From **Punta Sam** to **Isla Mujeres** (car ferry) 5 times a day.

From **Playa del Carmen** to **Cozumel** 3 times daily.

From **Puerto Morelos** to **Cozumel** (car ferry) once daily.

See Isla Mujeres and Cozumel for more details

Planes

Merida, Cancun and Cozumel all have busy international airports with several daily flights to Mexico City – Campeche and Chetumal also have daily direct services to Mexico City. Around the Caribbean coast various small companies fly light planes – very frequently from Cancun to Cozumel, less often from these places to Isla Mujeres, Playa del Carmen and Tulum.

Part three
CONTEXTS

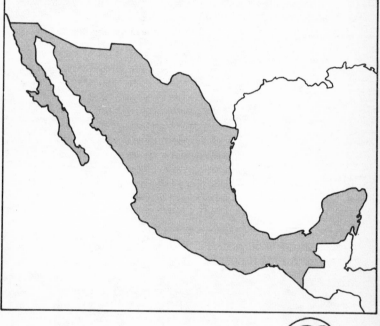

MEXÍCO

THE HISTORICAL FRAMEWORK

Mexico as we know it, with its present borders, has been in existence for less than 150 years. Real history, and a political entity known as Mexico, can be traced back before that, to the Spanish Conquest – but anything which pre-dates the sixteenth century is largely a matter of oral histories recorded long after the events, and of archaeological conjecture, for the Spanish were assiduous in their destruction of every trace of the cultures which preceded them. Such cultures were not confined to Mexico, but must instead be considered as part of **Meso-America**, which extends from the mid-north of Mexico well into Central America. To the north of this imaginary line the Indian tribes were essentially akin to those of North America, never abandoning their nomadic, hunter-gatherer existence; in the south, the Maya were spread all the way from south-eastern Mexico into what is now Honduras. Within Meso-America some of the world's most extraordinary societies grew up, creating – without the use of metal tools, draft animals or the wheel (used only in toys) – vast cities controlling millions of people, superb statuary and sculpture, and a mathematical and calendrical system more advanced than those known in the 'civilised' world.

The pre-history set out below is a synthesis of the theories which are generally, but by no means universally, accepted. There are still major puzzles – especially concerned with the extent and nature of the contact between the societies and their influence on each other – which, should they be solved, may overturn many existing notions. And there remain those determined to prove some of the theories first coined in the eighteenth century when serious investigation began – that Mexico is Atlantis, or that its cities were founded by Egyptians, Assyrians or Indians (or more recently space travellers). Mormon expeditions, for instance, continue to dig for proof that ancient Mexicans were in fact the lost tribes of Israel.

Prehistory

The **first inhabitants** of the Americas crossed the Bering Straits around 50,000BC, and successive waves of nomadic, stone-age hunters continued to arrive for the next 40,000 years, pushing their predecessors gradually further south. In Central Mexico, the earliest evidence of human life dates from about 20,000BC. In the period known as **Archaic**, from around 5000–1500BC, come the first signs of settled habitation: the cultivation of corn followed by the emergence of crude pottery, stone tools and even of trade between the regions. But the first real civilisation was established in the **Pre-Classic** era (1500BC–300 AD) with the rise of the Olmecs.

Still the least known of all the ancient societies, **Olmec** cities flourished in the low-lying coastal jungles of Tabasco and Veracruz. They are regarded by many as the inventors of almost every aspect of the cultures which are recognisably Meso-American – including the first calendar and hieroglyphic system in the western hemisphere, and a religion, based around the jaguar-god, which was spread by their traders throughout Central and Southern Mexico. Above all, though, and what you see of them in the museums today, is a magnificent artistic style exemplified in their sculpture and in the famous colossal heads. These, with their puzzling negroid (or 'baby-faced') features, were carved from monolithic blocks of basalt and somehow transported over 60 miles from the quarries to their final settings – proof in itself of a hierarchical society commanding a sizeable workforce.

Classic civilisations

The Olmec centres were already in decline by the end of the pre-Classic period – **La Venta**, the most important site, seems to have been abandoned about 400BC, and the rest followed in the next few hundred years – but by this time other cities were growing up throughout Central Mexico. The early phases of **Monte Alban**, near Oaxaca, show particularly strong Olmec influence. And in and around the great **valley of Mexico** itself (where Mexico City now stands, and an area known in pre-hispanic times as *Anahuac*) many smaller cities grew up. **Tlatilco** concealed a great horde of Olmec objects, and all of them must have had contact with the Olmecs through trade at least. Meanwhile there were hints of more important things to come: **Cuicuilco** (now in the capital's suburbs) was an important city until it was buried by a volcanic eruption around the beginning of the first century AD; and at the same time the first important buildings of **Teotihuacan** were being constructed.

Teotihuacan dominated the **Classic Period** (300–900AD) in Central Mexico as the first truly great urban society, and its architectural and religious influences are seen as far south as the Mayan heartlands of Guatemala. Even today the city, with its great pyramids of the Sun and Moon, is vast and chillingly impressive testimony to an urban-based society ruled by a demanding religious elite. Here for the first time appear many of the familiar gods – in particular *Tlaloc*, god of rain (and fertility), and *Quetzalcoatl*, the plumed serpent who brought civilisation to man. Historically, there's not a great deal to be said about Teotihuacan, for in the absence of written records we know almost nothing of its people or rulers, or even its true name (Teotihuacan was coined by the Aztecs – it means *the place where men became gods*). What is certain is that the city's period of greatness ended around 650AD, and that within a century it had been abandoned altogether: at the same time disruptions and often desertion seem to have affected societies throughout Meso-America, and in particular the Mayans.

The great **Mayan** centres, too, had reached the peak of their artistic, scientific and architectural achievements in the Classic period, above all in their cities in the highlands of Guatemala and Honduras. These survived longer than Teotihuacan, but by around 800 had also been abandoned. In the Yucatan the Maya fared rather better, their cities revived from about 900 by an injection of ideas (and perhaps invaders) from Central Mexico. The most famous structures at **Chichen Itza** mostly date from this later phase, around 900–1100AD.

In general, the Classic era saw development everywhere – in particular on the Gulf Coast at El Tajin and in the Zapotec areas around Monte Alban – followed by very rapid decline. There are numerous theories to account for this – and certainly the fall of Teotihuacan must

have affected its trading partners throughout Mexico severely – but none are entirely convincing. In all probability, once started, the disasters had a knock-on effect, and probably they were provoked by some sort of agricultural failure or ecological disaster which led to a loss of faith in the rulers, perhaps even rebellion.

Toltecs and Aztecs

At the same time, the start of the **Post-Classic** era (900–1520AD) saw the first of a series of invasions from the north which must have exacerbated any problems. Wandering tribes would arrive in the fertile valley of Mexico, like what they saw, build a city adopting many of the styles and religions of their predecessors in the area, enjoy a brief period of dominance, and be in turn subdued by a new wave of *Chichimeca*. In general, all such tribes were known as **Chichimec**, which implies barbarian (even if many of them were at least semi-civilised before they arrived), and all claimed to have set out on their journeys from the legendary seven caves of Chicomoztoc. Many cities were founded in the valley, and many achieved brief ascendancy (or at least independence), but two names stand out in this new warlike era – the Toltecs and the Aztecs.

The **Toltec** people, who dominated the central valleys from around 950–1150AD, were among the first to arrive – indeed some say that it was a direct attack by them which destroyed Teotihuacan. They assumed a mythical significance for the Aztecs, who regarded them as the founders of every art and science and claimed direct descent from Toltec blood. In fact, the Toltecs borrowed almost all their ideas from Teotihuacan, and their influence can never have been as pervasive as that city's (for the probabilities of Toltec invasions at Chichen Itza, see p. 333). Nevertheless, there were developments, and in particular the cult of **Quetzalcoatl** assumed new importance: the god was depicted everywhere at Tula, the Toltec capital (where he may have been embodied as a king or dynasty of kings), and it was from here that he was driven out by the evil god *Texcatlipoca*. The prediction of his return was later to have fatal consequences. The structure of Toltec society, too, was at least as militaristic as it was religious, and human sacrifice was practised on a far larger scale than had been seen before.

When the **Aztecs** (or *Mexica*) arrived in Central Mexico around the end of the twelfth century they found numerous small city-states, more or less powerful, but none in anything like a position of dominance. Even so it wasn't until 1345 – a period spent scavenging and raiding, often in semi-slavery to local rulers or working as mercenaries – that they found sufficient peace and the prophesied sign (an eagle perched on a cactus devouring a snake) to build their own city. This, **Tenochtitlan**, was to become centre of the most formidable of all Mexican empires, but its birth was still not easy. The chosen setting, an island in a lake (now Mexico City) was hardly promising, and the new city was at first a subject of its larger neighbours. By forming reed islands anchored to the lake bed by trees, the Mexica became self-sufficient in agriculture and expanded their base; they rebelled successfully against their former rulers, and around 1429 formed a triple alliance with neighbouring Texcoco and Tlacopan to establish the basis of the **Aztec empire**. Its achievements were remarkable – in less than a hundred years the Aztecs had come to control, and demand tribute and taxes from, the whole of Central and Southern Mexico. Tenochtitlan became huge – certainly the invading Spanish could not believe its size and grandeur – but however it grew, the Gods continued to demand more war: to suppress rebellious subjects, and to provide fresh victims for the constant rituals of human sacrifice.

Meanwhile other societies had continued much as before. In Oaxaca the Zapotecs were subjected to invasions by **Mixtecs** from the mountains in much the same way as was happening in the centre. By war and alliance the Mixtecs came eventually to dominate all their lands – developing the crafts of the potter and goldsmith as never before – and fell to the Aztecs only in the last years before the Spanish Conquest. In the Yucatan, the **Maya** were never conquered, but their culture was in decline and any form of central authority had long broken down. Nevertheless, they carried on trade all around the coasts, and Christopher Columbus himself (though he never got to Mexico) encountered a heavily laden boat full of Mayan traders, plying between Honduras and the Yucatan. On the **Gulf Coast** Aztec dominance was total by the time the Spanish arrived, but they were still struggling to subdue the West.

The Spanish Conquest

Hernan Cortes landed on the coast near modern Veracruz on April 21st 1519 – Good Friday. With him were just 550 men, a few horses, dogs and cannon; yet in less than three years they had defeated the Aztecs and effectively established control over most of Mexico. Several factors enabled them to do so. First was Cortes himself, as ruthless a leader as any in history – he burned the expedition's boats within days of their arrival, so that there was literally no turning back – and his men, who had little to lose and much to gain. Then, their metal weapons and armour were greatly superior to anything the Indians had (although many Spaniards adopted Aztec-style padded cotton, which was warmer, lighter and almost as protective) and their gunpowder and cannon could certainly wreak havoc with opposing armies – if mainly psychologically. The horses, too, terrified the Indians as well as affording greater manoeuverability, and the attack dogs, trained to kill, were almost as effective. None of these, though, in the end counted a fraction as much as Cortes's ability to form alliances with tribes who were fretting under Aztec subjugation and whose numbers eventually swelled his armies at least tenfold.

Even so, **Moctezuma**, had he chosen to do so, could certainly have destroyed the Spanish before they left their first camp, since his spies had brought news of their arrival almost immediately. Instead he sent a delegation bearing gifts of gold and jewels which he hoped would persuade them to leave in peace. They served only to inflame the imaginative greed of the Spanish. By all accounts Moctezuma was a morose, moody and indecisive man, but his failure to act against Cortes had deeper roots: he was also heavily influenced by religious omens, and the arrival of Cortes coincided with the predicted date for the return of **Quetzalcoatl**. The invaders were fair-skinned and bearded, as Quetzalcoatl, and they had come from the east, whither he had vanished – moreover it seemed they bore a peaceful message like that of the god, for one of their first acts was always to ban human sacrifice. So although he put obstacles in their way, tried to dissuade them, even persuaded his allies to fight them, when the Spanish finally reached Tenochtitlan in November 1519, Moctezuma welcomed them to the city as his guests. Hospitality which they promptly repaid by making him a prisoner within his own palace.

This 'phony war', during which Spanish troops skirmished with a number of other Indian tribes and made allies of many – most significantly the **Tlaxcalans** – lasted for about a year. In April 1520 news came of a second Spanish expedition, led by Panfilo Narvaez, which was under orders to capture Cortes and take him back to Cuba (the mission had always been unofficial, and many others hoped to seize the wealth of Mexico for themselves). Again, though, Cortes proved the more decisive commander – he marched back east, surprised Narvaez by night, killed him, and persuaded most of his troops to switch allegiance. Meanwhile the Spaniards left behind in Tenochtitlan had finally provoked their hosts beyond endurance by killing a group of their priests during a religious ceremony, and were under siege in their quarters. Cortes, with his reinforcements, fought his way back into the city on June 24th, only to find himself in the midst of a siege. On June 27th, Moctezuma (still a prisoner) was killed – according to the Spanish stoned to death by his own people while attempting to appeal for peace. Finally Cortes decided to break out on the night of the 30th – still commemorated as the **Noche Triste** – when the Spanish lost over half their number on the causeways across the lake; most of them so weighed down with gold and booty that they were barely able to move, let alone swim in the places where the bridges had been destroyed.

Once more, though, the Aztecs failed to follow up their advantage, and the Spanish survivors managed to reach the haven of their allies in Tlaxcala where they could regroup. The final assault on the capital began in January 1521, with more fresh troops and supplies, and more and more Indians throwing their lot in with the Spanish. Tenochtitlan was not only besieged (the Spanish built ships which could be sailed on the lake) but ravaged by an epidemic of smallpox among whose victims was Moctezuma's successor, Cuitlahuac. They held out for several more months under **Cuauhtemoc** – the only hero of this long episode in Mexican eyes – but on August 13th 1521 Tenochtitlan finally fell to the Spanish.

Although much of the country remained to be pacified, the defeat of the Aztec capital made it inevitable that eventually it would be.

Colonial rule

By dint of his success, Cortes was appointed Governor of **Nueva España** (New Spain) in 1522, although in practice he was watched over constantly by minders from Spain, and never to have much real freedom of action. There followed 300 years of direct Spanish rule, under a succession of sixty-one viceroys personally responsible to the king in Spain. By the end of the sixteenth century the entire country had been effectively subjugated, and its boundaries stretched by exploration from Panama to the western states of the USA (although the area from Guatemala down, including the Mexican state of Chiapas, was soon under separate rule).

The first tasks, in the Spanish mind, were of reconstruction, pacification and conversion. Tenochtitlan had already been destroyed in the war and subsequently pillaged, burned and its population dispersed: to complete matters – a conscious policy of destroying all reminders of Aztec power – the remaining stones were used to construct the new city, Mexico. At first there was quite remarkable **progress**; hundreds of towns were laid out (on a plan, with a plaza surrounded by a grid of streets, laid down in Spain); thousands of churches built, often in areas which had been sacred to the Indians, or on top of their pyramids (there were over 12,000 in Mexico by 1800); and with the first Franciscan monks arriving in 1524, mass conversions were the order of the day. In a sense the Indians were used to all this – the Aztecs and their predecessors had behaved in similar manner – but they had never experienced a slavery like that which was to follow.

When the Spanish arrived the **native population** of Central Mexico was at least 25 million; by the beginning of the nineteenth century the total population of Nueva España was just 6 million, and at most half of these were pure-blooded Indians. Some had been killed in battle, a few as a result of ill-treatment or simply from being left without homes or land to live on, but the vast majority died as a result of successive epidemics of European diseases to which the New World had no natural immunity. The effects were catastrophic, and not only for the Indians themselves. The few survivors found the burden of labour placed on them ever-increasing as their numbers dwindled – for certainly no white man came to Mexico to do manual labour – and became more and more like slaves. At the same time **the church**, which at first had championed their rights and attempted to record their legends and histories, and educate their sons, grew less interested, and more concerned with money. Any attempt to treat the Indians as human was in any case violently opposed by Spanish landowners, to whom they were rather less than machines (cheaper than machinery, and therefore more expendable). By the end of the colonial era the church owned more than half of all the land and wealth in the country, yet most Indian villages would be lucky to see a priest once a year.

In a sense Mexico remained a wealthy nation – certainly the richest of the Spanish colonies – but that sense would only have been understood by the rulers, or by those back home in Spain. For the governing philosophy was that 'what's good for Spain is good for Mexico', and to that end all **trade**, industry and profit was exclusively aimed. No local trade or agriculture which would compete with Spain was allowed, so the cultivation of vines or the production of silk was banned; heavy taxes on other products – coffee, sugar, tobacco, silver and other metals, cochineal – went directly to Spain or to still poorer colonies, and no trade except with Spain was allowed. Since the 'Spanish Galleon' (actually more of a convoy) sailed from Veracruz just once a year and was even then subject to the vagaries of piracy, this was a considerable handicap.

It didn't prevent the growth of a small class of extraordinarily wealthy *hacendados* (owners of massive haciendas) and mine-owners – whose growing confidence is shown in the architectural development of the colonial towns, from fortress-like huddles at the beginning of the colonial era to the full flowering of baroque extravagance by its end – but it did stop the development of any kind of realistic economic infrastructure, even of decent roads linking these towns. Just about the only proper road in 1800 was the one which connected Acapulco with Mexico City and Veracruz, by which goods from the far-eastern colonies would be transported across country before shipment on to Spain. Even among the wealthy there was growing **resentment**. Resentment which was fuelled by the status of Mexicans: only *Gachupines*, Spaniards born in Spain, could hold high office in the government or church. There were about 40,000 of them in Mexico in 1800 out of the 6 million population, and some 3 million Indians – the rest were *creoles* (born in Mexico of Spanish blood) who were in general educated, wealthy and aristocratic, and *mestizos* (of mixed race) who dominated the lower ranks of the church, army and civil service, and worked as shopkeepers, small ranchers or even bandits and beggars.

Independence

By the beginning of the nineteenth century Spain's status as a world power was in severe decline. In 1796 British seapower had forced them to open their colonial ports to free trade, and in 1808 Spain itself was invaded by Napoleon, who placed his brother Joseph on the throne. At the same time new political ideas were transforming the world outside, with the French Revolution and the American War of Independence still fresh in the memory. Although the works of such political philosophers as Rousseau, Voltaire and Paine were banned in Mexico, the opening of the ports made it inevitable that their ideas would spread – especially as it was traders from the new United States who most took advantage of the opportunities. Literary societies set up to discuss these books quickly became centres of political dissent.

The spark, though, was provided by the French invasion, as colonies throughout Latin America refused to recognise the Bonaparte regime (and the campaigns of Bolivar and others in South America began). In Mexico, the Gachupine rulers proclaimed their loyalty to Ferdinand VII (the deposed king) and hoped to carry on much as before, but Creole discontent was not to be so easily assuaged. The literary societies continued to meet, and from one, in Querétaro, emerged the first leaders of the Independence movement: Father **Miguel Hidalgo y Costilla**, a Creole priest, and **Ignacio Allende**, a disaffected junior army officer. When their plans for a coup were discovered, the conspirators were forced into premature action, with Hidalgo issuing the famous *Grito* (cry) from the steps of his parish church in Dolores on the 16th of September 1810 – *Mexicanos, viva Mexico!* The mob of Indians and mestizos who gathered behind the banner swiftly took the major towns of San Miguel, Guanajuato and others to the north of the capital, but their behaviour – seizing land and property, slaughtering the Spanish – horrified the Creoles who had initially supported the movement. In Spring 1811, Hidalgo's army, huge but undisciplined, moved on the capital, but at the crucial moment Hidalgo threw away a clear chance to overpower the Royalist army. Instead he chose to retreat, and his forces broke up as quickly as they had been assembled. Within months, Hidalgo, Allende and the other ringleaders had been captured and executed.

By this time most Creoles, horrified, had rejoined the ranks of the Royalists. But Indians and mestizos remained in a state of revolt, with a new leader in the mestizo priest **Jose Maria Morelos**. Morelos was not only a far better tactician than Hidalgo – instituting a highly successful series of guerrilla campaigns – he was also a genuine radical. By 1813 he controlled virtually the entire country, with the exception of the capital and the route from there to Veracruz, and at the **Congress of Chilpancingo** he declared the abolition of slavery and the equality of the races. But the royalists fought back with a series of crushing victories, Morelos was executed in 1815 and his forces, under the leadership of Vicente Guerrero, reduced to carrying out the occasional minor raid.

Ironically, it was the introduction of liberal reforms in Spain, of just the type feared by the Mexican ruling classes, which finally brought about Mexican Independence. Worried that such reforms might spread across the Atlantic, many Creoles once again switched their positions. In 1820 **Augustin de Iturbide**, a royalist general but himself a mestizo, threw in his lot with Guerrero: in 1821 he proposed the Iguala Plan to the Spanish authorities, who were hardly in a position to fight, and Mexico was independent. With **Independence**, though, came none of the changes which had been fought over so long – the church retained its power, and one set of rulers had simply been changed for another, native, set of rulers.

Foreign intervention

In 1822 Iturbide had himself proclaimed emperor; a year later he was forced to abdicate, a year after that he was executed. It was the first of many such events in a century which must rank among the most confused – and disastrous – in any nation's history. Not only had independence brought no real social change, it had left the new nation with virtually no chance of successful government: the power of the church and of the army were far greater than that of the supposed rulers, there was no basis on which to create a viable internal economy, and if the state hadn't already been bankrupted by the Independence Wars, it was to be cleaned out time and again by the demands of war and internal disruption. There were no less than fifty-six governments in the next forty years. In what approaches farce, the name of General **Santa Ana** stands out as the most bizarre figure of all, becoming president or dictator on eleven separate occasions and masterminding the loss of more than half Mexico's territory.

His first spell in office followed

immediately on Iturbide – Santa Ana declared Mexico a Republic (although he himself always expected to be treated as a king, and addressed as His Most Serene Majesty) and called a constitutional convention. Under the auspices of the new constitution, the Republic was confirmed, the country divided into thirteen states, and **Guadalupe Victoria**, a former guerrilla general, elected its first president. He lasted three years, something of a record. In 1829 the Spanish attempted a rather half-hearted invasion, easily defeated, after which they accepted the fact of Mexican Independence. In 1833 Santa Ana was elected president (officially) for the first time, the fifth thus far.

In 1836 a rather more serious chain of events was set in motion when **Texas**, Mexican territory but largely inhabited by migrants from the USA, declared its independence. Santa Ana commanded a punitive expedition which besieged **the Alamo** in the famous incident in which Jim Bowie and Davy Crockett, along with 150 other defenders, lost their lives. Santa Ana himself, though, was promptly defeated and captured at the battle of San Jacinto, and rather than face execution he signed a paper accepting **Texan Independence**. Although the authorities in Mexico City refused to accept the legality of its claim, Texas was, de facto, independent. Meanwhile, in 1838, the French chose to invade Veracruz demanding compensation for alleged damages to French property and citizens – a small **war** which lasted about four months, and during which Santa Ana lost a leg.

In 1845 the United States annexed Texas, and although the Mexicans at first hoped to negotiate a settlement, the redefinition of Texas as including most of Arizona, New Mexico and California made yet another war almost inevitable. In 1846 clashes between Mexican troops and US cavalry in these disputed western zones led to the declaration of the **Mexican-American War**. Following defeat for the Mexicans at Palo Alto and Resaca, three small US armies invaded from the north. At the same time General Winfield Scott took Veracruz after a long bombardment, and commenced his march on the capital. Santa Ana was roundly defeated on a number of occasions, and in September 1847, after heroic resistance by the *Niños Heroes*

(cadets at the military academy) Mexico City was captured. In 1848, by the **Treaty of Guadalupe Victoria**, the US paid $15 million for most of Texas, New Mexico, Arizona and California, along with parts of Colorado and Utah: in 1854 the present borders were established when Santa Ana sold a further strip down to the Rio Grande for $10 million.

Reform

Mexico finally saw the back of Santa Ana when, in 1855, he left for exile in Venezuela. But its troubles were by no means at an end. A new generation had grown up who had known only an independent Mexico in permanent turmoil, who had lived through the American humiliation, and who espoused once more the liberal ideals of Morelos. Above all they saw their enemy as the church; vast, self-serving, and far wealthier than any legitimate government, it had further sullied its reputation by refusing to provide funds for the American war. It was an extraordinarily reactionary institution, its position enshrined in the Constitution, bleeding the peasantry for the most basic of sacraments (few could afford official marriage, or burial) and failing to provide the few services it was charged with. All education was in church schools, which for 95 per cent of the population meant no education.

Benito Juarez, a Zapotec Indian who had been adopted and educated by a priest, and later trained as a lawyer, became the leader of this liberal movement through several years of civil war in which each side became more bitterly entrenched in increasingly extreme positions. When the liberals first came to power following Santa Ana's exile they began a relatively mild attempt at reform – permitting secular education, liberating the press, attempting to distance the church from government and instituting a new democratic Constitution. The church responded by obstruction and by threatening to excommunicate anyone cooperating with the government. In 1858 there was a conservative coup, and for the next three years **internal strife** on an unprecedented scale: with each new battle the liberals proclaimed more drastic reforms, churches were sacked and priests shot; while the conservatives responded by executing anyone suspected of liberal tendencies.

In 1861 Juarez emerged, at least temporarily, triumphant. Church property was confiscated, monasteries closed, weddings and burials became civil affairs, and set fees were established for the services of a priest. It wasn't until 1867 that most of these **Reform Laws** were to be fully enacted – for the conservatives had one more card to play – but most are still in force today: priests in Mexico, for example, are forbidden to wear their robes in public.

The conservatives' final chance was to appeal for outside help. At the end of the civil war, with the government bankrupt, Juarez had suspended payment of all foreign debts, and in 1861 a joint British, Spanish and French expedition occupied Veracruz to demand compensation. It rapidly became clear, however, that the French were after more than mere financial recompense. Britain and Spain withdrew their forces, and Napoleon III ordered his troops to advance on Mexico City. The aim, with the support of Mexican conservatives, was to place **Maximilian**, a Habsburg archduke, on the throne as emperor.

Despite a major defeat at Puebla on May 5th 1862 (now a national holiday), the French sent for reinforcements and occupied Mexico City in 1863. The new emperor arrived the following year. In many ways, Maximilian cuts a pathetic figure. He arrived in Mexico with no knowledge of its internal feuds (having gleaned most of his information from a book on court etiquette), expecting a triumphal welcome. Proving to be a liberal at heart – he refused to repeal any of Juarez's reforms – he promptly lost the support of even the small group which had initially welcomed him. While no-one doubts his good intentions, few believe that he would have been capable of putting them into practice even in the best of circumstances. And these were hardly ideal times. With Union victory in the US civil war, the authorities there threw their weight behind Juarez, providing him with arms and threatening to invade unless the French withdrew (on the basis of the Monroe doctrine, America for the Americans). Napoleon, already worried by the growing power of Bismarck's Prussia back home, had little choice but to comply. After 1866, Maximilian's position was hopeless.

His wife, the **Empress Carlota**, sailed to Europe in a vain attempt to win fresh support, but Napoleon had taken his decision, the Vatican refused to contemplate helping a man who had continued to attack the church, and the constant disappointments eventually drove Carlota mad. She died, insane, in Belgium in 1927. Maximilian, meanwhile, was at least salvaging his pride. He stayed at the head of his hopelessly outnumbered troops to the end – May 15th 1867 – when he was defeated and captured at Querétaro. A month later, he faced the firing squad.

Juarez re-assumed power, managing this time to ride the worst of the inevitable bankruptcy. The first steps towards economic reconstruction were taken, with the completion of a railway from Veracruz to the capital, encouragement of industry, and the development of a public education programme. Juarez died in office in 1872, having been re-elected in 1871, and was succeeded by his vice-president Lerdo de Tejada, who continued on the same road, though with few new ideas.

Dictatorship

Tejada was neither particularly popular nor spectacularly successful, but he did see out his term of office. However, there had been several Indian revolts and plots against him, the most serious of them led by a new radical liberal leader, **Porfirio Díaz**. Diaz had been a notably able military leader under Juarez, and in 1876, despite the re-election of Tejada, he proclaimed his own candidate president. The following year he assumed the presidency himself, and was to rule as dictator for the next thirty-four years. At first his platform was a radical one – including full implementation of the Reform Laws and no re-election to any political office – but it was soon dropped in favour of a brutal policy of modernisation. Diaz did actually stand down at the end of his first term, in 1880, but he continued to rule through a puppet president and in 1884 resumed the presidency for an unbroken stretch until 1911.

In many ways the **achievements** of his dictatorship were remarkable: some 10,000 miles of railway were built, industry boomed, telephones and telegraph were installed, and major towns, reached at last by reasonable roads, entered the modern era. In the country, Diaz established a police force – the notorious *rurales* – which finally stamped out banditry. Almost every city in Mexico seems to have a grandiose theatre and elegant public buildings from this era. But the costs were high: rapid development was achieved basically by handing over the country and its people to **foreign investors**, who owned the vast majority of the oil, mining rights, railways and natural resources. At the same time there was a massive policy of land expropriation: formerly communal village holdings being handed over to foreign exploitation or simply grabbed by corrupt officials.

Agriculture, meanwhile, was ignored entirely. The owners of vast haciendas could make more than enough money by relying on the forced labour of a landless peasantry, and had no interest in efficiency or production for domestic consumption. By 1900 the whole of Mexico was owned by some 3–4 per cent of its population. Without land of their own, peasants had no choice but to work on the haciendas or in the forests, where their serfdom was ensured by wages so low that they were permanently in debt to their employers. The rich became very rich indeed, the poor had lower incomes and fewer prospects than they had a century earlier. Once the *rurales* had done their job of making the roads safe to travel, they became a further burden – charging for the right to travel along roads they controlled and acting as a private police force for employers should any of their workers try to escape. In short, slavery had been re-introduced in all but name, and up to a quarter of the nation's resources came to be spent on internal security. The press was censored, too, education strictly controlled, and corruption rife.

Revolution

With the onset of the **twentieth century**, Diaz was already old and beginning to lose his grip on reality. He had every intention of continuing in power until he dropped. But a real middle-class opposition was beginning to develop, concerned above all by the racist policies of their government (which favoured foreign investors above native ones) and by the lack of opportunity for themselves – the young educated classes. Their movement revived the old slogan of '*no reeleccion*', and in 1910 **Francisco Madero** stood against Diaz in the presidential election. The old dictator responded by imprisoning his opponent and declaring himself victor at the polls by a vast majority. Madero, however, escaped to Texas where he proclaimed himself president, and called on the nation to rise in his support.

This was an entirely opportunist move, for at the time there were no revolutionary forces, but several small bands immediately took up arms. Most important were those in the northern state of Chihuahua, where **Pancho Villa** and **Pascual Orozco** won several minor battles, and in the south-west, where **Emiliano Zapata** began to arm Indian guerrilla forces. In May 1911 Orozco captured the major border town of Ciudad Juarez, and his success was rapidly followed by a string of revolutionary victories. By the end of the month, hoping to preserve the system if not his role in it, Porfirio Diaz had fled into exile. On October 2nd 1911, Madero was elected president.

Like the originators of Independence before him, Madero had no conception of the forces he had unleashed. He freed the press, encouraged the formation of unions and introduced genuine democracy, but failed to do anything about the condition of the peasantry or land redistribution. Zapata prepared to rise again. **Zapata** was perhaps the one true revolutionary in the whole long conflict to follow, and his battle cry of *Tierra y Libertad* (Land and Liberty) and insistence that 'it is better to die on your feet than live on your knees' make him still a revered figure among the peasants. By contrast, the rest were mostly out for personal gain: **Pancho Villa**, a cattle rustler and bandit in the time of Diaz, was by far the most successful of the more orthodox generals, brilliantly inventive, and ruthless in victory. But his motivation, though he came from peasant stock, seems to have been personal glory – he appeared to love fighting, and at one stage, when a Hollywood film crew was travelling with his armies, would allegedly arrange his battles so as to ensure the best lighting conditions and most impressive fight scenes.

In any case Madero was faced by a more immediately dangerous enemy than his own supporters – **US Business Interests**. Henry Lane Wilson, US ambassador, began openly plotting with **Victoriano Huerta**, a government general, and Felix Diaz, a nephew of the dictator who was held in prison. Fighting broke out between supporters of Diaz and those of Madero, while Huerta refused to commit his troops to either side. When he did, in 1913, it was to proclaim himself president. Madero was shot in suspicious circumstances (which few doubt were sanctioned by Huerta) and opponents on the right, including Diaz, either imprisoned or exiled. The new government was promptly recognised by the States and most other foreign powers, but not by the important forces within the country.

Villa and Zapata immediately took up arms, and in the north Villa was joined by **Alvaro Obregon**, governor of Sonora, and **Venustiano Carranza**, governor of Coahuila. Carranza was appointed head of the Constitutionalist forces, though he was always to be deeply suspicious of Villa, despite Villa's constant protestations of loyalty. At first the revolutionaries made little headway – Carranza couldn't even control his own state, although Obregon and Villa did enjoy some successes raiding south from Chihuahua and Sonora. But almost immediately the new US president, Woodrow Wilson, withdrew his support from Huerta and, infuriated by his refusal to resign, began actively supplying arms to the Revolution. In 1914, the **Constitutionalists** began to move south, and in April of that year US troops occupied Veracruz in their support (though neither side was exactly happy about the foreign presence). Huerta, now cut off from almost every source of money or supplies, fled the country in July, and in August Obregon occupied the capital, proclaiming Carranza president.

Renewed fighting broke out straight away, this time between Carranza and Obregon, the Constitutionalists on one side, and the rest of the revolutionary leaders on the other, so-called **Conventionalists** whose sole point of agreement was that Carranza should not lead them. The three years of fighting which

followed were the most bitter and chaotic yet, with petty chiefs in every part of the country proclaiming provisional governments, joining each other in factions and then splitting again, and the entire country in a state of anarchy. Each army issued its own money, and each press-ganged any able-bodied men they came across into joining. By 1920 it was reckoned that about one eighth of the population had been killed. Gradually, however, Obregon and Carranza gained ground – Obregon defeated Villa several times in 1915, and Villa withdrew to carry out border raids into the United States, hoping to provoke an invasion (which he nearly did; US troops pursued him across the border but were never able to catch up, and following defeat in a skirmish with Carranza's troops they withdrew). Zapata, meanwhile, had some conspicuous successes – and occupied Mexico City for much of 1915 – but his irregular troops tended to disappear back to their villages after each victory. In 1919 he was tricked into a meeting with one of Carranza's generals and shot in cold blood; Villa retired to a hacienda in his home state, and was assassinated in 1923.

Meanwhile Carranza continued to claim the presidency, and in 1917 set up a **Constitutional congress** to ratify his position. The document they produced – the present constitution – included most of the revolutionary demands, among them workers' rights, a mandatory 8-hour day, national ownership of all mineral rights, and the distribution of large landholdings and formerly communal properties to the peasantry. Carranza formally elected in May 1917 and proceeded to make no attempt to carry out any of its stipulations, certainly not with regard to land rights. In 1920 Carranza was forced to step down by Obregon, and was shot while attempting to escape the country with most of the contents of the treasury.

Obregon, at least, was well intentioned – but his efforts at real land reform were again stymied by fear of US reaction: in return for American support, he agreed not to expropriate land. In 1924 **Plutarco Elias Calles** succeeded him, and real progress towards the ideals of the Revolutionary Constitution began to be made. Work on large public works schemes began – roads, irrigation systems, village schools – and about 8 million acres of land were given back to the villages as communal holdings. At the same time Calles instituted a policy of virulent anti-clericalism, closing churches and monasteries, forcing priests to flee the country or go underground. It provoked the last throes of a backlash, as the Catholic **Cristero movement** took up arms in defence of the church. From 1927 until about 1935 isolated incidents of vicious banditry and occasional full-scale warfare continued, eventually burning themselves out as the stability of the new regime became obvious, and religious controls were relaxed. In 1928 Obregon was re-elected, but assassinated three weeks later in protest at this breach of the '*no re-eleccion*' clause of the Constitution. He was succeeded by Portes Gil and then Ortiz Rubio, both of whom followed the hard line established by Calles.

Modern Mexico

By 1934 Mexico enjoyed a degree of peace, and a remarkable change had been wrought. A new culture had emerged – seen nowhere more clearly than in the great murals of Rivera and Orozco which began to adorn public buildings throughout the country – in which native heroes like Hidalgo, Morelos, Juarez and Madero replaced European ideals. Nowadays everyone in the Republic would claim Indian blood – even if the Indians themselves remain the lowest stratum of society – and the invasion of Cortes is seen as the usurpation of the nation's march to its destiny, a march which resumed with Independence and the Revolution. At the same time there was a feeling in these early days that Calles was attempting to promote a dynasty of his own.

With the election of **Lazaro Cardenas** in 1934, such doubts were finally ended. As the spokesman of a younger generation, Cardenas expelled Calles and his supporters from the country, at the same time setting up the single broad-based party which still rules today as the **PRI** (Party of the Institutionalised Revolution). Cardenas set about an unprecedented programme of reform, redistributing land on a huge scale, and relaxing controls on the church to appease internal and international opposition. In 1938 he nationalised the oil companies, an act which has proved one of the most significant in shaping modern Mexico and bringing about its industrial miracle. For a time it seemed as if yet more foreign intervention might follow, but a boycott of Mexican oil by the major consumers crumbled with the onset of World War II, and was followed by a massive influx of money and huge boost for Mexican industry as a result of the war. By the time he stood down in 1940, Cardenas could claim to be the first president in modern Mexican history to have served his full six-year term in peace, and handed over to his successor without trouble.

Through the war **industrial growth** continued apace under Avila Camacho, and Mexico officially joined the Allies in 1942. Miguel Aleman (1946–52) presided over still faster development, and a further massive dose of public works and land reform – major prestige projects, like the University City in the capital, were planned by his regime. Since then massive oil incomes have continued to stimulate industry, and the PRI have managed to maintain a masterly control of all aspects of public life without apparently losing the support of a great majority of the Mexican public. Of course it is an accepted fact of life that governments will line their own pockets first – a practice which, if current reports are to be believed, reached its height under the last president, **Lopez Portillo** – but the unrelenting populism of the PRI, its massive powers of patronage, and above all its highly visible and undoubted achievement of progress, seem set to preserve it in power for a good while yet.

Which is not to say that real **problems** don't persist. Internal dissent became most dramatically visible in 1968, when massive student demonstrations, highlighted by the Mexican Olympics, culminated in hundreds of deaths as troops and tanks opened fire on the crowds. At present the unrest is less visible, but it is perhaps even more widespread – the government of **Miguel de la Madrid** tacitly acknowledges that it is involved in a race between economic recovery and the open outbreak of social disorder. Above all, the international economic crisis, and Mexico's foreign debt (of almost $100 billion), exacerbated by falling oil revenues, have forced severe austerity measures. Such policies have won widespread acclaim from international bankers (Jesus Silva Herzog was voted 'finance minister of the year' after his first year in office), but at home have produced drastically reduced standards of living and a huge degree of unemployment. An exploding population only adds to the problems, and even the huge scale of illegal emigration to the US can have little impact on it. The business community has suffered too – outraged by the nationalisation of the banks in 1982, they have been further hit by a series of bankruptcies and devaluation which has made imported materials impossible to afford. Unless economic recovery can take off, there seems a danger that some of the vast panoply of interests covered by the PRI – from the all-powerful unions to the top businessmen – will begin to split off.

Already the opposition **PAN** has won a string of victories in the north, while in the south a socialist/peasant alliance held power in Juchitan (Oaxaca) before being ousted with traditional (but nowadays rare) strong-arm tactics. These two also highlight a further danger – the increasing polarisation of the country. In the north, life is heavily influenced by the USA and right-wing business interests hold sway. In the south, where peasants continue to press for more land redistribution, opposition is far more radical and left-wing: alternately inspired and intimidated by events in Central America. It seems unlikely that any serious threat to the PRI will emerge, or that Mexico will lose its new reputation as the most stable nation in Latin America, but if dissent does increase it seems quite possible that the PRI will revert from its current modernistic, technocratic image, to a more authoritarian role.

MONUMENTAL CHRONOLOGY

20,000BC	First waves of stone-age migrants from the north.	Earliest evidence of man in the central valleys.
C6–C2BC	Archaic period	First evidence of settlement – cultivation, pottery and tools in the Valley of Mexico.
1500BC–300AD	Pre-Classic period. Rise and dominance of the **Olmecs.**	The first simple pyramids and magnificent statuary at their Gulf Coast sites – San Lorenzo, La Venta and Tres Zapotes. Olmec influence on art and architecture everywhere, especially Monte Alban.
		Early evidence of new cultures in the Valley of Mexico – Cuicuilco (buried by volcano) and Teotihuacan.
300–900AD	Classic period. **Teotihuacan** dominates Central Mexico, with evidence of its influence as far south as Kaminaljuyu in Guatemala.	Massive pyramids at Teotihuacan, decorated with stucco reliefs and murals. Monte Alban continues to thrive, while El Tajin on the Gulf Coast shows a new style in its Pyramid of the Niches.
	Mayan cities flourish in the highlands of Guatemala and Honduras, as well as Mexican Yucatan.	All the great sites – Uxmal, Palenque, Chichen Itza, Edzna, Kabah – at their peak. *Puuc*, *Chenes* and *Rio Bec* styles are perhaps the finest pre-hispanic architecture.
900–1500AD	Post-Classic. In Central Mexico, a series of invasions by warlike tribes from the north.	**Toltecs** make their capital at Tula (c.900–1150), new use of columns and roofed space – chac-mools and atlantean columns in decoration.
987	Toltec invasion of the Yucatan?	New Toltec-Mayan synthesis especially evident at Chichen Itza.
C10	**Mixtecs** gain control of Oaxaca area.	Mixtec tombs at Monte Alban, but seen above all at Mitla.
C11	League of Mayapan.	Mayan architecture in decline, as Mayapan itself clearly demonstrates.
C13	Arrival of the Mexica in Central Mexico, last of the major 'barbarian' invasions.	Many rival cities in the Valley of Mexico, including Tenayuca, Texcoco and Culhuacan.

1345	Foundation of Tenochtitlan – rapid expansion of the **Aztec Empire**.	Growth of all the great Aztec cities, especially Tenochtitlan itself. In the east cities such as Cholula and Zempoala fall under Aztec influence, and in the south the Mixtecs are conquered. To the west, Tarascan culture developing, with their capital at Tzintzuntzan. Mayan culture survives at cities such as Tulum.
1519	Cortes lands.	
1521	Tenochtitlan falls to Spanish.	Spanish destroy many ancient cities. Early colonial architecture is defensive and fortress-like; churches and mansions in Mexico City and elsewhere, monasteries with huge atriums for mass conversions. Gradually replaced by more elaborate renaissance and plateresque styles – seen above all in churches in the colonial cities north of the capital.
1524	First Franciscan monks arrive.	
1598	Conquest officially complete.	
C17–C18	Colonial rulers grow in wealth and confidence.	Baroque begins to take over religious building – great cathedrals at Mexico City and Puebla, lesser ones like Zacatecas. Towards the end the still more extravagant Churrigueresque comes in: magnificent churches around Puebla, and at Taxco and Tepotzotlan.
1810	Hidalgo proclaims Independence.	The development of the neoclassical style through the influence of the new San Carlos art academy, but little building in the next fifty chaotic years.
1821	Independence achieved.	
1836	Texas declares independence – battles of the Alamo and San Jacinto.	
1838	Brief French invasion.	
1845	Texas joins USA – Mexican-American War.	
1847	US troops occupy Mexico City.	
1848	Half of Mexican territory conceded to US by treaty.	

1858–61	Reform Wars between liberals under Benito Juarez and church-backed conservatives.	Many churches damaged or despoiled.
1861	Juarez triumphant; suspends payment of foreign debt. France, Spain and Britain send naval expedition.	
1862	Spain and Britain withdraw – invading French army defeated May 5th.	
1863	French take Mexico City. Maximilian becomes emperor.	Brief vogue for French styles Paseo de la Reforma and Chapultepec Castle in the capital.
1866	French troops withdrawn.	
1867	Juarez defeats Maximilian.	
1876	Porfirio Diaz accedes to power.	The Porfiriano sees a new outbreak of neo-classical and grandiose public building. Palacio de las Bellas Artes and Post Office in Mexico City.
1910	Madero stands for election – revolution starts.	Another period of destruction rather than building.
1911	Diaz flees into exile.	
1911–17	Vicious revolutionary infighting continues.	
1920 on	Modern Mexico.	Modern architecture in Mexico is among the world's most original and adventurous, combining traditional themes with modern techniques. Vast decorative murals are one of its constant themes. The National Archaeology Museum and University City in the capital are among its most notable achievements.

BOOKS

Mexico seems to have attracted more than its fair share of famous writers, and has inspired a vast literature and several classics. Most big American bookshops will have a vast array of books about, from or set in Mexico. Some of the best and most widely available are listed below.

Travel

Sybille Bedford *A Visit to Don Otavio* (Eland £3.95). An extremely enjoyable, often hilarious, occasionally lyrical and surprisingly relevant account of Ms Bedford's travels through Mexico in the early 1950s.

John Lincoln *One Man's Mexico* (Century £4.95). Lincoln's travels are about ten years more recent, and very different – travelling alone, often into the jungle, always away from tourists.

Paul Theroux *The Old Patagonian Express* (Penguin £2.50). The epic journey from Boston to Patagonia by train spends just three rather bad-tempered chapters in Mexico, so don't expect to find out too much about the country. A good read nonetheless.

Graham Greene *The Lawless Roads* (Penguin £1.95). In the late 1930s Greene was sent to Mexico to investigate the effects of the persecution of the Catholic church. The result (see also his novel below) was this account of his travels in a very bizarre era of modern Mexican history.

Charles Macomb Flandrau *Viva Mexico!* (Eland £3.95). First published in 1908, Flandrau's account of life on his brother's coffee farm is something of a cult classic. Dated in places, it's extremely funny in others.

D. H. Lawrence *Mornings in Mexico* (Penguin £1.95). A very slim volume, half of which is devoted to the Hopi Indians of New Mexico, this is an uncharacteristically cheerful account of Lawrence's stay in southern Mexico, and beautifully written.

Aldous Huxley *Beyond the Mexique Bay* (Penguin o/p). Again, only a small part of the book is devoted to Mexico, but the descriptions of the archaeological sites around Oaxaca, particularly, are still worth reading.

Frances Calderon de la Barca *Life in Mexico* (1840). Still available in libraries, this is the diary of a Scotswoman who married the Spanish ambassador to Mexico and spent two years observing life there.

Fiction

Malcolm Lowry *Under the Volcano* (Penguin £1.95). A classic since its publication and recently appallingly filmed, Lowry's account of the last day in the life of the British Consul in Cuernavaca – passed in a Mescal-induced haze – is totally brilliant.

B. Traven Traven's true identity is still unknown but he wrote a whole series of compelling novels set in Mexico. Among the best known are *Treasure of the Sierra Madre* and *The Death Ship*, but of more direct interest if you're travelling are such works as *The Bridge in the Jungle* and the six books of the Jungle series: *Government, The Carreta, March to the Monteria, Trozas, The Rebellion of the Hanged* and *General from the Jungle* (Allison & Busby). These latter all deal with the state of the peasantry and the growth of revolutionary feeling in the last years of the Diaz dictatorship, and if at times they're over polemical, as a whole they're enthralling.

Jorge Ibargüengoitia *The Dead Girls* (Chatto £3.50) and *Two Crimes* (Chatto £3.95). One of the few modern Mexican novelists translated into English, Ibargüengoitia was killed in a plane crash in 1983. These two are both blackly comic thrillers, superbly told, the first of them based on real events.

Carlos Fuentes *The Death of Artemio Cruz* (Penguin £1.75). Fuentes has a far more established reputation and this novel shows why – in many ways predating the complex layered style of Garcia Marques. Some of his other works, though, are plain obscure: they include *Distant Relations* (Abacus £2.95), *A Change of Skin*, and *Terra Nostra*.

Haniel Long *The Marvellous Adventure of Cabeza de Vaca* (Picador). Two short stories in one volume – the first the account of a shipwrecked conquistador's journey across the new continent, the second the thoughts and hopes of Malinche, Cortes's interpreter.

Graham Greene *The Power and the Glory* (Penguin £1.95). Inspired by his investigative travels, this story of a doomed whisky priest on the run from the authorities makes a great yarn. It was a wonderful film too.

D. H. Lawrence *The Plumed Serpent* (Penguin £1.75). One of Lawrence's own favourites, the novel reflects the intense dislike of the country which followed on the brief honeymoon period of *Mornings in Mexico*. Fans of his heavy spiritualism will love it.

Other authors whose books are at least partly set in Mexico include a whole clutch of modern Americans, including **Jack Kerouac's** *Desolation Angels* and several of **Richard Brautigan's** novels. And of course there's **Carlos Castaneda's** *Don Juan* trilogy – a search for enlightenment through peyote.

Poetry

An anthology of modern Mexican poets in translation, edited by **Octavio Paz** (perhaps the leading man of letters of the post-revolutionary era) is published as *New Poetry of Mexico* (Secker & Warburg).

History

Bernal Diaz *Historia Verdadera de la Conquista de la Nueva España*. Diaz, having already been on two earlier expeditions to Mexico, accompanied Cortes throughout his campaign of conquest, and this magnificent eyewitness account still makes compulsive reading. The best available translation is the heavily abridged version by J. M. Cohen (Penguin Classic £2.25).

William Prescott *History of the Conquest of Mexico*. Written in the mid-nineteenth century, and drawing heavily on Diaz, Prescott's history is still the standard text, although it makes for pretty heavy reading.

John Reed *Insurgent Mexico* (New World 2.75). This collection of his reportage of the Mexican Revolution was put together originally by Reed himself. He spent several months in 1913 and 1914 with various generals of the Revolution – especially Villa – and the book contains great descriptions of them, their men, and the mood of the times. It's far more anecdotal and easy to read than the celebrated *Ten Days that Shook the World*.

James D. Cockcroft *Mexico – Class Formation, Capital Accumulation and the State* (Monthly Review Press $12.50/£7.60). The most up to date and compre-

hensive history of Mexico, with a wealth of minute detail and consistent Marxist analysis.

Adolfo Gilly *The Mexican Revolution* (Verso £6.95/$11.50). Written in Mexico City's notorious Lecumberri jail (Gilly was later granted an absolute pardon), this is regarded as the classic work on the Revolution. Again, heavy-going and highly theoretical.

More **general histories** include Henry Bamford Parkes's *History of Mexico* (Eyre & Spottiswoode 1960); *The Course of Mexican History* by Michael Meyer and William Sherman (OUP 1979), and Atkins's *Revolution Mexico* (Panther).

Archaeology and architecture

Nigel Davies *The Ancient Kingdoms of Mexico* (Penguin £2.95). Although there's no single text which covers all the ancient cultures, this comes pretty close, covering the central areas from the Olmecs through Teotihuacan and the Toltecs to the Aztec Empire. An excellent mix of historical, archaeological, social and artistic information, but it doesn't cover the Maya. Davies is also the author of several more detailed academic works on the Aztecs and Toltecs.

Michael Coe *The Maya* (Penguin £2.95). This, or the Gallenkamp book below, is the ideal companion to fill the gaps: Michael Coe's is the more academic of them although still very readable. Coe, too, has written a whole series of weightier tomes.

Charles Gallenkamp *Maya* (Penguin £2.50). Gallenkamp's version takes a historical view of the development of Mayanism, from the earliest discoveries to recent rethinking of many theories. Anecdotal and easy to read.

John L. Stephens *Incidents of Travel in Central America, Chiapas and the Yucatan* (Dover, 2 vols). Stephens was the man who really 'discovered' the Maya in the early nineteenth century. His reprinted journals are as much travel book as archaeological source, but despite being rather turgid in places they're full of fascinating moments as he uncovers lost cities.

Ignacio Bernal *Mexico Before Cortes* (Doubleday $3.95). The leading Mexican archaeologist of the century, and one of the inspirations behind the National Museum of Anthropology, Bernal did important work on the Olmecs and on the restoration of Teotihuacan, and has written many important source works. This book covers much the same ground as Davies's, though in less detail and more dated, but it has the advantage of being widely available in Mexico.

There are, of course, hundreds of **other studies** of ancient Mexico. Names to look out for include **Eric S. Thompson**, an authority on the Maya (especially *The Rise and Fall of Maya Civilisation*, University of Oklahoma Press), Jacques Soustelle, Eric Wolf, Ralph Roys, E. Wyllys Andrews, and Richard Diehl. Coffee table picture books include *The Aztecs* (Cottie Burland and Werner Forman; Orbis £12.50) with good photography but poor text. *Ancient Mexican Architecture* and *Mayan Architecture* (Macdonald, living architecture series) both have detailed technicalities on **architecture** and superb black-and-white photos. **George Kubler's** *Art and Architecture of Ancient America* (Pelican £17.50) is a massive work and amazingly comprehensive, covering not only Mexico but Colombia, Ecuador and Peru as well. Architecture since the Conquest is less well documented, but **Sacheverell Sitwell's** *Southern Baroque Revisited* (Weidenfeld & Nicholson 1967) does have a chapter on the development of baroque in Mexico

Society and politics

Oscar Lewis *The Children of Sanchez* (Penguin £4.95). These oral histories of a working-class family in the Mexico City of the 1940s are regarded as a seminal work in modern anthropology. The book doesn't read as an anthropological text, though but as the most gripping of novels. Lewis's other works, including *Pedro Martinez* (Penguin £2.95), *A Death in the Sanchez Family* (Penguin £1.50) and *Five Families*, use the same first person narrative technique.

Gregory G. Reck *In the Shadow of Tlaloc* (Penguin 1978). Reck attempts a similar style in his study of a Mexican village, and the effects on it of encroaching modernity. Often seems to stray over the border into fiction, but interesting nonetheless.

Octavio Paz *The Labyrinth of Solitude* (Grove Press 1961). A series of philosophical essays exploring the social and political state of modern Mexico.

Miguel Covarrubias *Mexico South* (KPI £7.95) Superb book on the people and culture written by the well known Mexican artist and anthropologist.

Specific guides

Hilary Bradt and Rob Rachowiecki *Backpacking in Mexico and Central America* (Bradt Enterprises, 41 Nortoft Rd, Chalfont St Peter, Bucks. £5.95; or 95 Harvey St, Cambridge, Mass.). Only a couple of the major hikes described are actually in Mexico, but the general information is nonetheless extremely useful if you plan to do any serious hiking.

R. J. Secor *Mexico's Volcanoes* (The Mountaineers, 715 Pike St, Seattle WA 98101 £5.95). Detailed routes up all the big volcanoes, and full of invaluable information for climbers.

Carl Franz *People's Guide to Mexico* (John Muir £7.95). Not a guidebook as such, more a series of anecdotes and words of advice for staying out of trouble and heading off the beaten track. Perennially popular, but more entertaining than practical.

In Mexico itself, the best and most complete series of guides is that published by *Guias Panorama* – they have small books on all the main archaeological sites, as well as more general titles ranging from *Wild Flowers of Mexico* to *Pancho Villa – Truth and Legend*.

ONWARDS FROM MEXICO

For European travellers, heading north to **the USA** is the easiest onward move. So long as you have a valid visa, crossing the border is no problem at all, and I'm not going to attempt here to describe the multi-various attractions of the States. Do, however, get your visa before you leave home – queues at the US embassy in Mexico City are often several days long, and although non-Mexicans can usually circumvent them the immigration officials are likely to be even less helpful than those elsewhere. If you're arriving in the States, travelling into Mexico and then going back, you'll need a visa which is good for multiple entry.

Continuing south to Central America,

too, remains easy enough, but the explosive political situation makes it a less attractive proposition than it was a few years ago. **GUATEMALA** is still the most stunningly beautiful country in the entire continent: physically similar to Mexico's Chiapas but even greener, more mountainous and with yet more lakes. But I wouldn't choose to go there now: politically, it's more akin to pre-Revolution Mexico, with vast wealth and landholdings concentrated in a few hands, backed up by the muscle of the army. Most of the native population, of direct Mayan descent (Guatemala has a higher proportion of Indians than any other American nation), live in poverty, a condition made worse by the persistent army campaigns against the 'subversive' elements in their midst. If you do go, the main routes from Mexico are the rather dull coastal route from Tapachula, or the Pan-American Highway down from San Cristobal. The latter is by far the more attractive, from which you can visit the Indian towns of Huehuetenango and Quetzaltenango, the obscenely picturesque Lake Atitlan and, on the way to the capital, Chichicastenango. You can also get to Guatemala via Belize. To get into the country, virtually everyone except US citizens needs a visa, obtainable from Guatemalan Consulates anywhere. You'll find one in Mexico City, or with rather more delay visas can be obtained at Comitan or Tapachula.

BELIZE is the third country to share a land border with Mexico, and crossing from Chetumal is a simple enough operation – British, American and Commonwealth citizens need no visa. Only recently independent from Britain, Belize remains the most bizarre of nations. Extremely poor, it relies on a major British army presence to fend off Guatemalan claims to its territory. The feel is far more that of a Caribbean than a Latin country, with a substantially black, English-speaking population – even the major tourist attraction, the beautiful offshore islands (*Cays*), reinforce the impression. Apart from these, and the hopelessly, terminally run-down feel of the place, there's little to stay for. Crossing into Guatemala, however, you're very close to the fabulous Mayan site of Tikal, even more impressive than anything in Mexico. To get from there to Guatemala City, you'd be well advised

to fly, since the bus, which costs little less, has been known to take days. Occasionally there have been problems – especially for Britons – getting into Guatemala from Belize, but at present relations seem reasonably stable. In any event it's better to get your Guatemalan visa before arriving – there is a Guatemalan consul in Belize City, but delays tend to be long.

On from Guatemala, **EL SALVADOR** is riven by the activities of the death squads and guerrillas: it was never the most attractive place anyway, highly Americanised and industrialised. **HONDURAS** is at least relatively peaceful, despite an occasionally high-profile US military presence and training camps for El Salvadorean troops and the Nicaraguan *contras*. But there's not a great deal there, except for some virtually unknown, and quite undeveloped, Caribbean beaches, and the Mayan site of Copan, which is most easily visited from the Guatemalan town of Zacapa. Britons need no visa to visit Honduras; Americans, Australians and most other nationalities must have one. In **NICARAGUA**, of course, the problems are very different, but even here, although you can travel around in relative freedom, it's doubtful whether being a tourist is either particularly helpful or very rewarding. But you could always join the large band of *simpatico* foreigners who are lending their skills, or simply their physical presence, to the future of the country.

Continuing, **COSTA RICA** remains something of a haven – the army was abolished in 1948, and recent threats to revive it have not yet come to pass, the electoral system is at least nominally democratic, and if the country is poor, its wealth is relatively equitably distributed. After Guatemala, it was always the second most popular destination for Central American travellers. **PANAMA** is tiny, and dominated in every way by the Canal and the Canal Zone. Few people get this far, since there's no overland link across the Darien Gap into South America, and getting there this way requires a major and well-equipped expedition.

It is far easier, if **SOUTH AMERICA** is your goal, to fly. From Mexico there are regular connections to just about every major South American nation, and from most Central American capitals it's also easy enough to fly in – usually to Cartagena or Bogota in Colombia. *The South American Handbook* (Trade & Travel Publications £14.95) covers the whole of Central and South America, and even if its information isn't particularly easy to use, nor as comprehensive and up to date as it might at first appear, as a whole it remains unrivalled for sheer volume and number of places covered.

LANGUAGE

Once you get into it, Spanish is the easiest language there is – and in Mexico people are desperately eager to understand and to help even the most faltering attempt. English *is* widely spoken, especially in the tourist areas, but you'll get a far better reception if you at least try to communicate with people in their own tongue. You'll be further helped by the fact that Mexicans speak relatively slowly (at least compared with Spaniards in Spain) and that there's none of the difficult lisping pronunciation here.

The rules of **pronunciation** are pretty straightforward and, once you get to know them, strictly observed:

A somewhere between the A sound of back and that of father
E as in get
I as in police
O as in hot
U as in rule
C is soft before E and I, hard otherwise: *cerca* is pronounced serka.
G works the same way, a guttural H sound (like the *ch* in loch) before E or I, a hard G elsewhere – *gigante* becomes higante.
H is always silent
J has a guttural H sound similar to that of G: *jamon* is pronounced hamon.
LL sounds like an English Y: *tortilla* is pronounced torteeya.
N is as in English unless it has a tilde (accent) over it, when it becomes NY: *mañana* sounds like manyana.
QU is pronounced like an English K.
R is rolled, RR doubly so.
V sounds more like B, *vino* becoming beano.
X is slightly softer than in English – sometimes almost S – except between vowels in place names where it has an H sound – i.e. Mexico or Oaxaca.
Z is the same as a soft C, so *cerveza* becomes servesa.

Below is a list of a few essential words and phrases, though if you're travelling for any length of time some kind of dictionary or phrase-book is obviously a worthwhile investment – some specifically Latin-American ones are available (see below). If you're using a **dictionary**, bear in mind that in Spanish CH, LL and N count as separate letters and are listed after the Cs, Ls and Ns respectively.

Basics

Yes, No	Si, No	Open, Closed	Abierto/a, Cerrado/a
Please, Thank you	Por favor, Gracias	With, Without	Con, Sin
Where, When	Donde, Cuando	Good, Bad	Buen(o)/a, Mal(o)/a
What, How much	Que, Cuanto	Big, Small	Gran(de), Pequeño/a
Here, There	Aqui, Alli	More, Less	Mas, Menos
This, That	Esto, Eso	Today, Tomorrow	Hoy, Mañana
Now, Later	Ahora, Mas tarde	Yesterday	Ayer

Greetings and responses

Hello, Goodbye	Ola, Adios	See you later	Hasta luego
Good morning	Buenos dias	Sorry	Lo siento/
			disculpeme
Good afternoon/	Buenas tardes/	Excuse me	Con permiso/perdon
night	noches		

How are you?	Como esta (usted)?
Not at all/You're welcome	De nada
I (don't) understand	(No) Entiendo
Do you speak English?	Habla (usted) Ingles?
I (don't) speak Spanish	(No) Hablo Español
What (did you say)?	Mande?
My name is . . .	Me Llamo . . .
What's your name?	Como se llama usted?
I am English/American	Soy Ingles(a)/Americano(a).

Needs – Hotels and Transport

I want	Quiero	Do you know . . .?	Sabe . . .?
I'd like	Quisiera	I don't know	No se
There is (is there?)	Hay (?)	Give me . . .	Deme . . .
Do you have . . .?	Tiene . . .?	(one like that)	(uno asi)
. . . the time	. . . la hora		
. . . a room	. . . un cuarto		

. . . with two beds/double bed	. . . con dos camas/cama matrimonial
It's for one person (two people)	Es para una persona (dos personas)
. . . for one night (one week)	. . . para una noche (una semana)
It's fine, how much is it?	Esta bien, cuanto es?
It's too expensive	Es demasiado caro
Don't you have anything cheaper?	No tiene algo mas barato?
Can one . . .?	Se puede . . .?
. . . camp (near) here	. . . acampar aqui (cerca)
Is there a hotel nearby?	Hay un hotel aqui cerca?
How do I get to . . .	Por donde se va a . . .
Left, right, straight on	Izquierda, derecha, derecho
Where is . . .	Donde esta . . .?
. . . the bus station	. . . el central camionera
. . . the railway station	. . . el estacion de ferrocarriles
. . . the nearest bank	. . . el banco mas cercano
. . . the post office	. . . el correo (la oficina de correos)
. . . the toilet	. . . el baño/sanitario
Where does the bus to . . . leave from?	De donde sale el camion para . . .?
Is this the train for Merida?	Es este el tren para Merida?
I'd like a (return) ticket to . . .	Quisiera un boleto (de ida y vuelta) para . . .
What time does it leave (arrive in . . .)?	A que hora sale (llega en . . .)?
What is there to eat?	Que hay para comer?
What's that?	Que es eso?
What's this called in Spanish?	Como se llama esto en Español?

Numbers and days

1 un(o)/a	9 nueve	20 veinte	90 noventa
2 dos	10 diez	21 veintiuno	100 cien(to)
3 tres	11 once	30 treinta	101 ciento uno
4 cuatro	12 doce	40 cuarenta	200 doscientos
5 cinco	13 trece	50 cincuenta	500 quinientos
6 seis	14 catorce	60 sesenta	700 setecientos
7 siete	15 quince	70 setenta	1000 mil
8 ocho	16 diez y seis	80 ochenta	2000 dos mil

1985 mil novocientos ochenta y cinco
First – primero/a;   second – segundo/a;
third – tercero/a
Monday, lunes; Tuesday, martes; Wednesday, miercoles; Thursday, jueves; Friday, viernes; Saturday, sabado; Sunday, domingo.

Any good Spanish phrasebook or dictionary should see you through in Mexico; Spanish Travelmate *(Drew £1) is particularly easy to use. A specifically Latin-American one would be a help though: Berlitz and Pan both publish such a phrasebook, or try the* University of Chicago dictionary (Pocket, $1.95).

INDEX

Acapulco 241
Agua Prieta 39
Aguascalientes 85
Alamos 43
Alvarado 276

Barra de Navidad 253
Bonampak 307

Cabo San Lucas 36
Campeche 313
Cancun 341
Casas Grandes 57
Chalma 222
Chapala 106
Chetumal 351
Chiapa de Corzo 297
CHICHEN ITZA 332
Chicomoztoc 84
Chihuahua 58
Cholula 234
Ciudad Juarez 55
Ciudad Victoria 71
Coatzacoalcos 295
Coba 350
Colima 256
Comitan 301
Copper Canyon Railway 59
Cordoba 265
Cozumel 346
Creel 60
Cuernavaca 223

Dolores Hidalgo 131
Durango 63
Dzibilchaltun 324

Edzna 315
El Tajin 272

Felipe Carillo Puerto 351
Fortin de las Flores 264
Fresnillo 77

Guadalajara 95
Guanajuato 124
Guaymas 40
Guerrero Negro 33

Hermosillo 39
Hidalgo del Parral 52

Isla Mujeres 343
Ixtaccihuatl 235
Ixtapa 258

Jalapa 265
Janitzio 116
Juchitan 295

Kabah 330

Labna 331
Lagos de Moreno 88
Lagunas de Montebello 302
Lake Chapala 106
La Paz 34
Lazaro Cardenas 258
Leon 89
Loreto 34
Los Mochis 43

Malinalco 331
Manzanillo 254
Matamoros 71
Matehuala 89
Mayapan 331
Mazatlan 45
Merida 317
Mexicali 37
MEXICO CITY 150
    Alameda 175
    Anthropology Museum 182
    Chapultepec 179
    Coyoacan 191
    Food 201
    Guadalupe 199
    Hotels 162
    Listings 201
    Markets 204
    Nightlife 206
    San Angel 190
    Transport 157
    University 193
    Xochimilco 195
    Zocalo 165
Mitla 291
MONTE ALBAN 288
Monterrey 66
Morelia 118

Navojoa 42
Nogales 38

Oaxaca 281
Orizaba 264

PALENQUE 304
Papantla 271
Paracho 110
Paricutin 112

Patzcuaro 113
Pinotepa Nacional 248
Popocatépetl 235
Poza Rica 274
Progreso 325
Puebla 230
Puerto Angel 294
Puerto Escondido 293
Puerto Vallarta 249
Punta Maldonada 248

Querétaro 139
Quiroga 118

Real de Catorce 89
Rosarito 31

Salina Cruz 295
Saltillo 70
San Andres Tuxtla 276
San Blas 50
San Cristobal de las Casas 298
San Ignacio 33
San Juan del Rio 144
San Jose de Cabo 36
San Luis Potosí 91
San Miguel de Allende 133
San Patricio 254
San Quintin 32
Santa Rosalia 33
Sayil 330
Sonoita 37

Tapachula 296
Tapalpa 108
Taxco 227
Tehuacan 281
Tehuantepec 295
Teotihuacan 211
Tepic 49
Tepotzotlan 219
Tepoztlan 226
Tequila 107
Tijuana 30
Tlaquepaque 104
Tlaxcala 234
Toluca 220
Torreon 52
Tula 217
Tulum 349
Tuxpan 275
Tuxtepec 281
Tuxtla Gutierrez 297

Uruapan 110
UXMAL 326

Valladolid 340
Valle de Bravo 221
Veracruz 266
Villahermosa 303

Xochicalco 226

Zacatecas 77
Zempoala 270
Zihuatanejo 258

HELP US UPDATE

Every effort has been made to ensure that the information in **The Rough Guide to Mexico** is accurate. However things do change – especially opening hours which are notoriously erratic – and in time mistakes inevitably creep in. If you think you've spotted an error, or feel more should be said about a particular place, or simply feel the need to make some comment about the book, please write and tell us. We'll send copies of the next edition – or one of the other Rough Guides if you prefer – for the most useful accounts.

Send them to: John Fisher,
RKP Rough Guides,
14 Leicester Square,
London WC2H 7PH.

Keep These Handy When You're Travelling

For those who want to travel independently, at your own pace, seeing what you wish to see and keeping to a budget, The Rough Guide series are invaluable, something to keep near the top of your travel bag.

STA Travel works exclusively for the independent traveller. We offer the greatest selection of low fares in the world and we follow it up with accommodation, insurance and group tours especially designed for people who want more than the usual package.

So when you've read the book and you want to go travelling, make your first call an STA office.

Telephone Enquiries
01-581-1022

STA OFFICES:

74 OLD BROMPTON RD, LONDON SW7
117 EUSTON ROAD, LONDON NW1
ULU TRAVEL — BRANCHES AT MALET ST
QUEEN MARY COLLEGE, IMPERIAL COLLEGE
KINGSTON POLYTECHNIC TRAVEL BUREAU
KENT UNION TRAVEL, UNIVERSITY OF KENT

Government Bonded under ATOL 822 in Association with SATAC Charterers Ltd.